King Lear

Is *King Lear* an autonomous text, or a rewrite of the earlier and anonymous play *King Leir*? Should we refer to Shakespeare's original quarto when discussing the play, the revised folio text, or the popular composite version, stitched together by Alexander Pope in 1725? What of its stage variations? When turning from page to stage, the critical view on *King Lear* is skewed by the fact that for almost half of the four hundred years the play has occupied the stage, audiences preferred Nahum Tate's optimistic adaptation, in which Lear and Cordelia live happily ever after. When discussing *King Lear*, the question of what comprises 'the play' is both complex and fragmentary.

These issues of identity and authenticity across time and across mediums are outlined, debated, and considered critically by the contributors to this volume. Using a variety of approaches, from postcolonialism and New Historicism to psychoanalysis and gender studies, the leading international contributors to *King Lear: New Critical Essays* offer major new interpretations of the conception and writing, editing, and cultural production of *King Lear*. This book is an up-to-date and comprehensive anthology of textual scholarship, performance research, and critical writing on one of Shakespeare's most important and perplexing tragedies.

Contributors include: R.A. Foakes, Richard Knowles, Tom Clayton, Cyndia Susan Clegg, Edward L. Rocklin, Christy Desmet, Paul A. Cantor, R.V. Young, Stanley Stewart and Jean R. Brink.

Jeffrey Kahan is Associate Professor of English at the University of La Verne in California, and completed his Ph.D at the Shakespeare Institute, University of Birmingham. He is the author of *Reforging Shakespeare* (1998), and *The Cult of Kean* (2006) and editor of *Shakespeare Imitations, Parodies and Forgeries, 1710–1820* (3 vols. Routledge, 2004).

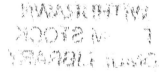

Shakespeare Criticism
Philip C. Kolin, *General Editor*

Romeo and Juliet
Critical Essays
Edited by John F. Andrews

Coriolanus
Critical Essays
Edited by David Wheeler

Titus Andronicus
Critical Essays
Edited by Philip C. Kolin

Love's Labour's Lost
Critical Essays
Edited by Felicia Hardison Londré

The Winter's Tale
Critical Essays
Edited by Maurice Hunt

Two Gentlemen of Verona
Critical Essays
Edited by June Schlueter

Venus and Adonis
Critical Essays
Edited by Philip C. Kolin

As You Like it from 1600 to the Present
Critical Essays
Edited by Edward Tomarken

The Comedy of Errors
Critical Essays
Edited by Robert S. Miola

A Midsummer Night's Dream
Critical Essays
Edited by Dorothea Kehler

Shakespeare's Sonnets
Critical Essays
Edited by James Schiffer

Henry VI
Critical Essays
Edited by Thomas A. Pendleton

The Tempest
Critical Essays
Edited by Patrick M. Murphy

Pericles
Critical Essays
Edited by David Skeele

The Taming of the Shrew
Critical Essays
Edited by Dana E. Aspinall

The Merchant of Venice
New Critical Essays
Edited by John W. Mahon and Ellen Macleod Mahon

Hamlet
New Critical Essays
Edited by Arthur F. Kinney

Othello
New Critical Essays
Edited by Philip C. Kolin

Julius Caesar
New Critical Essays
Edited by Horst Zander

Antony and Cleopatra
New Critical Essays
Edited by Sara M. Deats

All's Well, that Ends Well
New Critical Essays
Edited by Gary Waller

Macbeth
New Critical Essays
Edited by Nick Moschovakis

King Lear
New Critical Essays

Edited by Jeffrey Kahan

Shakespeare Criticism Volume 33

Routledge
Taylor & Francis Group
NEW YORK AND LONDON

First published 2008
by Routledge

711 Third Avenue, New York, NY 10017
Simultaneously published in the UK
by Routledge

2 Park Square, Milton Park, Abingdon, Oxfordshire OX14 4RN

First issued in paperback 2014

Routledge is an imprint of the Taylor and Francis Group, an informa business

Typeset in Times New Roman by
Swales & Willis Ltd, Exeter, Devon

Library of Congress Cataloging in Publication Data
King Lear : new critical essays / edited by Jeffrey Kahan.
p. cm.—(Shakespeare criticism)
Includes bibliographical references and index.
1. Shakespeare, William, 1564–1616. King Lear. I. Kahan, Jeffrey, 1964–
PR2819.K495 2008
822.3′3–dc22
2007044175

British Library Cataloguing in Publication Data
A catalogue record for this book is available from the British Library

ISBN 978-0-415-77526-7 (hbk)
ISBN 978-1-138-01151-9 (pbk)
ISBN 978-0-203-09008-4 (ebk)

Contents

List of figures and acknowledgements vii
General Editor's introduction ix

1 **Introduction: Shakespeare's *King Lear*** 1
JEFFREY KAHAN

2 **The reshaping of *King Lear*** 104
R.A. FOAKES

3 **The evolution of the texts of *Lear*** 124
RICHARD KNOWLES

4 ***King Lear* and early seventeenth-century print culture** 155
CYNDIA SUSAN CLEGG

5 **"The injuries that they themselves procure": justice poetic and pragmatic, and aspects of the endplay, in *King Lear*** 184
TOM CLAYTON

6 **What does Shakespeare leave out of *King Lear*?** 208
JEAN R. BRINK

7 **The cause of thunder: nature and justice in *King Lear*** 231
PAUL A. CANTOR

8 **Hope and despair in *King Lear*: the gospel and the crisis of natural law** 253
R.V. YOUNG

9 ***Lear* in Kierkegaard** 278
STANLEY STEWART

10 **The smell of mortality: performing torture in *King Lear* 3.7** 297
EDWARD L. ROCKLIN

11 **Some *Lear*s of private life, from Tate to Shaw** 326
CHRISTY DESMET

12 **If only: alternatives and the self in *King Lear*** 351
JEFFREY KAHAN

Notes on contributors 363
Index 365

List of figures and acknowledgements

1.1 John Philip Kemble (King Lear), playing opposite his sister, Sarah Siddons (Cordelia). By kind permission of the Harry Ransom Center. 21
1.2 Edmund Kean as King Lear. By kind permission of the Harry Ransom Center. 23
1.3 Edwin Forrest as King Lear. Personal Collection. 24
1.4 Playbill for Macready's 1838 re-launching of Shakespeare's *King Lear*. By kind permission of the Harry Ransom Center. 27
1.5 William C. Macready as King Lear. By kind permission of the Harry Ransom Center. 28
1.6 Henry Irving's set for his 1892 Lyceum production of *King Lear*. By kind permission of the Harry Ransom Center. 31
1.7 Henry Irving as King Lear. By kind permission of the Shakespeare Birthplace Trust. 49
1.8 John Gielgud as King Lear (1950). Angus McBean. By kind permission of the Shakespeare Birthplace Trust. 50
1.9 Theory 3: Shakespeare as revisionist, his texts recopied, reworked and censored. 67
1.10 Paul Scofield as King Lear (1971). By kind permission of the Harry Ransom Center. 72
1.11 Antony Sher as the Fool (1982). Joe Cocks Studio Collection. Copyright Shakespeare Birthplace Trust. 75
1.12 Diana Rigg as Cordelia (1962). She later played Regan in Oliver's 1982 made-for-TV version. Angus McBean. By kind permission of the Shakespeare Birthplace Trust. 78
1.13 Scene from *The Yiddish King Lear*, performed by members of the Yiddish amateur theater at the Jewish Community Center, Resistencia, 1959. By kind permission of the Beth Hatefutsoth, Visual Documentation Center. 80
1.14 Poster for Jean-Luc Godard's 1987 film *King Lear*. Personal Collection. 83

1.15 Henry Fuseli's rendering of King Lear for Boydell Shakespeare (published 1792). By kind permission of the Harry Ransom Center. 86
1.16 John Hamilton Mortimer's King Lear (1776). Personal Collection. 87
11.1 Lear and Cordelia in Prison (*ca.* 1779) by William Blake. By kind permission of ARTRES. 332
11.2 Lear and Cordelia (1848–49) by Ford Maddox Brown. By kind permission of ARTRES. 341
11.3 The Northwest Passage (1874) by Sir John Everett Millais (1829–96). By kind permission of ARTRES. 347

Every effort has been made to trace and contact copyright holders. The publishers would be pleased to hear from any copyright holders not acknowledged here, so that this acknowledgement page may be amended at the earliest opportunity.

General Editor's introduction

The continuing goal of the Shakespeare Criticism series is to provide the most significant and original contemporary interpretations of Shakespeare's works. Each volume in the series is devoted to a Shakespeare play or poem (e.g. the sonnets, *Venus and Adonis, Othello*) and contains eighteen to twenty-five new essays exploring the text from a variety of critical persepectives.

A major feature of each volume in the series is the editor's introduction. Each volume editor provides a substantial essay identifying the main critical issues and problems the play (or poem) has raised, charting the critical trends in looking at the work over the centuries, and assessing the critical discourse that has linked the play or poem to various ideological concerns. In addition to examining the critical commentary in light of important historical and theatrical events, each introduction functions as a discursive bibliographic essay citing and evaluating significant critical works—books, journal articles, theater documents, reviews, and interviews—giving readers a guide to the vast amounts of research on a particular play or poem.

Each volume showcases the work of leading Shakespeare scholars who participate in and extend the critical discourse on the text. Reflecting the most recent approaches in Shakespeare studies, these essays approach the play from a host of critical positions, including but not limited to feminist, Marxist, new historical, semiotic, mythic, performance/staging, cultural, and/or a combination of these and other methodologies. Some volumes in the series include bibliographic analyses of a Shakespeare text to shed light on its critical history and interpretation. Interviews with directors and/or actors are also part of some volumes in the series.

At least one, sometimes as many as two or three, of the essays in each volume is devoted to a play in performance, beginning with the earliest and most significant productions and proceeding to the most recent. These essays, which ultimatley provide a theater history of the play, should not be regarded as different from or rigidly isolated from the critical work on the script. Over the last thirty years or so Shakespeare criticism has understandably been labeled the "Age of Performance." Readers will find information in these essays on non-English speaking productions of Shakespeare's plays as well as landmark performances in English. Editors and contributors also include photographs from productions across the world to help readers see and further appreciate the ways a Shakespeare play has taken shape in the theater.

Ultimately, each volume in the Shakespeare Criticism series strives to give readers a balanced, representative collection of the most engaging and thoroughly researched criticism on the given Shakespeare text. In essence, each volume provides a careful survey of essential materials in the history of the criticism for a Shakespeare play or poem as well as cutting-edge essays that extend and enliven our understanding of the work in its critical context. In offering readers innovative and fulfilling new essays, volume editors have made invaluable contributions to the literary and theatrical criticism of Shakespeare's greatest legacy, his work.

Philip C. Kolin
University of Southern Mississippi

1 Introduction

Shakespeare's *King Lear*

Jeffrey Kahan

Like virtually all of Shakespeare's plays, *King Lear* is now thought of as a masterpiece. As of this writing, it is safe to say that in the public's mind the story of Lear's physical and spiritual suffering, and, above all, his heartbreaking end, aptly sum up the human condition:

> When we are born, we cry that we are come
> To this great stage of fools.
>
> (Scene 20.171–72)[1]

However, *King Lear* has not always been considered a profound, if bleak, meditation on the human experience. The Poet Laureate Naham Tate thought that the play was so deeply flawed that it could only be staged after radical revision. In his new and improved version, King Lear did not die but reigned victorious over his vanquished foes, an oddly happy conclusion for a tragedy! Whereas we would today think that any attempt to modify Shakespeare so fundamentally should have been met with contempt, audiences embraced Tate's version, which held the stage from 1681–1838.

Even with the return of Shakespeare's play, many very respectable artists and critics have continued to voice some unease. As Jan Kott (1964)[2] wrote: "The attitude of modern criticism to *King Lear* is ambiguous and somehow embarrassed. . . . *King Lear* gives one the impression of a high mountain that everyone admires, yet no one particularly wishes to climb" (87). Over the last four hundred years, many writers and artists have tried to scale its heights, and each essay has left its mark. In this Introduction, we will retrace these scholarly and theatrical paths, some of which are still fresh, others well-trodden, and still others now all but forgotten. Let's start with what we know about Shakespeare's source materials and what he did with them, and then turn to what various poets, novelists, academics, directors and actors have made of *King Lear*.

Origins

Setting the stage: Shakespeare and his actors

Because we often think of Shakespeare as ageless and his plays as timeless, it's sometimes difficult to remember that many of this man's most famous plays were written during the short span of 1599 to 1609. In that period, he—aided in various ways by his fellow actors—built the largest playhouse in London, The Globe, secured the protection of the king, and embarked upon a decade of playwriting that has never been equaled: the classic comedies such as *As You Like It*, *Much Ado About Nothing*, *Twelfth Night*, *Measure for Measure*, and *All's Well that Ends Well*; the historical war epic: *Henry V*; the Greco-Roman plays: *Julius Caesar*, *Troilus* and *Cressida*, *Timon of Athens*, *Pericles*, and *Coriolanus*; and the great tragedies upon which much of his posthumous reputation has been built: *Hamlet*, *Macbeth*, *Othello*, and, of course, *King Lear*.

In short, when composing *King Lear* (*ca.*1605–6), William Shakespeare was at his peak, but so too were his players. Richard Burbage, one of the chief tragedians of the era, played the part of Lear. Burbage came from an acting family. His father, James, owned The Theater, Renaissance London's first custom-built playhouse, and Richard's elder brother Cuthbert, who died in 1597, was an actor of some note. Burbage himself is often described as short and stocky, although his portrait shows he was in later life thin of face. The parts he played he made his own, so much so that when Shakespeare died in 1616 audiences hardly noticed, but when Burbage died in 1619, one poet lamented that the world had lost a whole host of tragic heroes:

> No more young Hamlett, ould Hieronymoe;
> Kind Lear, the grieved Moore, and more besyde
> That lived in him, have now for ever dy'de.
> (Qtd. in Stopes 118)

The reference to "Kind Lear" and to "the grievèd Moor" may suggest that Burbage played these tragic roles in the key of a victim. Certainly, "Kind Lear" sees himself as unjustly treated:

> I will forget my nature. So kind a father!
> (Scene 5.32)

> Who comes here? O heavens,
> If you do love old men, if your sweet sway
> Allow obedience, if yourselves are old,
> Make it your cause!
> (Scene 7.347–50)

> No I will weep no more.—
> In such a night as this! O Regan, Gonoril,
> Your old kind father, whose frank heart gave you all. . . .
> (Scene 11.17–19)

> I tax not you, you elements, with unkindness.
> I never gave you kingdom, called you children.
> You owe me no subscription. Why then, let fall
> Your horrible pleasure. Here I stand your slave,
> A poor, infirm, weak and despised old man. . . .
> (Scene 9.16–20)

> I am a man more sinned against than sinning.
> (Scene 9.60)

Likewise, the references to Hamlet and Hieronimo may tell us something about Burbage's histrionics. Both parts call for fits of madness, whether feigned or real. In *Lear*, Shakespeare played upon audience expectations by noting not the king's madness, but his repeated efforts to retain his fading sanity:

> O, let me not be mad, sweet heaven!
> I would not be mad.
> Keep me in temper. I would not be mad.
> (Scene 5.45–47)

> You heavens, give me that patience, patience I need . . .
> (Scene 7.430)

> No, I will be the pattern of all patience.
> (Scene 9.37)

> O, that way madness lies. Let me shun that.
> No more of that.
> (Scene 11.20–21)

It seems clear that Richard Burbage was a master of pathos, but, when circumstances dictated, he could also be downright menacing. On 16 November 1590, his father, James Burbage, found himself embroiled in a legal dispute with his sister-in-law, Margaret Brayne, who had hired one Robert Myles and some muscle to intimidate the family. When Myles presented the Burbages with what appeared to be legal documents on Margaret Brayne's behalf, James Burbage told him he'd sooner "wipe his tail" with the paper than read it. And how did Richard Burbage react to all of this? No doubt emboldened by his audience—he was, after all, performing before his father—Richard Burbage picked up a broom and, using it as a staff, marched up to the hired gang and threatened to take them all on. He then "scornfully and disdainfully" grabbed Robert Myles by the nose and said he "would beat him also, and did challenge the field of him at that time." He then began to beat Myles with a broom and called him a "murdering knave" and "other vile and unhonest words" (Wallace 115).[3]

The action is that of an experienced and gutsy street fighter—Richard Burbage literally getting in Robert Myles' face, insulting him with coarse language, grabbing and twisting the man's nose and daring him to do something about it; then, sensing Myles had no real fight in him, humiliating him physically. But the passage also has a theatrical edge to it—"challenge the field of him" sounds like something out of *Henry V*. Certainly, Burbage must have used his command of both voice and body to intimidate Myles and his gang, and he was successful in playing the part. Faced with Burbage's violence, Myles, bloodied and browbeaten, backed off. To be sure, this passage does not tell us anything about the costume he wore when playing King Lear, nor does it suggest the way he addressed Cordelia, nor the way he raged against the gods themselves in the heath scene, nor is this vignette as evocative as, say, Coleridge's description of Edmund Kean—"To see him act is like reading Shakespeare by flashes of lightning"—but it does suggest some of his fearsome power in *King Lear*. Recall, for example, the king's daunting, dramatic command:

> Come not between the dragon and his wrath.
> (Scene 1.114)

or his grim promise of sword and fire:

> I will have such revenges on you both
> That all the world shall—I will do such things—
> What they are, yet I know not; but they shall be
> The terrors of the earth.
> (Scene 7.438–41)

or, still later, Edgar's awestruck reaction when looking upon the infuriated king:

> Look where he stands and glares.
> (Scene 13.19)

The part of the Fool was most likely performed by the dwarfish Robert Armin, for whom Shakespeare had already written the parts of Touchstone and Feste.[4] Armin had been trained in the art of fooling by the famed Court jester, Richard Tarlton (Chettle 22).[5] As for the casting of the other parts, including which—if any—character Shakespeare himself played, we know nothing, though it has been suggested that he played the ever-truthful Albany (Ackroyd 234). What we can say is that even the minor actors who played in the original production of *Lear*—think of the boy actors who were called upon to play the female parts of Regan, Goneril and Cordelia—must have been extremely skillful.

Then again, calling these actors "boys" is something of a misnomer. Some of the "boy" actors of the era were older than Shakespeare when he got married. William Barksted was still performing in boys' companies at age twenty, Hugh Attewell was at least twenty-one; Joseph Taylor was twenty-three. Moreover, many of these actors were highly seasoned. Some had been performing professionally for over ten years (Munro 40–41).

The point is that, given the skills of his company, Shakespeare was free to write to his actors' strengths, though defining exactly how receptive Shakespeare was to his players remains unknown. The theater historian G.E. Bentley (1981) rather comically imagined Shakespeare as deaf or indifferent to his company's complaints. Roars Burbage: "Aw, come on Will! You can't expect me to do that!" Armin, equally upset with his role, chimes: "What the hell! Don't I come on in the last two acts at all?"(60)

King Leir *and Shakespeare's early works*

Surprising as it may seem to many, Shakespeare and his contemporaries did not value originality. Whereas we might dismiss a work as derivative or unoriginal, Shakespeare's audience saw no issue with someone taking well-known materials and revising or updating them. Before Shakespeare wrote *King Lear*, Elizabethans were familiar with another play called "king leare." On 6 April and then again on 8 April 1594, a troupe of actors at the Rose playhouse performed this play. We have the details from Philip Henslowe's records, which we often refer to as "Henslowe's Diary." Henslowe was a practical man, who tracked his business with precision. He regularly commissioned new plays and dutifully noted their premières. Since he did little more than record the title, dates and earnings of "king leare," we can assume that this play was not brand new. However, Henslowe did record one other important detail: the play was performed "by the Quenes men & my lord of Sussexe to geather" (I:17). If Shakespeare was, as most scholars suspect, a member of one or both companies, it's likely that he performed in this early and anonymous drama, a drama very much like the play he would write some eleven years later.[6]

Certainly, "king leare," or as it was re-titled upon publication, *King Leir*, continued to work upon Shakespeare's imagination. While most scholars and teachers are aware that Shakespeare regularly borrowed from other books and plays, his debt to *King Leir* is, perhaps, underappreciated. The ties between *King Leir* and early Shakespeare are intriguing:

King Leir (composed *ca.* 1593–4)

. . . proceed to execution.
But see thou faint not; for they will speak fair.

(4.5.51–52)

Richard III (composed *ca.* 1593)

But sirs, be sudden in the execution,
Withal obdurate; do not hear him plead,
For Clarence is well spoken, and perhaps
May move your hearts to pity, if you mark him.

(1.3.344–46)

King Leir (composed *ca.* 1593–4)

Did never Philomel sing so sweet a note.

(1.3.74)[7]

When will this scene of sadness have an end[?]

(4.4.3)

As easy it is for the blackamoor
To wash the tawny colour from his skin . . .

(4.4.42–44)

I am no cannibal, that I should delight
To slake my hungry jaws with human flesh . . .

(5.4.38–39)

Titus Andronicus (composed *ca.* 1593–4)

Did ever raven sing so like a lark[?]

(3.1.158)

When will this fearful slumber have an end?

(3.1.251)

For all the water in the ocean
Can never turn the swan's black legs to white,
Although she lave them hourly in the flood.

(4.2.100–2)

Why, there they are, both bakèd in this pie,
Whereof their mother daintily hath fed,
Eating the flesh that she herself hath bred.

(5.3.59–61)

King Leir (composed *ca.* 1593–4)

For she would rather die than give consent
To join in marriage with the Irish king.

(1.2.93–94)

Merchant of Venice (composed *ca.* 1595)

If I live to be as old as Sibylla, I will die as chaste as Diana. . . . I pray God grant them a fair departure.

(1.3.103–4, 107–8)

Given our inability to know exactly when Shakespeare wrote these plays, we cannot say that all these parallels mean Shakespeare borrowed from *King Leir*. It's possible that the anonymous author of *King Leir* had, in some instances, borrowed from Shakespeare. At the least, it seems safe to assume that Shakespeare knew of the play in the early 1590s. Why, then, did he wait over a decade to write his own version?[8] It's possible that the printing of a quarto of *King Leir* in 1605 reawakened his interest in the play and its dramatic potential.[9] This is certainly the belief of the eighteenth-century editor Edward Capell (1767), who acknowledged that Shakespeare had "done him [the anonymous author of *King Leir*] the honour to follow him in a stroke or two" (Malone, I: 160).

King Leir *and* King Lear

Capell had understated the matter. There can be no doubt that Shakespeare borrowed heavily from *King Leir* when writing *King Lear*:

Anonymous *King Leir* (composed *ca.* 1593–94; published 1605)	Shakespeare's *King Lear* (composed *ca.* 1605–6; published 1608)
I will provide him a piece of bread and cheese . . . (3.3.17)	. . . this toasted cheese will do it . . . (Scene 20.89)
. . . carry thou these letters to my sister, which contain matter quite contrary to the other. There shall she be given to understand, that my father hath detracted her . . . (3.5.88–92)	You bring letters against the King . . . (Scene 7.32–33)
And think me but the shadow of myself. (4.2.17)	Who is it that can tell me who I am? Lear's shadow? (Scene 4.225–26)
. . . his coming he shall curse, And truly say he came from bad to worse . . . (4.2.56–57)	O gods! Who is't can say "I am at the worst?" I am worse then e'er I was. (Scene 15.23–24)
Camest thou from France of purpose to do this [murder]? (4.7.129)	If you have poison for me, I will drink it, I know you do not love me . . . (Scene 21.69–70)

The heav'ns are just and hate impiety . . . (5.2.30)	This shows you are above, You justicers, that these our nether crimes So speedily can venge. (Scene 16.77–79)
Why, say the worst: the worst can be but death . . . (5.3.88)	And worse I may be yet. The worst is not As long as we can say, "This is the worst." (Scene 15.25–26)
God, world and nature say I do you wrong . . . (5.4.221)	You do me wrong to take me out o'th' grave. (Scene 21.43)
Knowest thou these letters? (5.10.77)	Know'st thou this paper? (Scene 24.156)[10]

Shakespeare didn't follow the old plot to the letter. *King Leir*, after all, contains no Gloucester, no Edgar or Edmund, and no Fool. But for all the things this old play lacks, it does flesh out one vital character that Shakespeare mentions only in passing: Lear's deceased queen. In Shakespeare's version, Lear, on meeting Regan, is sure she is happy to see him:

> If thou shouldst not be glad
> I would divorce me from thy mother's shrine,
> Sepulchring an adultress.
> (Scene 7.292–94)

Of course, we'd like to know more about this queen: when she died, how she died, and what rapport she had with her husband, and, perhaps more centrally, with her daughters. Shakespeare might have assumed his audience had some memory of the old play, in which King Leir not only mentions his wife but also explains why he needs to know which daughter loves him best:

> Of our too late deceas'd and dearest queen,
> Whose soul, I hope, possess'd of heavenly joys,
> Doth ride in triumph 'mongst the cherubims,
> Let us request your grave advice, my lords,
> For the disposing of our princely daughters. . . .
> (1.1.2–6)

Apparently, Leir had left the management of his daughters to his wife. Since her recent death, he has to do it himself, and he finds that he's out of his depth, especially in matters concerning marriage. We soon learn that Leir has big plans for his youngest daughter, Cordella. But how to convince her to do as he asks? The counselor Scalliger comes up with the idea of demanding which daughter loves him best. The king agrees, not because he needs to be flattered, but because he thinks he can use the question to force his youngest daughter to marry. He'll begin by asking if Cordella loves him; when she replies that she does, Leir will demand that she demonstrate her love by agreeing to wed the king of Brittany.

In this version, none of the sisters are married, and, jealous of their father's affection for their young and beautiful sister, they plan to out-vie her in protestations, with the hope that she will be cheated out of a husband:

Regan. Do you not see what several choice of suitors
She daily hath, and of the best degree?
Say amongst all she hap to fancy one,
And have a husband whenas we have none;
Why then, by right, to her we must give place,
Though it be ne'er so much to our disgrace.
Gonoril. By my virginity, rather than she shall have
A husband before me,
I will marry one or other in his shirt. . . .
(1.2.19–27)

As in Shakespeare's play, Cordella fails the test, but unlike Shakespeare's play, she is thrust out-of-doors, penniless and friendless. (Shakespeare shifts this aspect of the old play into the Gloucester subplot.) Soon after Cordella's banishment, Regan and Gonoril marry the lords of Cornwall and Cambria.

The old king now decides that he will live with Gonoril permanently, though when she cuts off his pension he quickly moves in with Regan. As in Shakespeare, a series of letters are exchanged between the two sisters, though the Messenger in the old play has some of the characteristics we normally associate with the brash and flirtatious Edmund, not the obsequious and cowardly Oswald:

Regan. Hast thou the heart to act a stratagem,
And give a stab or two, if need require?
Messenger. I have a heart compact of adamant,
Which never knew what melting pity meant.
I weigh no more the murd'ring of a man,
Than I respect the cracking of a flea
When I do catch her biting on my skin.
If you will have your husband or your father

Or both of them sent to another world,
Do but command me do't; it shall be done.

Regan. It is enough; we make no doubt of thee.
Meet us tomorrow here at nine o'clock;
Meanwhile, farewell, and drink that for my sake. *Exit*

Messenger. Ay, this is it will make me do the deed.
Oh, had I every day such customers,
This were the gainful'st trade in Christendom!
A purse of gold giv'n for a paltry stab!
Why, here's a wench that longs to have a stab.
Well, I could give it her, and ne'er hurt her neither. *Exit*
(4.3.51–69)

Edmund's character is not simply the Messenger reworked. He also has elements of Regan in him:

Regan in *King Leir*

How may I bless the hour of my nativity
Which bodeth unto me such happy stars!
How may I thank kind Fortune, that vouchsafes
To all my actions, such desir'd event!
(3.4.1–4)

Edmund in *King Lear*

. . . my nativity was under Ursa Major, so that it follows I am rough and lecherous.—Fut! I should have been that I am had the maidenliest star in the firmament twinkled on my bastardizing.
(Scene 2.124–28)

Regan, reading the letters, quickly decides that the old man must be murdered. In the meantime, the beggarly Cordella has met the Galician king, who has come to England disguised as a commoner. When hearing of Cordella's ill-treatment, he offers his hand in marriage. Though she thinks he is a pauper, she agrees to be his wife.

Meanwhile, Leir is aided by the loyal Perillus—the prototype for Shakespeare's Kent. But unlike Kent, Perillus is never banished and, thus, is not in disguise as the blunt Caius. Still, for reasons which may suggest Leir's impaired judgment, the old king does not seem to know who Perillus is and remains surprised by his unsolicited kindness.

The Messenger comes across Leir and Perillus and plans to kill them both but is converted by the old king's piety—an aspect Shakespeare saved for Edmund's deathbed conversion. Cordella sends an ambassador to Regan, inquiring after her father. The ambassador is physically manhandled by Regan, a scene which broadly suggests Kent's stocking and, albeit only faintly, Gloucester's blinding. Meanwhile, Leir and Perillus have made it to France, where, dressed like peasants, they are reunited with Cordella and her husband, who, for reasons that remain hazy, are in disguise. Revealing herself to her father, she kneels in repentance. (In Shakespeare's play, we recall, it is Edgar who remains incognito until he cures his father of despair.)

When the French king hears how Leir has been treated, he raises an army. Although ignorant of their wives' attempted patricide, invasion is invasion, and Cambria and Cornwall quickly move to counter the threat. But the people rally to the old king. Cornwall and Cambria are easily defeated. We never learn what becomes of them or their wives, but there is no indication that they are punished by the victorious Leir. In Shakespeare's play, of course, there is far more mayhem. Gloucester suddenly dies of unknown causes; Edgar kills Edmund; Regan poisons her sister and then kills herself; Cordelia is hanged; Lear kills a guard and dies, again of unknown causes, though probably of a heart attack. And at the close, Kent threatens to kill himself.

Source for the Fool

The early and anonymous *King Leir* has no courtly fool attending the king. Why did Shakespeare add this character? When discussing the cast, we noted that Shakespeare customized his text to take advantage of Richard Burbage's skills; he probably did so with other actors as well, among them the highly-talented Robert Armin. In addition to being one of the chief comic actors of the era, Armin was also the author of several humorous books, including *Tarltons Newes Out of Purgatorie* (1590), *Quips upon Questions* (1600), and *Foole upon Foole; or, Six Sortes of Sottes* (1600); in the latter, he discussed the differences between natural-born and studied "foolosophers."[11] Shakespeare seems to have thought the distinction worth bearing in mind when writing Armin's lines:

Fool. Dost know the difference my boy, between a bitter fool and a sweet fool?
Lear. No, lad. Teach me.
Fool. [*sings*] That Lord that counselled thee
    To give away thy land,
  Come, place him here by me;
    Do thou for him stand.
  The sweet and bitter fool
    Will presently appear,
  The one in motley here,
    The other found out there.

(Scene 4.132–42)

Armin's *Foole upon Foole* was reprinted in 1605, a year before *King Lear* was performed at Court, and then again in 1608, the year the First Quarto of *King Lear* was published. Enid Welsford (1935) wrote that the Fool "does not merely raise a laugh or score a point, he sets a problem" (257).[12] Indeed, as Armin explained in his 1608 edition, a first-rate courtly fool will use severe, even malicious, humour to stimulate a philosophic discussion: "fooles questions reach to mirth, leading wisdome by the hand as age leads children by one finger, and though it houlds not fast in wisedome, yet it points at it" (Armin I: [F4v]).[13]

H.F. Lippincott (1975) denies that Shakespeare was at all influenced by Armin's writings (252); other scholars, including J.P. Feather, suggest that *Quips Upon Questions* was based upon Armin's stage parts and training (Introduction, *Collected Works of Robert Armin*, I:[2]). Perhaps the direct verbal echoes between Armin's works and *King Lear* are faint, but there is no doubt that Armin's *Foole upon Foole* offers a ready-made explanation for the behavior of Shakespeare's character. Certainly there are some passages in *Foole upon Foole* that echo not only the Fool's scenes but also the plot as a whole. In one passage of Armin's book, Jacke Oates, a professional jester, scolds a minstrel for dressing up like a fool. His garments, however, are not the motley associated with clowning. Rather, he enters in tattered clothes, more in keeping with a Poor-Tom beggar than a courtly jester. When Jacke sees him, he seizes upon him. His violence recalls Cornwall's attack on hapless Gloucester: "My poore Minstrill with a fall had his head broake to the scull against the ground, his face scracht, that which was worst of all his left eye put out" (Armin B1v).[14]

Source for the Gloucester subplot: Sir Philip Sidney's novel, Arcadia

While Armin's *Foole upon Foole* may or may not have influenced Shakespeare's play directly, all scholars agree that the main source for the Gloucester–Edgar–Edmund story is Sir Philip Sidney's novel *Arcadia* (1590), which features Pyrocles and Musidorus, who, in their travels, come upon Prince Leonatus and his blind father. As in Shakespeare's tale, the father is betrayed by his bastard son, Plexirtus, who, wanting to inherit his father's lands, has poisoned his father's mind against the legitimate Leonatus. But unlike Shakespeare's story, the Gloucester-figure of *Arcadia* is not a faithful counselor to the king, but a king himself—the ruler of the mythical Paphlagonia. The difference is worth bearing in mind: Plexirtus' displacement of his brother leads to his ruling the kingdom, described as "a fit place enough to make the stage of any tragedy" (184). In Shakespeare's version, Edmund also aims to rule the kingdom, but, lacking royal blood, he must do so by marrying one of Lear's daughters.

To return to Sidney's story: once Leonatus is out of the way, Plexirtus strips his father of power, until he was "left . . . nothing but the name of king" (182). Plexirtus then blinds his father and throws him out-of-doors. The well-loved king is abandoned by his subjects, who, fearful of Plexirtus, refuse to aid him.[15] As in Shakespeare's version, the blinded man is eventually reunited with his faithful son. The old man begs for death, but Leonatus refuses. Upon hearing the tale, Pyrocles and Musidorus aid Leonatus in overthrowing Plexirtus, but the bastard escapes with the aid of his childhood friends, Tydeus and Telenor. However, Plexirtus is no longer a direct threat, and the old king is restored to power just long enough to bequeath his kingdom to Leonatus. Thereafter, Plexirtus, feigning contrition, appears before his brother and begs forgiveness. Amazingly, Leonatus pardons him. Together, they then punish Plexirtus' former allies.[16]

Other minor sources: Holinshed and Spenser, Gorboduc

The former poet laureate Ted Hughes suggested that Shakespeare may have also had in mind a variety of histories and myths, ranging from the Welsh epic *The Mabinogion* to Geoffrey of Monmouth's *History of the Kings of Britain* (265–68). Certainly, Shakespeare would have come across other versions of the *Lear* story. In his play *As You Like It*, Shakespeare famously describes a boy carrying his satchel of books to school. One book doubtless put in Shakespeare's own schoolbag was Raphael Holinshed's *History of England* (1577), Shakespeare's mainstay for plots concerning English kings. Among the monarchs discussed in Holinshed is King Leir.

In this version, the king's daughters, named Gonorilla, Regan, and Cordeilla, are asked to express their love. As in Shakespeare's version, the elder daughters do so readily and effusively, but Cordeilla's reply is perfunctory and frosty:

> I maie not answere you otherwise than I thinke, and as my conscience leadeth me . . . I protest . . . I loue you as my naturall father. And if you would more vundertand of the loue that I beare you, assertaine your selfe, that so much as you haue, so much you are worth, and so much I loue you, and no more.
>
> (226)

This Lear-figure does not mean to divest himself of his entire kingdom. Instead, he divides it in two, one half going to his two eldest daughters, one half remaining in his power. And while suitors are present for Gonorilla and Regan, no prospective match is made for Cordeilla until she is disinherited. In fact, the king of France, here named Aganippus, takes her both penniless and sight unseen, on the basis, presumably, of her honesty. (Shakespeare, on the other hand, dispossesses Lear of his entire kingdom and presents not one but two suitors for Cordelia; further, his Goneril and Regan begin the play married—rather unhappily, but married nonetheless.)

As the king ages, he relies more and more on his elder daughters, who quickly seize power. Upset, the old king steals out of his kingdom to France, where he is reunited with his youngest daughter. Aganippus raises an army and invades Britain. After a successful campaign, he reinstalls Leir, who rules for five more years before dying. Cordeilla then rules the kingdom—what happened to Aganippus is not explained—until the sons of Gonorilla and Regan, "disdaining to be under the government of a woman," overthrow their aunt. Overcome by grief, Cordeilla hangs herself.

Both the overthrow and suicide of Cordeilla are repeated in Book II, Canto X.32 of *The Fairie Queene* (1590), though in Spenser's poem her name is Cordeill:

> Till that her sisters children, woxen strong
> Through proud ambition, against her rebeld,
> And ouercommen kept in prison long,
> Till wearie of that wretched life, her selfe she hong.

In Shakespeare's version, Cordelia is murdered, but the idea of suicide was apparently too dramatic for Shakespeare to give over altogether. Edmund, we remember, plans to tell the world that, overcome with "her own despair," she "fordid herself" (Scene 24.240–41).

In terms of still yet other admittedly minor sources for the *Lear* plot, Harry Levin (1959) argued that we might find useful parallels in Thomas Norton and Thomas Sackville's play *Gorboduc* (performed 1561; published 1565), but the parallels are, at best, general: King Gorboduc divides his land between his two sons, Ferrex and Porrex. Porrex soon murders Ferrex, prompting the queen to murder Porrex. The people thereafter rise in rebellion and kill both the king and queen. A long and bloody civil war ensues. The play ends with a warning that Englishmen should never let their country fall under the "Unnatural thralldom of stranger's reign." Soon after Levin's study, the magnificently named Barbara Heliodora Carneiro de Mendonça (1960: 44) mapped a variety of word incidences, which, on first reading, do suggest that Shakespeare consulted *Gorboduc*, but the findings are preliminary.

Restoration to the Long Eighteenth Century

Tate's revision of King Lear

Shakespeare died in 1616. In 1642, a civil war broke out in England, and London's theaters were closed until 1660. When they reopened, theatrical tastes had changed. The new king, Charles II, was an Englishman who had spent much of the war exiled in France. Not surprisingly, he preferred the French theater, which was governed by rather restrictive Neoclassical principles. "The Three Unities," as they were called, consisted of:

1. the Unity of Action: the strong moral message of tragedy should not be enervated by comedy;
2. the Unity of Place: the play's action was to be limited to a single location, no hopping, for example, to and from England and France;
3. the Unity of Time: the events dramatized were not to exceed a time span of

twenty-four hours, and should certainly not, as in many of Shakespeare's plays, present a story that unfolds over several months or even years.

While some English playwrights scrambled to please Charles II with entirely new plays, a small number of poets set about rewriting Shakespeare for the new Court aesthetic. William Davenant and John Dryden, for example, rewrote *The Tempest* and renamed it *The Enchanted Isle* (1667); working alone, Dryden reworked *Antony and Cleopatra* into a play dubbed *All for Love* (1677), and Naham Tate rewrote *King Lear* and called it, well, *King Lear* (1681).

Tate described his difficulties in rewriting *King Lear*. At first, he limited himself to patching the play, taking care to "comply with my Author's Style," but he found himself unable to write with such "Quaintness of Expression" (III). He soon found himself involved in a full-scale revision, retaining only those few passages which, though "unstrung, and unpolisht"—i.e. unmetrical and uneducated—"were the only Things in the World that ought to be said on those Occasions" (II). Tate also rejected large chunks of Shakespeare's plot, particularly the all-important fifth act. Anyone could strew the stage, as Shakespeare had, with corpses—a sight, Tate feared, which would only elicit laughter, or what he called "unseasonable Jests" (III). It took a real artist to find a way to retain fear and pity while reassuring the audience that good always triumphs over evil:

> Neither is it of so Trivial an Undertaking to make a Tragedy end happily, for 'tis more difficult to Save than 'tis to Kill: The Dagger and Cup of Poyson are alwaies in Readiness; but to bring the Action to the last Extremity, and then by probable Means to recover All, will require the Art and Judgment of a Writer, and cost him many a Pang in the Performance.
>
> (III)

And since Neoclassical theory declared clowns, fools and bawdy jokes to be undignified and inappropriate in a tragedy, Tate was forced to cut the entire role of the Fool.

But Tate had also to balance aesthetic considerations against practical concerns. He was sure of his Lear, to be played by Thomas Betterton, the chief tragedian of the era—Pepys called him "the best actor in the world" (*Diary* II: 207)—but, without the Fool's antics, the play was simply too grave to please an audience that had just come through twenty years of bloodshed.[17] Something would have to be added to lighten the overall mood of this very depressing play.

Over at the King's Theatre in Bridge Street, rival Thomas Killigrew had no such problems. Now that the stage had done away with boy actors playing women's roles, men were flocking to see Nell Gwyn, the most famous actress of the era. A self-declared "protestant whore," Gwyn was illiterate and often botched serious roles. But men loved the look of her. Arthur Irwin Dasent

(1924) suggested that Pepys was so captivated by her "tiny foot peeping beneath her petticoat" that he "forgot to notice" she was an abominable actress (44–45). Her beauty even captivated the king, who made her his mistress (*Dictionary*, XXIII: 402). An actress of Nell Gwyn's skills would have been wholly incapable of playing Cordelia.

Fortunately, Tate could rely upon the talents of Betterton's wife, Mary Saunderson, an actress of great depth and skill who had already played Miranda, Beatrice, and Ophelia. Revolving how he might use her, Tate hit upon an expedient to improve the play:

> 'Twas my good Fortune to light on one Expedient to rectifie what was wanting [by adding] . . . *Love* betwixt *Edgar* and *Cordelia*, that never chang'd word with each other in the Original. This renders *Cordelia's* Indifference and her Father's Passion in the first Scene probable. It likewise gives Countenance to *Edgar's* Disguise, making that a generous Design that was before a poor Shift to save his Life.
>
> (II)

With Saunderson's talents available Tate was free to exploit her dramatic skills, rather than her physical charms. And, after all, a pretty girl might still be added. Cordelia's pure love for Kent could be set off against Regan's unpardonable lust for Edmund. Perhaps a grotto scene—in which Regan is "amorously Seated" opposite Edmund (Act IV, p. 40)—could be added?

This would also entail modifying Edmund's character as well. Shakespeare's Edmund is motivated by his desire to overcome his own illegitimacy. Tate's Edmund, on the other hand, wants to spread his illegitimacy around: thus, when mulling over whether he should marry Goneril or Regan, Edmund rejects Regan because he has already "enjoy'd her," while Goneril remains "untasted" (Act V, p. 54). But the unappeasable Edmund has already decided that two women will not be enough. He therefore turns his attention to bedding the last of Lear's daughters, the chaste Cordelia:

> . . . then in th'Field
> Where like the vig'rous *Jove* I will enjoy
> This Semele in a Storm, 'twill deaf her Cries
> Like Drums in Battle, lest her Groans shou'd pierce
> My pittying Ear, and make the amorous Fight less fierce.
>
> (Act III, p. 28)

This plot-turn is rather shocking and demonstrates how Tate harnessed sexual energy, not to titillate but, returning to Neoclassical dictates, to instruct. As Tate's play draws to a close, virtue, embodied by the prim-and-proper Edgar, triumphs over vice. Wagging his finger, Edgar reminds us that nothing good can come from infidelity. Indeed, Edgar makes it clear that the real villain of the piece is not Edmund but his bed-hopping mother:

. . . from thy licentious Mother
Thou draw'st thy Villany; but for thy part
Of *Gloster*'s Blood, I hold thee worth my Sword.
(Act V, p. 60)

With Edmund slain and Goneril and Regan dead (both poison each other), Albany then turns over the kingdom to Lear, who then turns it over to Edgar, on the condition that he marry Cordelia. Kent, Gloucester, and the king then pack up for some nice retirement villa, leaving the young couple to rule in peace.

There is no doubt that Tate's rewrites of Shakespeare are, to say the least, extensive, and some scenes, at least from our perspective, seem preposterous. In Shakespeare's play, for example, Shakespeare emphasizes the fact that the blinded Gloucester can no longer shed tears:

Lear. If thou wilt weep my fortune, take my eyes.
I know thee well enough: thy name is Gloucester.
(Scene 20,165–66)

But Tate bends the laws of physical science to allow for a maudlin display of affection:

Glost. Let me embrace thee, had I Eyes I now
Should weep for Joy, but let this trickling Blood
Suffice instead of Tears.
(Act IV, p. 43)[18]

Weeping blood may be a biologically impossible act, but it is not a designedly *funny* moment. The scene, given Neoclassical dictates, is not as refined as we would expect, but it is certainly not humorous. (In the next section we will return to the problem of unwanted laughter, which, even in Tate's play, remained a concern.)

Above all, it is Tate's ending—again, not a *funny* ending but a *joyful* ending—which exasperated so many nineteenth- and twentieth-century critics. Charles Lamb (1811), for example, saw Tate's version on stage and remarked scornfully:

> A happy ending!—as if the living martyrdom that Lear had gone through,—the flaying of his feelings alive, did not make a fair dismissal from the stage of life the only decorous thing for him. If he is to live and be happy after, if he could sustain this world's burden after, why all this pudder and preparation,—why torment us with all this unnecessary sympathy?
>
> (IV: 206)

To many, Lamb's "why" seemed simple enough to answer: Tate's ending was indispensable to any decent Englishman who expected virtue to triumph over vice. Wrote Charles Gildon (1710) approvingly:

> The King and *Cordelia* ought by no means to have dy'd, and therefore Mr Tate has very justly alter'd that particular, which must disgust the Reader and Audience to have Vertue and Piety meet so unjust a Reward.
>
> (406)

Even renowned Shakespeare scholars embraced Tate's Neoclassical revision. Reflecting upon his own experience with Shakespeare's play, Samuel Johnson (1765) wrote:

> And, if my sensations could add any thing to the general suffrage, I might relate, that I was many years ago so shocked by *Cordelia*'s death, that I know not whether I ever endured to read again the last scenes of the play till I undertook to revise them as an editor.
>
> (161–62)

In Johnson's mind, Shakespeare's version was not just dramatically flawed, it was also ethically inferior: "He [Shakespeare] sacrifices virtue to convenience, and is so much more careful to please than to instruct, that he seems to write without any moral purpose . . . he makes no just distribution of good or evil" (20–21). He wasn't just referring to the death of Cordelia. Johnson was thoroughly repulsed by the blinding of Gloucester, which was "an act too horrid to be endured in dramatick exhibition" and even by King Lear's test of love: "Such preference of one daughter to another, or resignation of dominion on such conditions, would be yet credible, if told of a petty prince of *Guinea* or *Madagascar*" (160).[19] Thus, Johnson's preference for Tate's rewrite, which allowed justice to prevail:

> A play in which the wicked prosper, and the virtuous miscarry, may doubtless be good because it is a just representation of the common events of human life: but since all reasonable beings naturally love justice, I cannot easily be persuaded that the observation of justice makes a play worse; or that, if other excellencies are equal, the audience will not always rise better pleased from the final triumph of persecuted virtue.
>
> (161)[20]

Besides, wrote Johnson, any debate on Tate's version was moot, since the audience had long ago settled the matter: "In the present case the publick has decided. *Cordelia*, from the time of *Tate*, has always retired with victory and felicity" (161). Even Coleridge (1811–12), a Romantic poet whose aesthetics often preferred gloomy endings, could not find it in his heart to accept

Shakespeare's agonizing fifth act. "If we want to witness mere pain," he wrote, "we can visit the hospitals" (ed. 1856: 25).

Garrick to Kean

Tate's neoclassical rewrite may have aimed for tragic decorum, but, as John Shebbeare (1755) described, most actors following Betterton unintentionally turned the play into something akin to French farce: "actors speak [Lear's lines] with that kind of rage, with which a drunken shoemaker curses his daughter that has secretly taken his money from him, and prevented his from going to the alehouse; it is indeed a sheer scolding" (II: 286–87). Given these involuntary comic responses, it's not entirely surprising that actors shied away from anything which might further encourage their audiences to snicker. In 1756, David Garrick, the leading actor of his era, toyed with the idea of adding Shakespeare's comic Fool to Tate's rewrite of Shakespeare but decide against it, for fear that the Fool's jesting might "counteract the agonies of Lear" (Wingate 77). Spectators had no reason to cavil. With no comedy to distract audiences, Garrick could be mesmerizing. When Garrick fell to his knees, the first two rows of the audience, unwilling to miss even a second of his acting, rose to their feet, but did so silently, afraid their racket would ruin the actor's concentration. Cast members such as Jack Bannister and Kitty Clive watched him from the wings and often burst into tears at the sublimity of his genius.

In some ways, Garrick's preparation for the role seems startlingly modern. The actor made no secret that his portrayal of Lear was based upon the sufferings of a man he had met round the streets of east London:

> he [Garrick] was acquainted with a worthy man, who lived in Leman Street, Goodman's Fields; this friend had an only daughter, about two years old; he stood at his dining-room window, fondling the child, and dandling it in his arms, when it was his misfortune to drop the infant into a flagged area, and killed it on the spot. . . . Garrick frequently went to see his distracted friend, who passed the remainder of his life in going to the window, and there playing in fancy with his child. After some dalliance, he dropped it, and, bursting into a flood of tears, filled the house with shrieks of grief and bitter anguish. He then sat down, in a pensive mood, his eyes fixed on one object, at times looking slowly round him, as if to implore compassion. Garrick . . . was ever after used to say, that it gave him the very first idea of *King Lear*'s madness.
>
> (Davies I: 49–50)

Although Leigh Woods (1981) stated that Garrick internalized Lear's pain (74), theatrical anecdotes suggest otherwise. Even as the audience applauded a particularly fine moment of acting, Garrick would break from his role-playing and whisper to fellow actor Tom King: "Hang me, Tom! it will do; it will do" (Wingate 68). Yet, for someone so interested in acting technique, Garrick was remarkably unconcerned with stage attire. In fact, Garrick might just as well have worn his Lear costume in a comedy (Wingate 69). Needless to say, the actor was equally indifferent to what we now call "special effects."

Garrick's successor, John Philip Kemble, premièred his *Lear* on 21 January 1788. Kemble was an actor known far more for his tragedies than for his comedies. A political and artistic traditionalist, Kemble's Shakespearean interpretations were aimed at curbing all rebellious tendencies and antisocial activities, including regicide and sexual license. Even his tall, slim figure was a physical model of aristocratic self-restraint. (See Figure 1.1.) William Hazlitt described Kemble as "the very still-life and statuary of the stage; a perfect figure of a man; a petrifaction of sentiment, that heaves no sigh, and sheds no tear; an icicle upon the bust of Tragedy" (V: 304). Unsurprisingly, he excelled at playing calm, self-possessed heroes and well-mannered princes. John Howard Payne vividly recalled Kemble's Coriolanus:

> His person derived a majesty from a scarlet robe which he managed with inimitable dignity. The Roman energy of his deportment, the seraphic grace of his gesture, and the movements of his perfect self-possession displayed the great mind, daring to command, and disdaining to solicit, admiration.
>
> (*The Kembles*, 85–86)

Anxious to distance his characters from any taint of working-class vulgarity, Kemble regularly bowdlerized words: country "whoring" gave way to urbane "wenching." Even inoffensive phrases were subject to his overly-severe prudery: "i'th' name of Venus" became " 'i'th' name of wonder" (Baker 115). Offstage, Kemble lived, as it were, with "the cloak of the 'noble Roman' round him" (Kelly 103). As one praising theatergoer put it, "Who can like Kemble dignify the stage?" (*Actors and Editors* 33)

Kemble refashioned *King Lear* to reflect his neo-Puritan sensibilities. He cut the sexually-charged "grotto scene" between Edmund and Regan and even expurgated Tate's curtain closer, in which Edgar connects his phallic potency to the stability of the country:

> Our drooping Country now erects her Head,
> Peace spreads her balmy Wings, and Plenty Blooms.
>
> (Tate, Act V, p. 67)

Despite playing Lear as an old man—Kemble, according to his own promptbook, dressed in a "white bald wig"—he was, at points, surprisingly athletic. Within moments of the first act, Kemble's Lear rushed upon Kent, intent upon stabbing him for his impudence. When saving Cordelia—remember, we're dealing with Tate's adaptation here—Kemble snatched a

Figure 1.1 John Philip Kemble (King Lear), playing opposite his sister, Sarah Siddons (Cordelia). By kind permission of the Harry Ransom Research Center, The University of Texas at Austin.

sword from an officer and struck down the two "Ruffians" who threatened her. But Kemble's athleticism was to some extent overshadowed by his good breeding. Wrote Leigh Hunt: "He [Kemble] never rises and sinks in the enthusiasm of the moment; his ascension, though grand, is careful, and when he sinks it is with preparation and dignity" (*The Kembles* 85). Lear was never among his favorite roles, and, after his initial run, he rarely performed it (Shattuck, vol. 5: I–II).

During the Regency, audiences favored the flamboyant acting of Edmund Kean. (See Figure 1.2.) For the 1820 première of his *King Lear*, it "was widely reported that he was studying the character with great care, even visiting lunatic asylums to observe the effects of madness. . . . He disturbed [his wife] Mary by wandering about the house with his eyes alternately vacant and filled with fierce light" (FitzSimons 138). *The New York Post*, covering Kean's performance of 15 December 1820, was particularly struck with Kean's portrayal of lunacy:

> Nature, writhing under the poignancy of feeling, and finding no utterance in words or tears found a vent at length . . . in a spontaneous, hysterical, idiot laugh. The impressions made upon all who were present, will never be forgotten. His dreadful imprecations upon his daughters, his solemn appeals to heaven, struck the soul with awe.—But no adequate conception can be conveyed, by words, of Mr. Kean's representation of his high-drawn and arduous character. . . . When we lately . . . said, upon seeing the second representation of [Kean as] Richard [III], that "acting could go no further," it was because we had not then witnessed his Lear.
>
> (Odell, 1927, II: 588)

Kean's powerful Romantic performances spawned a number of imitators. The best of the lot was probably the American player Edwin Forrest. (See Figure 1.3.) Like Kean, Forrest "possessed the great power of making the spectator feel that the acting was real, not mimic of life, and even caused shudders and tears by his performance" (Wingate 97). So real seemed Forrest's agonies that one spectator refused to look upon him for more than a scene or two. Asking in a trembling whisper whether Forrest had yet left the stage, and told he had, our patron sighed in relief: "A moment more and I should have been a dead man. I know it. That terrible acting overcame me" (Wingate 100).

Like Kean, Edwin Forrest made a study of insanity, visited asylums for the insane "and with artistic exactness, carried out in his renditions all those mental peculiarities and eccentricities that critics recognize as truthful, and not as the mere ebullitions of a disposition and temper naturally fiery and irritable" (Rees 168). His rage gave way to sorrow in the last act when he looked into the lifeless eyes of his Cordelia, pressed her pulseless heart, stared upon her dumb lips, and then, as reality sank upon him, whispered in a broken, unsteady voice, "Cordelia! Cordelia! stay a little!" (Rees 171).

Figure 1.2 Edmund Kean as King Lear. By kind permission of the Harry Ransom Research Center, The University of Texas at Austin.

Figure 1.3 Edwin Forrest as King Lear. Editor's personal collection.

William Charles Macready and the return of Shakespeare's play

The poet Longfellow and the critic Leigh Hunt were greatly impressed by Forrest's acting; Douglas Jerrold called him "a man of genius" (Barrett 132). But William Charles Macready saw Forrest's King Lear in 1826 and then again in 1843 and remained unimpressed. In his diary, he recorded:

> I could discern no imagination, no original thought, no poetry at all in his acting. . . . there was throughout nothing *on* his mind, fastened *on* and tearing and convulsing it with agony, and certainly his frenzy "was not like madness."
>
> (Entry for 21 October [1843], II: 229)

Macready's main complaint did not concern the quality of Forrest's acting, but Forrest's continued partiality for Tate's text over that of Shakespeare's:

> The audience were very liberal, very vehement in their applause; but it was such an audience!—applauding all the disgusting trash of Tate as if it had been Shakspeare, with might and main. But an actor to speak the words of Tate—with Shakspeare's before him—I think criticizes his own performance; and of Forrest's representation I should like to say that it was like the part—false taste. In fact, I did not think it the performance of an artist. . . . His recognition of Cordelia the same. *He did not fully comprehend his poet.*
>
> (II: 229)

Given Macready's aversion to Tate's adaptation, it's not surprising that he worked hard to convince theater impresarios that the time had finally come to perform all of Shakespeare's *King Lear*. But the restoration of Shakespeare's play cannot be credited to Macready alone. In 1768, the playwright George Colman the Elder mounted a partial restoration of the play. In an advertisement accompanying the printed version, Colman explained his decision to cut the romantic subplot:

> Now this very expedient of a *love* betwixt Edgar and Cordelia, on which Tate felicitates himself, seemed to me to be one of the capital objections to his alteration: for even supposing that it rendered Cordelia's indifference to her father more probable (an indifference which Shakespeare has no where implied), it assigns a very poor motive for it; so that what Edgar gains on the side of romantick generosity, Cordelia loses on that of real virtue. The distress of the story is so far from being heightened by it, that it has diffused a languor over all the scenes of the play from which Lear is absent . . . [Overall,] the embraces of Cordelia and the ragged Edgar . . . would have appeared too ridiculous for representation, had they not been mixed and incorporated with some of the finest scenes of Shakespeare.
>
> (II–III)

Although the "embraces of Cordelia and the ragged Edgar" were done away with, Colman still thought it best to omit the Fool: "After the most serious consideration, I was convinced that such a scene [the comedy of the Fool] would [to quote Thomas Warton] 'sink into burlesque' " (V).[21] Despite a text which featured far less Tate and far more Shakespeare, critics reacted harshly: "we doubt very much whether humanity will give him her voice in preference to Tate" (*The Theatrical Review* [1772] in Odell 1920, I: 213). Another commented that Colman had marred the play more than he had polished it:

> We have only to observe here, that Mr. *Colman* has made several very judicious alterations, at the same time that we think his having restored the original distressed catastrophe, is a circumstance not greatly in favour of humanity or delicacy of feeling, since it is now, rather too shocking to be borne; and the rejecting the Episode of the loves of *Edgar* and *Cordelia*, so happily conceived by *Tate*, has, beyond all doubt, greatly weakened the Piece, both in the perusal and representation.
>
> (Odell, 1920, I: 381).

Though Colman's version was not altogether successful, Tate's hold on the play was slipping. By 1774, the London theaters were "judiciously blending" Tate and Shakespeare (Shakespeare [and Tate] Introduction, *King Lear*, *Bell's Shakespeare*, II: 3).

In 1820, Edmund Kean and Robert Elliston tinkered with Tate's text. They reinstalled the language from two Folio passages: the storm scene in Act III and the recognition scene between Lear and Cordelia in Act V. In 1823, Kean went still further, restoring all of Shakespeare's tragic fifth act. Unfortunately, both productions were spoiled by hard luck. For the 1820 production, Elliston insisted on using a new-fangled wind-machine for the heath scene. While this contraption added a new level of verisimilitude, Kean's voice, which was none-too-strong, was drowned out by all the mechanical whirling. As for the restored fifth act, Kean's Cordelia was played by the heavy-set Mrs. West, and Kean, who suffered from gout, was scarcely strong enough to carry her. Tottering onto stage with his bulky load, the audience erupted in laughter (Austin and Ralph 205).

No such comic business interrupted William Macready's *King Lear*, which debuted on 25 January 1838. (See Figures 1.4 and 1.5.) One reviewer praised the actor-director:

> On Thursday evening—and the date will be marked in the annals of the stage—the tragedy of *King Lear* was brought out, freed from the interpolations which have disgraced it for nearly two centuries, and with the aid of scenic adjuncts, which honoured the stage and became the author. The text spoken was, to a word, that of the poet, and the conducting and

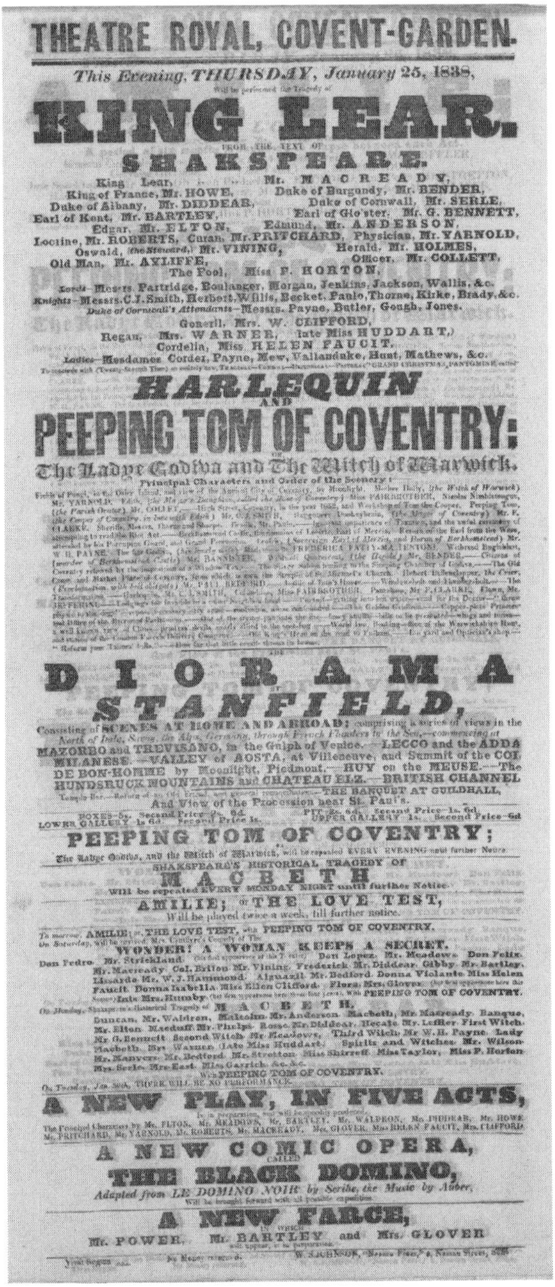

THEATRE ROYAL, COVENT-GARDEN.

This Evening, THURSDAY, January 25, 1838,

KING LEAR.

SHAKSPEARE.

King Lear, Mr. MACREADY,
King of France, Mr. HOWE, Duke of Burgundy, Mr. BENDER,
Duke of Albany, Mr. DIDDEAR, Duke of Cornwall, Mr. SERLE,
Earl of Kent, Mr. BARTLEY, Earl of Glo'ster, Mr. G. BENNETT,
Edgar, Mr. ELTON, Edmund, Mr. ANDERSON,
Locrine, Mr. ROBERTS, Curan, Mr. PRITCHARD, Physician, Mr. YARNOLD,
Oswald, (the Steward,) Mr. VINING, Herald, Mr. HOLMES,
Old Man, Mr. AYLIFFE, Officer, Mr. COLLETT,
The Fool, Miss P. HORTON,
Lords—Messrs. Partridge, Boulanger, Morgan, Jenkins, Jackson, Wallis, &c.
Knights—Messrs. C. J. Smith, Herbert, Willis, Becket, Paulo, Thorne, Kirke, Brady, &c.
Duke of Cornwall's Attendants—Messrs. Payne, Butler, Gough, Jones.
Goneril, Mrs. W. CLIFFORD,
Regan, Mrs. WARNER, (late Miss HUDDART,)
Cordelia, Miss HELEN FAUCIT,
Ladies—Mesdames Cordez, Payne, Mew, Vallandake, Hunt, Mathews, &c.

HARLEQUIN
AND
PEEPING TOM OF COVENTRY;
OR
The Ladye Godiva and The Witch of Warwick.

Principal Characters and Order of the Scenery:

DIORAMA
BY
STANFIELD,

Consisting of SCENES AT HOME AND ABROAD; comprising a series of views in the North of Italy, Savoy, the Alps, Germany, through French Flanders to the Sea,—commencing at MAZORBO and TREVISANO, in the Gulph of Venice.—LECCO and the ADDA MILANESE.—VALLEY of AOSTA, at Villeneuve, and Summit of the COL DE BON-HOMME by Moonlight, Piedmont.—HUY on the MEUSE.—The HUNDSRUCK MOUNTAINS and CHATEAU ELZ.—BRITISH CHANNEL

—THE BANQUET AT GUILDHALL,
And View of the Procession near St. Paul's.

BOXES 5s. Second Price 2s. 6d. PIT 2s. 6d. Second Price 1s. 6d.
LOWER GALLERY 1s. 6d. Second Price 1s. UPPER GALLERY 1s. Second Price 6d.

PEEPING TOM OF COVENTRY;
The Ladye Godiva, and the Witch of Warwick, will be repeated EVERY EVENING until further Notice.

SHAKSPEARE'S HISTORICAL TRAGEDY OF
MACBETH
Will be repeated EVERY MONDAY NIGHT until further Notice.

AMILIE; or THE LOVE TEST,
Will be played twice a week, till further notice.

To morrow, AMILIE; or, THE LOVE TEST, with PEEPING TOM OF COVENTRY.
On Saturday, will be revived, Mrs. Centlivre's Comedy of The
WONDER! A WOMAN KEEPS A SECRET.
Don Lopez, Mr. Meadows. Don Felix, Mr. Macready. Col. Briton, Mr. Vining. Frederick, Mr. Diddear. Gibby, Mr. Bartley. Don Pedro, Mr. Strickland. Lissardo, Mr. W. J. Hammond. Alguazil, Mr. Bedford. Donna Violante, Miss Helen Faucit. Donna Isabella, Miss Ellen Clifford. Flora, Mrs. Glover. Inis, Mrs. Humby. With PEEPING TOM OF COVENTRY.

On Monday, Shakspeare's Historical Tragedy of MACBETH.
Duncan, Mr. Waldron. Malcolm, Mr. Anderson. Macbeth, Mr. Macready. Banquo, Mr. Elton. Macduff, Mr. Phelps. Rosse, Mr. Diddear. Hecate, Mr. Leffler. First Witch, Mr. G. Bennett. Second Witch, Mr. Meadows. Third Witch, Mr. W. H. Payne. Lady Macbeth, Mrs. Warner (late Miss Huddart). Spirits and Witches, Mr. Wilson, Mr. Manvers, Mr. Bedford, Mr. Stretton, Miss Shirreff, Miss Taylor, Miss P. Horton, Mrs. Serle, Mrs. East, Miss Garrick, &c. &c.
With PEEPING TOM OF COVENTRY.

On Tuesday, THERE WILL BE NO PERFORMANCE.

A NEW PLAY, IN FIVE ACTS,

A NEW COMIC OPERA,
CALLED
THE BLACK DOMINO,
Adapted from LE DOMINO NOIR by Scribe, the Music by Auber,

A NEW FARCE,
IN WHICH
Mr. POWER, Mr. BARTLEY and Mrs. GLOVER

Figure 1.4 Playbill for Macready's 1838 re-launching of Shakespeare's *King Lear*. By kind permission of the Harry Ransom Research Center, The University of Texas at Austin.

Lear.
Here I disclaim all my paternal care,
Propinquity and property of blood,
And as a stranger to my he and me
Hold thee, from this, for ev
MACREADY AS KING LEAR, AND MRS. STIRLING AS CORDELIA.

Figure 1.5 William C. Macready as King Lear. By kind permission of the Harry Ransom Research Center, The University of Texas at Austin.

> machinery of the play were conceived in a noble and liberal strain, worthy a lofty art and a genuine artist.
>
> (Odell, 1920, II: 194)

But this restoration almost never happened. In his diaries, Macready recorded:

> Went to the theatre, where I went on a first rehearsal of *King Lear*. My opinion of the introduction of the Fool is that, like many such terrible contrasts in poetry and painting, in acting representation it will fail of effect; it will either weary and annoy or distract the spectator. I have no hope of it, and think that at the last we shall be obliged to dispense with it.
>
> (Diary entry, 4 January 1838, I: 437)

Macready registered a concern that can be traced back to Tate: that the Fool's inappropriate mirth would ruin all. Tate's solution had been to add a love story to, in effect, offset tragedy not with comedy but with romance. The success of Tate's play had also made audiences want and expect more of Cordelia. In Shakespeare's play, Cordelia has only one appearance in the first act and does not return except for brief lines in the fourth and fifth act; but in Tate's version, Cordelia was a much more impressive character. Indeed, it was not unheard of for an actress playing Cordelia to steal the show. Ann Barry's Cordelia (1758), for example, was a critical favorite:

> When she raised to heaven her large eyes, glistening with tears, said an old critic, and stood speechless, wringing her hands, it seemed as if she could claim "the aureole of a saint." "It is the grandest thing of the kind I have ever seen an actress do," the old play-goer cries in ecstasy; "my fancy still feeds on it, and the recollections of it will go with me to my grave."
>
> (Wingate 81)

At one performance, a gent was so taken with Peg Woffington's "pretty Cordelia" (1742) that he jumped onto the stage and gave her a "hearty kiss" (Wingate 73).

Macready faced a difficult problem. How to cut the love scenes but maintain the Tate-esque female presence audiences now expected in any production of *King Lear*? In one of those "Eureka" moments, Macready and his cast hit upon a solution:

> Speaking to Willmott and Bartley about the part of the Fool in *Lear*, and mentioning my apprehensions that, with Meadows, we should be obliged to omit the part, I described the sort of fragile, hectic, beautiful-faced, half-idiot-looking boy that he should be, and stated my belief that it never could be acted. Bartley observed that a woman should play it. I

> caught at the idea, and instantly exclaimed: "Miss P. Horton is the very person." I was delighted at the thought.
>
> (Diary entry, 5 January 1838, I: 438)[22]

Miss Priscilla Horton, consequently, was chosen for the part. *John Bull*, on 4 February 1838, remarked that her rendition was "perhaps not that of Shakspeare. . . . Still her's is a most pleasing performance, giving evidence of deep feeling; and she trills forth the snatches of song with the mingled archness and pathos of their own exquisite simplicity" (Odell, 1920, II: 195). As we shall see, Macready's casting of a female fool was prescient of late twentieth-century criticism, which argued that Cordelia and the Fool should be played by the same actor.

Stonehenge Shakespeare

While Macready's restoration of Shakespeare's text was a significant event, his choice of scenery also had a lasting impact. A reviewer for *John Bull* was awestruck by the chthonic grandeur of Macready's stage:

> the scenery of the piece . . . corresponds with the period, and with the circumstances of the text. The castles are heavy, sombre, solid; their halls adorned with trophies of the chase and instruments of war; druid circles rise in spectral loneliness out of the heath; and the "dreadful pother" of the elements is kept up with a verisimilitude which beggars all that we have hitherto seen attempted.
>
> (Odell, 1920, II: 210–11)

Following suit, Charles Kean (1845)—son of the aforementioned Edmund Kean—staged the play in a vaguely 800AD setting. No detail was too small; watching Samuel Phelps' Edmund, Charles Kean said that the actor needed to keep in mind historical accuracy, even in the most prosaic of circumstances. When Phelp's Edmund gave his Edgar a key, Kean criticized the action thus: "Good heavens! you give it to him as if it was a common room-door key. Let the audience see it, sir; make 'em feel it; impress upon 'em that it is a *key of the period*, sir" (Wingate 93).

Henry Irving (1892) also set the play in a world of cold wind and hewn granite. His Lear ruled over a battle-hardened horde, camped among Roman ruins; another backdrop featured "huge stones roughly laid upon each other in the Stonehenge fashion" (Odell, 1920, II: 446). (See Figure 1.6.) Indeed, Macready's Stonehenge-setting still holds imaginative sway. Note Winifred M.T. Nowottny's (1957) description: "The total impression [of the play] is one of primitive simplicity, of solid rock unfretted by the artist's tool" (90). Likewise, John Holloway (1961) thought it self-evident that *Lear* should be set "in the legendary pre-history of Britain, . . . a world which is remote and primaeval" (75); Victor Kiernan (1996) took it for granted that *King Lear* is

Figure 1.6 Henry Irving's set for his 1892 Lyceum production of *King Lear*. By kind permission of the Harry Ransom Research Center, The University of Texas at Austin.

set in "bleakness, grimness, barbarity, as of a boundless desert" (106). Later, we will see how Macready's Stonehenge concept has even affected recent film productions of the play.

But was it really Shakespeare's play?

Although we generally say that Shakespeare's version finally regained the stage with Macready, this is not entirely correct, for the play had been transmuted yet again. *King Lear*, we recall, was published in both quarto and folio. The bulky Folios, with their dedicatory poems, had, even by the Restoration, acquired reverential status. The slim, single text Quartos were another matter. When the poet-laureate Nicholas Rowe edited the plays in 1709, he was either ignorant of or indifferent to them. But Alexander Pope (1723) studied both the First Folio—often referred to as the Folio or F or F1—and a First Quarto—variously referred to as the Quarto or Q or Q1. (There is also a Second Quarto—referred to as Q2, but that text will be dealt with in a later section.)

Pope found that the Quarto text, called *The History of King Lear*, had only scene divisions; the Folio, called *The Tragedy of King Lear*, had act and scene divisions. Moreover, the Folio lacked some of the Quarto's passages, among them, a political dialogue between Lear and the Fool (Scene 4.135–51), a description of the French invasion (Scene 8.21–33), Lear's mock trial of his two eldest daughters (Scene 13.16–51), a dialogue in which Gloucester's servants discuss Gloucester's blinding (Scene 14.96–105), much of Albany's complaints concerning the treatment of the king (found throughout Scene 16), a discussion of Cordelia's grief upon seeing the condition of her father (all of Scene 17), Lear awaking to music (Scene 21.1–26), and Edgar's account of his meeting with Kent (Scene 24.201–18). Pope also found about 100 lines in the Folio that were not in the Quarto, among them, Kent's statement that the French had spies within both Albany's and Cornwall's households (3.1.14–20), and the Fool's recitation of Merlin's prophecy (3.2.79–96). Lastly, he found that a variety of lines were shifted from one character in the Quarto to another in the Folio.

Even this list, however, cannot give the reader a true sense of the differences between the two texts. The reader would be well-served in comparing the two separate versions available in the Wells and Taylor Oxford edition (1986), but I herein provide a short example:

The History of King Lear	*The Tragedy of King Lear*
Lear. Of all these bounds even from this line to this, With shady forests and wide skirted meads, We make thee lady. To thine and Albany's issue Be this perpetual.—What says our second daughter? Our dearest Regan, wife to Cornwall, speak. (Scene 1.58–62)	*Lear*. Of all these bounds even from this line to this, With shadowy forests and with champaigns riched, With plenteous rivers and wide-skirted meads, We make thee lady. To thine and Albany's issues Be this perpetual.—What says our second daughter? Our dearest Regan, wife of Cornwall? (1.1.63–68)

The point here is that, being unable to print one version without abandoning the beauties of the other, Pope adopted a simple enough expedient—to combine as much of the two as possible. Thus, Pope mixed both of the above passages to produce the following:

> Of all these bounds, ev'n from this line to this,
> With shadowy forests and with champions rich'd,
> With plenteous rivers and wide-skirted meads,
> We make thee lady. To thine and *Albany*'s issue,

> Be this perpetual,—What says our second daughter?
> Our dearest *Regan*, wife of *Cornwall*? speak.
>
> (I.ii.p. 3)

Note the first three lines are based on the Folio, the last three are based on the Quarto. In addition, Pope also silently emended "champaigns" (meaning: farmland) to the more martial "champions." Despite fixing what was clearly not broken, subsequent editors, such as Samuel Johnson (1765) acknowledged Pope's restoration, and complimented the editor on his discernment:

> I have retained all his notes, that no fragment of so great a writer may be lost; his preface, valuable alike for elegance of composition and justness of remark, and containing a general criticism on his authour, so extensive that little can be added, and so exact, that little can be disputed . . . that every reader would demand its insertion.
>
> (45)

Not everyone agreed with Pope's choices, however. Lewis Theobald, who edited Shakespeare's plays in 1633, called Pope a "blockhead" who seldom "corrected the text but to its injury" (Malone, I: 32, 31). Nonetheless, Theobald continued to fine-tune Pope's conflated text and justified his activities by blaming Shakespeare's actors for mutilating the original play:

> When the players took upon them to publish his works entire, every theatre was ransacked to supply copy; and parts collected, which had gone through as many changes as performers, either from mutilations or additions made to them. Hence we derive many chasms and incoherances in the sense and matter. Scenes were frequently transposed, and shuffled out of their true place, to humour the caprice, or supposed convenience, of some particular actor. Hence much confusion and impropriety had attended and embarrassed the business and fable. To these obvious causes of corruption . . . his works were published from the faulty copies, without the assistance of any intelligent editor.
>
> (I: 33)

Edward Capell (1767), went still further, arguing that Heminge and Condell, the two actors from Shakespeare's company who put together the Folio of 1623, had deliberately forged passages in *King Lear* so that their "lame edition" was markedly different from the rival Quarto edition (I: 10–11).

In short, almost everyone agreed that the editorial challenge was to reconstitute most, if not all, of Shakespeare's play by sifting through the various corrupted versions and linking all the best parts together. Admittedly, this project was highly interpretative, so much so that William Kenrick (1765) contended that recent editions of Shakespeare had been tainted by editorial error or, worse, were pure fabrications: "there is not one of Shakespeare's commentators who would make any scruple of substituting one word for the other, reciprocally, and alternately, as he thought the case might require" (V).

From our perspective, Kenrick's critique seems valid. After all, without consulting Shakespeare's long-lost original manuscript of *King Lear*, how was someone to prove that one passage was more "Shakespearean" than another? But in his era, Kenrick was pretty much on his own. Most critics agreed that an editor's major skill was his tastefulness; bibliographical or even historical knowledge was a secondary consideration. As Thomas Warton (1782) explained:

> It is not from the complexion of ink or of parchment, from the information of cotemporaries [*sic*], the tales of relations, the recollections of apprentices, and the prejudices of friends, nor even from the doomsday-book, pedigrees in the herald's office, armorial bearings, parliamentary rolls, inquisitions, indentures, episcopal registers, epitaphs, tomb-stones, and brass-plates, that this controversy is to be finally and effectually adjusted. Our arguments should be drawn from principles of taste, from analogical experiment, from a familiarity with antient poetry, and from gradations of composition.
>
> (124)

Given the contempt most eighteenth- and nineteenth-century editors had for the textual purity of the Quarto and First Folio, it's not entirely surprising that subsequent editors felt justified in adopting Pope and Theobald's shared methodology, and they often tried to explain their selections and adjustments. Johnson's (1765) notification was particularly confusing:

> the following lines inclosed in crotchets are in the quarto, not in the folio. So that if the speech be read with omission of the former, it will stand according to the first edition; and if the former are read, and the lines that follow them omitted, it will then stand according to the second. The speech is now tedious because it is formed by a coalition of both.
>
> (Malone, X: 136cf)

Aiming to simplify matters, the 1821 Malone–Boswell the Younger edition used asterisks and footnotes to indicate whether a particular word or phrase came from the Folio or the Quarto:

> Five* days we do allot thee, for provision
> *Quartos, *four*.
>
> (X: 19)[23]

Capell (1774) encouraged his readers—whom he referred to as "men of judgment"—to read his version, then sort through the variants and "pronounce on them, and upon the editor's choice" (I.2: 142).

More often than not, the resulting editions were stylistically awkward and, in extreme cases, nearly unintelligible, but at least these editors were plain about their substitutions. Other editors silently added Quarto passages or explained their decisions in long, tedious and, at least for the lay-reader, impenetrable footnotes or appendices. As we shall see in a later part of this essay, Pope's conflation would cause untold confusion for the many casual readers (and even some critics), who simply assumed that the *King Lear* they read in their *Complete Works of Shakespeare* was actually and unproblematically Shakespeare's *King Lear*.

Reforging King Lear

Given the universally acknowledged principle that Shakespeare's texts had been corrupted, there was only one way to clear up the matter once and for all. Shakespeare's original manuscripts had to be recovered. In 1794, they were. Sort of.

William-Henry Ireland, a seventeen-year-old law clerk, said that he had come upon a trunk of Shakespeare's Papers. Over the next year, he slowly emptied the treasure trove, each document examined and validated by experts: legal papers, love letters, lost poems, portraits, correspondences between Shakespeare and Leicester, Shakespeare and Southampton, Shakespeare and Queen Elizabeth, Shakespeare and his printer, signed and annotated books from Shakespeare's library, a fragment of the original *Hamlet* and the entire text of Shakespeare's *King Lear*.

By mid-February 1795, both the *King Lear* and some of the other papers were on display at his house at 8 Norfolk Street, London. Visitors lined up to see them, among them James Boswell, who had recently helped Edmond Malone with his edition of 1790. Boswell inspected the papers at the Ireland house on 20 February 1795. Being satisfied as to their antiquity, as far as the external appearance would attest, he proceeded to examine their style and language from the fair transcripts. Upon the completion of his examination, he requested a tumbler of warm brandy and water. Having nearly finished his drink, Boswell could no longer contain himself. "I shall now die contented, since I have lived to witness the present day." Falling to his knees, and bringing his lips close to the papers, he whispered reverentially: "I now kiss the invaluable relics of our bard: and thanks to God that I have lived to see them!" (W.H. Ireland 96). There was only one problem. The papers were all forgeries.

When rewriting *King Lear*, Ireland did his homework. The forger studied the 1608 Quarto, to which, he says, he had access by "being at liberty to resort to his [father's] library whenever . . . [he] thought proper"—for instance, when nobody was around (W.H. Ireland 116). (Almost certainly, this was not an original Quarto, but a copy produced in 1766 by George Steevens. But what's the difference between an original and a copy, especially to a forger?)

William-Henry Ireland did not just recopy the printed Quarto text of *King Lear* in his "Shakspeare hand"; he, not unlike Pope and Theobald, also made numerous alterations. However, unlike Pope and Theobald, Ireland had no need to rely on guesswork. Since he claimed to have Shakespeare's original manuscript, Shakespeare could now be used to correct Shakespeare:

> As it was generally deemed extraordinary that the productions of Shakspeare should be found so very unequal, and in particular that so much ribaldry should appear throughout his dramatic compositions, I determined on the expedient of rewriting, in the old hand, one of his most conspicuous plays, and making such alterations as I conceived appropriate.
>
> (W.H. Ireland 115)

Ireland also felt comfortable adding entirely new passages. Whereas Shakespeare had written, "What is't thou say'st— Her voice was ever soft, / Gentle and low; an excellent thing in woman," the forger rewrote and extended the verse to read:

> Whatte ist thou sayst her Voyce was everre softe
> And lowe sweete musyck oere the ryplynge Streame
> Qualytye rare ande excellente inne Womanne
> O Yesse bye heavennes twas I kylld the slave
> Thatte dydde rounde thye softe necke the murderouse
> Ande damnedde Corde entwine.
>
> (Samuel Ireland [ed.], 105)

James Boaden dismissed these additions as "childish amplification" (33), but these and other like-minded alterations intimate that Ireland was, at least in terms of aesthetics, on the same page as Pope and Theobald. Just like those editors, Ireland corrected according to his inclinations. For example, where Shakespeare wrote, "leave thy drink and thy whore," the rather prudish Ireland wrote, "leave thye drinke and thye hope" (Samuel Ireland [ed.] 26). Amazingly, some even considered Ireland's text an improvement on the original; Shakespeare was judged "a much more finished writer than had ever before been imagined" (W.H. Ireland 118).

Ireland's forgeries were exposed by Edmond Malone, who squashed Ireland like a bug. Malone noted that Ireland's odd spellings more resembled the recent forgeries of Thomas Chatterton than they did any text dating to the time of Queen Elizabeth, and that many of the words in Ireland's papers did not yet exist in Shakespeare's day, etc., etc. Malone is often described as a sort of Shakespearean white knight, a champion of facts. His 1790 edition collated one early text with another and often disputed long-standing emendations which had been based purely on principles of taste. His demolishment of the Ireland forgeries further forced editors to accept his editorial principles—chronology and dispassionate comparison. After Malone's exposure of Ireland, a "better" reading was no longer defined by poetic merit or social circumstance. Editorial decisions had to be made on the basis of historical accuracy and physical evidence.

His principles were initially adopted by John Payne Collier, who dedicated himself to archival scholarship. However, some of Collier's "scholarship" turns out to have been invented. In 1852, J.P. Collier, by then among the most respected Shakespeareans in the world, announced the discovery of the "Perkins": a second edition of Shakespeare's plays, which contained literally thousands of handwritten corrections. The handwriting style and spellings of these annotations dated to the reign of Charles I, and Collier asserted that only someone with an intimate knowledge of the plays could have made these immensely insightful improvements; the inference was that the "Old Corrector," as Collier called him, must have worked on or with the original copies of the plays either in the playhouse or the print house.

But how to explain the errors found in the Folio? After all, if the Old Corrector had personal knowledge of the original texts, so too had Heminge and Condell. Looking at the Old Corrector's emendations in *King Lear*, Collier noted that many of them seemed to be based on a switch of consonants. For example, where the Folio printed:

> Do you mark how this becomes the house[?]

Collier asks, "What has 'the *house*' to do with it?" But the Old Corrector supplied a new reading:

> Do you mark how this becomes the *mouth*[?]

But an *h* and an *m* even in Elizabethan hand, don't look much like each other. Why would the compositor so badly misread the manuscript? Studying the Old Corrector, Collier developed a theory to explain these sorts of errors: the original manuscripts were fine, but the print house compositor had not read the play; *someone had read it to him*. The errors recorded in the Folio were the result of a reader who either could not read Shakespeare's hand or a compositor who did not carefully attend to the reader's words. To explain the Old Corrector's preference for "mouth" over "house," Collier wrote: "We have here an instance of mishearing on the part of the scribe, which has occasioned an indisputable blunder" (1852: 439).

This theory was later accepted by H.H. Furness (1880) in his variorum edition of the play: "it is extremely probable that the copyist, or the compositor, misheard the word" (II.iv.149n); but, as Douglas Brooks pointed out to this writer in an email dated 3 June 2005, Collier's solution makes no sense. Compositors had to set all words on a manuscript page backward. When the compositor sees (or, if we believe Collier, hears) the word "STOP," he must set it as "POTS." In Collier's system, the compositor would have had to hear a word, then reverse it in his head, and then set it that way. It was much easier to see the letters on a page and set them backward.

In any case, Collier's evidence was phony. There was no "Old Corrector"; Collier had forged the entries himself. It didn't take long for some scholars to dismiss Collier as a mere imitator of Ireland—that is, as an imitator of a forger. Samuel Weller Singer (1853) for example, wrote:

> It would not be the first time that such knavish ingenuity had misled a well-trained Shakespearian antiquary and commentator; witness the Ireland forgeries, which, clumsy as they were, had numerous believers and apologists. I am in possession of several written sheets of a strenuous defence of them by one of the learned antiquaries of the time, who afterwards became convinced of the fraud.
>
> (VI)

Alexander Dyce went still further, dismissing not just Collier's work but the entire concept of emending by taste:

> I consider Mr. Collier's volume as useless to the future editors of Shakespeare: my opinion is, that while it abounds with alterations ignorant, tasteless, and wanton, it also occasionally presents corrections which require no authority to recommend them, because common sense declares them to be right.
>
> (Dyce 1853: [V])

The new readings were clearly forgeries, since they agreed with many of the corrections proposed by "his [Collier's] predecessors Rowe and Pope" (Dyce 1859: 194). Likewise, the aforementioned Singer concluded that the discovered "corrections" must be forgeries because they corresponded to emendations found in eighteenth-century editions of Shakespeare: one correction, he noted, was "adopted from Warburton" (273), another has "long since been suggested by Johnson" (272). Hamilton (1860) traced more of the "Old Corrector's" rectifications to the fairly recent works of Hanmer, Theobald, Steevens and Capell (42, 45, 46, 54). Even Collier himself didn't permanently adopt most of his "corrections." When he re-edited the plays in 1878, "mouth" again reverted to "house."

The good and bad Lears

After Ireland's and Collier's forgeries, guesswork, even if such guesswork actually improved the play, was no longer valid. Bibliographical emphasis now turned to the Quarto. Two copies of the Quarto of *King Lear* were known to George Steevens in 1766; three were known to James Boswell the Younger in 1821. By 1885, six copies had been found, all bearing the date 1608 (Daniel VI). But in many regards these copies differed with each other, and when William G. Clark and William Aldis Wright (1866) made a study of them, the editors concluded that there were, in fact, *two* sets of quartos, which we now refer to as Q1 and Q2. They initially assumed that the more faulty set was the older version, and that the more precise set was the newly-corrected edition. But, going over the data, these scholars soon reversed their conclusions. The inferior quarto text was set after and possibly from the first (VIII: XV).[24]

If there were two quartos and one was markedly better than the other, how good was the "good" Quarto? The aforementioned William G. Clark and William Aldis Wright (1866) collectively argued that passages of Q1 were not written by Shakespeare at all: "internal evidence is conclusive against the supposition that the lines were written by Shakespeare" (VIII: 433). Similarly citing the many "nonsense words" in the text, P.A. Daniel (1885) speculated, perhaps with a nodding glance to Collier's near-deaf compositor, that the Quarto was probably set by "a foreigner, imperfectly acquainted with English" (IV). Alfred W. Pollard (1909) thought that Q1's compositor had done his best, but that he had worked from an "unusually illegible playhouse copy" (53). In 1931, Madeleine Doran argued that the Quarto was merely a first draft; which had been marred by the "excrescences which have crept into the text through the medium of actors" (145). W.W. Greg (1933 and 1940) suggested that Q1's compositor or press corrector had worked with "remarkable incompetence" (1933: 261); "Indeed, it may be said without fear of contradiction that the quarto text is a very bad one, both in comparison with that of the folio and with any of the more reputable quartos of other Shakespearian plays" (1940: 137). It was not just the printers who were careless. The manuscript was itself an error-riddled transcription of a live performance (1940: 138).

Following Greg's lead, Leo Kirschbaum (1945) described Q1 as a "memorial perversion" (9). Cataloguing the sins of first quarto, Kirschabum wrote:

> Q vulgarizes. Q adds unnecessary words. Q substitutes the well-worn phrase for the Shakespearean phrase. Q misunderstands the meaning of lines. Q misunderstands and misinterprets the action. Q spoils fine touches of characterization. Q does not know who the speaker is and guesses. Q runs together two different speakers' lines. Q, in short, stands solidly in the way of Shakespeare.
>
> (10)[25]

If Q1 was put together by someone other than Shakespeare, who was the culprit? George Ian Duthie (1949[a]) doubted whether an audience member or members could have made even a short-hand transcription of the play while it was being performed (I). In a *King Lear* edition published that same year (1949[b]), Duthie favoured memorial reconstruction (21). Why writing fast would be more difficult that keeping the entire play in one's head was not explained. Undeterred, Alice Walker (1953) argued that Q1 was based upon the sometimes faulty memory of the boy actor who played Goneril, aided by the equally inaccurate boy actor who played Regan (48–49).

There was also some concern over who wrote or rewrote the Folio text. Madeleine Doran (1931) was certain that it had undergone "careful revision, *perhaps* by Shakespeare" (145; emphasis my own). R.H. Case (1931) suspected another writer was involved: "we have no evidence that from the time he [Shakespeare] handed over the play to his company, leaving them to deal with it at their pleasure, he took any further care of it" (XV). W.W. Greg (1940) compounded our fears by arguing that the manifestly bad First Quarto was somehow, in some way, used by the Folio compositors, probably because the Folio manuscript was in sections "damaged or illegible" (141). Thus, both Q1 and F1 were in varying degrees corrupted.

And let's not forget about that poorly-set Second Quarto. Although bearing the date 1608, the text was actually printed in 1619. Why the misdate? Fraud: in 1619, Thomas Pavier started to publish his own complete works of Shakespeare. When Heminge and Condell got wind of Pavier's project, they appealed to William Herbert—the Lord Chamberlain—who wrote to the Stationers' Company, demanding that "no playes that his Ma^{tyes} players do play shalbe printed wth out consent of som*me* of them" (Jackson 110). Pavier did abandon the project, but not before *King Lear* was already in press. Rather than destroy the extant copies, Pavier simply printed up a title-page with the wrong date (Somogyi XXX).

While the relationship between these three texts would undergo radical reassessment in the coming years—detailed in a later section—for now we might note the ongoing constraints: attempting to avoid the excesses of Pope, Theobald, Ireland, and Collier, nineteenth-century scholars had recommitted themselves to a detailed study of the Folio and the Quarto. By the late nineteenth century, scholars had identified two sets of Quartos and dismissed the second of the two as derivative. Then in the early twentieth century, Pollard, Greg and a variety of textual scholars proposed new theories that called into question the legitimacy of the Quarto. And while these experts conceded that the Quarto had been used for sections of the Folio, the underlying point was that if the Quarto was a reconstructed and inaccurate text which had been put together without Shakespeare's input or approval, then it could only be used with extreme caution by textual scholars.

This wary approach remained the gold standard, if not necessarily always the operative norm, during the "New Bibliography" (*ca.* 1900–50), until W.W. Greg, ironically one of the champions of that movement, proposed a return to eclectic editing. In 1946, when John Berryman began to edit a new conflation of *King Lear*, Greg wrote to him admitting that he was "no longer . . . prepared to maintain the position I took up . . . in 1940" (28 February 1946, Berryman 239). In fact, Greg offered that if he were to edit the play anew, he'd do so with an artistic freedom not seen since Collier's forgery of 1852:

> I should not myself hold too fast to F. We know that in some cases it took over errors from Q, & it very probably did so in many others. Where Q & F agree an editor has, in my opinion, considerable freedom of emendation, and to adhere to the reading whenever sense can be made of

> it is uncritical. Q + F has not *much* more authority than those passages for which Q is our only text.
>
> (6 January 1946, Berryman 234)

It was not until 1951 that Greg publicly came out against "the old fallacy of the 'best text' " (24) and "the tyranny of the copy-text" (26).

We shouldn't oversell Greg here. After all, he still believed that Q1 was a reported text, "whose accidental characteristics can be of *no authority whatever*" (1951: 35; italics my own). And Greg did not endorse a return to Collier's recklessness. Still, his reassessment eventually led to a revolutionary reevaluation of what if anything constituted a "good" or "bad" text. Indeed, Greg should be seen as the godfather of present editorial practice. In 1942, he argued that Q1, while inaccurate, still held valuable information concerning staging: "we find in the quarto all the usual stigmas of a reported text: [including] . . . actors' introduction of vocatives, expletives, or connective phrases, or through their lapsing into looser and more commonplace phraseology" (90).

For his part, Berryman was relieved by Greg's position, but it hardly made his task any easier. As he discovered in his readings of the play, even the Folio version, based on Shakespeare's final, recorded thoughts on the play, was a mess. For example, at 3.1.25–27, Kent sends a verbal message to Cordelia. Upon its delivery, Cordelia is supposed to tell the messenger the true identity of Caius. But this set-up is lost somewhere in the shuffle, since we never see the letter delivered. At 3.1.28–33, Kent and a Gentleman decide to search for Lear. The one who finds him first is supposed to immediately notify the other. Yet when Kent finds him (3.2.37), he seems to forget his mission. More problems: Lear leaves Goneril for Regan's house (1.4.31–33). For reasons that are unclear, he ends up at Gloucester's house. In 2.2, the Fool tells Kent that half his train has deserted the king (lines 237–50), yet Lear and his daughters do not seem to be aware of any reduction. At 3.4, Lear leaves Gloucester's house with only Kent, the Fool and no other followers. In the same scene, he meets Edgar and Gloucester. At 3.7.14, we learn that "some five- or six-and-thirty of his knights" are looking for him. How and why did Lear and his entourage give them the slip? What happened to Lear's Fool, who is last seen in 3.6? True, Lear tells us that he was hanged (5.3.281), but why, by whom, and when? If Lear is, as some critics argue, referring to Cordelia as his "poor fool," then we have no explanation for the Fool's sudden absence. Did he abandon Lear, was he killed in the war, or was he just forgotten by Shakespeare? In short, for any editor (or director) wanting a cohesive text, revisions of Shakespeare's revisions may be necessary.[26]

In a letter to his mother, Berryman half-jokingly offered his own solution to the play's textual knots, one in which Shakespeare himself forged his own play as part of a mischievous prank played upon posterity:

> My new theory is that Shakespeare, disloyal at heart and divided against himself, in a fit of amnesia "reported" his own play, sold the copy to the

> printer after carefully destroying all the distinctions in it between prose & verse, and is now merry with wicked joy peeping over Olympus at sorrowful scholars.
>
> (3 October 1952, 253)

Berryman worked on the textual complexities of *King Lear* for over twenty-five years. On 7 January 1972, he committed suicide.

Regency to modern: explorations of theme and character

Is King Lear *untheatrical?*

Despite his feeling that "It is almost blasphemy to say that a play of Shakespeare's is bad," the Victorian novelist William Makepeace Thackeray found *King Lear* in performance to be "a bore" (II: 292). He was not alone. Charles Lamb (1811) told us that *King Lear* "cannot be acted. The contemptible machinery by which they [the theatres] mimic the storm . . . is not more inadequate to represent the horrors of the real elements, than any actor can be to represent Lear" (IV: 205).

We might argue that Lamb and Thackeray lived in a mechanically clunky era. Today, flying witches look real enough with *Harry Potter*-esque CGI, but look at the *Wizard of Oz*. You can see the wires holding aloft the Wicked Witch of the West. Imagine how primitive things were a hundred or two hundred years ago! That being said, the core of their criticism—that Shakespeare's play is essentially untheatrical—cannot be so readily dismissed. After all, if *King Lear* is designedly theatrical, and people who go to the theater are bored by it, then that must mean that Shakespeare's so-called theatrical masterpiece is a failure.[27]

Certainly, few actors or critics have been entirely at ease with the restored, conflated text. Charles Kean's 1858 production of *King Lear* followed Macready's version, but in the last scene, with Lear dying, he and his actors declaimed the following:

Lear. Mine eyes are none o'the best. I'll tell you straight.
Kent. If fortune brag of two she lov'd and hated, one of them we behold!
Lear. Are you not Kent?
Kent. The same: your servant Kent.
Where is your servant Caius?
Lear. He's dead and rotten.
Kent. No, my good lord, I am the very man.
Lear. I'll see that straight.
Kent. That from your first step of difference and decay,
Have followed your sad steps.

Despite Charles Kean's declared interest in historical accuracy, this passage was *not* a full restoration of Shakespeare's text. In fact, he carefully cut two lines that were originally in both Shakespeare's Quarto and Folio versions—namely, Lear's remarks on Caius: "He's a good fellow, I can tell you that./He'll strike, and quickly too." The entire passage was also expunged in Charles Kean's 1858 and 1860 printed versions. Why the lines were cut remains unexplained, but we can guess that Kean did not want to remind his audience that Lear was, seemingly to the last, sanguinary, admiring of brutality.

Henry Irving (1892) thought less *King Lear* might satisfy his audiences more. He cut some 1,507 lines, or 46 percent of the text (Alan Hughes 118). A.C. Bradley (1904) liked the idea of expurgating whole chunks of the play, especially the Gloucester subplot. As he pointed out, when we read the play, we can ignore the duke of Gloucester's blinding, but in the theater, there is no escape from his plight:

> The blinding of Gloster on the stage has been condemned almost universally; and surely with justice, because the mere physical horror of such a spectacle would in the theatre be a sensation so violent as to overpower the purely tragic emotions, and therefore the spectacle would seem revolting or shocking. But it is otherwise in reading. . . . Thus the blinding of Gloster . . . is a blot upon *King Lear* as a stage-play.
>
> (203)[28]

And the problem of Cordelia's death remained. Bradley admitted that when he read the play "simply as a drama," he longed for a Tate-esque finale: "I find that my feelings call for this 'happy ending.' " Further, he believed that most playgoers shared in this guilty indulgence:

> What they wish, though they have not always the courage to confess it even to themselves, is that the deaths of Edmund, Goneril, Regan and Gloster should be followed by the escape of Lear and Cordelia from death, and that we should be allowed to imagine the poor old King passing quietly in the home of his beloved child to the end which cannot be far off.
>
> (204)

We can see his somewhat overly-paternal point. With women and children in attendance, the theater had a responsibility to provide an enriching and uplifting experience. As far as Bradley was concerned, it was only as a private, meditative experience, away from the staged violence of the playhouse, that the dark profundity of Shakespeare's play could or should be contemplated: "there is something in its very essence which is at war with the senses, and demands a purely imaginative realisation" (201). Yet, even when communing with the play in the privacy of his study, Bradley was sorely disenchanted. *King Lear*, he wrote, lacked a "dramatic clearness even when the play is read, and in the theatre not only refuses to reveal itself fully through the senses but seems to be almost in contradiction with their reports" (200–1).

Winifred M.T. Nowottny (1960) also wondered whether the play's dramatic and literary strengths matched its reputation:

> Perhaps one reason why *King Lear* has been mistaken for an unactable play is that it is so nearly an unreadable play: taken passage by passage, it is so flat and grey that . . . the style alone might lead one to suppose that what happens in *King Lear* happens in some realm of the imagination beyond ear and eye.
>
> (49)

Ivor Brown (1946) agreed that the play was a disappointment, but only because Shakespeare's recent directors and critics were too squeamish. *King Lear*, in his view, was not a philosophical thesis but a gory spectacle: "Let the hurricane whistle and roar, let Gloucester's eyes be gouged out like jellies, let mortals die like flies beneath the thumbs of wanton boys; Britain can take it" (3). Maynard Mack (1965) also argued that audiences, inured by two world wars and Auschwitz, had little to fear watching a Shakespeare play. Directors should explore the "play's jagged violence, its sadism, madness, and processional of deaths, its wild blends of levity and horror, selfishness and selflessness, and the anguish of its closing scene." However, rather than advise that we stage *King Lear* in an Auschwitz-like setting; he suggested a return to "the virtues of the bare unlocalized Elizabethan platform stage" (25).[29]

What followed, however, was not an attempt to unleash the full genius of the play. Rather, a variety of archivally-minded scholars used history to excuse *Lear*'s so-called flaws. John Reibetanz (1977), for example, linked the play's extreme characters, illogical actions, spatial and temporal discontinuities to theatrical conventions of the period, particularly the dramatic uses of fools and madmen (81–107). John L. Murphy (1984) despaired that without a firm grasp of Shakespeare's contemporaries and source materials, any attempt to understand *King Lear* was a "hopeless enterprise" (216).[30]

Other critics, unable to find coherence within the play itself, searched for it in Shakespeare's other tragedies. G. Wilson Knight (1930) traced the grotesqueries of *King Lear* to Shakespeare's first tragedy, *Titus Andronicus*, ironically a play which scholars also see as deeply flawed: "These ghoulish horrors, so popular in Elizabethan drama, and the very stuff of the *Lear* of Shakespeare's youth, *Titus Andronicus*, find an exquisitely appropriate place in the tragedy of Shakespeare's maturity which takes as its especial province this territory of the grotesque and the fantastic which is Lear's madness" (186). Kenneth Muir also charted a variety of *Lear–Titus* parallels (1952; rev. 1959; XLII). So did Maynard Mack (1965): in his view, *Lear* "is the only Shakespearean tragedy . . . in which a number of the characters are conceived in terms of unmitigated goodness and badness, and the only one, apart from the early *Titus*, where the plot is made up of incidents each more incredible" (5); "No other Shakespearean tragedy, not even *Titus*, contains more levels of raw ferocity, physical as well moral" (87). A.C. Bradley (1904), who thought little of *Titus*, found parallels in two other Shakespeare plays. Bradley maintained that Edmund was a great character because he was cut from a length of Iago's cloth: "The gulling of Gloster . . . recalls the gulling of Othello" (198). But, he added, *King Lear* was a failure because it was too much like *Timon of Athens*, a play he thought "weak, ill-constructed and confused" (199).

King Lear's (spiritual) suffering

Whether they read in relation or in isolation, the abovementioned critics agreed that the heart of the play was Lear's anguish, an idea that can be traced back as far as William Richardson (1784), who posited that the old king's sufferings made him a better person. Lear's:

> misfortunes correct his conduct; they route reflection, and lead him to that reformation which we approve. We see the commencement of this reformation, after he has been dismissed by Goneril, and meets with symptoms of disaffection in Regan. He who abandoned Cordelia with impetuous outrage, and banished Kent for offering an apology in her behalf; seeing his servant grossly maltreated, and his own arrival unwelcomed, has already sustained some chastisement: he does not express that ungoverned violence which his preceding conduct might lead us to expect.
>
> (80)

The German critic A.W. Schlegel (1811) also thought the play was principally about pain: "in *King Lear* the science of compassion is exhausted. The principal characters here are not those who act, but those who suffer" (411).

Fine, Lear suffers, but are critics right in thinking that Lear suffers into truth, and, if he does, what truth is that? According to A.C. Bradley (1904), Lear's misery leads to religious epiphany: "To us, perhaps, the knowledge that he is deceived [in thinking Cordelia alive] may bring a culmination of pain: but, if it brings *only* that, I believe we are false to Shakespeare, and it seems almost beyond question that any actor is false to the text who does not attempt to express, in Lear's last accents and gestures and look, an unbearable *joy*" (233–34). He even suggested that a better title for the play would be *The Redemption of King Lear* (228).

Bradley's sublime vision of the play was endorsed by a variety of religiously-oriented scholars. Thomas Carter (1905) traced Shakespeare's use of Scripture in the play (432–43). R.W. Chambers (1940) described *King Lear* as "a vast poem on the victory of [God's] true love" (49). Granville-Barker (1946) described King Lear's "spiritual death and resurrection" (I: 266). John M. Lothian (1949) posited that the play was centrally about Lear's growing knowledge of "things unseen and eternal" (96). M.C. Bradbrook (1952) was sure that the play "must have had a Biblical origin" (163). The Gnostic-minded Paul N. Siegel (1957) argued that Lear and Cordelia "become reunited in eternal bliss" (186). Likewise, Irving Ribner (1960) affirmed that the play soothingly offers a vision of "a harmonious system ruled by a benevolent God" (117). Barbara Everett (1960) had her doubts that *King Lear* was best read as a morality play but acknowledged that it was valid to see Lear as a kind of Christ figure: "The old Lear died in the storm. The new Lear is born in the scene in which he is reunited with Cordelia. His madness marked the end of the wilful, egotistical monarch. He is resurrected as a fully human being" (325). In short, he loses the world and gains his soul.

On a less upbeat note, George W. Williams (1951) argued that the storm scene borrowed heavily from biblical passages concerning the Last Judgment (67); Holloway (1961) thought that Lear's "special part is best understood by dwelling upon something which has seldom received much attention: the clear parallel . . . between the condition of Lear, and that in the Old Testament of Job" (85). Jan Kott (1964: 106); Ruth Nevo (1972: 260–61) and Steven Marx (2000: 59–78) also argued that Lear was a Job-like figure. Jonathan Bate (1989) inferred that King Lear, holding the body of his dead child, is an anti-Job, a man who curses heaven for its ill will (141).

Yet other critics contended that we were wrong to focus solely on Lear's redemption; Cordelia's sacrificial love is just as important. Thus, A.C. Bradley called her a "thing enskyed and sainted" (252); G. Wilson Knight (1930) added that Cordelia "represents the Principle of Love" (220); S.L. Bethell (1944) was sure that Cordelia "from first to last is associated with theological terminology and Christian symbol" (59); Geoffrey L. Bickersteth (1946) compared Lear's grief over the death of Cordelia to "some old master's painting of the crucifixion of a saint" (16). George Ian Duthie (1960) conceived her as a "Christ-like figure" (p.XX).

King Lear *and the crisis of faith*

While Bradley's Christian reading was adopted by a variety of critics, others questioned whether Lear's pain taught him anything. Derek Traversi (1938), although sympathetic to such pious readings, admitted that Lear's world is "consistently indifferent to the spiritual intuitions which suffering itself has brought so painfully to birth" (213). William Empson (1951) could not dispute the logic of Traversi's argument but objected that without a spoonful of Bradley the play "would become sickly" (154). John Holloway (1961) granted that Bradley's critique had no textual justification but could not bear to read *King Lear* otherwise: "It is better to see the play thus, than to regard its close as the embodiment only of cynicism, chaos and despair" (91). S.L. Goldberg (1974) offered faint hope: "we *are* left with a sense that something is 'affirmed' . . . [though] whatever the 'something' is, it may be impossible to define" (162).

Secular-minded critics had the courage to break with Bradley. George Orwell (1945) held that the play was incompatible with a belief in God (40). Maynard Mack (1960) questioned Lear's spiritual depth:

> the man before us . . . who sweeps Kent aside, rakes all who have helped him with grapeshot . . ., exults in the revenge he has exacted for Cordelia's death, and dies self-deceived in the thought she still lives—this man is one of the most profoundly human figures ever created in a play; but he is not, certainly, the Platonic ideal laid up in heaven, or in critical schemes, of regenerate man.
>
> (38)

Similarly, Robert Ornstein (1960) posited that King Lear is forced to face the "vanity of his metaphysical formulations" and the "vast inscrutable universe which surrounds him" (273). C.J. Sisson (1962) declared that the play destabilizes our theological and moral assurances, "a devastating thought" (90).[31] Northrop Frye (1967) also opined that the play deconstructs old religious certainties: "The thunder in *King Lear* is the tragically authentic voice of nature crumbling into chaos, though Lear himself half hopes that it is making a comment on his situation" (116).

The idea that the audience was on various levels aware of the crumbling of order both in the play and in their own lives was endorsed by William R. Elton (1966). In his view, the play was written for an audience in theological crisis (338). Paul J. Alpers (1962) removed God entirely from the conversation and, presumably, from the minds of Shakespeare's audience: "Cordelia is Cordelia. Surely there is no need to identify her with the abstraction Love in order to say that she is extraordinarily loving" (152). Thomas P. Roche Jr. (1981) agreed: "I can see no Biblical source to justify Shakespeare's changing the end of the Lear story"—remember, in the source Cordelia rules England, until she is overthrown and commits suicide—"it is Shakespeare and Shakespeare alone who creates the defeat of Lear" (151).

Over the last forty years or so, however, many Christian critics have reinvented the redemption of King Lear: Francis G. Schoff (1962) preferred a play of fire-and-brimstone: *Lear* is neither about politics nor ethics, but "the fearful power of evil, into whose grip, through some misstep or accident, even the wisest and noblest man may plunge himself and us" (172). Robert G. Hunter (1976) felt that Lear was somehow reenacting the Passion of the Christ (183). James P. Driscoll (1977) preached that *King Lear* "brings us as close as poetry can to seeing the faces of God" (186). René Fortin (1979) consoled us that the Lear's painful struggles were a brief but necessary condition, resolving in eternal salvation:

> The lesson that Lear learns in his suffering is that he has been morally callous; it is a lesson that he learns by becoming himself poor, naked, and—symbolically though his madness—blind. The suffering of Lear, seen against this background is at once punitive and propaedeutic, a necessary condition to his redemption.
>
> (119)

Fredson Bowers (1980: 19) and Mary Lascelles (1982: 55–65) resurrected still more Christian elements in their respective studies of the play's structure and source materials. James Stampfer (1982) despaired that "penance [for Lear and for mankind] is impossible, that the covenant, once broken, can never be re-established" (86); likewise, Paul Kahn (2000) compared Lear to Saint Paul, who preached the end of law and the reign of love; Marion D. Perret (1985) urged us to consider that the "gods [in the play] are just if not generous" (95). Stephen J. Lynch (1986) brightened with the belief that the play demonstrates aspects of Christian doctrine, namely patience, fortitude, humility and charity (173). William F. Martin (1987) declared that no matter what religion was at the core of the play, *King Lear* was centrally about "enlightenment, self-knowledge, and moral edification" (80). Ian J. Kirby (1989) will have no cloudy doubts darkening his beatific reading: King Lear, fully aware that he is going to heaven, "dies of joy" because "he will never need to say goodbye to his beloved daughter again" (157).

Lear's dotage

In a play apparently containing contrary meanings, there is surprisingly little disagreement on how an actor should play King Lear—a grumpy old man, sliding into senility. While we know nothing about the way Shakespeare's company dressed Burbage for the part, we do know that Tate's King Lear was a "little old white-haired man" with a spindlelegged gait, and "great shoes upon the little feet" (Wingate 69). Kemble (1788), while initially favoring athleticism, eventually played Lear as agèd and infirm (Wingate 85). Henry Irving's Lear (1892) was "a scared, eccentric, lunatic shamble" (Rosenberg 281). (See Figure 1.7.) Sir Laurence Olivier, after playing the role in 1983, wrote: "Lear is easy. He's like all of us, really: he's just a stupid old fart" (1986: 137).

The German critic A.W. Schlegel (1811) also preferred his Lear dotty and suggested that the king's senility and fragility were essential devices to gain and to maintain the audience's interest and pity:

> the old Lear, who out of a foolish tenderness has given away every thing, is driven out to the world a wandering beggar; the childish imbecility to which he was fast advancing changes into the wildest insanity . . . and all that now remains to him of life is the capability of loving and suffering beyond measure.
>
> (411)

The play's reception history suggests that young actors are just not convincing in the role. When seeing a twenty-six-year-old John Gielgud play Lear, the critic James Agate complained: "the pathos of this [Lear's] death-scene had less to do with Lear than with a talented young actor's comments upon an old man's passing" (196).[32] (See Figure 1.8.) Still, Agate recognized that all

Figure 1.7 Henry Irving as King Lear. By kind permission of the Shakespeare Birthplace Trust.

Figure 1.8 John Gielgud as King Lear (1950). Angus McBean. By kind permission of the Shakespeare Birthplace Trust.

great actors, no matter what their age, have been drawn to the role, despite its hazards: "There is a sense in which a very young player Shakespeareanly bent is not ill-advised to tackle Lear; nobody is to be blamed for not climbing Everest, whereas he is a fool who falls off Skiddaw" (199).

While we cannot dispute that older actors have made the most successful Lears, emphasis on his age alone does tend to reduce the play to Lear's disordered search for a good nursing home. Keep that thought in mind when reading Charles Lamb's critique of the play:

> to see Lear acted,—to see an old man tottering about the stage with a walking-stick, turned out of doors by his daughters in a rainy night, has nothing in it but what is painful and disgusting. We want to take him into shelter and relieve him. That is all the feeling which the acting of Lear has ever produced in me. . . . On the stage we see nothing but corporal infirmities and weakness, the impotence of rage.
>
> (IV: 205)

Later in this study we will be looking at alternative responses to the play in some detail. We might here note that Lamb's interpretation has had a long shelf life and has even affected adaptations of the play.

Defending Edmund

If there has been surprisingly little diversity concerning the casting, costuming and playing of Lear, the same cannot be said of Edmund. We might have expected his having always been played or read as calculating, charismatic, and villainous. But some of Shakespeare's greatest critics have actually rallied to his defense. Wrote Coleridge (1810–11) sympathetically:

> From the first drawing up of the curtain he [Edmund] has stood before us in the united strength and beauty of earliest manhood. . . . But alas! in his own presence his own father takes shame to himself for the frank avowal that he is his father—has "blushed so often to acknowledge him that he is now braz'd to it". He hears . . . the circumstances of his birth spoken of with a most degrading and licentious levity—[his mother] described as a wanton by her own paramour. . . . Need it be said how heavy an aggravation the stain of bastardy must have been, were it only that the younger brother was liable to hear his own dishonor and his mother's infamy related by his father with an excusing shrug of the shoulders, and in a tone betwixt waggery and shame.
>
> (ed.1959: 179–80)

We might add that there is something rather childlike about Edmund. As the play opens, he is, as Coleridge noted, subjected to his father's narrative concerning his whorish mother. He is told that he is the offspring of lust, not love. And yet, as he dies, his greatest joy is that he can claim that "Edmund was beloved" (24.236). "*That* is what he wanted to know, and he can acknowledge it now, when it cannot be returned, now that its claim is dead" (Cavell, 1987: 70). Indeed, it is directly after the self-realization that he was loved that Edmund decides to save Cordelia:

> I pant for life. Some good I mean to do,
> Despite of my own nature. Quickly send,
> Be brief in it, to th' castle; for my writ
> Is on the life of Lear and on Cordelia.
>
> (24.239–42)[33]

If Edmund was a villain because his daddy didn't hug him enough, A.C. Bradley (1904) tried a different approach. Edmund was graceful, even magnanimous, in defeat:

> with no more ill-will to anyone than good-will, it is natural that, when he has lost the game, he should accept his failure without showing personal animosity. But he does more. He admits the truth of Edgar's words about the justice of the gods, and applies them to his own case. . . . He shows too that he is not destitute of feeling; for he is touched by the story of his

> father's death, and at last "pants for life" in the effort to do "some good" by saving Lear and Cordelia.
>
> (241)

According to Richard Matthews (1975) Edmund is actually like Lear, someone who suffers and creates suffering, but, to his credit, ends his life newly-frocked in saintly regret and compassion: "It might be objected that such a learning process as Edmund's (snatching grace from the jaws of lust) is utterly repugnant; but surely Lear's journey to grace is no less so" (29). Edwin Muir (1947) saw Edmund as an idolater, faithful in his own way to the "gods of the new age": interest and force (24). Implying that Edmund was impish rather than evil, Harold Skulsky (1966) proposed that Edmund worshipped "moral randomness" (9). R.C. Sharma (1975) also had a soft-spot for this villain: "Edmund has been callous, ruthless, utterly unscrupulous and even unnatural . . . but he is not altogether wanting in some vestiges of nobility" (272).

Many of the most sympathetic readings of Edmund are somehow connected to our respect for self-made men, including Shakespeare. It was a time when a monarch ruled the country, but it was also a time of free enterprise, when a man born in one trade might rise to great success in another— Shakespeare, we recall, was the son of a glover in a provincial town, yet ended up an actor and playwright who, along with his business partners, owned a theater company in London and rubbed, if only at command performances, shoulders with royalty. Thus, John F. Danby (1949) tried to persuade readers that Edmund was a positive role model, a natural-born capitalist, someone who exemplified the "impulse to acquire, to provide for one's security, to extend one's prestige" (41). The idea was later championed by Arnold Kettle (1988), who heralded Edmund as "the new man of the incipient bourgeois revolution, the private enterprise man, the man who thinks he has got to be a phoenix, the individualist go-getter . . ." (72).

In what is perhaps the oddest defense of Edmund, Janet Adelman (1992) asks, "What literally kills Cordelia?" (127). No, it's not Edmund's orders or even the guard's noose that finishes off Cordelia. In her view, Lear himself is somehow behind the fatal complot, for having been emasculated by his daughters, reduced to choking tears by Goneril, Cordelia's "own death by choking enacts a talion punishment, the terrible recuperation of male individuality from the threat of the overwhelming mother within" (128). Going still further, Adelman begins not only to treat Cordelia and Lear as if they were flesh and blood, but introduces Shakespeare not as a author but as Lear's co-conspirator: "Shakespeare is complicit in Lear's fantasy, rewarding him for his suffering by remaking for him the Cordelia he had wanted all along; Shakespeare too requires the sacrifice of her autonomy. This is a very painful recognition for a feminist critic, for any reader who reads as a daughter" (125).

Edgar

According to A.C. Bradley (1904), of all the characters in the play "Edgar excites the least enthusiasm" (244). Then again, A.C. Bradley thought that the entire Edmund-versus-Edgar plot was a needless distraction, a plot that "fails to excite a tithe of . . . interest" (206). We have seen such arguments before; in particular, Garrick's concern that restoring the Fool would "counteract the agonies of Lear." Northrop Frye (1967) marginalized Edgar's role as inconsequential. His function in the play was merely to hold Lear's hand when necessary:

> No one can study *King Lear* without wondering why Edgar puts on this Poor Tom act for Lear's benefit. He has to go into disguise, of course, but none of Cornwall's spies are likely to be listening, and elsewhere on the heath open conspiracy is discussed under the storm's cover. . . . Poor Tom is the providence or guardian spirit that shows Lear the end of his journey to find his own nature.
>
> (106)

If so, Frye must have agreed with Bradley that everything Edgar did subsequently, including his leading Gloucester to the cliffs and his defeat of Edmund, was just so much distractive filler. Fortunately, poor Edgar was saved from further critical contempt by a variety of critics, among them, Leonard Tennenhouse (1986), who argued that the duel between Edgar and Edmund highlighted "the dissymmetrical power relations between bastard and legitimate son" (141). William C. Carroll (1987) advanced the theory that Edgar's transformations from heir to beggar to restored heir, and perhaps, finally, to king, point to his being vital to Shakespeare's overall design.

Goneril and Regan

William Hazlitt (1817) passed over Goneril and Regan in one breath. They were "so thoroughly hateful that we do not even like to repeat their names" (IV: 258). Edwin Muir (1947) dismissively described them as seeming to "come from nowhere and to be on the road to nowhere" (17). Helen Gardner (1967) thought of them as sour and strident: "They sound like the unsympathetic matrons of an old people's home"(13). Likewise, Terry Eagleton (1986) lumped them together: the sisters were in his view "fundamentally passive in this sense, unable after their initial dissembling to falsify what they are" (80). They're ambitious and bad, the equivalent of Cinderella's step-sisters, and that's all we need to know. Or is it?

A.C. Bradley (1904) argued that Goneril was the worse of the two evil sisters:

> Regan did not commit adultery, did not murder her sister or plot to

> murder her husband, did not join her name with Edmund's on the order for the deaths of Cordelia and Lear, and in other respects failed to take quite so active a part as Goneril in atrocious wickedness.
>
> (239)

But Algernon Charles Swinburne (1909) played no favorites, describing Regan as a "Gadarean sow," "Beast," and "she-devil" (9–10). Likewise championing Goneril, Peter Brook (1968) tried to persuade us that, out of context, her lines read as both elegant and sympathetic: "her villainy and Lear's martyrdom are neither as crude nor as simplified as they might appear" (14).

The least compassionate rendering of these sisters is surely found in Orson Welles' film (dir. Peter Brook, CBS TV, 1953), which cut Goneril and Regan's conference concerning Lear's growing unruliness, and their own need to defend themselves. The result was that their actions seemed far more malicious, if only because they seemed less rational. In sororal defense, Carol Rutter (1997) offered a new approach: it was not that Goneril and Regan were so bad and Cordelia so good, but that we had been misled by traditionalists to read the play through Lear's eyes. She proposed an alternative in which all three daughters work to sustain their father's mental acuity: Cordelia rejects her father's attempts to "child-change himself back to infancy" (175);[34] "Cordelia brutally exposes the myth; it is left to Goneril and Regan to root it [Lear's desired infantilism] up with boar fangs" (176).

Incest?

This interpretation might shock many readers, but the fear that Lear had committed or wished to commit incest can be traced back to Tate's revision of the play. Tate, we recall, was concerned with the logic of "Cordelia's Indifference, and her Father's Passion" (II). Edgar's love of Cordeila was evidently not enough to protect our heroine. Tate had to make sure that Lear, even in prison, was never alone with his daughter. Note the addition of Kent:

Lear. No, no, they shall not see us weep,
We'll see them rot first,—Guards lead away to Prison;
Come, *Kent*, *Cordelia* come,
We Two will sit alone, like Birds i'th Cage,
When Thou dost ask me Blessing, I'll kneel down
And ask of Thee Forgiveness; Thus we'll live,
And Pray, and Sing, and tell old Tales, and Laugh
At gilded Butter-flies, hear Sycophants
Talk of Court News, and we'll talk with them too,
Who loses, and who wins, who's in, who's out,

And take upon us the Mystery of Things
As if we were Heav'ns Spies.
(Act V, p. 58)

Even with Kent chaperoning, Tate's Lear still maintains that he is entitled to all of Cordelia's love.

Tate's casting of the husband-and-wife tandem Betterton and Saunderson as Lear and Cordelia may have further fueled the fear that there was something sexual between these two characters. But even after Betterton and Saunderson had retired from the stage, indeed, even after Tate's play had been replaced by Shakespeare's, critics continued to worry about Lear's perverted impulses. J.W. Ashton (1932) grieved that Lear "covets the love of his daughters, is filled with self-love and perhaps most fatal of all, has too much curiosity" (532). While not discussing Lear's relationship with Cordelia specifically, William Empson (1951) grumbled that Lear's interest in sex was "ridiculous and rather sordid" in so elderly a man (138). C.L. Barber (1978) allied himself with this school of dirty thoughts: Regan and Goneril "pretend to meet Lear's demand for love in all but incestuous terms" (118). More recently, Stephen Greenblatt (1990) alerted us that Lear "wants something" from Cordelia and her sisters "more than formal obedience, something akin to the odd blend of submission to authority and almost erotic longing" (82). Jeffrey Stern (1990) added that in Lear's mind, Cordelia serves the dutiful role, if not physical function, of wife and mother (308). Harry Berger Jr. (1997) also reads the relationship as incestuous in nature: "Even as she distinguishes the role of daughter from that of wife, she slips into the marriage formula. She acknowledges the father's right to compete with the husband but feels it oppressive and strains away from it" (43). In Maureen Quilligan's *Incest and Agency in Elizabeth's England* (2005), she speculates that Cordelia could not express her "love" for her father, because he demands a transgressive blurring of boundaries between father and husband (2, see also 232–35). Thus, there is no need to blame Cordelia, or even Goneril and Regan, for Lear's heartache. To excuse the daughters, we need only think of King Lear as depraved.

That being said, seeing the play as a struggle of gender does allow for a variety of new insights and counter-readings. Leonard Tennenhouse (1986) suggested that *King Lear* reflected James' anxieties concerning masculinity and authority (141–42).To Coppélia Kahn (1986), the play is about Lear's acceptance of his own femininity: Lear's "progress" culminates with his acknowledgement "of the woman in himself," that is, his ability to be in touch with his emotions (46).[35] Taking a more political stance, Kathleen McLuskie (1985) argued that Cordelia was a traitor to her gender: "Cordelia's saving love, so much admired by critics, works in the action less as a redemption for womankind than as an example of patriarchy restored" (98–99).

Doubling Cordelia and the Fool

We have already seen that many critics and adaptors have felt that Cordelia should have a significant role in the play. But in Shakespeare's version, she is a minor character who only appears in four scenes and speaks scarcely more than a hundred lines. Tate added love-scenes to bolster her role. While this was a workable solution, in the last hundred years or so others have dismissed Tate's bulking of Cordelia as unnecessary. Alois Brandl (1894) argued that, given the brevity of Cordelia's role in Shakespeare's play, it was logical to assume that whoever played Lear's youngest daughter also played another part in the play. In essence, the audience would have understood that Cordelia's presence was somehow retained whenever the boy playing Cordelia reappeared in another role. Thus, Shakespeare would not have just doubled one part with another, but would have found meaningful or thought-provoking doublings. Brandl therefore suggested that Shakespeare had written Cordelia and the Fool with a view to having one actor play both parts (Stroup 127).

While not endorsing the doubling outright, A.C. Bradley (1904) noted a "confused association in Lear's mind between his child and the Fool" (251). Thomas B. Stroup (1961) argued that such associations made the pairing of these parts "all the more probable" (132). Gamini Salgādo (1984) also endorsed, albeit with some hesitation, the doubling and suggested a "special relationship between the two characters" (65); Peter Ackroyd (2005), accepted the theory as a straightforward fact: "in doubling he [Shakespeare] could also create some wonderful effects. Thus the doubling of Cordelia and the Fool in *King Lear*—the Fool mysteriously disappears when Lear's good and faithful daughter reappears in the plot—allowed for deeper ironies beyond the reach of words" (265).

Fact is not theory, however, and, as theory goes, this one has its issues. To begin with, scholars generally assume that an adult, Robert Armin—the accomplished comic actor who had written time and again on or about fools—was cast as the Fool. David Wiles (1987) pointed out that Armin did have some experience in doubling parts (140). And he was dwarfish. Perhaps he was no taller than a boy actor? If so, he might have played Cordelia and the Fool. However, since women's roles were played by boys, and Armin was 42 years old at the time the play premièred, it's difficult to accept that he played Lear's youngest daughter.

Alright then, if Cordelia and the Fool were played by the same boy actor, perhaps Armin played some other part? Martin Holmes (1978) speculated that Armin had outgrown comedy and wanted to try more serious roles (185). William A. Ringler Jr. (1981) promptly cast him as Edgar (190–93). Again, there are difficulties: Armin continued to write comedic material, including *The History of the two Maids of More-clarke* (1609) and *The Italian Taylor* (1609); why would performing comedy bore him when writing it did not? Further, even if Armin had wanted to expand his range of parts, there is no reason to assume that the company would have complied with his request. After all, he was hired to play fools. Given these issues, Stephen Booth (1978) dismissed the proposed doubling as mere "student ingenuity" (104);[36] Ralph Berry (1993), an expert on Shakespearean direction and staging, called it sheer "academic fancy, based on the premise that because doubling is technically possible it is worth doing" (17).

The Fool

Of course, we can discuss the Fool and his role without necessarily linking the part to Cordelia. Most critics agree that the Fool functions as Lear's touchstone. With Kent and Cordelia banished for speaking their minds, the king is surrounded by liars (his remaining daughters) and sycophants (his attending knights). Even Caius (the banished Kent in disguise) refuses to criticize him. Only the Fool is willing to tell Lear the unflattering truth. Shakespeare liked this aspect of the Fool so much that he took care to amplify it in his rewrite, giving the Fool the wisdom to say what Lear himself originally suggested only in jest:

History of King Lear (1605–6)	*Tragedy of King Lear* (*ca.* 1609)
Lear. Doth any here know me? Why this is not Lear. Doth Lear walk thus, speak thus? Where are his eyes? . . . Who is it that can tell me who I am? Lear's shadow? I would learn that . . . (Scene 4.220–21, 225–26)	*Lear.* Does any here know me? This is not Lear. Does Lear walk thus, speak thus? Where are his eyes? . . . Who is it can tell me who I am? *Fool.* Lear's Shadow. (1.4.208–9, 212–13)

Given the Fool's importance, especially in Shakespeare's rewrite, it is odd that he disappears after the heath scene. G. Wilson Knight (1930) turned to philosophy to solve the problem: the Fool, even when he is not on stage, is never forgotten, since, from the start, the play is filled with exactly "the stuff of which humour is made" (179); the audience walks a "tight-rope of . . . pity over the depths of bathos and absurdity" (185). Even the king, he notes, displays "foolish misjudgment" (177) and seems, to his eldest daughters and to us, "a cruelly ridiculous figure" (177).

Paul A. Jorgensen (1967) agreed that there was no need to account for the Fool's disappearance. True, "the Fool is closely associated in Lear's mind with the lost Cordelia" but "if we accept the interpretation of some critics, that the Fool is one aspect of Lear's own nature, the quest for the Fool is really a quest for a part of himself; and the Fool disappears from the play once that part has been found" (111). While not dealing with the Fool's vanishing, Kathleen McLuskie (1985) approved in principle that the Fool was more a symbol than a character: "In an important sense the Fool is less an *alter ego* for Lear than for his daughters: like them he reminds Lear and the audience of the material basis for the change in the balance of power" (105).

But these ideas are difficult to transmit theatrically. In his rehearsals for the 1982 performance of the Fool for the Royal Shakespeare Company, actor Anthony Sher hit upon one possible exit strategy. While having one of his rants, Lear begins to stab a pillow; as his fit becomes homicidal, he accidentally kills his Fool (163). Sher's solution works on stage, but there is no textual evidence in support. The same may be said of James L. Calderwood's explanation (1986) that "the Fool cannot endure" Lear's insanity and so "escapes madness by disappearing" (13).

Gloucester

We recall that Samuel Johnson was horrified by Gloucester's blinding, a moment he thought unworthy of the stage. Going still further, we might ask how important Gloucester is to the play? He appears, for the most part, in a subplot. Would *Lear* be a better play without him? A.W. Schlegel (1811) considered the character Gloucester to be a critical component in the play:

> And with what ingenuity and skill are the two main parts of the composition dovetailed into one another! The pity felt by Gloster for the fate of Lear becomes the means which enables his son Edmund to effect his complete destruction. . . . The two cases resemble each other in the main: an infatuated father is blind towards his well-disposed child, and the unnatural children, whom he prefers, requite him by the ruin of all his happiness.
>
> (412)

A.C. Bradley (1904) agreed that the subplot "repeats the theme of the main story" (211); "His [Gloucester's] sufferings, like Lear's, are partially traceable to his own extreme folly and injustice" (235).[37] However, whereas Schlegel found proof of Shakespeare's genius, Bradley was unimpressed with what he considered slipshod work. Gloucester's character was, in his estimation, neither "very interesting [n]or very distinct." He is a kind of nothing. We have no sense of him as a person: "He often gives one the impression of being wanted mainly to fill a place in the scheme of the play" (235).

The Russian novelist Leo Tolstoy (1906) also found the Gloucester subplot to be contrived:

> The fact that Lear's relations with his daughters are the same as those of Gloucester with his sons, makes one feel yet more strongly that in both

> cases the relations are quite arbitrary and do not flow from the characters nor the natural course of events.
>
> (35)

But Robert B. Heilman (1948) responded by arguing that Shakespeare—not Tolstoy—knows best:

> the master, being the master, has not erred in his duplicity of plot; so Gloucester's family situation and experiences, we are told, heighten the effect produced by Lear's family situation and experiences; and again, the two plots come together in the dealings between Lear and Gloucester, and between Edmund and the two sisters who desire him; and again, in these interrelationships inhere some remarkable ironies which otherwise the play would be without.
>
> (169)

Mark Van Doren (1939) maintained that the Gloucester-plot was essential: "woe piled on woe, music answering to music" (205). Irving Ribner (1960) suggested that Gloucester was a Lear for the middle class: "The double action offers us another hero who is Lear on a slightly lower social plane, and his career by paralleling closely that of Lear reinforces the universal validity of the play's theme" (117). Stephen Greenblatt (1990) also noted their correspondences, though not their comparative stations in life: Lear is as blind to the intentions of his daughters as Gloucester is to the perfidy of Edmund (85). Stanley Cavell (1987) did not dwell so much on the correspondences of blinding as on Lear's sudden insight that he, like Gloucester, must bear the responsibility for his own actions and their unhappy consequences. In seeing Gloucester:

> Lear is confronted here with the direct consequences of his conduct, of his covering up in rage and madness, of his having given up authority and kingdom for the wrong motives, to the wrong people; and he is for the first time confronting himself. . . . Gloucester has by now become not just a figure "parallel" to Lear, but Lear's double.
>
> (52)

Yet other critics read Gloucester and Lear in counterpoint: William R. Elton (1966) suggested that Gloucester dies happy, knowing that Edgar is safe, whereas Lear dies without redemption, "only suffering, tears, pity, and loss—*and* illusion" (334). Howard Felperin (1977) argued that Gloucester embraces pious and unproblematic Christian virtues, whereas the old king comes to realize that the world is more complex than the hierarchy of God–angels–king–adoring servants (94–96); according to Jonathan Goldberg (1988), Gloucester finds peace in the grave, whereas Lear remains "deprived of that ultimate rest" (246). David Hare, who directed the play for a National

Theatre production (1986, starring Anthony Hopkins), assured us that "Gloucester's story has an urgency which, even if it doesn't quite match, certainly echoes Lear's. This makes a special difficulty, as there are no 'unimportant' scenes. There is no relaxation. Every bit fits."

Oswald

Gordon Craig (1930) recalled that when he played Oswald, he "wondered what the devil it was all about." Reading the name over and over in the *dramatis personae* list ("Oswald—a Steward—hmm"), his mind "went at once towards thoughts of Atlantic liners," but he found this of little help (109). Finally Granville-Barker suggested that he play the role as if Malvolio from *Twelfth Night* had walked into Lear's world. "With *that* in my pocket I knew what to do, and didn't hesitate" (Craig 110). But few others have seen Oswald as a Puritan stick-in-the mud. H.T. Hall (1879) described him as a "faithful servitor" (29), and Phyllis Rackin (1970) argued that Oswald was the last and most obvious vestige of the feudal order: "he is completely the creature of the social and political hierarchy" (31).

Hugh MacLean (1960) dismissed Oswald as a fop who was created to provide "slapstick" for Kent (54). Nearly forty years later, Judy Kronenfeld (1998) argued that it is Oswald, just as much as Edmund, who represents the new world of no-holds barred capitalism, and Kent, not Edgar, who represents the traditional world of aristocratic decorum and self-control (239–43). This latter argument is worth considering, given that both Edmund and Oswald were probably derived from the character of the avaricious Messenger in the anonymous *King Leir*. But, given the dates of her criticism, it seems more likely that Kronenfeld was directly influenced by Orson Welles' film (dir. Peter Brook, CBS TV, 1953), which cut Edmund altogether. Rather, it is Oswald who plays the cheat and betrays Gloucester, plans Cordelia's murder, and offers himself to both Regan and Goneril.

Cornwall and Albany

At first glance, these characters seem nearly as interchangeable as their wives. According to Harry Berger Jr. (1997), Lear sees himself threatened initially by both Albany and Cornwall: "Lear assumes that both dukes are anticipating an unequal distribution and waiting to start something—against each other or against him" (28). His plan is "to use, deceive, and humiliate Goneril and Regan in order to accentuate Cordelia's triumph and his partiality" (31). There is some irony here. In an attempt to sustain the peace, Lear purposefully planned to cut up his land unfairly and unequally. It is only his equal division of the kingdom that causes the potential for war. While in the short term his division caused the war he sought to avoid, by the play's close, the king gets what he wanted: three kingdoms whose rulers are unlikely to make war.

When dealing with Cornwall and Albany, one aspect or parallel worth bearing in mind is that James I, for whom the play was performed in December of 1606, had two sons, the dukes of Albany and Cornwall. According to Victor Kiernan (1996), Shakespeare, always eager to please his capricious patrons, may have added an Albany and a Cornwall as a compliment to the royal family (104–5). But this reader remains unconvinced. It's true that Albany gets more lines in the Quarto version, which was performed before the king. But Shakespeare's Albany is a hen-pecked cuckold. Worse yet, Cornwall is a sociopath, or, as Margot Heinemann (1992) describes him, a "Nazi-type brute" (80). And his own servants think he is an immoral despot:

Second Servant. I'll never care what wickedness I do
If this man come to good.
(Scene 14.97–98)

It's difficult to believe that Shakespeare wanted to suggest that James' sons were in any way like these characters, but that hasn't stopped the argument from gaining ground. Thus, Hugh Grady (1996) matter-of-factly accepted that "Albany's slow conversion . . . [is] a compliment to King James" (177), while Alexander Leggatt (1988) goes so far as to call Albany the "moral spokesman of the Quarto" (54). Andrew Gurr (2004) finds in the use of the names of Albany and Gloucester a celebration of James's bestowing these dukedoms on his sons (182–84).

The Politics of King Lear *declassified*

Reading between the lines of *King Lear*, Algernon Charles Swinburne (1880) glimpsed Shakespeare's politics:

> surely as the author of *Julius Caesar* has approved himself in the best and highest sense of the word at least potentially a republican, so surely has the author of *King Lear* avowed himself in the only good and rational sense of the words a spiritual if not political democrat and socialist.
> (175)

Charles Creighton (1913) suggested that Shakespeare, unable to write about the Henry VIII's Court, used code names: Burgundy was Erasmus, Kent was Sir Thomas More, the Fool was John Skelton, and Oswald was Cardinal Wolsey (8). Since Shakespeare went on to write a play on Henry VIII, it's difficult to see why he would have resorted to such maneuvering. To J.W. Draper (1937), *King Lear* was a dramatic "series of studies in statecraft" designed to educate James I, who had claimed the English throne in 1603 (184). Again, since James had been the king of Scotland since 1567, it's hard to believe that he needed the pointers.[38]

Emerging from World War II with England's political, military and cultural future very much in doubt, George Orwell (1945) read *King Lear* and concluded that Shakespeare was not, as Swinburne had hoped, a socialist:

> It is clear, for instance, that he [Shakespeare] liked to stand well with the rich and powerful, and was capable of flattering them in the most servile way. He is also noticeably cautious, not to say cowardly, in his manner of uttering unpopular opinions.
>
> (48)[39]

John Danby (1949) thought that Shakespeare's good characters agreed with the theological and moral order of a John Hooker or a Francis Bacon, while his bad characters were cut-throat pragmatists, not unlike Niccolo Machiavelli (31–36).

D.G. James (1949) also thought that his close reading of *King Lear* had led him to an understanding of Shakespeare himself:

> Lear was contained in the Shakespeare who gave him birth; his passions, and the passions of the other characters, were felt and realized in Shakespeare who suffered in them. Therefore, the idea of *King Lear* we have is also the life of Shakespeare as he was then; and in contemplating the play we become what we behold; as he was what he created.
>
> (149)

In 1949, the Freudian therapist Ella Freeman Sharpe argued that the play was Shakespeare's attempt to dramatize "an old conflict, a conflict not of age but of childhood and infancy re-activated in the poet's maturity. . . . The poet in childhood . . . felt as King Lear feels" (218–19).

It seems rather obvious that these (often diametrical) reactions to the play tell us more about the critics and their respective eras than they do about Shakespeare's soul, psyche or voting record. We recognize that *King Lear* is by Shakespeare, to be sure, but it is also the product of source materials, actors, market forces, political, spiritual and social movements, etc. Graham Holderness (1988) explains: "When we deconstruct the Shakespeare myth what we discover is not a universal individual genius . . . but a collaborative cultural process" (13). Here, we might invoke Judy Kronenfeld's warning that "to assume that *Lear* is about the transition from the feudal to the bourgeois, the moral to the market economy, the patriarchal to the materialist" is to impose a retrospective structure of understanding—the clarity of hindsight—on to a much more complicated, nuanced—or simply confused—situation. "When we dichotomize hierarchical/feudal versus individualist," we invent "categories" arguably inconsistent with the "implicit perceptions and feelings of Jacobeans" (1998: 97).

Not surprisingly, our view of *King Lear* has continued to reflect our ever-shifting interests. R.A. Foakes linked an interest in *King Lear* during the

1960s to "the final decline of Britain as an imperialist and economic power, with the dissolution of the empire, much of it [like Lear's power] given away in a withdrawal from or a division of the many colonies once dominated from London" (1993: 213). In the 1980s—just as then-President Regan was calling the Soviet Union an "evil empire"—many academics in America were seeing capitalism, not communism, as the source of the world's injustice. Reflective of such views, Arnold Kettle (1988), read the play as a meditation on the evils of capitalism:

> On the one hand are those who accept the old order (Lear, Gloucester, Kent, Albany) which has to be seen as, broadly speaking, the feudal order; on the other hand are the new people, the individualists (Goneril, Regan, Edmund, Cornwall) who have the characteristic outlook of the bourgeoisie.
>
> (70)

We've seen this argument before. Remember John F. Danby's idea that Edmund was a proto-capitalist? This is the same thesis but blackened and broad-brushed to include the middle class and, presumably, Shakespeare himself, who, like Edmund, reinvented himself and rubbed shoulders, albeit only on special occasions, with royalty.

McLuskie (1985) thought of King Lear not as a feudalist but as a property-rights attorney. She pointed out that that King Lear's agreement states that he is to retain the title and trappings of majesty, all to be paid for by his daughters, but they, corrupt accountants, renege on their arranged "mathematical computation" (105). Since they have broken the terms of their agreement, the king is quite right to exercise his legal loophole to reclaim the kingdom. Leonard Tennenhouse (1986) likewise read the play in terms of property values and the competitive virtues of the free market:

> it [property] can be divided, willed, used as surety for a loan, and—as the play takes pains to demonstrate—treated as dowry to be divided equally among the three daughters for their jointure. As property, it could be subjected to laws governing the distribution of property or even be seized by force. . . . [T]rue power displays itself in the effective exercise of physical force through competition and is subsequently ratified by an outpouring of popular support for the displaced king.
>
> (133)

With the Soviet Union presiding over its own dismantling—it was completely mothballed in 1991—Kiernan Ryan (1989) stated that conservatives often read the play, if they read it at all, as a melancholy farewell to "the accustomed ordering of things" (46). Stephen Greenblatt (1990) dwelled on the fact that "Lear's claim to unbounded power" comes "even at the moment of his abdication" (97). From a cultural perspective, we might say that these latter critics, whether pro-Marxist or capitalist, used *King Lear* to voice their own apprehensions concerning the abrupt end of the Cold War and the resulting imbalance in East–West relations.

Postmodernist revisions

Textual revolutions

By the early 1980s, textual scholars were of three minds concerning *Lear*. There were the traditionalists, such as P.W.K. Stone (1980), who continued to believe that the First Quarto was bad. "Questionable readings," he wrote, "meet the eye on nearly every page, many of them obviously wrong, and some of them egregious nonsense" (2). Since the Second Quarto is considered by traditionalists to be an even worse knock-off of the First Quarto, it too could be dispensed with.

Other scholars continued to support the Pope–Theobald composite text. This group, now reconstituted around Greg's call for more eclectic texts, included Arden editor Kenneth Muir (1952; rev. 1959), who felt free to use any passage he felt was "palpably superior" (XIX). However, Muir did not believe that there was a single lost archetype—Shakespeare's perfect manuscript—behind the Folio and First Quarto. Signaling the beginning—albeit the *very beginning*—of the end of the "good" and "bad" text theory, Muir looked at the quarto not as a "bad" version but as an important snap-shot in the play's development. For example, Muir argued that the trial scene in the Quarto had been cut from the finished version of the Folio because the play was running long; alternatively, Shakespeare may have made the cut because the original audiences found the scene to be funny (XLVIII).[40] We recall that Tate feared that Shakespeare's ending would be met with laughter, and that Garrick and, later, Colman had each refused to restore the Fool for the same reason. Now that same logic was being used to suggest that a scene was "bad" at least in its dramaturgy, if not its authorship.

Finally, there were some, like Michael Warren (1978) and Steven Urkowitz (1980), who believed that there were two legitimate versions of the play: (I) the Quarto, which was based on an early text and (II) the Folio, which was a revision of the Quarto. The conflated Pope–Theobald text was dismissed as a "modern version" constructed on the unsound theory of a single "lost original" (Urkowitz 3). The idea of Shakespeare as reviser was further explored in a book of landmark essays, *The Division of the Kingdoms: Shakespeare's Two Versions of King Lear* (Taylor and Warren: 1983), which, as the title suggests, argued that the Quarto and Folio were so dissimilar as to constitute virtually different plays.

When Warren first presented his idea in 1975, his work was received with scholarly skepticism. *PMLA*, a leading academic journal, rejected it; a report by one of the journal's readers concluded that "This paper ought not to be published anywhere" (Holderness, 1995: 16), not because it was a badly argued paper but because its implications were so far-reaching. Warren's idea, however, was not new. Despite his endorsement of Pope's conflated text, Johnson (1765) believed that the Folio was Shakespeare's final, though somewhat hasty, revision (Furness, III.vi.100n). Johnson further believed that some Quarto lines had been cut from the Folio due to censorship (Furness, 1880: I.iv.135–50n, III.vi.100n). And, as we have seen, Madeleine Doran (1931) and M.R. Ridley (1935: X) had already argued that the Quarto was Shakespeare's authentic first draft; Kenneth Muir (1952, rev.1959) also believed that the Quarto represented an early performance text, and the Folio a more mature version.

Nonetheless, ripeness is all, and revision and censorship by the mid-1980s were suddenly in vogue. In 1986, Wells and Taylor included the two versions of *Lear* in their Oxford edition of Shakespeare, with a short accompanying essay outlining their thinking. In 1996, Laurie E. Maguire tried to put an end to the last vestiges of the "good" and "bad" text theory by taking a fresh look at the premise of memorial reconstruction. Like Duthie (1949[a]), Maguire found little evidence to support the theory of shorthand transcription.[41] Further, she found that W.W. Greg, often thought of as the chief proponent of the shorthand theory, also had his doubts (Maguire 70–77). It seemed as if we were heading for some sort of consensus: there were two *Lear*s and they were both legitimate.

In reality, textual matters were just getting interesting. To begin with, the problem of who had revised the Folio text had returned. P.W.K. Stone (1980) argued that the revision was done in 1618, two years after Shakespeare's death. In his view, Philip Massinger had revised the play on Shakespeare's behalf. Stone also left the door open to other dramatists having been involved, among them, Jonson and Fletcher (127). Gary Taylor (1980: 34) argued that the revision could only have been undertaken by Shakespeare but later (1983[b]) conceded that we "have no right to assume Shakespeare's responsibility" for all of the Folio text (352).[42] In another piece published in 1983, Gary Taylor argued that some of the Folio changes may have been made by Shakespeare, who cut politically delicate passages in anticipation of a thin-skinned Court censor (Taylor 1983[c]: 82 and 101).

The possibility that Shakespeare or someone else had made changes to the play to avoid the wrath of a Court censor was also investigated by Leah Marcus' 1988 essay "Retrospective: 'King Lear' on St Stephen's Night, 1606." Marcus returned to the title page of Q1, which states that it was performed at Court, but she argued that elements of the quarto *King Lear* appear to criticize King James' "high notions of his own prerogative" (149). Rather than finding the kowtowing Shakespeare that Orwell expected, Marcus found a Shakespeare who was quietly ambivalent, both endorsing and indicting James' rule. Might this mean that censorships played no role in the 1608 quarto after all?[43] One possible solution: the text printed as Q1 was not, in fact, based on the royal command performance text. It is likely that there were at minimum two manuscripts floating around Shakespeare's playhouse. One went to the censor for this special, one-off, Court-approved performance, but the other standard playhouse text—the one that was evidently printed as Q1—did not record those special Court performance cuts (Wells, 2000: 3–4).

Another problem. Most scholars agree that the Quarto was used as the base copy for the Folio text. Some even suggest that Shakespeare penned his changes directly into a printed Quarto. But, as scholars point out, the Quarto was poorly printed and contained many corruptions. Why would Shakespeare work from an inaccurate version of his own play when the precise original was available in the playhouse? Here we have what really looks like a leap of faith: Gary Taylor (1983[b]) speculated that Shakespeare undertook the revision while on vacation in Stratford; consequently, he could not have used the promptbook, owned by the company, nor the version sold to the printer, so he had no choice but to buy a copy of Q1 (365). Fanciful—we can imagine Shakespeare walking over to a bookseller to purchase a copy of his own play!—but the proposal does explain why Shakespeare seems to have worked from a Quarto copy.

On the other hand, the fact that the Folio was set up from a copy of the Quarto may indicate that Shakespeare was not involved at all. Perhaps sending Shakespeare away on vacation is just too far-fetched. If he was in London throughout 1609, he could have written the play out again, or simply borrowed the promptbook. Only a writer outside the company, someone who had no access to the promptbook, would be forced to buy a copy of the Quarto. But if *that* was what happened, then how did it end up in Heminge and Condell's hands, and why did they print that version, rather than their own promptbook copy? Maybe Shakespeare or the company needed to buy and use a Quarto copy because of an unanticipated circumstance. Was the original promptbook destroyed somehow (a fire?), necessitating their having to buy and adopt Q1 as their performance text?

More problems: maybe Q1 was involved in the printing of F1, but there must have been yet another intermediary text, so argued a group of upstart scholars who looked anew at Q2. As early as 1964, Charles Hinman suggested that F was set up from a transcript of a promptbook, itself made up of corrected leaves from Q1 and Q2, but he also admitted that the evidence for his theory was not "altogether convincing" ([6]). Steven Urkowitz (1980) argued for a looser association: the compositors who set Q2 also set "a large part" of the Folio text (11). Gary Taylor concurred that the Folio showed signs of being set from a marked up copy of Q2, one that recorded both Shakespeare's rewrites of 1609 and the performance cuts of 1606 (1983[b]: 357; see also Taylor 1983[a]: 48). Peter Blayney (1982) promised to discuss Q2's influence on F in the follow-up to his *The Texts of King Lear and Their Origins* (245). More than twenty years later, we're still waiting, though other scholars have followed up on Blayney's work: T.H. Howard-Hill (1997) raised the "likelihood that Q2 was used in the printing of the [First Folio] in some manner" (34).[44] R.A. Foakes (Arden ed., 1997) and Richard Knowles (1997) acknowledged the possibility that F was set from an annotated Q2, though the latter stressed that the "exact relationships" of the texts involved in the making of the Folio "remains still a mystery" (75).[45] While no editor has yet to base an edition on the Second Quarto, it is increasingly of scholarly interest, so much so that, at least in relation to the Folio, the First Quarto, once a critical favorite, seems to be on its way to being banished, Cordelia-like, from the textual kingdom.

All this is enough to confuse Confucius. Assuming all recent investigations have some validity, Figure 1.9 may clarify this admittedly complex sequence of events.

Given the complexities of these options, and the ongoing spirited disagreements between (and sometimes within) the aforementioned theoretical camps, it's not surprising that even within academia, the matter is far from settled. While most editors still prefer to base their texts on the Folio, Stanley Wells (2000), Jay L. Halio (1994), and Graham Holderness (1995) have

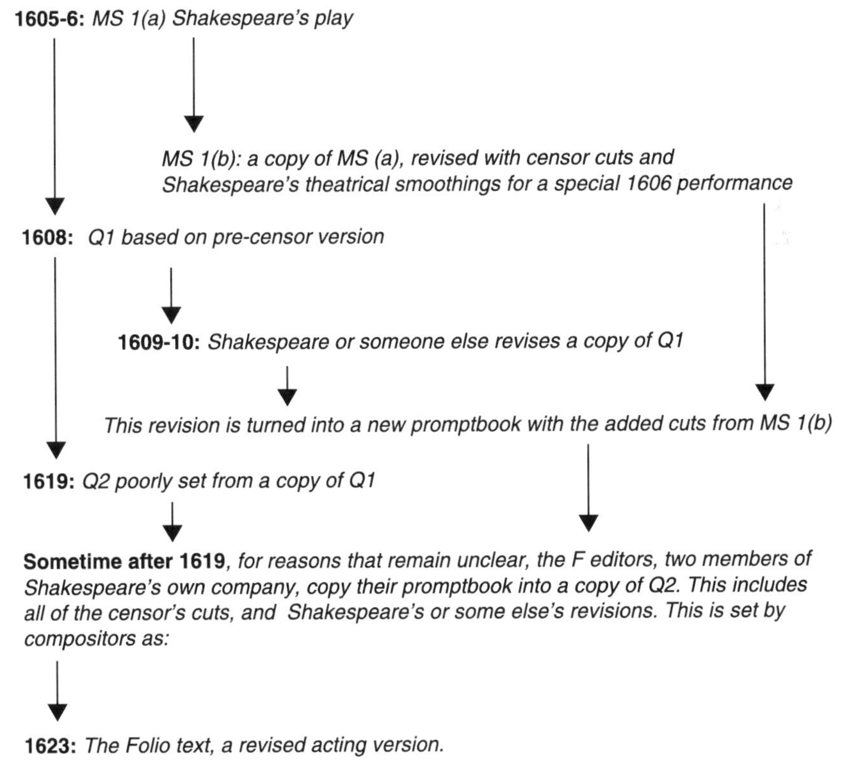
1605-6: MS 1(a) Shakespeare's play
MS 1(b): a copy of MS (a), revised with censor cuts and Shakespeare's theatrical smoothings for a special 1606 performance
1608: Q1 based on pre-censor version
1609-10: Shakespeare or someone else revises a copy of Q1
This revision is turned into a new promptbook with the added cuts from MS 1(b)
1619: Q2 poorly set from a copy of Q1
Sometime after 1619, for reasons that remain unclear, the F editors, two members of Shakespeare's own company, copy their promptbook into a copy of Q2. This includes all of the censor's cuts, and Shakespeare's or some else's revisions. This is set by compositors as:
1623: The Folio text, a revised acting version.

Figure 1.9 Theory 3: Shakespeare as revisionist, his texts recopied, reworked and censored.

produced editions based on the Quarto; R.A. Foakes (1997) and Douglas Brooks (2007) have opted for conflationary texts; Michael Warren (1989) and Stephen Orgel (2000) have tendered parallel texts of both the Folio and the Quarto; Nick de Somogyi (2004) has published a Folio text with a parallel modern edition. Further, many well-established critics remain reluctant to change their interpretations of the play to reflect the two-text paradigm. Marjorie Garber (2004), for example, writes that she "will continue to include [in her discussions] all scenes and passages that have become [i.e.—since Pope and Theobald] customarily associated with the play over the years" (652). Note her insistence that there is only *one* play, although she admits that it is merely customary to regard the play/plays as so.

Garber's aversion to multiple *Lear*s is, perhaps, reasonable, given that undergraduates and armchair readers have a hard enough time following *one* version; offering *two* plays seems to compound the problems we all face. But, as Jonathan Goldberg (1986) pointed out some twenty years ago, a conflated text which borrows from one version of the play and then another creates a depth of character and meaning that is constructed by the editor, not the playwright: "That in the two *Lear*s different characters may speak the same lines, that the same characters (characters with the same proper names) speak different lines, suggests the radical instability of character as a locus of meaning in the Shakespearean text" (215). Going still further, Goldberg asserted that "there never was *a* [singular] *King Lear*" (213).

Certainly, conflation can lure us into a false sense of security. Even the addition of a few letters can make a huge difference. In the Quarto, for example, Lear's last utterance begins with the dying groan: "O, o, o, o" and is followed by "Break heart, I prithee break" (24.304,306). Lear, dying, hastening his own body to break, is committing a form of suicide, a sin, punishable by damnation. Or is he rejecting the existence of God altogether? Recall that in *Hamlet*, the princely Dane wanted to commit suicide but decided against it because "the Everlasting had . . . fixed/His canon 'gainst self-slaughter" (1.2.131–32). If Lear is hastening his death, is he tacitly stating that he no longer believes in God? How does the Folio handle the matter? Lear dies in a sort of ecstasy, thinking that Cordelia's lips are moving, that she is alive:

> This feather stirs. She lives. If it be so,
> It is a chance which does redeem all sorrows
> That ever I felt.
>
> (5.3.240–43)

> Do you see this? Look on her. Look, her lips,
> Look there, Look there. *He dies*
>
> (5.3.286–87)

In this version, it is Kent who is given the line "Break heart, I prithee break"

(5.3.288), a line that clearly echoes Horatio's "Now cracks a noble heart" (*Hamlet* 5.2.312).

It's true that what follows does not seem extremely Christian on its own:

Kent. Vex not his ghost. O, let him pass. He hates him
That would upon the rack of this tough world
Stretch him longer.
(5.3.289–91)

Then again, compare it to Horatio's:

Good night, sweet prince,
And flights of angels sing thee to thy rest.
(*Hamlet* 5.2.312–13)

Neither Kent nor Horatio mention "heaven," but both are sure that good souls are rewarded with eternal rest.[46]

Not surprisingly, Pope omitted the Quarto's murky ending in favor of the Folio's upbeat spirituality. But, to confirm the Christian piety of the Folio ending, Pope had also to import some earlier Quarto exchanges which confer upon Cordelia a saintly quality, including this description of Cordelia weeping for her father:

There she shook
The holy water from her heavenly eyes.
(Scene 17.30–31; or IV.iii.p.79 in Pope)[47]

The issue here is not whether the Quarto's ending is superior, but that people who read a conflationary text are seldom aware that there is a starkly alternative—and quite possibly equally legitimate—ending.

It is perhaps natural at this point to indulge in "what-if" scenarios: What if Bradley had only read the Quarto, in which Lear seems to hasten his own death, would he be so sure of Lear's redemption? On the other hand, since the conflation contains both the Folio ending and the reference to a "holy" Cordelia, might we wonder why Orwell was so adamant that King Lear's world was essentially godless? But this is to belabor the point. No matter what scholars read, they make arguments. Some critics, like Bradley or Orwell, may have such a powerful sense of what they wish *King Lear* to be and are so persuasive in their arguments, that they not only seduce us with their polemic, they also seem to seduce themselves.

Twentieth-century **Lear*s***

It may look like we are entering into an endgame in which Shakespeare's *King Lear* is being pushed aside so that scholars and editors can pursue their own ideological agendas. Reading criticism with some skepticism is probably a good thing. But the multiplicity of meanings derived from *Lear* is not necessarily a bad thing, just ask anyone who goes to the theater. No one wants or expects to see the same production of *King Lear* time after time. In fact, long before the "Shakespeare as Revisionist" theory came into vogue, theater companies large and small had matter-of-factly revised the various *Lear* texts into a single *King Lear*, suited to the economic constraints of their companies and the aesthetic interests of their audiences.

While we have already looked at a variety of seventeenth-, eighteenth-, and nineteenth-century productions of *King Lear*, the following recent examples may give readers a greater sense of the play's (or plays') ongoing flexibility.

Peter Brook, director, Royal Shakespeare Company, Stratford-upon-Avon, 1962

Recalling Macready's Stonehenge staging, Peter Brook's 1962 RSC production was set in what J.C. Trewin called "a rusting Iron Age" (*Birmingham Post*, 7 November 1962). The costumes were simple. Only Lear wore a robe; the rest of the men sported jackets and pants. When divested of his power, Lear dressed like a servant. When reunited with Cordelia, Paul Scofield, who played the king, was re-robed, but in simpler garb, indicative that, despite courtly ceremony, the king and his power were not as they had been.

Efforts were made to eradicate what Charles Marowitz (1963) called "aesthetic shelter" from this version of the play:

> To remove the tint of sympathy usually found at the end of the Blinding Scene, Brook cut Cornwall's servants and their commiseration of Gloucester's fate. Once the second "vile jelly" has been thumbed out of his head, Gloucester is covered with tattered rags and shoved off in the direction of Dover. Servants clearing the stage collide with the confused blind man and rudely shove him aside.
>
> (114)

As we might remember, Robert Elliston (1820) tried to heighten the drama of the storm scene with machinery. The result was that the speech itself was often drowned out in the whirling and hammering of mechanical parts. But Brook used the storm as a sort of chorus to Lear. The end of "I am a man more sinned against than sinning" (9.60) was punctuated with a rattle of thunder. Not everyone was impressed with the effect. The *Evening News* (7 November 1962) described it as "a thousand servant girls dropping a thousand tin trays." His most telling sound effect, however, was that of Cordelia's neck in the hangman's noose, which was heard to snap.

Brook also set up some character differences between Goneril and Regan. Goneril wore boots, indicative of her masculinity, Regan a skirt, suggestive of her feminine wiles. Cornwall (Tony Church) revealed his own violent nature when he methodically tapped his riding crop on Kent's cheek or calmly set his shining boot spur on Gloucester eye, as if he were doing no more than putting out a cigarette underfoot. Cornwall's violence was all the more shocking, considering Alan Webb's deliberately comic, and thus non-threatening, Gloucester. Alexander Leggatt (2004) recalled that when Gloucester said "we have seen the best of our times" (1.2.110) he sounded like the laughable Justice Shallow, saying "We have heard the chimes at midnight" (51–52). Later, when Gloucester pulled off the king's boots, he cried like a child. Gloucester's candid virtues were reflected by others in members of the supporting cast. When Lear wondered aloud whether he was going mad, Alex McCowen's Fool tenderly held his master's hand.

In the dying moments of the final scene, Scofield's Lear seemed to accept Orwell's stark truth that there was no God, and even, half-smilingly, half-weepingly confirmed the cosmic farce in which he had played:

> Why should a dog, a horse, a rat have life,
> And thou no breath at all? Thou'lt come no more.
> Never, never, never, never, never.
>
> (5.3.282–84)

Yet, this same Lear remained to many unsympathetic. The *Birmingham Post* (7 November 1962) stated that Scofield had the "voice of a man to be feared"; the reviewer for the *Nottingham Guardian Journal* (7 November 1962) thought that Lear acted like a "general in Tzarist Russia": the *Wolverhampton Express and Star* (7 November 1962) referred to him as an "old sea dog"; Harold Hobson complained that Scofield's Lear reminded him of a man given to "insulting the servants and cursing his relations" (*Sunday Times*, 11 November 1962).[48] This version was put to film in 1971 and retained Scofield as Lear. (See Figure 1.10.) It is now available on DVD; a version of Brook's 1953 made-for-TV version, starring Orson Welles, is also available, though, as of this writing, only on VHS.

James Earl Jones, King Lear, New York Shakespeare Festival, dir. Joseph Papp, 1974

In this version, Lear, his elder daughters, and his servants were dressed in vaguely biblical robes, their colours black and maroon. The two exceptions were Edmund (played by Raul Julia, later of *Kiss of the Spiderwoman*) and Cordelia (played by Lee Chamberlain). Edmund, dressed in bright orange robes, was a kind of Judas brightened by his ambition; Cordelia, in garments of white and grey, was a neophyte, not yet too-deeply stained by the Court's murky politics.

Jones entered slowly, concentrating on placing one foot before the other, his voice husky, a weak old man, were it not for the sword he held

Figure 1.10 Paul Scofield as King Lear (1971). By kind permission of the Harry Ransom Research Center, The University of Texas at Austin.

determinedly in his hand. As his anger against Cordelia and Kent rose, so too did his strength. Recalling Kemble's performance of 1788, this Lear rushed on Kent, intent on peppering him with his long blade. Still later in the same scene, Jones seemed to turn himself into marble when explaining to Burgundy and France that, since his daughter could offer "nothing" in the way of expressing her love, he likewise offered "nothing" in return. Later, on the heath, he shook his fists defiantly at the heavens and swore that, come what may, he would endure. Yet, as the play wore on, this Lear seemed a changed man, no longer the sport of heaven, but a conduit for its pity. Cleansed and restored by Cordelia, he appeared in yellow and tan, an angel among the black spectacle of armed soldiers. At his death, Kent and Albany (played by Douglass Watson and Robert Stattel, respectively) traced their fingers across the sky, seemingly tracking Lear's ghost as it ascended to heaven.

Gloucester (Paul Sorvino, later in Baz Luhrmann's *Romeo and Juliet*) was in many ways a mirror of Lear. Pulling out spectacles to read Edgar's supposed letter, he seems very much a man on the downward slope of life, but, being roused by the contents of the letter, flashed his sword and demanded to know where Edgar was, ready to execute the villain. Later, blinded by Regan and Cornwall (played by Ellen Holly and Robert Lanchester, respectively), he came to realize that his passions were his undoing.

Edgar (played by Rene Auberjonois, later of *Deep Space Nine* and *Boston Legal*), was easy-going, open, and, like Cordelia, a little naïve. But, by the time he donned his Poor-Tom disguise, he had learned that in many ways he had been played a fool. His brother Edmund was an Iago-figure, playful, confident, but never jovial. The Fool, meanwhile (played by Tom Aldridge) was a pointedly caustic politician, rather than a courtly entertainer. When the king confessed that he had "done her [Cordelia] wrong" (5.24), he said so not to his own conscience but as an admission to his trusted counselor and friend. This version is available on DVD.

Robin Philips, director, starring Peter Ustinov, Stratford, Ontario, 1979

Peter Ustinov starred as a kind but increasingly erratic (suffering from Alzheimer's?) Lear. Here, the set was Victorian and the acting disarmingly prosaic. King Lear did not descend from a high throne to unfurl a ceremonial map the size of a goodly Turkish carpet; instead, Ustinov slung himself out of his desk chair and then signed and stamped an order, as if he were a midlevel clerk in an import/export firm. Later, Gloucester was tortured in his own study, his eyes pierced with a letter opener.

Gina Mallet, of the *Toronto Star*, accurately described it as "a Victorian morality tale" (*Toronto Star*, 15 September 1980), but Jay Carr, of the *Detroit News*, preferred to grumble about what the play was not: this Lear was "not nearly massive, resonant or archetypal enough" (*Detroit News*, 9 October 1979); similarly, the New York critic Clive Barnes regretted that the production lacked "the special desperation of man against destiny."[49] Ustinov, who thought of Lear as more Willy Loman than Sisyphus, ignored these reviews. His acting in *King Lear* confirmed his intuition that Shakespeare remains "the most modern of playwrights" (Good ix).

Adrian Noble, director, Stratford-upon-Avon, Royal Shakespeare Company, 1982

In Adrian Noble's 1982 RSC production, Michael Gambon's Lear played opposite Antony Sher's Fool, the latter dressed as if he were a clown who had just tumbled out of a three-ring circus. (See Figure 1.11.) With his red plastic nose, Sher's Fool was a revelation, in that he was able to extract belly-laughs from speeches that often seemed pointedly serious and philosophical:

> The first breakthrough came in a rehearsal of the heath scenes when Adrian asked each of the actors involved to find an animal to play, in order to release the savagery and wildness of the situation. I chose a chimpanzee, chattering and clapping hands, hurling myself around in forward rolls, and found this very liberating for the role.
>
> (Sher 154–55)

As the play progressed, so did its setting, from traditional fairy-tale majesty to increasingly modern dress. Oswald appeared in a neo-WWI uniform, with briefcase under arm and high leather boots on foot. In later scenes, the once-regal Lear appeared in pajamas. Likewise, by Act V, horses and swords gave way to flashes of heavy artillery shells. Edgar, like a fugitive P.O.W., dodged detention center floodlights.

Alice Krige's Cordelia was a tower of strength but oddly lacking in emotional warmth, "all too clearly her father's daughter" (Judith Cook, *The Scotsman*, 30 June 1982).[50] Critics were mildly disappointed with Gambon's Lear. *Times* reporter Ned Chaillet objected that the actor communicated little of Lear's anguish or bewilderment (30 June 1982); Stanley Wells complained that Gambon lacked "inwardness"; his "Madness is only lightly sketched in" (*TLS*, 16 July 1982, 764). The king's emotional depth seemed to be transferred to Antony Sher, who in Scene 4 sat on Lear's knee, as if he were a dummy mouthing the king's muted conscience.

Jonathan Miller, director, BBC TV, 1982

Miller attempted to fit the play within the limits of the television box. There can be no doubt that TV does many things well, especially close-ups, effective for transmitting the emotions of Shakespeare's characters. But acting for television is not the same as acting for the stage. A theater, especially big theaters, requires actors to project their voice. Even experienced actors find themselves sweeping their hands to and fro, attracting and keeping the audience trained on them. Television makes no such demands. The viewer cannot say to themselves, "Gee, Lear's pretty good, but I'm focused on the Fool right now." The television cuts out such options. We see what we're told to see. But Shakespearean actors too often perform their TV-version Shakespeare as if they were performing for a theatrical audience. It was a welcomed relief,

Figure 1.11 Antony Sher as the Fool (1982). Joe Cocks Studio Collection. Copyright Shakespeare Birthplace Trust.

therefore, that Miller avoided sweeping gestures and large-scale hectoring in favor of naturalistic movements and people talking quietly in their own voice. The result was a production that was more family saga than regal tragedy. Lear (Michael Hordern) entered the throne room without pageantry or musical accompaniment. He wore no crown, and, even when railing, did not shout so much as express a "schoolmasterly exasperation" (Leggatt 2004: 127). Likewise, Frank Middlemass's Fool was the same age as the king, and treated him with a sense of parity that he felt his age entitled him to (Fenwick 173).

But the Fool's counsel, though dipped in the tradition of Armin's "foolosopher," was somewhat inappropriate here, especially when the king finally gave into madness, described thus by Alexander Leggatt: "tetchy, jumpy, and totally off his head" (2004: 128). This was not a man who had lost his wits because his world-view had suddenly crumbled before him. Rather, Lear's madness was "a picture of dotage . . . one can almost see his tears and smell his urine."[51]

While realism was the byword of the production, Miller also attempted to resurrect some of the play's spiritual themes. When Cordelia said that she went about her father's business (4.3.24), it was God the Father, and actress Brenda Blethyn crossed herself reverently while saying it. Adding to the religiosity of the production, Edgar, disguised as Poor Tom, wore a crown of thorns (Willis 127–28). Recalling Brook's production, Goneril and Regan seemed to take pleasure in cruelty. Goneril (Gillian Barge) giggled while helping her husband pluck out Gloucester's eyes, and Regan (Penelope Wilton) thought that Gloucester smelling his way to Dover was hilarious (Leggatt 2004: 125). This version is widely available on DVD.

Sir Laurence Olivier, starring, made-for-TV movie, 1983

Describing Lear, Olivier said: "He's just a selfish, irascible old bastard . . . he's got just that sort of ridiculous temper, those sulks. Absolutely mad as a hatter sometimes" (Cowie, 1983, rpt. 1991: 188). Lear's temperament aside, there is a melancholy that hangs over this production. Olivier, who had previously portrayed a variety of vigorous heroes, Henry V (1944), Hamlet (1948), and Othello (1965), was suddenly and shockingly old, someone the viewer might think of as an emotionally needy parent, one who requires of us more time than we have to give. Suddenly, his acting took on an added dimension: so old and frail an actor was not long for the world, and, given that he was playing an old man who was himself in the last throes of life, his every movement took on an extended significance. Granville-Barker wanted his Lears to be old, and Olivier certainly was that, but would he have the stamina for the part? (Consider that most film units shoot twelve- to fourteen-hour days.) But he was surprisingly vigorous, especially in the early scenes, when he seemed genuinely anguished by Cordelia's "Nothing."

This version seemed to take inventory of *Lear*'s reception history. Recalling Macready's 1838 production, emphasis was placed on a primitive, Iron Age Britain. The play opened on a Stonehenge-style set. Edmund recited his "nature, art my goddess" (Scene 2.1) speech with the sun rising behind him, suggesting that he was, above all, a pagan. Reduced from king to peasant, we see Lear snaring a rabbit and enjoying a leisurely cookout or passing the time by putting flowers in his hair, a Celtic hippie at one with nature. Leo McKern's Gloucester gloated that Edmund's mother had been fine sport, prompting hurt feelings from Edmund, played by the always interesting Robert Lindsay (later Capt. Pellew in the *Horatio Hornblower* series). Was McKern (famous for his cantankerous lover of Wordsworth, Rumpole of the Bailey) backing up Coleridge's and Bradley's defense of Edmund? Later, on the heath, the rain flattening Lear's wispy hair, his arms shaking arthritically, it was difficult not to share in Lamb's assessment of the play: "to see an old man tottering about the stage with a walking-stick, turned out of doors by his daughters in a rainy night, has nothing in it but what is painful and disgusting. We want to take him into shelter and relieve him."

Not surprisingly, Olivier won the last of his several Emmy Awards for his Lear. However, director Michael Elliot seemed at a loss as to how to get the best from the stellar supporting cast.[52] John Hurt—Caligula in *I Claudius* and later Mr. Ollivander in *Harry Potter and the Sorcerer's Stone*—was underused as the Fool. His role seems to have been to stand around looking venerable. Brian Cox—who later played Lear for Deborah Warner at the National (1990) but is best known to young audiences as William Stryker in the second *X-Men* film—was badly miscast as the money-wise Burgundy. Diana Rigg, who had played Cordelia in a 1962 Royal Shakespeare Company production (See Figure 1.12), played a surprisingly convincing Regan but often overshadowed Dorothy Tutin's Goneril. Elliot's directorial hand steadied when dealing with Edgar and Edmund's showdown, which clanged and clashed with the vigor of a gladiator movie. This version is available on DVD.

Richard Eyre, director, BBC TV production, 1998

Lear (Ian Holm) played the king with a "short fuse" (Leggatt, 2004: 165) and, in places, recalled the fury of Scofield and the senility of Ustinov. Goneril (Barbara Flynn) was an "exasperated housewife," who characteristically kept her arms folded. Her sister Regan (Amanda Redman) was a "sexy society hostess with an eye for the younger guests" (Leggatt, 2004: 157). Recalling Tony Church's performance in Brook's 1962 production, this Cornwall (Michael Simkins) was excited by the torture of Gloucester (Timothy West), a pleasure he shared with his equally sadistic wife.

Eyre kept the fate of the Fool a mystery but did leave us a clue. Upon his first entrance, the Fool (Michael Bryant) scolded Lear for giving away his crown and promised to train the king in the art of courtly jesting. In Scene 20, Lear enters wearing the Fool's garb. Missing or dead, the Fool has apparently

Figure 1.12 Diana Rigg as Cordelia (1962). She later played Regan in Olivier's 1982 made-for-TV version. Angus McBean. By kind permission of the Shakespeare Birthplace Trust.

fulfilled his promise and Lear his training; as the king himself informed Cordelia (Victoria Hamilton): "I am a very foolish, fond old man" (Scene 21.57). Recalling James Earl Jones' Lear some twenty years before, this Lear dies in ecstasy, his fingers tracing Cordelia's spirit as it soars to heaven.

As poignant as such moments were, the production was marred by its setting. The cold, almost plastic walls of the sound stage looked cheap, and the costumes looked like they might have come from any number of episodes of *Star Trek: The Next Generation*. Worse yet, watching Ian Holm in this production, it's difficult not to recall John Shebbeare's warning that all-too-often King Lear comes across like "a drunken shoemaker [who] curses his daughter that has secretly taken his money from him." From the start, this Lear was in too-high a rage. The result was that his rantings soon wore thin. When he promised to bring down "the terrors of the earth," it was all Regan and Goneril could do to hold back the giggles.[53]

Adaptations and foreign versions

King Lear has also inspired a number of offshoots, among them William Moncrieff's *The Lear of Private Life* (1820), a conflation of Shakespeare's play with Amelia Opie's novel *Father and Daughter*. In Opie's novel, Agnes Fitzroy elopes with a rich libertine, who soon after deserts her. Pregnant, she returns home to find her father insane with grief. She nurses him until he dies. In Moncrieff's stage version, instead of the father dying of a broken heart, he is reunited with his daughter, and they live happily-ever-after in a Tate-like fantasy (Bratton 39–40).

Jacob Gordin's *The Yiddish King Lear* (1892) begins at a Purim feast given by David Moishele, a wealthy Russian Jewish merchant living in mid-nineteenth century Vilna. (See Figure 1.13.) He gives all his daughters expensive gifts, but his youngest daughter, Telbele, refuses his present, a brooch valued at 80 rubles, as overly lavish. Upset, Moishele banishes her from his house. He then informs his wife and his remaining daughters that he intends to give away his goods and set off for the holy land, where he hopes to spend his remaining years in Talmudic study. Jaffe, a teacher, warns him not to divest himself of his possessions and draws a parallel between his actions and those of King Lear. Moishele takes no heed. Returning from Palestine, he finds that his wife is now a drudge to both daughters. Meanwhile, Telbele has graduated from medical school and plans to marry Jaffe. She is informed that her father has returned and is now blind. This detail heightens our sympathy for the old man who, taking a moment's rest, is set upon by one of his drunken sons-in-law, who throws the old man from a chair and then proceeds to beat him like a dog. Wandering the streets, Moishele cries out, "Give alms to the new beggar! Give alms to the new King Lear!" However, Gordin's play ends with a Tate-esque celebration: David Moishele and his wife take refuge in a synagogue, where, as it happens, Telbele and Jaffe are about to be married. Reconciled with his youngest daughter, Moishele declares that love is the greatest thing in the world ("The Jewish King Lear," *The New York Times*, 26 May 1901). *The Yiddish King Lear* was a cornerstone of Yiddish Theater. Between 1894 and 1989, it was performed over 400 times (" 'King Lear' in Hebrew"). The play was revived in 1920 and filmed in 1934.[54]

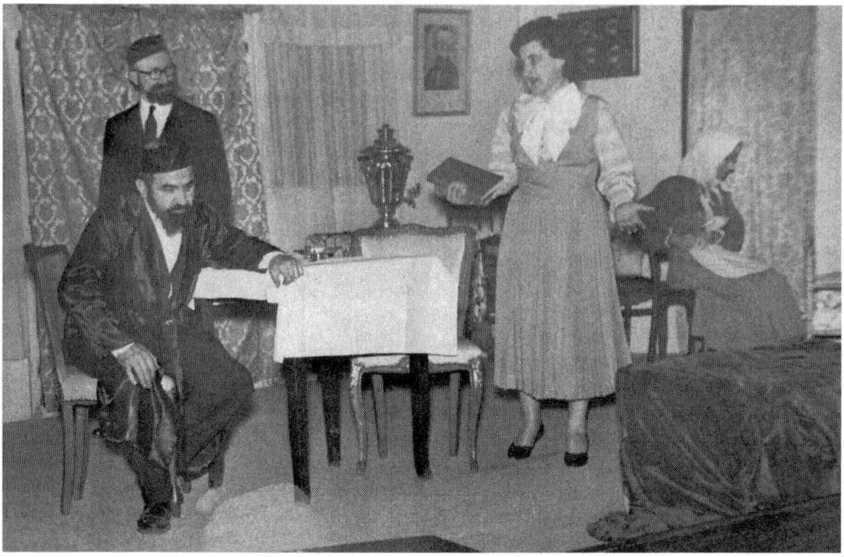

Figure 1.13 Scene from *The Yiddish King Lear*, performed by members of the Yiddish amateur theater at the Jewish Community Center, Resistencia, 1959. By kind permission of the Beth Hatefutsoth, Visual Documentation Center.

As Gordon Bottomley's play *King Lear's Wife* (1915) opens, Lear's wife, Queen Hygd, is on her deathbed. But Lear is more concerned with his mistress, the commoner, Gormflaith, who assumes she will soon be queen. Goneril kills Lear's mistress, but the father puts his family first and refuses to punish his daughter. The division of the kingdom, then, is a peace offering, blood-money for his years of infidelity.[55] In 1956, Somerset Maugham, who described himself as "in the very first row of the second-raters," published *Mister Lear*, in which a famous writer, Walter Craine, deals with his three daughters. Following Shakespeare's plot, the two eldest are schemers, the youngest (Jane) is a shining example of virtue. Craine's best friend is Harold Kent, who once saved the famous writer's life in World War I; the Edgar-figure is Peter Stacey, Craine's secretary, who, following Tate's rewrite, ends up marrying Jane.

Cordelia's happiness also figures in Edward Bond's *Lear* (1971), in which she marries the Gravedigger's son. This marriage suggests some knowledge of Shakespeare's source materials. Remember that in *King Leir*, the banished princess accepts the hand of a man she thinks is a commoner. But this Cordelia marries as much for love as for politics, and unlike Shakespeare's princess, hates her father, whom she equates with the worse excesses of a police state:

> *Cordelia* [to *Lear*]. You were here when they killed my husband. I watched them kill him. I covered my face with my hands, but my fingers

> opened so I watched. I watched them rape me, and John kill them, and my child miscarry. I didn't miss anything. I watched and I said we won't be at the mercy of brutes anymore, we'll live a new life and help one another.
>
> (Scene III, p. 83)

A darkly comic King Lear pops up in an early draft version of Tom Stoppard's *Rosencrantz and Guildenstern Are Dead* (1966) or, as it was initially titled, *Rosencrantz and Guildenstern Meet King Lear*. Toward the end of the play, the mad king comes across Hamlet:

Lear. I knew your father. He did not have daughters.
Hamlet. No, my lord.
Lear. Then he died happy.

(p. 42)

Later in the same scene, King Lear enters and, filled with homicidal rage, attacks Rosencrantz and Guildenstern:

Lear. As I am a King, these twin mockers who have dispatched their warrant, I'll warrant them dispatched to hell, and now.
Ros. Treachery, (*He draws his sword*)
Hamlet. Will out for traitors.
Guil. We did but play.
Hamlet. Go to it. And I to Elsinore.
Lear. Kill, kill, kill. (*The swords of the attendants etc stab. . . . Ros and Guil scream and fall*)

(p. 43)

King Lear has also inspired significant and popular foreign films such as Grigoriy Kozintsev's bleak *Korol Lir* (1969), which features a film score by Dmitri Shostakovich and a script by Boris Pasternak. It begins with an emphasis on the austerity of the landscape. Peasants, many of them lacking a limb or racked with age, trudge toward Lear's castle. The sheltered Lear (Yari Yarvet) lives a surprisingly happy life, laughing jovially with and at his fool. It is only when he is thrown into the wilds of his own land that he confronts the sufferings of his subjects.[56] But what follows suggests that the new order will be just as uncaring. The play closes with soldiers carrying away the king's body. One pallbearer, seeing the Fool, belligerently kicks him.

Unlike most interpretations, which favor a well-meaning, if emotionally unstable, king, Akira Kurosawa's *Ran* (1984) follows the fortunes of Hidetora, a merciless ruler. His elder sons (Taro and Jiro) are equally merciless to him, prompting the king to take refuge with his youngest son, Saburo. But, departing from Shakespeare's play, Taro is assassinated, and Jiro commits suicide after his forces are defeated by Saburo's army. So far, it looks like a happy ending is at hand, but, returning from the battle, Hidetora and Saburo are ambushed. A shot is fired, and Saburo dies. His father cradles him in his arms:

> He is dead. I know when one is dead. He is dead. You and I live but Saburo is dead. Saburo . . . You cannot die. I have tales to tell you . . . forgiveness to ask. Is this justice? Saburo, are you gone forever? It grows dark. Senile old man . . . Saburo!
>
> [*Clutches his chest and dies.*]

In Jean-Luc Godard's arty *King Lear* (1987), Shakespeare's descendant, William Shaksper Junior the Fifth (played by Peter Sellars, not to be confused with Peter Sellers of *Pink Panther*-fame) takes the play to Hollywood to have it filmed. Along the way, he meets with Burgess Meredith (best remembered as Rocky Balboa's boxing coach), Molly Ringwald (the rich, spoiled, moody, awkward, brainy or angst-filled girl in any number of John Hughes movies), as well as the perpetually quirky and uncomfortable Woody Allen, who plays someone named "Mr. Alien." (See Figure 1.14.) The film was much excoriated by critics.

Shakespeare's play has also generated a variety of mainstream American updates, among them, the recent *King of Texas* (2002), a made-for-TV film starring Patrick Stewart (a perfectly respectable Shakespearean ruined by seasons of Star Trek-related schlock). The film takes place in the American Wild West. Stewart stars as John Lear, a wealthy landowner who divides his property among his daughters only to be rejected by them once they have it. The film seems to be a rehashing of both Shakespeare's play and another Lear-inspired movie: *A Thousand Acres* (1997), based upon Jane Smiley's sentimental novel of the same name (1991), in which Rose/Regan (Michelle Pfeiffer) and Jenny/Goneril (Jessica Lange) share the farm with "Daddy" (Jason Robards). The youngest daughter Caroline/Cordelia (Jennifer Jason Leigh) goes off to college to get a law degree. When the aging patriarch sniffs his own mortality, he decides to set up a corporation, which, he says, will avoid death taxes. But Caroline expresses doubts. Despite her legal training, her advice is rejected, and she is cut out of his plans. Explains daughter Jenny: "she [Caroline] spoke as a lawyer when she should have spoken as a daughter." Rose and Jenny then fight over Jessie/Edmund (Colin Firth), and then over who owns the land. Jenny is eventually pushed out and ends up working as a waitress at a Denny's. As for their turning on their father, Smiley chooses to see Rose as the hero of the film. Her hatred of their father is readily explained: "Daddy" is, to pick up on an aforementioned strand in the play's critical history, an incestuous pedophile. Nonetheless, Caroline takes him in and nurses him until he dies.

For those interested in a study of Smiley's novel, Julie Sanders has a superb chapter in her book *Novel Shakespeares: Twentieth-Century Women Novelists and Appropriation* (2001). Sanders' study also looks at other

Figure 1.14 Poster for Jean-Luc Godard's 1987 film *King Lear*. Editor's personal collection.

Lear-inspired novels, including Valerie Miner's *A Walking Fire* (1994), which, like Edward Bond's aforementioned play, is highly political. In Miner's re-interpretation, "Cora" is not exiled to France but to Canada, where she hides from the F.B.I., whose agents want her in connection with some fires she set as an anti-war activist. As we can already imagine, her father, Roy Casey—*roy* reflects the French word "roi," which means "king"—supports the police action.

In Anne Tyler's comic novel *Ladder of Year* (1996), the protagonist, Cordelia Grinstead, is the youngest and favorite daughter of the domineering Dr. Felson. Cordelia has married a doctor (incest by profession) but flirts with the grocery boy. Her sisters, Eliza (an aromatherapist) and Linda (divorced with two children Marie-Claire and Therese), depend upon her emotionally. Her husband annoys her, and she longs for a world in which her responsibilities amount to "nothing." Davidson Garrett's *King Lear of the Taxi: Musings of a New York City Actor / Taxi Driver* (2006)—a finalist in the 2000 Gival Press Chapbook—is a philosophical glimpse of an ever-changing city by an actor who must drive a taxi for survival. Often quoting from *King Lear*, "Garrett documents his thespian dreams and artistic struggles from behind the wheel of a cab as he glances at humanity in his rearview mirror" (backcover blurb).

There are *Lear*-inspired poems. In "On Sitting Down to Read *King Lear* Once Again" (1818), John Keats, perhaps comforted by the Tate adaptation, enters into a "fierce dispute" with the "bitter-sweet" of Shakespeare's play:

O golden-tongued Romance with serene lute!
Fair plumed Syren! Queen of far away!
Leave melodizing on this wintry day,
Shut up thine olden pages, and be mute:
Adieu! for once again the fierce dispute,
Betwixt damnation and impassion'd clay
Must I burn through; once more humbly assay
The bitter-sweet of this Shakespearian fruit.

After her father's death in 1994, Margaret Atwood penned "King Lear in Respite Care," a poem that reworks the Folio's "The weight of this sad time we must obey, / Speak what we feel, not what we ought to say" (5.3.299–300). The penultimate stanza of Atwood's poem reads:

The sun goes straight down. The trees bend,
they straighten up. They bend.
At eight the youngest daughter comes.
She holds his hand.
She says, *Did they feed you?*
He says no.

He says, *Get me out of here.*
He wants so much to say *please.*
but he won't.

Similarly, in Lucas McClure's play *The Lear Project* (1998), Lear suffers from dementia. Confined to a convalescent hospital, he imagines his two nurses to be his pitiless daughters and a young intern to be Cordelia.

King Lear has also been appropriated by musicians and artists. In 1858 (revised 1901), Mily Alexeyevich Balakirev wrote a classical overture to the play, as did the more widely-known Hector Berlioz in 1931. Both pieces have been variously recorded and performed. A fairly popular folk-rock band, Cordelia's Dad, flirted with some success in the mid–1990s. In 1991, the talented Morrissey released "King Leer" on his *Kill Uncle* album. The song doesn't deal directly with Shakespeare's play, however—unless he's making a rather veiled reference to Edmund's sexual appetite:

Your boyfriend, he
Has displayed to me
More than just a
Real hint of cruelty
I tried to surprise you
I crept up behind you
With a homeless chihuahua
You "coo"-ed for an hour
You handed him back and said:
"You'll never guess—I'm bored now."

Painters inspired by *King Lear* run the alphabet, from Edward Austin Abbey to Benjamin West. While this book cannot reproduce every-and-all pictures inspired or related to the play, a reproduction of Henry Fuseli's rendering of *King Lear* for the illustrated *Boydell Shakespeare* (published (1795–1805) and John Hamilton Mortimer's splendid *King Lear*, part of his "Twelve Heads" Shakespeare series, are appended. (See Figures 1.15 and 1.16.)[57]

In 1914, Charles Bernard Lear, a baseball player who studied at Princeton, named himself "King Lear," but his career in the majors lasted scarcely a year. Writing in 1998 for *Forbes* magazine, Laura Saunders suggested that the mayhem in *King Lear* might have been avoided with proper estate planning. Perhaps the oddest appropriation of the play was by The Beatles: John Lennon sampled a bit of a BBC radio performance of *Lear* and added it to the song "I Am the Walrus," released in the States as part of *The Magical Mystery Tour* album and film (1967). Fans latched onto Oswald's catchphrase "bury my body" (20.239) as well as his bewailed "O, untimely death!" (20.242) as confirmation that Paul McCartney was dead.

Figure 1.15 Henry Fuseli's rendering of King Lear for Boydell Shakespeare (published 1792). By kind permission of the Harry Ransom Research Center, The University of Texas at Austin.

Our role in The History (and) Tragedy of King Lear

The above-cited adaptations and appropriations may not tell us much about the play, though they certainly document the ways artists in various disciplines have attempted to investigate its profundity. Indeed, there are few works in our collective history with sufficient power to inspire so many generations of artists, actors, directors and critics. Devoting some 400 pages to looking over various scholarly and theatrical responses to the play, Marvin Rosenberg (1972) accepts that no one theory can shed light on all aspects of this play:

> The dark, deadly, grimly comic world of *Lear* evokes so wide and intense a range of responses on so many levels of consciousness . . . that it must defeat any attempt to enclose its meaning in limited formulae such as redemption, retribution, endgame, morality, etc.
>
> (328)

Terry Eagleton (1986) agrees that *King Lear* is an intellectual and spiritual puzzle unlikely to be solved by any one interpretative reading: "no poetic symbolism is adequate to resolve it" (83).

Figure 1.16 John Hamilton Mortimer's King Lear (1776). Editor's personal collection.

Yet other critics stress not that theory is at a loss to solve the mystery of *Lear*, but that readers must first resolve their own moral stances before they can find any clarity in the play. Howard Felperin (1977), for example, argued that Shakespeare designed *King Lear* to force us to make our own ethical declarations:

Shakespeare has certainly not made things easy for us. For he leaves us in

> the end with not a choice of *either* morality and meaning *or* madness and absurdity, but more like an ultimatum of *neither* morality and meaning *nor* madness and absurdity, an ultimatum that becomes inescapable as a result of Lear's own strenuous and futile effort to remain within the realm of choice.
>
> (105)

Similarly, Derek Peat (1980) acknowledged that the play forces us "to choose between the contrary possibilities it holds in unresolved opposition" (43).

Where does all this leave us? To begin with, we can certainly acknowledge that *King Lear* has meant and will continue to mean different things to different people. But in this conclusion I want to argue that the play does not sanction any-and-all meanings. Rather, the play, even in its various adapted and conflated forms, generates an endless amount of responses to *a circumscribed set of questions*: Is there a God and, if there is, is he indifferent to our plight? Is death the end of our journey? What loyalty do we owe to our fathers, and what do we owe to ourselves? How should we recognize and value love? How do we cope with the outcasts of the world, with the sufferings of the innocent, the vulnerable, and the criminal? These are Lear's questions. They remain the questions that plague us still, for they are, like the titles of *King Lear*, both our history and our tragedy.

Jeffrey Kahan
University of La Verne

Notes

1 Unless otherwise stated, all *Lear* quotations are derived from *William Shakespeare: The Complete Works*, Gen. Eds. Stanley Wells and Gary Taylor. The edition published two versions of the play. Their differences and dates are explained in the main body of this text.
2 The parenthetical date refers to the date of first publication, not necessarily the date of the volume consulted. See Works cited for full volume citation.
3 I have modernized these quotations, which are extracted from the court deposition of Nicholas Bishop, who related the aforementioned encounter. Richard Burbage's mother also participated in the mêlée.
4 The description of his height is found in Stephen Greenblatt (2004: 293). The possibility that Armin did not play the Fool is detailed later in this study. His influence on Shakespeare, however, is beyond question. As M.C. Bradbrook (1972) notes: "From the time that Armin joined the company Shakespeare very noticeably began to give his clowns the catechism as a form of jesting" (228).
5 The attribution of *Tarlton's Jests* (1600) to Henry Chettle is circumstantial; the book is sometimes attributed directly to Tarlton, who died in 1588.
6 Shakespeare's connection to Sussex's Men is established by *Henslowe's Diary*. On 23 January 1594, Shakespeare had his first tragedy, *Titus Andronicus*, performed at the Rose playhouse by Sussex's Men (Gurr, 1970: 128). As for Shakespeare and the Queen's Men, the evidence is circumstantial. See Scott McMillin and Sally-Beth MacLean, *The Queen's Men and Their Plays*, 160–65. If, as some suspect, Robert

Armin replaced Tarlton in the Queen's Men, he may have also been a member of this "king leare" cast, but he is usually linked to Chandos' Men.

7 All *King Leir* citations are from the Globe Quartos edition of *King Leir* (ed.) Tiffany Stern.

8 Richard Knowles (2002) cites a number of studies which suggest that Shakespeare continued to use a manuscript of *King Leir* when writing plays as diverse as *As You Like It, Hamlet, Richard II*. Knowles, however, disputes the evidence: "there is no convincing evidence that the old play exerted a continuing influence on one play of Shakespeare's after another for the next ten or fifteen years" (35).

9 More recently, Steven Urkowitz (1980) has found evidence that Shakespeare also referred to the old play when revising *King Lear ca.* 1609 (91–92). On the other hand, Tiffany Stern (2002) has recently put forward that Shakespeare's play was written before 1605; therefore the availability of *King Leir* in quarto had no direct influence on Shakespeare's decision to write a play on the same subject. Indeed, she theorizes that the printing of *King Leir* was a hoax of sorts: "the anonymous *Leir* may have been printed in order to exploit interest in Shakespeare's *Lear* (or even in order to gull potential readers into thinking they were buying Shakespeare's play)" (IX). On the dating of Q1, see Wells 2000: 9–14.

10 A fuller comparison of passages is undertaken by Kenneth Muir in his edition of the play (XXX–XXXI).

11 David Wiles goes so far as to call Armin an "intellectual" (136). James Shapiro speculates that Armin might have been hired after Shakespeare perused the actor's manuscripts (221). The attribution of *Tarltons Newes Out of Purgatorie* to Armin is circumstantial but accepted by most libraries.

12 Leslie Hotson (1952) agreed that the Fool's role was not to torture the king but to help him with "sharp truths" (96). M.C. Bradbrook (1972) notes that "From the time that Armin joined the company Shakespeare very noticeably began to give his clowns the catechism as a form of jesting" (228).

13 This third, heavily-revised edition was printed with the title *A Nest of Ninnies*.

14 Armin was also influenced by *King Lear*. In his poem *The Italian Taylor* (1609), a daughter refuses to give a magic ring to her father-king, echoing Lear's "Better thou hadst not been born than not to have pleased me better" (2.226–27): "Goe chaine her head vnto her knees,/There let her pine and die;/Since their obedience giues to leese,/What children owe thereby./Shall I haue any in my land;/Nay, of my flesh and blood,/That will, nay dare, so soone withstand/The motion wee thinke good?" (*Collected Works*, vol. 2: Canto 6; sheet E). One last possible parallel: in Armin's play *The Valiant Welshman* (1615), Gloucester helps the bastard Codigune seize the throne.

15 This detail appealed to Shakespeare. At the close of *Titus Andronicus*, Lucius punishes Aaron and warns the subjects of Rome not to aid him in any way:

Set him breast-deep in earth and famish him.
There let him stand, and rave, and cry for food.
If anyone relieves or pities him,
For the offence he dies. This is our doom.
(5.3.178–82)

16 Arthur F. Kinney (1980) further speculates that Shakespeare borrowed from Sidney's *Arcadia* for the storm scene (13). Shakespeare also filed some other aspects of this story away for later use. For example, in *Cymbeline* a Leonatus fights against his country, only to beg and to receive forgiveness from King Cymbeline and his daughter, Innogen. But in *Cymbeline*, Leonatus is not a Machiavel; rather, he is misled by Jachimo, who also solicits and receives clemency from Leonatus.

17 In a brilliant critique of the period, Michael Dobson has surveyed how Shakespeare, while considered imperfect, could be improved with Neoclassical cutting, adapting, and altering. Although he suggests that Tate's adaptation of *Lear* was more informed by politics than by aesthetics, we agree that Tate was not a "neo-classical cissy who couldn't stand the sight of stage blood" (83).
18 Gloucester is here addressing Kent and Cordelia, not, as in 20.165–66, Lear.
19 Johnson's pronouncement on the play was echoed by A.B. Walkley (1909): "The people [of *King Lear*] remind you of some simple South Sea Islanders in some 18th century traveller's narrative—peering through the wrong end of a telescope, expressing their emotions by uncouth dances, and filled with delight by the present of some coloured beads" (qtd. Mack 24–25). Northrop Frye (1986) likened Shakespeare's artistry in the play to "certain primitive poets and magicians, like the 'shamans' of central Asia" (118).
20 There was, as ever, some dissent. Joseph Addison, writing in the *Spectator* (1711), argued that Tate's "notion of poetical justice," may have seemed like a good idea, but the end result was a play that had "lost half its beauty" (214).
21 Arthur John Harris (1971) argued that it was Garrick, not Colman, who had first started the process of deleting Tate's text in favor of Shakespeare's text, but his argument has yet to be adopted by most theater historians.
22 Echoing aspects of Macready's casting, William Poel (1909) suggested that the ideal Fool should be "very young and frail. He might even be lame or a dwarf, but the face should be beautiful and infinitely sad to look upon" (qtd. in Speaight, 1954: 229).
23 Similarly, R.A. Foakes (1997) created a rather eye-straining system involving superscripted Fs and Qs; Jay L. Halio (2002[b]) engaged in limited experimentation with bold type and spaces to indicate a Folio or Quarto passage (82–89).
24 For an overview of their date reversal of the Quartos, see Greg, 1940: 1.
25 Two critics had the temerity to buck this anti-Quarto trend: M.R. Ridley (1935), who argued that Q1 was an accurate version of Shakespeare's first draft, and Van Dam (1935), who stated that Q1 was "far superior" to the later corrupted version found in the Folio (Kirschbaum 3).
26 Richard Knowles (1999) suggested that the play's textual inconsistencies may have been a ploy by Shakespeare to maximize dramatic effect (50).
27 Harold Bloom, for all his Bardolatry, recently admitted that he loved reading *King Lear*, but disliked seeing it: "I have attended many stagings of *King Lear*, and invariably have regretted being there" (476).
28 This comment leads to a rather important question: Just what, if any, stage production of the play did Bradley see? As Jay Halio (1992[b]) points out, Irving's 1892 production cut the blinding of Gloucester. But even with the scene cut, the production was a failure and never toured (43–44).
29 Mack's idea was not exactly new. On 1 December 1904, the *New York Times* reported that a Parisian company had mounted just such a production. However, the audience only showed mild interest, and the revival, "though earnestly archaic, was anything but Shakespearean" (" 'King Lear' in Paris"). What this critic meant by "Shakespearean" is difficult to decipher. Certainly, a historically accurate staging would not look much like any other Shakespeare production of the early twentieth century.
30 Attempts to explore *King Lear* via Shakespeare's contemporaries were not entirely groundbreaking. Both Edmond Malone and J.P. Collier, among others, had undertaken similar studies.
31 Sisson added that it was a "confession of weakness" that led A.C. Bradley to wish Lear and Cordelia saved from the doom Shakespeare insisted upon at the play's end (78).
32 Agate was writing of Gielgud's Old Vic production of 1931. When the actor

returned to the part in 1940, director Granville-Barker still complained: "you are an ash and this part demands an oak" (Gielgud, 134).

33 The Folio version is identical.

34 Rutter's argument was anticipated by L.C. Knights (1959), who described Lear as "conspicuously infantile" and given to "tantrums and tears" (101). According to Janet Adelman (1992), Lear acts like an "abandoned child" (118).

35 Kahn also glimpsed Lear's incestuous desires, arguing that the "ceremony [of divestment] alludes to the incest taboo and raises a question about Lear's 'darker purpose' in giving Cordelia away" (39).

36 In his book *King Lear, Macbeth, Indefinition, and Tragedy*, Booth stepped back from his prior statement, suggesting that doubling was intriguing, though, given the extant theatrical evidence, impossible to prove (153–55).

37 Jay Halio (1992[a]) uncovered historical evidence that blinding was a punishment for fornication. The inference is that Shakespeare wanted his audience to see Gloucester as partially culpable for Edmund's actions.

38 Annabel Patterson (1989) also suggested that the play was designed to discuss, if not openly criticize, James: "the audience would have quickly realized that the archaic setting was a ruse to permit analysis of a particular style and ideology of monarchy, one that was . . . with James's accession, suddenly topical" (106).

39 Conveniently, Orwell claimed the right to decipher the author's thoughts, which were hidden so well that they were concealed even from Shakespeare himself: "it does not very much matter whether he was fully aware of it [his actual moral beliefs]" (46).

40 Stanley Wells (2000) also raised the possibility that the mock-trial scene might have elicited unwanted laughter (Oxford ed. 56). Both editors may have been aware of director Granville–Barker's earlier speculation that Shakespeare cut the mock-trial scene because "it was a question of time and a choice between two scenes, [and] doubtless his audience would be supposed to prefer the rhetoric of the storm" (I:293.n.14). Interestingly, Granville–Barker reinserted it, along with other quarto passages, for his 1940 production of the play (Salgado 72–73).

41 As is so often the case, total consensus is difficult to come by: Adele Davidson (1998) suggests that a Renaissance stenographer may have been capable of the feat and that, consequently, the matter needs to be reconsidered.

42 See also Richard Knowles (1997: 59) and Jay L. Halio (1992[b]: 76–77).

43 On censorship and the readying of manuscripts for performance, see also Tiffany Stern (2004: 145).

44 See also T.H. Howard-Hill, "The Problem of Manuscript Copy for *Hamlet, King Lear*, and *Othello*," *SQ* 34(1983): 44–61.

45 See also Richard Knowles, The Printing of the Second Quarto (1619) of *King Lear*," *Studies in Bibliography* 35 (1982): 191–206.

46 R.A. Foakes differs with a rather poignant reading in which Lear, looking at Cordelia's lips, dies not from joy but in remembrance of her speech in Act 1, when "he hoped she would speak and her lips said nothing" (1993: 219).

47 Modified by Pope to read: "then she shook/The holy water from her heav'nly eyes."

48 Excerpts of these reviews are recorded in Leggatt (2004: 56–57).

49 Excerpts of both of these reviews are found in Leggatt (2004: 65, 72).

50 This excerpt is also found in Leggatt (2004: 82).

51 Benedict Nightingale, *New Statesman*, 7 November 1969. Though referring to another production, Leggatt feels the quotation aptly summarized Hordern's 1982 portrayal (2004: 129–30).

52 Elliot's other stage credits include a TV version of *As You Like It* (1963) and an episode of something called *The Year of the Sex Olympics* (1968).

53 The question of mirth was revived in Brian Cox's 1990 performance for the National (dir. Deborah Warner). Said Cox, Lear is "a bit of a curmudgeon, a bit of a silly old boy . . . I do think there are a lot of laughs in *Lear*, it's a play with humour" (Oliver Ford Davies 75).

54 Gordin also wrote another play, *Mirele Efros*, which was initially titled *The Jewish Queen Lear*. For a study of that play, I refer the reader to Iska Alter's 2002 article.

55 More on Bottomley's play can be found in Richard Foulkes' 2002 article.

56 Dorothy Bussy (*ca.* 1918) anticipated this interpretation when she wrote, in a letter to André Gide: "Of course Lear is senile, gâteux, fat, sot. That is where the whole point of the work lies. He impersonates the luxury, folly, indifference and selfishness of the wealthy and powerful, who have never come into contact with reality and who are suddenly forced to experience all its horrors."

57 The reader is encouraged to consult a variety of *Lear* paintings and engravings at http://www.english.emory.edu/classes/Shakespeare_Illustrated/LearPaintings.html.

Works cited

Ackroyd, Peter. *Shakespeare: The Biography*. New York and London: Nan A. Talese/ Doubleday, 2005.

Actors and Editors, A Poem By An Undergraduate. London: W. Smith and Co., 1817.

Addison, Joseph. *Critical Essays From* The Spectator *by Joseph Addison With Four Essays By Richard Steele*. Ed. Donald F. Bond. New York and Oxford: Oxford University Press, 1970.

Adelman, Janet. *Suffocating Mothers: Fantasies of Maternal Origins in Shakespeare's Plays, Hamlet to The Tempest*. New York and London: Routledge, 1992.

Agate, James. *Brief Chronicles: A Survey of the Plays of Shakespeare and the Elizabethans in Actual Performance*. London: Jonathan Cape, 1943; rpt. New York: Benjamin Blom, 1971.

Alpers, Paul J. "*King Lear* and the Theory of the 'Sight Pattern'." *In Defense of Reading*. Eds. Reuben Browner and Richard Poirier. New York: E.P. Dutton and Co., 1962: 133–52.

Alter, Iska. "Jacob Gordin's *Mirele Efros*: King Lear as Jewish Mother." *Shakespeare Survey* 55 (2002): 114–27.

Armin, Robert. *The Collected Works of Robert Armin*. Ed. J.P. Feather. 2 vols. New York and London: Johnson Reprint Corporation, 1972.

Ashton, J.W. "The Wrath of King Lear." *The Journal of English and Germanic Philology* XXXI.4 (October 1932): 530–36.

Austin, Wiltshire Stanton (Jr.) and John Ralph. *The Lives of the Poets-Laureate, With an Introductory Essay on the Title and Office*. London: Richard Bentley, 1853.

Baker, Herschel. *John Philip Kemble: The Actor in His Theatre*. Cambridge Massachusetts: Harvard University Press, 1942.

Barber, C.L. "On Christianity and the Family: Tragedy of the Sacred." *Twentieth Century Interpretations of King Lear: A Collection of Critical Essays*. Ed. Janet Adelman. Englewood Cliffs, NJ: Prentice-Hall Inc., 1978: 117–20.

Barrett, Lawrence. *Edwin Forrest*. London: David Bogue, 1881.

Bate, Jonathan. "Ovid and the Mature Tragedies: Metamorphosis in *Othello* and *King Lear*." *Shakespeare Survey* 41 (1989): 133–44.

Bentley, G.E. "Shakespeare, the King's Company, and *King Lear*." *On King Lear*. Ed. Lawrence Danson. Princeton: Princeton University Press, 1981: 47–60.

Berger, Harry (Jr.). *Making Trifles of Terrors: Redistributing Complicities in Shakespeare*. Introduction by Peter Erickson. Stanford: Stanford University Press, 1997.

Berry, Ralph. *Shakespeare in Performance: Castings and Metamorphoses*. Houndmills, Basingstoke, Hampshire and London: St. Martin's/Macmillan Press Ltd., 1993.

Berryman, John. *Berryman's Shakespeare*. Ed. John Haffenden. New York: Farrar, Straus and Giroux, 1999.

Bethell, S.L. *Shakespeare and the Popular Dramatic Tradition*. Introduction by T.S. Eliot. 1944. 2nd edn. London: P.S. King and Staples Ltd., 1948.

Bickersteth, Geoffrey L. *The Golden World of "King Lear": Proceedings of the British Academy 1946*. Vol. XXXII. London: Geoffrey Cumberlege, [1947].

Blayney, Peter W.M. *The Texts of King Lear and Their Origins. Volume I: Nicholas Okes and the First Quarto*. Cambridge: Cambridge University Press, 1982.

Bloom, Harold. *Shakespeare and the Invention of the Human*. New York: Riverhead Books/Peguin Putnum, Inc. 1998.

Boaden, James. *A Letter to George Steevens, Esq. Containing a Critical Examination of the Papers of Shakspeare; Published by Mr. Samuel Ireland. To Which are Added, Extracts From Vortigern*. London: Martin and Bain, 1796.

Bond, Edward. *Lear*. New York: Hill and Wang, 1972.

Booth, Stephen. "On the Greatness of *King Lear*." *Twentieth Century Interpretations of King Lear*. Ed. Janet Adelman. Englewood Cliffs, N.J.: Prentice-Hall Inc., 1978. 98–111.

—— *King Lear, Macbeth, Indefinition, and Tragedy*. New Haven and London: Yale University Press, 1983.

Bowers, Fredson. "The Structure of *King Lear*." *Shakespeare Quarterly* 31.1 (1980): 7–20.

Bradbrook, M.C. "Robert Armin and *Twelfth Night*." *Twelfth Night: A Casebook*. Ed. D.J. Palmer. London: Macmillan Press Ltd, 1972: 222–43.

—— "Shakespeare and the Use of Disguise in Elizabethan Drama." *Essays in Criticism* II (1952): 159–68.

Bradley, A.C. *Shakespearean Tragedy*. 1904. Eighth Printing. New York: Meridian Books Inc./St. Martin's Press, 1960.

Bratton, J.S. *Plays in Performace: King Lear*. Bristol: Bristol Classical Press, 1987.

Brook, Peter. *The Empty Space*. New York: Atheneum, 1968.

Brooks, Douglas. Correspondence with Jeffrey Kahan (email, 3 June 2005).

—— *King Lear*. Naperville, IL.: The Sourcebooks Shakespeare, 2007.

—— "*King Lear* (1608) and the Typography of Literary Ambition." *Renaissance Drama* 30 (2001): 133–60.

Brown, Ivor. "The Old Vic *King Lear*." *The Masque: A Theatre Notebook: The Old Vic King Lear*. 1 December 1946: 1–16.

Bussy, Dorothy. Harry Ransom Center. Lake/Gide, André, *ca.* 1918: 86.2.

Calderwood, James L. "Creative Uncreation In *King Lear*." *Shakespeare Quarterly* 37.1 (1986): 5–19.

Campbell, Thomas. *An Essay on English Poetry; With Notices of the British Poets*. Notes by Peter Cunningham. London: John Murray, 1848.

Capell, Edward. *Notes and Various Readings to Shakespeare*. 3 vols. Vol. I: London: Edward and Charles Dilly, 1774; Vols. II–III: London: Henry Hughes: n.d.

—— (ed.) *Mr. William Shakespeare, His Comedies, Histories, and Tragedies*. 10 vols. London: D. Leach, for J. and R. Tonson, [1767–68].

Carroll, William C. " 'The Base Shall Top Th'Legitimate': The Bedlam Beggar and the Role of Edgar in *King Lear*." *Shakespeare Quarterly* 38.4 (1987): 426–41.

Carter, Thomas. *Shakespeare and Holy Scripture With the Version He Used*. London: Hodder and Stoughton, 1905.

Case, R.H. Introduction. *The Tragedy of King Lear. The Arden Shakespeare*. Ed. W.J. Craig. 5th edn. revised. London: Methuen and Co. Ltd., 1931.

Cavell, Stanley. *Disowning Knowledge in Six Plays of Shakespeare*. Cambridge: Cambridge University Press, 1987.

Chambers, R.W. *King Lear*. Foreword by David Baird Smith. Glasgow: Jackson, Son and Company, 1940.

Chettle, Henry. *Tarlton's Jests, and News out of Purgatory: With Notes, and Some Account of the Life of Tarlton*. Ed. James Orchard Halliwell. London: Shakespeare Society, 1844.

Clark, William G. and William Aldis Wright (eds.). *The Works of Shakespeare*. 9 vols. London and Cambridge: MacMillan and Co., 1866.

Coleridge, Samuel Taylor. *Coleridge's Writings on Shakespeare*. Ed. Terence Hawkes. Introduction by Alfred Harbage. New York: Capricorn Books/G.P. Putnum's Sons, 1959.

—— *Seven Lectures on Shakespeare and Milton*. Ed. John Payne Collier. London: Chapman and Hall, 1856.

Collier, John Payne. *Notes and Emendations to the Text of Shakespeare's Plays, From Early Manuscript Corrections in a Copy of the Folio, 1632*. London: The Shakespeare Society, 1852.

Colman, George. *The History of King Lear. As It Is Performed at the Theatre Royal in Covent Garden*. London: R. Baldwin and T. Becket, 1768.

Cowie, Peter. "In the Picture: The Olivier Lear." *Sight and Sound* 52.2 (Spring 1983), rpt. in *Reading Shakespeare in Performance: King Lear*. Eds. James P. Lusardi and June Schlueter. Rutherford: Fairleigh Dickinson University Press; London and Toronto: Associated University Press, 1991: 187–89.

Craig, Gordon. *Henry Irving*. New York and Toronto: Longmans, Green and Co., 1930.

Creighton, Charles. *An Allegory of King Lear*. London: Arthur L. Humphreys, 1913.

Danby, John F. *Shakespeare's Doctrine of Nature: A Study of King Lear*. London: Faber and Faber, 1949.

Daniel, P.A. (ed.). *M. William Shak-speare's King Lear: The First Quarto 1608*. London: C. Praetorius, 1885.

Dasent, Arthur Irwin. *Nell Gwyne 1650–1687*. London: Macmillan and Co., 1924.

Davidson, Adele. "*King Lear* in an Age of Stenographical Reproduction or 'On Sitting Down to Copy *King Lear* Again'." *Papers of the Bibliographical Society of America* 92 (1998): 297–324.

Davies, Oliver Ford. *Playing Lear*. London: Nick Hern Books, 2003.

Davies, Thomas. *Memoirs of the Life of David Garrick*. 2 vols. London: Longman, Hurst, Rees, and Orme, 1808.

Dictionary of National Biography. Eds. Leslie Stephen and Sidney Lee. London: Smith, Elder, & Co., 1885–1900.

Dobson, Michael. *The Making of the National Poet: Shakespeare, Adaptation and Authorship, 1660–1769*. Oxford: Clarendon Press; New York: Oxford University Press, 1992.

Doran, Madeleine. "The Text of King Lear." *Stanford University Publications. University Series; Language and Literature* IV.2 (1931): 99–244.

Doren, Mark Van. *Shakespeare*. 1939. Foreword by David Lehman. New York: New York Review of Books, 2005.

Draper, J.W. "The Occasion of *King Lear*." *Studies in Philology* (1937): 178–85.

Driscoll, James P. "The Vision of *King Lear*." *Shakespeare Studies* X (1977): 159–89.

Duthie, George Ian. *Elizabethan Shorthand and the First Quarto of King Lear*. Oxford: Basil Blackwell, 1949[a].

—— (ed.) *Shakespeare's King Lear: A Critical Edition*. Oxford: Basil Blackwell, 1949[b].

Duthie, George Ian and John Dover Wilson (eds.). *King Lear*. London and New York: Cambridge University Press, 1960.

Dyce, Alexander. *A Few Notes on Shakespeare: With Occasional Remarks on the Emendations of the Manuscript-Corrector in Mr. Collier's Copy of the Folio 1632*. London: John Russell Smith, 1853.

—— *Strictures on Mr. Collier's New Edition of Shakespeare, 1858*. London: John Russell Smith, 1859.

Eagleton, Terry. *William Shakespeare*. Oxford: Basil Blackwell, 1986.

Elton, William R. *King Lear and the Gods*. San Marino, California: The Huntington Library, 1966.

Empson, William. *The Structure of Complex Words*. Norfolk, Connecticut: New Directions Books/ London and Colchester: Spottiswoode, Ballantyne and Co. Ld., [1951].

Erne, Lukas. *Shakespeare as Literary Dramatist*. Cambridge and New York: Cambridge University Press, 2003.

Everett, Barbara. "The New *King Lear*." *Critical Quarterly* 2.4 (Winter 1960): 325–39.

Felperin, Howard. *Shakespearean Representation: Mimesis and Modernity in Elizabethan Tragedy*. Princeton: Princeton University Press, 1977.

Fenwick, Henry. "The Production." *King Lear: The BBC TV Shakespeare*. Eds. Peter Alexander *et al.* London: British Broadcasting Corporation, 1983: 19–34, rpt. in *Reading Shakespeare in Performance: King Lear*. Eds. James P. Lusardi and June Schlueter. Rutherford: Fairleigh Dickinson University Press, London and Toronto: Associates University Presses, 1991: 172–85.

FitzSimons, Raymund. *Edmund Kean: Fire From Heaven*. London: Hamish Hamilton Ltd., 1976.

Foakes, Reginald A. *Hamlet Versus Lear: Cultural Politics and Shakespeare's Art*. Cambridge: Cambridge University Press, 1993.

—— (ed.) *King Lear. The Arden Shakespeare*. Third Series. Cambridge, Walton-on-Thames, Surrey: Thomas Nelson and Sons, Ltd., 1997.

Fortin, René E. "Hermeneutical Circularity and Christian Interpretations of *King Lear*." *Shakespeare Studies* XII (1979): 113–25.

Foulkes, Richard. " 'How fine a play was Mrs Lear': The Case for Gordon Bottomley's *King Lear's Wife*." *Shakespeare Survey* 55 (2002): 128–38.

Frye, Northrop. *Fools of Time: Studies in Shakespearean Tragedy*. Toronto: University of Toronto Press, 1967.

—— *On Shakespeare*. Ed. Robert Sandler. Markham, Ontario: Fitzhenry & Whiteside, 1986.

Furness, Horace Howard. *King Lear: A New Variorum Edition*. 1880. Twelfth Impression. Philadelphia and London: J.B. Lippincott and Co., 1908.

Garber, Marjorie. *Shakespeare After All*. New York: Anchor Books/Random House, 2004.

Gardner, Helen. *King Lear: The John Coffin Memorial Lecture 1966*. London: The Athlone Press/University of London; New York and Toronto: Oxford University Press, 1967.

Garrett, Davidson. *King Lear of the Taxi: Musings of a New York City Actor/Taxi Driver*. New York: Advent Purple Press, 2006.

Gielgud, John and John Miller and John Powell. *An Actor and His Time*. London: Sidgwick and Jaskson, Ltd., 1979.

Gildon, Charles. *The Works of Mr. William Shakespear. Volume the Seventh. Containing, Venus & Adonis, Tarquin & Lucrece and His Miscellany Poems. With Critical Remarks on His PLAYS, &c. to which is Prefix'd An ESSAY on the Art, Rise and Progress of the STAGE in Greece, Rome and England*. London: E. Curll and E. Sanger, 1710.

Goldberg, Jonathan. "Perspectives: Dover Cliff and the Conditions of Representation." *Shakespeare and Deconstruction*. Eds. G. Douglas Atkins and David M. Bergeron. New York, Bern, Frankfurt am Main, Paris: Peter Lang, 1988: 245–65.

—— "Textual Properties." *Shakespeare Quarterly* 37.2 (1986): 213–17.

Goldberg, S.L. *An Essay on King Lear*. London: Cambridge University Press, 1974.

Good, Maurice. *Every Inch A Lear: A Rehearsal Journal of "King Lear" With Peter Ustinov and the Stratford Festival Company Directed by Robin Phillips*. Victoria, BC: Sono Nis Press, 1982.

Grady, Hugh. *Shakespeare's Universal Wolf: Studies in Early Modern Reification*. Oxford: Clarendon Press, 1996.

Granville-Barker, Harley. *Prefaces to Shakespeare*. 2 vols. Princeton, NJ: Princeton University Press, 1946–47.

Greenblatt, Stephen J. *Learning to Curse: Essays in Early Modern Culture*. New York and London: Routledge, 1990.

—— *Will in the World: How Shakespeare Became Shakespeare*. London and New York: W.W. Norton and Company Inc. 2004.

Greg, W.W. *The Editorial Problem in Shakespeare: A Survey of the Foundations of the Text*. Oxford: Clarendon Press, 1942.

—— "The Function of Bibliography in Literary Criticism Illustrated in a Study of the Text of 'King Lear.' " *Neophilogus* XVIII (1933): 241–62.

—— "The Rationale of Copy-Text." *Studies in Bibliography* 3 (1950–1): 19–36.

—— *The Variants in the First Quarto of "King Lear": A Bibliographical and Critical Inquiry*. London: Printed for the Bibliographical Society at the University Press, Oxford 1940 for 1939.

Gurr, Andrew. *The Shakespeare Company, 1694–1642*. Cambridge: Cambridge University Press, 2004.

—— *The Shakespearean Stage: 1574–1642*. Cambridge: Cambridge University Press, 1970.

Halio, Jay L. (ed.). *The First Quarto of King Lear. The New Cambridge Shakespeare: The Early Quartos*. Cambridge and New York: Cambridge University Press, 1994.

—— "Gloucester's Blinding." *Shakespeare Quarterly* 43.2 (1992[a]): 221–23.

—— (ed.) *The Tragedy of King Lear. The New Cambridge Shakespeare*. Cambridge and New York: Cambridge University Press, 1992[b].

Hall, H.T. *King Lear. Shaksperean Fly-Leaves. New Series*. Cambridge: H. Wallis for H.T. Hall, 1879.

Hamilton, N.E.S.A. *An Inquiry into the Genuineness of the Manuscript Corrections in Mr. J. Payne Collier's Annotated Shakspere, Folio, 1632; and of Certain Shaksperian Documents Likewise Published by Mr. Collier*. London: Richard Bentley, 1860.

Hare, David. Anne Busy interview with David Hare, in S. Hare, Director, *King Lear*. Harry Ransom Center HRC 31.4.

Harris, Arthur John. "Garrick, Colman, and *King Lear*: A Reconsideration." *Shakespeare Quarterly* 22.1 (1971): 57–66.

Hazlitt, William. *The Complete Works of William Hazlitt in Twenty-One Volumes*. 1817. Ed. P.P. Howe. London and Toronto: J.M. Dent and Sons, 1930–34.

Heilman, Robert B. "The Unity of *King Lear*." *Sewanee Review* (1948); rpt. in *Shakespeare: King Lear. Casebook Series*. Ed. Frank Kermode. London: Macmillan, 1969: 169–78.

Heinemann, Margot. " 'Demystifying the Mystery of State': *King Lear* and the World Turned Upside Down." *Shakespeare Survey* 44 (1992): 75–90.

Henslowe's Diary. Ed. W.W. Greg. 2 vols. London: A.H. Bullen, Vol I: 1904; Vol. II: 1908.

Hinman, Charles and W.W. Greg (eds.). *King Lear, 1608 (Pied Bull Quarto)*. Shakespeare Quarto Facsimiles Number 1. Second Impression. Oxford: Clarendon Press, 1964.

Holderness, Graham. "Bardolatry: or, The cultural materialist's guide to Stratford-upon-Avon." *The Shakespeare Myth*. Ed. Graham Holderness. Manchester: Manchester University Press/New York: St. Martin's Press, 1988: 2–15.

—— (ed.) *William Shak-speare, His True Chronicle Historie of the Life and Death of King Lear and His Three Daughters*. Hemel Hempstead, Herts.; Englewood Cliffs: Prentice Hall, Harvester Wheatsheaf, 1995.

Holinshed, Raphael. *Holinshed's Chronicle As Used In Shakespeare's Plays*. Eds. Allardyce and Josephine Nicoll. London: J.M. Dent and Sons, Ltd.; New York: E.P. Dutton and Co. Inc., 1927; rpt. 1959.

Holloway, John. *The Story of the Night: Studies in Shakespeare's Major Tragedies*. Lincoln: University of Nebraska Press, 1961.

Holmes, Martin. *Shakespeare and Burbage*. Introduction by J.C. Trewin. London and Chichester: Phillimore/New Jersey: Rowman and Littlefield, 1978.

Hotson, Leslie. *Shakespeare's Motley*. New York: Oxford University Press, 1952.

Howard-Hill, T.H. "The Two-Text Controversy." *Lear from Study to Stage: Essays in Criticism*. Eds. James Ogden and Arthur H. Scouten. Madison, Teaneck: Fairleigh Dickenson University Press; London: Associated University Presses, 1997: 31–44.

Hughes, Alan. *Henry Irving, Shakespearean*. Foreword by John Russell Brown. Cambridge: Cambridge University Press, 1981.

Hughes, Ted. *Shakespeare and the Goddess of Complete Being*. London: Faber and Faber Ltd., 1992.

Hunter, Robert G. *Shakespeare and the Mystery of God's Judgments*. Athens. GA: The University of Georgia Press, 1976.

Ireland, Samuel (ed.). *Miscellaneous Papers and Legal Instruments Under the Hand and Seal of William Shakspeare: Including the Tragedy of King Lear, and a Small Fragment of Hamlet, From the Original MSS. In the Possession of Samuel Ireland of Norfolk Street*. [Oversized folio version.] London: Cooper and Graham, etc., 1796.

Ireland, William-Henry. *Confessions of William-Henry Ireland. Containing the Particulars of His Fabrication of the Shakspeare Manuscripts; Together With Anecdotes and Opinions of Many Distinguished Persons in the Literary, Political, and Theatrical World.* London: Ellerton and Byworth, for T. Goddard, 1805; rpt. New York: Burt Franklin, 1874.

Jackson, William A. *Records of the Court of the Stationers' Company*. London: The Bibliographical Society, 1957.

James, D.G. *The Life of Reason; Hobbes, Locke, Bolingbroke*. London, New York: Longmans, Green and Co., 1949.

Johnson, Samuel. *Johnson on Shakespeare: Essays and Notes Selected and Set Forth With an Introduction*. 1765. Ed. Walter Raleigh. London: Henry Frowde, 1908.

Jorgensen, Paul A. *Lear's Self-Discovery*. Berkeley and Los Angeles: University of California Press, 1967.

Kahn, Coppélia. "The Absent Mother in 'King Lear.' " *Rewriting the Renaissance: The Discourses of Sexual Difference in Early Modern Europe*. Eds. Margaret W. Furguson, Maureen Quilligan and Nancy J. Vickers. Chicago and London: University of Chicago Press, 1986: 33–49.

Kahn, Paul W. *Law and Love: The Trials of King Lear*. New Haven and London: Yale University Press, 2000.

Kean, Charles (ed./dir.). *King Lear*, in *Selections from the Plays of Shakespeare. As Arranged for Representation at the Princess's Theatre, and Especially Adapted for Schools, Private Families, and Young People*. Vol. 2. London: Bradbury and Evans, 1860.

—— *King Lear Promptbook*, 1858. Copy of Promptbook in "Promptbook Collection," Harry Ransom Center.

—— *Shakespeare Tragedy of King Lear, Arranged for Representation at the Princess's Theatre, With Historical and Explanatory Notes By Charles Kean, F.S.A. As First Performed on Saturday, April 17, 1858*. London: John K. Chapman and Co., [1858].

Kelly, Linda. *The Kemble Era: John Philip Kemble, Sarah Siddons and the London Stage*. New York: Random House, 1980.

Kemble, John Philip. *King Lear, John Philip Kemble Promptbooks*. 1788. Ed. Charles H. Shattuck. 11 Vols. Charlottesville: The University Press of Virginia/The Folger Shakespeare Library, 1974.

The Kembles and Their Contemporaries: Actors and Actresses of Great Britain and the United States. Eds. Brander Mathews and Laurence Hutton. 1886. Boston: L.C. Page and Company, 1890.

Kenrick, William. *A Review of Doctor Johnson's New Edition of Shakespeare*. London: J. Payne, 1765.

Kettle, Arnold. *Literature and Liberation: Selected Essays Arnold Kettle*. Eds. Graham Martin and W.R. Owens. Introduction by Dipak Nandy. Manchester: Manchester University Press/New York: St. Martin's Press, 1988.

Kiernan, Victor. *Eight Tragedies of Shakespeare: A Marxist Study*. London and New York: Verso, 1996.

" 'King Lear' in Hebrew." *The New York Times*, August 13, 1899.

" 'King Lear' in Paris." *The New York Times*, December 1, 1904.

Kinney, Arthur F. "Some Conjectures on the Composition of 'King Lear.' " *Shakespeare Survey* 33 (1980): 13–25.

Kirby. Ian J. "The Passing of King Lear." *Shakespeare Survey* 41 (1989): 145–57.

Kirschbaum, Leo. *The True Text of King Lear*. Baltimore: The John Hopkins Press, 1945.

Knight, G. Wilson. *The Wheel of Fire: Interpretations of Shakespeare's Sombre Tragedies*. London: Humphrey Milford / Oxford University Press, 1930.

Knights, L.C. *Some Shakespearan Themes*. London: Chatto and Windus, 1959.

Knowles, Richard. "Cordelia's Return." *Shakespeare Quarterly* 50.1 (1999): 33–50.

—— "How Shakespeare Knew *King Leir*." *Shakespeare Survey* 55 (2002): 12–35.

—— "The Printing of the Second Quarto (1619) of *King Lear*." *Studies in Bibliography* 35 (1982): 191–206.

—— "Two *Lears*? By Shakespeare?" *Lear from Study to Stage: Essays in Criticism*. Eds. James Ogden and Arthur H. Scouten. Madison, Teaneck: Fairleigh Dickenson University Press; London: Associated University Press, 1997: 57–78.

Kott, Jan. *Shakespeare Our Contemporary*. Trans. Boleslaw Taborski. Garden City, New York: Doubleday and Co., Inc., 1964.

Kronenfeld, Judy. *King Lear and the Naked Truth: Rethinking the Language of Religion and Resistance*. Durham and London: Duke University Press, 1998.

Lamb, Charles. *The Life, Letters and Writings of Charles Lamb*. 1811. Ed. Percy Fitzgerald. The Enfield Edition. 6 vols. London: Bedford, [1875].

Lascelles, Mary. " 'King Lear' and Doomsday." *Aspects of King Lear: Articles Reprinted from Shakespeare Survey*. Eds. Kenneth Muir and Stanley Wells. Cambridge: Cambridge University Press, 1982: 55–65.

Leggatt, Alexander. *King Lear. Shakespeare in Performance*. Gen Eds. J.R. Mulryne and J.C. Bulman; Associate Ed. Margaret Shewring. 1991; rev. 2nd edn. New York and Manchester: Manchester University Press, 2004.

—— *King Lear. Twayne's New Critical Introductions to Shakespeare*. Boston: Twayne Publishers / G.K. Hall and Co., 1988.

Levin, Harry. "The Heights and the Depths: A Scene from 'King Lear.' " *More Talking of Shakespeare*. Ed. John Garrett. New York: Theatre Arts Books, 1959: 87–103.

Lippincott, H.F. "*King Lear* and the Fools of Robert Armin." *Shakespeare Quarterly* 26.3 (1975): 243–53.

Lothian, John M. *King Lear: A Tragic Reading of Life*. Toronto: Clarke, Irwin and Company, Ltd., 1949.

Lynch, Stephen J. "Sin, Suffering, and Redemption in *Leir* and *Lear*." *Shakespeare Studies* XVIII (1986): 161–74.

Mack, Maynard. "The Jacobean Shakespeare: Some Observations on the Construction of the Tragedies." *Jacobean Theatre*. Eds. John Russell Brown and Bernard Harris. London: Edward Arnold, 1960: 11–42.

—— *King Lear In Our Time*. Berkeley and Los Angeles: University of California Press, 1965.

MacLean, Hugh. "Disguise in *King Lear*: Kent and Edgar." *Shakespeare Quarterly* 11.1 (1960): 49–54.

McLuskie, Kathleen. "The Patriarchal Bard: Feminist Criticism and Shakespeare: *King Lear* and *Measure for Measure*." *Political Shakespeare: New Essays in Cultural Materialism*. Eds. Jonathan Dollimore and Alan Sinfield. Ithaca and London: Cornell University Press, 1985: 88–108.

McMillin, Scott and Sally-Beth MacLean. *The Queen's Men and Their Plays*. Cambridge: Cambridge University Press, 1998.

Macready, Charles William. *The Diaries of William Charles Macready 1833–1851*. Ed. William Toynbee. 2 vols. New York: G.P. Putnum's Sons, 1912.

Maguire, Laurie E. *Shakespearean Suspect Texts: The 'Bad' Quartos and their Contexts*. Cambridge: Cambridge University Press, 1996.

Malone, Edmond [and James Boswell the Younger] (eds.). *The Plays and Poems of William Shakespeare*. 21 vols. London, F.C. and J. Rivington, etc. 1821.

Marcus, Leah S. *Puzzling Shakespeare: Local Readings and Its Discontents*. Berkeley, Los Angeles, London: University of California Press, 1988.

Marowitz, Charles. "Lear Log." *Tulane Drama Review* 8.2 (Winter 1963): 103–21.

Martin, William F. *The Indissoluble Knot: King Lear As Ironic Drama*. Lanham, New York and London: University Press of America, 1987.

Marx, Steven. *Shakespeare and the Bible. Oxford Shakespeare Topics*. Gen. Eds. Peter Holland and Stanley Wells. Oxford and New York: Oxford University Press, 2000.

Matthews, Richard. "Edmund's Redemption in *King Lear*." *Shakespeare Quarterly* 26.1 (1975): 25–29.

Mendonça, Barbara Heliodora Carneiro de. "The Influence of *Gorboduc* on *King Lear*." *Shakespeare Survey* 13 (1960): 41–48.

Muir, Edwin. *The Politics of King Lear: The Seventh W.P. Ker Memorial Lecture delivered in the University of Glasgow 23 April, 1946*. 1947; rpt. Glasgow: Jackson, Son and Company, New York: Gordon Press, 1972.

Muir, Kenneth (ed.). *King Lear: The Arden Edition of the Works of William Shakespeare*. 8th edn. London: Methuen and Co. Ltd, 1952; revised and corrected 1959.

Munro, Lucy. *Children of the Queen's Revels: A Jacobean Theatre Repertory*. Cambridge: Cambridge University Press, 2005.

Murphy, John L. *Darkness and Devils: Exorcism and King Lear*. Athens, Ohio and London: Ohio University Press, 1984.

Nevo, Ruth. *Tragic Form in Shakespeare*. Princeton, NJ: Princeton University Press, 1972.

Nowottny, Winifred M.T. "Lear's Questions." *Shakespeare Survey* 10 (1957): 90–97.

—— "Some Aspects of the Style of *King Lear*." *Shakespeare Survey* 13 (1960): 49–57.

Odell, George C. D. *Annals of the New York Stage*. 10 vols. New York: Columbia University Press, 1927–49.

—— *Shakespeare From Betterton to Irving*. 2 vols. 1920; rpt. New York: Dover Publications, 1966.

Olivier, Laurence. *On Acting*. New York: Simon and Schuster, 1986.

Orgel, Stephen (ed.). *King Lear: The 1608 Quarto and 1623 Folio Texts*. New York: Penguin Books, 2000.

Ornstein, Robert. *The Moral Vision of Jacobean Tragedy*. 1960. 2nd edn. Madison and Milwaukee: University of Wisconsin Press, 1965.

Orwell, George. "Lear, Tolstoy and the Fool." *Shooting an Elephant and Other Essays*. 1945; rpt. New York: Harcourt, Brace and Company, 1950: 32–52.

Patterson, Annabel. *Shakespeare and the Popular Voice*. Oxford: Basil Blackwell, 1989.

Peat, Derek. " 'And That's True Too': 'King Lear' and the Tension of Uncertainty." *Shakespeare Survey* 33 (1980): 43–53.

Pepys, Samuel. *The Diary of Samuel Pepys*. Eds. Robert Latham and William Matthews. 11 vols. Berkeley and Los Angeles: University of California Press, 1970–83.

Perret, Marion D. "*Lear*'s Good Old Man." *Shakespeare Studies* XVII (1985): 89–102.

Pollard, Alfred W. *Shakespeare Folios and Quartos: A Study in the Bibliography of*

Shakespeare's Plays 1594–1685. London: Methuen and Co., 1909; rpt. New York: A Marandell Book / Cooper Square Publishers, Inc., 1970.

Quilligan, Maureen. *Incest and Agency in Elizabeth's England*. Philadelphia: University of Pennsylvania, 2005.

Rackin, Phyllis. "Delusion as Resolution in *King Lear*." *Shakespeare Quarterly* 21.1 (1970): 29–34.

Rees, James. *The Life of Edwin Forrest. With Reminiscences and Personal Recollections*. Philadelphia: T.B. Peterson and Brothers, 1874.

Reibetanz, John. *The Lear World: A Study of King Lear in Its Dramatic Context*. Toronto and Buffalo: University of Toronto Press, 1977.

Ribner, Irving. *Patterns in Shakespearian Tragedy*. London: Methuen and Co. Ltd., 1960.

Richardson, William. *Essays on Shakespeare's Dramatic Characters of Richard the Third, King Lear, and Timon of Athens*. London: J. Murray, 1784.

Ridley, M.R. (ed.). *King Lear. The New Temple Shakespeare*. London: J.M. Dent and Sons Ltd; New York: E.P. Dutton and Co., Inc., 1935.

Ringler William A. (Jr.). "Shakespeare and his Actors: Some Remarks on *King Lear*." *Shakespeare's Art from a Comparative Perspective*. Ed. Wendell M. Aycock. Lubbock: Texas Tech Press, 1981: 183–94.

Roche Thomas P. (Jr.). " 'Nothing Almost Sees Miracles': Tragic Knowledge in *King Lear*." *On King Lear*. Ed. Lawrence Danson. Princeton: Princeton University Press, 1981: 136–62.

Rosenberg, Marvin. *The Masks of King Lear*. Berkeley, Los Angeles, London: University of California Press, 1972.

Rutter, Carol. "Eel Pie and Ugly Sisters in *King Lear*." *Lear from Study to Stage: Essays in Criticism*. Eds. James Ogden and Arthur H. Scouten. Madison, Teaneck: Fairleigh Dickenson University Press; London: Associated University Press, 1997: 172–225.

Ryan, Kiernan. *Shakespeare*. Atlantic Highlands, NJ: Humanities Press International, Inc., 1989.

Salgādo, Gamini. *King Lear: Text and Performance*. Houndsmills, Basingstoke, Hampshire: Macmillan Publishers Ltd., 1984.

Sanders, Julie. *Novel Shakespeares: Twentieth-Century Women Novelists and Appropriation*. Manchester and New York: Manchester University Press, 2001.

Saunders, Laura. "*King Lear*, updated." *Forbes Magazine*. September 9, 1998.

Schlegel, Augustus William. *A Course of Lectures on Dramatic Art and Literature*. 1811; English trans. John Black; revised by Rev. A.J.W. Morrision. London: Henry G. Bohn, 1846.

Schoff, Francis G. "King Lear: Moral Example or Tragic Protagonist?" *Shakespeare Quarterly* 13.2 (1962): 157–72.

Shakespeare, William. *The Life and Death of King Lear*. Vol. 3 (1723) of *The works of Shakespear*. Ed. Alexander Pope. London: Jacob Tonson, 1723–25.

—— *William Shakespeare: The Complete Works*. Gen. Eds. Stanley Wells and Gary Taylor. Oxford: Clarendon Press, 1986.

Shakespeare, William [and Naham Tate]. *King Lear*, in *Bell's Edition of Shakespeare's Plays, As They Are Now Performed at the Theatres Royal in London; Regulated From the Prompt Books With Notes Critical and Illustrative; by the Authors of the Dramatic Censor*. 9 vols. London and York: John Bell, and C. Etherington, 1773–74.

Shapiro, James. *A Year in the Life of William Shakespeare: 1599*. New York: Harper-Collins Publishers, 2005.

Sharma, R.C. *An Approach to King Lear*. Delhi: The Macmillan Company of India, Ltd., 1975.

Shattuck, Charles H. See Kemble, John Philip. *King Lear, John Philip Kemble Promptbooks*.

[Shebbeare, John]. *Letters on the English Nation By Batista Angeloni, A Jesuit, Who Resided Many Years in London*. 2 vols. London: [S.N.], 1755.

Sher, Antony. "The Fool in *King Lear*." *Players of Shakespeare 2*. Eds. Russell Jackson and Robert Smallwood. Cambridge: Cambridge University Press, 1988: 151–65.

Sidney, [Sir] Philip. *The Countess of Pembroke's Arcadia (The New Arcadia)*. Ed. Victor Skretkowicz. Oxford: Clarendon Press, 1987.

Siegel, Paul N. *Shakespearean Tragedy and the Elizabethan Compromise*. New York: New York University Press, 1957.

Singer, Samuel Weller. *The Text of Shakespeare Vindicated From the Interpolations and Corruptions Advocated By John Payne Collier Esq. In His Notes And Emendations*. London: William Pickering, 1853.

Sisson, C.J. *Shakespeare's Tragic Justice*. Canada: W.J. Gage Limited, [1962].

Skulsky, Harold. "*King Lear* and the Meaning of Chaos." *Shakespeare Quarterly* 17.1 (1966): 3–17.

Somogyi, Nick de (ed.). *King Lear: The Tragedie of King Lear: The First Folio of 1623 and A Parallel Modern Edition*. London: Nick Hern, 2004.

Speaight, Robert. *William Poel and the Elizabethan Revival*. Melbourne, London, Toronto: William Heinemann Ltd., 1954.

Spenser, Edmund. *Spenser: Poetical Works*. Eds. J.C. Smith and E. de Selincourt. 1912; rpt. London, Oxford, New York: Oxford University Press, 1975.

Stampfer, James. "The Catharsis of *King Lear*." A*spects of King Lear*. Eds. Kenneth Muir and Stanley Wells. Cambridge: Cambridge University Press, 1982: 77–86.

Stern, Jeffrey. "*King Lear*: The Transference of the Kingdom." *Shakespeare Quarterly* 41.3 (1990): 299–308.

Stern, Tiffany (ed.). *King Leir*. Globe Quartos. London: Nick Hern Books Ltd., 2002.

—— *Making Shakespeare From Stage to Page. Accents on Shakespeare Series*. Gen. ed. Terence Hawkes. New York and London: Routledge/Francis and Taylor, 2004.

Stone, P.W.K. *The Textual History of King Lear*. London: Scolar Press, 1980.

Stopes, Charlotte Carmichael. *Burbage and Shakespeare's Stage*. London: Alexander Moring Ltd., 1913; rpt. New York: Haskell House Publishers, 1970.

Stoppard, Tom. *Rosencrantz and Guildenstern Meet King Lear*. Stoppard Collection, 23.11. Harry Ransom Center.

Stroup, Thomas B. "Cordelia and the Fool." *Shakespeare Quarterly* 12.2 (1961): 127–32.

Swinburne, Algernon Charles. *A Study of Shakespeare*. London: Chatto and Windus, 1880.

—— *Three Plays of Shakespeare*. London and New York: Harper and Brothers, 1909.

Tate, Naham. *The History of King Lear. Acted at the Duke's Theatre. Reviv'd with Alterations*. London: E. Flesher, and are to be sold by R. Bentley, and M. Magnes in Russel-street near Covent-Garden, 1681.

Taylor, Gary. "The Folio Copy for *Hamlet, King Lear*, and *Othello*." *Shakespeare Quarterly* 34.1 (1983[a]): 44–61.

—— "*King Lear:* Date and Authorship of the Folio Version." *The Division of the Kingdoms: Shakespeare's Two Versions of King Lear*. Eds. Gary Taylor and Michael Warren. Oxford: Clarendon Press, 1983[b]: 351–468.
—— "Monopolies, Show Trials, Disaster, and Invasion: *King Lear* and Censorship." *The Division of the Kingdoms: Shakespeare's Two Versions of King Lear*. Eds. Gary Taylor and Michael Warren. Oxford: Clarendon Press, 1983[c]: 75–119.
—— "The War in *King Lear*." *Shakespeare Survey* 33 (1980): 27–34.
Taylor, Gary and Michael Warren (eds.) *The Division of the Kingdoms: Shakespeare's Two Versions of King Lear*. Oxford: Clarendon Press, 1983.
Tennenhouse, Leonard. *Power on Display: The Politics of Shakespeare's Genres*. New York: Methuen, Inc., 1986.
Thackeray, William Makepeace. *Letters and Private Papers of William Makepeace Thackeray*. Ed. Gordon N. Ray. 4 vols. Cambridge, MA: Harvard University Press, 1946.
Tolstoy, Leo. *Tolstoy on Shakespeare*. 1906; English trans. London: Everett and Co. / Christchurch, Hants.: The Free Age Press, [1907?].
Traversi, Derek. *An Approach to Shakespeare*. 1938; 2nd edn., rev. and enlarged. London and Glasgow: Sands and Co., [1957?].
Urkowitz, Stephen. *Shakespeare's Revision of King Lear*. Princeton, NJ: Princeton University Press, 1980.
Walker, Alice. *Textual Problems of the First Folio*. Cambridge: Cambridge University Press, 1953.
Wallace, Charles William. "The First London Theatre: Materials for a History." *Nebraska University Studies* XIII.1–3 (January–April–July 1913): 1–297.
Warren, Michael. "Albany and Edgar," in *Shakespeare: Pattern of Excelling Nature*. Eds. David Bevington and Jay L. Halio. Newark: University of Delaware Press, 1978: 95–107.
—— (ed.) *The Parallel King Lear, 1608–1623*. Berkeley: University of California Press, 1989.
Warton, Thomas. *An Enquiry into the Authenticity of the Poems Attributed to Thomas Rowley*. London: J. Dodsley, 1782.
Wells, Stanley (ed.). *The History of King Lear*. Oxford: Clarendon, 2000.
—— "Lear in the fool's shadow." *TLS* (16 July 1982): 764.
Welsford, Enid. *The Fool: His Social and Literary History*. 1935. New York: Farrar and Rinehart, [1962].
Wiles, David. *Shakespeare's Clown: Actor and Text in the Elizabethan Playhouse*. New York and London: Cambridge University Press, 1987.
Williams, George W. "The Poetry of the Storm in *King Lear*." *Shakespeare Quarterly* 2.1 (1951): 57–71.
Willis, Susan. *The BBC Shakespeare Plays: Making the Televised Canon*. Chapel Hill and London: The University of North Carolina Press, 1991.
Wingate, Charles E.L. *Shakespeare's Heroes on the Stage*. New York: Thomas Y. Crowell and Company, 1896.
Woods, Leigh. "Crowns of Straw on Little Men: Garrick's New Heroes." *Shakespeare Quarterly* 32.1 (1981): 69–79.

2 The reshaping of *King Lear*

R.A. Foakes

This essay revisits a vexed question that has in recent years provoked much heat and dogmatic claims on both sides, namely, whether the numerous and important differences between the 1608 Quarto and 1623 Folio texts of *King Lear* indicate that someone, perhaps Shakespeare himself, deliberately reworked the play. In my edition of the play for the Arden Series 3, published in 1997, I found the evidence of revision by someone skilled in writing for the stage persuasive. Reviewing the treatment of the texts between 1980 and 2000 in *Shakespeare Survey* 55 (2002), Kiernan Ryan takes the side of those who reject the idea of deliberate revision, and indeed says that the revisionist hypothesis has been dealt "a series of body-blows from which it looks unlikely to recover"; he thinks changes found in the Folio might have been made by anyone, and "most of the cuts and revisions are not convincing on artistic or theatrical grounds anyway" (Ryan 3). This dismissive assertion led me to reconsider the evidence here, with, I trust, greater sharpness and clarity.

There are indications of revisions by someone in a number of Shakespeare's plays that exist in Quarto and Folio texts, but none of these has proved as controversial as the changes in the text of *King Lear*. In spite of increasing attention to texts that can be related to performance on the stage,[1] many textual critics and editors have preferred first Quarto versions because these are thought in general to be closer to the author's manuscript, usually his "foul papers." Like everyone else, scholars in general find binary oppositions attractive, white and black, good and evil, republican and democrat, labor and conservative, and, in textual matters, "foul papers," a term first recorded (in the form "foule sheet") by the playwright Richard Daborne in 1613, and "fair copy." This binary opposition assumes that dramatists always wrote only one draft of a play: " 'foul' seems to have been the contemporary descriptive term for authors' own papers, sheets or copies of the working draft of a play" (Ioppolo, 2006: 78–79),[2] while a "fair copy" made by the author or a scribe was what the censor desired to see in order to license a play, and the actors wished to have in order to perform it. The "fair copy" seems often to have been preserved by the company of actors for its use, and it is now thought that at least eighteen of Shakespeare's plays were printed from his "foul papers," which could be released for publication,[3] all of them works that "show to varying degrees similar authorial errors, false starts, loose ends, duplications, inconsistencies and other confusions in plot, setting, character, dialogue, speech-prefixes and stage directions" (Ioppolo, 2006: 183).

Ben Jonson and Shakespeare's fellow sharers John Heminge and Henry Condell praised him in the First Folio as one who left scarcely a blot in his papers, but this comment cannot be taken literally. A number of the early printed texts provide evidence that he altered, added or cut, and left loose ends, mislineations and inconsistencies in manuscripts. One such text is the first Quarto of *King Lear*, which, as the many press variants in surviving copies show, was printed from a manuscript that was probably "so messy as to be illegible at points," and which had many confusions and errors. These were compounded by the sloppy work of the printing house. The Quarto of the "True Chronicle Historie of the life and death of King Lear" was the first play printed in the workshop of Nicholas Okes, and was set by two compositors who were not familiar with the conventions of play-texts, so that they printed a good deal of verse as prose and they also made many mistakes that suggest their copy derived from a manuscript that was indeed often hard to decipher (Blayney, 1982: 184).

Any changes in later drafts or printings could have been made by scribes, printers or players, and are therefore treated by scholars with suspicion. It is true that Folio revisions and cuts could have been made by someone else, but there is no reason to suppose that Shakespeare, a sharer and senior member of his company of players, would let others rework his texts. He may well have had second thoughts or accepted advice from members of his cast who suggested alterations for the stage, but where substantive additions or alterations in the Folio are consonant with his style, they have been accepted as Shakespearean lines. As to "artistic or theatrical" values, these are matters for individual judgment, and are often affected by the wider convictions and assumptions critics hold. In any case, I am not concerned to argue here for Shakespeare's authorship of textual changes, which is a separate issue, but only to present the evidence for what seems to me a consistent pattern of revision in the Folio that subtly changes the dramatic shaping of the play as it is presented in the Quarto.

The study of Shakespeare's texts has been largely conditioned by a traditional assumption that he wrote only one draft of a play, or "foul papers," which was corrected and perhaps revised in a "fair copy." No manuscript text by Shakespeare survives (with the exception of some lines in the collaborative play of *Sir Thomas More*), and so we do not know whether he always composed by writing one draft before making, or employing a scribe to make, a copy that could be used in the playhouse for productions. Dramatists had to churn out plays rapidly for the daily repertory on Elizabethan stages, but there is no reason to assume that they invariably wrote only one draft. Some printed texts provide evidence that Shakespeare altered, added or cut, and left loose ends in manuscripts, for example, the copy from which the Quartos of

Romeo and Juliet are derived (Ioppolo, 2006: 176–83). He apparently did not prepare manuscripts for publication, but if he had done so he would, no doubt, have encountered the same difficulty as Tom Stoppard did with his play *Jumpers*:

> In preparing previous plays for publication I have tried with some difficulty to arrive at something called a "definitive text", but I now believe that in the case of plays there is no such animal. Each production will throw up its own problems and very often the solution will lie in some minor change to the text, either in the dialogue or in the author's directions, or both.
>
> (Stoppard 11)

It is also possible that more than one draft was made for some texts, and this could provide an explanation for the muddled nature of the Quarto (1608) and exceptional range of differences between this and the Folio (1623) texts of *King Lear*. It could be that the manuscript from which Q was printed was an early draft, and we can only speculate about how or why it came to be printed in 1608. One possibility is that a discarded draft no longer needed in the theater found its way into a printing house. The title-page advertised the play as it was staged before the King on St. Stephen's night in the Christmas holidays, but does not add that this performance took place in 1606; thus it may well be an advertising gambit, like the appearance of the author's name William Shakespeare in large capitals at the head of this page, to distinguish this play from the anonymous *True Chronicle History of King Leir* published in 1605.

Like variants in other plays that exist in two or more versions, the differences between the texts of *King Lear* have been regarded as evidence of textual instability. Some recent "Complete Works" editions, such as the *Norton Shakespeare*, "stress process over product," in conformity with much theorizing about editing.[4] Thus, the Norton edition seeks to exemplify the problem of instability by including multiple texts, Q, F, and a conflated text, of just one play, *King Lear*. This play has also been used to develop the idea that Shakespeare could have revised his own work, and some have even claimed that the Q and F texts should be regarded not as early and late versions of the same play but as separate versions (Warren 105).

The idea that Shakespeare revised some of his plays has proved persuasive to many, and has helped to foster an argument that all surviving versions of Shakespeare's plays have an equal standing and importance, since "The text in flux, the text as process, was precisely what Renaissance printing practice preserved. . . . Renaissance dramatic texts are designed to be unstable" (Orgel 23–25).[5] Shakespeare's eminence as a writer has fostered the further notion that editors should not publish conflated or eclectic texts of his plays, but treat the differing texts of plays such as the two texts of *King Lear* and the three texts of *Hamlet* (Q1, Q2 and F) as each of equal value. The effect of such treatment is to elevate the importance of each early version of the text and give each an independent authority. Each text is restored to stability even as the play is destabilized.

The problem of multiple texts may be seen from a different perspective as in many ways having to do with the nature of language. Words slip, slide, are subject to distortion, mishearing or misspelling, revision and misunderstanding. Printers may misread manuscripts, incorporate errors, accidentally omit passages. Authors revise, change, leave loose ends even as they copy their own work (Honigmann), and editors often have to make difficult choices where there is no "correct" decision. In the case of Shakespeare, however, it is increasingly common to treat every Shakespeare text as of equal stature and every word or variant as of vital importance. We might gain a better perspective on plays like *Hamlet* and *King Lear* if we worried less about making all the texts available, as in the case of Arden 3 *Hamlet* (Q1, Q2 and F) and the *Norton Shakespeare*, which, as noted earlier, includes three texts of *King Lear*, and more about providing users with what editors regard as the best version for their time. Most readers are not likely to worry about textual variants anyway, and there are no good solutions for all the problems of language.

Changes in meaning create various kinds of difficulty, as the compilers of the King James Bible found, which some regard as the word of God, and so unalterable. But how, for example, can present-day readers coming to 1 Corinthians 13 (Authorised Version) understand "now abideth faith hope and charity, these three; but the greatest of these is charity?" The committee of bishops in 1611 changed William Tyndale's "love" (in his translation from the Greek of 1534) to charity perhaps in order to ensure that it would not be confused with sexual love. But modern revised versions reinstate "love" for "charity," which draws attention to the difficulty Milton noticed when the Archangel Michael advises Adam in *Paradise Lost*, XII.584 to practise "love/ By name to come called Charity." English has only one all-embracing word for love, which for many has the primary meaning of sexual or erotic love. The Latin "caritas" (charitas in the Vulgate) is hard to translate, since charity has come to mean principally what the epistle specifically excludes in verse 3, bestowing one's goods to feed the poor.

In this case neither "charity" nor "love" seems quite right. There are, similarly, many instances of words that have changed meaning and create difficulties for modern readers in Shakespeare's plays. In plays that exist in two versions, a copyist, probably in some instances the author himself, substituted roughly equivalent terms that overlap in meaning, but are not identical, like "love" and "charity." Such variants may seem to an editor or reader to be indifferent alternatives, but it is worth asking in each case whether the author had some subtle shading in mind. Examples from the opening scene in *King Lear* include "protection" (Q) and "dear shelter" (F); "unclean" (Q) and "unchaste" (F), "respects" (Q) and "regards" (F). Shakespeare also exploits another kind of instability frequently in puns and double meanings. The editors of Arden 3 *Hamlet* (Thompson and Taylor 175) have chosen to print the first line of Hamlet's first soliloquy as "O that this too too sallied flesh would melt," because both Q1 and Q2 have "sallied," and they gloss it as "assailed, besieged." Neither the *Oxford English Dictionary* nor *Webster's Collegiate Dictionary* recognize a verb "to sally" with this meaning, and many editors have preferred to print "sullied," regarding the "a" as a mistake, or "solid," the reading in F, as more appropriate in a modernized text. I doubt if any actor in the theater today is going to puzzle his audience by pronouncing "sallied" here. Such complexities occur many times, as in Horatio's "In the dead waste and middle of the night" (1.2.198), where Q1 has "vast" and "waste" puns on and could be "waist" (a pun Shakespeare exploits in the Chief Justice's rebuke to Falstaff at *2 Henry IV*, 1.2.128: "Your means are very slender, and your waste is great"). Whatever choice an editor or an actor speaking the line makes, some shadowy further meaning haunts such lines. The instability of language, though sometimes confusing, is also often brilliantly energized by Shakespeare in ways that contribute to the rich texture of the plays.

Perhaps we should think of plays less in terms of instability than in terms of the evolution or development of response to the play, which allows us to take from it what we want? For many of Shakespeare's plays only one text survives, and no play other than *King Lear* exists in two texts that differ so markedly in important ways. The Quarto text has about 300 lines that are not in the Folio, which in turn has about 110 that are not in the Quarto. Hence the play has featured as a kind of test case. Rather than foregrounding the various texts, editions for ordinary users (including students) might offer a different perspective by describing the play in terms of evolution. This is not an easy matter to establish for several reasons. One is the sheer number and variety of changes between the two texts. For instance, in the 309 lines of the opening scene there are by my count 39 indifferent changes that could easily have been made by an author in copying his text and usually do little to vary the sense (e.g., "shady" and "shadowy;" "betwixt" and "between"), as well as thirteen instances in which a word, usually a noun, is singular in one text and plural in the other. Then there are 36 changes of phrases or words that affect the sense, if not usually in a drastic way (e.g., "of our state," Q becomes "from our age" in F; "Reverse thy doom" becomes "reserve thy state"). Some could be considered improvements, such as the alteration of "Covered with our curse" to "Dowered with our curse" in Lear's dismissal of Cordelia. In ten places a word or short phrase present in Q is omitted in F (mainly terms like "How," "Go to, go to," "Well," "Do," at the beginning of a speech), while one or two words not in Q are added in F. In addition there are five transpositions, e.g., "goes this with thy heart" changed to "goes thy heart with this," also such as an author might make in copying. At some fifteen places either Q (5 times) or F (ten times) is pretty clearly correct and the other text in error, and at one place both get it wrong ("mistresse" in Q, "miseries" in F, correcting Q but perhaps by oversight omitting "t" needed for "mysteries"). There are also differences in stage directions, which are fuller in F and may be drawn from a text prepared for performance, though it lacks the entry calling for "one bearing a coronet." It is now generally thought that F was based on an annotated Q2 (1619) or a scribal copy, and has no direct link with Q1, so that errors of transmission, actor's interventions, printer's mistakes, and the changes inevitably made in copying, all may have some responsibility.

The sheer number of changes might seem to support a belief that the differences between the texts are of the same kind and could be due to mistakes or corrections made by a scribe or by compositors in the printing house. Alterations made by actors could also have been incorporated into the printed text. A comparison of the scripts used for plays of Shakespeare televised by the BBC with the words spoken by the actors reveals that they made numerous substitutions, transpositions, and numerical errors (compare *King Lear*, 1.1.172 where "fifth" in Q (Scene 1.162) becomes "sixth" in F). They also made compound errors, omitted passages and made additions, usually of words like "truly," "then," "why," "come." The largest number (163) occurred in the performance of *I Henry IV* (Maguire 136–46; Holland 223–27). The interventions of actors may similarly account for some of the differences between the two texts of *King Lear*. But the additions in F of verse and prose that qualify the action and affect characterization, together with substantial omissions including one whole scene present in Q, are of a different kind and suggest deliberate reworking.

In the opening scene F intercalates thirteen-and-a-half error-free lines not in Q, lines that notably affect the role of Lear, and also reassigns the announcement of the entry of the King of France and Duke of Burgundy from Gloucester to Cornwall at 1.1.185 (*Cor.* is the speech-prefix in F, which the *Norton Shakespeare* interprets as *Cordelia*). These passages in F that are not in Q pose a problem of a different kind. No one, I think, disputes that they are remarkably consistent with the general quality of the verse and prose of the play, even if there is no way of proving whether Shakespeare was the author of them. But many critics treat them as if they are changes of the same kind as those described above in the first scene, that is to say as minor rewordings or alterations that could have been made by anyone (Ryan 3). The strongest argument for regarding them in this way has been made by Richard Knowles who wrote:

> No speech of any length is rewritten to make it substantially different in content or style, no new scenes or episodes are added, no changes made in the order of existing scenes or episodes or speeches, no new characters are added, no named characters are omitted (or renamed), no new speeches are made to introduce or elaborate upon themes or to provide new and different motives. The reassignment of speeches may represent no more than normal scribal or compositorial error. If F *Lear* represents a new "concept" of the play, it is remarkably limited in its means of revision.
>
> (Knowles 63–64)

This statement is, I think, incorrect in implying that no new themes or motives are introduced, and also misleading in its general claim. The exact relationship between the Quarto and Folio texts of *King Lear* remains speculative in the absence of manuscripts, but what these texts show may well be the evolution of the play as the author's overall conception changed. It is worth considering whether the cuts and additions are different from other changes in the effect they have on the design of the play, and can be seen as convincing on artistic grounds.

Most of the critical debates about these changes in *King Lear* have been affected by long-held beliefs and prejudices about the nature and relationship of the texts. Those who vigorously reject the notion that Shakespeare might have revised the play are usually convinced that the Quarto is based on an authorial manuscript and therefore must be superior artistically. Hence they dismiss the possibility that any changes in F might be for the better, and resist considering whether they modify the play and in what ways. I realize that this involves aesthetic judgments, about which there can be no final agreement. However, my concern will be with the integrity of the play as a whole, rather than with the quality of particular scenes. Nearly all Folio-based productions of the play, for instance, include the mock-trial scene, 3.6, much of which appears only in Q, because it is great theater, and critics are especially severe on F for omitting part of it. We still can ask whether there was a good reason why it might have been cut in the context of all the other cuts and additions.

The lines added in F in the first scene I think significantly affect the role of Lear, and, contrary to what Knowles implies, both "elaborate upon themes" and "provide new and different motives." One addition consists of the lines italicized here:

> 'tis our fast intent
> To shake all cares and business from our age,
> Conferring them on younger strengths, *while we*
> *Unburdened crawl toward death. Our son of Cornwall,*
> *And you, our no less loving son of Albany,*
> *We have this hour a constant will to publish*
> *Our daughters' several dowers, that future strife*
> *May be prevented now.* The princes, France and Burgundy—
> Great rivals in our youngest daughter's love—
> Long in our court have made their amorous sojourn,
> And here are to be answered. Tell me, my daughters—
> *Since now we will divest us both of rule,*
> *Interest of territory, cares of state—*
> Which of you shall we say doth love us most.
>
> (1.1.36–49)

These interpolated lines stitched into the text provide a motive other than retirement for what Lear is doing, in a desire to prevent "future strife," which brings home his blindness to the consequences of what he is doing, and is ironic in that he fails to realize that dividing his kingdom virtually guarantees strife to come. The lines also introduce Lear's idea of settling his affairs before dying, with a further irony in the hope that he may be "unburdened." In the event he is burdened by the body of the dying or dead Cordelia as he approaches his own death. In announcing his intention to divest himself of rule and cares of state, Lear's lines also introduce the clothing imagery that continues in his attempt to strip off his own garments in 3.4 (Q Scene 11) and culminates in his cry, "Pray you undo this button" at the end of the play. Another addition expands and alters the exchange between Lear and Cordelia, when he calls on her to express her love for him:

Lear. Now our joy,
Although our last and least, *to whose young love*
The vines of France and milk of Burgundy,
Strive to be interessed: what can you say to draw
A third more opulent than your sisters? *Speak.*
Cordelia. Nothing, my lord
Lear. *Nothing?*
Cordelia. *Nothing.*
Lear. Nothing will come of nothing. Speak again.
(1.1.80–88)

In Q Lear begins by speaking of his love for her: "But now our joy, / Although the last, not least in our dear love." F transfers question of love from father to suitors, and then adds, helpfully for an audience, an explanation as to why the King of France and the Duke of Burgundy have been summoned on stage. Also the repetition of "Nothing" both enhances Lear's incomprehension that anyone could confront his authority in this way, and points up Cordelia's inflexibility, as well as emphasizing the negatives that echo through the play and culminate in the lines in Lear's last speech, "Thou'lt come no more. / Never, never, never, never, never" (5.3.282–83).

Changes relating to the part of Lear in the rest of the play extend the sense of a reworking and deepening of his character. These changes include alterations in the roles of Goneril and Regan in relation to their father. In Q the short scene between Goneril and Oswald, in which she first complains about the disorder of her father and his knights has seven lines not in F (Scene 3.16–21, 24–25), in which she pours contempt on Lear as an "idle old man" in his second childhood, and reveals her intention to "breed from hence occasions" presumably to get rid of him. The effect is to sharpen our sense of her brutality, enhance sympathy for Lear, and put more emphasis on the riotous behavior of Lear's knights, his "insolent retinue" (1.4.167; Q Scene 4.180). The unruly actions of the knights become the theme of her complaints at 1.4.285–96, where an exchange between Goneril and Albany is added in

F to emphasize further her anxiety about the violence of the hundred knights. F also adds a speech for Regan when Lear proceeds to her house in which she speaks of Goneril restraining "the riots of your followers" (2.2.305–9). Both the daughters thus focus their anger in F on the knights by seeing them as a threat to their own stability and power.

Goneril's harsh treatment of him bewilders Lear and leads him in 1.4 to question his own identity as king. His self-questioning is treated differently in Q and F:

(Q) *Lear.* Who is it that can tell me who I am?
Lear's shadow? I would learn that, for by the marks
Of sovereignty, knowledge, and reason,
I should be false persuaded I had daughters.
Fool. Which they will make an obedient father.
(Scene 4.209–13)

(F) *Lear.* Who is it that can tell me who I am?
Fool. Lear's shadow.
(1.4.195–96)

In Q Lear answers his own rhetorical question, suggesting that Goneril's behaviour at once makes him conscious of a split in himself; he is at the same time Lear and a shadow of his former royal self. In F the question is left hanging by Lear, marking his incomprehension, and is mockingly answered by the Fool, expressing his own awareness, not Lear's. In the next scene the Fool needles Lear with images that bring him to the brink of awareness in his anxiety about going mad ("O, let me not be mad," 1.5.41; Q Scene 5.39), and it is only when he finds Goneril and Regan united against him in 2.2 (Q Scene 7) that he is at last forced to recognize that he has lost everything, and begins to show signs of madness. The change in F shows a more gradual development in Lear's understanding of his folly and his descent into madness.

Another subtle change is made in Scene 7, where Goneril enters in Q crying:

Goneril. Who struck my servant? Regan, I have good hope
Thou didst not know on't.
Lear. Who comes here? O heavens.
(Scene 7. 340–41)

She is referring to Oswald, who was struck by Lear at 1.4.72 (Q Scene 4.71), and possibly again at 2.2.352 (Q Scene 7.339), when Lear dismisses him, "Out, varlet, from my sight!" though there is no stage direction or indication in the text here. The reference to Regan in Q might have been intended to anticipate the split that develops between her and Goneril, but it is at once contradicted by Regan's action in taking her sister "by the hand" in harmony at line 383. F makes the confrontation here much more powerful and consistent with the development of the action. In this text Lear addresses Regan before he notices the entry of Goneril, with his demand:

Lear. Who stocked my servant? Regan, I have good hope
Thou didst not know on't. Who comes here? O heavens,

Lear refers not to Oswald, but to Kent, who was put in the stocks by Cornwall at 2.2.134 (Q Scene 7.140), and repeats a question he asked without getting an answer at line 347 and again at 353 in F, and which is answered at last by Cornwall at 364 (Q Scene 7.351). Goneril then enters on "Who comes here?"; further, in F the sisters are united in opposition to Lear, and ignore his anger at Kent being put in the stocks.

In Q Lear conducts in Scene 13 (3.6) an imaginary trial of his elder daughters in thirty-six lines which are omitted in F. This mock-trial is a fine piece of theater, but arguably superfluous in the flow of the action, which may explain why it was dropped from F. It gives prominence to Edgar, the Fool and Kent as Lear's "justicers," whose comic byplay distracts attention from the pathos of Lear's descent into madness. The mock-trial restores the Fool to prominence just before his unexplained disappearance from the play after this scene. The mock-trial here also anticipates and in some measure duplicates the grander "trial" of 4.5 (Q Scene 21), in which the mad Lear sees Gloucester as "Goneril with a white beard" (F text), and denounces adultery, ingratitude and all injustice. This scene is enhanced in F by a further addition of Lear's powerful lines:

Place sin with gold
And the strong lance of justice hurtless breaks;
Arm it in rags, a pigmy's straw does pierce it.
None does offend, none, I say none. I'll able 'em;
Take that of me, my friend, who have the power
To seal th'accuser's lips.
(4.5.155–60)

In this scene, the King dominates the stage with a misogynistic attack on all women, including his daughters among them, and a general onslaught on the corruptions of justice in his kingdom. The scene deals more profoundly with the issues at stake here, and with the cutting of the earlier mock-trial its dramatic force is strengthened in F.

At the end of the play another change significantly affects the character of Lear :

(Q) *Lear.* O thou wilt come no more,
Never, never, never—Pray you undo
This button. Thank you, sir. O, O, O, O!

Edgar. He faints. My lord, my lord.
Lear. Break, heart, I prithee break.
(Scene 24.301–5)

(F) *Lear.* Thou'lt come no more,
Never, never, never, never, never.
Pray you undo this button. Thank you, sir.
Do you see this? Look on her? Look, her lips,
Look there, look there. *He dies.*
Edgar. He faints. My lord, my lord.
Kent. Break heart, I prithee break.
(5.3.282–87)

The changes here notably enrich Lear's final moments. In Q he groans ("O, O, O, O!), and then summons death with his cry "Break heart." In F it seems likely that the "button" Lear wants undone is on Cordelia's costume rather than his own, for he draws attention to "her lips." We are left to imagine what it is he sees or thinks he sees, but "lips" suggests either breath or speech. Does he imagine the daughter who refused to say anything in the opening scene now speaks? Does he die, as the stage direction in F demands, even as he thinks she may be alive, or is it merely a delusion? Is death a welcome release in a reunion with his beloved, or a painful reminder of the death and destruction Lear has brought about? Is Kent thinking of himself or Lear with his cry, "Break heart?" The rich play of ambiguities in the ending for Lear in F is intensely moving. In Q, by contrast, Lear simply wants to die quickly, and the cry "Break heart, I prithee break" serves as his last words.

These modifications, none of them large, in the role of Lear, complicate his character in subtle ways. His relations with other characters are also reshaped, notably with Goneril and Regan, with the Fool, and with Cordelia, as the changed ending of the play shows. It would be possible to consider most of the major characters in this way, but it is difficult to hold all the details in mind, and easy to lose sight of the larger picture. So I will sketch more briefly a number of other significant differences between Q and F in order to show that they may be interpreted as effectually altering the design of the play. The character most affected by changes between Q and F is the Fool (Foakes 1985), of whose 225 lines in six scenes, fifty-four are cut or added or altered. It seems that Shakespeare initially thought of him as a professional court Fool wearing motley, but the lines that mention his costume (Q Scene 4.123–37), are omitted in F. In Q the Fool presents himself as "sweet" in contrast to the "bitter" Fool in mocking Lear. In the Folio the Fool is more consistently a "pestilent gall" (as Lear calls him at 1.4.99; Q Scene 4.99), during the first part of the play, as is seen in the lines added in F at 2.2.216–23 (Q Scene 7), a scene in which Fool speaks mainly to Kent in Q, but in F twists the knife in Lear with lines that include the rhyme:

Fathers that wear rags
  Do make their children blind,
But fathers that bear bags
  Shall see their children kind.
            (2.2. 217–20)

The Fool's role as social commentator is enhanced in F by his ironic "prophecy" added at 3.2.78–94 (Q Scene 9), after Lear and Kent go in search of shelter, foreseeing "confusion" in the realm if greed and corruption cease. The Fool's role then changes. Edgar enters as Poor Tom in 3.4 (Q Scene 11) and at once displaces the Fool, taking over much of his role in relation to Lear. From here onwards Lear now pays almost no attention to the Fool, who in F himself answers the riddling question he puts to the old king at 3.6.8–12 (Q Scene 13), "whether a madman be a gentleman or a yeoman?" This riddle remains unsolved in Q, where at this point Lear abruptly begins the mock-trial. After the mock-trial the Fool speaks no more in Q, but in F he is given a notable exit-line to cap Lear's "We'll go to supper i'th'morning" with "And I'll go to bed at noon" (3.6.39).

From this scene onwards, Edgar, Kent and Albany all have notably less to say in F than in Q, as their roles are subtly changed (Warren 95–107). Both Edgar and Kent are present in Q's mock-trial, omitted from F. Edgar's moralizing at Scene 13.91–104 (3.6) is cut from F, as also his report of meeting Kent and hearing Kent's "piteous tale" of Lear at Scene 24.200–17 (5.3). But if Edgar loses two choric speeches in this way, he gains in authority by taking over three brief but important speeches of Albany. One change is especially affecting. In F it is Edgar,[6] not Albany as in Q, who responds to the gentleman who rushes in at 5.3.196–97 (Q Scene 24.218–19) crying "Help" by asking "What kind of help?" and "What means this bloody knife?" (The text in F deliberately misleads us into thinking for a moment that he is reporting the death of Cordelia rather than Goneril). It is Edgar, not Albany, who in F gives the order "Haste thee for thy life" (5.3.225; Q Scene 24.246), sending someone to try to save the lives of Lear and Cordelia; also Edgar, not Albany as in Q, has the last four-line speech in the play, suggesting he may take control of future events. Albany loses some of his moral authority in F, which lacks his denunciations of Goneril at Q Scene 16.31–49 and 61–66; 4.2), including his vision of anarchy to come ("Humanity must perforce prey on itself/Like monsters of the deep"). His lines in Q explaining that he is in arms to repel a French invasion, not to fight Lear (Q Scene 22.25–29) also disappear from F. But he gains in authority of command, for in Q Edmund is bolder and seizes control of his duel with Edgar in 5.3. Edmund calls for a herald, and after the first sounding of the trumpet he intervenes twice more to demand the second and third soundings. In F Albany is firmly in charge and gives the herald his orders.

Kent's role is also diminished in the later scenes in F, and he has little to say between the end of 3.6 (Scene 13), where in Q he calls on others to help him support Lear off stage, and the final scene. F, as noted, omits Q Scene 17 (4.3) altogether, the scene in which Kent and a gentleman sympathetically report on Cordelia and Lear. An exchange between the disguised Kent and (the same?) gentleman at the end of Scene 22 (4.7) is also not present in F, and could have been cut because the latter speaks of a rumour that Kent is in Germany. This makes no sense because Cordelia has recognized and named Kent in the opening line of this scene. Since Edgar's account at 5.3.195–217 of meeting Kent is not in F, Kent is not heard of after 4.7 in this text until he enters at 5.3.226 to bid farewell to his "King and master." Here he regains a strong presence, and has eleven speeches in the last seventy lines of the play (one more than in Q), including the moving exchange with Lear at lines 256–67 (Scene 24). In F Kent thus effectively vanishes with the Fool after 3.6, but unlike the Fool is restored to prominence at the very end. The changes in the parts of Edgar, Albany and Kent reduce or remove much moralizing commentary from the last two acts and arguably strengthen the dramatic effect by empowering the audience or readers to judge for themselves. The dialogue between two servants that closes Q Scene 14, who comment on the wickedness of Cornwall and Regan in blinding Gloucester, and speak of getting Poor Tom to lead him, may have been omitted from F 3.7 partly for the same reason, if also to lessen the number of actors needed, and avoid an inconsistency—Gloucester next appears led by an old man, not by Edgar as Poor Tom.

Many of the minor differences between Q and F may be due to accident or error, but those I have outlined here seem to me deliberate, often neatly incorporated into the blank verse, and part of a pattern of revisions intended to reshape the design of the play. Some of these revisions show a minute attention to detail, most strikingly in the alterations that affect the dramatization of Lear's death in the final scene. Their effect on the design of the play can only be appreciated in relation to another series of important alterations concerning the French connection.[7] In the opening scene Cordelia is taken off by the King of France to be his Queen. He never appears again in Q or in F, but there are indications in Q that in drafting the play Shakespeare kept open the idea of his return. References to France in the opening scene in Q and F may be to the country or to the King. Cornwall (Gloucester in Q; *Cor.*, which the Oxford Shakespeare interprets as Cordelia, in F) announces the entry of the King, "Here's France and Burgundy" at 1.1.185 (Q Scene 1. 175), but later the King takes Cordelia as "queen of us, of ours, and our fair France" (1.1.259; Q Scene 1.245). From the end of Act 2, however, all references in Q to France which might be to the King rather than the land are omitted or changed in F, as follows.

Q Scene 8 (3.1)

Immediately after Lear goes off into the storm at the end of Act 2 there is a scene between Kent and a Gentleman in which Kent reports impending civil war. Here is where alterations that remove possible references to the King of France begin, and it seems that at this beginning a compositor may have misunderstood handwritten notations for what he was being asked to do. This is the only scene in which there are two different versions in Q and F of a substantial speech in 3.1. Scholars differ on the interpretation of the texts, but it seems clear that a major concern of the substitution in F was to replace the lines in Q, Scene 8.17–33 that for the first time mention a war with France:

> There is division,
> Although as yet the face of it be covered
> With mutual cunning, 'twixt Albany and Cornwall;
> But true it is from France there comes a power
> Into this scattered kingdom, who already
> Wise in our negligence have secret feet
> In some of our best ports, and are at point
> To show their open banner.
> (Scene 8.18–25)

These lines, which might be interpreted as referring to an invasion led by the King of France, are replaced in F by a more guarded allusion to potential civil war that might influence France in some unspecified way, lines in which Kent says only that Albany and Cornwall have servants at their courts who are acting as spies and passing intelligence to France:

> There is division,
> Although as yet the face of it is covered
> With mutual cunning, 'twixt Albany, and Cornwall,
> Who have—as who have not, that their great Starres
> Thron'd and set high—servants, who seem no less,
> Which are to France the spies and speculations
> Intelligent of our state.

Gloucester is revealed as such a spy by the letter Edmund delivers to Cornwall that shows his father to be "an intelligent party to the advantages of France" (3.5.9; Scene 12.8–9).

Q Scene 10 (3.3.13)

Gloucester tells Edmund in Q that the injuries to Lear will be revenged: "There's part of a power already landed." In F the word "landed," implying an invasion from abroad, is changed to "footed," a term that avoids signaling the identity of the forces, and suggests rather the prospect of civil war. Gloucester begins the speech by saying, "There is division between the dukes, and a worse matter than that," and in F this "worse matter," an invasion by French forces, is reported first by Goneril in 3.7.2 (Q Scene 14).

Q Scene 16 (4.2.56–58)

In a passage found only in Q Goneril calls on Albany to raise an army:

> Where's thy drum?
> France spreads his banners in our noiseless land,
> With plumed helm, thy state begins to threat.

The last few words emend the Q text ("thy slayer begin threats" press corrected to "thy state begins thereat," neither of which phrases makes sense), but the reference is clearly to the King of France and his "plumed helm."

Q Scene 17 (4.3)

This scene is omitted from F. It begins with Kent asking a Gentleman "Why the King of France is so suddenly gone back, know you no reason?" The gentleman responds by referring vaguely to "something imperfect in the state."

Q Scene 17

At lines 8–9 Kent asks the Gentleman, "Who hath he left behind him. General?" and is told, "The Maréchal of France, Monsieur la Far." Nothing more is heard of this Marshal.

Q Scene 22 (4.7.91–93)

In another conversation between Kent and a Gentleman, present only in Q, the following exchange takes place:

First gentleman. They say Edgar his banished son is with the Earl of Kent in Germany.
Kent. Report is changeable, 'tis time to looke about,
The powers of the kingdom approach apace.

As noted above, the disguised Kent has been identified and named by Cordelia in the opening line of this scene, so this would have been a reason for omitting these lines from F. But at the same time the omission in F neatly removes Kent's reference to "the powers of the kingdom," which might point to the French kingdom, since England is divided between Albany and Cornwall.

Q Scene 22 (5.1.26–29)

At the head of his own forces, Albany protests in Q that he is concerned only to repel an invasion by the King of France, and is not fighting against Lear. These lines are omitted in F.

> For this business,
> It touches us as France invades our land,
> Yet bold's the King, with others whom I fear
> Most just and heavy causes make oppose.

These references in Q from Scene 8 (3.1) onwards to a French invasion, or to the presence of the King of France in England, are omitted or changed in F. It would seem that as initially conceived the play may have been intended to have had an ending more like that in the old play of *King Leir*, with the King of France returning with Cordelia to restore Lear to his throne, and that traces of this remain in Q. If the changes between Q and F were owing to scribal or compositorial errors, it is inconceivable that they would have produced the consistent excision in F of all references to the King of France from Act 3 to the end of the play. Other allusions in Q to the French from 3.7 onwards are kept in F, but to quite different effect. In both texts Cornwall reports that "the army of France is landed" (3.7.2; Q Scene 14), and Oswald has also told Albany at 4.2.4 (Q Scene 16) "of the army that was landed." Cordelia is grateful for the army "great France" has provided her (4.3.24; Scene 18), and we learn in 4.6 that a battle is "toward" between English and French armies, but that Cordelia has remained behind for her father's sake while "Her army is moved on" (4.5.209–10; Q Scene 20.203–4). These references to France remind us that Cordelia is heading an invasion as if she were an enemy of her native country, and so reinforce our sense of the chaos that has resulted from Lear's actions.

Certain changes in stage directions also provide a different emphasis in F. We do not know who wrote these directions, which are generally fuller in the text in F. This may be an acting version, and its stage directions possibly relate to performances of the play at the Globe. But two of them, in 4.4 and 5.2, appear to embody deliberate changes that alter our perception of Cordelia and Lear, are consistent with the pattern outlined above, and suggest authorial intervention. In Q a scene not in F, Scene 17, stresses Cordelia's sorrow, tears and pity for the sufferings of her father, and prepares for her entry in the next scene accompanied by a "*Doctor and others*" as she seeks out the wandering Lear in order to minister to him.[8] In F, by contrast, she appears abruptly with no preparation at the head of an army, "*with drum and colours . . . Gentlemen and soldiers.*" Here she is visibly present as Queen of France leading the invading army that in Q was to be headed by the King of France, who in that text "spreads his banners" in England in 4.2. In Q the emphasis seems to be on Cordelia's immediate concern to relieve Lear's "distress" than in F, where her military appearance relates more to her determination to restore her father to the throne:

> No blown ambition doth our arms incite,
> But love, dear love, and our aged father's right.
> (4.3.28–29; Q Scene 18)

Here Cordelia's anxiety is to restore Lear to his "right" as King of England. There is no indication of status or costume for Cordelia when at last she meets her father in 4.6 (Q Scene 21), but Lear wakes to suppose he may be in France (4.7.69; Q Scene 22.73) which might imply that French colours are displayed again. The text of this scene is much the same in Q and F, but it is noticeable that Cordelia treats Lear as King, and does not address him as father ("How does my royal lord? How fares your majesty?" 4.7.37 (Q Scene 21.42), again as if she is anxious to restore him to the throne, to a role he no longer wants.

The entry in 4.3 (Q Scene 18) in F calls for Cordelia to enter "*with drum and colours*" at the head of her army, whereas in Q she enters with "*Doctor, and others.*" In F Edmund and Regan enter with drum and colours leading the English army in 5.1 (Q Scene 22) and so do Lear and Cordelia in 5.2 (Q Scene 22). The colours of the banners or flags would have identified for an audience the different armies, and their use might be taken for granted in Q. However, the direction in F at 5.2, where the French army processes across the stage and goes off, is significantly different from that in Q:

Q: *Alarum. Enter the powers of France over the stage, Cordelia with her father in her hand.*

F: *Alarum within. Enter with drumme and colours, Lear, Cordelia, and soldiers, over the stage, and exeunt.*

In Q Cordelia and Lear bring up the rear, as she draws him by the hand following the French army (perhaps reluctantly on his part?). In F, by contrast, Lear and Cordelia lead the soldiers of France, in accordance with her desire to restore his rights as king (except that, ironically, he is leading a French army here). The alterations in the stage directions in 4.3. and 5.2 are consistent with the other changes in F listed above that together remove any hint that the King of France is present in the play, and transform Cordelia from a weeping embodiment of compassion in Q into a fighting Queen at the head of a French invading army in F. The "colours" on stage, "banners" with French or English emblems, which Goneril speaks of in Q, are those of the King of France, which in F are used to establish Cordelia instead of the King of France as the leader of the French invasion.

All considerations of the texts of *King Lear* are speculative, since there is not enough evidence to explain the origins of the two texts or the relationship between them. This has not prevented critics from being stubbornly dogmatic on both sides of the matter, some insisting that Shakespeare revised the play, others opposing such claims with equal or stronger assurance. Textual critics are like theologians in converting their articles of faith into dogma. My concern is not to insist on authorial revision, though it remains the most economical explanation of the changes between Q and F, which otherwise require us to invent one or more people with Shakespeare's power to write blank verse and a consistent concern to reshape the play. The evidence presented above in my view makes it implausible that the cuts and revisions in F I have outlined could have been made "by several people at different times" (Ryan 3).

In this essay I have set out reasons for thinking that while many changes between Q and F are likely to be errors on the part of a copyist or a compositor, or alterations of the kind Tom Stoppard accepted as inevitable in the performance of *Jumpers*, there are also cuts and additions in F, together with many other often small changes, that form a pattern of deliberate reworking. Some of the major characters and their relationships with others are significantly modified, as, for instance, we see Lear deepened and made more complex, Cordelia transformed late in the play from an emblem of pity into a fighting Queen of France, the Fool changed from a sweet to a bitter critic of Lear, Goneril and Regan given stronger reasons to demand that their father dismiss his followers, and Edgar gaining more prominence than Albany in the final scene. Moreover, references to the King of France, who hovers in the background of Q without actually appearing after Act 1, are systematically removed or changed in F, sharpening the dramatic irony as Cordelia, Queen of France, leads her soldiers with Lear in the invasion of his own kingdom. It is not possible to prove this or any other argument about the relationship between the texts of Q and F *King Lear*, but the evidence is strong enough to be taken seriously, not simply dismissed. The changes I have described are often in small details, such as the reassignment of a speech to a different character, and the omission or insertion of lines or short speeches, but they accumulate to affect in subtle but consistent ways the dramatic shaping of the play and of the relations between the characters. The most plausible explanation for them is that someone (probably Shakespeare) skillfully reshaped the play by cuts, additions and numerous small changes accordant with a detailed overall view. In the absence of external evidence critics, editors and producers will no doubt continue to interpret the variations between the texts according to their preferred model. But we should take very seriously thc possibility that the differences help us to trace the evolution of the dramatist's conception of one of his greatest plays.

Notes

1 The Oxford edition of 1986, edited by Stanley Wells, Gary Taylor and John Jowett, on which the Norton Shakespeare of 1997 was based, led the way in this respect. The choice was described by Stephen Greenblatt, general editor of the Norton version as "the text immersed in history, that is, in the theatrical embodiment for

which it was intended by its author" (*The Norton Shakespeare* 72). Line references and quotations are from the modernized texts of Q and F as printed in this edition.

2 The transmission of Shakespeare's texts is a disputed matter, dealt with in Ioppolo's chapter on dramatists and foul papers; but see also the recent essays by Henry Woudhuysen on "Editors and texts, authorities and originals," and Paul Werstine on "Housmania: episodes in twentieth-century 'critical' editing of Shakespeare" in *Textual Performances*, eds. Lukas Erne and Margaret Kidnie, 21–48 and 49–62.

3 Printed plays did not usually sell well, and were not good investment opportunities as a rule, so it is remarkable that so many of Shakespeare's plays found their way into print; see Peter W.M. Blayney, "The Alleged Popularity of Playbooks," *Shakespeare Quarterly* 56 (2005): 33–50, especially 45–46.

4 Many textual theorists argue that "multiple or indeterminate texts that provoke resistance should be preferred to unproblematic, stable texts" (Foakes, 1998: 1322).

5 Stephen Orgel, "What is an Editor?" (1996). Henry Woudhuysen, in *Textual Performances* (2004), 43, offers what from the user's point of view is a council of despair in arguing that the debate over revision in the case of *King Lear* has led "to a too rarely articulated sense that *Lear* as a work can never be recovered (because it never was a single work), and that only the relevant documents which preserve versions of it can be edited." In reading and performing the play users desire a coherent text and are not obligated to stick with Q or with F. Probably no early staged plays can be recovered as "works," including those published by Ben Jonson under that title, since they were modified in rehearsal and in performance, affected by licensing and censorship, and subject to revision of various kinds.

6 The presence of two prominent characters with the initial "E" created problems for the compositors in Q, who wrongly printed "Edgar," corrected to "Edmund" in F in the text, at 4.2.15 (Q Scene 16), and "*Edmund*" instead of "*Edgar*" in a stage direction, the entry at 4.5 (Q Scene 20), again corrected in F. On the text's demand for capital "E", as in directions like "Exit" and "Enter," see Blayney, 1982: 129–30, and also Peter Stallybrass, "Naming, renaming and unnaming in the Shakespearean quartos and folio," in *The Renaissance Text*, ed. Andrew Murphy, 108–34, especially 124–31.

7 In his essay, "The War in *King Lear*," *Shakespeare Survey* 33 (1980): 27–34, Gary Taylor argued that Q presents an invasion by the French, whereas F stages a civil war. He is right to draw attention to the omission in F of some references to a French invasion, but mistaken, as I argue in the main body of this essay, in claiming that F shows "not an invasion, but a rebellion."

8 In *Revising Shakespeare*, 167–83, Grace Ioppolo argues that Cordelia is more "powerful and active" in Q, and her view has been endorsed by Graham Holderness in *Textual Shakespeare*, 138–39. The description of her in 4.3 (Q) as a weeping figure of compassion, and her entry in 4.4. with a doctor in that text, not as a military Queen, seem to me to soften her into more of a romance figure, perhaps bearing traces of a conception of the play as ending with the restoration of Lear to his throne and the survival of Cordelia.

Works cited

Blayney, Peter W.M. "The Alleged Popularity of Playbooks." *Shakespeare Quarterly* 56 (2005): 33–50.

—— *The Texts of King Lear and their Origins*, Vol.1: *Nicholas Okes and the First Quarto*. Cambridge: Cambridge University Press, 1982.

Foakes, R.A., ed. "Heavyweight Shakespeare." *Renaissance Quarterly* 51 (1998): 1320–29.

—— *King Lear*. The Arden Shakespeare, Series 3. London: Thomas Nelson and Sons, Ltd., 1997.

—— "Textual Revision and the Fool in *King Lear*." *Trivium* 20 1985): 33–47, reprinted in *Lear from Study to Stage*, eds. James Ogden and Arthur H. Scouten. Madison and Teaneck, Fairleigh Dickinson University Press; London: Associated University Presses, 1996: 109–22.

De Grazia, Margreta and Peter Stallybrass. "The Materiality of the Shakespearean Text." *Shakespeare Quarterly* 44 (1993): 255–84.

Greenblatt, Stephen. General Editor. *The Norton Shakespeare*. New York and London: W.W. Norton and Co., 1997.

Holland, Peter. "On the gravy train: Shakespeare, memory and forgetting." *Shakespeare, Memory and Performance*, ed. Peter Holland. Cambridge: Cambridge University Press, 2006: 207–34.

Honigmann, E.A.J. *The Stability of Shakespeare's Text*. London: Edward Arnold, 1965.

Ioppolo, Grace. *Dramatists and their Manuscripts in the Age of Shakespeare, Jonson, Middleton and Heywood: Authorship, authority and the playhouse*. London and New York: Routledge, 2006.

—— *Revising Shakespeare*. Cambridge, MA: Harvard University Press, 1991.

Knowles, Richard. "Two Lears? By Shakespeare?" *Lear from Study to Stage: Essays in Criticism*, eds. James Ogden and Arthur H. Scouten. Madison and Teaneck: Fairleigh Dickinson University Press; London: Associated University Presses, 1996: 57–78.

Maguire, Laurie. *Shakespeare's Suspect Texts: The "bad" quartos and their contexts*. Cambridge: Cambridge University Press, 1996.

Marcus, Leah. *Unediting the Renaissance: Shakespeare, Marlowe, Milton*. London and New York: Routledge, 1996.

Orgel, Stephen. "What is an Editor?" *Shakespeare Studies* XXIV (1996): 23–25.

Ryan, Kiernan. "*King Lear*: A Retrospect." *Shakespeare Survey*, 55 (2004): 1–11.

Stallybrass, Peter. "Naming, renaming and unnaming in the Shakespearean quartos and folio." *The Renaissance Text*, ed. Andrew Murphy. Manchester and New York: Manchester University Press (2000): 108–34.

Stoppard, Tom. *Jumpers*. London: Faber and Faber, 1972.

Taylor, Gary. "The Folio Copy for *Hamlet, King Lear*, and *Othello*." *Shakespeare Quarterly* 34 (1983): 44–61.

—— "The War in *King Lear*." *Shakespeare Survey* 33 (1980): 27–34.

Taylor, Gary and Warren, Michael J., eds. *The Division of the Kingdoms*. Oxford: Oxford University Press, 1983.

Thompson, Anne and Taylor, Neil, eds. *Hamlet*. The Arden Shakespeare, Series 3. London: Thomson Learning, 2006.

Warren, Michael J. "Quarto and Folio *King Lear*: The interpretation of Albany and Edgar." *Shakespeare Pattern of Excelling Nature*, eds. David Bevington and Jay L. Halio. Newark, Delaware: Associated University Presses, 1978: 95–105.

Werstine, Paul. "Housmania: episodes in twentieth-century 'critical' editing of Shakespeare." *Textual Performances: The Modern Reproduction of Shakespeare's Drama*, eds. Lukas Erne and Margaret Jane Kidnie. Cambridge: Cambridge University Press, 2004: 49–62.

Woudhuysen, Henry. "Editors and Texts, authorities and originals." *Textual Performances* (2004): 21–48.

3 The evolution of the texts of *Lear*

Richard Knowles

Once one could speak of "establishing" the text of *King Lear*. Beginning with Alexander Pope in 1725, editors believed that, however imperfectly, they could reconstruct from the earliest printed editions a text that would represent Shakespeare's intentions for the play's presentation to the world and posterity. The Globe edition of 1864, culminating a century and a half of such attempts, effectively fixed the shape and texture of the play for more than another century. That form of the play is still found in most modern editions, such as the Riverside, Penguin, Bantam, Folger, and New Arden.

Today, however, in response to new textual studies and a recent emphasis on theatrical criticism, editors are more aware of how the play of *Lear* has always been in constant flux, in the theater and in print, evolving from one state or version to another. Consequently one now finds in the Oxford, Cambridge, and Pelican editions not one fixed *Lear* but two variant versions, and three versions in the popular Norton edition for students: one purporting to represent an early Shakespearean draft, a second presenting a later, revised version supposedly as played by Shakespeare's company, and the third a traditional editorial combination of parts of the other two versions. Here, depending on one's point of view, is either deconstruction or enrichment; where once was one play, now a trilogy; where once one king, triplets.

In very recent years a still more subversive idea has begun to take hold: that *none* of these versions was ever seen on the stage in Shakespeare's day. According to this theory, modern editions never represent the play that Shakespeare could have seen or expected to see acted in the Globe or Blackfriars theaters. Indeed, the argument goes, it is probably impossible to know or to represent in a modern edition anything but a very indefinite approximation of the *Lear* that Shakespeare's audiences saw. In addition to, or instead of, the two or three versions now represented in recent editions, there may have existed in the theater an unknown number of other, significantly different versions, changing from one theatrical season to the next, or even from one month or day to the next. Our scrupulously edited texts are each valuable for critical discussion, but they may not represent what we have come to think they do—the play as conceived or as played.

In the following essay I wish to review what we now think we know about the origin and nature of the early printed versions of *Lear*, and then to construct a very general, partly factual and partly speculative narrative describing how the play has continually changed—in Shakespeare's mind, in production, and in print—since its beginnings in the author's imagination down to its latest appearance in editions and stage revivals. The word "evolution" in my title implies neither teleology nor Darwinian struggle, but simple mutability. More than ample documentation exists for the play's metamorphoses after its posthumous publication in the Folio of 1623, and these may be summarized briefly. Since, however, we have neither authorial nor original theatrical manuscripts of *Lear*, its forms and vicissitudes before 1623 can be only partly and doubtfully inferred from two earlier printed editions and from our general knowledge (such as it is) of theatrical and publishing practices of the time. The best one can hope for is an account of its career that is coherent within itself and consistent with facts presently known and opinions generally accepted. There is no certainty that such a theoretical narrative coincides closely with what actually happened.

Playing time

Because I will refer to it from time to time in my discussion of the original printed texts of the play, I wish to begin by briefly recounting the "subversive" new theory that I have mentioned. Although it had its beginnings some three-quarters of a century ago, its significance is only now being more widely recognized, and readers of this essay may not be familiar with it. In the 1930s Alfred Hart counted the number of lines in several hundred Elizabethan and Jacobean plays and found that the vast majority of those plays fell within a range of from 2,000 to 2,800 lines and averaged about 2,400 lines. Furthermore, from 1614 the average length of plays declined, and by 1620 it was about 2,250 lines, at which length it remained steady for over twenty years (Hart, 1934: 77–153; 1942: 132–6). That is to say, it was normal for plays to be playable within the "two-hours traffic" on the stage often cited by contemporary witnesses.

Why the majority of plays conformed to these limits and to this norm is not entirely clear. When in 1594 the Lord Chamberlain proposed to the Lord Mayor that his players "begin at two, & have don between fower and five," he was probably naming "the standard accommodation to the earlier arrival of darkness in wintertime" (Gurr, 2005: 75). Although there is no record of any attempt to enforce those limits, the line counts make clear that almost all surviving plays could easily have been performed within those times. Perhaps such limits became a convention and general expectation, convenient because of their predictability: audiences going to a play could expect it to begin and end at customary times. And of course they may have found that physical conditions—the strain of standing for two to three hours in cold weather, the loss of daylight, the time needed to cross the Thames before and after the performance, and the like—conspired to make three hours seem a comfortable maximum, and mid- to late afternoon a convenient part of the day for play-going. Actors in turn might have found two to three hours of projecting their voices into a large amphitheater sufficient to the need thereof, and have been content to observe limits that their audiences found convenient.

The striking exceptions to the norm were several long plays of Ben Jonson and Shakespeare. Hart's figures show that when the First Folio was published in 1623, the average length of a play written and performed at that time was about 2,200 lines; a number of Shakespeare's longer plays (including *Lear*) published at that time in their Folio versions were almost half as long again. Hart notes that the six longest plays in the Shakespeare Folio average almost 1,000 lines longer than plays being written in 1623. He has no doubt about the reason for this anomaly: "The folio text [of *Lear*] is not an acting version, because this abridged version would be five hundred lines longer than the maximum length of a two-hour play" (1942: 132). He finds the same true of the original Quarto version: "[I] think it most improbable that either the quarto text or the folio text . . . was itself an acting version. . . . The total amount of curtailment is far too small" (136). This conclusion was immediately seconded by the most knowledgeable Shakespearean of the century, E.K. Chambers: "The full texts of Shakespeare's longest plays, as we have them, including at least eleven plays of over 3,000 lines, were no more likely than Ben Jonson's to have been actually presented at the Globe or Blackfriars" (1944: 40).

Remarkably, this very plausible explanation of the facts has been resisted for the better part of a century. As Stephen Orgel has observed,

> The plays Shakespeare's company performed were shorter than the plays Shakespeare wrote for them. . . . But most editors and critics go to extraordinary lengths to avoid dealing with the notion. . . . It is often claimed, for example, that two hours is an approximate figure, which in the sixteenth century could mean anything up to four hours; that if you read very fast you can get through the text of most Shakespeare plays in around two hours; even that the Elizabethans spoke twice as fast as we do. (1994: 251–52)

Trials have been conducted to see whether Q or F or a conflated *Lear* could be read within the outer limits of three hours. Harley Granville-Barker reports (1927: 146 n.) that Nugent Monck, in his Maddermarket Theatre, performed a *Lear* cut down to 2,590 lines, with a ten-minute interval, in two hours and a half. At that rate the Quarto version of about 3,063 lines would take a full three hours. Similarly Chambers (40) reports that Lewis Casson expected his 3,071-line acting text (evidently containing both Folio and some Quarto lines) to take two and a half hours in performance at the Old Vic; in fact it took three hours and eleven minutes. Chambers also cites Levin Schücking's report that a *Hamlet* of 3,762 lines performed at the Old Vic without act-intervals took four hours and twenty-two minutes; at that rate a Q *Lear* without intervals would take more than three hours and a half. None of these experiments makes allowance for the slower rate of speech required in a large amphitheater like the Globe, or several act-intervals in the Blackfriars, or time for a final jig, or time to clear the house.

The usual explanation now for so many overlong plays in the Folio is that that collection, produced with readers and posterity in mind, sought to preserve all the lines that Shakespeare wrote, whether they were ever played or not. Hart surmises that "Heminge and Condell tried to offer [Sh.'s overlong plays] to the readers 'cur'd, and perfect of their limbes.' " Similarly Kristian Smidt (1964: 161–62; compare 1988: 25) surmises that the printed versions "may derive from a 'book' [i.e., playbook] marked with theatrical omissions, some of which were observed in the printing and some not." Andrew Gurr has recently proposed (1999: 69 ff.) that the company kept in its archives a "maximal" text of a play, preserving all the lines that were regularly omitted to produce the "minimal" texts heard in performance, and that the printed version represents the uncut original "poem" approved by the Master of the Revels rather than the acted text. "It was from the basis of that ideal text that the more minimal reality [the 'play'] was drawn out for performance. The minimal versions changed according to the local and immediate conditions of performance." That is, actual performances would have contained fewer lines than in the maximal allowed manuscript, and the actual lines spoken might have differed from one production, and possibly from one performance, to the next. F1 *Lear*, evidently derived from the "maximal" playbook, is longer than any version of the play ever seen in contemporary performances.

Why Shakespeare should repeatedly have presented his company with plays much longer than he could have expected to see performed has often been speculated upon. He may simply have felt that weighty tragic and historical subjects needed "adequate length" (Aristotle's term) to be sufficiently developed, and so wrote fully articulated poems for the theater of the mind, knowing that the actors would necessarily have to trim them for performance as plays. More recently the idea has been advanced that from the very beginning of his career Shakespeare (like Jonson) wrote with an eye not simply on contemporary playing but on immortality in print. Chambers first broached the idea:

> Are we to infer that Shakespeare, like Jonson, wrote for publication, and let the players, in the meantime, do their worst? . . . For whom . . . did he write? For himself? It follows, if this is so, that we must to some extent qualify Dr. Granville-Barker's view of the plays as "raw material for acting." And perhaps, after all, we may have to resort to our firesides when we wish to capture the full significance of their tragic or comic intentions.
>
> (40–41)

More recently both Giorgio Melchiori (1992: 200 ff.) and Richard Dutton

(1996: 82 ff.) have argued that Shakespeare's long plays survive in two forms, a longer one intended for readers and one or more shorter adaptations for stage performance. Most recently Lukas Erne has taken the unplayable length of perhaps a third of Shakespeare's plays as evidence of his lifelong ambition for immortality in print: "The tragedies and histories are of a length far exceeding what is necessary for a stage play because Shakespeare simultaneously conceived of them as literary drama with which he hoped to increase his reputation" (2003: 143).

Like many of our theories about Renaissance texts, these are founded more on speculation than on hard evidence. Only a handful of theatrical playbooks survive in manuscript, only one or two actors' "parts," and no playwright's rough draft. We are therefore unable to provide anything like Hart's line-counts to demonstrate the amount of cutting that was customarily done. Still, Erne and others cite a number of contemporary witnesses to the fact that printed editions restored considerable amounts of text that had been cut for performance; extant playbooks show how those cuts could be indicated without obliterating text; and Folio *Lear*, apparently based on a playbook version, does omit some 300 lines originally present in the earlier Quarto version. That playwrights frequently provided companies with more lines than they expected to see performed, and that printed editions often published more lines than were played, seem to be reasonable conclusions, and will be accepted as such in the following discussion.

Beginnings and the First Quarto (1608)

Obviously the earliest changes in the evolution of the text occurred in the mind of *Lear*'s creator as he conceived and developed his masterpiece. Of that process we can know next to nothing. We know that he relied extensively on a few major sources—the old *King Leir* play published in 1605, Sir Philip Sidney's *Arcadia*, Samuel Harsnett's satirical *Declaration* (1603), probably a few of Montaigne's *Essais* (tr. John Florio, 1603)—and on countless other sources that also affected many of his other plays—the Bible, proverbs, Ovid and Seneca, contemporary playwrights and pamphleteers, folklore, topical events, and so on. These and many other sources and influences have been identified, and we may see in any version of the finished play how they have been "coalesced" and "fused" (to use Coleridge's words) into a whole.

But to describe the steps or stages or processes by which Shakespeare's dramatic and literary genius transmuted the many into the one is of course beyond anyone's ability. Madeleine Doran (1933) attempted to identify places in the Q1 text where breaks in the metrical and linguistic texture revealed (she thought) Shakespeare in the process of revising his earliest version; similarly Hardin Craig (1961; 1962) found the greatest disruption of the verse in the places where the Gloucester subplot was fitted into the main plot; and recently Kristian Smidt (1990: 129 ff.) has argued that certain "unconformities"—loose ends in the plot, changing conceptions of character, odd repetitions, misalignment of verse—show "Shakespeare's revising hand" in the copy underlying Q1. Perhaps because there might be many causes for such formal discontinuities in a draft besides revision, such arguments have not been widely embraced. In any case, we cannot begin to imagine the myriad details, ideas, images, turns of phrase, and the like that the author rejected in favor of others as he revised and perfected the whole in his mind and in his manuscript. Barbara Everett eloquently describes a process of composition and constant revision too complex for anyone to reconstruct from the printed record:

> Defining a play by Shakespeare as a dramatic script only, and laying it down that differing Quarto and Folio texts illuminate the writer's struggle to adjust his words to the stages of his time, revisionists reduce the poet's astonishing imagination to the two or three printed versions they have in front of them. *King Lear* must have existed in Shakespeare's head not as two or three versions but a thousand: ideas, gestures, names, rhymes, songs, buttons, curses and courtesies, thunder and lightning, weeds, blank verse, gods and toasted cheese, bodies, boys, a girdle, kneeling and dying and speaking. To get this turned into the agonizing and brutal and beautiful world of *King Lear* as we have it—or almost have it—must have required from him acts of formative balance that stun imagination.
>
> (1998: 230)

At some point—probably in mid-to-late 1606, certainly before the first recorded performance at court on 26 December 1606—Shakespeare had in a hand a manuscript containing a version of *King Lear* that he was content to deliver to his company. The manuscript no longer exists; the closest we can come to it is apparently the first printed text of the play, the First Quarto (Q1) published in 1608. The text that we find there is so full of error and nonsense (e.g., "a nellthu night more and her nine fold/bid her, O light and her troth plight/and arint thee, with arint thee") that editors and bibliographers have labored for more than a century to determine how accurately it may reflect either Shakespeare's finished draft or the text played at court in 1606.[1] The following account focuses on the crucial advances made by three modern scholars: Walter Greg, Madeleine Doran, and Peter Blayney.

It was a fairly ordinary procedure for a playwright to provide a "fair copy" of his play to his company, so that when it was submitted to the Master of the Revels to be "allowed" for playing it would be easily legible, and so that the company's bookholder or scribe would have an accurate text from which to prepare a playing version and actors' parts. Admittedly some extant playbooks reveal that the players could sometimes work from fairly rough and inaccurate copy. In the case of *Lear*, however, there is little doubt that a fair copy was needed and was produced. When Walter Greg (1940) minutely compared all twelve extant copies of Q1, he discovered that the book had been subject to an unusual amount of stop-press correction. On sheet after sheet the proof-corrector in the printing house had discovered textual errors that required an interruption of the machining of the sheets and correction of the mistakes—a laborious and time-consuming process involving the loosening of the wedges that held the bed of types tightly together, location and replacement of the offending types, and re-locking the types together again before printing could be resumed. Moreover, Greg's collations of the uncorrected and corrected versions of the sheets revealed that in many cases the proof-corrector had failed to make proper corrections, apparently baffled by what he found in his copy. The obvious conclusion was that the manuscript from which the play was being set was frequently so illegible or disordered that neither printer not proof-reader could completely decipher it. In all probability it would not have been suitable for submission to the players or the Master of the Revels, and would have been transcribed into a fair copy.

In her detailed comparison (1931) of the Quarto and Folio texts, Madeleine Doran provided clear evidence that a clean transcript was in fact prepared, presumably for use by the playing company. No one today seriously doubts that the text in the First Folio (1623) is derived closely if not immediately from the company's playbook. Doran found copious evidence that erroneous readings in Q1 and F1 were obviously derived from the same manuscript—that is, from the same badly formed letters in the handwriting of the original draft. The person preparing clean copy for the company's use, despite producing a superior text in general, was often misled by the same bad script that misled the Q1 printers and proofreader. The person making that transcript could not have been Shakespeare, since he would not so often have been so baffled by his own hand that he could not recognize his own recently written words and lines. In one swoop Doran established two important facts: that a scribe other than Shakespeare had produced the relatively clean manuscript which soon became the basis of the company's playbook, and that the printers of Q1, two years later, were working from the same original manuscript used earlier by that scribe.

Unfortunately, Doran was opposed repeatedly and implacably by Greg, who for several decades championed one rival theory of Q1's provenance after another, until she gave in, partly disowning the explanation that virtually all textual scholars today accept as correct. In order to explain the miserable quality of the Q1 text, and to show that it was a less authoritative text than that found in F1, Greg and other textual scholars proposed that Q1 had been printed from an unauthorized manuscript acquired by surreptitious means. The various means proposed included shorthand notes taken down in the theater (or even at court!) and later expanded into a full text; reconstruction from memory by one of the actors; reconstruction by the whole company, perhaps while on tour; dictation by one or more actors to another actor who, from his memory of previous performance, substituted words other than those being read from the playbook; longhand copying during repeated performances; and so on. Eventually all of these theories languished from their own over-ingenious complexities and inconsistencies. Significantly, an argument used against most of them was that the play represented in Q1 was too long to have been performed; a play taken down in performance should have resembled in length that in the Folio, derived from the playbook; but instead it was some 200 lines longer.

Besides its large number of verbal errors, two other features of the Q1 text bred resistance to the idea that it was an authorial manuscript: its woefully inadequate punctuation, and its extensive mislining of blank verse. In fact neither kind of difficulty in itself rules out an authorial holograph: extant manuscripts reveal the same kinds of inadequate and casual punctuation found in Q1—the almost total reliance on commas, as often as not missing or misplaced—and verse lines lacking initial capitals and sometimes wrongly divided or undivided, so as to be often indistinguishable from prose. These features may readily be seen in authorial hands in the nearly contemporary manuscript of *Sir Thomas More*, some pages of which are reproduced in both facsimile and modern transcript in the *Riverside Shakespeare* (ed. Evans, 1974: 1686–1700). All of these kinds of faults were considerably remedied in the much-improved text of F1, perhaps in part by the scribe who made the transcript from Shakespeare's draft. In Q1, however, they have not been corrected, and the verse and prose lineation may even (as I suggest below) have been made worse by the printers than it was in the original. Since compositors frequently improved upon both the punctuation and verse lining in their copy—as did the typesetters later copying the Second Quarto (1619) of *Lear* from Q1—the survival of so much error of these kinds in Q1 seemed to imply a manuscript more disordered than we should expect an author to give to a printer. The unusual degree of error is the reason for the persistence of theories about a surreptitiously acquired manuscript and about a text taken down by ear from performance or dictation: presumably the reporter of the text could not reproduce by ear either the punctuation or the versification of the original, let alone get all its words right.

With the publication in 1982 of Peter Blayney's exhaustive study of the printing of Q1 the onus shifted significantly from the manuscript to its printers. Some early speculations about the shortcomings of Q1's printers had verged on the comic: that the book had been typeset in Germany, or in England by a German or by a Fleming who knew French, possibly composing by ear from the dictation of an illiterate assistant from the rural districts of England. Blayney's study established that its newly established printer, Nicholas Okes, had never before printed a play and so was inexperienced with the setting of dramatic verse; that he unwisely attempted to set *Lear* seriatim, thus tying up many pages of type at a time and causing type shortages that forced unusual expedients affecting the text; and that he assigned the composition to two very young and inexperienced employees.

> [Thomas] Corneforth and [John] Reynolds were probably about 21 and 17 respectively. Corneforth had been an apprentice for two and a quarter

> years, and Reynolds for eight months, while Okes himself [just turned 28] had been a master printer for only ten months. It is not very surprising to find occasional signs of inexperience in Okes's early books.
>
> (187)

The unusual and ill-advised method of seriatim printing, Blayney suggests, reflects the state of the manuscript: it was too disorderly and illegible to allow the more usual process of "casting-off" necessary for "setting by formes." In order to set the four non-consecutive pages printed on one side of a quarto sheet—in the outer forme these would be pages 1, 4, 5, and 8—the printer would have to "cast off" or mark off in advance which and how much text would be set on each of those pages. If the copy were too messy to allow of such estimates, all eight pages would have to be set consecutively into type before that outer forme could be printed off, thereby tying up eight pages of standing type (in addition to any others being printed concurrently). Another printer might have spent two or three shillings on a clean transcript; Okes evidently let his compositors struggle with the messy original. That decision would help account for the often garbled text and the unusual amount of stop-press correction.

The extraordinary amount of false lineation of verse (as bad verse or as prose) has always been the feature of Q1 most difficult to explain; indeed, Doran abandoned her theory because she became increasingly unwilling to imagine that Shakespeare had written out his verse in something that resembled rhythmic prose. Now that we know that the compositors setting Q1 *Lear*'s verse were novices, it is relatively easy to imagine that the mislining in Q1 was due largely to their inexperience, not simply to their manuscript. Since they were able to set two-thirds of the verse correctly, a majority of the verse lines in the manuscript were evidently distinguishable from prose. Repeatedly each man, having set several overlong or incorrectly divided lines, was able to recover from his mistake and proceed with the correct verse lineation, which must therefore have been clear enough in the manuscript.

It has not been previously noted that one kind of error in particular shows the compositors' ignorance of a basic convention of dramatic verse, and is responsible for a great many erroneously divided lines: they did not know how to handle part-lines of verse. In Elizabethan and Jacobean dramatic verse a part-line beginning a speech is often meant to link metrically with a part-line ending the previous speech (or standing by itself); these part-lines were usually lined separately in dramatic manuscripts, but would be spoken by actors as comprising one continuous line of verse. For the first third of the play the compositor who set most of the play failed (with three early anomalous exceptions) to set these beginning or ending part-lines as separate lines. Instead, he repeatedly ran a concluding part-line up into the preceding typographic line, making a hypermetric final verse; or (more seriously) he would run a speech's initial part-line down into the succeeding line, beginning mislineation that would sometimes continue for several lines, until he recovered the verse pattern. This kind of error occurs several dozen times throughout the play. At line 1303 and from line 1426 onwards, however, first one compositor and then his partner began to set some of these initial part-lines correctly, giving about three dozen of them typographic lines of their own. Either they had been instructed to follow their copy more closely or had learned the principle of linking part-lines, for they began to set them properly, though missing a number of later instances. The cause of such erratic lining of part-lines must be found in the inexperience of the compositors rather than in their copy; an experienced dramatist such as Shakespeare would not have neglected to indicate separate linking lines in the first two-fifths of his play and have indicated them only sporadically thereafter. The compositor who set most of the play seems also to have had a poor ear for verse, since he turned prose into some sixty lines of false verse, failed repeatedly to recognize rhyming lines, and was responsible for most of the 500 lines of verse throughout the play set as prose. In short, the manuscript's lineation may not have been so inadequate as the printers were unskilled.[2]

One more obstacle to the idea that Q1 *Lear* was printed from Shakespeare's draft of the play is the puzzling question of how the publishers would have acquired such a manuscript. At about the turn of the century Shakespeare's company had sold a number of their plays to stationers for publication, but after *Hamlet* was sold to James Roberts in 1602 and issued in 1603 and in a different edition in 1604, they seem to have abruptly reversed that practice, and showed little or no interest in publishing Shakespeare's plays until the appearance of the First Folio in 1623. Besides *Lear*, only *Troilus and Cressida* (1609), *Pericles* (1609), and after a long hiatus *Othello* (1622) found their way into print, perhaps none of them at the wish of the King's Men. Lukas Erne has remarked (2003: 109) the company's striking new reluctance to publish:

> The four-year period from 1605 to 1608 saw the publication of no fewer than fifty-two plays written for the commercial stage. . . . While Shakespeare's plays account for more than 18 percent of all the (commercial) plays printed in the ten years prior to 1603, that figure is down to less than 4 percent for the ten years after 1603.

Moreover, it is doubtful that the company could have sold Shakespeare's draft to a publisher even if they had wished to (or, according to older theories, that a "piratical" publisher could have suborned a company member to convey it by surreptitious means). Greg convinced two or three generations of textual scholars that Shakespeare's company routinely received from its playwrights both a fair copy (which became the official playbook) and "foul papers" (which they kept as insurance). The belief that they kept an archive of rough drafts has now come to be generally doubted, for lack of any evidence.[3]

How then could Shakespeare's rough but complete "final" draft have found its way to publishers who had apparently not dealt regularly with the company in the past, and to a new and unknown printer wholly inexperienced in printing plays? It is impossible to imagine that Shakespeare, contravening his company's new reluctance to publish, would have consigned his greatest tragedy to the mercies of such a consort as acquired, printed, and published it. Nor is it easy to imagine why he would not have provided better copy. As Erne observes (107), "What appears to have been the state of the manuscript from which *King Lear* was set up does pose a problem . . . if we wanted to assume that Shakespeare cared about its publication." Thought is free, and one may imagine several possibilities—e.g., improbably, that Shakespeare gave away his rough draft to a friend, who out of admiration undertook to make it more available. Since no adequate explanation has ever been proposed for how Nicholas Okes came to print the first edition of *King Lear*, I wish to offer here (as I have elsewhere) one possibility which may not be entirely improbable.

A Stationers' Register entry for 26 November 1607 announces that Nathaniel Butter and John Busby then owned and (evidently) planned to publish "A booke called. Mr Willm Shakespeare his historye of Kynge Lear as yt was played before the king*es* maiestie at Whitehall vppon St Stephans [*deleted* k]night at xp̃istm̃s Last by his mai^{tes} servant*es* playinge vsually at the globe on the Banksyde." John Busby's previous connection, if any, with Shakespeare's company had been at best remote: in 1600 and 1602 he had printed two "bad quartos," apparently corrupt and unauthorized versions, of the Chamberlain's Men's *Henry V* and *Merry Wives*. He had sufficient traffic with the theater world to acquire between 1599 and 1609 ownership (usually joint, twice with Butter) of seven play manuscripts. Since his name appears on the title pages of only two of these, he was apparently mainly interested in acquiring those manuscripts and then transferring them (presumably for a fee or a share) to someone else who would publish them. It may be that he acted typically in the case of *Lear*, acquiring the manuscript and transferring it to Butter. Since 1604 Nathaniel Butter had published several plays; only one of these, *The London Prodigal* (1605), was from the repertory of the King's Men, and since its title-page erroneously announces William Shakespeare as its author, it may not have come from the company. Butter had recently hired Nicholas Okes to print several of his (non-dramatic) titles, and continued their business association by hiring him to print *Lear*. All of these transactions, including the entry in the Stationers' Register, would have been perfectly regular, offering no whiff of "surreptitious" dealing.

But how could Busby have acquired Shakespeare's draft of the play? By the time he would have done so, either the company or Shakespeare himself would have engaged a scribe to make a clean transcript for presentation to the company and the Master of the Revels (for permission to play). It is hard to imagine that, contrary to recent company practice, either the King's Men or Shakespeare himself would have directed the scribe after copying the rough authorial draft to convey it to John Busby for publication. It is possible, however, that the scribe was unable immediately to return that draft to either its author or the company, and held it for a year, knowing that in the meantime the company's clean transcript made its return unnecessary. If Leeds Barroll's estimates (1991: 173) are correct, the plague may have closed the playhouses for all but three months in 1605–6 and for all but one in 1606–7. Andrew Gurr (1996: 304–5) records that in 1606–7 Shakespeare's company were often touring outside of the city; Shakespeare may have spent much of his time on tour with them or in Stratford working on *Macbeth* and *Antony*. Between the time when Shakespeare was finishing his play (probably in the second half of 1606) and the time when Butter published it early in 1608, the scribe may have had little opportunity, and may have felt no urgency, to return a now superseded rough draft, and could eventually by the fall of 1607 have agreed to make some use of it by selling it to Busby, who in 1606–8 was acquiring play manuscripts from several companies. Busby's speculative purchase of an available manuscript of his third Shakespearean play may well have seemed, to him and to the scribe, simply an ordinary and straightforward business investment. The play, not having been purchased or entered for publication by another stationer, would have been fair game.

Our hypothetical narrative, so far, may be summarized thus: Shakespeare in the second half of 1606 had in hand (in London or in Stratford) a much-reworked and therefore often illegible draft of his new play of *King Lear*, in a state finished enough for presentation to the company. Either Shakespeare or the company arranged for a scribe to prepare a clean copy for company use and submission to the Master of the Revels. That clean copy was presented by the scribe to the company and became the basis of the official playbook of the play. After transcription that original draft was not immediately returned by the scribe to either Shakespeare or his company, both being much of the time absent from London. Eventually a stationer who regularly acquired dramatic manuscripts for publication bought from that scribe the rough draft of *King Lear*, which was now of no use to the company and which, since it had not been retrieved by its author for a year, seemed of no great interest or use to him either. The partner of that stationer hired a printer who, doubtless despite good enough intentions, lacked the experience and means to produce from that disorderly manuscript a better book than the notoriously bad First Quarto of *Lear*. That such a chain of events happened there is no proof nor any possibility of proof; at best such a scenario is reasonably possible in its details and is able to account for the first publication, in such an astonishingly disreputable form, of Shakespeare's great tragedy.

The Playbook and First Folio (1623)

Shakespeare's play probably began to change its shape in the transcript made from his finished draft. In all probability a professional scribe hired by Shakespeare or his company (presumably because of his experience with dramatic texts) would have known how to align correctly most of the dramatic verse and would have done so, out of faithfulness to his copy and as an aid to the actors; he would have produced much if not most of the correct lineation of, and distinction between, verse and prose found later in the Folio. He may also, as he went along, have instinctively, even unconsciously, made small improvements in punctuation, spelling, and grammar, out of a habitual professional interest in producing a better text than he found in his copy. It is entirely likely that from time to time, carrying phrases in his mind, he unconsciously made small verbal changes—occasional errors, substitutions of synonyms or homonyms, transpositions, additions or omissions of particles. Some of the several hundred minor verbal variants by which the Folio differs from the Quarto may have begun to appear in the text at this time.

The first date of performance is unknown. Shakespeare's main source, the old play of *King Leir*, was entered for publication on 8 May 1605; he could not have had access to the published book for another month or more, in the summer of that year.[4] He had apparently not finished writing his play by the Christmas season of 1605–6, since it was not performed then at court; had it been, it would not have been repeated the following Christmas (on St. Stephen's Day, 26 December 1606). According to Leeds Barroll (1991: 154–5), the plague would have allowed almost no time for mounting a play earlier in 1606. "Plague had closed the playhouses throughout the late spring of 1606, the entire summer, and even the autumn. . . . Indeed, no holiday plays by any city company were presented before the king in autumn and winter 1606 until that St. Stephen's Day." If *Lear* had first opened in the narrow window between Easter and late spring of 1606, it would have been ready for performance before the court at Greenwich or Hampton Court for the King of Denmark's visit in late July and early August; but it would not have been presented at Whitehall at Christmas if it had been one of the three unnamed plays performed for the court only four months earlier. Plays performed for the court were usually drawn from the recent repertory in the public houses, but possibly *Lear* was first seen at court in December 1606, or at the Globe only very shortly before.

In any case, before the company could perform the play, they needed permission from the Master of the Revels, who would screen it to remove any dangerous or offensive matter, usually anything suggesting blasphemy, sedition, or satire of important persons. The Folio lacks some three hundred lines that are present in the Quarto, and whether or not some of these were removed by the censor, Sir George Buc, has been much (and inconclusively) debated. A number of the cut lines might be seen as reflecting obliquely on topical matters—the King's attempts to unify Britain, his wish to avoid foreign war, his liberal granting of knighthoods and monopolies, his love of the hunt, possible tensions within the royal family, and so on. But while many critics have detected censorship of such matters at a few places, others have found the allusions, if any, to be too general and unpointed to give offense, and have denied much, if any, censorship.[5] Indeed Andrew Gurr (2004: 182–84) argues strongly for an absence of censorship: the play, chosen by the Master of the Revels (the censor himself) for Christmas performance in 1606, "was the most explicitly loyal of all the plays Shakespeare wrote for the company's royal patron"; it "flaunted the company's allegiance" and "caused no uproar." Perhaps the most one may say is that censorship *may* have shaped the text, in a limited way in a few places. In any case, almost no one today suggests that the uncut text in Q represents the version played before the court or any other audience: it contains too many errors and obscurities, it lacks a number of stage directions (especially sound and music cues supplied by the Folio), and it is too long for an ordinary public (if not court) performance.

How and why the text was altered within or without the theater during the next seventeen years is almost entirely a matter of conjecture. It was probably shortened almost immediately. The Folio omits some 300 of Q's lines, and many or most of these omissions have been thought to represent theatrical cutting of static or reflective material that does little to move the action forward; most of the cuts occur in the last two acts of the play, a fact suggesting that they were intended to move the action as quickly as possible to its conclusion. Because the play would still be far longer than the theatrical norm, other passages may have been omitted as well, at different times, despite their later inclusion in the printed Folio text. In playbooks, omissions were frequently indicated not by blotting out or cross-hatching but by the drawing of a vertical line in the margin to the left of the lines to be omitted from performance; passages so lightly marked would have been easy to restore in the Folio years later. Other passages may have remained unrecoverable or at least unrecovered, as have the 300 Q lines missing from F. The *Lear* that King's Men audiences saw may have been much shorter than that in F, and may have been changed from one revival or even one week to the next, by different hands for different occasions. Shakespeare may have been responsible for some or all of these cuts, or he may, from his remove in Stratford, have trusted his company as usual to trim down his overlong play. No one can identify the author or authors of the cuts nor do more than infer their causes. It does seem probable that, given the excessive length of the play, a good deal of cutting would have been done immediately, before the first performance.[6]

The Folio text also makes it clear that at some time or times the text in the playbook was added to. The 110 lines unique to the Folio text are now generally agreed to be later additions to the Quarto text, and since the Folio evidently derives from the company's playbook, these additions almost certainly represent changes made to the play during one or more playing seasons. There is no guarantee that all of these additions were staged, and others may have been made and staged which were not recorded in the playbook or, if they were recorded, did not survive in F. In comparison to the large-scale additions made in some other contemporary plays, those printed in F are relatively modest; most of them are brief enough to have been interlined or added in the margin. Only four passages are longer than five lines, and some sixty other additions consist of only a word or a phrase of four syllables or less, amounting to about fifteen lines in sum. Twenty-three new speeches are added, often of no more than a word or two, and averaging about two lines per speaker; and another sixty lines amplify by at least a half-line twenty-five speeches aleady present in Q, adding an average of 2.4 lines per speech. The Fool is given four new speeches (one of a half-line); Lear, Albany, and Goneril are given three new speeches apiece; Gloucester, Kent, Cornwall, and Edgar receive two apiece, and Regan and Cordelia one each. Except for the Fool, Goneril, and Regan, no character is given a new speech of more than one pentameter line, and no Q speech of a half-line or more is rewritten or replaced by a new one. On the face of it, such a miscellany of short additions does not strongly suggest a thoroughgoing attempt to revise the play, by the author or a hired playwright; most or all of the additions could have been local improvements, added piecemeal by several hands on several occasions for a variety of reasons.

A cluster of several short additions in the opening scene (TLN 45–50, 54–55, 69–70, 90–91, 94–95) seem designed to make exposition of its action clearer, and especially to make Lear's motives more explicit; from then on the additions are spread out fairly evenly over the play. Almost half of the new lines are given to the Fool (twenty-five) and Lear (twenty-three); Goneril gets about thirteen lines plus a two-word sarcasm ("An enterlude"), Kent and Edmund both about nine lines, Gloucester seven, Regan six, Albany and Edgar about two and a half, Cornwall two half-lines, and Cordelia one word ("Nothing"). The two longest added speeches have both been suspected of being spurious: the Fool's "Merlin's prophecy" (TLN 1734–49), despite its admirers, has often been thought to be an intrusive irrelevance, and Kent's ruminations in 3.1 about French spies and domestic disturbances (TLN 1631–8) have recently come under suspicion for their uncharacteristically clotted style and un-Shakespearean vocabulary.[7] Most of the additions to Lear's part range from a half-line to no more than two, and are mainly small local additions to existing speeches, often mere expostulations or repetitions which point up his distress; the most significant to critics is his dying third expression (3282–3283; cf. 3227, 3236) of an earlier hope that Cordelia may still be alive. Goneril is given two long speeches of self-justification (TLN 842–57) when she goes on the warpath against her father (and her husband), and Regan is given a shorter counterpart speech (1420–24) in her sister's defense. The Fool's part has been expanded the most, in four fairly characteristic fool's routines—his jingle and puns about wild geese (1322–27), his mock prophecy (1734–49), his joke about a mad yeoman (2010–12), and his final quip (poignant in retrospect) about going to bed at noon. Because none of these is essential to advancing the action, they have often been suspected to be padding of the Fool's part, perhaps by Robert Armin himself, to compensate for his uncharacteristically foreshortened role, truncated after only three acts.[8]

Another possible cause of alteration might be adaptation to a different playing space. If *Lear* was revived after the King's Men acquired and began playing in the small indoor Blackfriars, then changes may have been made and recorded in the playbook. It is quite possible that the division into five acts found in the Folio reflects act intervals observed in the Blackfriars. If so, the text may have been even further reduced to provide time for trimming candles between acts and for entre-acte singing and dancing, a final jig, and other diversions. Two changes in staging between Q and F have often been attributed to adaptation to a theater with more limited stage resources than the Globe or Blackfriars offered. In 2.2 the stocks may be revealed in a discovery space in Q1, in F1 they are specifically "*brought out*"; in 4.7 Lear is apparently discovered asleep to the sound of music in Q1, but in F1 he enters "*in a chaire carried by Seruants*," without mention of music. There would have been no need to make such adaptations for performance at court, where both a retiring space and music could have been easily supplied. On tour, however, the company might regularly have had to play in guildhalls, rooms in provincial schools or inns, the halls of great houses, and other such improvised staging spaces lacking a rear alcove. On tour they might also have found it easy to provide (perhaps from among the actors) the occasional trumpeter and drummer required in *Lear*, but would have thought it unnecessary to bring along or hire a consort of viols or recorders for a single scene. The King's Men's customary touring routes had in the past, as recently as 1606, included Dover and other places nearby in Kent. In 1607, when the plague offered continual inducement for touring outside the city, a new tragedy set partly in Dover would have been a natural offering in towns thereabout. Unfortunately, touring records never specify play titles.

Because of the length of the text in Shakespeare's first finished draft (as represented in Q1), considerable omissions from the text—perhaps those cuts reflected in F1, perhaps not—would have happened early on, before the first performance. Experience in later performances may have led to later cuts and to restorations of material earlier omitted. As for the score of miscellaneous new speeches, usually brief, and many small and local augmentations of existing speeches by a few words or a few lines, these require almost no revision of surrounding lines, and could easily have been added piecemeal over time. The speeches and actions of the characters remain on the whole unchanged by them, as do the substance and sequence of the scenes. The clarifications of Lear's motives in the first scene might have been added early; the filling-out of the Fool's part might have taken place more gradually, after Armin or his successor had tried out the role in performance and experimented with it, improvising an occasional bit of "gag" that got recorded in the playbook for future use. The dozens of short phrases interspersed in existing lines, and even the whole lines not suspected of being spurious, are mostly unremarkable in language and rhetoric; they are not beyond the reach of any competent playwright or even some actors associated with Shakespeare's theater. A few changes in details of staging may reflect adaptation to a stage at court, or at the Blackfriars, or on tour. We cannot reconstruct a chronology for these changes; at most we can say that they are such as could have been made at any time between the preparation of scribal copy in 1606 and preparation for publication in the Folio of 1623. We may also recall, as performance criticism continually reminds us, that it is common experience in the theater for a text to be modified over time, adjusted to audience response, changing tastes and topical interests, new and different actors, and so on. G.E. Bentley (1971: 263) observes that, owing to the "universal" practice of theatrical revision 1590–1642, "Almost any play first printed more than ten years after composition and known to have been kept in active repertory . . . is most likely to contain later revisions by the author or, in many cases, by another playwright working for the same company."

Those who have urged that F1 *Lear* represents Shakespeare's own revision of the play must assume the contrary—that all of the changes were made at one time by the same person. But the playbook on which F1 is based could have been modified at any time between 1606 and 1623; during the last ten of those years Shakespeare would not have been in the company, nor would he have been alive during the last seven. Perhaps the best kind of argument for coherent rather than piecemeal revision is that introduced in 1913 by W.D. Moriarty, who argued that changes in Q and F are interrelated—e.g., omissions from Q are compensated for by additions elsewhere in F. This form of argument has been repeatedly applied more recently in order to demonstrate in F new conceptions of the characters of Albany, Edgar, the Fool, and Kent, and of the French invasion, as well as "streamlining," improved pacing, rhythm, dramatic effects, and the like.[9]

Such arguments for each of the Folio changes, and counterarguments resisting them, have been thoroughly vented in the past thirty years and are familiar to most Shakespeareans; they are all recorded in the line-by-line commentary of the forthcoming Variorum and will not be rehearsed here. Suffice it to say, in support of the idea of ongoing theatrical rather than one-time authorial revision, that in the minds of many critics some of the cuts in F1 seem too clumsy or ruthless to be authorial, particularly the sacrifice of the brilliant mock-trial in 3.6, the servants' kindness after Gloucester's blinding, and the whole of 4.3, which prepares for Cordelia's reappearance.[10] Company members other than Shakespeare could have made such cuts; Eric Rasmussen (1997: 445–46) points out that in *Hamlet*, phrases and lines are cut by artful, "surgical" excision from within speeches, whereas in *Lear* they are "trimmed" off the ends of speeches and scenes, suggesting different hands and purposes. In *Lear*, the main intent would seem to be to shorten the play by lopping off lines and passages—probably not only the 300 Q1 lines missing from F1, but also (because the F text is still too long for normal performance) additional passages, marked for cutting in the playbook but preserved in F. A number of F additions have seemed suspiciously un-Shakespearean. Despite exquisite reasons defending it, the Fool's mock-prophecy in 3.2, a stand-up routine suddenly breaking dramatic illusion, seems to many an irrelevance un-Shakespearean in manner; and several of the added passages (1631–38, possibly 439–44, 842–55, 2608–12), besides being turgid and clotted in style, contain a much higher than usual number of words found nowhere else in Shakespeare, suggesting later revisions by another hand than his.[11] Other non-Shakespearean features of style and meter in F are discussed below. A major reason to doubt a one-time, comprehensive revision by Shakespeare himself, however, is that it preemptively excludes from F all the other kinds of changes, made for a variety of reasons by a variety of agencies, that were not simply normal but probably inescapable in the theater. Of course it is possible that Shakespeare made many or most of the changes in *Lear*; but no compelling reason has yet been given to believe that he made any.

The many hundreds of small verbal changes from Q that are found throughout F give fairly compelling evidence of non-authorial and even of non-theatrical intervention. Most of these changes are explainable as editorial, scribal, or compositorial error, correction, or sophistication, and the vast majority of them make no practical difference. Some F variants correct erroneous words in Q, a few add new errors; even the handful of changed speech prefixes, significantly reassigning speeches, have seemed to editors to be in most cases either the corrections of errors or new errors. Occasionally old-fashioned words, such as *rash* and *dearne* (2130, 2135), are replaced by more modern ones (*sticke*, *sterne*). Scores of other changes, serving no practical purpose in the theater, seem both uncharacteristic of Shakespeare and likely to be someone else's trivial, even pedantic, modernizations or improvements. F consistently changes Q's *towards*, *sometime*, *farther*, and adverbial *beside* to *toward*, *sometimes*, *further*, and *besides*. The Folio repeatedly modernizes the older forms *hath* and *hast* to *has* or *haue*, as well as *a* to *he* and *and* to *if*, and sometimes changes the older second-person subjunctive to the indicative in -st (*be* to *be'st*, *loue* to *lou'st*, etc.). F frequently corrects *thy* to *thine* before a vowel, and (inconsistently with Shakespeare's known style elsewhere) alters *that* to *which*, *who*[*m*], and *which*; *who* to *which*; *what's* to *who's*; and the like—all more rigidly regular in matters of grammatical usage than Shakespeare customarily was.

Neither are these many small particular improvements or sophistications habitual to the two F compositors; rather, they seem more likely to reflect the habits of a scribe accustomed to turn rough drafts into smooth copy. It is evident from recent textual study that for quite a number of plays either the King's Men or Jaggard were willing to invest the two to three shillings (less than $50 in modern currency) that a transcript would cost in order to supply good printer's copy and to keep the playbook out of danger of loss or damage in the printshop. Besides the several transcripts prepared by Ralph Crane (of *The Tempest*, *Two Gentlemen of Verona*, *Merry Wives of Windsor*, *Measure for Measure*, *The Winter's Tale*, probably *Cymbeline*, and possibly *2 Henry IV* and *Othello*), transcripts by other scribes have been detected behind (among others) *As You Like It*, *Twelfth Night*, *Henry VIII*, and especially several plays in the Tragedies section of F1—*Julius Caesar*, *Hamlet*, *Macbeth*, *Antony and Cleopatra*, and *Coriolanus*, as well as *Othello*. The originals of these transcripts have seemed in most cases to be theatrical documents, most likely the playbooks. Ernst Honigmann (1996: 74–75) even surmises that

Hamlet, *Lear*, and *Othello*, placed consecutively in F1, may have been transcribed, "perhaps simultaneously," by three different scribes who might on occasion have shared work on the same play.

That a scribal copy of the playbook was prepared for the printers of F1 *Lear* is now, I think, a warranted assertability. F *Lear* is filled with minor changes of spelling and elision that would serve no purpose in the theater and are not characteristic of the F compositors, but that resemble similar changes in other texts known or thought to be set from scribal transcripts. Some examples are the persistently repeated abbreviations and elisions *'em*, *o'th*, *i'th'*, *th'*, *th'hast*, *ha's*, *do's*, *I'ld*, and the spelling *Oh*. For more than a century F1 *Lear* was thought to have been typeset from a marked-up copy of Q1; more recently a marked-up copy of Q2 has been proposed. The theory has always met resistance because printer's copy in which thousands of small variants from the playbook had been written marginally would be very difficult to read, and hardly easier or cheaper to prepare than a fresh transcript. Having given evidence (1982) that F1 *Lear* was set from a manuscript, not printed copy, Trevor Howard-Hill (1986) argued convincingly that no substantive reading need to have derived from Q1, and that no "collator" marking up either quarto would have transferred to it hundreds of additional *un*substantive, meaningless changes of elision, spelling, and the like. In all likelihood these represent the habitual linguistic and orthographic style of the scribe himself, who entered them in his transcript, either intentionally or unconsciously as he went along, copying directly from the playbook.

This latter scribe, like his predecessor who made fair copy in 1606, is yet another agent in the evolution of the text. Like the earlier scribe he may be responsible for some relining of verse, substitutions of synonymous words, or of erroneous ones, or for corrections of apparent errors, regularization of spelling and punctuation, and so on. He very possibly copied the act-and-scene divisions that he found marked in the playbook, probably indicated there after the company moved to the Blackfriars playhouse, where act intervals were observed. He is probably the person responsible for the confusion in 3.1, where one or two additions to Kent's instructions to the Gentleman, very likely tipped into the playbook on a separate slip of paper, have been mistaken for a substitution for part of Kent's speech. He may also have erroneously substituted other F for Q material at 823, 1016, 1294+1–1296, and 2538–39. He is very likely the source of the majority of small verbal changes of number and case agreement, interchanges of synonymous prepositions or relative pronouns, modernizations of forms of verbs, etc. which a scribe might intentionally or unconsciously introduce into a text that he knew was meant for readers but which are changes pointless for a theatrical reviser to make. F's spelling *Gonerill,* found neither in the quartos nor in any of the sources, is probably scribal.

Whether it was this scribe, or the company bookholder, or an experienced company member with literary abilities, or Heminge and Condell, or another playwright known to and enlisted by them, clearly someone undertook the job of thoroughly editing or vetting the playhouse manuscript. Q lacks a great many entrances and exits, and contains a number of irregular (vague, inconsistent, missing, or erroneous) character designations; these have been thoroughly (if not perfectly) supplied and regularized in F. Textual scholars would once have thought such improvements to be the work of the bookholder, but recent studies of extant manuscript playbooks (e.g. Long, 1985, 1999) reveal that regularization of entrances, exits, and character descriptions seldom occurred in them. If the playbook was not regularly used as a "promptbook" during performances, but was instead a "maximal" record of all the lines approved by the Master of the Revels (whether acted or not), there would have been no pressing need for recording in it the clarifications of stage business that would have been attended to in performance. Such changes in F1 therefore more probably represent editing for a reading edition than theatrical regularization. Normalizations of names in the accessories from *Bastard* to *Edmund*, *Oswald* or *Gentleman* to *Steward*, *Duke* to *Albany* or *Cornwall*, and the like would have served no purpose in performance, since each actor knew from memorizing his part which lines he spoke when, no matter how his character had been variously designated in speech prefixes or stage directions in Q or its transcript. Any real ambiguities or confusions would have been straightened out when the parts were written out or during the first days of production; there was no urgent practical need to transfer these disambiguations to the playbook. Such regularization (and the correction of actual errors) would, however, have been a real help to a first-time (or one-time) reader of the text in F1, and would very naturally have been provided in a final, pre-publication editorial review.

Either that editor or a dramatist hired earlier to make revisions for a revival is probably responsible for one other kind of non-Shakespearean alteration to the text in F—a consistent attempt throughout the play to polish its verse. In at least 130 places throughout the play individual words or phrases have been omitted, added, or substituted in F in order to smoothe the meter, and in most cases for no other apparent reason. Some such emendations elsewhere in the play do not improve the meter, but the totality of such changes in F result in greater metrical regularity three times as often as in disruption; and if changes due to relining or consequent upon other revision are excluded, metrical improvement results five times as often as not. Continual verbal emendation intended to regularize an author's verse would not normally be expected of a scribe making a transcript of the playbook; neither do the two F compositors who set F *Lear* make such changes in other plays. These alterations seem to derive from revisions made in the playbook itself, either by the author between 1606 and his retirement or, more probably, by someone else. It is scarcely to be credited that such metrical polishings are Shakespeare's. The jagged rhythms throughout both Q and F *Lear* have often been admired as perfectly suiting the moods of the speakers or the stresses of the occasion; and in his later plays Shakespeare's verses became increasingly free and irregular for the same kinds of reasons. Yet here in F *Lear* we find, in some 130 places, the smoothing out and polishing of the rhythm. It is far easier to imagine a hired reviser or an editor attempting to supply such correct (and more pedestrian) regularity to *Lear* while vetting it, than to imagine Shakespeare, late in his career, working so contrarily to his own recent habits in order to undo his own characteristic and vigorous verse.[12]

The last agents of changes to the text in F1 were the two compositors, called B and E, who set their transcript into galleys and pages of type. Their habits and preferences have been studied extensively and minutely. The older and more experienced of the two, Compositor B, was for a long time unjustly maligned as unreliable, given to making careless or high-handed alterations from his copy; in fact he was trustworthy enough to set more lines in F than any other compositor, in 35 of 36 plays, and his work required no unusual amount of press-correction. He can be shown to have made errors, substituted and transposed words, imposed some of his preferences of spelling and punctuation, and from time to time adjusted the lineation of his text to fit the page—perhaps omitting or possibly even inventing occasional lines and phrases in order to do so. Compositor E, on the other hand, was evidently a young and inexperienced recent apprentice; before setting a majority of the lines in *Lear* he had worked on only two tragedies and three or four pages of other plays, and after *Lear* he set parts of only three more. He was not experienced enough to set complicated typography such as title pages, he worked slowly, and his rate of error required frequent and repeated press-correction. More often than B he was guilty of omitting, substituting, and transposing words (even possibly omitting whole lines), and he was especially prone to adding or omitting *-s* and *-es* at the ends of words. Before *Lear* he had worked almost wholly from printed copy; the number of literal errors in his work suggests that he had some trouble reading from the manuscript copy for *Lear*, and as an aid continually consulted printed copy, the Second Quarto (Q2) edition of *Lear* that Jaggard had printed four years earlier. Compositor B also consulted Q2 frequently.[13] Both F compositors therefore, in different degrees, repeated alterations made by the three earlier compositors of Q2, which is our last identifiable source of changes in the text of F.

Because for the better part of a century a marked-up copy of Q1 had been thought to be the printer's copy for F1, editors had been puzzled to find (increasingly) that words, spellings, and marks of punctuation from Q2 were duplicated in F.[14] During the past quarter-century Q2's influence on F1 has been frequently exaggerated, and claims have been made that a marked-up Q2, instead of or in addition to Q1, was printer's copy for F1. It can now be shown that such claims are untenable; F rejects some 1,300 substantive readings found in Q2, and seems to accept a mere 90. Moreover, the 90 agreements between the texts need not show any substantive influence from Q2, since the F readings could all have been arrived at independently by such natural means as the substitution of obviously correct readings for Q1 misreadings. Both F compositors obviously derive their substantive readings from elsewhere—i.e., from a manuscript, not from Q1 or Q2.

Nonetheless, Q2 seems to have had a significant influence on the "accidentals" of F1, particularly its punctuation and to a lesser extent its spellings, elisions, and the like. The three compositors who copied Q2 from Q1, perhaps simply following Jaggard's customary house style, had made occasional improvements in words, orthography, and meter, and extensive changes in punctuation. In hundreds of places Q2 replaces Q1's light and inadequate punctuation marks (mainly commas) with heavier stops, especially colons, semicolons, and periods. While F's punctuation does not exactly correspond with Q2's, in many places it obviously derives from it. Moreover, the inexperienced Compositor E adopts several times as many of Q2's accidentals as does his more experienced co-worker Compositor B—almost twice as many marks of punctuation, and four or five times as many of some other features.[15] Obviously compositor E consulted Q2 constantly, and consciously or unconsciously adopted its readings, while Compositor B consulted it less frequently and adopted fewer. The reason for this pattern is not hard to imagine: Compositor E, just beginning to set from manuscript copy, constantly resorted to the earlier printed edition for guidance in reading and interpreting his transcript; since Q2 was at hand, Compositor B also consulted it from time to time, but he felt less need for it. Both compositors, in any case, were agents in bringing yet another influence to bear upon F1, the improvements made four years earlier in Q2; in so doing they affected the syntax, meter, and rhetorical texture of F1 *Lear*.

After the Folio

With the publication of the First Folio the ability to shape the received text of *Lear*, theatrically or editorially, passed out of the hands of his company. Their officially sanctioned reading text of the play, F1, remained substantially unchanged for a century in the reprints F2 (1632), F3 (1663–64) and F4 (1685); most of the unauthoritative emendations made in F2 by an intelligent anonymous editor were repeated in the two later Folios. In 1655 a Third Quarto (Q3), a reprint of Q2, was published, adding a great many textual errors; its title page, copied from the original quartos, still repeats, in the interregnum, long after the companies had been disbanded and the theaters torn down, Q1's advertisement of performance before the "kinges maiestie at Whitehall" by his "servant*es* playinge vsually at the globe on the Banksyde." It is not an independent edition, and had no influence on the history of the text.

At the beginning of the eighteenth century the conventional synthetic text that readers and scholars used for the next three centuries began to take shape. The dramatist Nicholas Rowe was engaged to re-edit F4, and in his editions of 1709 and 1714 he changed it as one would expect a man of the theater to do, regularizing its act–scene divisions and character names, adding dramatis personae lists and numerous stage directions and indications of locale, and emending obscure words and lines. Alexander Pope, in his edition of 1725, emended words freely, rewrote much of the verse according to his neoclassic tastes, and "degraded" to the bottom of the page a number of passages that he considered unworthy of Shakespeare. But his most important contribution was restoring to his Folio-based text more than a hundred Quarto lines that had been omitted from F1: here beginneth the modern conflated edition of *Lear*. In his edition of 1733 Lewis Theobald, while rejecting a large proportion of Pope's "improvements," thereby winning himself a place in the *Dunciad*, restored the greater part of the remaining Quarto lines (unwittingly taking them from Q2). It remained for Edward Capell in his edition of 1768 and Charles Jennens in his of 1770 to restore a score more lines, and for Maurice Ridley in his edition of 1935 to salvage a remaining phrase or two.

The intention in these synthetic reconstructions from F and Q was a prudential one—to preserve from oblivion the lines that had been lost from the Folio because of theatrical cutting, and thus to recover the whole play that Shakespeare had originally written. The restoration of 300 Quarto lines went some way to achieving that end; the inclusion of 110 lines and hundreds of variants from the Folio, on the other hand, certainly added an amount of non-Shakespearean material to the edited version(s) of *Lear* that the reading public was to know for three centuries. Although occasionally a rare edition was based on the Quarto rather than the Folio, and a few parallel-text editions were produced exhibiting the Q and F texts on facing pages, the idea that those two original texts represented discrete and distinct authorial versions, deserving separate modern editions, was not realized until the Oxford *Works* of 1986.

The text in the theater has proved to be much more protean. Apart from a performance of the Q text by a local troupe in Yorkshire in 1611, and of a German translation by a traveling English troupe in Dresden in 1626, no performance of *Lear* is recorded between its original court presentation in 1606 and the closing of the theaters; if there was a revival in that period, it was presumably based on the company's playbook. When in 1660 Sir William Davenant was granted exclusive right to produce the play, it was described as one of "the most ancient Playes that were playd at Blackfriers." Davenant's company performed it at Lincoln's Inn Fields in January 1664; it may have been performed there again in 1665, and was given a revival at Dorset Garden, again by the Duke's Company, in 1675. Although no playscript for Davenant's productions survives, a contemporary witness, John Downes, reported that the play was "as Mr. *Shakespear* Wrote it."

All that changed when a recently established playwright, Nahum Tate, rewrote *Lear* so as to suit the theatrical fashions, political ideas, and neoclassic tastes of the Restoration audience. Although professing to strengthen and polish his original, Tate produced in his *History of King Lear* (1681) quite a different play. In giving Shakespeare's tragedy a happy ending, he played to his royalist audience's aversion to regicide, foreign invasion, and civil war, and probably expected them to see parallels between the ambitions of Edmund the Bastard and of Charles's illegitimate son the Duke of Monmouth. To capitalize on the return of actresses and feminine charms to the London stage he invented a love affair between Cordelia and Edgar, added a female companion Arante, and staged an adulterous tryst and an attempted rape. To preserve semi-tragic decorum and avoid old-fashioned theatrical taste for clowning he cut the part of the Fool. He added further disguises, mistaken identity, tearful scenes of pathos, and abstract moralizing.

Though aimed at the Restoration audience, Tate's revision was a long-lasting success, completely replacing Shakespeare's text of *King Lear* on the London stage for more than a century and a half and on the American stage for almost a half-century more. The dozens of theater or "acting" editions of *Lear* published from the late eighteenth century until the beginning of the twentieth century all reveal that the performances that made Garrick, Kemble, Kean, Booth, and Forrest famous Lears were all completely or mostly based on Tate's version. Not until Macready's revival of 1838 did a completely Shakespearean (though still truncated) version, including the Fool and the tragic ending, begin to return to the stage. For several decades thereafter the play bearing Shakespeare's title kept changing its shape with each production, as more of Shakespeare's original lines were restored and more vestiges of Tate were removed.

Only seldom has anything resembling either the original Quarto or Folio version returned to the modern stage. The play's length has always been a problem, and has invited cutting more drastic than that found in the already considerably shortened Folio text. Henry Irving omitted almost half of the lines, causing George Bernard Shaw to remark that if Mr. Irving were to present himself in as maimed a condition as his *Lear*, his public would run from him shrieking in horror. Kenneth Muir reported having to cut enough from a production to allow the audience to catch the last train. The Victorian taste for lavish stage sets also dictated the combining, rearranging, shortening, and omission of scenes, to reduce their number and thereby the time needed for scene-shifting. Directors re-shaped the play according to their dramaturgic judgments, streamlining it, heightening the part of one star actor or another, removing speeches obscure to a modern audience, and the like. Since the rise to dominance in the twentieth century of "director's theater," audiences have come to accept the trimming and reshaping of the play to fit a director's "concept" as only to be expected, while complete fidelity to a full and unmediated authorial text may seem the exception.[16] Not much new there; as this survey reminds us, both players and editors have continually reshaped *Lear* in one way and degree or another since before its first presentation at the Globe and Whitehall in 1606.

Inconclusion

In the 1980s the *Lear* revisionists—those asserting that Q1 and F1 represented two equally authorial versions of the play—often disparaged the conventional synthetic or "conflated" text, declaring that it was an editorial fiction, embodying a version of the play that Shakespeare never intended and that no contemporary audience ever saw. True enough, I think: but exactly the same claims can be made of the texts in both Q1 and F1. Both the First Quarto and the First Folio present "documentary texts" of *Lear*, and like any other document their texts may be edited in a variety of formats—facsimile, diplomatic reprint, critical old-spelling edition, modernized critical edition, and so on. In recent years a considerable number of editions of the separate, unconflated texts have been published, wholly useful for teaching, criticism, and scholarship, as any edited document may be. The question that needs to be faced, however, is what kind of entity these texts are documents of. Each can be defended as presenting a distinct, coherent version of the play having an integrity that would be compromised by contamination with any part of the other. But that either text represents Shakespeare's final intention or a version seen on the Jacobean stage is anything but certain. Each presents a momentary snapshot of a play that from the beginning down to the present has been in constant flux, in print and on the stage. Each original text presents an ideal rather than an actually presented version of the play. Among other things, each version is several hundred lines longer than could have been presented within the normal playing limits, and it is doubtful that Shakespeare intended or expected that all of its lines would be performed.

As for Q1, it presents an "ideal" text in more than one sense. For whatever reason—artistic thoroughness, expectation of publication in print, hope for literary as well as theatrical fame, creative momentum resulting in overkill—Shakespeare wrote a first complete draft longer that he could have expected to be staged; he knew that it would have to be considerably shortened, and (to judge from F's cuts) it was. That draft seems to have been "maximal," presenting the players with more material than they needed; it provided optimal resources from which they could make their preferred selection of scenes, episodes, and speeches, omitting some parts while leaving most of the play intact. The text in Q1 is ideal (rather than actual) in another sense: when it was published it had already been made obsolete by a year of actual stage practice and alteration. No one believes that it ever served as an acting text: it is too long, too full of error, and too lacking in necessary stage directions. It does not represent what had actually been performed on the stage in 1606–8. It therefore does not reflect any censor's cuts, or record any additions to speeches to clarify motive, or additions to the clown's part, any adjustments for performance on tour, or any other such changes; in all likelihood Q1 offers only an incomplete approximation of what was or could have been staged in 1606, 1607, and 1608. And of course Q's text is ideal in the sense of imaginary, unreal, illusionary; it gives a partly false representation of Shakespeare's intentions and even of his manuscript because of all the distortions of language and meter invented by its incompetent printers. Formerly it was classed among the "bad quartos"; now, because of its closeness to Shakespeare's original manuscript, it has undergone a remarkable rehabilitation and may in time (as I expect it will) replace F1 as the preferred base text for modern editions. Nonetheless, one cannot claim with any confidence that Q1 represents accurately either what Shakespeare intended for the stage or what the players acted.

As for F1, even if one believes that most of the cuts, additions, and occasional rewordings represent Shakespeare's own wholesale revision of the play—and there is nothing like general agreement that they do—there is copious evidence that a great many people other than or in addition to Shakespeare affected the text: at least two scribes and five compositors (three in Q2, two in F1); company members, possibly Shakespeare, possibly not, who made cuts; a bookholder who may have recorded incidental changes in lines or action; one or more persons who added a few speeches, repeatedly modernized language, grammar, and orthography, and rewrote meter, thus adding nuances of style and language other than Shakespeare's; probably an editor or redactor or "dresser of plays" (if not the bookholder, then possibly Heminge or Condell, possibly a company volunteer or hireling) who vetted the text before publication, regularizing names and speech prefixes, providing stage directions, inserting act and scene divisions, possibly adding or cutting or rewriting an occasional line. Because the text in F1, though 200 lines shorter than that in Q1, is still hundreds of lines longer than the contemporary norm, it probably preserves more lines and speeches than were ever spoken in any actual performance. As with Q, the result is a text which can hardly be wholly Shakespeare's or represent settled stage practice.

Until recently editors strove to fix—determine, establish, stabilize—the text of *Lear*, and in accordance with the editorial assumptions of their times they succeeded in doing so. Meanwhile actors and (eventually) directors, beginning with Shakespeare's own company, exercised great freedom—grotesquely so when Tateification was at its height—to do the opposite, reshaping the text in countless ways to suit their own purposes. Readers, scholars, and critics naturally prefer to base their judgments and discussions upon one standard agreed-upon text or texts; people in the theater have instead always worked from scripts of the greatest diversity. Recent volumes in the New Variorum series include a comprehensive and detailed essay on the history of the play's text on the stage; each of these essays lists, analyzes, and interprets all the significant changes recorded in dozens of printed acting editions and available promptbooks from the past three centuries.[17] It is easy to abstract from the textual data in these surveys an essential core of playable scenes and speeches that actors have found indispensable, and conversely the speeches and episodes that many different directors have found expendable; but much of the play comes and goes from one production to the next, in a bewildering and unpredictable variety of ways. *Lear* on the stage has been the opposite of a monolith.

It is interesting to me, therefore, to hear calls recently from theater people for a return to a conventionally conflated text—to something resembling the familiar, stable text of the past—as the grounds for theatrical interpretation (and normal dramaturgic reshaping). To those who insist on the integrity of the Q1 and F1 texts, the idea of blurring their distinctions by merging them in a synthetic edition is anathema. But the theatrical use of such a text would be practical, not initially or primarily conceptual. The conflated text is certainly an editorial invention, but it is not entirely an artificial or arbitrary one. Of course a Folio text that omits 300 lines (including the mock trial in 3.6 and the whole of 4.3), that reassigns an occasional speech, and sprinkles more than a hundred new lines or part-lines throughout the text offers a significantly different text for playing than that in the Quarto; and there are good reasons for editing the two texts separately, to illuminate and preserve their differences. A conflated edition, on the other hand, shows both how much of the play remains unchanged between the one version and the other, and how much logic can connect the parts of a reconstituted whole. A repeated argument against the claim of a wholesale authorial revision in F is that so little has been changed—there are no new characters, scenes, events, no rewritten speeches—that the intention behind the alterations seems mainly to be theatrical shortening and local adjustment, not true revision. A conflation shows fairly accurately how much, and how little, has been changed from Q to F, and how well their separate parts hang together. When a conflated text restores or preserves the 300 Quarto lines, it simply puts them where Shakespeare originally had them; when it includes the 110 new Folio lines and phrases, it places them where one or more revisers, possibly including Shakespeare, put them. Some variants of words and phrases may make a significant difference, but in overall outline and substance the two versions are not that different: almost 90 percent of the lines and their sequence are virtually the same.

In effect a conflation of Q and F reconstitutes something like the complete "maximal" playbook owned by Shakespeare's company (though including even 300 more lines than survived from it into F). A number of editors—e.g. Furness, Ridley, Foakes—have been scrupulously careful to indicate, as that playbook would have done in its own way, which lines were original, which marked for omission, which added later. This kind of textual amalgam of two original versions may be unsuitable for many critical and scholarly purposes, but for a man of the theater it may be more useful than separate editions of either Q or F—which themselves do not, as I have been arguing, give us completely satisfactory Shakespearean or Jacobean acting texts to begin with. Giorgi Melchiori explicitly makes "a plea in favour of conflated texts. Men of the theatre should be provided with as full texts, including variants, as are available in the original printings. It is their task to choose, select, and cut in order to suit the circumstances in which the plays are to be staged" (2003: 25). The advantage of a conflated edition for directors is that, like the original maximal playbook, it provides an archive of possibilities, arranged as coherently as may be, from which actors and producers will, as they always have done, make a selection—continuing the theatrical evolution of the play we call *King Lear*. What kind of text the future general reader will prefer remains to be seen.

Notes

1 A full survey of their attempts may be found in the forthcoming New Variorum edition, and a useful annotated reading list of their studies may be found in Michael Warren's *Complete King Lear* (1989, 1: xxiii–xxxiii).

2 The evidence is discussed in greater detail in the forthcoming New Variorum.

3 See, e.g. Bowers (1955: 15; 1966: 17); Werstine (2000: 32–36).

4 Shakespeare almost certainly worked from the published book of *Leir*; earlier theories that he had once acted in the play as a member of the Queen's Men, or that he later had access to a manuscript, are all lacking in evidence and probability. See Knowles (2002).

5 For representative arguments see Taylor (1983: 75 ff.), Patterson (1984: 58–73), and Clare (1990: 132 ff.).

6 This likelihood would contradict the fundamental belief of those who think that all the major cuts, additions, and verbal changes were made all at once, by Shakespeare, perhaps in 1610. See also n. 11 below.

7 See in particular Stone (1980: 72–75, 127) and Knowles (1995: 45; 1997: 60). Stone proposes as the author of these and other added lines one of the King's Men's regular playwrights, Philip Massinger, who is known for his "involuted syntax, his fondness especially for periodic sentences and for every kind of parenthetic construction" (127). Taylor's attempt to disqualify Massinger (1983: 443, n. 97), on the grounds that F1 *Lear* lacks a handful of Massinger's favorite words and contains a few forms uncharacteristic of him, is unconvincing: there is no occasion for any of the words (embryon, scarabs, imp feathers, etc.), and the un-Massingerian forms (has, i'th', ye) in all likelihood originate in the scribal transcript used as printer's copy.

8 Many commentators who have suspected that the Fool's part was padded by Armin or another actor, among them Charles and Mary Cowden Clarke, A.C. Bradley, Harley Granville-Barker, E.K. Chambers, Madeleine Doran, Thomas M. Parrott, Tucker Brooke, Charles S. Felver, and Peter Stone, are quoted in the notes on these and other passages, and in the appendix on the play's sources, in the forthcoming New Variorum.

9 The showpiece of the method, cited as a model by many of the contributors to Taylor and Warren (1983), is Taylor's argument (1980) that Q1 presents a foreign invasion, F1 a civil war. So impressionistic a form of argument is open to the dangers of exaggeration and special pleading; even a critic sympathetic to the idea of authorial revision has rejected Taylor's proof (see Foakes, 1993: 107, 206), and Knowles (1999: 270 ff.) details its misuses of evidence.

10 E.g. Ryan (2002: 3): "The problem is that most of the cuts and revisions are not convincing on artistic or theatrical grounds anyway."

11 These non-Shakespearean words are identified and discussed briefly by Knowles (1995: 45; 1997: 60). Though a search through the data banks of LION turns up many incidences of these words in other writers, I have not yet found that they are all the favorites of any particular dramatist, who might therefore be suspected of authoring some of the additions to *Lear*. The date of circulation of these words is of interest. Taylor speculated that Shakespeare rewrote his play at about 1610; these words seem to have become current rather later than that, suggesting a later date for the additions. Brian Vickers, who used vocabulary tests extensively in his *Shakespeeare, Co-Author*, has generously communicated the following: "I asked my asistant, Dr Marcus Dahl, to run those [ten] rare words through his data base of 450 texts, some non-dramatic. . . . I did a little dating test, using the Harbage *Annals*, and found that, of the drama instances, 3 fell in the decade 1600–1610, 5 in 1611–1620, 13 in 1621–1630, and 3 in 1631–1640. Not conclusive, of course, but it further weakens the theory of an authorial revision in 1610." The question needs more work.

12 A list identifying these lines, too long to be included here, and commentary notes on each line, may be found in the forthcoming New Variorum. Their significance has been briefly discussed by Knowles (1997: 74–5; 1999: 282).

13 It was long believed that Jaggard's Compositor B, four years before setting much of F1, had set all or most of the Pavier Quartos of 1619, including all of *Lear*. That idea has now been discredited and abandoned: among others questioning it, Knowles (1982) gave evidence that not one but three compositors set Q2 *Lear*, none of them showing the characteristic setting style of Compositor B.

14 The problem was long compounded by the false date (1608) on the title page of Thomas Pavier's 1619 quarto, and by the fact that its text closely resembled that in Q1, from which it had been copied. Q1 and Q2 were still being confused as late as the Cambridge edition of 1863–66.

15 Exhaustive counts of the relative frequency of spellings and punctuation marks in Q1, Q2, and F1 *Lear* are provided by Andrews (1971) and Stone (1980). I have supplemented them with my own computer-aided comparison of the three texts.

16 An exhaustive tabulation of all the changes to the text found in several dozen printed theater editions and promptbooks spanning three centuries is provided by Halstead (1977–83). His data are not always accurate, and are somewhat difficult to use because they are keyed to an obsolete text. A full discursive survey of the same and additional theatrical texts has been written for the forthcoming New Variorum by Dr. Paula Glatzer.

17 Such surveys have appeared in the volumes for *As You Like It*, *Antony and Cleopatra*, and *The Winter's Tale*, have been completed for the forthcoming volumes for *The Comedy of Errors* and *King Lear*, and will be part of all future volumes in the series.

Works cited

Andrews, John F. "The Pavier Quartos of 1619—Evidence for Two Compositors." Vanderbilt diss., 1971.

Barroll, [J.] Leeds. *Politics, Plague, and Shakespeare's Theater: The Stuart Years*. Ithaca and London: Cornell University Press, 1991.

Bentley, Gerald E. *The Profession of Dramatist in Shakespeare's Time 1590–1642*. Princeton: Princeton University Press, 1971.

Blayney, Peter W.M. *The Texts of* King Lear *and their Origins*. Vol. I: *Nicholas Okes and the First Quarto*. Cambridge University Press, 1982. (Vol. 2 not yet published.)

Bowers, Fredson. *On Editing Shakespeare*. Rpt., with additions. Charlottesville: University Press of Virginia, 1966. (First pub. as *On Editing Shakespeare and the Elizabethan Dramatists*. Oxford: Oxford University Press, 1955.)

Chambers, E[dmund] K. *Shakespearean Gleanings*. Oxford: Oxford University Press, 1944.

Clare, Janet. *"Art made tongue-tied by authority": Elizabethan and Jacobean Dramatic Censorship*. Manchester: Manchester University Press and New York: St. Martin's, 1990.

Craig, Hardin. "The Composition of *King Lear*." *Renaissance Papers 1961*. Ed. George W. Williams. Durham, NC: Renaissance Meeting in the Southeastern States, 1962: 57–61.

—— *A New Look at Shakespeare's Quartos*. Stanford: Stanford University Press, 1961.

Doran, Madeleine. "Elements in the Composition of *King Lear*." *Studies in Philology* 30 (1933): 34–58.

—— *The Text of* King Lear. Stanford University Publications, University Series, Language and Literature 4.2. Stanford and London: Stanford University Press, 1931.

Dutton, Richard. "The Birth of the Author." *Elizabethan Theater: Essays in Honor of S. Schoenbaum*. Eds. R.B. Parker and S.P. Zitner. Newark and London: Associated University Presses, 1996: 71–92.

Erne, Lukas. *Shakespeare as a Literary Dramatist*. Cambridge: Cambridge University Press, 2003.

Evans, G. Blakemore, (ed.). *The Riverside Shakespeare*. Boston: Houghton Mifflin, 1974.

Everett, Barbara. "Shakespeare in the Twentieth Century: Finding a Way Out." *Shakespeare and the Twentieth Century*. Eds. Jonathan Bate, Jill L. Levenson, and Dieter Mehl. Newark, DE, and London: Associated University Presses, 1998: 215–30.

Foakes, R.A. *Hamlet Versus Lear*. Cambridge: Cambridge University Press, 1993.

Granville-Barker, Harley. *Prefaces to Shakespeare: First Series*. London: Sidgwick and Jackson, 1927. (First pub. in *The Players Shakespeare*.)

Greg, W[alter] W. *The Variants in the First Quarto of "King Lear."* Oxford: Oxford University Press, 1940.

Gurr, Andrew. "Henry Carey's Peculiar Letter." *Shakespeare Quarterly* 56 (2005): 51–75.

—— "Maximal and Minimal Texts: Shakespeare v. the Globe." *Shakespeare Survey* 52 (1999): 68–87.

—— *The Shakespeare Company 1594–1642*. Cambridge: Cambridge University Press, 2004.

—— *The Shakespearian Playing Companies*. Oxford: Oxford University Press, 1996.

Halstead, William P. *Shakespeare as Spoken*. 14 vols. Ann Arbor and Washington: American Theatre Association and University Microfilms, 1977–83.

Hart, Alfred. *Shakespeare and the Homilies and Other Pieces of Research into the Elizabethan Drama*. Melbourne: Melbourne University Press, 1934.

—— *Stolne and Surreptitious Copies: A Comparative Study of Shakespeare's Bad Quartos*. Melbourne: Melbourne University Press and London: Oxford University Press, 1942.

Honigmann, E.A.J. *The Texts of* Othello *and Shakespearian Revision*. London and New York: Routledge, 1996.

Howard-Hill, Trevor H. "The Problem of Manuscript Copy for Folio *King Lear*." 6 *Library* 4 (1982): 1–24.

—— "Q1 and the Copy for Folio *Lear*." *Papers of the Bibliographical Society of America* 80 (1986): 419–35.

Knowles, Richard. "The Case for Two Lears." *Shakespeare Quarterly* 36 (1985): 115–20.

—— "How Shakespeare Knew *King Leir*." *Shakespeare Survey* 55 (2002): 12–35.

—— "Merging the Kingdoms: *King Lear*." *The Shakespearean International Yearbook 1: Where are we now in Shakespearean Studies?* Eds. W.R. Elton and John M. Mucciolo. Aldershot and Brookfield, VT: Ashgate, 1999: 266–86.

—— "The Printing of the Second Quarto (1619) of *King Lear*." *Studies in Bibliography* 35 (1982): 191–206.

—— "Revision Awry in Folio *Lear* 3.1." *Shakespeare Quarterly* 46 (1995): 32–46.

—— "Two *Lears*? By Shakespeare?" Lear *from Study to Stage: Essays in Criticism*.

Eds. James Ogden and Arthur H. Scouten. Madison, NJ: Associated University Presses, 1997: 57–78.

Long, William B. " 'Precious Few': English Manuscript Playbooks." *A Companion to Shakespeare*. Ed. David S. Kastan. Oxford and Malden, MA: Blackwell, 1999: 414–33.

—— "Stage-directions: a Misunderstoood Factor in Determining Textual Provenance." *Text* 2 (1985): 121–37.

Melchiori, Giorgio. "The Continuing Importance of New Bibliography." *In Arden: Editing Shakespeare*. Eds. Ann Thompson and Gordon McMullan. London, Arden Shakespeare, 2003: 17–30.

—— "*Hamlet*: The Acting Version and the Wiser Sort." *The* Hamlet *First Published (Q1, 1603): Origins, Form, Intextualities*. Ed. Thomas Clayton. Newark, DE, London and Toronto: Associated University Presses, 1992: 195–210.

Moriarty, W.D. "The Bearing on Dramatic Sequence of the Varia in *Richard the Third* and *King Lear*." *Modern Philology* 10 (1913): 451–71.

Orgel, Stephen. "Acting Scripts, Performing Texts." *Crisis in Editing: Texts of the English Renaissance*. Ed. Randall M[c]Leod. New York: AMS, 1994: 251–91. (Paper given 1988.)

Patterson, Annabel. *Censorship and Interpretation*. Madison: University of Wisconsin Press, 1984.

Rasmussen, Eric. "The Revision of Scripts." *A New History of Early English Drama*. Eds. John D. Cox and David S. Kastan. New York: Columbia University Press, 1997: 441–60.

Ryan, Kiernan. "*King Lear*: A Retrospect, 1980–2000." *Shakespeare Survey* 55 (2002): 1–11.

Smidt, Kristian. "The Quarto and Folio *Lear*: Another Look at the Theories of Textual Deviation." *English Studies* 45 (1964): 149–62.

—— "Repetition, Revision, and Editorial Greed in Shakespeare's Play Texts." *Cahiers Elisabéthains* 34 (1988): 25–37.

—— *Unconformities in Shakespeare's Tragedies*. New York: St. Martin's Press, 1990.

Stone, P[eter] W.K. *The Textual History of* King Lear. London: Scolar, 1980.

Taylor, Gary. "*King Lear*: The Date and Authorship of the Folio Version." *The Division of the Kingdoms*. Eds. Gary Taylor and Michael Warren. Oxford: Oxford University Press, 1983: 351–468.

—— "Monopolies, Show Trials, Disaster, and Invasion: *King Lear* and Censorship." *The Division of the Kingdoms*. Eds. Gary Taylor and Michael Warren. Oxford: Oxford University Press, 1983: 75–119.

—— "The War in 'King Lear.' " *Shakespeare Survey* 20 (1980): 27–34.

Taylor, Gary and Michael Warren. *The Division of the Kingdoms*. Oxford: Oxford University Press, 1983.

Vickers, Brian. *Shakespeare, Co-Author*. Oxford: Oxford University Press, 2002.

Warren, Michael (ed.). *The Complete* King Lear, *1608–1623*. 4 Parts. Berkeley, Los Angeles and London: University of California Press, 1989.

Werstine, Paul. "Editing Shakespeare and Editing Without Shakespeare: Wilson, McKerrow, Greg, Bowers, Tanselle, and Copy-text Editing." *Text* 13 (2000): 27–53.

4 *King Lear* and early seventeenth-century print culture

Cyndia Susan Clegg

William Shakespeare arrived in London nearly a century after Wynken de Worde set up his printing establishment in nearby Westminster and within a decade of the opening of London's first two commercial theaters, the Theatre in Shoreditch and the Curtain. At a time when theatrical playing companies were beginning to realize their commercial potential and to formulate procedures and practices within London's religious, political and social culture, publishers and printers followed time-honored practices. The Stationers' mysterie or guild had existed even before the first printers arrived from the Continent although its incorporation, in 1557, had been fairly recent. Despite the theater's comparative novelty, for the past four hundred years when scholars and editors have taken interest in London publishing during Shakespeare's time, it has largely been for its role in transmitting the texts of canonical authors. In the case of Shakespeare, according to Peter W.M. Blayney, such scholarship has engaged in extraordinary flights of fantasy to account for the disparity that exists among the early textual witnesses to his genius ("Playbooks" 283–84). Shakespearean textual studies have told tales of piratical printers and unscrupulous actors intent on constructing and printing "unauthorized" versions of the bard's plays. The problem, Blayney contends, is that this scholarly tradition has accorded insufficient attention to London print culture per se. In recent years, this has been changing. Important scholarship on the history of the book, including Blayney's, is providing a revised understanding of the contexts in which Shakespearean printed texts appeared. It is the purpose of this essay to consider *King Lear* from the perspective of this expanded knowledge of print culture in early modern England.

Before considering how studies in print culture might reshape our thinking about *King Lear*, it will be useful to revisit the premises that long dominated Shakespearean textual studies. The question of textual "authority" lies at the center of the work of generations of editors and scholars, beginning with Nicholas Rowe in 1709. Any given printed text, or various features of it, may or may not possess "authority," that is, it may or may not represent Shakespeare's authorial intentions. Had authorial manuscripts survived, this search for authority would be moot—but they did not, with the possible exception of a part of "Sir Thomas More" that has been ascribed to Shakespeare (Merriam 65–66). Instead, authority must be defined and discerned independently. The question of authority may be the focus of questions of canon—of whether or not a play attributed to Shakespeare was, indeed, written by him—or it may be a matter of text. The title-page of the first printed edition of *The Yorkshire Tragedy*, for example, claimed W. S. as its author, but the play was omitted from the first collection of Shakespeare's plays printed in 1623, *Mr William Shakespeares Comedies, Histories & Tragedies* (the First Folio). On the other hand, the First Folio omitted plays that today are considered authoritative, *Pericles* and *Two Noble Kinsmen*. It also included plays that if Shakespeare had any part in them, it was as a collaborator.

Indeed, the presence of one collaborative play, *Henry VIII*, in the First Folio illustrates how being "authoritative" works. Stanley Wells and Gary Taylor decided to include *Henry VIII* in their edition of Shakespeare's works for Oxford University Press, a move which is, in itself, not unusual. However, in the accompanying *Textual Companion* to that volume, the editors admitted, "Our only authority for this play is the text of the First Folio"—in which the play was printed for the first time (Wells and Taylor 618). (Fredson Bowers, on the other hand, included the play in his edition of *The Dramatic Works in the Beaumont and Fletcher Canon*.) In the case of this play, for Taylor and Wells and their other Oxford co-editor, William Montgomery, the real question of "authoritative" is not a matter of canon but of title. From contemporary references they conclude, "it seems probable that 'All is True' was the play's original title, and that the Folio alternative [*The Famous History of the Life of King Henry the Eight*, shortened to *The Life of King Henry the Eighth* in the Folio's 'Catalogue'] was either a subtitle, or, more likely, an unauthoritative one imposed by the compilers of that volume" (Wells and Taylor 618). The Oxford editors titled the play as *All is True*, despite contemporary references to it as "the play of Hen: 8" and "the play, viz. of Henry the 8" (Wells and Taylor 618, n.). Implicit, in this statement, are two principles that have governed editing and textual studies since Rowe: first, that which is "authoritative" reflects the author's original intention; second, that in the face of alternative or multiple witnesses, it is the responsibility of textual scholars and editors to recover and to restore authoritative text that may have been lost or mangled in transit from Shakespeare's pure intention and the printed witnesses to that intent.

Shakespeare and the New Bibliography

Discerning the authoritative Shakespearean text has been a principal task for textual scholarship for the past one hundred years. At the beginning of the twentieth century Graham Pollard, R.B. McKerrow, and W.W. Greg in their New Bibliography established a narrative to account for the character of the printed texts of Shakespeare's plays that not only judged the quality of quarto texts ("good" and "bad") but also described the various states of manuscript copy in relation to composition and performance. Greg further introduced "scientific" principles that discerned what kind of textual variants could be introduced at every state of textual text transmission. In essence, then, the practice of discerning a true "authoritative" text engages the textual scholar in the task of regressively purging irregularities that can be identified with the reprinting of texts, with compositor errors for each textual witness, with scribal error in transmitting Shakespeare's text, and even with the irregularities of authorial spelling and script. Even when bibliographers and editors ascertained that the manuscript upon which a given witness is based may have been Shakespeare's own (his "foul papers"), they have insisted upon consistency between apparent irregularities and Shakespeare's "usual" practices in "better" texts. Thus, they presumed that in many instances the authorial texts that formed the basis for printed copy were necessarily early drafts that were ill-written and/or illegible. There was for every Shakespeare play, as the New Bibliographer Bowers would have it, an "ideal text," and every modern editor's job was to make editorial decisions that would assure that the text he produced represented that ideal as it was conceived by Shakespeare—free from the interventions of censors and publishers and from the kinds of errors that Shakespeare himself may have made as he hurriedly penned his inspiration, or that the most careful scribe made in reading and transcribing Shakespeare's rushed writing, or that even experienced compositors made in casting type. The goal of nearly four-hundred years of Shakespeare editing has been to produce a text that can claim, as the First Folio did, to be the "True Original."

Multiple copies or True copies

For many of the plays included in the First Folio, approximating the "True Original" has posed less of a problem than for others. Sixteen of the thirty-six plays appeared in print for the first time in the 1623 Folio, so for them the First Folio's text is "authoritative."[1] The remaining twenty plays had been previously printed (and reprinted) in texts of varying quality. *King Lear* is one of these, and the "authority" of its texts has particularly vexed scholars.

Two printed texts of *King Lear* existed prior to the 1623 First Folio—a 1608 quarto and a 1619 quarto imprinted with the same date as Q1. Textual scholars have for some time agreed that Q2 derived from Q1. The question of the relationship between the folio text and the quartos is somewhat more complicated since F contains both distinctive Q1 and Q2 textual variants along with substantive omissions, additions, and changes. While current scholarship generally concedes that Q1 and F are valid representations of different stages in the play's composition, this was not always so. In his study of early quartos W.W. Greg identified Q1 *Lear* as a "bad" quarto printed without "authority" and derived from memorial reconstruction. Greg's use of "authoritative" introduced a problem that has bedeviled Shakespeare scholarship. From his narrative, texts that were printed by authority were made available for print by either the author or the acting company. Any other text was "unauthorized." This assumes that notions of copyright and intellectual property like our own existed in early print culture, which is problematic since the recognition of authors' proprietary interests in their writing did not exist in England before the eighteenth century.

The idea of "authorized" texts, also a difficulty, derives from Pollard's presumptions about textual transmission. In his study on the origins of manuscript copy, Paul Werstine recounts (and repudiates) Pollard's myth:

> Pollard argued (1) that Shakespeare would turn over to his company manuscripts of his plays in his own hand—not scribal transcripts of them. . . . Then, according to Pollard, (2) the bookkeeper would annotate Shakespeare's holograph, which would serve as the "Booke," the theatrical document (often called anachronistically the "promptbook") upon which performance would be based . . . Finally, (3) when the company decided to print the play, it would hand over the holograph—there was no other copy—to the printer, who was poor enough at his trade to introduce a quantity of errors in spite of having such fine copy before him.
>
> (Werstine 68)

The underlying principle of this narrative is that acting companies, especially those with which Shakespeare was associated, allowed only one manuscript copy of a play to exist in order to prevent "theft." Werstine dismisses Pollard's narrative by reminding us that there is no evidence for a theatrical manuscript ever being stolen from Shakespeare's company. He also doubts that authorial holographs served as promptbooks (Werstine 68). Allowing potentially multiple manuscripts, however, does not make the question of an "authorized" manuscript moot. One important step in the transition from page to stage was the requirement that a play be "authorized"—that is licensed for performance by the Master of the Revels. As long a play was being performed in repertory, whatever other manuscripts may have existed that witnessed to all or part of a play, the playbook authorized by the Master of the Revels was retained by the acting company bookkeeper as witness to the version approved for performance.

Licensing of plays and issues of authority

Initially, the Master of the Revels was responsible only for overseeing performances at court. This remained his central responsibility, even after the Revels Office assumed oversight for all licensed adult acting companies and, after 1610, the children's companies as well. His ties to the court meant that the Master of the Revels was sensitive to contemporary issues that, if referenced too openly, would prove unacceptable for court performance. Even when he licensed plays for the public playhouse, he was directed by the tastes and anxieties of the court (Dutton 158). A manuscript copy of a play as it was to be performed had to be presented to the Master of the Revels for his approbation prior to performance, and his recommendations or requirements for change appeared on this "licensed" book. This would have been the manuscript copy of the play that an acting company would have needed to preserve in case any question might later arise about the relationship between a performance and what had been authorized. According to Richard Dutton, while the Master of the Revels, was fairly lenient in terms of what might be allowable—the personation of living persons being one dominant concern—he conscientiously protected his own authority by intervening when unapproved material was inserted after licensing, or plays were performed without license (Dutton 158). Given that the "booke"—the licensed book—was preserved as a record of performance, we cannot be sure of the status of the manuscript so authorized.[2] The only thing of which we can be certain is that whatever manuscript was presented for approval would have reflected the intended performance. Thus, while the authorized book may have been a scribal copy, it also could have been an unmediated link between authorial holograph and performance. In which case, those "non-theatrical" features textual scholars associate with authorial manuscripts ("ghost" characters, speech attribution errors, minimal stage directions, etc.) also may have appeared in performance texts. Indeed, as Laurie Maguire reminds us, the kind of tidiness and order that the New Bibliographers envisioned in playbooks—the texts upon which performances were based—is a myth (Maguire 23–24).

From stage to page

If we can thus be uncertain about the provenance and state of the manuscript upon which a performance was based, we can be even less certain about the manuscript upon which a printed text was based—or, indeed, how manuscripts potentially became copy texts. Blayney proposes several alternatives: a holograph containing a late draft of "final" copy, a copy of that holograph made for authorization and performance (the playbook, which Blayney persists in calling the "promptbook"), an old playbook if a new one had been made for performance, or even an authorial copy of a current playbook to whose publication "the players had merely consented" ("Playbooks" 392). Even while admitting these possibilities, Blayney persists in the traditional mythology of authority. By suggesting the necessary complicity between the author and company for any "authorized" publication, especially when the playbook was kept for plays in repertory, he subscribes to Pollard's single manuscript principle. He also implies that manuscripts of different provenances might not simultaneously exist, unless the acting company allowed it. Denying multiple manuscript witnesses poses an interesting problem for Shakespeare studies. In the rush to overturn the New Bibliographers, editors and textual scholars have revisited the "authority" of the extant quartos. According to Werstine, "So strong is the will to Will that it has invested 'foul papers' with such narrative power that nowadays all the 'good' quartos of Shakespeare's plays are said to have been printed *directly* from his 'foul papers' " (Werstine 75). Even though recent scholarship has repudiated many old myths, both the old language and the old dreams of authorship persist. It is Shakespeare's holograph or nothing.

Werstine proposes instead that the journey from stage to page might have multiple narratives. He finds one alternative in the example of Thomas Heywood's claim in the preliminaries to the 1608 *Rape of Lucrece* that while he preferred only to sell his labors to the stage, he has brought this play to the printer because a "mangled" printed version of it has brought him "shame" (quoted in Werstine 84). According to Werstine, in providing the printer with copy, Heywood's story

> differs rather widely from currently accepted accounts regarding the publication of Shakespeare's plays that have the acting companies both jealously guarding playscripts (including drafts and all) from stationers, and paradoxically, being the only agents who could and did release "authoritative" playscripts to the stationers—giving the stationers only "foul papers" because the companies could easily afford to part with these but not with their "promptbooks".
>
> (84)

In reality, according to Werstine, Shakespeare's dramatic texts were open to "penetration and alteration" by multiple agents, and this should be kept "in play" when we read multiple text works.

The Stationers' Company

Before turning to the authority of *King Lear*'s texts, we need to consider the last kind of authority that affected plays—that of the London Company of Stationers by whose authority plays were printed. The "authority" that mattered most to printers and publishers was that which assured them ownership of their titles. This right to copy, obtained by securing permission to publish a title from the Master and Warden of their own company, constituted the Company's license, for which its members paid a small fee. Stationers who desired evidence of this license could pay an additional fee to have it recorded in the Company's register book. Even if a title was not entered, the Stationer—publisher or printer—who obtained the Company's license retained the exclusive right throughout his or her life to publish that title, unless he or she chose to assign the title to another Company member. Titles (or "copies" as Company records refer to them) became part of a Stationers' estate and could be retained, sold or assigned by his heirs.

In addition to the Stationers' Company's requirement that no book be printed without its license, the state called for official oversight of printed texts to prevent heresy and sedition. As a condition for granting the Company's license, the Master and Wardens, could (and for many categories of texts did) require evidence of official approbation. Surviving manuscripts bear the words of approval and signatures of their official authorizers, usually chaplains to either the bishop of London or the archbishop of Canterbury in the early seventeenth century.[3] Beginning in 1606, Sir George Buc was granted sole authority to approve plays for publication—an authority distinct from the post of Master of the Revels, though Buc also worked for Edmund Tilney, Master of the Revels from (1579–1610) (Dutton 148–50).

From a contemporary perspective, then, a play which was "authorized" for print was one that obtained the Stationers' Company's license. Additionally, if the Company officials required it, it might also have been "authorized" by an ecclesiastical official, or, after 1606, George Buc. It would not have been the business of the Stationers' Company officials to determine whether the writer of a play willed it to print or not, nor would they have been terribly concerned about whether or not the acting company that had either purchased or commissioned the play encouraged or objected to its publication.

As Blayney points out, a Stationer's right to a copy was distinct from later notions of copyright that concerned intellectual property:

> the right to a copy, being conferred by and existing only within the company itself, could extend no farther than the Company's jurisdiction. Unlike copyright, it was not a generalized right to an intellectual property: the publisher of a book had no control over any form of dissemination (acting, public reading, manuscript copying, etc.) other than publication for print.
>
> ("Playbooks" 398)

An acting company's "right" to a play was similarly proprietary. As Andrew Gurr reminds us, "it was not the author but the company that controlled everything to do with his plays. The company bought the play from the author and did with it whatever they pleased" (*Shakespeare Company* xiv). Like the Stationers' Company, however, the acting company's jurisdiction extended no "farther than the Company's jurisdiction," so they had little means to prevent the publication of plays. Once Buc assumed responsibility for licensing plays for print, however, the acting companies would have had an intermediary between playhouse and printing house who had the actors' interests in mind. After James I came to the throne and Shakespeare's Lord Chamberlain's Men were brought under royal patronage as the King's Men, they worked closely with the Masters of the Revels—first Sir Edmund Tilney, then between 1610 and 1622, Buc—who were responsible for all performances before the king. It seems entirely reasonable to conclude that any play in the King's Men's repertory that Buc approved for print would not have been sold to its publisher against the company's wishes.

Q1 *Lear*

What now, may we ask, do the printed texts of *King Lear* look like in a world that did not privilege "good" and "bad" quartos, "foul," "fair," and "prompt-book" copy, or "authorized" versions? As Peter Blayney's *The Texts of King Lear and their Origins. Volume I: Nicholas Okes and the First Quarto* clearly demonstrates, the problems of the Q1 text derive predominantly from the job done in Okes's printing house, where it was "the only play quarto which can fairly claim a place among Okes's half-dozen worst-printed books of 1607–1609" (184–85).

> *Lear* was set . . . from a play-manuscript which required the compositors to impose conventions differing quite substantially from those in most of Okes's other books, and it is perfectly evident that the manuscript itself was a difficult one. *Lear* was set seriatim (quite probably because the manuscript was difficult to cast off for the more customary setting by formes), and this fact caused unprecedented problems of type-supply. (184)

Few other texts, according to Blayney, have so many "self-evident blunders" (184). Blayney's study of textual variants, Okes's printing house and its output, and the bibliographical descriptions present in his checklist of books printed between 1604 and 1609 lends considerable support to the position that Q1 *Lear* represents an early version of Shakespeare's play—a position subscribed to by the essays in Gary Taylor and Michael Warren's influential *The Division of the Kingdoms: Shakespeare's Two Versions of King Lear*. The actual nature of that version, however, is still being debated. Drawing upon Blayney's assessment that Q1 reflected a "difficult" manuscript, Jay Halio in his introduction to the Cambridge edition of *King Lear* argues: "If Q derives from Shakespeare's own rough draft—his foul papers in some state or other—it can be argued that this version, as reflected in Q, was not a finished product but just a stage in the development of the play" (*Tragedy* 69). Halio proposes that Shakespeare's "foul papers" provided the source both for a fair copy prepared for the King's Men's 1606 performance at court and for Q1 (whose irregularities derive from the particularly unreadable state of Shakespeare's holograph). Both Q1 and the fair copy represented *Lear* "As it was played before the Kings Maiestie at Whitehall upon S. Stephans night in Christmas Holidayes. By his Maiesties seruants playing vsually at the Gloabe on the Bancke-side." Even though Halio subscribes to the "two-text hypothesis," he sees a different relationship between Q1 and performance than that advanced by the influential Oxford edition, based on a text prepared by Gary Taylor.

Taylor denies that Q1 could have related to the play's performance at Whitehall in 1606 because it contains a passage that necessarily would have been censored for a court performance. Q1 contains this interchange between Lear and the fool (absent in F):

Foole. That Lord that counsail'd thee to give away they land,
Come place him here by mee, doe thou for him stand,
The sweet and bitter foole will presently appeare,
The one in motley here, the other found out there.
Lear. Do'st thou call mee foole boy?
Foole. All thy other Titles thou hast given away, that thou
Wast borne with.
Kent. This is not altogether foole my Lord.
Foole. No faith, Lords and great men will not let me, if I had
A monopolie out there, they would haue part'an't, and lodes too, they
will not let me haue all the foole to may selfe, they'l be snatching.
(C4v–D1r)

From Taylor's perspective:

> Any one of these features . . . the knights, the jokes about monopolies, or courtiers, or promiscuous ladies, or bad advisers, or giving away titles—might, in isolation, have passed unnoticed; their conjunction, in one brief passage, even the blindest censor could hardly overlook. But even if Buc were half asleep when he first read the submitted manuscript of *King Lear*, one line alone would have been enough to wake him up: "Do'st thou call mee foole boy?" The king's licensed fool calls the king, to his face, a fool. Such sentiments would have been dangerous in any circumstances, but particularly so in 1605–6.
> ("Censorship" 104)

According to Taylor, the Master of the Revels would have ordered this passage removed for the 1606 court performance of the play; therefore, "the Quarto text of *King Lear* must have been set from manuscript which contained material the censor had ordered removed" ("Monopolies" 109). Since Q1 could not have been based on the play as it was acted before the king, Taylor posits two performances with public performance preceding the court performance—even though we have no evidence that this was the case.

In the Oxford edition of *King Lear*, which privileges Q1 as its text and accepts Taylor's dating, Stanley Wells offers this history of *Lear*:

> Not long after Shakespeare first wrote the play, and before the script was printed, the company of players, the King's (formerly the Lord Chamberlain's) Men, in which he was an actor and shareholder, and for which he had already written at least twenty plays, put it into performance. They are likely to have done so first at their regular theatre, the Globe. . . . The title-page of the Quarto gives us the only precise date of an early

> performance, stating that "His Majesty's servants playing usually at the Globe on the Bankside" acted the play before King James, not in a public theatre but in his palace at Whitehall. The year must have been 1606.
>
> (3–4)

Q1 *Lear* accordingly is the printed script of *King Lear* as it was first performed at the Globe. In this, Wells turns Taylor's hypothesis in to fact.

While many scholars have accepted the "two-text hypothesis," others remain skeptical. In his introduction to the 1997 Arden edition of *King Lear*, R.A. Foakes observes that the essays in *Division of the Kingdoms:*

> may well have been right to argue that Shakespeare could have been involved in reworking the play, but [were] less justified in their over-confident assertion that the Quarto and Folio texts of the play "are distinct", "that the later [i.e. Folio] is the better play", and that new editions should attempt "to restore each text to an authentic and independent state".
>
> (128–29)

Further in this introduction, Foakes sees *King Lear* as a "single work that is extant in two versions that differ in various ways" and rejects the idea that all the substantive differences between Q1 and F reflect revision (129). Indeed, since some of the differences "raise questions about the nature of the manuscript from which it was derived," Foakes proposes "that Q offers some intermediate stage in the development of the play rather than an author's final draft" (121). He also questions why the play would have been printed at all:

> It was generally in the interest of companies of players to keep the fair copies made for prompt use in the theatre as long as a play was likely to be in repertory, so that the King's Men could have passed on to a printer an author's draft or foul papers. However, it is hard to understand why they would have handed over a manuscript to an unfamiliar and inexperienced printer, especially as the only hitherto unprinted text the King's Men certainly authorized for publication between 1600 and 1619 was the 1604–5 Quarto of *Hamlet*, published in response to what was probably a pirated "bad" quarto of 1603.
>
> (122)

Foakes suggests that the company may have paid a scribe to make a fair copy of Shakespeare's draft and then "made a deal with Okes for the foul papers," but he also reminds us that, "Much remains obscure about the nature of the manuscript, in particular, why so much verse was interpreted by the compositors as prose" (125).

While most of the editors of the most important recent editions of *King Lear* do not subscribe to a fully conflated Q1 and F, as had long been the tradition, their assimilation of the two-text scholarship is curious. Taylor, Wells, Halio and Foakes all subscribe to Blayney's "difficult" manuscript. For Halio and Foakes, however, "difficult" becomes "messy," and the "foul papers" represent the play as "unfinished" or in a very early stage in the authorial project. The question too of the text's relationship to performance is troublesome. While all subscribe to the theory that Q1 represents Shakespeare's holograph, they also link that holograph to performance, which would seem to contradict the idea of a rough draft or early version. We may further wonder why the King's Men would have sold a play assumed to be in current repertory to any publisher. Placing the printing of Q1 within its theatrical and publishing contexts should help to resolve some of these difficulties.

Q1's publishers

Before I proceed to speculate—as inevitably anyone must in the face of non-existent authorial manuscripts—about the nature of the manuscript behind Q1 and the motivations for the King's Men's sale of their play, it will be useful to review the actual evidence. First, the King's Men, who played "vsually at the Gloabe [sic] on the Bancke-side," performed *King Lear* "before the Kings Maiestie at Whitehall upon S. Stephans night in Christmas Holidayes" (26 December). Based on distribution of type in other texts that Okes printed, Blayney has demonstrated that Q1's printing began in December 1607, so even without information we gain from the Stationers' Register entry (to which I will return shortly), the performance would have occurred during the previous Christmas season, so 1606. Second, Nathaniel Butter and John Busby entered *King Lear* as their copy on 26 November 1607 in an entry that reads:

> Entred for their copie vnder th' hands of Sir George Buck knight & th' wardens A booke called. Mr William Shakespeare his historye of Kinge Lear as it was played before the Kings maietie at Whitehall vppon St Stephans night at Christmas Last by his maiesties servantes playinge vsually at the globe on Banksyde [.]

The performance information is consistent with Q1's title-page, but we learn that Butter and Busby (not Okes) are the play's publishers. They procured the manuscript which they would give to Okes to print. They also obtained George Buc's allowance to print the play. While the manuscript is not extant, Buc's "hand" (signature) would have appeared on the copy of the manuscript they presented to Company officials to obtain the Company license this entry reflects. Besides this scant evidence, the rest we know about Q1 *Lear* comes from Blayney's formidable work on its printing—it was printed from a "difficult" manuscript in a printing house unaccustomed to printing playtexts. Its compositors besides being careless were unaccustomed to such conventions as stage directions, speech headings, blank verse, and even to the spelling of the "Gloabe" theater! That Okes was a "rookie" in publishing plays is firmly established. Why Butter and Busby would have been handed *King Lear* is not.

John Busby occupied a distinctive position in the London book trade. Aside from publishing two murder pamphlets, most of his trade was in plays, which he usually entered in the Stationers' Register with another publisher. Between 1600 and 1609 he published only thirteen titles. His earliest publication, in 1595, was the Catholic poet Robert Southwell's *Triumph over death*, which was printed by Valentine Simmes and went through multiple editions. He jointly entered *Henry V* with Thomas Pavier, who retained the right. He entered *Merry Wives of Windsor* in 1602 and immediately assigned it to Arthur Johnson. Busby and John Trundle entered Sharpham's *The Fleare* in May 1607, and Trundle assigned his interest to Johnson, who with Busby also published Sharpham's *Cupid's Whirligig* the same year. In 1608 Busby and Nathaniel Butter published Thomas Heywood's *Rape of Lucrece* and Shakespeare's *Lear* (entered in 1607). The pattern of assignments suggests that Busby may have had connections with the playing companies by which he obtained play-texts and then he either sold his right or traded it for printed copies to sell in his shop. Such a business strategy minimized the risks in what, as Blayney has reminded us, was not the most profitable part of the book trade since

> a bookseller would normally have to sell about 60 percent of a first edition to break even. Fewer than 21 percent of the plays published in the sixty years under discussion [1580–1620] reached a second edition inside nine years. What this means is that no more than one play in five would have returned the publisher's initial investment inside five years.
>
> ("Playbooks" 389)

Busby's first partnership with Nathaniel Butter was in 1607, for *Lear* and a drama-related pamphlet, *The Jesuits Play at Lyon*.

Busby had been active in the booktrade for more than a decade when his partner in the publication of *King Lear*, Nathaniel Butter, first became involved in publishing. In 1605, Butter partnered with William Welby to publish Thomas Bell's *The Regiment of the Church*. Butter's first venture into dramatic publication, also in 1605, was to be one of the unusual successes in play publication: Thomas Heywood's *If You Know Not Me*, part 1, a play about Queen Elizabeth. According to Blayney, it was one of only eleven plays that went through five or more editions in twenty-five years ("Playbooks," 388). Two editions appeared in 1605, with others in 1606, 1608, and 1613. In 1606, he published the second part of Heywood's play, which was reprinted in 1609. Unlike Busby, play-texts represented a small part of his interests. In the first three years in business, Butter published thirty titles, seven of which were plays. While the title pages of the Elizabeth plays do not mention where they were performed, other plays written by Heywood in 1605–8 indicate that the

Queen's Men acted them at the Red Bull. Samuel Rowley's *When You See Me You Know Me* (1605), about Henry VIII, and Thomas Dekker's *Whore of Babylon* (1607) were performed by the Prince's Men, and *Lear* and *The London Prodigal*, whose title-page claims Shakespeare's authorship, belonged to the King's Men. Publishing plays acted by the major companies in venues with large audiences—as well as diversification—was Butter's strategy for success in the London booktrade.

Given Busby's and Butter's experience with play publication, that the King's Men should offer them *Lear* is entirely reasonable. Why Busby and Butter subcontracted the actual printing of the play to Okes is another matter. While Butter worked with several printers, Edward Allde, Thomas Purfoot, William Braddock, and Valentine Simmes were his usual choices. Very busy throughout 1607, Allde's shop printed more than twenty titles including two almanacs (which printed in large runs) for the Stationers' Company's English Stock. Thomas Purfoot, far less busy than Allde, printed only nine titles and for one-third of these he was both publisher and printer. That he did not enter these titles in the Stationers' Register suggests he may have been having financial problems. Furthermore, he printed nothing between 1607 and 1610, unless he printed as a journeyman. Perhaps some personal problem like illness interfered with his printing business, so he would have been unavailable to print *Lear*. Like Purfoot, William Braddock only printed a few titles in 1607–8 but most of those that he did print were large projects, two of them being large-run items for the English Stock. Beginning late in 1607 and extending into 1608, Braddock was printing Marthurin Cordier's *Colloquiorum Scholasticorum*, a Latin–English textbook, usually printed in runs of 3,000. Simmes, who often printed plays, printed fourteen titles in 1607, and would have been a likely candidate if he had been available.

Sometime during 1607, Butter first made the acquaintance of Okes, who had just that year begun his printing enterprise. The second edition of a volatile (and apparently popular) political pamphlet reporting a courtroom speech on political corruption by Lord Chief Justice Edward Coke indicated that it was printed for Butter (Robert Pricket, *The Lord Coke his speech and charge. With a discouerie of the abuses and corruption of officers*). *The Short Title Catalogue* identifies Robert Raworth and Nicholas Okes as its printers. Later that year Butter employed Okes to print a jest book, *Jests to make you merrie*, which was entered in the Stationers' Register on 6 October 1607. This and two late November entries, *Lear*, and a sermon, were the only printing jobs for which Butter would employ Okes until 1614. *King Lear*, then, appeared under very regular publishing and rather unusual printing circumstances.

Manuscript source for Q1

Given both that Okes's printing operation was so new that he had never before printed a play, we can perhaps now resolve one of the principle problems that scholars have with Q1: its setting of so much verse in prose. Besides the obvious matter of saving paper, Okes's compositors probably did not understand the nature of the text they were setting. Furthermore, based on the manuscript of "Sir Thomas More," Shakespeare's hand would have posed its own special problem for compositors: its use of both capitalization and punctuation throughout are sparse, and the first words of blank verse lines are not capitalized. Most scholars agree that the manuscript hand from which Q1 was set was "difficult," but difficult need not necessarily mean an early and much blotted draft. Of a Thomas Heywood holograph manuscript, Werstine remarks:

> The manuscript is not "an original draft" but almost entirely a reproduction, with some revisions, of scenes from Heywood's earlier plays *The Golden Age* and *The Silver Age*. There are few corrections to render the manuscript untidy, and the characters are uniformly designated in speech prefixes and directions.
>
> (73)

Heywood's hand, however, would be one that could vex a compositor. It was, according to Anthony Petti, "probably the least legible of all those extant in Elizabethan dramatic documents" (55) By comparison, based on "Sir Thomas More," Shakespeare's hand is quite clear, although it does possess idiosyncrasies.

Petti describes Shakespeare's hand as "a facile / rapid Elizabethan secretary" that is not "especially distinctive." It is "firm, even-stroked and very cursive, and ably combines boldness and freedom with compactness and economy" (87). The boldness can be seen in thick heavy strokes on both ascending and descending letters, so bold indeed that the descenders in *h*, *g*, and *y* frequently obscure letters in words below them. Additionally the ends of words frequently contain irregular flourishes. Among the particular features Petti finds are superfluous minims, upright lines in such letters as *m*, *n*, *u*, *i* and the frequent appearance of different forms of letters, especially *a*, *b*, *g*, *h*, *p*, *s* and *t*. I also notice the frequent use of ligatures in initial and terminal positions. This is especially problematic when the ligature involves *s* or *g*. Discarding the possibility that the manuscript had gone through stage revision, Shakespeare's hand alone would have made the copy from which Q1 was set difficult enough for Okes's compositors.

How the features of Shakespeare's hand might have been misinterpreted by the compositors may be seen in a brief comparison of seven consecutive lines in Q1 and F (1.iv.297–304), keeping in mind that Q is not set as verse.

Q1 that these hot teares that breake from me perforce,
F That these hot teares, which breake from me perforce

Q1 should make the worst
F Should make thee worth them.

Q1 blasts and fogs vpon the
F Blastes and Fogges vpon thee:

Q1 vntender woundings of a fatherscursse,
F Th'untented woundings of a Fathers curse

Q1 peruse euery sence about the old fond eyes,
F Pierce euerie sense about thee. Old fond eyes,

Q1 betweepe this cause againe, ile pluck you out,
F Beweepe this cause againe, Ile pluck ye out,

Q1 & you cast with the waters that you make
And cast you with the waters that you loose

Q1 to temper clay, yea, I'st come to this?
F To temper Clay. Ha?

Certainly some of the changes reflect substantive revision (like *that* and *which* in the first line), but some differences may have arisen from the character of Shakepseare's hand. Capital letters and punctuation are much more prevalent in F than they are in either Q or the "More" manuscript. The substantative change in meaning that appears in "thee worth them. Blasts and Fogges vpon thee" (F) and "the worst blasts and fogs vpon the untender woundings" (Q) could have arisen when Q's compositors compressed the blank verse that lacked capitalization at the beginning of lines and was infrequently punctuated. "Worst" might easily be substituted for a scribal "worth," since in "More" the abbreviated *th* as *h* was employed and both *t* and *h* in a final position sometimes resembled a final elongated *s*. A stop-press correction shows that "untented" was intended rather than "untender." In the next line "pierce" and "peruse" would not be likely to arise from confusion of secretary *c* and *s*. If, however, "pierce" were spelled "pierse" a common spelling substitution of *s* and *c*, confusing medial *r*/*u*, especially before the long *s* Shakespeare used, the misreading could produce "peruse."

George Buc: licensing *Lear*

These few examples suggest that a "difficult" manuscript did not necessarily mean early, frequently revised, or messy—especially given Q1 *Lear*'s compositors' questionable skills. Perhaps the most valuable evidence we have—that the play was allowed for print by George Buc—offers further insight into the state of Q1's manuscript source. Whatever copy Buc reviewed and to which he set his hand—and he reviewed it not as the Master of the Revels but as the press authorizer—needed to have been legible enough for Buc to read. That Buc actually wrote his approbation on the manuscript copy provided to him—and which would subsequently go to the printer—is apparent from a Stationers' Register entry that contains his judgment that another play, "The

Hector of Germany," was a harmless thing. The clerk copied Buc's words into the Register and then drew a line through them (Arber 3: 566). The copy to which Buc set his hand was the copy the printer's would have used to set the play.[4]

Buc's role as a licenser has been misunderstood. As we have seen, Taylor has argued that Q1 could not have been based on the play as it was acted before the king because it contains a passage that would have been excised for such a performance. This is to confuse the licensing of plays for stage with the licensing of plays for print.

Although Buc is often associated with Edmund Tilney, who served as Master of the Revels from 1579–1610, it does not follow that George Buc approved of or even saw the text of *Lear* as performed at court in 1606. As we have seen, he did license the manuscript copy for Q1, and for this he allowed the offending Fool/Lear interchange to stand. Given Buc's familiarity with the world of the court and the acting companies—even before he served as Master of the Revels—it is unlikely that Buc would have allowed the play to be printed containing a passage that would have embarrassed the King's Men by offending the king. Nor would he have approved a play for print against the King's Men's wishes. We probably should accept at face value the claim made both on the title page of Q1 *Lear* and in the Stationers' Register that Q1 is the play as it was presented at Whitehall—especially since the statement in the Register is rather unusual. No other play was entered in the Register with such detailed information. Indeed for the fifty plays entered in the Stationers' Register between 1604 and 1615, only nine give any kind of performance information, and two of these entries were for plays performed at Cambridge for a royal visitation. For the other five, outside of *King Lear*, either the company or the venue appears but not both. Except on two occasions, the Register identifies authors only in entries for plays by or attributed to Ben Jonson, George Chapman, and Shakespeare. The information that *Lear* was performed by the King's Men before the king, that it was at Whitehall "upon St. Stephans night at Christmas Last," that the acting company usually performed at the Globe on Bankside, and that the play was written by Master William Shakespeare is unique. The copy presented at Stationers' Hall for licensing which then went to the printer clearly contained the information. Blayney proposes that a trial layout of the title page may have been added to the manuscript, but the information is clearly less formulaic than Blayney suggests—simply put, both the title page and the Register entry contain far greater detail than was usual, even for title-pages.

Competition, topicality and *Lear*'s publication in 1608

The unusual Register entry and the title page suggest why the King's Men may have given *Lear* to its publishers—to advertise the Company and its venues. For many years, scholars assumed that when acting companies sold their plays to publishers, they did so for financial reasons that arose from suspension of playing usually due to plague. Blayney disagrees. Between 1585 and 1604, he finds a regular (and low) rate of play printing (from none, up to five plays per year), except for two seventeen-month periods when twenty-seven plays appeared. The first of these peaks, between December 1593 and May 1595, occurred not during a plague closure but afterwards when the acting companies returned to London and were advertising their return ("Playbooks" 385–87). Roslyn Knutson associates the second peak, May 1600–October 1601, with the kind of competition that existed among the London acting companies (Knutson 66)—on this occasion with the opening of the Admiral's Men at the new Fortune Theatre. According to Knutson, "It is plausible that businessmen in the company decided to generate interest in that new playhouse by getting plays into print that advertised the company and its repertory" (70). In response, the managers of the Chamberlain's Men [Shakespeare's Company] may have entered the fray by deciding "to sell some of their plays, imitating the Admiral's Men in advertising their business" (71). A few years later *King Lear* appeared in print under similarly competitive circumstances.

While the links between Shakespeare's *King Lear* and the anonymous *King Leir* are central to source studies for Shakespeare's play, the participation of the two plays in a "cultural contest" has not been considered. In 1605 *The true chronicle history of King Leir, and his three daughters, Gonorill, Ragan, and Cordella As it hath bene diuers and sundry times lately acted*, a play that had been performed in the 1590s, was printed by Simon Stafford. We cannot be certain why *Leir* was currently being revived in print and, likely in repertory, but there seems to have been some interest in history plays around this time, including Thomas Heywood's play on Queen Elizabeth, If *you knovv not me, you know no bodie: or, The troubles of Queene Elizabeth* (1 and 2), Thomas Dekker's *Famous Histories of Thomas Wyat*, Samuel Rowley's *When you see me, you know me. Or the famous chronicle historie of King Henry the eight, with the birth and vertuous life of Edward Prince of Wales*, Chapman's *Bussy d'Ambois*, and revivals of Shakespeare's *Richard II, Henry V*, and possibly *Henry IV, part 1*. The title-page of Q1 *Lear* clearly intended to distinguish Shakespeare's play from *Leir*, but it also appears to be competing for the audience's current interest in history:

> M. William Shak-speare: his true chronicle historie of the life and death of King Lear and his three daughters With the vnfortunate life of Edgar, sonne and heire to the Earle of Gloster, and his sullen and assumed humor of Tom of Bedlam: as it was played before the Kings Maiestie at Whitehall vpon S. Stephans night in Christmas hollidayes.

It is, I think, no accident of the printing house that what we regard as one of Shakespeare's greatest tragedies is billed as "his true chronicle history," clearly to imply that the other *Leir* is not the true story and to participate in the current vogue for history plays.

The cultural importance of Shakespeare's play was not merely that it intended to capitalize on the chronicle vogue. It contained a pointed topicality that would have provided serious competition to performances by the boy companies that traded in contemporary allusion and satire (Dutton 7). Leah Marcus argues that the play directly addressed the question of parliamentary resistance to James I's much-desired union between England and Scotland by showing the dangers of a divided kingdom. In light of the project for union, *King Lear* shows the perils of division, and Lear himself serves as anti-type to James. While many critics have resisted seeing Shakespeare's drama as openly political, Marcus's contention that in writing the play, Shakespeare was indeed being a "King's Man" who served King James's political interests, is persuasive in light of contemporary references in the play that the King might otherwise have found offensive.[5] The mere use of names, for example, may have caused some frisson (Prince Henry being the Duke of Cornwall and Prince Charles the Duke of Albany), as surely did Lear's speech, "Know, that we have divided/In three our kingdom." Marcus finds the contemporary political reference even more pointed: "The 1606 *King Lear* performed before King James I was, in contemporary political terms, a demand for what had not been offered generously and freely," that is, union (Marcus 148–59).

Even if Shakespeare did not write *Lear* at James I's behest, the play's position that a divided kingdom was a perilous thing, must have appealed to the Master of the Revels as he prepared the Christmas entertainments in 1606. Andrew Gurr considers *King Lear* the "most explicitly loyal" of all the plays Shakespeare wrote for "the King's Men's patron, James I" and finds the use of the names of Albany and Gloucester to be a celebration of James's bestowing these dukedoms on his sons (*Shakespeare Company* 182). I find Gurr's position plausible since the use of these names not only serves as a reminder of the antiquity of the titles, but also joins the princes with King James as anti-types to the characters in the play—strengthening the case for Union. Gurr finds in the play's support for the King's position on the divided kingdoms—"the most contentious political issue of the day"—an expression of the King's Men's "blatant and self-confident bravado" (*Shakespeare Company* 182–84). Even with this "daring use of 'application,'" Gurr concurs with the widely held assumption that Shakespeare probably wrote *Lear* in 1605 and that it was part of their 1606 repertory for public performances, where the King's Men would have perfected the play before bringing it to court. *Lear*'s engagement with the issue of Union with Scotland also helps to explain why the King's Men may have offered the play to the printers: its appeal as a repertory piece was much diminished by the defeat Parliament handed to King James on the Union.

The King's Men, of course, could simply have buried *Lear* deep in a chest for some more opportune season, and they probably would have except that 1607–8 was an unusual time in the intersection of theater and print culture—it was another "peak" period for play printing like the ones Blayney and Knutson described in 1593–95 and 1600–1, only this time, instead of twenty-seven playbooks appearing in print, 1607–8 saw the publication of thirty-eight plays, two masques, and two classical (probably closet) dramas. Ten of these plays had been performed by Paul's Boys, a company that had cultivated the London citizens with its city comedies and then offended them with Thomas Middleton's portrayal of hypocritical Puritans in *The Puritan*. According to Gurr, Paul's Boys last performed at court during the 1605–6 Christmas season, and disbanded by July 1606 (*Playing Companies* 336–46). Discounting this ten, the 1607–8 peak still saw the publication of twenty-eight plays—two performed by the Queen's Men, one by the Prince's Company, five from the Boys of the King's Revels, and nine from the King's Men. The title pages of two of the plays from the King's Men, the two that began and ended the King's Men's 1606–7 season at court—more than all the other plays printed in these years—point to advertising. Barnabe Barnes's *The Devil's Charter*, printed sometime after October 1607, proclaims, "As it was plaid before the Kings Maiestie, vpon Candlemass [February 2] night last: by his Maiesties Servants."[6] *Lear*'s title page, of course, also had such detail, but adds the information about the King's Men usually playing at the Globe upon Bankside—nice advertising for the acting company that may have been especially useful in 1607–8.

As part of the King's Men's 1606 repertory, *Lear* would have played during what Gurr says may have been a "lengthy tour with some sea travel around the coast," an experience that was repeated during the summer of 1607 (Gurr, *Shakespeare Company* 60). After these extended absences, the company may have felt the need to remind their London audience of their customary venues. They also may have felt some pressure from the printing of controversial plays that had been acted by the boy companies at the Blackfriars. Among the plays that appeared in print in 1606–7 after Paul's Boys disbanded was John Day's *Isle of Gulls*, which achieved some notoriety and landed some of the actors in Bridewell prison (Dutton 179). The title-pages for both *Lear* and *The Devil's Charter* not only remind the frequenters of the book-stalls that the King's Men are back playing at the Globe, but also that their work (played before the king) was legitimate and respectable—unlike that of the boy companies. The title-pages may even have been performing a third task, one that was similar to the printing of Admiral's Men's plays in anticipation of moving to the Fortune: they bolstered the King's Men's image in anticipation of a prospective move to the Blackfriars. In 1605 the manager of the Blackfriars, Henry Evans, had approached his landlords, the Burbages, about surrendering his lease (Gurr, *Playing Companies* 345). By 1607 shareholders in the King's Men may have been readily considering the prospect of opening in another venue; by August 1608 the Burbages finally purchased the remaining lease from Evans and intended it as the King's Men's venue (Gurr, *Shakespeare Company* 255).

According to Blayney, "one of the most important facts about *Lear* is that, in whatever context one attempts to place it, it is *not* typical" (*Texts* 185). Perhaps one of the best responses to all that is extraordinary in *Lear* is to accept the simplest narrative of its transmission: Q1 *Lear* represents the play as it was performed at court before the king at Christmas 1606 and probably as it had been performed publicly in 1605–6 while the issue of the Union with Scotland was forefront. Given multiple pressures in both theatrical and print culture—competition from the boy companies both in repertory and in employing plays for advertising, the need to use their position to reassert theatrical legitimacy, and the necessity of keeping themselves before the public after two summers of lengthy touring—the King's Men decided to procure the publication of several plays, but especially of two performed before the king during the 1606–7 season. *King Lear*, the most topical of all of Shakespeare's plays, by fall of 1607 not only had lost its currency, but continuing to perform a play that had advanced the King James's now lost cause might prove embarrassing to the monarch. Expecting not to perform the play again and not wishing to incur the costs of having the play newly copied, the King's Men gave the company's book—probably an authorial holograph—to the publishers, Busby and Butter, with distinct instructions about how the title-page should read. Buc approved the play for print, and it was printed in a relatively new printing house and set by compositors who were not only unfamiliar with play-texts but who were fairly inept. This simple narrative explains why an authorial holograph would have been in the printing house, why the King's Men did not have a copy of their book when they prepared a revision for a later revival (something considered below), and, thanks to Blayney's impressive analysis or the printing of Q1, why a play printed with the King's Men's blessings, would have appeared in so mangled a form.

Q2 *Lear*

In 1619, another text of *King Lear* was published, this time by Thomas Pavier, who, according to W.W. Greg, intended to publish a collection of Shakespeare plays but aborted the plan when the Lord Chamberlain intervened on behalf of the players. Not that this did much good. Pavier circumvented the order by assigning to his quartos a series of false dates, apparently with the intent to pass them off as remainders (*First Folio* 9–16). This detection of "fraud . . . with the consequent naming of the texts as the 'Pavier quartos', has assured Pavier of a notoriety that has obscured the rest of his career in the booktrade" (Johnson 12).

In his study of Pavier, which focuses on his position in the London Company of Stationers and on his publishing practices, Gerald D. Johnson expresses considerable skepticism about the fraudulent nature of these publications and about the Lord Chamberlain's directive to the Stationers. Johnson's caution, I think, is justified, especially since none of the title-pages of the so-called Pavier quartos misrepresents copy ownership, all dates correspond to this ownership except one (and that could have been unintentional), and the real common denominator among the quartos is not Pavier but the printing house of William Jaggard.

Whatever role Pavier played in the quartos printed by Jaggard, Johnson demonstrates that he would have been unlikely to have risked his prominence by perpetrating a fraud. Rather than the scoundrel that he is so often portrayed, Pavier was a respected member of the Stationers' Company's livery with shares in both the English and the Latin Stock. He succeeded as a publisher largely through publishing "popular books that went though multiple editions . . . whose copyrights he had taken over from other men, either by outright purchase or through an arrangement by which he paid the copyright-holder a certain amount for the copies published" (13). By 1619, Pavier rarely published plays. He did, however, possess the rights to many of the plays Jaggard printed in 1619. As noted above, the right to copy "belonged" to whatever Stationer either entered the title in the Stationers' Register or to whom an entered title had been assigned, even if the title had been published long ago. Either through initial entry or assignment Pavier held the rights to *The first part of the Contention of York and Lancaster* and *The True Tragedy of Richard Duke of York* (which Jaggard printed together with the title *The Whole Contention*), *Pericles, Henry the Fifth, Titus Andronicus* (not reprinted in 1619), and two plays attributed to Shakespeare, *Sir John Oldcastle* and *The Yorkshire Tragedy*. Since Pavier often published books in special relationships with other publishers—some of which were not entirely transparent—Johnson posits similar relationships behind the 1619 quartos. With regard to *Lear*, Johnson observes that:

> Among the copyright holders was Nathaniel Butter, with whom Pavier had collaborated in the publication of *If You Know Not Me* in 1608 and 1610 and who owned the rights to *King Lear* and *The London Prodigal.* In view of this and later connections between these two publishers, it appears likely that Butter agreed to the reprinting of *King Lear*.
>
> (37)

Besides *Lear*, Johnson traces patterns of associations to argue that the so-called Pavier quartos were legitimate publications (although he puzzles over how John Roberts, now dead, transferred his rights to *A Midsummer Night's Dream* and *The Merchant of Venice*).

Looking more closely at copy ownership and transfer should further clarify the 1619 title-page records of ownership that perplexed Johnson. John Roberts's name appears on the title pages of *The Merchant of Venice* and *A Midsummer Night's Dream*, whose first editions he had printed. When Roberts died, his printing materials and the titles he owned exclusively passed to William Jaggard, so when Jaggard named Roberts on the 1619 title page of *Merchant* (and gave the date when he first printed the play), in some respects he was being scrupulous. To have claimed the title for himself could have produced a challenge in the Stationers' Court of Assistants. Reprinting a title to which he had a customary claim would have reaffirmed Jaggard's rights. Although Roberts had printed *A Midsummer Night's Dream*, its title had been entered in the Stationers' Register to Thomas Fisher and Humphrey Lownes. By 1619, only Lownes survived, and he may have become a silent partner in the Jaggard/Pavier enterprise, allowing them to print his title, one he may not have wished publicly to own. (Lownes may have felt his reputation could be tarnished by printing a play quarto since in 1617–18 he published and printed Richard Hooker's *Laws of Ecclesiastical Polity*, Spenser'*s Faerie Queene*, and important Latin works). Jaggard may have had a similar agreement with Butter, who in 1616–17 was printing books for important Calvinist authors, including Nicolas Byfield, Joseph Hall, and Miles Smith, men who did not hold the theater in high regard. Butter probably assented to *Lear* being printed, but only if it bore the original date. Lastly, *The Merry Wives of Windsor* belonged to Arthur Johnson, a London bookseller, but he too apparently cooperated with Jaggard and Pavier, and the title-page properly names him: "Printed for Authur Johnson, 1619." Perhaps the most remarkable feature of the so-called Pavier Quartos was that in every case, even with their unusual dates, their title pages properly ascribed ownership!

The other aspect of the Pavier quarto narrative, the assignment of false dates in response to the Lord Chamberlain's letter to the Stationers' Company ordering that none of the King's Men's plays be printed without the consent of "somme of them," Gerald D. Johnson accepts with reservation. The practice of false dating, according to Johnson, usually infringed the copyholders' rights, but on this occasion it was the King's Men who were the "intended dupes" (40). Only one date, however, is actually false. If going on date of first publication, then all the dates recorded on the 1619 quartos are correct, except for *Henry the Fifth*, which was first published in 1600, and not, as the Pavier Quarto asserts, in 1608. According to the printing order for these quartos established by W.W. Greg, *Henry the Fifth* was printed immediately after *Lear* (cited in Johnson 48). The title-page date of 1608 may have been an error. Perhaps the title-page from which the 1619 quarto was set was missing, so that Jaggard did not know the correct date. Perhaps a piece of paper with play names in columns under the dates was misread. Or the compositor was careless when he broke down the forme for *Lear*, and he retained the 1608 date. If we assume the date for *Henry V* was an honest error, we have no evidence of fraud at all.

What was the point, then, in restating the earlier dates of publication? If, as has been long thought, in 1619 word was out that the Kings' Men were planning to publish a collection of Shakespeare's plays, for members of the Stationers' Company to reaffirm their rights in titles they owned by reprinting them would make good business sense. Such publication would make it very clear to the Kings' Men that they would have to gain the actual owner's permission to include these plays in their collection. Just because, for example, the Kings' Men owned a manuscript copy of *Henry V*, even if it was a "good" text and the 1619 [1608] was not, did not mean that they could publish the play without Pavier's permission. Likewise, if the King's Men had a manuscript copy of *King Lear*, indeed, even if it was a different version, they would have to negotiate with Nathaniel Butter to obtain permission to print this title, which he owned.

While the tendency has been to refer to these ten plays as the "Pavier Quartos," they should more properly be called the Pavier–Johnson–Butter–Jaggard quartos, since the 1619 quartos affirmed their rights to the titles of these plays. Or perhaps, they should be called the "Jaggard Quartos" since he printed all of them while Pavier only "published" four. If the publication of the 1619 quartos were done to exert pressure on the King's Men, who were planning to publish the collection we now call the First Folio, the plan was successful. These titles could be included in the King's Men's collection if Jaggard and his partner Edward Blount became the official publishers not just of the "Pavier Quartos" but of all the remaining Shakespeare plays in the possession of the King's Men. The King's Men apparently offered their unpublished plays to Jaggard and Blount as their share in the project, and Jaggard and Blount provided the titles they owned, including the "Pavier" quartos, along with labor and, most likely, capital. On 8 November 1623, Blount and Jaggard entered in the Stationers' Register their proprietary right to all of Shakespeare's plays that "were not entered to other men." The First Folio, published by Jaggard and Blount and printed in Jaggard's printing house, appeared in the bookseller's stalls by the end of the year.

First Folio *Lear*: the textual puzzle

The influence of both Q1 and Q2 on the folio text or *Lear* has puzzled textual scholars. Throughout most of the twentieth century, Q1, although regarded as a debased text, was accepted as a source for F (Greg *First Folio*, 138–39). On the other hand, studies of compositor stints for F have led to the conclusion that the compositors in Jaggard's printing house relied in some way on Q2. Trevor Howard-Hill proposes that F was printed from a manuscript that was derived from Q2 and a damaged copy of the prompt book ("The problem of manuscript copy for Folio *King Lear*). Noting relationships between F and Q1, Gary Taylor offers this different explanation:

> Sometime after 1603 Shakespeare began to spend less time in London acting, and more time in Stratford with his family. If, at some point in or after 1608, he decided to revise *Lear* during one of these sojourns in Stratford, he could hardly have taken the prompt-book with him: the company might need it in his absence, or he might lose it, and in any case he had no advance guarantee that the company would approve of his mutilating it. If he could not take the prompt-book, and could not take the foul papers (which had been sold), the only text of the play he could have taken with him was an exemplar of Q1—printed, he would have known, from his own foul papers. He could annotate, revise, blot, and dirty a copy of Q1 as much as he wanted, without committing himself or the King's Men to anything; and if, when he had finished, the result

> seemed to him worth presenting to his fellow sharers as a new version of the play, then at some point he or someone else would have had to transcribe a new fair copy from Shakespeare's own heavily marked-up exemplar of Q1.
>
> ("Date and Authorship" 365)

In his forthcoming second volume on the origins and texts of *King Lear*, Blayney negotiates the evidence Howard-Hill and Taylor considered. Blayney agrees with Howard-Hill that F is based on a manuscript and not on printed copy, but the manuscript, according to Blayney, was not a prompt-book nor a transcription of it. Instead the manuscript source for F was a transcription of an annotated copy of Q1, not Q2. This transcription became a new prompt-book. When the compositors set this manuscript, however, they constantly referred to Q2 for punctuation (Halio, *King Lear* 67). Blayney's account of the manuscript source for F, outside of the jaunt down to Stratford, concurs with Taylor's. Halio reminds us, however, that the relationship of the manuscript source for F to the prompt-book is "still unclear" given that "several prompt book-indicators are missing, such as the names of actors, duplicated stage directions, and warnings for the use of some stage properties" (67–68). Halio's skepticism about the prompt book raises an interesting possibility for the manuscript source of F that has not been considered before:

> Whether the manuscript was the prompt-book itself or a transcription of it made by consulting Q2 or possibly even an autograph or scribal fair copy (made for presentation or some other purpose), we shall probably never know for certain, but both a manuscript and an exemplar of Q2 influenced the setting of the F.
>
> (67–68)

True, we may not know for certain, but the details concerning Jaggard and Q2 suggest that it would not have been unreasonable for Jaggard's compositors to introduce features of Q2 when setting the folio text. That Jaggard was recasting "his" own play may be seen as adding to the legitimacy of that process. It's even possible that Jaggard saw the manuscript provided by the King's Men for the First Folio as less authoritative than his own version, printed in 1619.

The revised topicality of the folio version

Like many other scholars, I believe that the substantitive differences that arise between the quarto and folio versions of King Lear derive from revision. Many have argued that these revisions were undertaken for purely artistic reasons, that Shakespeare, or some other playwright, rewrote *King Lear* with an eye toward publishing a literary, rather than performative version. In my view, during the 1607–8 season the King's Men sold *Lear* to the Stationers because they did not intend further performances that may have proven embarrassing to King James after the Union failed. A few years later, however, Shakespeare and the King's Men may have decided to revive the play for an important occasion at court—this time to be part of the entertainments for the wedding of Princess Elizabeth and Frederick, the Elector Palatine, who were married on 14 February 1613.

The marriage contract for Elizabeth and Frederick was signed on 16 May 1612 in the presence of the duc de Bouillon, the French Protestant leader and ambassador for the Queen Regent, Marie de Medici (Gardiner 2: 52). According to James M. Sutton, Prince Henry had been the force behind a strong Protestant marriage for his sister. Throughout the summer and fall of 1612, Prince Henry, a great lover of both theater and court ceremony, personally attended to preparations for Frederick's visit (Sutton).[7] The King's Men played a prominent role in the festivities Henry arranged for the occasion. Between October and mid-February, they performed nineteen plays. For the February wedding festivities they were joined by the Whitefriars Boys, who presented masques. If we accept Shakespeare's own evidence from *A Midsummer Night's Dream* that several proposals for plays for wedding festivities were put forth before the festivities, and that the Master of the Revels, with advice from the ruler, selected from among them, then it would not be unreasonable to believe that Shakespeare revised *King Lear* as one of the proposed options for the King's Men's December 1612–February 1613 performances. An authorial revision depending on Q1 and then copied out "for presentation," as Blayney envisions, offers a plausible—and simple—explanation for the peculiarities of the manuscript on which the Folio is based. The kinds of revisions that appear in F may be seen as being appropriate for the ceremonies honoring James's only daughter to a foreign ruler.

Why, we may wonder, would the Kings' Men have thought that *King Lear* might have been appropriate for the wedding festivities? Even before revision, the story of *King Lear* is a domestic tragedy about an arrogant, irrational father and a loyal, candid daughter separated by the business of marriage (dowries and suitors) and reunited by the daughter's efforts to save her father and his kingdom. In the course of the play, its hero comes to understand his deep love for his daughter—and she for him. In nearly all critical accounts, the folio *Lear* gives both Lear and Cordelia greater prominence and attends more closely to the subtleties and complexities of their characterization. Furthermore, far more than the Quarto, as Thomas Clayton argues, the Folio text, however fragilely, offers the prospect that Cordelia's death is not entirely in vain and that Lear, like Gloucester, may experience a hopeful death (Clayton 138). This shift in both characterization and tone might be seen not only as appropriate for wedding festivities but also as an implied compliment to a father-king and daughter-subject. Along with the enhancement of Lear and Cordelia, the folio revisions, which as Michael Warren has shown, diminished the roles of Kent and Albany may have considered the occasion ("The Diminution of Kent" and "Q and F *King Lear* and the Interpretation of Albany and Edgar").

The 1606 performance of *King Lear* had titillated audiences with allusions to the royal princes as the dukes of Albany and Cornwall. Making Albany more of a cipher lessened the frisson of contemporary reference that had belonged to the moment in 1605–6, before James' disappointment over the failed Union. On the other hand, one folio revision creates a new topicality:

> There is diuision
> (Although as yet the face of it is couer'd
> With mutuall cunning) 'twixt Albany, and Cornwall:
> Who haue, as who haue not, that their great Starres
> Thron'd and set high; Seruants, who seeme no lesse,
> Which are to France the Spies and Speculations
> Intelligent in our State. What hath bin seene,
> Either in snuffles, and packings of the Dukes,
> Or the hard Reine which both of them hath borne
> Against the old kind King; or something deeper,
> Whereof (perchance) these are but furnishings.
> (3.1.11–21)

Besides the fact that it places the dukes of Cornwall and Albany (Princes Henry and Charles) on equal ground, and likens their interests one to the other, this passage relates to a favorite activity of Prince Henry. According to Sutton, Prince Henry, who was principally interested in chivalric and military endeavors, so "scrutinized" Continental affairs that "He encouraged friends to send him secret reports on French fortifications." Folio *Lear*'s nod to Prince Henry's interests may have been made as part of an effort to reproduce in the revisions a play as relevant to contemporary royal interests, or at least to the interests of the prince involved in orchestrating the wedding festivities, as Q1 had been. I think, too, this may be said of the removal of passages on the French invasion of England. After 1610, France and England had a mutual defense treaty. Referring to a French invasion in a play that hopefully would be performed before European dignitaries, including the French ambassador, would be inconsonant with current politics.[8]

Alas, *King Lear* was not part of the revivals for the royal wedding. While it might be tempting to view this as some sort of gross censorship, that would not have been the case. However much Shakespeare and the King's Men may have desired to perform a play with poignant contemporary relevance to the loss of a daughter, it would not be *King Lear* but other plays in their repertory that confirmed their status as King's Men. The King's Men's court performances during this period included four comedies, four tragedies, two history plays, and four tragicomedies or romances. Since four of the plays have been lost ("Cardenio," "Bad Beginning," "Captain," and "Twins Tragedy"), it is not absolutely certain that thematic interests dictated the dramatic choices, but the extant plays gravitate towards certain themes. They warn about the dangers of jealousy and marital incontinence and, conversely, the necessity of chastity (*Much Ado about Nothing*, performed twice, *A Winter's Tale*, *Philaster*, *The Maid's Tragedy*, and *The Tempest*). Even though the play's evil characters share a common bond of lust, *King Lear* does little to warn its protagonists about the political dangers of such behavior. Both *The Tempest* and *A King and No King* contend that good political alliances rest on good marriages. F *Lear* virtually erases whatever references Q had to the relationship between marriage and political alliance. *The Maid's Tragedy*, *Henry IV*, parts 1 and 2, *The Tempest*, and *Julius Caesar* equate good government with good moral governance. While *Lear*'s villains enact incomparable moral degeneracy, their moral failings are not associated with their bad governance of the state. Finally, and I'm not sure quite what to do with this, three of the plays have sorcery and magic at their core—*The Alchemist*, *The Merry Devil of Edmonton*, and *The Tempest*—except to note that their nod to some of James's special interests appeared in plays that must have offered a welcome comic relief to the themes of the rest of the repertory.

In conclusion, I wish to return to Blayney's observation that there is nothing usual about the texts of *King Lear*. While this is indeed the case, what I have tried to suggest here is that the conditions in which those texts were produced represented the customary practices of both the Stationers' Company and the acting companies. If *King Lear* was unusual, it was more than those conditions in theatrical and print culture that complicated its textual transmission. More than any other Shakespeare play, in its 1605–6 performances, *King Lear* was bound to local circumstance—the Union and the implications of a divided kingdom. The kinds of revision that appear in F reflect a brilliant effort to free the play from these moorings and possibly to attach it to a new occasion at court. As brilliant as this effort was, *King Lear* did not share the thematic interests of the plays that dominated the marriage festivities—nor could revision really elide the question of the division of the kingdom without *Lear* becoming an entirely different play. As for the two texts of *King Lear*, the hopes for union belong to the past and the kingdom's division remains inescapable.

Notes

1 A 1623 entry in the Stationers' Register listed the plays intended for the First Folio that had not been previously printed. The listed comedies included *The Tempest*, *The Two Gentlemen from Verona*, *Measure for Measure*, *Comedy of Errors*, *As You Like It*, *All's Well that Ends Well*, *Twelfth Night*, and *A Winter's Tale*. The histories were *Henry VI, part 1*, *Henry the Eight*, *Coriolanus*, and *Timon of Athens*, and the tragedies were *Julius Caesar*, *Macbeth*, *Antony and Cleopatra*, and *Cymbeline*. (The word "Tragedies" appears slightly below *Julius Caesar* and above *Macbeth*, but the "Catalogue" lists *Julius Caesar* as a tragedy. For an explanation of the function of this entry, see Peter W.M. Blayney, *The First Folio of Shakespeare* (Washington, DC: Folger Library Publications, 1991): 18–21.)

2 In one instance where an authorial holograph was presented for licensing, Henry Herbert, Master of the Revels, dictated to the acting company that "hereafter" he

should be presented with a "faire Copy" (Werstine 69). But Herbert was Master of the Revels from 1623–42, so it cannot tell us about practices circa 1606, the year *Lear* was performed at court.

3 See, for example, Add. Ms. 4378 f. 1v; Add. Ms. 27,936 f. 62; Add. Ms. 27,936 f.64. The British Library.

4 While the New Bibliography rejected the possibility that this copy could also have been the playbook, Werstine's example of Heywood's holograph indicates that we cannot rule out the possibility that the final authorial draft and the playbook indeed might be the same thing (73).

5 With James I's royal patronage of Shakespeare's acting company, the Lord Chamberlain's Men had become the King's Men.

6 In English tradition since Lent usually began sometime in February, some Candelmas traditions became associated with Lent, and Candlemas became the final feast of the Christmas season.

7 Frederick arrived in England in October. On 6 November Henry died and his body lay in state until his funeral on 7 December. The funeral obsequies having been duly observed, Elizabeth and Frederick were betrothed on 27 December, and married on 14 February 1613.

8 For full consideration of the problems with contemporary reference and their potential for provoking censorship as a cause of alterations between Q and F Lear with regard to France, see Madeleine Doran, *The Text of King Lear* (Stanford: Stanford University Press, 1931); Gary Taylor "The War in King Lear," *Shakespeare Survey* 33 (1980): 27–34; and Gary Taylor "Monopolies, Show Trials, Disaster, and Invasion: King Lear and Censorship" in Taylor and Michael Warren *The Division of the Kingdoms* (Oxford: Oxford University Press, 1983): 75–119.

Works cited

Arber, Edward (ed.). *A Transcript of the Registers of the Company of Stationers of London*. 5 vols. Birmingham, 1875–94.

Blayney, Peter W.M. *The First Folio of Shakespeare*. Washington, DC: Folger Library Publications, 1991.

—— "The Publication of Playbooks." *A New History of Early English Drama*. Eds. John D. Cox and David Scott Kastan. New York: Columbia University Press, 1997: 383–422.

—— *The Texts of King Lear and their Origins. Vol I: Nicholas Okes and the First Quarto*. Cambridge: Cambridge University Press, 1982.

Bowers, Fredson (ed.). *The Dramatic Works in the Beaumont and Fletcher Canon*. 10 vols. Cambridge: Cambridge University Press, 1966–96.

Clayton, Thomas. "'Is this the promis'd end?' Revision in the Role of the King." Taylor and Warren: 121–41.

Dutton, Richard. *Mastering the Revels: The Regulation and Censorship of English Renaissance Drama*. Iowa City: University of Iowa Press, 1991.

Foakes, R.A. (ed.). *King Lear*. The Arden Shakespeare. Walton-on-Thames: Thomas Nelson and Sons Ltd., 1997.

Gardiner, S.R. *History of England from the Accession of James I to the Outbreak of the Civil War 1603–1642*. 10 vols. 1883–84.

Greg, W.W. *The First Folio*. Oxford: Clarendon Press, 1955.

—— *The Variants in the First Quarto of King Lear: A Bibliographical and Critical Inquiry*. London: Printed for the Bibliographical Society at the University Press, Oxford, 1940.

Gurr, Andrew. *The Shakespeare Company, 1694–1642*. Cambridge: Cambridge University Press, 2004.

—— *The Shakespearian Playing Companies*. Cambridge: Cambridge University Press, 1996.

Halio, Jay (ed.). *The First Quarto of King Lear*. Cambridge: Cambridge University Press, 1994.

—— *The Tragedy of King Lear*. Cambridge: Cambridge University Press, 1992.

Howard-Hill, Trevor. "The problem of manuscript copy for Folio *King Lear*." *The Library*. 6th series, 4 (1982): 1–24.

Johnson, Gerald D. "Thomas Pavier, Publisher, 1600–1625." *The Library*. 6th series, 14 (1992): 12–48.

Knutson, Roslyn Lander. *Playing Companies and Commerce in Shakespeare's Time*. Cambridge: Cambridge University Press, 2001.

Maguire, Laurie. *Shakespearean Suspect Texts: The "Bad" Quartos and Their Contexts*. Cambridge: Cambridge University Press, 1996.

Marcus, Leah. *Puzzling Shakespeare: Local Reading and its Discontents*. Berkeley: University of California Press, 1988.

Merriam, Thomas. "Some Further Evidence for Shakespeare's Authorship of Hand D in *Sir Thomas More*." *Notes and Queries* 53, 250, 1 (March 2006): 65–66.

Petti, Anthony G. *English Literary Hands from Chaucer to Dryden*. Cambridge, MA: Harvard University Press, 1977.

Sutton, James M. "Henry Frederick, Prince of Wales (1594–1612)." *Oxford Dictionary of National Biography*. Eds. H.C.G. Matthew and Brian Harrison. Oxford: Oxford University Press, 2004; online edn., ed. Lawrence Goldman, January 2007, http://www.oxforddnb.co.m/view/article/12961 (accessed 5 June 2007).

Taylor, Gary. "King Lear: The Date and Authorship of the Folio Version." Taylor and Warren: 351–470.

—— "Monopolies, Show Trials, Disaster, and Invasion: King Lear and Censorship" Taylor and Warren: 75–119

—— "King Lear: The Date and Authorship of the Folio Version." Taylor and Warren.

Taylor, Gary and Michael Warren (eds.). *The Division of the Kingdoms: Shakespeare's Two Versions of King Lear*. Oxford: Clarendon, 1983.

Warren, Michael. "The Diminution of Kent." Taylor and Warren: 59–73.

—— "Q and F *King Lear* and the Interpretation of Albany and Edgar." *Shakespeare, pattern of excelling nature: Shakespeare criticism in honor of America's Bicentennial: from the International Shakespeare Association Congress, Washington, D. C., April 1976*. Eds. David Bevington and Jay L. Halio. Newark: University of Delaware Press, 1979, c1978.

Wells, Stanley (ed.). *The History of King Lear*. Oxford: Clarendon, 2000.

Wells, Stanley and Gary Taylor, *et al. William Shakespeare: A Textual Companion*. Oxford: Oxford University Press, 1987.

Werstine, Paul "Narratives About Printed Shakespeare Texts: 'Foul Papers' and 'Bad' Quartos." *Shakespeare Quarterly* 41 (1990): 64–86.

5 "The injuries that they themselves procure"

Justice poetic and pragmatic, and aspects of the endplay, in *King Lear*

Tom Clayton

Epigraphs

In general, I recommend the Arden Shakespeare, but frequently I have followed the Riverside or other editions. I have avoided the New Oxford Shakespeare [1986, 2005], which perversely seeks, more often than not, to print the worst possible text, poetically speaking.

(Harold Bloom xi)

In the second rank comes the kind of tragedy which some place first. Like the *Odyssey* it has a double thread of plot, and also an opposite catastrophe for the good and for the bad. It is accounted the best because of the weakness of the spectators; for the poet is guided in what he writes by the wishes of the audience. The pleasure, however, thence derived is not the true tragic pleasure.

(Aristotle, *Poetics* 13.8 / 1453a.30–36)

Lear. Poor naked wretches, wheresoe'er you are,
That bide the pelting of this pitiless storm,
How shall your houseless heads and unfed sides,
Your loop'd and window'd raggedness, defend you
From seasons such as these? O, I have ta'en
Too little care of this! Take physic, pomp,
Expose thyself to feel what wretches feel,
That thou mayst shake the superflux to them,
And show the heavens more just.

(3.4.28–36)

I hope that this edition [based on Q 1608] will seem complementary to other modern editions, offering insight into the text of Shakespeare's greatest play as he first conceived it.

(Stanley Wells 7)

A play in which the wicked prosper and the virtuous miscarry may doubtless be good, because it is a just representation of the common events of human life; but since all reasonable beings naturally love justice, I cannot easily be persuaded that the observation of justice makes a play worse; or that, if other excellencies are equal, the audience will not always rise better pleased from the final triumph of persecuted virtue.

(Samuel Johnson, on *King Lear*)

Gloucester. Here, take this purse, thou whom the heavens' plagues

heauens Q; heau'ns F[1]

Have humbled to all strokes. That I am wretched

Makes thee the happier; heavens, deal so still!
Let the superfluous and lust-dieted man,
That slaves your ordinance, that will not see
Because he does not feel, feel your pow'r quickly;
So distribution should undo excess,
And each man have enough.
(4.1.63–70)

Since the general acceptance of the hypothesis that the Folio version of *King Lear* represents Shakespeare's own revising, in the main if not in the case of every last cut, addition, or substitution, there now are two versions of *King Lear*. Disagreement continues over the authorship of some if not all of the changes in the revised Folio text, and the Quarto—once a "bad" quarto but now viewed as just a very messy but authoritative quarto—has come to be recognized much as Stanley Wells describes it in the epigraph quoted above, "offering insight into the text of Shakespeare's greatest play as he first conceived it." For millions a conflated text continues to be the primary source of reading—as well as of theater and film experience—of *King Lear*, and perhaps that is not altogether a bad thing, as Harold Bloom implies in the passage quoted as epigraph. Another perspective is that of René Weis, editor of a parallel-text *King Lear*, who concludes his introduction, "It is the task of the editor to present them ['every reader and audience'] with the best possible text. For the time being, that may have to be a Q/F parallel *Lear*" (40): *et voilà*![2] He adds, magnanimously and soundly, "While it seems unlikely that a conflated text of *King Lear* can in the future form a satisfactory basis for discussion, conflated *Lears* (as currently available in a number of excellent single editions by Muir 1989 and Hunter 1972, and in prestigious complete Shakespeares such as the Alexander, Riverside and Bevington texts) will undoubtedly continue to inspire readers and audiences" (5). This may appropriately be called the received edition.

This received edition presents a synthetic *King Lear*, but its conflated whole is not greatly amplified by what it adds from F. Furthermore, with modest differences between individual editions, it has been the basis of criticism and scholarship since the time of Pope,[3] and it is hard to believe that the world is the worse for all of that, even if the labors of love and intellect were expended on a synthetic text. In addition, *King Lear* has been thought Shakespeare's greatest tragedy, even his greatest play, for a very long time—on the basis of the received text. Was everyone wrong who thought so well of it? Harold Bloom's criticism of the Oxford Shakespeare is obviously erroneous as well as hyperbolic (see epigraph), but one can understand his preference for the received edition. I confess that, much as I admire the latest scholarly editions of *King Lear*—only one of them conflated—by scholars I hold in the highest regard (Messrs. Foakes, Halio, Weis, and Wells),[4] I have a downright and abiding affection for the late Kenneth Muir's New Arden edition (in which I have long since hand-bracketed Q's and F's add–omissions for easier recognition as such than the fine print of the critical apparatus affords), and I turn to it often for comfort and reassurance. I can't help but believe that some such edition remains the best for both readers and the theater, in some respects, and an honest conflation with its seams in evidence (as in Foakes's edition) has no need to feel embarrassment or issue more than a modest explanation.

My aim in this essay is to discuss poetic justice in *King Lear*, including its Western dimension; the endplay (or catastrophe or dénouement), coda, and conclusion; the preparations for these in relation especially to the convergent loyal survivors Albany, Edgar, and Kent; and the hypothetical prospect beyond the play at the end.[5] I shall take account of Q and F separately or together and intertextually according to the individual aspect and the state of the text(s).[6] The endplay, coda, and conclusion are both the epitome and the puzzle of the play, in some ways. Some critics are certain of what they are all about; I confess that I am not. Hence the present enquiry.

Justice poetic and pragmatic

King Lear abounds in instances of poetic justice, but the fact is not often noted or dwelt on as such, perhaps because it is diminished in effect by the kind, amount, and timing: too little, too late, in one perspective, the worst getting their just deserts at last with death for the lot, the most deserving *not* receiving theirs: Cordelia and, partly if not entirely because of the final loss of Cordelia, Lear, the man who would be king again, if he were fit. By "pragmatic justice" I mean the real thing, in life, justice with actual results. Poetic justice uplifts as fictional example, and by supplying reward and retribution where they deserve to be, rather than where they are likely to be, a kind of wish-fulfillment and imaginative compensation for the limits of justice in real life, which Dr. Johnson refers to in the epigraph; this kind is called illicit by some as facile, sentimental, unrealistic, and accommodating to the status quo, a sophisticated position related to Aristotle's in the epigraph from the *Poetics*. By contrast with that poetic justice is the pragmatic justice it cannot confer, because the needs of the truly suffering, not the fictional but the historical, cannot be met by fiction *and* are not likely to be met in life, for reasons the play powerfully suggests and at least one it does not: that in almost every society in which there is a wealthy class, the wealth depends upon the deprivation of the underclasses, in part for absolute economic reasons, in part because the contrast is necessary for wealth to be seen as something enviable—which for those with little or nothing it definitely is.[7] In both Q and F, Lear's and Gloucester's apprehensions of real-life injustice in (and out of) the play ring out loud and clear, and the spectacle of poverty and want is synecdochically expressed in the beggared king, two earls, a fool, and an ad-hoc madman.[8]

Among the ironical and unsettling effects of *King Lear* is the fact that one of its profound perennial truths—"O, sir, to willful men, / The injuries that they themselves procure / Must be their schoolmasters"—is expressed, with serene smugness if not malignant satisfaction, by Regan of her aged father (2.4.300–2), who has just gone out of doors in a winter downpour.[9] And, she might have added, to wilful women, too, in this tragedy in which the suffering and passing of the better—even the great—are complemented, tempered in degree, by the violent retribution accorded the base: Cornwall at the hand of his own servant; Oswald and Edmund by the wronged brother Edgar; Goneril poisoning Regan and stabbing herself to death, the last three all together, as Edmund has the wit to say in extremis, "I was contracted to them both; / All three now marry in an instant" (5.3.204–5); and last and not least impressive, Lear's killing "the slave that was a-hanging" Cordelia, an epic achievement for a man of fourscore and upward. Scant compensation for the tragic losses,[10] perhaps, but with the survival of the fittest left, no cold comfort, either: a not ungenerous measure of poetic justice, in short, taking the form primarily of dispensing capital punishment to the malefactors rather than rewards to the good beyond the merit of the doing. But that happens in some degree in this play, too, even if the "reward" is little more visible than survival and recovery of identity and title, and whatever reward awaits in whatever afterlife.[11]

Related to poetic justice in action is, as suggested by Regan's hypocritical moralizing, the expression of sentiments and principles that underscore or reinforce the cause of the good. Q alone contains several passages usually stigmatized as sententious—and so they are; but I am not so sure as those who fault them that they were held in low regard by all of Shakespeare's audience or even their successors. Among such passages *not* cut in F are those concerned with the justice lacking to the masses of the poor that Lear cries out for in inspired monologues (reason in madness mixed), and Gloucester speaks for, too (see the third pair of epigraphs). One such speech by Lear begins with a remonstration, "O reason not the need"; carries on to imprecation, "No, you unnatural hags"; and ends with a declaration, "No, I'll not weep" (2.4.266–88), Lear trying to defend his *need* for his knights—his *companions*. At the point where he ends his speech, F supplies a strong and significant stage direction, "*Storm and tempest*,"[12] as though the heavens wept for him, as later Gloucester says that he, "poor old heart, he holp the heavens to rain" (3.7.62), sympathetic nature in both directions:

Lear. O! reason not the need; our basest beggars
Are in the poorest thing superfluous:
Allow not nature more than nature needs,
Man's life is cheap as beast's. Thou art a lady;
If only to go warm were gorgeous,
Why, nature needs not what thou gorgeous wear'st,
Which scarcely keeps thee warm. But, for true need—
You Heavens,[13] give me that patience, patience I need!—
You see me here, you Gods, a poor old man,
As full of grief as age; wretched in both!
If it be you that stirs these daughters' hearts
Against their father, fool me not so much
To bear it tamely; touch me with noble anger,

And let not women's weapons, water-drops,
Stain my man's cheeks! No, you unnatural hags,
I will have such revenges on you both
That all the world shall—I will do such things,
What they are, yet I know not, but they shall be
The terrors of the earth. You think I'll weep;
No, I'll not weep:
I have full cause of weeping, but this heart
Storm and tempest.
Shall break into a hundred thousand flaws
Or ere I'll weep. O Fool! I shall go mad.
[*Exeunt Lear, Gloucester, Gentleman, and Fool.*
Corn. Let us withdraw, 'twill be a storm.
(2.4.264–87)[14]

King Lear's transcendently compelling speeches ring changes on perennial urgencies.[15] The importance of these speeches in the play and their relevance directly to our condition and the collective human condition can scarcely be exaggerated. Their imaginative power of articulation, their piercing clarity, their substance as well as their figurative elaboration, remain little less expressive than they were at first writing, and their context gives them special power.

Reasons for many edits are obvious enough in an accelerated text, whatever its designs otherwise: dialogue inessential to the plot goes, reflective or elaborate expression first. Edgar's speech in heroic couplets at the end of 3.6 ("When we our betters see bearing our woes, / We scarcely think our miseries our foes," etc. 99 ff.) is nowhere near the depth and height of any of Lear's extraordinary monologues, and may easily be dismissed as pedestrian and banal—partly because it is, in one perspective. In another—in its favor—it expresses Edgar's insight into human nature and powers of observation, markers of his maturing—morally as well as experientially—into understanding the ways of the world. In a third perspective—another possible reason for the cut—is that the comfort Edgar finds in his own lot seeing even the King suffering belongs to the "uneasy lies the head that wears the crown" line of sentiment and runs rather counter to the thrust of Lear's and Gloucester's speeches.[16] In Q Edgar is shown learning or observing what his younger brother already knows, having learned the more quickly and easily, one infers, for his being undetained by altruism or morality, and quite satisfied with his ability to manipulate others to his advantage: stock psychopathy. The brothers have similar native powers, but Edgar—who may also have the mental advantage of the elder—has Gloucester's human decency and compassion, and expresses it in "what will hap tonight, safe 'scape the King" (117). There may even be a touch of humor in his concluding "Lurk, lurk" in Q (118). Since Edmund has not been neglected though raised abroad, there may be a hint that he took on alien ballast in his bastardizing, a possibility not precluded by anything Gloucester says appreciatively of Edmund's mother: she was "fair" and "there was good sport at his making" (1.1.22–24). Moreover, as Edgar says to Edmund near his end,

> The gods are just, and of our pleasant vices
> Make instruments to plague us:
> The dark and vicious place where thee he got
> Cost him his eyes.
>
> (5.3.171–74)

The unallegorically inclined may not believe this, but it seems not offered for instant incredulity. Edgar's soliloquy ending 3.6 in Q gives access to a certain kind of character whose identity without it is somewhat different, but some of the essence is retained in what he subsequently *does* and in his (QF) answer to Gloucester's question, in 4.6, "Now, good sir, what are you?"

> *Edgar.* A most poor man, made *lame by* fortune's blows, tame to *F*
> Who, by the art of known and feeling sorrows,
> Am pregnant to good pity.
>
> (221–24)

That is the essential sentiment expressed by Lear and Gloucester, congruent with his soliloquy in couplets cut, but deeper, stronger in expression, and closer to Edgar's heart than to his head.

Another subscene cut, and with it a patch of moralizing in blank verse (not the usual idiom for servants), has dialogue between the Second and Third Servants after the blinding of Gloucester and, in a sword fight between them, the wounding of Cornwall by the First Servant, whom Regan slays with a borrowed sword. It begins with the Second Servant's saying, "I'll never care what wickedness I do,/If this man come to good" (3.7.100–8). There is instrumental if not necessary matter here in the proposal to have Edgar as Bedlam lead Gloucester, but the major emphasis is on the moral order of the world, where if injustice prevails it will be the example for more injustice by all, women asserted, men implied, by the Second Servant's hypothetically never caring as noted in the first line just quoted. And on the Servants' kindness to Gloucester, the Third to tend his wounds and asking heaven to "help him." Without this exchange, the scene ends with stress on Cornwall's overarching brutality and his wound, richly deserved and "Untimely," as he calls it (94–97), only to the extent that it did not prevent Gloucester's blinding.

Kent the Loyal in the Lear plot

Loyalty as such is not a virtue in this ethically circumspect play: Oswald, too, is loyal, to the death; he could honestly say he was "just obeying orders," but whose? He is consistently a "serviceable villain," quite ready to kill the blind Gloucester to advance his status. The ever-loyal Kent's role is diminished in F, as Michael Warren has shown: his part is reduced especially in 3.6 the Trial Scene, and in 4.3, which in F is missing in its entirety (56 ll.); in it Kent hears a lyrical and moving report of Cordelia by a Gentleman who comes from her, and in turn tells the Gent. that "A sovereign shame . . . elbows" Lear (4.3.43–48a), reflecting that "It is the stars, / The stars above us, govern our conditions; / Else one self mate and make could not beget such different issues" (4.3.33b–36a), a comment on the contrast between Cordelia and the other two daughters "tried" in 3.6 by Lear in his passionate dementia. Kent's last speech in 4.3 Q performs a function especially in anticipating and explaining his forthcoming absence:

> Well, sir, I'll bring you to our master Lear,
> And leave you to attend him. *Some dear cause*
> *Will in concealment wrap me up a while*;
> When I am known aright [as Kent, not "Caius"], you shall not grieve
> Lending me this assistance. I pray you,
> Go along with me.
>
> (4.3.51–56a, emphasis added)

He is then absent from 4.4–6 (QF). But his character was so firmly established at his first appearance and strenuously maintained through 3.4 that there is no shock or even surprise in store for readers and spectators at his return in 4.7 with Cordelia for Lear's resurrection, one of the greatest scenes in literature, and reduced in F by very little until the end—though importantly there.

Q 4.7 *is* a resurrection scene akin to such scenes in the Romances, and all the stops are pulled out to make it a powerful and moving one, involving as it does the agencies of sleep, change of garments, the ministrations of a doctor, music, and finally the kiss of one who is a princess (often the formulary identity in folk tale) and his loving daughter. F has a "Gent." in place of the Q's Doctor and eliminates music altogether by cutting the (Doctor's) call for "Louder the music there!" (4.7.25), where music in Q was clearly part of the therapy as it is in *Pericles* 3.2 / sc. 12, when Cerimon revives Thaisa cast overboard in a storm; and again in 5.1 or 2 / sc. 21, when Marina plays and sings to Pericles and he, on recognizing her as his daughter, hears the music of the spheres. Music figures also in *The Winter's Tale* 5.3 at the restoring of Hermione to Leontes. Though the music departed with the Doctor, the rest was left in F, including Cordelia's QF speech that in Q immediately follows "Louder the music there":

> O my dear father! Restoration hang
> Thy medicine on my lips, and let this kiss
> Repair those violent harms that my two sisters
> Have in thy reverence made!
>
> (4.7.26–29)

and so it does, not only in Q but in F, which oddly adds "not an hour, more or lesse" (high precision) to Lear's "Fourscore and upward" (broad approximation).

The absence in F of the closing dialogue between Kent and Gent. pointedly gives Lear the scene's last word, which must be so in many a director-edited, non-F-based production: "You [Cordelia] must bear with me. / Pray you now, forget and forgive: I am old and foolish" (4.7.82b–83). The lines omitted from F for its own reasons effectively serve their purposes in Q, especially the martial lines preparing for the coming battle; and these lines are arguably the greatest loss to Kent:

Gent. Holds it true, sir, that the Duke of Cornwall was so slain?
Kent. Most certain, sir.
Gent. Who is conductor of his people?
Kent. As 'tis said, the bastard son of Gloucester.
Gent. They say Edgar, his banish'd son, is with the Earl of Kent in Germany.
Kent. Report is changeable. 'Tis time to look about, the powers of the kingdom approach apace.
Gent. The arbitrement is like to be bloody. Fare you well, sir. [Exit.]
Kent. My point and period will be throughly wrought,
Or well or ill, as this day's battle's fought. [Exit.]
(4.7.84–96)

So in F Kent is out of sight and presumably out of mind from 3.6 to 4.7.4–6 ("To be acknowledged, madam, is o'erpaid," etc.). From 4.7 he is again absent until late in act 5, when Edgar says "Here comes Kent" (228) and Kent himself speaks: "I am come / To bid my King and master aye good night; / Is he not here?" (5.3.234–36) which lines initiate his final act of loyalty in the endplay. With his character already fully known and well fortified, though long absent, he makes a felicitous and powerful return, however brief, possibly even more so in F, after long absence and silence from a character who at the beginning elicited instant sympathy and admiration. Kent in disguise, in order to continue his service to Lear, characterizes himself not only for Lear but for us in 1.4.14–42, and that character is reinforced repeatedly later, especially by contrast with his counterpart, Oswald, and more interestingly with Edmund as an attractive character (as Oswald never was)—but only for a time: the distance between Kent's unflinching loyalty and Edmund's undeviating self-aggrandizement is beyond measure.

Edgar the Loyal in the Gloucester subplot

The changes in Edgar's part between Q and F were first addressed in detail in recent times by Michael Warren in "Quarto and Folio *King Lear* and the Interpretation of Albany and Edgar," and they have subsequently been recorded and further analyzed by Steven Urkowitz and the editors of scholarly editions. What might well be regarded as Edgar's signal achievement in the play—defeating and fatally wounding Edmund in a duel—often goes all but unnoticed, however, for reasons that escape me, since it is a showdown long-anticipated and an exciting moment in productions that observe its importance. This is the central matter of the subscene beginning with Albany's throwing down the gauntlet and vowing,

> Thou art arm'd, Gloucester; let the trumpet sound:
> If none appear to prove upon thy person
> Thy heinous, manifest, and many treasons,
> There is my pledge; [*Throws down a glove.*] I'll make it on thy heart,
> Ere I taste bread, thou art in nothing less
> Than I have here proclaim'd thee.
>
> (5.3.89–94)

and the subscene ends much later, after line 221, with "*Enter one with a bloudie knife* Q/*Enter a Gentleman* F. The highlights of a thrilling focal episode are Edmund's falling to end the duel; the recognition, reconciliation, and "The wheel is come full circle; I am here" (174); "I was contracted to them both: all three/Now marry in an instant" (228–29); Albany's "The Gods defend her!/Bear him hence awhile" (255–56); and an officer's announcing that "Edmund is dead, my Lord" and Albany's replying with apt dismission, "That's but a trifle here" (295).

Much of the positive attention paid to Edgar has centered understandably on his best qualities: his endurance, his care of his father, his life as a make-believe madman, his maturing with experience, his moral and philosophical observations (especially in Q), and his status at the end of the play. But two of his most striking actions are cases of justified violence, first in dispatching Oswald, who, coming upon the blind Gloucester in the charge of an apparent peasant, rejoices in

> A proclaim'd prize! Most happy!
> That eyeless head of thine was first fram'd flesh
> To raise my fortunes. Thou old unhappy traitor,
> Briefly thyself remember: the sword is out
> That must destroy thee.
>
> (4.6.227–31)

This leads to an altercation in which Edgar mocks Oswald in Mummerset culminating in "Chill pick your teeth, zir. Come; no matter vor your foins" (4.6.246) followed by a mortal blow to Oswald, who survives long enough to request burial and delivery of Goneril's letters to Edmund. Oswald dies, and Edgar delivers the eulogy: "I know thee well: a serviceable villain;/As duteous to the vices of thy mistress/As badness would desire" (254–56).

Whether Oswald is buried ever, one may doubt, but he has real claim to the dunghill to which Cornwall consigned his servant. The scene ends with Edgar's rousing "Give me your hand:/Far off, methinks, I hear the beaten drum./Come, father, I'll bestow you with a friend" (288).

The duel of Edgar and Edmund is the showdown in the Western manifestation of the play's poetic justice, and it is important in the same way if not the same degree as the showdown scene in a Western film or a classical epic, beginning with the first Western, *The Iliad*, in which the showdown between Achilles and Hector is brewing from before the beginning of the epic like that between Edgar and Edmund in its own way, since each is the champion of the fighters for his culture. In the epic, after Achilles refuses to fight the Trojans because he has been arrogantly mistreated by the general Agamemnon (book 1), and his dear friend Patroclus, wearing Achilles' armor, is killed in battle by Hector (16), the showdown is assured: Achilles returns to battle (21–22) and kills Hector (23). In the last book, Hermes escorts King Priam, father of Hector, to Achilles' shelter beside the tall ships of the Achaians to plead for the return of the body of his son. The scene of his meeting with Achilles is profoundly affecting (24.471–676) and shares place of honor with the reunion of Lear and Cordelia in 4.7. Only extreme self-restraint prevents my quoting a few lines here. The showdown in *King Lear* is finely timed by all concerned, including Shakespeare: Albany arrests Edmund "on capital treason" and with him the "gilded serpent" Goneril (5.3.83–84), assuring Edmund (as quoted above) that he will see to him if no other champion appears. Regan has been poisoned by Goneril, who will soon kill herself: she has been arrested with Edmund for treason (her boast that "the laws are mine, not" Albany's is vain; 5.2.82–84, 157–58), and Edmund has been mortally wounded. Edmund holds his own as worthy antagonist to the very end and finally shows enough remorse to try to do "some good . . ./Despite of mine own nature," but too late to effect more than half of the good that needs to be done, cancel "my writ/. . . on the life of Lear and on Cordelia" (243–46), and that is the wrong half. Had Lear died and Cordelia lived—ah, but that way lies not *Lear* but some other virtual world and, worse, Nahum Tate, in whose adaptation both live.

Showdowns in Westerns take various forms—*High Noon* being the type and some think prime example—and there is no need to flog a dead horse over them here, since most readers will be familiar with one or more, and many are cited in a book that had to be written and now has been, Stevie Simkin's *Early Modern Tragedy and the Cinema of Violence* (2006), which sums up *High Noon*: "There is a clear genealogical link between the urban vigilante movie [notably Clint Eastwood's *Dirty Harry* series] and the 'lone wolf' of the Western tradition, epitomized by Marshall Will Kane in Fred Zinnemann's *High Noon* (1952), which found Gary Cooper's lawman abandoned by the townsfolk, standing alone against the outlaws" (40). In *Lear* it is of course the lone lamb, Edgar. Such works are not solely about such showdowns, but without them there would be no show: they are intersections of inevitability where irreconcilable opposites, each the other's obstacle to progress, meet to determine passage and direction (the pattern is familiar in Oedipus's encounter at the crossroads before *Oedipus the King* begins). In pre-1950s Westerns, the victor typically wears a white hat and drinks only milk. After World War II, a stronger kind of Western (with whiskey) developed in which the victor was not necessarily a pillar of virtue but yet was the exponent of real justice without the support of law, because the law itself, certainly authority, was a seat of injustice, as not infrequently even in what we think of as real life. The *Iliad* as the first of Westerns was the archetype and remains the model.[17]

Edgar's conduct in the showdown is exquisitely restrained, frank but ironically enigmatic: "Know, my name is lost; / By treason's tooth bare-gnawn, and canker bit; / Yet am I noble as the adversary / I come to cope" (121–24). And his speech accusing Edmund as "A most toad-spotted traitor" is strong and fraught with bristling particulars (126–41). Edmund's response is equally strong, both sons reflecting credit on their courageous father (141–50). The combat takes place in protracted but unmapped time in 5.3 *between* lines 150 and 151, with Albany's "Save him! save him!" to mark Edmund's defeat. Q has no SD, F has "Alarums. Fights." The reckonings and reconciliations follow, with Edmund dying after Goneril, after Cordelia.

The endplay

I use *endplay* in place of *dénouement* and especially *catastrophe*, as neutral, not limited to tragedy, and broadly applicable. In *King Lear* it includes all that follows "*Enter Lear with Cordelia in his armes*" (QF) after 5.3.255 to the end of the play (325). The *coda* includes all that follows the death of King Lear to the conclusion—the play's last speech, the quatrain spoken by Albany or Edgar.

While the deaths of King Lear and Cordelia are devastatingly sad, two of the most moving in literature, King Lear's is especially so because he must endure the death of his most loved child and so soon after being reunited and reconciled with her, and forgiven. There can be very little more painful in life than to lose a beloved child, for reasons evolutionary as well as human in any perspective. With Lear's death, not just the best of it but the very line of Lear itself is at an end, which may not in itself cause grief: what is supremely great does not necessarily breed true or viable, as witness the three daughters, Cordelia too good for this world, the other two sisters ultimately too wicked. If Cordelia had lived, her living would "redeem all sorrows / That ever I have felt" (267), says Lear, and we believe him. For him and more "all's cheerless, dark, and deadly," in Kent's assessment (290). The only emotional response humanly possible to Lear's last moments is grief, and it takes stern stuff indeed not to feel and show it. I confess to being made of no such stuff, and I cannot read the endplay aloud or usually even in silence without tearing: the griefs gather to a head for the dearest one has lost, as though they were incarnate in Cordelia and we with Lear were missing them in his final agony. This response must be related to what Aristotle meant by a catharsis of pity.

For Cordelia herself, it pays to recall both the ancient proverb, "Whom the gods love die young,"[18] which is referred to in several plays including *Pericles*; and Kent's blessing on her: "The gods to their dear shelter take thee, maid" (1.1.182). And there is often a quite different feeling accompanying the grief that has been analyzed very well by the philosopher D.D. Raphael in *The Paradox of Tragedy* and exemplified in *Macbeth*:

> The tragic hero, even though he be a villain like Macbeth, attracts our admiration because of some *grandeur d'âme* [greatness of spirit], a greatness in his effort to resist, and our pity for his defeat. Although he must be crushed in his conflict, since his adversary is necessity, yet he does not yield the victory on all counts: *Capta ferum victorem cepit.*[19] His *grandeur d'âme* is sublime and wins our admiration. Herein lies the satisfaction, the elevation, produced by Tragedy.
>
> (25–26)

The balance of sympathies and emotions elicited by the endplay and terminal events immediately preceding it, very much including the visiting of poetic justice upon the malefactors (itself a source of some ambivalence since so much arrives so late), is such that the reader and the spectator are not left with a sense only of utter and irreparable loss where there is no future. Such ambivalence is not unique to *King Lear*, but because the desolation is so great in it, many tend to think and feel that it is the ultimate endgame in which even the King leaves the board, a conviction not easily contested. But beyond the bitter end, the survivors are the best that could be hoped for, and the foreseeable future, bleak as it may be, is theirs.

"O, o, o, o . . . Break, heart, I prithee break" (5.3.312) and the coda (–322)

Last page of the Quarto (H4)

Kent. That from your life of difference and decay,
Haue followed your ſad ſteps. *Lear.* You'r welcome hither.
Kent. Nor no man elſe, als chearles, dark and deadly,
Your oldest daughters haue foredoome themselues,
and deſperatly are dead. *Lear.* So thinke I to.
Duke. He knows not what he ſees, and vaine it is,
That we preſent vs to him. *Edg.* Very bootleſſe. *Enter*
Capt. *Edmund* is dead my Lord. *Captaine.*

Last page of the Folio (ſſ3)

That we present vs to him.

Enter a Messenger.

Edg. Very bootleſſe.
Meſſ. Edmund is dead my Lord.
Duke. That's but a trifle heere :
Your Lords and noble friends, know our intent,
What comfort to this great decay may come,

Last page of the Quarto (H4)

Duke. Thats but a trifle heere,you Lords and noble friends, Know our intent, what comfort to this decay may come, shall be applied : for vs we wil refigne during the life of this old maiefty, to him our abfolute power, you to your rights with boote, and such addition as your honor haue more than merited, all friends shall taft the wages of their virtue,and all foes the cup of their deseruings. O fee,fee.

Lear. And my poore foole is hangd, no, no life, why fhould a dog, a hofre, a rat of life and thou no breath at all, O thou wilt come no more, neuer,neuer,neuer, pray you vndo this button, thanke you fir, O, o,o,o. *Edg.* He faints my Lord,my Lord.

Lear. Breake hart,I prethe breake. *Edgar.* Look vp my Lord.

Kent. Vex not his ghoft, O let him paffe,
He hates him that would vpon the wracke,
Of this tough world ftretch him out longer.

Edg. O he is gone indeed.

Kent. The wonder is, he hath endured so long,
He but vfurpt his life.

Duke. Beare them from hence, our prefent bufines
Is to generall woe, friends of my foule, you twaine
Rule in this kingdome, and the goard ftate fuftaine.

Kent. I haue a iourney fir, fhortly to go,
My maifter cals, and I must not fay no.

Duke. The waight of this fad time we muft obey,
Speake what we feele, not what we ought to fay,
The oldeft haue borne moft, we that are yong,
Shall neuer fee fo much, nor liue fo long.

FINIS

Last page of the Folio (ʃʃ3)

Shall be appli'd. For vs. we will refigne,
During the life of this old Maiefty
To him our abfolute power, you to your rights,
With boote, and such addition as your Honours
Haue more than merited. All Friends shall
Tafte the wages of their vertue,and all Foes
The cup of their deseruings : O fee,fee.

Lear. And my poore Foole is hang'd: no,no,no life?
Why fhould a Dog,a Horfe,a Rat haue life,
And thou no breath at all? Thou'lt come no more,
Neuer,neuer,neuer,neuer,neuer.
Pray you vndo this Button. Thanke you Sir,
Do you fee this? Looke on her? Looke her lips,
Looke there,looke there *He di[e]s.*

Edg. He faints,my Lord,my Lord.,

Kent. Breake heart,I prythee breake.

Edg. Looke vp my Lord.

Kent. Vex not his ghoft,O let him pafe,he hates him,
That would vpon the wracke of this tough world
Stretch him out longer.

Edg. He is gon indeed.

Kent. The wonder is,he hath endur'd fo long,
He but vfurpt his life.

Alb. Beare them from hence,our prefent bufineffe
Is generall woe: Friends of my foule, you twaine,
Rule in this Realme,and the gor'd ftate fuftaine.

Kent. I haue a iourney Sir,fhortly to go,
My Mafter calls me,I muft not fay no.

Edg. The waight of this fad time we muft obey,
Speake what we feele,not what we ought to fay:
The oldeft hath borne moft, we that are yong,
Shall neuer fee fo much, nor liue fo long.

Exeunt with a dead March.

The effects of the spectacle of Lear's passing are much the same, but it matters where and how he dies, and what he is saying. In Q there is no SD. F is precise, to a point: "Looke there, looke there. *He dies*," with Edgar's pentameter-completing "He faints, my Lord, my Lord" following in the next line. Of recent scholarly editions, F-based (and conflated) texts follow F (Foakes, Halio F, Muir, Oxford F, Weis F). Weis's Q-based text has editorial "[*Dies*]" after "Break, heart, I prithee break," but Halio Q, Wells, and Oxford Q place "[*Lear dies*]" after Kent's "Vex not his ghost: O! let him pass; he hates him / That would upon the rack of this tough world / Stretch him out longer," several lines later than the others and just before Edgar's "O, he is gone indeed" (no "O" in F), the prompting for Lear's death to be editorially set where it is, probably. In Q "He faints my Lord, my Lord" follows—and completes a pentameter—with "O, o, o, o," which has the sound and look of Lear's last utterance in Q.[20] I suspect it was *intended* to be his last utterance, and therefore should have had—and should have an editorial—"[*He dies*]" placed after it, with the correlative assigning of "Breake hart, I prethe breake" to Kent, who has it very appropriately in F and would have it not less appropriately in Q.[21] All the dialogue in the coda is the same except for Lear's last fourteen words added in F (and the dropping of "O[, he is gone indeed]"), and an erroneous speech prefix in Q for "Breake hart, I prethe breake" seems more likely than that this awkward, quasi-posthumous self-expostulation was intended to be Lear's. Ockham's razor seems to favor this interpretation as the simpler and more plausible than the readings in Q, where Lear "faints" (says Edgar) immediately after his "O,o,o,o" but then revives and says "Breake hart, I prethe breake," an anticlimactic and redundant last line no matter how effectively it could be played on stage or rationalized in the study. "Lear" is not a very likely misreading of "Kent," although less of a stretch in Shakespeare's not-always-legible Secretary Hand (as in the *More* MS) than one might suppose. It *is* an easy eye-skip to pick up the "*Lear*. [And my poore fool is hangd]," etc., above, before the "Edgar" of "He faints my Lord, my Lord," and repeat it before (intended Kent's?) "Break, heart, I prithee break."

Edgar's continuing ministration, attempts to revive Lear, and "Look up my Lord" imply no change in Lear's condition after his "He faints my Lord, my Lord," which, indeed, one would hardly expect without more explicit business—if not an SD (though Q is sparing of SDs)—and referential dialogue. Likewise Kent's "Vex not his ghost" (QF). What seems common to QF—everything but Lear's last lines that were supplied in F in place of "O, o, o, o"—falls into place by giving to Kent in Q his F line. "Look up my Lord" after "He faints" does not seem to imply that, having fainted, he is looking anywhere. And Kent's "Vex not his ghost" surely says that he has already died in Q as in F, giving up the ghost with his last breath, which one would have thought that "O, o, o, o" signifies in this context as it does explicitly in F *Hamlet*.[22] Kent's "The wonder is, he hath endured so long, / He but usurpt his life" concludes the part of the coda centered on

Lear and shifts focus with the "Duke"'s (Q) taking charge again; he went silent after his earlier speech ending "O see, see" that redirected attention to Lear.

The three prominent survivors are the best the play's world has to offer and its final showing of poetic justice. Given this world—and it extends to nameless officers and soldiers, and an imaginable population of the sort materialized in Grigori Kozintsev's film—could one ask for better, aside, of course, from the King, Cordelia, and the Fool? This is where poetic justice's brighter side comes in. Kent rises to whatever occasion presents itself throughout. Albany and Edgar have in common—in both Q and F—that for different reasons they are slow to take the initiatives of power into their hands, but both also rise to the occasion as circumstances permit or demand; and perhaps either could be seen as capable of exercising kingship past the end. Worse luck and better that Kent will follow Lear, but Kent's nature is such as reflexively to heed the call where he recognizes true authority, and now he is to follow Lear the second time into—this time permanent—exile. Are we *meant* to regard "My master calls" as not primarily figurative but a summons that he hears? Whatever Lear's perception of Cordelia's state when he dies (in F; his attention is not explicitly directed to Cordelia in Q), Kent's is unequivocal, and we are implicitly asked to share it. Or not. It *may* be only figurative, after all, auditory hallucination (though not hinted at), or personification from his feelings. It is at all events vivid and compelling; it may even be the real thing.

The conclusion (5.3.322–25): Albany? Edgar? Does it matter?

Alb.	Friends of my soul, you twain,	
	Rule in this *kingdom* and the gored state sustain.	realm *F*
Kent.	I have a journey, sir, shortly to go;	
	My master calls, *and* I must not say no.	me, *F*
Alb.	The weight of this sad time we must obey,	*Edg. F*
	Speak what we feel, not what we ought to say:	
	The oldest *have* borne most; we that are young	hath *F*
	Shall never see so much, nor live so long.	

The primary mechanical reasons for assigning the speech (almost regardless of content) derive from decorum and have been around for a long time. (1) In Shakespeare's histories and other tragedies the major authority figure has the play's last speech, and it should accordingly go to the Duke of Albany. But (2) Edgar should speak the speech because he has been addressed with Kent and Kent has already replied. Finally, (3) whoever speaks last is ipso facto the major authority figure. Aside from that questionable supposition, precedent notwithstanding, what are the claims, what is the meaning, and what are the effects of the speech's being given by Albany or Edgar, respectively?

An important consideration is surely that from his coming to the fore in 4.2 virtually to the end of the play Albany is *the* authority figure. Although much of his dialogue in 4.2—addressed to Goneril and brilliantly imaginative, doctrinal, and analytical as well as damning—is not in F (4.2.31–50, 62–67), the new Albany newly arrived *is*, in F as in Q, announced by Oswald as

never man so chang'd.
I told him of the army that was landed;
He smil'd at it. I told him you were coming;
His answer was, "The worse." Of Gloucester's treachery,
And of the loyal service of his son,
When I inform'd him, then he call'd me sot,
And told me I had turn'd the wrong side out.
What most he should dislike seems pleasant to him;
What like, offensive.

(4.2.3–11)[23]

And even with the cuts he has lines fit enough though few in the scene to bear out what Oswald has said of him and prepare us for his generalship and whatever else may come thereafter. He is assertive, authoritative, and general-like in his conduct of the war from what we see in 5.1. In fact, almost everything about Albany's actions toward the end in F as in Q shows him in charge, and that role arguably continues to the very end, even *if* Edgar has the last speech.

Albany's status is strongly articulated in the regal speech he makes to the officers and soldiers present, using the royal "we" throughout in lines that could by themselves conclude a play:

Alb. You lords and noble friends, know our intent.
What comfort to this great decay may come
Shall be applied. For us, we will resign,
During the life of this old majesty,
To him our absolute power. [*To Edgar and Kent.*] You, to your rights,
With boot, and such addition as your honors
Have more than merited. All friends shall taste
The wages of their virtue, and all foes
The cup of their deservings.

(297–305)

On the subject of this speech in general, it is easy for a reader to forget that there are others present throughout the last scene, in which at the beginning F has "*Enter in conquest with Drum and Colours, Edmund, Lear, and Cordelia, as prisoners, Souldiers, Captaine.*" Q has only "*Enter Edmund, with Lear and Cordelia prisoners*," but Edmund's very first line implies others present: "Some officers take them away, good guard," etc. And just before line 40, "*Flourish. Enter Albany, Gonerill, Regan, Soldiers*" (F), for Q's "*Enter Duke, the two Ladies, and others.*" It would seem that all or a number of "You lords and noble friends" are addressed throughout this relatively formal speech, including "you, to your rights, / With boot and such addition as your honours / Have more than merited." For these last lines, however, editors invariably supply the apparently hereditary but almost certainly erroneous editorial SD, "[*To Edgar and Kent*]," which is in the Variorum (ascribed to Malone; Rowe had it as "To Edgar"), where the absence of a note implies that the specification is universally accepted as ungainsayable. But Kent and Edgar unquestionably *are* addressed by Albany in 318–19, as "Friends of my soul," an altogether different and more personal expression. This is also what one would expect: Albany's speech commends those whose "boot" and "addition" their "honours / Have more than merited" in their fighting, presumably, while Kent and Edgar, especially, were otherwise engaged and are to be singled out later, not here. The remedy is easy: drop the SD.

> The weight of this sad time we must obey;
> Speak what we feel, not what we ought to say.
> The oldest hath borne most: we that are young — have *Q*
> Shall never see so much, nor live so long.
>
> (322–25)

At the end of Q there would be no question of the propriety of Albany's having the last speech: (1) as "Duke" (SP) he is the ranking person left; (2) after a beginning-and-middle as a milquetoast—according to Goneril, and he does and says nothing to contradict her description, meaning that he was not forthcoming in the circumstances—he has come forcefully into his moral and authoritative own in 4.2; (3) in 5.3 he has just exercised his authority with the royal "we" in a speech to the officers and soldiers; and (4) he invites the "friends of my soul" to "rule in this realm, and the gor'd state sustain," which only "absolute power" could offer, whatever he meant thereby. In F, he has little less claim in the immediate context of the endplay. Only (2) has limited application, owing to the absence of his *extended* dialogue to Goneril in 4.2; but Oswald's description of the new Albany, as noted, and Albany's remaining dialogue to Goneril assert his status more than sufficiently. And, by contrast with Edgar's felt and youthful emotional efforts to revive Lear, Albany's patience and authority, silence during Lear's passing, and resumption of authority after Kent's quasi-epitaph are entirely congruent with his speaking the last speech in Q—and also in F, one would think. And it seems odd that Albany, of superior rank, the general, and the King's surviving heir, should on the gad, as it were, give away the crown, especially just after he has asserted regal authority before the troops.

It seems likely that if Edgar had not been assigned the last speech in F he would not be a candidate for it. The critical comments in the New Variorum anticipate most of the more recent arguments and include a few untenable ones and some that are entertaining, like Theobald's "Being a more favourite actor than he who performed Albany, in spite of decorum it was thought proper he should have the last word" (this is *not* untenable but would be hard to prove); and Walker's "It seems to me just possible,—yet hardly so,—that the Folio might be right" (349).

Just what is Albany inviting Kent and Edgar to *do*? Most commentators assume that it is some variant of "do be kings in place of me," in effect, also an odd *dual* assignment; and some, including Harold Bloom, have no doubt that Edgar becomes King. At least one related but different possibility turns on, for example, "Kingdom" here (Q) together with "kingdom*s*" in 1.1.4Q, where Gloucester speaks of the "division of the kingdom*s*," which might be taken to mean that Albany is asking Edgar and Kent to rule over the part, "*this* kingdom" or "realm"—of the whole united kingdom—where the battles have been fought. I find that explanation not unattractive. Lear himself does not refer to kingdom*s* (37), however, and the rest of the play uses "kingdom" singular in the sense of the entire realm ruled over originally by Lear. But Lear *did* divide the kingdom into parts of "perpetual" possession (67), originally three: Regan is explicitly given an "ample *third* of our fair kingdom" (80) and Cordelia asked what she can say "to win [draw *F*] / A third more opulent than your sisters?" (85–86). And the parts are implicitly associated with coronets, since after the banishment of Cordelia Lear directs "Cornwall and Albany, / With my two daughters' dowers, digest this third" (129–30) and "This [Cordelia's] coronet part between you" (1.1.140). All things considered, Kent and Edgar's being asked to rule a part seems viable. It might also seem that one reason for asking both Kent and Edgar to rule, wherever it is, is that Kent is the experienced and seasoned earl (48+) and Edgar the very worthy and talented but less court-experienced (?) earl untried in the exercise of authority and rule—as Kent's apprentice, as it were. Nothing is said or even implied to this effect, but it fits. In such a perspective, if Edgar *were* to speak the last speech, it need not be a speech asserting the authority of the speaker beyond the limits of a certain kind of experience, which Edgar has had in spades; and it would be particularly appropriate for him, as younger than Albany (who unlike Edgar was married and had no living father in the play).

Edgar's *having* the play's last speech is usually thought to complete the aggrandizing of his character in the latter part of the play in F, and of course it does, whatever his future, so that could have been the main reason for the speech's being reassigned to him in the text behind F—if not just that it "seemed a good idea at the time." René Weis "would maintain that Edgar's speaking the last lines in *Lear* (as he does in F and perhaps should in Q) is the result of an intense creative immersion in Q by someone (quite possibly Shakespeare) who elsewhere repeatedly seems to have cut and rearranged material in less than felicitous ways" (27). My own inference is that any "intense creative immersion in Q by someone (quite possibly Shakespeare)" would involve a bit more at this point in the play than the mere change of a speech prefix; but I am bound by my own hypothesis about "Break, heart, I prithee break" to concede the possibility even of Albany's being given the speech in error in Q, and I readily do. But Lear's last speech was drastically altered by an addition in F, and it is hard to believe that anyone but Shakespeare would have written "Do you see this? Looke on her? Looke her lips,/ Looke there, looke there" (F),[24] a profound substantive change in only fourteen words and a line-and-two-fifths of blank verse. Accordingly, if the play's final speech in F were intended to be spoken not by Albany but by Edgar, one would expect some adjustment to be made beyond a change of speech prefix—depending on the intention, of course.

Edgar as hypothetical future king seems to be inferred mainly from his *having* the last speech in F, but the actual line that most "qualifies" him for the crown and the last speech, perhaps, is Albany's "Methought thy very gait did prophecy/A royal nobleness" (5.3.17)—but that is in Q as well as F, and "royal nobleness" is not "noble royalty," nor is a courtesy an anointment. To some the shift to Edgar in F may seem arbitrary, a perfunctorily assigned production-value (cf. Theobald). Although most seem to take the last speech, if Edgar's, to be a circumlocutory expression of assent to Albany's invitation, it is not self-evident how that is so. The first couplet, "The weight of this sad time we must obey;/Speak what we feel, not what we ought to say," seems to be a comment on Kent's frank if not brusque response to Albany's invitation, whoever says it. It is an expression of approval on principle of what Kent has just said not diplomatically but honestly where circumstances call for candor. This fits Albany well enough, Edgar arguably a bit less well, because it represents the assertion and judgment of established authority, too: "we *must* obey." It has been suggested that the royal "we" is present in the closing quatrain, but it must be the plural and inclusive "we" in the first couplet; in the second "we that are young" cannot refer to Kent (48+), so it must refer to the other young persons present (Albany or Edgar, officers, soldiers?) and elsewhere in the kingdom(s) who may yet be generalized about in the same terms; in other words, the epoch of giants has ended.

As for the closing couplet itself, "we that are young" fits Edgar well enough, and somewhat better than Albany, perhaps (though he is not certainly *much* older than Edgar), but could an *Edgar* who says we must "Speake what we feele, not what we ought to say"—as Kent has just done—truly *mean* "*we* . . ./Shall never see so much, nor live so long?" This sounds suspiciously like "what we ought to say," especially since Edgar, as we have seen, has seen plenty. How soon we forget? The argument from one kind of decorum that because both Kent and Edgar are addressed both must answer seems not necessarily true, but the first two lines as Edgar's make good enough sense as an immediate and candid response to Kent's frankness; likewise for Albany's speaking it. "The oldest *have* borne most" would better fit Edgar as including Gloucester, but the textual change went in the other direction, from "have" (Q) to "hath" (F), presumably to focus the line on Lear alone. In short, the case in both versions seems stronger for Albany than for Edgar, although the latter can be defended, especially in F. A problem for any speaker is just what sort of sense "we . . . / Shall never see so much, nor live so long" is supposed to make, and how. It has an acceptable if somewhat Orphic resonance and can be delivered with and to awe, but it needs noting that New Variorum commentators are somewhat readier than recent ones to weigh in on the closing couplet: for example, "Jennens: The last two lines, as they stand, are silly and false; and are only inserted that anyone may alter them for the better if they can. Hanmer has not made them a jot better" (350).

It is and is not surprising that any engagement with Shakespeare's *King Lear* is hugely rewarding, whether with one text, two texts, or no text, since the memory and experience of this play, by whatever route it made its way into place, is indelible and sharp enough in its mimesis that it stays with one while memory holds a seat in this distracted globe. In one way, it seems the very archetype of imaginative reality. In another, at the base of such experience and on the way to bringing it home, the value of their being two texts, versions, is that they demand renewed attention. The received text was and is by many, often and for too long, taken for granted. When such comfortable familiarity is ruptured by awareness that it wasn't altogether as we thought, the language comes alive anew with renewed attention; poetic justice rises, half triumphant, in the coda; and the ultimate King Lear both in and beyond these extraordinary literary and dramatic texts comes into his own again. And again. And again. And, finally, however we divide it inventorially, there is one and only one *King Lear*.

Notes

1 heavens' *Halio, Muir* (heav'ns'), *Weis* (QF), *Wells*; heaven's *Foakes*. Here and throughout I use "F" to refer to the 1623 Folio and "Q" to refer to the 1608 Quarto texts of the play. I use "SD" for stage direction and "SP" for speech prefix. Finally, I use "subscene" to refer to a part of a scene in which the same persons are present, another subscene beginning when the stage is not cleared but one or more leaves or enters; each such subscene has its own focus and formal organization. I am grateful to Jay L. Halio, as often, for comments, corrections, and suggestions at two stages in the writing of this essay.

2 How the two texts should be presented is not as simple a matter as it may seem. Both of Weis's texts are edited, and made somewhat more alike in the editing than they are in their first printings; the edition is valuable for its notes and supplementary materials as well as for the texts. Michael Warren's *Parallel "King Lear" 1608–1623* (1989) is indispensable for its placing photofacsimiles of the corresponding lines of Q and F opposite each other. But a student of the two texts *still* needs to see them as they were first printed, and that means juxtaposing separate facsimiles. Both Foakes and Halio show in effect what is to be gained by seeing the texts as they were first printed: Foakes shows on 76–77 the end of the play in Q and F, respectively, and on 394–95 "two different versions of a substantial speech" (3.1.17–39); and Halio shows photofacsimiles of passages unique to Q and F, respectively, and also parallel passages (Textual Analysis, Part II: 265–88).

3 Production was another story: the Restoration revision by Nahum Tate held the stage for nearly two centuries after it was first perpetrated in 1681.

4 The sentiment holds for the scholarly work on *King Lear* by Blayney, Richard Knowles, Urkowitz, and Warren, and by all my fellow contributors to *The Division of the Kingdoms*. Foakes's conflated Arden 3 edition clearly differentiates origins by superscript [Q] and [F].

5 In the obvious way, *nothing* follows the end of the play—unless there is a sequel. But all the plays have a hypothetical continuation, and few readers or spectators fail to think about it. The "prospects" are brighter in the histories (*Henry VIII*, *King John*, the last play of the tetralogies, *Richard III* and *Henry V*, respectively) and the tragedies other than the later three Roman plays and *Timon of Athens*, which take place in the world of realpolitik more than in that of poetic justice.

6 I quote extensively as a matter of principle. No matter how one paraphrases or describes while condensing, the subject of analysis and the evidence—which are one and the same—are lacking without quotation, and the play speaks best for itself, though for critical purposes with assistance. Where the text is virtually the same in Q and F (much of it), I often quote Kenneth Muir's New Arden edition. I also quote from other texts (including my own mental ones) without identifying them individually so long as the substantives are those of the received text and the punctuation is reasonable; whenever a quotation is textually unusual, I say so and note the particulars. In quoting from Q and F I reproduce the spelling and punctuation but not the typography.

7 One is not supposed to say this sort of thing in criticism except by way of propagating a particular ideology in general and usually (New) "historical" terms, but it is at least as important in "real life" as in the play to call attention to it unequivocally and often. If it is a breach of academic freedom to say such things as a matter of principled conviction, there is no academic freedom. In what might seem an unlikely quarter, *Business Week* (21 May 2007: 57–64) has a Special Report on "The Poverty Business: Inside U.S. companies' audacious drive to extract more profits from the nation's working poor." The reciprocal causes of wealth and poverty could hardly be clearer: if inequity comes, can iniquity be far behind? Not in *King Lear*, either.

8 One of the strengths of Grigori Kozintsev's film (1970) is that it could *show* the masses of the milling poor, with a small and dispossessed King Lear quickly lost among them, like a stone dropped into a quarry.

9 The "school of hard knocks" is a modern colloquial expression of the truism that many learn only from experience and painfully.

10 I say "tragic loss*es*" because Cordelia too dies tragically in attenuated form, her death dwelt on less for its own sake than because we see and are made to feel Lear's reaction to it.

11 This claim assumes that drama has poetic license to effect justice—with or without revenge—beyond what courts might pronounce, and find some deaths right enough in the fiction, Oswald's being such a case in this play and Polonius's, and Rosencrantz and Guildenstern's, in *Hamlet*. Hamlet says he repents even as he thinks he has been made heaven's scourge and minister. He recognizes, at all events, a turning point with the stabbing of Polonius through the arras: "Come, sir, to draw toward an end with you" (3.4.217); but Rosencrantz and Guildenstern "are not near my conscience; their defeat/Does by their own insinuation grow" (5.2.58–59) and poetic justice is duly theirs.

12 Some editors tone down the F SD—e.g., "*Storm heard at a distance*" (Muir 2.4.282), presumably as suggested by Cornwall's "Let us withdraw, *'twill be* a storm" (285, emphasis added).

13 The word is monosyllabic in this metrical context, but nothing in the substantive or modern texts signifies this. Until about the 1960s there were more or less consistent differences in punctuation between British and American practice in indicating sounded and silent syllables, but such indications were no more

comprehensive by either than they were in Early Modern practice. Persons concerned to get the stresses—and with them the sense—right simply have to learn to scan.

14 Muir's altered SD immediately follows "cause of weeping." Much is said in the play about the gods, and the late William R. Elton wrote an excellent scholarly study of "*King Lear*" *and the Gods*. The only evidence there is in the play of the intervention of gods in human affairs is the "*Storm and tempest*" (F only) here, and the deeds of humans "that show the Heavens more just" by projection. "*Storm and tempest*" at just the moment Lear refuses to weep suggests a sympathetic manifestation of nature but, given Cornwall's " *'twill be* a storm," seems premature and more willed than thoughtful—but likely to be effective in the theater, where sound effects would drown out Cornwall, anyway.

15 If there were such conviction (and the gift of such articulation) among our politicians at this trying time (October 2007), we Americans should hear more such sentiments in Congress, if not in the White House; but propaganda-generated aversion to federal programs, taxes, and "big government," and the mania for wealth and against "redistribution," are so great and so little exposed or countered that there is scant prospect of amelioration of the lot of the poor anytime soon, and their ranks will very likely swell with accelerating downward mobility and upward CEO salaries. According to the U.S. Census Bureau, in fact, in 2006 "the percentage of people without health insurance hit a high," and "Average wages . . . declined for the third straight year" (*New York Times*, 29 Aug. 2007: A1). And on 3 October 2007 President George W. Bush vetoed a children's health-insurance bill that would have extended health care to more children than were previously eligible, on the grounds that it was a step toward "socialized medicine," a shibboleth routinely produced to exorcise health care for all—or more, even. These sentiments come to mind not through what I.A. Richards called "mnemonic irrelevance" but because they are the current referents of Lear's speeches, including "Reason not the need" (2.4.262–68) and especially "Take physic, Pomp" (3.4.28–36, epigraph); and Gloucester's "Here, take this purse" (4.1.63–70, epigraph).

16 "Uneasy," etc. *Henry IV, Part 2*, 3.1.31, concluding a soliloquy by King Henry IV.

17 The *Odyssey* was the second, of the type of *Gunfight at the O.K. Corral*, with multiples on either side when Odysseus, Telemachus, and the swineherd confront the parasitic suitors.

18 Dent, Oxford, Tilley G251. The first recorded instance is in Menander.

19 I.e., "*Graecia capta*": "the conquered [Greece] has conquered the savage victor." Horace, *Epistles*, 2.1.156.

20 In F *Hamlet*, Hamlet's "the rest is silence" is followed by "O,o,o,o. *Dyes*."

21 Charmian says "O break, o break" while Cleopatra is applying the asps in *Antony and Cleopatra* (5.2.311), written not long after *King Lear* in which Cleopatra's passing is in a way very like Lear's in F.

22 Not all (including me) are convinced that Hamlet's "O, o, o, o" is Shakespeare's (editors uniformly eschew it), but if his here, why not there?

23 Steven Urkowitz does not quote, paraphrase, or refer to this speech in his long chapter on "The Role of Albany" (v, 80–128) in *Revision*, which contributed seminally to the dialogue on the two texts of *King Lear*. In it he was concerned to show that the whole of F represents authorial revision, so he had to motivate every change in F to show intention and effect, in particular to present a negative "reading of Albany's character . . . utterly and irreconcilably at odds with the conventional view" (126), which is that generally accepted here as the one the evidence of the text of F as well as of Q most strongly supports.

24 Especially considering the great similarity to Cleopatra's end, and Lear's end in F may have come after Cleopatra's (if revised in 1610, as Gary Taylor has strongly argued) and been influenced by Shakespeare's discovery there.

Works cited and consulted

King Lear, *Scholarly editions*

—— Ed. R.A. Foakes. Arden 3 Shakespeare. Walton-on-Thames: Thomas Nelson, 1997.

—— Ed. H.H. Furness. New Variorum Edition. 1880. New York: Dover, 1963.

—— Ed. Jay L. Halio. New Cambridge Shakespeare. Cambridge: Cambridge University Press, 1992.

—— Ed. G.K. Hunter. New Penguin Shakespeare. Harmondsworth: Penguin, 1972.

—— Ed. Kenneth Muir. New Arden Shakespeare. 9th edn. London: Methuen, 1972.

—— Ed. Stanley Wells; text prep. Gary Taylor. Oxford Shakespeare. Oxford: Oxford University Press, 2000.

King Lear, *Parallel-text editions*

"King Lear": A Parallel Text Edition. Ed. René Weis. Longman Annotated Texts. London: Longman, 1993. Edited texts.

The Parallel "King Lear" 1608–1623. Prep. Michael Warren. Berkeley and Los Angeles: University of California Press, 1989. Facsimile arranged by parallel passages and lines.

King Lear, *Complete Facsimiles of early substantive editions*

The First Folio of Shakespeare. Prep. Charlton Hinman. Norton Facsimile. New York: Norton, 1968.

"King Lear," 1608 (Pied Bull Quarto). Ed. W.W. Greg. Shakespeare Quarto Facsimiles No. 1. 1939. Oxford: Clarendon Press, 1964. Note to Second Impression, Charlton Hinman.

King Lear, *Edited substantive edition*

The First Quarto of "King Lear." Ed. Jay L. Halio. New Cambridge Shakespeare: Early Quartos. Cambridge: Cambridge University Press, 1994.

Complete Works (conflated except as otherwise noted):

The Complete Works of William Shakespeare. Ed. Peter Alexander. 1951. Introd. Peter Ackroyd. New York: HarperCollins, 2006.

William Shakespeare: Complete Works. Ed. Jonathan Bate and Eric Rasmussen. RSC Shakespeare. New York: Modern Library-Random House, 2007. Folio based, theater oriented.

The Complete Works of Shakespeare. Ed. David Bevington. 5th edn. London: Longman, 2003.

The Riverside Shakespeare. Ed. G. Blakemore Evans. 2nd edn. Boston: Houghton, 1997.

William Shakespeare: The Complete Works. Ed. Stanley Wells and Gary Taylor, with

John Jowett and William Montgomery. Oxford Shakespeare. 2nd edn. Oxford: Clarendon Press, 2005. Prints two texts of *King Lear*, based respectively on Q and F. "For other plays which we believe Shakespeare to have revised, we have attempted to provide edited texts which, so far as possible, represent the text as it stood after Shakespeare revised it" (509).

Works by others

Blayney, Peter W.M. *The Texts of "King Lear" and Their Origins: Nicholas Okes and the First Quarto*. Cambridge: Cambridge University Press, 1982.

Bloom, Harold. *Shakespeare: The Invention of the Human*. New York: Riverhead-Penguin, 1998.

Booth, Stephen. *"King Lear," "Macbeth," Indefinition, and Tragedy*. New Haven: Yale University Press, 1983.

Dent, R.W. *Shakespeare's Proverbial Language: An Index*. Berkeley and Los Angeles: University of California Press, 1981.

Elton, William R. *King Lear and the Gods*. Lexington: University Press of Kentucky, 1988.

Honigmann, E.A.J. *The Stability of Shakespeare's Text*. London: Arnold, 1965.

The Oxford Book of English Proverbs. Comp. William George Smith. Ed. F.P. Wilson. 3rd edn. Oxford: Clarendon Press, 1970.

Raphael, D.D. *The Paradox of Tragedy*. Bloomington, Indiana University Press, 1960.

Simkin, Stevie. *Early Modern Tragedy and the Cinema of Violence*. Basingstoke: Palgrave-Macmillan, 2006.

Taylor, Gary and Michael Warren. *The Division of the Kingdoms: Shakespeare's Two Versions of "King Lear."* Oxford: Clarendon Press, 1983.

Tilley, Morris Palmer. *A Dictionary of the Proverbs in England in the Sixteenth and Seventeenth Centuries*. Ann Arbor: University of Michigan Press, 1950.

Urkowitz, Steven. *Shakespeare's Revision of "King Lear."* Princeton: Princeton University Press, 1980.

Warren, Michael J. "Quarto and Folio *King Lear* and the Interpretation of Albany and Edgar." *Shakespeare: Pattern of Excelling Nature*. Ed. David Bevington and Jay L. Halio. Newark: University of Delaware Press, 1978: 95–107.

Wright, George T. *Shakespeare's Metrical Art*. Berkeley and Los Angeles: University of California Press, 1988.

6 What does Shakespeare leave out of *King Lear*?

Jean R. Brink

An unwritten convention underlies the make-up of modern editions of Shakespeare. The editor identifies the possible sources, and, in the case of *King Lear*, the anonymous *Leir* play is described as Shakespeare's immediate source (Halio 1992; Wells 2000). The *Leir* play is labeled a chronicle play and/or a tragi-comedy, but little attention is paid to it per se except as one of several Shakespearian sources for *King Lear*. In keeping with the methodology of traditional source studies, the text of the "source," in this case *Leir*, is subjected to scrutiny principally to identify elements of plot, character, or language that Shakespeare adapted for use in his version of the Lear story. At its most simplistic, this structural analysis aims at demonstrating the influence of *Leir* on *King Lear* and attempts to reach conclusions regarding Shakespeare's indebtedness to the earlier play.

My purpose in this reexamination of the two plays and their contexts is to raise diachronic as well as synchronic issues or, to phrase the strategy differently, to consider historical context as a function of intertextuality. Instead of focusing on the influence of one text, a pre-existing structure, on another text to demonstrate indebtedness, I want to posit an inventory of Lear source texts, consisting of the dramas, chronicles, and poems that tell the Lear story. This adjustment of traditional methodology will enable me to consider what choices have been made within this inventory and then to analyze the social and political implications of those choices. My objective is to isolate and compare structural elements in the texts and then to examine those elements in relation to their respective historical contexts. From the perspective of literary criticism, the tragic conclusion of *King Lear* is one of the most important differences between *Leir* and *King Lear* but the happy ending of *Leir* has never, to my knowledge, been historically contextualized. This historicized approach to intertextuality will enable me to focus on lack of indebtedness—as well as indebtedness. I can more easily ask: What does Shakespeare leave out of *King Lear* and why?

First, I will explore the implications of two kinds of specific omissions affecting action and then characterization. Shakespeare omits much of the introductory material present in the *Leir* play—the action and dialogue that give plausibility to the staging of the love test in Act 1. In addition, he reduces and blurs the psychological explanations for the actions of Gonorill and Ragan. These omissions make the behavior of Leir's two older daughters less explicable in human terms and, conversely, suggest that their actions may be directed by a nameless evil in the macrocosm. Shakespeare's use of cosmic imagery foregrounds philosophical issues, such as "Is there justice in the universe?" and his reduction of psychological probability intensifies this questioning. To conclude the comparison of *Leir* with *King Lear* I will reopen the issue of Shakespeare's historical relevance and comment briefly on the debate over Shakespeare's topicality—whether he wrote about contemporary politics or for the ages. By virtue of his status in the canon, Shakespeare is associated with the view that great art is timeless and speaks to universals in the human condition. Definitions of what makes Shakespeare great nearly always appeal to his persistent relevance, to his capacity to speak to one generation after another. His voice is understood to be philosophical, to be an autonomous statement of enduring truth. In her early study of the "crisis of the aristocracy" in *King Lear*, Rosalie Colie, for example, felt obligated to make the disclaimer: "I do not want to seem to take the play as reportage on current political and social conditions" (217, n. 17) even though, in fact, she was relating the play to "current political and social conditions." As Colie's apology indicates, claims that Shakespeare's plays are topical are considered reductive. Although I will argue that Shakespeare turns away from the very specific political relevance characteristic of the *Leir* play, I will show that he was aware of and deeply affected by his own political context. Shakespeare, however, manifested his political awareness by an indirect and allusive approach to topicality, an approach that left interpretation to the audience.

The *Leir* play: 1594 to 1605

Anonymous plays, like *Leir*, typically are given short shrift in literary criticism. This is particularly true in the case of traditional source study because an author-centered methodology highlights what the author owed to a pre-existing source. If we focus on the audience or reader, then we can more easily accommodate anonymity and multiple authors. The reader of a set of analogous texts with similar plots, characters, and themes will observe adaptations or omissions. This reader or viewer will think about *King Lear* while watching a performance of *Leir* and vice versa. We need not summon up the poststructuralist authority of Kristeva and Genette to legitimize descriptive analysis of a text from the perspective of later treatments of the same plot, characters, and themes.[1] In "Tradition and the Individual Talent," T.S. Eliot anticipates this theoretical concept when he mentions that later treatments of a story can also affect our response to an earlier version (Eliot 13–14). We need not distort historical probability to consider how the playgoer responded to *Leir* after seeing *King Lear*. *Leir* was performed in the seventeenth century at the same time that *King Lear* was in repertoire. In terms of the stage history, a playgoer might well have seen Shakespeare's *King Lear* and then attended a performance of the earlier *Leir* (Ioppolo 2005).

The *Leir* play is considered anonymous, but has been attributed to Michael Drayton as well as the less distinguished usual suspects, Anthony Munday and Henry Chettle. Several commentators have expressed surprise that it is an interesting play, but with one noteworthy exception (Sams 58), few have thought it worthy of attribution to Shakespeare. No one doubts that Shakespeare's *King Lear*, both quarto and folio versions, is a tragedy, even though the quarto describes the play as a history (Perkinson 315). The genre of the *Leir* play is less transparent (Law 112). The story of Lear and his daughters was transmitted and adapted principally by Geoffrey of Monmouth, John Higgins, Holinshed's *Chronicles*, and, notably, Edmund Spenser in the *Faerie Queene*. Not one of these versions of the story prepares a reader for a dénouement in which Leir is restored to the throne, declares his youngest daughter to be his heir, and rewards the loyalty of retainers and supporters. Not surprisingly, given the poetic justice of this ending, in which justice is meted out to all and sundry, Tolstoy preferred the *Leir* play to Shakespeare's *King Lear*. Nahum Tate, whose version Samuel Johnson preferred, introduced a marriage between Edgar and Cordelia. The *Leir* play, though lacking Tate's wedding of Cordelia to Edgar, may be closer to Tate than it is to Shakespeare (Legatt 4–5).

The known facts about the *Leir* play and its composition are few. It was entered in the Stationers' Register to Adam Islip, but Islip's name was crossed out. Edward White's name was substituted. The date of the entry was 14 May 1594. Even a cursory investigation of the records for 1594 demonstrates that White was interested in stage plays and is likely to have had ties with the professional companies. In the same year, George Peele's *The Love of King David and Fair Bathsheba* was also entered to him. When Shakespeare's *Titus Andronicus* was entered in the Stationers' Register, it was to be sold at his shop, as was the latest imprint of Kyd's *Spanish Tragedy*. He was also engaged in printing or selling Marlowe's *Massacre of Paris* and Robert Greene's *Friar Bacon and Friar Bungay*. The *Leir* play is recorded in Philip Henslowe's papers, and two performances at the Rose are noted in April 1594; the performances were combined productions of the Queen's Men and Sussex's Men (Henslowe 21). It has been argued that the *Leir* play was part of the repertoire of the Queen's Men and that Shakespeare belonged to this company before he joined the Chamberlain's Men in 1594 (McMillin and MacLean 145–46).

This 1594 *Leir* seems to have been the first version of the Lear story to be adapted for the stage, and it produced receipts of thirty-eight and twenty-six shillings when performed in April of that year. Though it was entered in the Stationers' Register a month later on 14 May, no copy seems to have been actually printed until more than a decade later. In the seventeenth century the *Leir* play was reentered in the Stationers' Register on 8 May 1605 to Simon Stafford as the "tragicall historie of King Leir and his three daughters" with the note "as it was latelie acted" (*Transcript of the Registers*, III: 289). An additional note reassigning the play to John Wright is important: "Entred for his Copie by assignement from Simon Stafford and by consent of Master Leake . . . Provided that Simon Stafford shall haue the printing of this booke." John Wright was apprenticed to Edward White, the bookseller and printer, who first entered the play in the Stationers' Register in 1594. These connections among the people involved in the two entries in the Stationers' Register make it likely that we are dealing with substantially the same play.

Previous source studies

Scholarship on the *Leir* play has almost exclusively centered on its relationship to Shakespeare, but not just on its relationship to *King Lear*. There is a cottage industry of source studies that attempt to document the influence of *Leir* on Shakespeare's early and later work. W.W. Greg summarized the consensus that Shakespeare saw the early performances or read a manuscript so closely that *Leir* lodged in his memory: "It would seem that as he wrote, ideas, phrases, cadences from the old play still floated in his memory below the level of conscious thought, and that now and again one or another helped to fashion the words that flowed from his pen." (Greg 1940: 397).

Kenneth Muir thought that Shakespeare might have acted in *Leir* (1978). Geoffrey Bullough in his authoritative collection on Shakespearian sources notes parallels between *Leir* and Shakespeare's *As You Like It* (7.299). Stanley Wells finds correspondences between *Leir* and *The Taming of the Shrew*, *Richard II*, *Much Ado About Nothing*, and *Hamlet* (12). Meredith A. Skura and Thomas P. Harrison point out the influence of *Leir* on *Titus Andronicus* and *Richard II* (Skura 285–86; Harrison 121–30). M. Mueller sees resemblances with *Richard III*, *Merchant of Venice*, *As You Like It*, and *Hamlet* and concludes that "the pervasive presence of the *Leir* play in Shakespeare's memory" is "evidence of a long-standing intention to write a play about Lear" (198–202). What are we to make of this long list of plays influenced by the *Leir* play? Those of us who by disposition are tidy might well want to establish boundaries for this perceived limitless intertextuality. Are similarities in plot line and verbal echoes enough to constitute influence? In the realm of poststructuralist theory, though any text can be compared with any other text, some comparisons will still be inherently more useful.

Wells, the editor of *The History of King Lear* for the Oxford Clarendon Press, draws extensive comparisons between *The Two Gentlemen of Verona*, probably one of Shakespeare's first works for the stage, and *King Lear* (15–16). He first cites the similarities in basic situation. The Duke plans to marry his daughter Silvia to the foolish Thurio; Valentine, her successful suitor, asks if the Duke has been able to get Silvia's consent to the marriage. Wells then cites the Duke's response as evidence of similarities to *King Lear* (16):

> No, trust me. She is peevish, sullen, forward,
> Proud, disobedient, stubborn, lacking duty,
> Neither regarding that she is my child
> Nor fearing me as if I were her father.
> And may I say to thee, this pride of hers
> Upon advice hath drawn my love from her,
> And where I thought the remnant of mine age
> Should have been cherished by her child-like duty,
> I now am resolved to take a wife,
> And turn her out to who will take her in.
> Then let her beauty be her wedding dower,
> For me and my possessions she esteems not.
> (3.1.68–79)

Wells cites verbal parallels, such as the Duke's desire to be "cherished by her child-like duty" and Lear's "thought to set [his] rest on [Cordelia's] kind nursery." The Duke says "let her beauty be her wedding dower" and Lear later says "Thy truth then be thy dower." Both the Duke and Lear accuse their daughters of being too proud. Wells then summarizes (16):

> As this passage looks forward to Shakespeare's play of *King Lear*, so also it looks backwards—or at least sideways—to the anonymous play of *King Leir*, because in that play too the King is planning to marry his youngest daughter to a man whom "she ne'er could fancy".
> (l. 141)

Although Wells seems to be serious in this curious attempt to point out resemblances between *Two Gentlemen of Verona* and *King Lear*, he adopts a one-dimensional view of influence. He argues that "a complete catalogue of minor variations on the [chronicle] story would be of little critical value" because it would not "necessarily demonstrate indebtedness since Shakespeare himself might have introduced changes independently of other writers" (20). This statement is important for our theoretical purposes because it assumes that the rationale for looking at "sources" or "analogues" is to demonstrate "indebtedness."

Because source study is conceptualized as a one-sided perspective on influence, Wells and other critics have focused on Shakespeare's indebtedness to the earlier *Leir*. We, for example, are repeatedly told that Shakespeare is responsible for adding the Gloucester subplot from Sidney's *Arcadia* and the character of the fool to the traditional version of the story. We hear little about what he leaves out or the way he blurs the psychological motivation of the characters. Shakespeare subtracts as well as adds, and too little attention has been paid to what he leaves out. In consequence, marked differences in the beginnings of the two plays have been ignored.

Shakespeare's reconsideration of *King Leir*

The author, or authors, of *Leir* made very different choices from those made by Shakespeare when he fashioned the play from the chronicle story. In the *Leir* play King Leir consciously plans the love test in Act 1 as a strategy for manipulating circumstances so that Cordella will be forced to marry a man of his choice rather than her own.

Shakespeare, significantly, chose not to use this very plausible explanation for why King Leir decides to convene the court and have his daughters proclaim their affection for him. In *Leir* the king plans to use this public ceremony to entrap Cordella into marriage with the neighboring king of Ireland:

> Yet, if my policy may her beguile,
> Ile match her to some King within this Ile,
> And so establish such a perfit peace,
> As fortune's force shall ne're prevail to cease.
>
> (A2V)[2]

In *Leir* when Cordella proclaims her affection, her father and king will ask her to demonstrate her love and duty by submitting to his choice of her husband. Shakespeare omits this motivation for staging the love test from *King Lear*. Shakespeare's independence from both his own *Two Gentlemen of Verona* and the anonymous *Leir* play is noteworthy in this respect.

In addition to omitting Lear's political motivation for the love test, Shakespeare also blurs and reduces the psychological motivation of the two older sisters, Gonorill and Ragan. And, as we shall see, he complicates the character development of Cordelia, who is far less pious than the Cordella of the *Leir* play. From the moment that we are first introduced to Gonorill and Ragan in the *Leir* play we are made aware that they intensely resent Cordella:

> *Gonorill.* I marvell, Ragan, how you can indure
> To see that proud pert Peat, our youngest sister,
> So slightly to account of us, her elders,
> As if we were no better than herselfe!
>
> (A3R)

Gonorill accuses Cordella of attempting to detract attention from her sisters and make herself more fashionable:

> We cannot have a quaint device so soone,
> Or new-made fashion, of our choice invention;
> But if she like it, she will have the same,
> Or study newer to exceed us both.
>
> (A3R)

Her own censure of Cordella reveals that it is not her younger sister's fashion, but her sister's courtesy that has won her the admiration of the court:

> Besides, she is so nice and so demure;
> So sober, courteous, modest, and precise,
> That all the Court hath worke ynough to do,
> To talke how she exceedeth me and you.
> (A3V)

Like Gonorill, Ragan realizes that Cordella, though their younger sister, outshines them. Observing that she has numerous suitors, Ragan is eager to "dimme the glory of her mounting fame" (A3V) for fear that she will find a worthy suitor, marry first, and then take precedence over her two older sisters. Gonorill swears by her virginity that she will not let this happen even if she has to marry a man "in his shirt" (A3V). The implication is that she is even willing to compromise her dignity and chastity in order to maintain her precedence over Cordella.

After we are introduced to the two older sisters and shown their resentment of Cordella, Lord Skalliger enters and betrays Leir's confidence. Skalliger resembles Oswald in Shakespeare's *King Lear* and is a variation on the stock figure of the unctuous, overly compliant servant. In Shakespeare's play, however, no one warns the sisters' of the approaching love test; they, like Cordelia, are taken by surprise. In *Leir* Skalliger reveals to the sisters that Ragan is to be married to the Prince of Cambria and Gonorill to the King of Cornwall; he adds that Leir wishes to marry Cordella to the rich King of Hibernia, but fears that she will not consent. He hints that there is a "further mystery" that he will reveal only if they promise to keep it secret and then warns them of the approaching love test:

> *Skalliger.* He earnestly desireth for to know,
> Which of you three do beare most love to him,
> And on your loves he so extremely dotes,
> As never any did, I thinke, before.
> He presently doth meane to send for you,
> To be resolv'd of this tormenting doubt:
> And looke, whose answere pleaseth him the best,
> They shall have most unto their marriages.
> (A4R)

Skalliger's revelation is somewhat puzzling because it misrepresents the preceding scene in which Leir revealed his strategy for settling the succession. In this scene it is Skalliger, not Leir, who supports giving a larger portion to the daughter who wins the love contest and protests the most love for her father; in contrast, Leir favours treating his daughters equally:

Skalliger. . . . since your Grace hath licens'd me to speake,
I censure thus; Your Maiesty knowing well,
What several Suters your princely daughters have,
To make them eche a Jointer more or lesse,
As is their worth, to them that love professe.
(A2R–A2V)

Skalliger proposes that Leir distribute his lands to his daughters in accordance with their performances in the love test, but Leir rejects this proposal:

Leir. No more, nor lesse, but even all alike,
My zeale is fixt, all fashiond in one mould:
Wherefore unpartiall shall my censure be,
Both old and young shall have alike for me.
(A2V)

Since it seems unlikely that the playwright could have forgotten what had transpired in the previous scene, it is possible that we have here an example of hasty revision. For our purposes, it is most important that Shakespeare omits these repeated assertions that someone other than Lear was the author of the love test.

In the *Leir* play Skalliger does not mention that Leir himself insisted that he would treat his daughters equally, but he does reveal that Leir intends to use the love test as a strategy for obtaining Cordella's consent to a marriage with the Hibernian king. Ragan immediately recognizes that the love test offers them "a fit occasion . . . [t]o be reveng'd upon her unperceiv'd" (A4R). Gonorill responds that their "revenge . . . shall be accounted piety" (A4R). Cunningly, since she knows that her father intends her to marry her to the King of Cornwall, she decides that she will protest that she loves her father so much that she would be willing to marry a beggar if he wished. Likewise, Ragan, secure in mind that she will "injoy the noble Cambrian Prince" (A4R) will protest that she will be content with anyone he selects. Gonorill rejoices in the "woeful plight" (178) that she and Ragan will create for Cordella:

For she will rather die, then give consent
To joine in marriage with the Irish King:
So will our father think, she loveth him not,
Because she will not graunt to his desire,
Which we will aggravate in such bitter termes,
That he will soone convert his love to hate.
(A4V)

The two sisters are motivated by their desire to outshine Cordella in the eyes of the court and to maintain their precedence over Cordella. As in Shakespeare's version, they seem aware of Leir's "extremes" in temperament (A4V).

One of the most interesting differences between *Leir* and *King Lear* has been overlooked. Just prior to the love test, the king, whose motivation has always been concern for his kingdom, has a deep sense of foreboding. He feels torn between "childrens love, and care of Common weale!" (A4V). He muses over his affection for his daughters and hopes that in the future they will securely sleep on beds of down. Pushing back his foreboding, he reassures himself that "the world/Affords not children more conformable" (A4V). In these opening scenes, we are introduced to a Leir who acts principally as a king concerned about his kingdom, but who remains a father genuinely worried about his children. Shakespeare omits these hints of humanity: his Lear lacks the altruistic "care of Common weale" and paternal devotion of Leir.

In the scene that follows, Leir puts the terms of the love test somewhat differently than in Shakespeare's play because he asks his daughters if they are willing to yield to his will:

> Which of you three to me would prove most kind;
> Which loves me most, and which at my request
> Will soonest yeeld unto their father's hest.
>
> (B1R)

Both Gonorill and Ragan depict themselves as willing to yield to any request from their father. Ragan, for example, suggests a scenario in which she has a fondness for a particular noble suitor, but then insists that she would be ruled by her father's wishes:

> Yet, would you have me make my choice anew,
> Ide bridle fancy, and be ruled by you.
>
> (B1V)

In *Leir*, as opposed to *King Lear*, the sisters actively attempt to discredit Cordella. After each of her sisters' protestations, Cordella accuses them of flattery, presumably in asides though they are not identified as such in the text. Her speech, as in Shakespeare, is very plain:

> *Cordella.* I cannot paint my duty forth in words,
> I hope my deeds shall make report for me:
> But looke what love the child doth owe the father,
> The same to you I beare, my gracious Lord.
>
> (B1V)

As if to cue their father's response, Gonorill and Ragan immediately condemn Cordella's response:

Gonorill. Here is an answer answerlesse indeed:
Were you my daughter, I should scarcely brooke it.
Ragan. Dost thou not blush, proud Peacock as thou art,
To make our father such a slight reply?
(B1V)

Leir accuses Cordella of being proud and describes her speech as "peremptory." He makes it clear that he has been deeply wounded:

But, didst thou know, proud girle,
What care I had to foster thee to this,
Ah, then thou wouldst say as thy sisters do:
Our life is lesse, then love we owe to you.
(B1R)

In her defense Cordella asserts that her "tongue was never used to flattery" and begs that her "plaine meaning" not be "misconstrued" (B2R). Gonorill and Ragan swiftly testify to their sincerity, support each other, and cast doubt on Cordella's affection for her father:

Gonorill. You were not best say I flatter: if you do,
My deeds shall shew, I flatter not with you.
I love my father better than thou canst.
(B2R)

Cordella interjects that Gonorill's assertion is self-serving and would be more compelling if it came from an impartial observer. Ragan immediately confirms her sister's true and filial love:

Ragan. Nay, here is one, that will confirme as much
As she hath said, both for myselfe and her.
I say, thou dost not wish my fathers good.
(B2R)

As in *King Lear* the king divides his kingdom between Gonorill and Ragan and disinherits Cordella. Before the members of the court exit, the sisters, however, have the last words. Gonorill reiterates that Cordella's pride has caused their father to disinherit her: "I ever thought that pride would have a fall" (B2R). Ragan, still smarting over Cordella's reputation for beauty, taunts her:

Ragan. Plaine dealing, sister: your beauty is so sheene,
You need no dowry, to make you be a Queene.
(B2R)

Disinherited by her father and abandoned by her sisters who "triumph in [her] woe," she piously says that she will put her faith in God who "doth protect the just" (B2R). The Cordella of the *Leir* play is entirely the victim of her unscrupulous sisters' jealousy and the conniving of Lord Skalliger.

In contrast, the Cordelia of Shakespeare's Act 1 seems more complicit in her own downfall. In Shakespeare's *King Lear* the two older sisters do not have a clear advantage over their younger sister. At least as far as the audience knows, Lear's three daughters are caught unaware by the love test. None of them suspects that he plans to stage a formal test of their love in front of the court. In keeping with the ceremonial tone of the occasion, both Goneril and Regan protest their love in extravagant terms. Cordelia's asides directed against her sisters' insincerity suggest that she despises flattery, but hint that she may also feel sibling rivalry. Her comment "Nothing" (1. 80) smacks of impertinence, and when she finally answers her father, she seems as interested in censuring her sisters as in protesting her love:

> Why have my sisters husbands if they say
> They love you all?
> . . .
> Sure, I shall never marry like my sisters,
> To love my father all.
> (11.90–92, 94–95)

Shakespeare gives his characterization of Cordelia an edge that Cordella lacks in the *Leir* play.

Shakespeare's Goneril and Regan, in contrast, are less deliberately hateful than in *Leir*. Neither of them actively attempts to turn Lear against Cordelia, and they seem surprised that he has disinherited her. When France tells her to bid her sisters farewell, she chides them. In the quarto Goneril tells her not to "prescribe" their "duties" (1.265), and then Regan prescribes Cordelia's duty, telling her to "study" to "content" her lord because he has taken her at "fortune's alms" (1.267–68). When they are left alone, they immediately switch from blank verse to prose as though to signal that they feel secure in revealing their actual feelings. Their candid perceptions of their father are far from flattering. They agree that flaws in his character are likely to be exacerbated by age. Regan comments that Lear has "ever but slenderly known himself" (1.280–81). Goneril signals her lack of sympathy with Lear by personifying his age as "unruly waywardness" and "infirm and choleric years" (1.285–87). Since we have just witnessed Lear disinherit his favorite daughter and banish a trusted councilor, Goneril and Regan's censure of their father seems just, even if it is disquieting.

In later scenes, when they have the kingdom and the power, Goneril and Regan become actively malevolent, and their unkindness, cloaked in a rational indifference, grows increasingly monstrous. In Coleridge's famous phrase, they, like Iago, have a motiveless malignity. To Lear they become "pelican daughters" because they seem to wish to feed on his flesh. In the storm scene the Gentleman describes Lear as the victim of "impetuous blasts" and "eyeless rage" (8.7). The greater order of nature, the macrocosm, does not feel or see his suffering, but his daughters knowingly inflict their cruelty on their father. Their rational indifference to their father's suffering is far more chilling than the hostility they exhibit in *Leir*.

As Goneril and Regan become ever more vicious in their treatment of their father, Cordelia's forgiveness of Lear comes to seem ever more generous. At the conclusion of the play, Lear has learned the emptiness of words, the vanity of pomp and wants only to be with Cordelia and "sing like birds in th' cage" (24.9). Cordelia, however, has not achieved Lear's indifference to the world, his desire to "take upon's the mystery of things / As if we were God's spies" (24.16–17). When they are taken to prison, she comments that she sorrows only for her father, but remains interested in confronting Goneril and Regan:

> For thee, oppressed King, am I cast down,
> Myself could else outfrown false fortune's frown.
> Shall we not see these daughters and these sisters?
> (24.5–7)

Lear shrugs away this suggestion of a confrontation with his two older daughters and wants only to reenact the moment of his reunion with Cordelia. She will ask his blessing, and he will "kneel down / And ask of thee forgiveness" (24.10–11). Shakespeare's Cordelia is not saintly. She remains hostile toward Goneril and Regan and reveals the same resentment that we saw in the first scene; she says: "Shall we not see these daughters and these sisters?" (24.7).

In *Leir* the political divisions are healed and peace is achieved; in Shakespeare's *King Lear* the succession is unresolved, and peace is uncertain. Rather than simply prefer Shakespeare's version, which is also the more historically accurate, we may ask why a peaceful settlement to the succession was more congenial to a playwright and his audience in the 1590s. The audience of 1594 lived in a period so uncertain that even the staged end of a dynasty might have been intolerable. It was probably much better business to supply the audience with the dramatic panacea of Leir and Cordella's victory.

Political contexts for *King Leir*

If we imagine an Elizabethan playgoer watching a dark stage in April 1594, we can be sure that he would have regarded the single most important political issue confronting the government in 1594 as the succession to the throne of England. The Leir play begins with this precise political dilemma. The king in the play has no male heir; he has three daughters, but even though he has three legitimate female heirs; neither he nor his courtiers are sanguine about a peaceful succession. In the case of our playgoer, his queen has no heirs of her body. James VI of Scotland will almost certainly claim the crown when the queen dies, but there are other possible domestic and foreign claimants. To this playgoer civil war, perhaps accompanied by a foreign invasion, seems inevitable. This civil war, like those raging on the continent, is also likely to be a war of religion. Many Englishmen—some would even argue most—are Roman Catholic in 1594; a number are radical Protestants or Puritans; the Anglican establishment is by no means secure. In early 1594 Father Robert Parsons had published his *A Conference about the Next Succession to the Crowne of England*. This tract produced by the Catholic underground argued that the Spanish Infanta had a strong claim to the throne and was dedicated to Robert Devereux, Earl of Essex. An increasingly popular political figure, Essex had inherited the puritan mantle of leadership from his stepfather and Elizabeth's long-time favorite, Robert Dudley, Earl of Leicester. Essex, however, appealed as well to the Catholics because he opposed religious persecution. Parsons had vividly pointed out—what our playgoer already knew—that if the succession were not settled to their satisfaction, English Catholics might support the intervention of a foreign power and the leading domestic and foreign claimants then might well engage in a bloody civil war. The new civil war, fueled as it would be by religious zeal, would be far more disastrous than the Lancaster and York civil war so successfully staged in Shakespeare's *Henry VI*.

The political context in 1594 mirrors the dramatic situation in the *Leir* play. In this version of the Lear story, lack of an obvious heir to the throne is the initiating political issue. The division of the kingdom occurs only because Leir has no male heir. In the *Leir* play the king's lack of a male heir and his age are both made explicit and linked to the problem of the succession. For our Elizabethan playgoer this would have translated into concern about his aging queen and the uncertain succession to the English throne. In his opening speech, Leir has just lost his wife, a wife unmentioned in the chronicles. He emphasizes his age and his lack of a male heir, and it is these two considerations that prompt him to divide his kingdom:

> A sonne we want for to succeed our Crowne,
> And course of time hath cancelled the date
> Of further issue from our withered loines:
> One foote already hangeth in the grave,
> . . .
> And I would fain resigne these earthly cares,
> And thinke vpon the welfare of my soule:
> Which by no better meanes may be effected,
> Then by resigning vp the Crowne from me,
> In equall dowry to my daughters three.
>
> (A2R)

The lords in attendance are aware that the king's lack of a male heir bodes ill to an orderly succession. The position of Elizabeth was far worse; she had no surviving legitimate siblings, and she lacked any legitimate heir of her own body.

An unnamed nobleman seems to voice the general apprehension over what will transpire after Leir's death:

> My gracious Lord, I hartily do wish,
> That God had lent you an heir indubitate,
> Which might have set upon your royall throne,
> When fates should loose the prison of your life,
> By whose succession all this doubt might cease;
> And as by you, by him we might have peace.
>
> (A2V)

A son would have been "an heir indubitate," and his existence would have insured that the kingdom would have peace. A male heir was associated with political stability. Henry VIII, Elizabeth's father, thought that only a male heir would guarantee a peaceful succession. The Elizabethan audience was well aware that Henry Tudor's quest for a male heir had helped to fuel the English Reformation.

The nobleman in *Leir* is concerned about foreign intervention, presumably from the continent, and so he advocates that Leir marry his daughters to local British lords:

> Wherefore, my Liege, my censure deemes it best,
> To match them with some of your neighbour Kings,
> Bord'ring within the bounds of Albion,
> By whose united friendship, this our state
> May be protected 'gainst all forraign hate.
>
> (A2V)

It could be argued that this passage in the *Leir* play seems to favor a Scottish succession because James VI of Scotland was a neighboring king. Early in Elizabeth's reign the Scottish succession had been a problem because Mary, Queen of Scots, was Roman Catholic. That religious tension climaxed in Mary's execution in 1587 and led to the invasion of the Spanish armada in 1588.

The succession of James VI of Scotland and James I of England was also complicated by constitutional issues. Henry VIII had gone to parliament to settle the succession: first on his son Edward and then on his elder daughter Mary, followed by Elizabeth. In the unlikely event that all three of his children were to die without heirs, then the throne was to succeed to the children of his younger sister Mary Tudor rather than his older sister, Margaret, who was by primogeniture the legal heir. Mary, widow of the French king, had married as her second husband, the English-born Charles Brandon, who was then created the Duke of Suffolk by Henry VIII. After the death of Edward VI, there had been an abortive attempt to make Lady Jane Grey, the Protestant Suffolk heir, queen rather than the Catholic Mary, but Mary prevailed and Jane was executed. The Greys, descendants of Mary Tudor, were taken seriously as claimants to the throne even though Elizabeth had declared the marriage of Catherine Grey to the Earl of Hertford illegal and imprisoned Catherine.

The Elizabethan succession also involved constitutional questions. When Henry VIII asked parliament to vest the succession in the descendants of his younger sister, he had ignored the superior claim of the offspring of his older sister Margaret. Margaret had married the King of Scotland, and her heirs were Scots. If primogeniture could be ignored in order to favor the Suffolk claimants over the Stuarts, then constitutionally it might be possible for parliament to use its own wisdom and establish an alternate line of succession. Conceivably, then, parliament might even elect a popular military leader, such as Essex, king.

Religion intensified the importance of these constitutional and dynastic considerations. Recent Tudor historiography has emphasized the fragility of the Elizabethan religious settlement; Protestantism under Edward VI gave way to Roman Catholicism under Mary and Philip, but returned under Elizabeth. Until the execution of Mary, Queen of Scots, in 1587, many people regarded Mary, a Catholic, as Elizabeth's legitimate heir. By 1594 the claim had passed to Mary's son, James VI of Scotland. James was considered a foreign heir, but presumably less foreign than the Spanish Infanta whom Parsons' *Conference on the Succession* had promoted as a claimant. The Earl of Derby and his son were also English claimants, but the earl and his son Ferdinando Stanley had both recently died. The younger Stanley's death in 1593 under mysterious circumstances was rumored to have resulted from a Catholic conspiracy carried out by Jesuits.

The events depicted in *Leir* offered a possible exemplum of England's future after the queen's death. Nevertheless, it would be a mistake to assume that *Leir* is a propaganda play about the Elizabethan succession. The play invites the audience to make parallels between the story that it tells and the contemporary political situation, but it does not endorse a particular claimant to the throne. The Elizabethans were concerned about the invasion or civil war that might ensue after the death of their aging queen, and that concern made the political circumstances at the beginning of *Leir* highly relevant in 1594. The play dramatizes these fears, acting out the internal dissension and the foreign invasion feared by the audience, but assuages them with a happy ending.

In the *Leir* play Leir formulates a policy for preventing foreign invasion by attempting to engineer a succession from within the British Isles. He has already determined to marry his older daughters to the neighboring kings of Cornwall and Cambria (Wales), but Cordella is thwarting his plan by insisting on marrying for love. She lacks interest in neighboring lords and kings and indeed in his choice for her, the king of Ireland. Nevertheless, he has a plan that will cause her to fall in with his strategy and accept a neighboring suitor:

> She is sollicited by divers Peeres;
> But none of them her partiall fancy heares.
> Yet, if my policy may her beguile,
> Ile match her to some King within this Ile.
> (A2V)

Leir wants to establish a "perfect peace" after his exodus from this world, and it is care for the welfare of his kingdom that motivates him to stage the love test.

Perillus, later the Kent figure in Shakespeare's *King Lear*, acknowledges Leir's "gracious care" for his kingdom and people and exclaims that it "deserves an everlasting memory, / To be enrolled in Chronicles of fame, / By never-dying perpetuity" (A2V). He praises Leir for his concern for the commonwealth, but is reluctant to see Cordella forced into a loveless marriage against her will and warns Leir that "streams, being stopped, above the banks do swell" (A3R). Leir brushes aside this warning because he does not connect the future of his kingdom with his daughter's domestic happiness. In the *Leir* play the king engages in the love test principally because he plans to use the pressure of the ceremonial occasion to manipulate Cordella into marriage with a neighboring prince. When Cordella says that she loves him most, he plans to ask her to grant him one request and use that request to "triumph in [his] policy, / And match her with a King of Britanny" (A3R).

The political topicality of the *Leir* play may help to explain why it was not printed in 1594—even though it was produced and entered in the Stationers' Register. Immediately following the publication of Parsons' *Conference on the Succession*, the authorities were alert to commentary on the succession, and in this climate it may have seemed wiser not to go on with the play's publication. In the early scenes the anonymous *Leir* play accommodates to this political climate by a careful ambiguity regarding the succession, but like *Gorbuduc* it could be interpreted as a play about contemporary politics. We know that the anonymous *Leir* was staged in the theater, but never printed. It may have been voluntarily suppressed by its anonymous author, and such a suppression would not be surprising. We know of a number of discussions of the succession that were composed in the late 1590s but left in manuscript by their authors. Official reactions to the publication of Parsons' *Conference on the Succession* and later to Sir John Hayward's *History of Henry IV* show that the government frowned on any work that might be interpreted as debate on the succession question. We do not know if the deposition scene in Shakespeare's *Richard II* was ever staged, but we do know that it was never included in printed editions of the play during the lifetime of Elizabeth

Tudor. It may well be that the clear emphasis upon the succession at the beginning of the *Leir* play led the author(s) to suppress its printing during the reign of Elizabeth.

Publication on the succession question was even illegal in 1594. An act passed in 1571 specifically prohibited discussion of claims to the throne except by parliament. Since the queen could and did prevent parliamentary discussion, this act in effect had made any printed commentary on the succession illegal. When Peter Wentworth, a stalwart Puritan, attempted to bring the succession question before the Parliament of 1593, Wentworth and his supporters were all imprisoned (Neale). His tract on the succession was suppressed, and Wentworth, who was sixty-nine, remained in the Tower from 1593 until his death in 1597. After his death in 1597 *A Pithie Exhortation to her Majesty for Establishing her Successor* was printed posthumously in Scotland in 1598. Like Wentworth, Sir Walter Raleigh had carefully worked out his views on the succession. His recommendations seem to have been in accord with Elizabeth's policy of not identifying a successor, but even so his manuscript was never published (Lanfranc, 38–46). Likewise, Sir John Harington, the queen's godson, prepared an elaborate manuscript entitled, "A Tract on the Succession to the Crown" (1602) but this manuscript tract was not published until the nineteenth century when a descendant thought it safe to make his ancestor's views public (Harington, ed. Markham, 1880).

Leir and other Lear stories

It is almost certain that the political topicality of *Leir* explains why the playwright ignored chronicle history and supplied a happy ending. The *Leir* play pays no attention to the unhappy endings of the chronicle story in Holinshed's *Chronicles* and Edmund Spenser's *Faerie Queene*, the two versions likely to be most familiar to an Elizabethan audience. In Holinshed's *Chronicles*, the sons of Cordelia's sisters, Margan and Cunedag, "disdaining to be vnder the gouernment of a woman, leuied warre against hir" (Bk. 2, Ch. 5, 448). After she is taken prisoner, Cordelia "tooke suche griefe, being a woman of a manlie courage, and despairing to recouer libertie, there she slue hirselfe" (2.6.448). Spenser's *Faerie Queene* also glides over Lear's restoration to the throne and dwells on Cordelia's imprisonment at the hands of her sisters' sons:

> So to his crowne she him restord againe,
> In which he dyde, made ripe for death by eld,
> And after wild, it should to her remaine:
> Who peaceably the same long time did weld:
> And all mens harts in dew obedience held:
> Till that her sisters children, woxen strong,
> Through proud ambition against her rebeld,
> And ouercommen kept in prison long,

> Till weary of that wretched life, her selfe she hong.
> (Book 2, Canto 10, stanza 32)

Although Cordelia commits suicide in other versions, Spenser introduces the idea that Cordelia dies by hanging. From this detail, we know that Shakespeare consulted Spenser. Since Spenser's treatment of the Lear story was published in the 1590 *Faerie Queene*, it was readily available to the author of the 1594 *Leir*, but he ignores Spenser's bleak conclusion to the story of the fortunes of Lear and his daughter Cordelia.

It is important to emphasize that the *Leir* play ignores the tragic dénouement of the chronicle story and superimposes a happy ending on a tale that had ended unhappily in every previous account. Cordelia, in fact, had committed suicide in both *The Mirror for Magistrates* and Spenser's *Faerie Queene*. In *Leir* both Cordella and her husband are still alive at the conclusion of the play, and Leir thanks his son-in-law, the king of Gaul, for his service in restoring him to the throne:

> First to the heavens, next, thanks to you, my sonne,
> By whose good means I repossess the same:
> Which if it please you to accept yourselfe,
> With all my heart I will resign to you.
> (I3V)

Leir says that his kingdom belongs to Gaul because he raised an army at his own expense and ventured his own body in Leir's defense. The king and Cordella assure Leir that they are pleased by his restoration to the throne. The plays conclude with this scene in which Leir bids his daughter Cordella and her husband to stay with him for a while before they return to France. Both the kings of Cornwall and Cambria (Wales) have fled along with their wicked wives; the people rejoice in having their old king restored. Moreover, in spite of the concern about foreign marriage expressed at the beginning of the play, there is now no hint that anyone will object to having the king of Gaul and his wife Cordella succeed to the English throne after Leir's death.

> Come, sonne and daughter, who did me advannce,
> Repose with me awhile, and then for Fraunce.
> (I4V)

In the *Leir* play staged in 1594 but not printed until 1605 the king is concerned about the succession; it is made to seem plausible that his concern for the welfare of his kingdom after his death motivates the love test. Shakespeare omits all of this concern about the succession and focuses upon Lear's pride and his interest in staging a public ceremony in which his daughters pay tribute to him as their royal father.

There is no doubt that Shakespeare was thoroughly familiar with the *Leir* play; "in nearly a hundred significant details" he shows a close familiarity with the old play (Knowles 12–35). His most significant deviations from it occur at the beginning and the end of the play. He omits entirely Lear's motivation for staging the love test. There is no discussion of the king's lack of a son, no expressed concern over marrying Goneril and Regan to neighboring princes, and, most striking of all, we hear nothing about Lear's having a strategy to marry Cordelia to a suitor within the British Isles. Her suitors, France and Burgundy, are both foreign princes, and their foreign nationalities are not represented as a bar to marriage with Cordelia. In Shakespeare's *King Lear* the king is given little or no motivation for requiring his daughters to declare their affection in public. Critics have commented on James and his support of a unified kingdom (Marcus 148–50, Patterson 58–73, Axton 131–47, Taylor and Warren 75–119, 351–468), but this theme is more implicit than explicit to the politics of the play. It would be impossible to prove that Shakespeare chose to omit the psychological underpinning of this scene specifically because the succession question was no longer relevant to his audience; nevertheless, its irrelevance in 1606 may have been a consideration. From the perspective of fidelity to the contemporary scene, superficially at least, we would expect Shakespeare to maintain the happy ending of *Leir*. Certainly, the succession question no longer looms large in 1606. James has succeeded to Elizabeth's throne, and the Stuart line is secure.

The accession to the throne of James I was not the bright beginning of a new age that Shakespeare and his contemporaries may have initially anticipated. The Stuart succession was at best a mixed success. James's succession was peaceful, but we know that by 1606 there was already nostalgia for the old queen; phrases such as Jacobean melancholy have been invented to describe the malaise of the early seventeenth century. Those who, like Shakespeare, could look back on the decorum and brilliance of performances before the Elizabethan court were disillusioned with the new milieu. The title page of his *True Chronicle Historie of the life and death of King Lear* states that this version of the play was performed "before the Kings Maiestie at Whitehall upon S. Stephans night in Christmas Hollidayes" (Wells 4). No account of that performance survives, but we do have two accounts of the Jacobean court that compare its atmosphere with that of its Elizabethan counterpart.

Six months after Shakespeare's *King Lear* was staged at court during the Christmas season of 1606, James entertained Christian IV in England from 17 July to 11 August 1606. To mark this occasion an entertainment was arranged in which the Queen of Sheba brought gifts to the two kings. Speeches were also to be presented by the theological virtues, Faith, Hope, and Charity, and by the civic values of Victory and Peace. An account of this court entertainment was written by Sir John Harington to Secretary Barlow; it is dated 1606 and was probably written shortly after the conclusion of the visit. Harington, author of *The Metamorphosis of Ajax*, and translator of Ariosto, was hardly a prude, but he is dismayed by the lack of decorum:

> The Lady who did play the Queens part, did carry most precious gifts to both their Majesties; but . . . overset her caskets into his Danish Majesties lap, and fell at his feet, tho I rather think it was in his face. . . . His Majesty then got up and would dance with the Queen of Sheba; but he fell down . . . and was carried to an inner chamber and laid on a bed of state; which was not a little defiled with the presents of the Queen which had been bestowed on his garments; such as wine, cream, jelly, beverage, cakes, spices, and other good matters. The entertainment and show went forward, and most of the presenters went backward, or fell down; wine did so occupy their upper chambers.

Those representing the cardinal virtues were also intoxicated: "Hope did assay to speak, but wine rendered her endeavours so feeble that she withdrew" . . . Faith was then all alone, for I am sure that she was not joined with good works, and left the court in a staggering condition. Harington concludes that he has "much marvalled at these strange pageantries":

> they do bring to my remembrance what passed of this sort in our Queens days . . . but I neer did see such lack of good order, discretion, and sobriety, as I have now done. I have passed much time in seeing the royal sports of hunting and hawking, where the manners were such as made me devise the beasts were pursuing the sober creation, and not man in quest of exercise or food.
>
> (352)

He tells his correspondent that if he wishes to see "howe folly dothe grow," he should come quickly to court; otherwise he can stay home and meditate: "on the future mischiefs of those our posterity, who shall learn the good lessons and examples helde forthe in these days" (353).

Five years later in 1611 Lord Thomas Howard, one of the Howard family who fared very well under James I, wrote to Sir John Harington, describing the king's attraction to handsome young men like Robert Carr, whom Howard accurately prophesies will be knighted and given a title. With obvious irony, Howard tells Harington to concentrate on the king's "heart and most delightful subject of his mind" his roan jennet. He, too, feels nostalgic about Elizabeth's reign:

> You have lived to see the trim of old times, and what passed in the Queen's days. These things are no more the same. Your Queen did talk of her subjects love and good affections, and in good truth she aimed well; our King talketh of his subjects fear and subjection, and herein I think he dothe well too, as long as it holdeth good.
>
> (394–95)

Howard tells Harington that his scholarship and wit might receive attention for a while at court, "as strangers at such a place," but adds that flattery is what "men live by now a days" (395). He asks Harington if he is prepared to say "that the stars are bright jewels fit for Carr's [James's favourite] ears? That the roan jennet surpasseth Bucephalus, and is worthy to be bestridden by Alexander? That his eyes are fire, his tail is Bernice's locks" (396). At the conclusion of the letter he assures Harington that he is sending his letter by his son so that "no danger may happen from our freedom" (397).

We need not belabor the obvious. This is the Jacobean court that Shakespeare would have known. When he wrote his version of the Lear play in the early seventeenth century, he, like Sir John Harington and Lord Thomas Howard, may well have looked back nostalgically to the Elizabethan age of his youth. The most gifted nondramatic writers, Sir Philip Sidney and Edmund Spenser, had died young; the charismatic Robert Devereux, Earl of Essex, had been executed after a misguided rebellion. The new generation seemed less inspired and inspiring to their older contemporaries. There is less anxiety about the future in Shakespeare's *King Lear*, but more darkness than in *Leir*. In Shakespeare's quarto Albany seems to relinquish power to Kent and Edgar, "friends of my soul, you twain/Rule in this kingdom, and the gored state sustain" (24. 313–15). The Duke's last speech is bleak:

> The weight of this sad time we must obey,
> Speak what we feel, not what we ought to say.
> (24.318–19)

The Duke of Albany does not appear in *Leir* where Gonorill's husband is the "Cornwall King" and Ragan's "the noble Cambrian Prince" (A4R). If Shakespeare substituted the Duke of Albany for the Cambrian Prince as a compliment to James, he stopped short of endorsing Elizabeth's successor. There is no suggestion that Albany, who is associated with Scotland and so with James, may prefigure a unified Britain.

Notes

1 In his *Paratexts: Thresholds of Interpretation* Gerard Genette reformulates Kristeva's intertextuality as transtextuality. Of Genette's subcategories, the three most allusive are architextuality (genre), metatextuality (critical commentary of one text on another), and hypertextuality (text that transforms a preceding hypotext, e.g., parody, sequel, translation). Genette's reformulation may not focus specifically on the author, but either a reader or an author is implicit in these conceptualizations of intertextuality. Of the above concepts, it is metatextuality that is most adaptable to the process of reintroducing historical contextualization into poststructuralist discourse on intertextuality.

2 All references to *The True Chronicle History of King Leir, and his three daughters* will be to the 1605 edition preserved at the Henry E. Huntington Library, San Marino, CA. Signatures will be cited parenthetically in the text. For clarity I have modernized the spelling for "u" and "v" and "i" and "j."

Works cited

Axton, Marie. *The Queen's Two Bodies: Drama and the Elizabethan Succession.* London: Royal Historical Society, 1977.

Bullough, Geoffrey. *Narrative and Dramatic Sources of Shakespeare.* 7 vols. London: Routledge and Kegan Paul, 1973.

Colie, Rosalie L. "Reason and Need: *King Lear* and the 'Crisis' of the Aristocracy." *Some Facets of* King Lear. Eds. Rosalie Colie and F.T. Flahiff. Toronto: University Press Toronto, 1974: 185–219.

Eliot, T.S. *Selected Essays, 1917–1932.* London: Faber and Faber, 1932.

Genette, Gerard. *Paratexts: Thresholds of Interpretation.* Cambridge: Cambridge University Press, 1997.

Greg, W.W. "The Date of *King Lear* and Shakespeare's Use of Earlier Versions of the Story." *The Library*, Fourth Series 20 (1940): 377–99.

Halio, Jay L. (ed.). *The Tragedy of King Lear.* Cambridge: Cambridge University Press, 1992.

Harington, Sir John. *A Tract of the Succession to the Crown by Sir John Harington, Kt.* Ed. Clements R. Markham. London: J.B. Nichols and Sons, 1880.

Harrison, Thomas P. "*Titus Andronicus* and *King Lear*: A Study in Continuity." *Shakespearean Essays.* Eds. Alvin Thaler and Norman Sanders. Knoxville, TN: University of Tennessee Press, 1964: 121–30.

Henslowe, Philip. *Henslowe's Diary.* Eds. R.A. Foakes and R.T. Rickert. Cambridge: Cambridge University Press, 1961.

Holinshed, Raphael. *Chronicles of England, Scotland, and Ireland.* 6 vols. London: Johnson, Rivington, Payne, *et al.*, 1807.

Ioppolo, Grace. "The Idea of Shakespeare and the Two Lears." *Lear from Study to Stage: Essays in Criticism.* Eds. James Ogden and Arthur H. Scouten. London and Cranbury, NJ: Associated University Presses, 1997: 45–56.

—— " 'A Jointure more or less': Re-measuring *The True Chronicle History of King Leir and His Three Daughters.*" *Medieval and Renaissance Drama in England* 17 (2005): 165–79.

—— *William Shakespeare's King Lear: A Sourcebook.* London: Routledge, 2007.

Knowles, Richard. "How Shakespeare Knew *King Leir*." *Shakespeare Survey* 55 (2002): 12–35.

Lanfranc, Pierre, "Un inedit de Ralegh sur la Succession." *Etudes Anglaises* 13 (1960): 38–46.

Law, Robert Adgar. "*King Leir* and *King Lear*: An Examination of the Two Plays." Studies in Honor of T.W. Baldwin. Ed. Don Cameron Allen. Urbana: University of Illinois Press, 1958: 112–24.

Leggatt, Alexander. *King Lear: Twayne's New Critical Introductions to Shakespeare.* Boston: G.K. Hall, 1988.

Marcus, Leah. *Puzzling Shakespeare: Local Reading and its Discontents.* Berkeley, Los Angeles, London: University of California Press, 1988.

McMillin, Scott and MacLean, Sally-Beth. *The Queen's Men and their Plays.* Cambridge: Cambridge UP, 1998.

Mueller, M. "From Leir to Lear." *Philological Quarterly* 73 (1994): 195–217.

Muir, Kenneth and Stanley Wells (eds.). *Aspects of King Lear.* Articles reprinted from *Shakespeare Survey.* Cambridge: Cambridge University Press, 1982.

—— *The Sources of Shakespeare's Plays.* New Haven: Yale University Press, 1978.

Neale, J.E. "Peter Wentworth." *English Historical Review* (1924): 36–54; 175–204.
Patterson, Annabel. *Censorship and Interpretation: The Conditions of Writing and Reading in Early Modern England.* Madison, Wisconsin: University of Wisconsin Press, 1984.
Perkinson, Richard H. "Shakespeare's Revision of the Lear Story and the Structure of *King Lear.*" *Philological Quarterly* 22 (1943): 315–29.
Sams, Eric. *The Real Shakespeare: Retrieving the Early Years, 1564–1594*. New Haven: Yale University Press, 1995.
Shakespeare, William. *The First Folio of Shakespeare*. Ed. Charlton Hinman. Norton facsimile. 2nd edn. London and New York: W.W. Norton, 1996.
Skura, Meredith Anne. *Shakespeare the Actor and the Purpose of Playing*. Chicago: University Press Chicago, 1993.
Spenser, Edmund. *The Faerie Queene*. Ed. A.C. Hamilton. Text edited by Hiroshi Yamashita and Toshiyuki Suzuki. Edinburgh: Pearson Education, 2001.
Stafford, Helen. *James VI of Scotland and the Throne of England.* New York, D. Appleton-Century Co., Inc., 1940.
Taylor, Gary and Michael Warren (eds.). *The Division of the Kingdoms: Shakespeare's Two Versions of King Lear*. Oxford: Clarendon Press, 1983.
A Transcript of the Registers of the Company of Stationers' Register. Ed. Edward Arber. Reprinted Gloucester, MA: Peter Smith, 1967.
The True Chronicle History of King Leir, and his three daughters. London: S. Stafford for J. Wright, 1605.
Wells, Stanley (ed.). *The History of King Lear*. Oxford: Oxford University Press, 2000.

7 The cause of thunder

Nature and justice in *King Lear*

Paul A. Cantor

As many critics have recognized, the central themes of *King Lear* are nature and justice (Heilman 10–11, 26; Danby 15; Moseley 69; Hunter 17; Lowenthal 78; Craig 113), and in exploring their relation, the play investigates the nature of justice and the justice of nature. At the very center of the play, Act 3, scene 4, the king in his madness believes that he has been given the rare opportunity to consult a philosopher in the person of a beggar named Poor Tom (in reality, the young nobleman Edgar masquerading as a hapless lunatic). The first question Lear asks his philosopher is: "What is the cause of thunder?" (3.4.155).[1] Ever since Aristophanes' *The Clouds*, with its dialogue between Socrates and the dim-witted rustic Strepsiades, this question has pointed to the larger question of divine justice. Puzzled by Socrates' claim that Zeus does not exist, Strepsiades wants to know who, then, creates thunder and lightning, and therefore who can be counted on to strike down malefactors and see that justice prevails in the city? What Aristophanes' Socrates presents as purely a question of natural science—he gives Strepsiades a meteorological explanation of thunder and lighting in terms of the physics of clouds—the old farmer insists on treating as an ethical and political matter. Strepsiades' understanding of nature is intimately bound up with his understanding of the social and political order because it is intimately bound up with his understanding of the gods. Strepsiades worries that if Zeus is *not* the cause of thunder, the natural order has no basis in any kind of ethical principle, and, among other evil consequences, children will feel free to beat up their parents. Strepsiades' concerns help us understand Lear's obsession with the storm and suggest that when the mad king asks about the cause of thunder, he is really asking whether the gods exist and whether justice can be said to exist by nature (Lowenthal 88; Craig 182; Kahn 80).

Whether or not Shakespeare knew *The Clouds*, he re-creates in his tragedy the basic problem Aristophanes poses in his comedy. In Lear's monumental self-assurance as a reigning monarch, he has always assumed that the political order is rooted in the natural, that nature supports human justice and in particular his own decrees as king (McDonald 15). That is why he swears "by the sacred radiance of the sun" and "all the operation of the orbs" (1.1.109–11) when he banishes Cordelia in the first scene, and why in calling down a curse on Goneril, he invokes natural and divine forces at once: "Hear, Nature, hear, dear goddess, hear!" (1.4.275). As a pagan, Lear believes that the natural and the divine orders are one and the same, and both are aligned with human justice and law. One reason he is certain that his plan for disposing of his kingdom will work is that he has no doubt that his authority as a father is independent of his political position and will consequently survive his abdication of power. For Lear, the power of a father does not require the support of law and social convention; it is rooted in the very order of nature; in his view, children who disobey their parents are "unnatural hags" (2.4.278), and nature will accordingly punish them without any need for human intervention on his behalf.

However, the tragic sequence of events set in motion by Lear's decision to renounce political power has the effect of shattering his confidence that nature supports human justice. He learns that once he no longer has the forces necessary to restrain the ambition and desires of his daughters, Goneril and Regan can behave unjustly toward him with impunity. Unconstrained by the normal dictates of law and social convention, they reveal the depth of evil in their natures. The outbreak of the storm in Act 3 only confirms what Lear has come to suspect about the fundamental injustice of the natural world. Instead of punishing "ingrateful man" (3.2.9), the thunder and the lightning have conspired with Lear's daughters to make innocent people suffer. In one of his most moving speeches, Lear comes to see the cruelty of the natural elements as emblematic of the unjust way the poor and downtrodden are oppressed by the rich and powerful (3.4.28–35), leading him to wish that he could "show the heavens more just" (3.4.36). For the pagan Lear, losing faith in the justice of nature goes hand in hand with losing faith in divine justice as well.

As Lear later explains to Gloucester, the storm teaches him that nature does not automatically obey his commands as king: "When the rain came to wet me once, and the wind to make me chatter, when the thunder would not peace at my bidding, there I found 'em, there I smelt 'em out. . . . they told me I was every thing. 'Tis a lie, I am not ague-proof" (4.6.100–5). Lear finally realizes that the king is not by nature superior to other human beings but instead shares the physical limitations of humanity. Thus, there will always be an element of arbitrariness and conventionality in the rule of one human being over another, and, hence, in any claim to administer justice. As Lear puts it: "change places, and handy-dandy, which is the justice, which is the thief?" (4.6.153–54) In Lear's eyes, the conventional social and political hierarchy lacks any basis in nature. Having begun the play as a firm believer in the identity of nature and convention, Lear comes to believe in their complete disjunction. What exists by convention does not exist by nature, and for Lear, justice and law are prime examples of what exists only by convention, by human decree (McDonald 5, 160–61).

Many commentators on *King Lear* are content to leave the play's examination of the relation of nature and justice at this conclusion.[2] The play does seem to offer the most corrosive critique possible of the conventional order of society and to leave us with a sense of the arbitrary character of social hierarchy and conventional conceptions of justice. And yet, as if to warn against identifying Lear's understanding of society with his own, Shakespeare makes the king commit a glaring error in the midst of his seemingly insightful speech on the nature of justice (Craig 180):

> Let copulation thrive; for Gloucester's bastard son
> Was kinder to his father than my daughters
> Got 'tween the lawful sheets.
>
> (4.6.114–16)

Even though Lear does not at this moment know the truth about Edmund, we as viewers or readers do, and cannot help thinking that Gloucester's bastard son was just as cruel to his father as Goneril and Regan were to theirs. If Lear in his madness can be mistaken about such an important matter, perhaps his overall understanding of justice is defective, or at least incomplete. Moreover, Lear's defense of the "bastard son" evokes disquieting associations—it echoes Edmund's soliloquy in Act 1, scene 2, in which he too argues for a complete disjunction between the natural and the conventional order, and for the superiority of the natural over the conventional (Heilman 103). Edmund speaks with contempt for "the plague of custom" (1.2.3) and asserts that the illegitimate son will always by nature have more energy than the legitimate. For Edmund, the distinction codified in law between legitimate and illegitimate offspring is an example of the arbitrariness of conventional society.

The fact that Shakespeare has a villain first articulate the position that conventional legal distinctions have no basis in nature should give us pause and make us wonder if this view can be identified as the playwright's own. However forcefully this position may be expressed in words in the play, when it is expressed in deeds, we see repeatedly that it can have horrific consequences, especially for Lear and Gloucester. The characters who scorn conventional laws as merely arbitrary distinctions turn out to behave criminally, even among themselves. Of course, the fact that an ideological position can have harmful consequences is not in itself an argument against its validity, but in a drama all ideas must be interrogated in light of the outcome of the action. And the fact is that the ideas in Edmund's soliloquy are not confirmed by the plot of *King Lear*. The play does not demonstrate the superiority of the illegitimate son Edmund over the legitimate son Edgar (McDonald 44), even in the Machiavellian terms of political efficacy that provide Edmund's standard. In the end Edgar defeats Edmund, beating him at his own game of disguise and trickery. Perhaps society's conventional preference for the legitimate son does have some basis in nature after all.[3]

To understand the relation of nature and justice in *King Lear*, we must look to the play as a whole, not just to Lear's speeches in isolation, especially when his views on the matter keep changing. Lear begins with one view of the relation of nature and justice in the first scene, and is powerfully driven to the opposite view by the middle of the play. But this is not necessarily his final understanding of nature and justice, let alone Shakespeare's. Having argued in Act 4 for pardoning all offenders against the law, in Act 5, Lear executes the soldier who killed Cordelia in what the king no doubt regards as a supreme act of justice. Having rejected all orders of rank as purely arbitrary in Act 4, in Act 5 Lear goes to his death asserting Cordelia's superiority over the lower orders of nature: "Why should a dog, a horse, a rat have life, / And thou no breath at all?" (5.3.307–8). In the end, Lear forcefully rejects the view he expresses in the middle of the play that human beings are no better than animals.

King Lear certainly calls into question and ultimately puts to rest any naïve notion that the political order can simply reflect the order of nature and not involve any arbitrary or conventional elements. But that does not mean that justice has no basis in nature whatsoever, or that one political order might not be more natural—closer in touch with nature—than another. The play shows how arbitrary justice and law can become, and yet at the same time it shows that justice and law are necessary to society and in that sense integral to its nature (Craig 149). In the absence of any notion of justice and law, society becomes bestial and self-destructive and thus no longer *human* society at all. Albany offers a frightening vision of what life would be like if the sense of human justice were not grounded in some sense of a larger order in the world:

> If that the heavens do not their visible spirits
> Send quickly down to tame these vild offenses,
> It will come,
> Humanity must perforce prey on itself,
> Like monsters of the deep.
>
> (4.2.46–50)

In Albany's view—and the action of the play seems to confirm his perception—a society without justice and law would be monstrous and, in that sense, unnatural. The issue of nature and justice in *King Lear* is more complicated than at first appears. Although not identical, nature and justice may not be complete opposites either, and a given society may involve a complex mixture of natural and conventional elements. To sort out the complicated understanding of nature and justice in *King Lear*, we need to look at the whole of the play and above all its dramatic movement, and that means its dramatic structure as a whole.

At the risk of being schematic, but in an effort to get a grasp on the whole of *King Lear* in a brief essay, I will argue that the play is structured around four attempted acts of justice, specifically four trial scenes: 1) Lear's trial of his daughters' love in Act 1, scene 1; 2) Lear's imaginary trial of Goneril and

Regan in Act 3, scene 6; 3) the impromptu trial of Gloucester for treason in Act 3, scene 7; and 4) the trial by combat between Edmund and Edgar in Act 5, scene 3.[4] The play begins and ends with trial scenes, and has two trial scenes roughly at its center. Of course the meaning of "trial" varies from scene to scene but that may be just the point. Each of these "trials" captures some but not all of the aspects of the nature of justice, and hence a fuller grasp of Shakespeare's understanding of the phenomenon can be gained only by thinking through all four cases, as well as the movement from one to the other. The scenes are paired and contrasted in ways that illuminate the interplay between nature and justice within the borders of society and beyond.

King Lear is framed by two grand public scenes, filled with rituals and ceremonies that call attention to the conventional aspects of political justice as customarily practiced. The first scene takes place indoors at a peaceful court; the last takes place outdoors on or near a battlefield immediately following a war. Peace and war: these are the poles between which politics moves and where justice is normally exercised. The first scene deals with justice in the attempt to perpetuate a regime; the last with justice in the attempt to found or re-found a regime. In Act 1, scene 1, Lear tries to go beyond the limits of conventional justice, while still maintaining the cover of ritual and ceremony to implement his plan. The unintended result is to set in motion the dissolution of the conventional regime, and to lead Lear and other characters out into the world of nature, where justice becomes at once more philosophic and more barbaric, if we are to judge by the juxtaposition of the two trial scenes in Act 3. The last scene of the play represents an attempt to re-impose a conventional order, once the dangers of a "return to nature" have become evident. The overall movement of *King Lear* is from a conventional world to a more natural world and then back again to the conventional world, although that world has been profoundly altered by the intervening convulsions.

Act 1, scene 1 of *King Lear* dramatizes a royal court in all its ceremonial and ritualistic grandeur (Moseley 69; Garber 692). With years of practice under his belt, Lear masterfully plays the role of king, and until Cordelia disrupts the proceedings, everyone in court seems willing to play their conventional roles too—as obedient daughters, loyal subjects, ardent suitors, and so on. The power of convention is at work in this opening scene; indeed Lear is counting upon it. But despite the conventional role he adopts, Lear is actually attempting to do something quite unconventional in this scene. He has summoned his court to deal with the problem of the succession and is clearly not content to follow the customary path. Given the fact that Lear has no sons, the matter of the succession is murky, but custom would normally dictate that in the event of his death, the crown would pass to the eldest of his children, Goneril.[5] If Lear were the doddering old fool many take him to be,[6] he would simply let this result come to pass. But he evidently is smart enough to foresee problems if Goneril becomes his sole successor. To ensure "that future strife/May be prevented now" (1.1.44–45), Lear has come up with an unconventional scheme for dividing up his kingdom and managing the succession while he is still alive to supervise it. His plan apparently is to give Goneril and Regan limited portions of the realm, while reserving the largest section for his youngest daughter, Cordelia. At the same time, he will ally Cordelia with a foreign power—most likely Burgundy but perhaps France[7]—thus strengthening her position vis-à-vis her sisters and their husbands, Albany and Cornwall. In order to strengthen Cordelia even further and ensure that she can maintain her superior position, Lear plans on dwelling with her after the division of the kingdom, thus lending his prestige and authority to her rule.[8]

Lear is thus pursuing a kind of natural justice in the opening scene, even amidst the conventional trappings of the court (Jaffa 135). Rather than accepting the conventional pattern of succession, which leaves the outcome to the arbitrary principle of order of birth, Lear is taking into account the differing natures of his daughters in disposing of his kingdom (Kahn 91). But Lear evidently realizes that this kind of natural justice is not publicly defensible in the conventional world of the court, where Goneril has claims according to time-honored custom that take precedence over Cordelia's. Thus Lear decides to mix a little convention with nature in his plan, and hopes to accomplish his political purposes under the cover of a family drama. He stages a love test, in which he appeals to the conventional attachment of children to their parents as a principle. Although he has already divided up the kingdom and even had a map prepared to show the new boundaries (Muir 55), he pretends that the division will depend on something conventional, public displays of affection from his daughters. He undoubtedly is not aware of the depths of evil in Goneril and Regan, but he does know his daughters well enough to have pinned his hopes for the future on Cordelia and her love for him. He has every reason to expect that she will easily outdo her sisters by simply expressing her genuine love for him when called upon to do so in public.

The opening scene thus suggests that justice may involve a complex interplay of the natural and the conventional. Lear wishes to bring about the naturally just outcome—the outcome that takes into account the differing natures of his daughters—by securing the bulk of his kingdom for the morally superior Cordelia. But to make this outcome publicly defensible, he has to find a conventional justification for what might otherwise appear to be a violation of custom. Hence the love test, which is cleverly contrived to maneuver Goneril and Regan into publicly ratifying a division of the kingdom that is to their disadvantage and that they might have claimed is unconventional and unjust. Lear's scheme is to turn the political into the personal. Once he makes the division of the kingdom appear to turn, not on careful political calculations that even involve foreign alliances, but on his daughters' love, he thinks that he will trap Goneril and Regan. They cannot profess their unbounded love in public, and then turn around and haggle over their inheritance (Jaffa 127). Lear is relying on the public nature of the scene and thus on the weight of convention being brought to bear on his daughters. If his daughters will simply say what custom dictates in the situation, he will succeed in giving the appearance of being guided by considerations of convention when he is really being guided by considerations of nature (Jaffa 140: note 19). The naturally just outcome will be ratified by convention in a public setting. In sum, the way Lear proposes the love test is in itself unconventional, but he relies on the power of convention to make the love test work to implement his plan for the succession.

What Lear does not anticipate is that Cordelia will be put off by the conventionality of the scene he stages, and balk at speaking what she ought to say in public, precisely because the scene occurs in public. Cordelia objects to the hypocrisy of her sisters, the way they simply say what is conventionally demanded by the situation in order to gain as much of the kingdom as they can. She refuses to be put in the same class with them, and thereby confused with them in public (ironically, Lear's plan is actually based on his understanding of how she differs from her sisters). Cordelia rejects precisely the way Lear's scheme runs together nature and convention, working to confuse her genuine love for her father with her sisters' artificial expressions of a purely customary affection (Garber 656; McDonald 27). Unfortunately Cordelia's refusal to tell her father what he wants to hear triggers the worst possible response in him, leading him to confuse nature and convention further in ways that bring on his tragedy. It is here that we first see Lear's tendency to identify his own commands with the dictates of nature, as he banishes Cordelia and claims that, as king, he can overrule all blood ties and natural affection: "Here I disclaim all my paternal care, / Propinquity and property of blood" (1.1.113–14). As we have seen, Lear carefully thought through his original plan for dividing the kingdom (Kinney 112). From the opening lines of the play we know that his trusted counselors Kent and Gloucester are already familiar with the details of the plan and see nothing to object to in it; if anything, they are struck by its even-handedness (1.1.1–7; Muir 10; Jaffa 118–20; Lowenthal 75; Craig 119; Kahn 2). But now, on the spur of the moment and in anger, Lear improvises a new division of the kingdom, an ill-considered plan that will prove to be a formula for disaster and provoke the very conflicts he had hoped to avoid (Kinney 142–43). Leaving himself without allies and therefore at the mercy of Goneril and Regan, Lear relies fatally on the principle that a father's authority over his children is rooted in nature, even though he has just demonstrated that someone with political power can abrogate any familial relation. Lear pays dearly for failing to understand the conventional component of a father's authority—the fact that in a family crisis, the law must support paternal power or it will inevitably yield to superior force.

Lear's hastily devised second plan for dividing the kingdom leads to a catastrophic breakdown of political order, culminating in civil war and foreign invasion. The chaos that ensues produces many disastrous consequences—Lear is forced out unprotected into the storm and goes mad, while Gloucester is blinded. But the loss of political order results in a gain in political wisdom. Moral distinctions among the characters that were initially obscured come to light. Indeed Lear regards this moment as a time for moral clarification:

> Let the great gods
> That keep this dreadful pudder o'er our heads,
> Find out their enemies now.
>
> (3.2.49–51)

With the conventional restraints on ambition and desire removed, the evil characters—Goneril, Regan, Cornwall, Edmund—begin to show their true colors after long concealing them, while the good characters—Cordelia, Kent, the Fool—are able to demonstrate what true loyalty and love can be. Above all, Lear learns to distinguish what he initially confused. The difference between his power as a king and his power as a father becomes painfully evident once he finds that children with political authority get to turn the tables and rule their parents. Moreover, as we have seen, he comes to recognize how arbitrary and conventional kingly authority can be. As Lear and other characters are thrust out of the comfortable and conventional world of the court, they move into closer contact with the harsh world of physical nature and that proves to be an enlightening experience for them. They learn to criticize convention in the name of nature.

The central scenes of *King Lear* move as far away as possible from the world of conventional political justice, and present in quick succession two contrasting attempts at practicing a more natural kind of justice. As opposed to the grand opening and closing scenes of the play, scenes 6 and 7 of Act 3 are intensely private. The movement from convention to nature in *King Lear* is related to a movement from public to private. At the very center of the play, Lear holds a conversation with his "noble philosopher" that is so private, we as audience do not even hear it ("Let me ask you one word in private," Lear says to Poor Tom [3.4.160]). As we saw in Act 1, scene 1, the fact that a scene takes place in public brings the weight of social convention to bear on the characters. By contrast, the more private a scene is, the freer the characters are from public pressure and hence from conventional modes of thinking and behavior. The trial of Goneril and Regan virtually takes place within the privacy of Lear's mind. Although other characters on stage witness it and to some extent participate in it, its meaning and even its reality are evident only to Lear. As for the trial of Gloucester, Cornwall and Regan want as few people as possible to witness it. They make a point of even getting their partners in crime, Goneril and Edmund, out of the way.[9]

The private character of these two trials means that in both cases the niceties of conventional courtroom procedure are not observed, since the "judges" do not have to answer to any higher authority. Lear in effect tries

Goneril and Regan in absentia, denying them all customary legal rights, including the right to confront their accuser and the witnesses against them.[10] Cornwall and Regan barely allow Gloucester to defend himself. Both trials are biased because the injured parties themselves control the proceedings and are complainant, prosecutor, and judge all at once. From a formal point of view, both trials thus seem arbitrary and the verdicts arrived at are cruel and even savage. This is obvious in the way Cornwall and Regan, after a perfunctory inquisition, tear out Gloucester's eyes on the spot. But Lear's trial of Goneril and Regan is even briefer. He has passed sentence on them before the trial begins, and if he had his way at this moment, their punishment would be even crueler than Gloucester's: "To have a thousand with red burning spits / Come hizzing in upon 'em" (3.6.15–16).

For all this savagery, in both cases the trials somehow arrive at a kind of truth about the matter under investigation. Goneril and Regan have in fact mistreated Lear, and, as much as we may hesitate to admit it, Gloucester is guilty of a kind of treason. He has been dealing surreptitiously with a foreign power intent on invading Britain (Kahn 100–1). The unconventional character of these trials means that the judges get at the truth quickly, without "the law's delay" of which Hamlet famously complains (3.1.71). Cornwall and Regan display a kind of animal cunning in exposing Gloucester's conspiring against them, as they force him to admit his guilt. Their bestial behavior in blinding him points to the savage origins of justice in the animal nature of humanity, the brute craving for revenge (Heilman 148). Lear's trial of Goneril and Regan points to a higher dimension of justice (Heilman 145, 149; Moseley 72). It follows upon his encounter with Poor Tom as the "noble philosopher" and the enquiry into nature it inaugurates. In interrogating Goneril and Regan, Lear may be seeking for revenge, but he is also searching for the truth, the truth about their natures. His questioning in scene 6 is clearly linked to his questioning in scene 4: "Is there any cause in nature that make [*sic*] these hard hearts?" (3.6.77–78) and is profoundly related to his earlier enquiry: "What is the cause of thunder?" (Heilman 129; McDonald 119).

If the tyrants Cornwall and Regan exercise a kind of low justice in scene 7, Lear gives a glimpse of a higher kind of justice in scene 6, a justice rooted in a philosophic enquiry into the truth about nature. Both trial scenes in Act 3 are extreme cases of justice, and together they define the upper and lower limits of the phenomenon. We move between a kind of higher, philosophic justice and the low animal justice of tyrants, the law of the jungle. As we witness philosophers and tyrants at work—two classes of human beings beyond the pale of conventional society—the trial scenes of Act 3 seem to take us from the world of convention to the world of nature and thus to provide an image of natural justice. But that image is not as benign as we might have hoped. In offering forms of natural justice that are lower as well as higher than ordinary or conventional justice, Act 3 cautions us against simply embracing nature as an alternative to convention.

Moreover, even in Act 3, separating nature completely from convention proves impossible. Even the savage Cornwall and Regan do not descend completely to the level of beasts, but feel that they have to observe some formalities and give the appearance of acting justly in conventional terms (Moseley 72–73; McDonald 131). Cornwall shows that he is aware of the pressure of public opinion in the very act of scorning it:

> Though well we may not pass upon his life
> Without the form of justice, yet our power
> Shall do a court'sy to our wrath, which men
> May blame, but not control.
>
> (3.7.24–27)

Although Cornwall just wants to kill Gloucester as quickly as possible, he still feels he must pay lip service to "the form of justice." Lear too observes some formalities. Whereas he earlier celebrates Poor Tom's nakedness, he now feels that he has to cloak him in the conventional robes of the judicial profession (3.6.36). He dilutes the pure philosophic constitution of his courtroom—the wise foolishness of Poor Tom and the Fool—by adding the conventional Kent to the bench (Kahn 188: note 7). Thus even the examples of natural justice Shakespeare offers have some of the trappings of a conventional courtroom. In Act 3, Shakespeare calls our attention to the defects of conventional justice, but he also makes us aware of its virtues. We may admire the ability of people to get at the truth swiftly and directly when they disregard all conventional judicial procedures, but we can also see that this kind of unconventional and seemingly natural justice is barely distinguishable from tyranny—the height of arbitrary power and hence of injustice as customarily understood.[11]

Thus for all the criticism of convention in *King Lear*, one cannot reduce the play to some kind of primitivist message of "back to nature." Shakespeare is not Rousseau. In the center of the play, we get a glimpse of truths about human nature that are ordinarily obscured in the settled circumstances of a conventional community. But, however uplifting this glimpse may be, at times it also involves looking into an abyss, and we become aware of how dangerous it is to remove all conventional restraints on human passions. The heights reached at the center of the play are simultaneously depths. In Act 3, *King Lear* takes us probably as far as possible in drama into the state of nature, but that realm turns out to be strangely bifurcated. From one perspective it seems primitive, the lower limit of humanity, a world of pitiful beggars in rags and tyrants acting like beasts to their fellow human beings. But from another perspective, the state of nature appears to be hypercivilized, the upper limit of humanity, a world of noble philosophers, decked out in Persian finery (3.6.80–81). Given the way Act 3 moves between the lowest and the highest in human nature, Aristotle's *Politics* provides a formula for the center of *King Lear* and its ambivalent portrait of the dissolution of the political community: "A man without a city is either a beast or a god."[12]

Lear obviously learns a great deal from his mad encounter with his philosopher, Poor Tom, but it is a profoundly disorienting experience, and the pressure of events prevents him from ever fully digesting or integrating what he discovers about humanity on the heath. Thus, for all his isolated insights, the Lear of Acts 3 and 4 in varying ways recapitulates his errors in the earlier acts. Taking appearances for reality in Act 1, scene 1, Lear momentarily fails to appreciate what distinguishes Cordelia from her sisters. But he overreacts to his mistake and goes to the opposite extreme in Act 4, scene 6. In the grip of his bitter disillusionment with conventional appearances, Lear generalizes from a few powerful examples to conclude that all women are deceitful animals:

> Down from the waist they are Centaurs,
> Though women all above;
> But to the girdle do the gods inherit,
> Beneath is all the fiends'.
>
> (4.6.124–27)

In this pronouncement about all women, Lear once again fails to take Cordelia's virtue into account. Having once been blind to the savagery in his other daughters, Lear now just as falsely takes it as the norm of womankind.

Lear's insight into the animal nature of humanity thus proves to be ultimately as misleading as his uncritical acceptance of conventional appearances at the beginning of the play. To be sure, he is reunited with Cordelia in Act 4, scene 7, and he learns to appreciate her virtue once again. But he never finds a way to integrate his rediscovery of her moral superiority into his total image of humanity. Having been baffled by the hard hearts of Goneril and Regan, Lear is equally unable to give an account of nature that would explain the transcendent goodness of Cordelia's heart (Craig 180; Nuttall 309). Despite his fitful insights into human nature, Lear cannot come up with a comprehensive understanding that would embrace the extremes of humanity and inhumanity he encounters in the central acts. That is perhaps the deepest reason why his wisdom can only take the form of madness, and why he alternates in scenes 6 and 7 of Act 4 between images of immoral baseness and moral elevation (Heilman 128–29, 214).

As the literal storm on the heath and the metaphorical storm in Lear's mind suggest, nature appears in *King Lear* as a dangerous and disorienting force, a threat to both the safety of the body and the composure of the soul. For all the gains that result from the journey from the world of convention to the world of nature in *King Lear*, the characters find that they must return to the political community by the end of the play (Hunter 44–45). As Lear reaches the heart of the natural world on the heath in Act 3, scene 4, he offers the naked beggar Poor Tom as an emblem of humanity in the state of nature: "Thou art the thing itself: unaccommodated man is no more but such a poor, bare fork'd animal as thou art" (3.4.106–8). But the Fool tries to stop Lear from taking off all his garments in imitation of Tom, having previously noted that even a natural man in his basest state retains a scrap of conventional clothing: "he reserv'd a blanket, else we had been all sham'd" (3.4.65–66). And from this point—at once the summit and the nadir of the pursuit of nature in the play—its movement begins to reverse in the direction of the conventional world. In his next scene, scene 6, Lear enters a hovel, the barest form of human shelter, but still a step away from the barren heath, a step that eventually leads him back to the political world in Act 5. By Act 4, scene 7, Lear's attendants have "put fresh garments on him" (4.7.21). In terms of the significant pattern of clothing imagery in the play (Heilman 67–87; Craig 182–87), this moment carries a great deal of weight, counterpointing Lear's earlier attempt to strip himself of all customary trappings and indicating his return to the world of convention. But *King Lear* would be the deeply nihilistic work some critics claim it is,[13] if after all the torment the characters have gone through, they found themselves simply back where they started. Although the plot returns them to the world of convention in Act 5, it is a world that has been altered, for better and for worse, by all their encounters with the natural world in Acts 3 and 4.

The British regime must be refounded at the end of the play and to some extent reconstituted. Whether it has been fundamentally changed is questionable[14]—after all, it is still a monarchy—and whether it can incorporate the sort of lessons Lear learned on the heath is even more doubtful. But one change for the better is clear: by the end of the play, Goneril, Regan, Cornwall, and Edmund are all dead. If nothing else, the regime has been purged of its most evil elements, clearing the way for the surviving good characters to prevail. The restoration of the conventional world is predicated on the fact that the nature of the evil characters finally became manifest in the political chaos Lear inadvertently unleashed. That is the principal political benefit of the process of clarification that is integral to the movement toward nature in the middle of the play.

One must not, however, expect that the new regime founded in Act 5 will be able to maintain forever the clarity about the nature of its subjects that emerged at the end of Lear's reign. The same forces that led in Lear's regime to the obscuring of the truth about human nature and the differences among human beings will be at work in any regime that succeeds it. Lear's errors did not result simply from his personal mistakes, but in a profounder sense were the consequence of the inherent limitations of his position as a powerful ruler (Jaffa 131–32; Kahn 10, 48; Craig 132; Cantor 1996a: 216–20). Whoever succeeds him will still face the problem of being surrounded by hypocrites and flatterers, as happens to all rulers. Thus, any optimism about the future of the British regime at the end of *King Lear* must be guarded. The play ends with an overwhelming sense of loss and diminished expectations (Kernan 101). Edgar's final words (5.3.324–27) virtually guarantee that the new regime cannot encompass the depth of Lear's experience (Heilman 63, 332: note 6).[15]

Still, some hope can be found in the bare fact that the British regime has been refounded and perhaps to some extent revitalized. At the beginning of the play, Lear is searching for a way to perpetuate his regime while avoiding a convulsion. The course of the action suggests that the regime cannot revitalize itself without undergoing some form of catastrophe, some kind of tragic conflict. Lear and his regime have become complacent by the time the play begins (Heilman 279–80). In his secure state, he has among other things lost sight of a fundamental fact of political life, the need for military force to maintain his rights as king. Otherwise he would not recklessly allow his daughters to gain the military advantage over him. Perhaps this is what happens to any regime as it grows old and falls into the grip of habit—it gets out of touch with political reality and its own roots. In this limited but significant sense, the regime founded in Act 5 is more in touch with nature than the one we see in Act 1. At least its foundation in military power is now clear. The breakdown of Lear's regime unleashes violent forces in his kingdom of which he, and perhaps everyone else, was unaware. The release of this energy turns out to be highly dangerous, and threatens to tear the kingdom apart. These passions must once again be contained if political order is to be restored—partly as a result of the passions having played themselves out in an orgy of self-destruction that consumes Goneril, Regan, Cornwall, and Edmund (Lowenthal 96). The self-destructive character of evil reflects a kind of rough justice in the world of *King Lear*. In the way that evil actions eventually prove to have disastrous consequences for the evil-doers, the natural order is not completely indifferent to moral principles (Bradley 242–43). *King Lear* concludes with a very public act of justice in which legitimacy triumphs over illegitimacy. Even Edmund, who originally laughs at all notions of moral fitness in the world, sees a kind of moral logic to his defeat, a sense of a natural cycle: "The wheel is come full circle, I am here" (5.3.175; Hunter 306).

Accordingly, Act 5 builds up to the last of the trial scenes in *King Lear*, which in the overarching pattern of the play balances the trial scene in Act 1. The grandly public character of Act 5, scene 3 recalls the staging of Act 1, scene 1, and indeed all the characters from the first scene, with the exception of Gloucester, France, and Burgundy, reassemble for the final scene (Hockey 394; Kinney 105). Instead of a love trial, however, we now witness a trial by combat, and this ceremonial procedure is more successful than the earlier one (McDonald 191). The feudal pomp of the ritual combat between Edmund and Edgar reflects the need to return to the ordered world of civilization and its conventions. Although Edmund and Edgar must settle their differences by the sword, they must not fight savagely like rats in a hole. Rather, they fight by the book, like knights in shining armor, obeying the rules of chivalry and treating each other with courtesy. The recourse to ritual combat reminds us of the violence that ultimately lies at the basis of all political life, but the fact that the violence is carefully ritualized provides a contrast to the naked cruelty we witness in the middle of the play. We have come a long way from the brutal blinding of Gloucester in Act 3. Edgar's desire to return to the conventional order may explain his insistence on proclaiming in this scene: "The gods are just" (5.3.171) in what may seem like a tasteless reference to his father's blinding. Many critics have been put off by what strikes them as Edgar's pious moralizing in this scene (Bradley 244). In light of all the horrors Edgar has witnessed in the course of the play, this is an odd conclusion for him to draw. Nevertheless, it seems to be part of the convention–nature–convention pattern of *King Lear*. The characters begin the play with faith in the justice of the gods, come to question that faith in the middle, and finally struggle back to some form of belief at the end (Kahn 112).

The civilized and courtly behavior of the characters in the first and last trial scenes of *King Lear* contrasts favorably with the uncourteous and unceremonious behavior in the two trial scenes in Act 3. But this ceremoniousness has a drawback: in both Act 1 and Act 5 convention threatens to obscure nature. We have seen how this happens in the opening scene, as Lear's carefully planned scheme appears like the arbitrary whim of a wilful monarch and ends up obscuring the natural differences among his daughters. The trial by combat in Act 5 also appears to be arbitrary as a principle of justice. As it happens, the outcome of the combat between Edmund and Edgar corresponds to our sense of what is just by nature. But Edmund might just as well have been the victor; based on what we have seen of the two up to this point, we might in fact have expected Edmund to win the fight. As a principle of justice, trial by combat seems to be a pure convention. There is no natural correlation between strength of arms and the justice of someone's cause, unless one takes a strictly providential view of human life, and the plot of *King Lear* would seem to contradict such a view (Nuttall 308). The only thing one can say on behalf of trial by combat as a principle of justice is that it is a way of settling disputes that minimizes bloodshed. As long as everyone agrees by convention to accept the outcome of the combat as just, this form of trial can produce communal peace (which is no doubt the reason why the custom developed as it did). This is a good example of how conventions work, even when they seem to have little or no basis in nature. What matters is not the specific outcome, but the fact that everybody can agree to abide by it. If one thinks of societies as peaceful by nature, then a convention that works to produce peace can in some sense be thought of as natural to a human community. *King Lear* begins and ends in the world of politics and conventional forms of justice, and we see why political actors feel constrained to rely on convention when they seek peace and justice. At the same time, however, we should not forget the limits of convention when trying to achieve true, full, and perfect justice, justice by nature (Craig 147).

The final attempt to bring nature and convention together in *King Lear* is encapsulated in Edgar's coming to power by force of arms in Act 5, as he does a better job than Lear did of accomplishing his purposes under the cover of ceremony. The trajectory of Edgar's career in the play epitomizes its back-and-forth movement between nature and convention.[16] Edgar begins the play as a conventional and callow youth, easily duped by his half-brother and therefore an unpromising candidate for any position of authority. At the beginning of the play, he evidently does not have the nature of a king. Like Lear, Edgar must be thrust out of the comfort of his conventional role and into the world of nature in order for him to gain insight into himself and humanity. Because of the kaleidoscopic variety of roles the outlawed Edgar plays (Danby 190–91; Craig 189–90), by the end of *King Lear* he has been exposed in one way or another to the whole spectrum of humanity, from the king at the top to the basest beggar at the bottom, from the philosopher as the highest representative of human wisdom to the lunatic as the emblem of human folly. Armed with this better understanding of human nature in all its heights and depths, Edgar is prepared by Act 5 to resume his place in conventional society, now elevated to a position of leadership, first as the Earl of Gloucester, and then evidently as the new king. Clearly Edgar has grown in stature in the course of the play, and at the end he seems to incorporate some elements of a kingly nature (McDonald 8). Albany says to him in the last scene: "Methought thy very gait did prophesy / A royal nobleness" (5.3.176–77). Edgar's masquerading throughout the play resembles Prince Hal's strategy in the *Henry IV* plays. Like Hal, Edgar has the opportunity to survey and sample the wide range of human beings he will come to rule. Moreover, just as Hal absorbs the qualities of his rival Hotspur by defeating him in combat, Edgar may lay claim to having assimilated from his defeated brother the natural energy in which Edmund claims bastards excel. Edgar concludes the play by contrasting youth with age, ostensibly to the detriment of youth, but his own youthfulness is one of the few hopeful signs at the end of this bleak play, promising some form of renewal in the next regime and the next generation.

At the end of *King Lear* nature and convention are not wholly reconciled, but for the moment they have at least been brought somewhat closer together. The play of course raises serious doubts about the conventional political order, but it does not simply reject it as unnatural as many readings of the play imply. Rather, employing nature as a standard for judging convention, Shakespeare searches for ways in which convention could be brought more in line with nature. We see that conventions can get in the way of human nature and obscure it, but we also see that human beings cannot do without conventions completely. In political life, nature can never entirely displace convention, because it is in the nature of the human community to require conventions. Animals like bees and ants form communities naturally, that is, by instinct and without forethought. Human beings are different. Although it may be in their nature to form communities in the Aristotelian sense that they are unable to fulfill their potential in isolation, the human community requires some form of founding and the specific shape it takes will vary over time and space, involving different sets of conventions in different societies.

Human beings are those peculiar creatures whose nature is to produce conventions; indeed they need to establish conventions in order to fulfill their natures.[17]

In a later play, *The Winter's Tale*, Shakespeare develops a similar view of a parallel case, the seemingly sharp opposition between nature and art. In a rustic debate over the practice of grafting, the characters become concerned that the art of horticulture is interfering with nature. But Polixenes assures Perdita that it is in the nature of human beings to improve upon physical nature with their art, and therefore art is natural to humanity:

> Yet Nature is made better by no mean
> But Nature makes that mean; so over that art,
> Which you say adds to Nature, is an art,
> That Nature makes. You see, sweet maid, we marry
> A gentler scion to the wildest stock,
> And make conceive a bark of baser kind
> By bud of nobler race. This is an art
> Which does mend Nature, change it rather; but
> The art itself is Nature.
>
> (4.4.89–97)

Shakespeare's vision of a human art that is an extension of the power of nature, not its opposite, is a specific case of how he thought that nature and convention can be brought together (Craig 184).

Thus, Lear's most insightful observations on the subject of nature and convention may come, not in his madness, but in an earlier moment of sanity and clarity in Act 2. In one of the characteristically reductive movements in the play, Goneril and Regan compete to bid down the number of knights in Lear's train. Typically, they view the matter in light of the concept of mere necessity, and try to reduce Lear to the barest essentials, culminating in Regan's mean-spirited evaluation of Lear's requirements for followers: "What need one?" (2.4.263). Lear's answer, although uttered in great passion, manifests a profound and complex understanding of human nature:

> O, reason not the need! our basest beggars
> Are in the poorest thing superfluous.
> Allow not nature more than nature needs,
> Man's life is cheap as beast's. Thou art a lady;
> If only to go warm were gorgeous,
> Why, nature needs not what thou gorgeous wears't,
> Which scarcely keeps thee warm. But for true need—
> You heavens, give me that patience, patience I need!
>
> (2.4.264–71)

In rejecting the way Goneril and Regan calculate in terms of mere necessity and therefore the lowest common denominator of human nature, Lear exposes in advance the limitations of his own later vision of the beggar Poor Tom as the "thing itself," the emblem of "unaccommodated man" and the state of nature. In this speech, by contrast, Lear refuses to take his bearings on human nature from the example of the "basest beggars." He realizes that to define human beings in terms of the barest minimum that they need to live will result in an impoverished image of humanity. It will efface the line between the human and the animal, leaving us with the disillusioning and disheartening proposition: "Man's life is cheap as beast's."

Although in Act 3, scene 4 Lear justifiably criticizes the "superflux" with which powerful nobles indulge themselves at the expense of the poor, here he gives an equally eloquent defense of how essential the "superfluous" element in human life is to giving us a sense of our distinctive dignity. As Lear understands, only because human beings constantly strive to rise above the level of bare necessity are they truly human. Here Lear defends the human custom of clothing, viewing it as integral to human nature. Later, in Act 3, scene 4, Lear thinks differently—there he believes that one can get at human nature only by stripping off one's clothing and accordingly he tries to divest himself of his own garments. But Lear is in fact wrong about Poor Tom in Act 3. Since Edgar is masquerading as Poor Tom, his nakedness is actually a form of disguise, concealing, rather than, as Lear believes, revealing, his true nature. Poor Tom is *not* the thing itself—he is a sophisticated courtier only pretending to be the basest beggar (McDonald 116). In answer to Lear's anguished question about Poor Tom: "Is man no more than this?" (3.4.102–3), Shakespeare seems to reassure us: "Yes, he *is*."

Responding to Goneril and Regan in Act 2, Lear points out the paradoxical character of human behavior. If human beings actually behaved according to a strict standard of necessity, they would choose their clothing solely on the basis of utility, wearing simpler garments that would fulfill better the basic function of shielding the human body from the hostile elements. But clothing illustrates the fact that human beings are not content with merely living; they want to live *well*, to rise above the level of mere physical necessity (Kahn 65–66). As the custom of clothing has developed, it does not merely shield the body, but adorns it, allowing humans to make something beautiful of their bodies and, therefore, higher than that which physical nature provides. In fact, as Lear insists, in choosing their clothing, humans often disregard its elemental function, sacrificing utility to beauty (Craig 183–84).

Thus, the universal human custom of clothing, which seems to grow out of a physical necessity, actually points to the characteristically human urge to transcend the level of the mere body. From one point of view, the human impulse to luxury seems to reflect the injustice of the human condition, the unequal distribution of goods that Lear condemns in Act 3. But from another point of view, Lear shows that the desire for luxury is connected to the higher strivings of humanity, and is in that sense integral to human nature. What appears to be "superfluous" in human life may turn out to be the one thing needful, something that makes us feel above the level of mere animals and thus true to our distinctive nature. This complicated speech has of course a dramatic purpose. Lear is arguing that his claim to his retinue is just by nature, that his train of knights is not essential to his physical needs but it is to his dignity as a human being and a king, and thus reflects a higher need. That is why Lear concludes this speech by redefining need as involving the spiritual rather than the physical nature of humanity. He is trying to gain justice for himself, a justice based on considerations of nature, but a concept of nature higher than the one offered by Goneril and Regan. Indeed, at the end of Act 2, Lear skillfully navigates between the two conceptions of human nature that run throughout the play, one taking its bearings from the human body and its animal origins, the other from the human soul with its striving toward spiritual perfection (Heilman 115–16, 178; Danby 15–53). In the changes Lear rings on the word *nature* in this speech, he comes closest to arriving at an integrated image of the human condition in all its heights and depths. At the end of this speech, he hears the first rumblings of thunder, the beginning of the storm that will soon cost him his sanity. Lear never regains the balanced view of human nature he achieves at the end of Act 2. But in shaping his tragedy, Shakespeare presents the storm as only one moment in the life of Lear, a painful but still only temporary disruption of the natural order.[18] Thus Shakespeare's play as a whole offers what Lear can glimpse only partially and fitfully—a lasting image of the duality of the human condition and its paradoxical mixture of nature and convention.

Notes

1 All quotations from Shakespeare are taken from Evans, *The Riverside Shakespeare*, with act, scene, and line citations incorporated into the text. For an explanation of why this essay does not use the Oxford edition, see note 4, below.

2 For example, Harold Bloom's discussion of the play builds up to and ends with Lear's anti-convention speeches in Act 4, scene 6, and he concludes: "Lear's prophecy fuses reason, nature, and society into one great negative image, the inauthentic authority of this great stage of fools" (Bloom 515). Similarly, Heilman views Act 4, scene 6 as "the climax of the Gloucester plot and the climax of the Lear plot" (197) and he says that this is where "Lear comes to his most penetrating vision"; this scene is "his most important in the play" (198). Kahn also offers this scene as the "thematic climax" of the play (126); argues that Lear here achieves "complete vision" (134); and claims that "the play reaches its moment of greatest insight in Lear's transcendence of the political" (162). I will argue that the great tragic insight of *King Lear* is that human beings cannot ever completely transcend the political because they cannot do without the conventions politics underwrites.

3 For a subtle critique of Edmund's speech in favor of bastards, and a thoroughgoing justification of the conventional principle of legitimacy, see Craig 135–50.

4 Several critics have argued for a pattern of trial scenes in *King Lear*, beginning as far as I can tell with Hockey in 1959. Kahn builds a whole book around the trial scenes in *King Lear*; see especially xvii and 7. Moseley (50–51) speaks of five trial scenes in the play; to my list he adds "II.ii, where Cornwall, seconded by Regan,

'judges' and punishes Kent" (66). Warren suggests one more candidate for a trial scene, 4.6, another scene in which Lear conducts an imaginary judicial proceeding, this time issuing in clemency, not punishment: "I pardon that man's life" (4.6.109). By my count, Hockey discusses nine "trial" scenes in the play. To streamline my discussion, I am restricting myself to what I regard as the four principal trials scenes in terms of which *King Lear* is structured; I do not think my argument would be materially altered if I added other scenes to this pattern. As for Lear's imaginary trial of Goneril and Regan, I am aware that this passage is omitted from the Folio text of the play. Given my understanding of the play's structure, this omission convinces me that the Folio text does not represent Shakespeare's own revision of *King Lear*, but is the result of some adventitious factor, such as censorship or theatrical cutting by another hand or hands. I argue this point and give my view of the textual problems concerning *King Lear* in Cantor 1996c, especially 451–52. I develop my interpretation of *King Lear* further in Cantor 1996a and 1996b.

5 On the complicated question of how the law of primogeniture might operate in the case of a king with three daughters and no sons, see Craig 343 (note 36), Kinney 140, and McDonald 212.

6 For a classic statement of this view, see Goethe's evaluation: "in this scene Lear seems so absurd that we are not able, in what follows, to ascribe to his daughters the entire guilt. We are sorry for the old man, but we do not feel real pity for him" (Goethe 585). See also Kott 130: "Lear is ridiculous, naïve and stupid," and Nuttall 304, who speaks of "the uncritical simplicity of [Lear's] own mind."

7 Lear offers Cordelia to Burgundy first, and the Duke refers to the concrete terms of a dowry proposal Lear has already made to him: "Royal King/Give but that portion which yourself propos'd" (1.1.242–42; Craig 120). There is one other scene in Shakespeare in which the Duke of Burgundy and the King of France appear together with the King of Britain—Act 5, scene 2 of *Henry V* (a scene that also results in a political marriage). As this scene suggests, the Duke of Burgundy is well positioned to mediate and make peace between France and Britain. Today we may associate Burgundy largely with fine wine, but in Shakespeare's day the links between the House of Burgundy and the House of Habsburg (and hence the Holy Roman Empire) made Burgundy a significant factor in the power struggles of Europe. On the role of Burgundy in *King Lear* and the connection to *Henry V*, see McDonald 215–17. See also Jaffa 124–26, 139–40 (notes 16, 17, 18), and Hopkins 115–16.

8 The first thoroughgoing attempt to explicate Lear's original political plan is Jaffa 121–28; see also Lowenthal 74–77; Craig 120–24; Davis 6–8; and Kinney 142.

9 Their one mistake is to allow their servants to be present at the trial—one of the servants is so appalled by what he witnesses that he kills Cornwall (Kahn 103–4).

10 To oversimplify a typically complicated legal matter: the right to confront witnesses is rooted in the British common law tradition and is to some extent codified in clause 38 of Magna Carta. Of course the fact that this right could be traced back to the medieval era does not mean that it was always honored in British courts; some of the royal courts in Shakespeare's day, such as the Star Chamber, excluded oral testimony by witnesses entirely. The British legal tradition put a special emphasis on the need to produce witnesses in treason trials. This became the central procedural issue in the notoriously unfair trial of Sir Walter Raleigh for treason in 1603. Raleigh cited statute law and even biblical scripture in support of his right to confront the witnesses being used against him on the basis of written evidence alone. The controversy surrounding the Raleigh trial suggests that legal procedural issues, especially the right to confront witnesses, were very much on people's minds at the time Shakespeare wrote *King Lear*. On the Raleigh trial, see Greenblatt 1–2, 114–21. For the closest we have to a transcript of the trial, see

Jardine, especially what Raleigh says on 418: "But, my Lords, I claim to have my accuser brought here face to face to speak; and though I know not to make my best defence by law, yet since I was prisoner, I have learned that by the law and statutes of this realm in case of treason, a man ought to be convicted by the testimony of two witnesses if they be living." For clarifying these complex legal issues for me, I am indebted to Professor John Mansfield of Harvard Law School.

11 The legal irregularities in the two trials in Act 3 mirror the abuses of the royal courts in the Stuart era, especially those in the infamous Star Chamber. These abuses led to the eventual establishment of the right to confront witnesses throughout British courts by the end of the seventeenth century (Jardine 513–14). In view of the way royal courts like the Star Chamber became a byword for tyrannical injustice, it is ironic that they were originally regarded as providing a more efficient and equitable justice than was available in other courts in Britain. The virtues and defects of the trials in Act 3 of *King Lear* seem to reflect the mixed character of royal justice in Shakespeare's day.

12 See *Politics*, Book 1, 1253a in the standard Bekker numeration. Here is a fuller and more accurate translation of the Greek: "One who is incapable of participating or who is in need of nothing through being self-sufficient is no part of a city, and so is either a beast or a god" (Aristotle 37).

13 The classic reading of the play as nihilistic is Kott's essay "King Lear or Endgame," which interprets Shakespeare in light of Samuel Beckett (Kott 127–68). See also Harold Bloom, who speaks of "the ultimate nihilism of the play" (492) and its "profound nihilism" (493). See also Nuttall, 307, 312.

14 For an argument for a fundamental change in regime by the end of the play, see McDonald 19.

15 These words are given to Edgar in the Folio, but to Albany in the Quarto; whoever speaks them, they provide a bleak ending to the play.

16 For a good summary of Edgar's role in the play, see Muir 25–27 and Carroll 426–41.

17 Cf. Craig 170: "a valid idea of Nature, adequate for encompassing *human* nature, similarly must encompass conventions. Much about the particularities of how these or those people live is due to 'mere convention,' but this human capacity to frame and live in accordance with various conventions is not itself conventional: it is natural." See also Lowenthal 98 and Kahn 66: "It is man's—or woman's—nature to live unnaturally in a world of conventions."

18 For a contrary view, see Harold Bloom: "The play is a storm, with no subsequent clearing" (493). In contrast to Bloom, Heilman argues: "Yet the tragedy as a whole affirms the pre-eminence of order. There cannot be a breach in nature unless there is a nature" (91) and: "yet the storm is regarded regularly as a convulsion of nature—a disorder which interferes with but does not destroy an essential order which still *is*. There is chaos in the world; but tragedy sees chaos in perspective; it measures chaos by order" (116; see also 286–87 and Lowenthal 92, 103).

Works cited

Aristotle. *The Politics*. Trans. Carnes Lord. Chicago: University of Chicago Press, 1984.

Bloom, Harold. *Shakespeare: The Invention of the Human*. New York: Riverhead, 1998.

Bradley, A.C. *Shakespearean Tragedy*, 1904; rpt. New York: Meridian, 1955.

Cantor, Paul A. "Nature and Convention in *King Lear*." *Poets, Princes, and Private Citizens: Literary Alternatives to Postmodern Politics*. Eds. Joseph M. Knippenberg and Peter Augustine Lawler. Lanham, MD: Rowman and Littlefield, 1996a: 213–33.

—— "*King Lear*: The Tragic Disjunction of Wisdom and Power." *Shakespeare's Political Pageant: Essays in Literature and Politics*. Eds. Joseph Alulis and Vickie Sullivan. Lanham, MD: Rowman and Littlefield, 1996b: 189–207.

—— "On Sitting Down to Read *King Lears* Once Again: The Textual Deconstruction of Shakespeare." *The Flight from Science and Reason*. Eds. Paul R. Gross, Norman Levitt, and Martin W. Lewis. New York: New York Academy of Sciences, 1996c: 445–58.

Carroll, William C. " 'The Base Shall Top Th'Legitimate': The Bedlam Beggar and the Role of Edgar in *King Lear*." *Shakespeare Quarterly* 38 (1987): 426–41.

Craig, Leon. *Of Philosophers and Kings: Political Philosophy in Shakespeare's Macbeth and King Lear*. Toronto: University of Toronto Press, 2001.

Danby, John F. *Shakespeare's Doctrine of Nature: A Study of King Lear*. London: Faber and Faber, 1948.

Davis, Arthur G. *The Royalty of Lear*. New York: St. John's University Press, 1974.

Evans, G. Blakemore (ed.). *The Riverside Shakespeare*. Boston: Houghton Mifflin, 1974.

Garber, Marjorie. *Shakespeare After All*. New York: Pantheon, 2004.

Goethe, Johann Wolfgang von. "Shakespeare Ad Infinitum." Trans. Randolph Bourne. *The Permanent Goethe*. Ed. Thomas Mann. New York: Dial, 1953: 575–86.

Greenblatt, Stephen J. *Sir Walter Raleigh: The Renaissance Man and His Roles*. New Haven, CT: Yale University Press, 1973.

Heilman, Robert Bechtold. *This Great Stage: Image and Structure in King Lear*. Seattle: University of Washington Press, 1963.

Hockey, Dorothy C. "The Trial Pattern in *King Lear*." *Shakespeare Quarterly* 10 (1959): 389–95.

Hopkins, Lisa. *Shakespeare on the Edge: Border-crossing in the Tragedies and the Henriad*. Hampshire, UK: Ashgate, 2005.

Hunter, G.K. "Introduction." *King Lear*. Harmondsworth, UK: Penguin, 1972: 7–55.

Jaffa, Harry V. "The Limits of Politics: *King Lear*, Act I, Scene i." *Shakespeare's Politics*. Ed. Allan Bloom. New York: Basic, 1964: 113–45.

Jardine, David, (ed.). "The Trial of Sir Walter Raleigh." *Criminal Trials*. London: C. Knight, 1832. 1:389–520.

Kahn, Paul W. *Law and Love: The Trials of King Lear*. New Haven: Yale University Press, 2000.

Kernan, Alvin. *Shakespeare, the King's Playwright: Theater in the Stuart Court, 1603–1613*. New Haven: Yale University Press, 1995.

Kinney, Arthur F. *Shakespeare's Webs: Networks of Meaning in Renaissance Drama*. New York: Routledge, 2004.

Kott, Jan. *Shakespeare Our Contemporary*. Trans. Boleslaw Taborski. Garden City, NY: Doubleday, 1966.

Lowenthal, David. *Shakespeare and the Good Life: Ethics and Politics in Dramatic Form*. Lanham, MD: Rowman and Littlefield, 1997.

McDonald, Mark A. *Shakespeare's King Lear with The Tempest: The Discovery of Nature and the Recovery of Classical Natural Right*. Lanham, Maryland: University Press of America, 2004.

Moseley, Charles. "Trial and judgement: the trial scenes in *King Lear*." *Critical Essays On King Lear*. Eds. Linda Cookson and Bryan Loughrey. Harlow, Essex: Longman, 1988: 65–75.

Muir, Kenneth. *William Shakespeare: King Lear*. London: Penguin, 1986.

Nuttall, A.D. *Shakespeare the Thinker*. New Haven: Yale University Press, 2007.
Warren, Roger. "The Folio Omission of the Mock Trial: Motives and Consequences." *The Division of the Kingdoms: Shakespeare's Two Versions of "King Lear."* Eds. Gary Taylor and Michael Warren. Oxford: Clarendon Press, 1983. 45–57.

8 Hope and despair in *King Lear*

The gospel and the crisis of natural law

R. V. Young

King Lear has long been regarded as one of Shakespeare's greatest plays and is not infrequently judged to be perhaps the finest specimen of the Western dramatic tradition. Nevertheless, it has also been viewed as problematic both morally and aesthetically. The most powerful example of the discomfort caused by the play among audiences and critics is the revision by Nahum Tate, which has Cordelia surviving and marrying Edgar. This version was the basis of every theatrical production of *King Lear* from 1681 until 1838, and it was endorsed by no less a figure than Dr. Johnson:

> In the present case the public has decided. Cordelia, from the time of Tate, has always retired with victory and felicity. And, if my sensations could add anything to the general suffrage, I might relate, I was many years ago so shocked by Cordelia's death that I know not whether I ever endured to read again the last scenes of the play till I undertook to revise them as an editor.
>
> (Johnson 98)

While a twenty-first-century revival of Tate's rewriting of Shakespeare is improbable and would be unlikely to find favor, at least among professional scholars and critics, Johnson's demurral and the theatrical taste of more than a century and a half must not be lightly dismissed. Sharp disagreements over the import of the play's grim conclusion throughout the twentieth century and persisting even to the present are evidence of how terrible that ending seems even to the most cynical and sophisticated of readers and audiences.

Interpreters have generally sought to show either that the tragic close evinces a redemptive possibility, notwithstanding its horror, or that Tate was right, that *King Lear* in fact subverts a Christian or even Enlightenment world view and anticipates the absurd universe of existentialism or postmodern materialism. The redemptive readings, which dominated the middle of the twentieth century, often seem to assume the close of a Christian tragedy must be marked by an explicit affirmation of the human efforts of the more sympathetic characters. The relationship between Christian redemption and natural law, a theme obviously emphasized in the play, is regarded as unproblematic.

The anti-Christian readings, which have predominated over the past four decades, have concentrated on refuting this "optimistic Christian" reading. This essay is designed to show that "Christian Optimism," although promulgated by some "Christian" critics, reflects a misunderstanding of Christianity, which is not an optimistic religion; and that natural law and the meaning of "nature" is a critical theme in *King Lear* because its relation to grace was a contested concept at the turn of the seventeenth century. Regarded in this perspective, *King Lear* may be understood as a profoundly Christian vision of human reality unfolding in a decidedly non-Christian setting among pagan characters.

What might be called the *affirmative* view of the ending of *King Lear* goes back at least to some manuscript notes of Coleridge: "The affecting return of Lear to reason and the mild pathos preparing the mind for the last sad yet sweet consolation of his death" (Coleridge 188). In *A Study of Shakespeare* (1880), Swinburne countered by suggesting that the import of *King Lear* is summed up in the despair of the blinded Gloucester: " 'As flies to wanton boys are we to the gods;/They kill us for their sport'. [. . .] the words just cited," Swinburne remarks, "are not causal or episodical; they strike the keynote of the whole poem, lay the keystone of the whole arch of thought" (123).[1] A.C. Bradley's *Shakespearean Tragedy* (1904), a work that would influence everyone who approached the subject for decades to come, qualifies Swinburne's "pessimistic" reading (see 228–30) by remarking that the tragedy "presents the world as a place where heavenly good grows side by side with evil, where extreme evil cannot long endure, and where all that survives the storm is good, if not great" (271–72). Bradley even suggests that we might as justly refer to the play as "*The Redemption of King* Lear" as accept Swinburne's view (235). By the middle of the twentieth century, there were numerous accounts of *King Lear* maintaining that the final effect of the tragedy was exaltation at the spiritual transcendence of Cordelia and the redemption of her father, not despair over their suffering and death.

Robert Speaight puts the case rather forcefully in explicitly Christian terms:

> Cordelia's death must remain as a redemption, but also as a reproach. For her there can be no felicity except at her father's side in the immunity of eternal sleep. The Fool is there already, and Kent will follow shortly. Albany feels no title to authority and only Edgar remains. But in a metaphysical sense, [. . .] Edgar and Cordelia are one. They are the male and female, the active and the passive counterparts of a single redemptive process. They answer, for those who have ears, the tragic agnosticism of the play, although neither may fully understand the significance of their words and actions.
>
> (Speaight 129)

This solution sounds rather like Tate in "metaphysical" terms; Cordelia and

Edgar are, in a sense, "married" after all. But Speaight maintains that Cordelia transcends even this kind of continued life "in Edgar"; "she lives on also," he says, "in her own right. . . . She is Nature redeemed and remade; she is mercy and reconciliation; she is the pole around which all the movement of *King Lear* revolves" (129–30). Speaight thus typifies readings of *King Lear* that answer the unease of Dr. Johnson by asserting that the conclusion of the play as Shakespeare originally wrote it is sufficiently happy insofar as it suggests that the death of Cordelia is an image of saving grace, not a revelation of meaninglessness.[2]

To be sure, some of the critics who present generally affirmative readings are more cautious and offer more qualifications than Speaight. Reflecting on the dying Lear's last words, "Look on her! Look her lips, / Look there, look there!" (V.iii. 311–12),[3] Maynard Mack, for example, disparages "two ways of being sentimental" about the ending of the tragedy in *"King Lear" in Our Time*: "One is to follow those who argue that, because these last lines probably mean that Lear dies in the joy of thinking Cordelia lives, some sort of mitigation or transformation has been reached which turns defeat into total victory" (114). This, Mack maintains, "is too simple"; and he might have added that these apparently hopeful lines do not occur in the quarto version of the play. He rejects more emphatically, however, the opposite view, as presented by Judah Stampfer (10):

> The other sentimentality leads us to indulge the currently fashionable existentialist *nausée*, and to derive from the fact that Lear's joy is mistaken, or, alternatively, from the fact that in the Lear world "even those who have fully repented, done penance, and risen to the tender regard of sainthood can be hunted down, driven insane, and killed by the most agonizing extremes of passion", the conclusion that "we inhabit an imbecile universe". Perhaps we do,

is Mack's curt rejoinder "—but Shakespeare's *King Lear* provides no evidence of it that till now we lacked" (115).

Certainly Shakespeare's original audience would not have found profound suffering and pervasive evil to be proof of a godless world. In 1563 Alexander Neville prefaced a translation of Seneca's *Oedipus* with an explanation of its horrors that would serve nicely for Shakespeare's tragedy:

> As in this present tragedy, and so forth in the process of the whole history, thou mayst right well perceive, wherein thou shalt see a very express and lively image of the inconstant change of fickle fortune in the person of a Prince of passing fame and renown, midst whole floods of earthly bliss, by mere misfortune (nay rather by the deep hidden judgements of God) piteously plunged in most extreme miseries. The whole realm for his sake in strangest guise grievously plagued; besides the apparent destruction of the nobility, the general death and spoil of the communalty, the

> miserable transformed face of the city, with an infinite number of mischiefs more.
>
> (125–26)

This stern view was not confined to poetry. Only a little more than twenty years before the composition of *King Lear*, Justus Lipsius, in his popular philosophical dialogue *De Constantia*, had subjected a youthful version of himself to the admonitions of an elder Stoic sage for presuming that the sufferings of his native Low Countries in the civil war of the late sixteenth century were in anyway extraordinary or a cause to doubt divine providence.[4]

Still, when all the allowances and qualifications have been made, the closing scene of *King Lear* remains a terrible spectacle, and many commentators have maintained that it betrays an ultimate skepticism concerning a divine ordering of the universe or indeed any rational significance apart from what men and women can provisionally devise for themselves. Robert G. Hunter, who has investigated Shakespeare's encounter with Reformation theology quite thoroughly, finds in the close of *King Lear* a message "different from and rather worse even than" the "imbecile universe" rejected by Mack:

> It tells us nothing. It shows us that in a state of nature, without the knowledge or the grace of God, we are nothing—O's without a figure. And it suggests that perhaps we *are* in a state of nature. It suggests but does not say that our knowledge may be an illusion, that the faith and theology of the original audience, may, by analogy with the evasions within the play, be one more admirable evasion of whoremaster man. Indeed, any attempt to deal with the play's either/or statement of incomprehensibility and meaninglessness by resolving it in favor of one or the other is to evade the play's demonstration of our incertitude.
>
> (Hunter 190–91)

Hunter evokes Pascal's "wager"—after realizing that one can neither prove nor disprove the existence of God, *il faut parier*—only to dismiss it. "Of all the distractions," he says, "tragedy is the most nearly capable of confronting mystery without denying it. It can cope without evading and can take as its motto 'le juste est de ne point parier'. Art is above nature in that respect" (196). Hunter seems to arrive at the same conclusion as Mack: "Tragedy never tells us what to think; it shows us what we are and may be" (Mack 117). While their tone is very different, both critics finally excuse the playwright from any obligation to define a theological—or "atheological"—position.

The determined skeptics, however, are as insistent about recruiting Shakespeare to their company as their Christian counterparts who find a parable of regeneration in the conclusion of *King Lear*. In *The Structure of Complex Words* William Empson provides less a refutation of A.C. Bradley than a kind of subdued ridicule by incredulity. Bradley suggests that we are reconciled to Cordelia's death because "The 'gods', it seems, do *not* show their approval by 'defending' their own from adversity or death, or by giving them power and prosperity. These, on the contrary, are worthless, or worse; it is not on them, but on the renunciation of them, that the gods throw incense" (270–71). Empson at first admits that Bradley does not apply the remark about the corrupting effect of power and prosperity to Cordelia, but this concession is quickly dismissed:

> The main thing about this argument, no doubt, is that it succeeds in turning the blasphemies against the gods into the orthodox view held by Mrs. Gamp, that the world is a Wale. I do not know how seriously he took his last little twist of piety, the view that Cordelia was sure to become corrupt. It is curious how often the puritan high-mindedness can be found interlocked with an almost farcical cynicism.[5]
>
> (Empson 153–54)

Bradley, who sometimes wins Empson's praise, and who hardly qualifies as a champion of the "Christian Right," is nonetheless chided in a rather derisory fashion for insufficient stress upon the grimly subversive features of Shakespeare's tragedy.

Fifty years after the first edition of *The Structure of Complex Words*, the skeptical view of *King Lear* is still prominent and even more explicit, as attested by the example of Millicent Bell's *Shakespeare's Tragic Skepticism*:

> But their [Lear's and Cordelia's] own loving reconciliation before death does not look toward the heavenly afterlife religion promises. In his madness Lear had had a vision of himself in hell, "on a wheel of fire," and of Cordelia in heaven—but when he dies at last it is only the condition of recovered selfhood and sanity that can replace despair and confusion in a purely secular way.
>
> (189)

Like Empson, Bell attributes to Shakespeare a sardonic, modern vision that sees through all traditional pieties, and she is able to invoke Stephen Greenblatt and the New Historicists as further witnesses to her claim; in fact, Greenblatt becomes for her virtually a model for the playwright himself: "Shakespeare, one might almost propose, is an early-seventeenth [*sic*] century New Historicist of sorts, bounded by his own time and place yet enabled by his skepticism to view his culture with detachment" (xiv). High praise for the Bard indeed! He is enlisted among the ranks of knowing postmodern theorists who seem alone to escape the fate they ascribe to ordinary mortals of being helpless puppets of the currently regnant ideological hegemony.

The most important attack upon the redemptive view of *King Lear*, the work that presents the most relentless and scholarly refutation of what it calls "the currently widespread view that *Lear* is an optimistically Christian drama" (Elton 3), is W.R. Elton's King Lear *and the Gods*, which first appeared in 1966. Since its appearance, this book has been what might be called the "Unholy Writ" of the school of Shakespeare criticism that regards *King Lear* as a skeptical, radically subversive play, calling into question all the norms and pieties of the "Elizabethan World Picture," now perceived as a self-interested ideological imposition of the ruling classes of early modern England. Among its advocates Elton's work appears to be not merely definitive, but simply devastating. In *Radical Tragedy* Jonathan Dollimore maintains, "As William R. Elton has demonstrated in an important study, the Elizabethan–Jacobean period witnessed 'the skeptical disintegration of providential belief' " (38), and he later declines to "argue again the case against the Christian view [of *King Lear*] since, even though it is still sometimes advanced, it has been effectively discredited by writers as diverse as Barbara Everett, William R. Elton, and Cedric Watts" (190). According to Bell, "William Elton, in his learned *King Lear and the Gods* (1966) buried the idea that *King Lear* was optimistically Christian' " (xi). As these sample remarks show, Elton has been thought to have overwhelmed opposition so decisively that the matter requires no further investigation.

It is true that Elton's massive volume makes a formidable display of learning and, unlike many of its scholarly beneficiaries and supporters, delves deeply into the religious thought of Shakespeare's day. In some respects, however, the mountain of theological and philosophical details that Elton has so painstakingly amassed seems to occlude his vision of its significance, and his refutation of "Christian" readings of *King Lear* often accepts as "Christian" accounts of human nature and man's relation to providence that dubiously fit under that rubric. Further, his religious taxonomy of the various characters, especially his effort to show that Lear himself is not saved, tends to treat them as symbols for religious ideas rather than as agents of a tragic action in Aristotle's sense. Finally, although his argument stresses the rising current of skepticism, he pays little attention to the specific associations of the various characters with what we may call the crisis of natural law in the era of Elizabeth and James. Critics who rely on Elton's work to dismiss Christian interpretations of *King Lear* are thus heaping disdain on a sentimental, insubstantial version of Christianity. The Christian import of the play can only be grasped in terms of its complex relation to natural law.

It is an auspicious moment, then, for a fresh look at the theme of natural law in *King Lear*. Although this topic has been dealt with extensively in the critical literature for many decades, it will not be amiss to reconsider natural law as it interacts in a Christian culture with the doctrine of original sin and redemption through grace, as well as in relation to the notion of God's providential ordering of the creation. Moreover, it is important that the play be treated as a tragic drama, not a treatise. In Aristotelian terms, the διάνοια or "thought" or "theme" will emerge more clearly and persuasively if we begin with the representation of "a piece of action, of life, of happiness and unhappiness" (*Poetics* 1450a) rather than with the ideas as such. Regarded in this perspective, *King Lear* is most assuredly *not* an exposition of "Christian optimism," a phrase that is not even a paradox but rather a contradiction in terms. What Shakespeare offers us is an embodiment of the social disintegration that results when the philosophical and cultural foundations of a Christian community are undermined by radical skepticism about the nature and purpose of human life. Elton is very perceptive in remarking the crisis of belief figured forth in the play, but he treats the characters schematically in terms of fixed theological categories rather than attending to the overall effect of the drama. The "redemptive" interpretations are surely correct in seeing that our sympathy remains with the characters who adhere to natural law. They fail to see, however, that a crisis of natural law leaves only the naked Gospel, a "Good News" that offers a stark choice of hope and despair and reveals *optimism* to be a shallow presumption.

It is a critical commonplace that "natural," "unnatural," and their cognates are used more in *King Lear* than in any other play by Shakespeare. Theodore Spencer avails himself of a concordance in his 1942 study (142 n. 8), and Leon Harold Craig is still counting word occurrences almost sixty years later in *Of Philosophers and Kings* (133). The point of these observations is stated most plainly by Danby: "*King Lear* can be regarded as a play dramatizing the meanings of the single word 'Nature' " (15). These meanings are effectively reduced to two by a dichotomy between internal headings of the first chapter: "The Benignant Nature of Bacon, Hooker, and Lear" (20) and "The Malignant Nature of Hobbes, Edmund, and the Wicked Daughters" (31). "The idea of Nature, then, in orthodox Elizabethan thought, is always something normative for human beings" (21). This is the view of "the Lear party" with Cordelia as its "limiting expression" (20). It is the view that the moral law arises *naturally* out of the constitutive rationality of the souls of human beings situated in an intelligible created order. It is the practical antithesis of the "mechanical necessity" associated with modern scientifically determined "laws of nature":

> The law it [Reason] observed was felt more as self-expression than as external restraint. It was a law, in any case, which the creature was most itself when it obeyed. And rebellion against this law was rebellion against one's self, loss of all nature, lapse into chaos.
>
> (Danby 25)

The opposite vision of nature and the law of nature is voiced in Edmund's famous soliloquy at the beginning of the play's second scene, "Thou, Nature, art my goddess, to thy law/My services are bound" (I.ii.1–2). Edmund's notion of nature is individual rather than communal: "nature" for him means what distinguishes him as a particular being rather than what unites him to mankind by participation in a common human nature. What is "natural" is, in romantic fashion, opposed to what is social, traditional, conventional, or artificial—"the plague of custom" and "the curiosity of nations" (I.ii.3–4). Finally, his "nature" is defined by passion rather than reason, which is passion's servant. Edmund relishes his illegitimate status, asserting that the transgression of conventional morality involved in begetting a bastard is likely to produce more vigorous and aggressive sons:

> Who, in the lusty stealth of nature, take
> More composition and fierce quality,
> Than doth within a dull, stale, tired bed
> Go to th'creating a whole tribe of fops.
> (I.ii.11–14)

Danby catches the tone of this quite well: "Edmund is not a devil. He is, on the contrary, a normal, sensible, reasonable fellow; but emancipated. His knowledge of what Nature is like is a real knowledge of what she is really like" (34–35). And Danby likewise quite shrewdly observes that "The dualism of Reason *versus* the Passions is useless to explain Edmund. Though Edmund is Appetite, he is also a rationalist" (36–37). Noting that Shakespeare has presciently anticipated in Edmund the philosophy of Thomas Hobbes, he observes, "Reason is no longer a normative drive but a calculator of the means to satisfy the appetites with which we were born" (38).

Danby finds in the dramatic unfolding of the clash between the traditional classical and Christian view of natural law and the modern, Hobbesian view "not only our profoundest tragedy" but even "our profoundest expression of an essentially Christian comment on man's world and his society, using the terms and benefiting by the formulations of the Christian tradition" (204–5). His interpretation (especially in a summary) is rather schematic and seems vulnerable to Elton's disdainful disparaging of "Shakespearean neo-Christianizers" (263); it cannot be maintained, however, that Danby has simply failed to see the subversive tendencies toward skepticism that Elton finds proliferating at the end of the sixteenth century: "New orientations between man and the heavenly powers were, in several directions, formed during the Renaissance, disintegrating the relative medieval sense of security" (Elton 9). Nearly twenty years before the appearance of Elton's book, Danby arguing the opposite case, makes the same basic observation about the growing prevalence of the subversive outlook expressed in Edmund's soliloquy:

> The sentiments of Edmund's speech must have been fairly widespread in Shakespeare's society. There is no doubt that similar ethical views were implicit in the eminent generality of public conduct at any time during the sixteenth and seventeenth centuries. It was not, however, an acceptable view.
>
> (32)

The issue, then, is not whether *King Lear* dramatizes powerful doubts about the traditional orthodox doctrine of natural law and divine providence, but rather what the import of the play is regarding the contemporaneous challenge to orthodoxy.

If the usual "orthodox" interpretation is to be faulted, it is not for tying the debate about nature too closely to Christian doctrine, but for attributing too much latitude to natural law as such. As Russell Hittinger points out, "It is true that modern philosophy abandoned the metaphysics of participation, and thus wrestled with problem of whether law belongs properly to physical states of affairs or mental constructs, but it is entirely anachronistic to impose this dilemma on the older tradition" (xxii). In summing up his own argument Danby seems torn between the urge to see the natural law embodied in a "physical state of affairs" and the regret that it seems finally only a "mental construct":

> It has been argued that Shakespeare began by seeing a new thrustful godlessness attacking the pious medieval structure represented by the good King Henry VI. Regretfully, Shakespeare then comes to terms with "the times" such as he saw them to be under Elizabeth. Last, he recognized the iniquity of the times and of the machiavel's rule. To these he opposed the society that Lear's and Gloster's prayers demand, a transcendent society adequated to the necessity for a community of goodness in which Lear's regeneration and Cordelia's truth might be completed: a Utopia and a New Jerusalem.
>
> (202)

Writing half a century after Danby, R.S. White is even more explicit about how *King Lear* demands that the natural law be embodied in a specific political order: "Lear's sentiments in this part of the play [III.iv] are as communitarian, anti-individualistic, and anti-authoritarian as More's in his fictional version of Utopia" (210). White suggests that Shakespeare, like a seventeenth-century Jean-Jacques Rousseau, maintains that the norms of natural law could be realized by a kind of communitarian socialism that is prevented only by deeply established vested interests:

> The logic of *King Lear*, with its decisive celebration of virtue over vice and its equally decisive extinction of virtue, folds back to catch in its snare those who would impose any kind of positive law, literary or legal, over Natural Law. As in *Utopia*, no matter how splendid is the prospect of a world based on reason and conscience, that world may not be achievable, because human greed and power-seeking are too deeply entrenched in the existing structures of authority and power: but the effort of trying should still go on.
>
> (215)

This sounds more like the liberation theology of the twentieth century than what St. Thomas Aquinas or Richard Hooker would recognize as natural law.

Hobbes is, quite reasonably, the villain waiting in the wings to provide philosophical cover for the Edmunds of the world in both Danby and White, but in their insistence that natural law be embodied in a particular program that will somehow guarantee the poetic justice that Shakespeare's version of *King Lear* denies, they are to some degree embracing Hobbes's instrumental version of reason, much as Rousseau did in the eighteenth century, and endorsing Nahum Tate's revision of the play.[6]

It is important to bear in mind that the most explicit and thorough exposition of natural law in Shakespeare's time, Richard Hooker's *Of the Laws of Ecclesiastical Polity* (1593, 1597), was composed with the express purpose of refuting the Puritan view that the Church of England ought to be governed strictly according to Scriptural norms, identified with the Presbyterian form of church governance established by Calvin in Geneva. Taking continental Anabaptists as a negative exemplum, Hooker warns the Puritans against attempting to establish the realm of divine perfection on earth:

> Nothing more clear unto their seeming, than that a new Jerusalem being often spoken of in Scripture, they undoubtedly were themselves that new Jerusalem, and the old did by way of a certain figurative resemblance signify what they should both be and do.
>
> (I: 139)

Natural law is thus invoked, not as a template for the New Jerusalem or Utopia, but as a constraint upon the imprudent effort to embody these ideals literally in human institutions:

> These men, in whose mouths at the first sounded nothing but only mortification of the flesh, were come at the length to think they might lawfully have their six or seven wives apiece; they which at the first thought judgment and justice itself to be merciless cruelty, accounted at the length their own hands sanctified with being embrued in Christian blood; they who at the first were wont to beat down all dominion, and to urge against poor constables, "Kings of nations;" had at the length both consuls and kings of their own erection amongst themselves.
>
> (I: 139–40)

Natural law is not, then, the basis for an absolutely just polity or community, but rather a set of norms guiding the admittedly diverse and contingent political arrangements of fallen men in an uncertain world: "The case of man's nature standing therefore as it doth, some kind of regiment the Law of Nature doth require; yet the kinds thereof being many, Nature tieth not to any one, but leaveth the choice as a thing arbitrary" (Hooker, I: 191–92).

"The case of man's nature" raises a second point: Christians at the end of the sixteenth century were under no illusions about human nature. Human beings, along with angels, are rational agents and fulfill the law of their nature voluntarily: "God which moveth mere natural agents as an efficient only, doth otherwise move intellectual creatures" (Hooker I: 161). The result of this freedom is that men's apprehension of their good, of the object of their nature, may vary:

> There is in the Will of man naturally that freedom, whereby it is apt to take or refuse any particular object whatsoever being presented unto it. Whereupon it followeth, that there is no particular object so good, but it may have the show of some difficulty or unpleasant quality annexed to it, in respect whereof the Will may shrink and decline it; contrariwise (for so things are blended) there is no particular evil which hath not some appearance of goodness whereby to insinuate itself.
>
> (I: 171–72)

What is more, in actual human history, from the perspective not merely of Hooker but all Christians, the indeterminacy of the human will had led not merely to contingency, but to the depravity of original sin. Men may know by nature—even the heathen—"the shewe & effect of the Law written in their hearts" (Romans 2.15), but this knowledge serves only to justify their condemnation. The estate of men under merely natural law is described grimly by St. Paul in the Epistle to the Ephesians: "That ye were, I say at that time without Christ, & were aliantes from the commune welth of Israel, & were strangers from the covenants of the promes, & had no hope, & were without God in the worlde" (2.12).[7] Natural law may provide a pattern for the positive laws of commonwealths, but Hooker insists that the human legislator must take into account the effects of original sin:

> Laws politic, ordained for external order and regiment among men, are never framed as they should be, unless presuming the will of man to be inwardly obstinate, rebellious, and averse from all obedience unto the sacred laws of his nature; in a word, unless presuming man to be in regard of his depraved mind little better than a wild beast.
>
> (I: 188)

Hooker's account of natural law owes a good deal to St. Thomas Aquinas, and in his baleful view of human nature with its aversion "from all obedience unto the sacred laws of his nature," he differs from the Angelic Doctor not at all. R.S. White contrasts "Aquinas' idealism about people and the scepticism of Calvin and Hobbes" (185), but this view is rather short-sighted. In the first place, like Hooker, St. Thomas realizes that mankind is subject to original sin. Particular human laws are necessary since fallen human beings are incapable of grasping the natural law completely "because human reason is unable to participate in the full order of divine reason, but only in its own capacity and imperfectly" (*Summa Theologiae* I–II.91.3 ad 1); "hence it was necessary for the peace and virtue of men that laws be imposed . . .; because man has the weapons of reason for carrying out his concupiscence and his savagery, which other animals do not have" (I–II.95.2).[8] Most important, the "optimistic" St. Thomas denies that "anyone can be happy in this life." And it is not just that the goal "in which happiness specially consists, namely the vision of the divine essence," is unattainable in this life, but even the good of natural life:

> Now happiness, since it would be a perfect and sufficient good, excludes every evil and fulfills every desire. In this life, however, it is not possible that every evil be excluded. For the present life is subject to many evils, which cannot be avoided: to ignorance on the part of the intellect, to inordinate longing on the part of the appetite, and to many pains on the part of the body.
>
> (I–II.5.3)

Both Aquinas and Hooker, then, in expounding the natural law that St. Paul says is written in the hearts of all, are constantly aware that this inherent moral sense is of no avail to men and women under the curse of original sin and without grace—"who had no hope, & were without God in the worlde."

Such is precisely the situation that Shakespeare imagines in *King Lear*. The characters are pagans whose knowledge and understanding of natural law are real but imperfect or distorted. Edmund's view of human nature and the law that governs it is perverse according to the traditional standards of Shakespeare's society—or progressive if one takes the modern view, first fully articulated, perhaps, by Hobbes. Opposing Edmund's position most explicitly are the utterances of Lear and Gloucester, who both condemn their children for a failure of the filial love and loyalty required by natural law. Just as Edmund calls upon the "gods" associated with the "goddess" Nature to "stand up for bastards" (I.ii.1,22), thus giving shape to his ruthlessly individualistic and self-serving idea of human nature, so Lear calls upon the "dear goddess" Nature to punish Goneril for her transgression of natural *moral* law with a failure or defect of her *physical* nature:

> Suspend thy purpose, if thou didst intend
> To make this creature fruitful.
> Into her womb convey sterility,
> Dry up in her the organs of increase,
> And from her derogate body never spring
> A babe to honor her!
>
> (I.iv.276–81)

Or, alternatively, he demands that she be repaid in kind for ingratitude with a "child of spleen [. . .] that she may feel,/How sharper than a serpent's tooth it is/To have a thankless child!" (I.iv.282, 287–89). Although he *knows* that his paternal obligations are as binding as his daughter's filial obligations, his practical conduct is as selfish as Edmund's without the latter's explicit rationalization of selfishness as only "natural." Even when his rage and frustration with Goneril lead him to regret his treatment Cordelia, he does not yet acknowledge the extent of his injustice:

> O most small fault,
> How ugly didst thou in Cordelia show!
> Which, like an engine wrench'd my frame of nature
> From the fix'd place, drew from my heart all love,
> And added to the gall.
>
> (I.iv.266–70)

It is a "most small fault" but it is still Cordelia's *fault* that caused the displacement of his "frame of nature." Lear's conduct provides some basis for Regan's assertion that "he hath ever but slenderly known himself" (I.i.294).

Gloucester provides an even clearer example of how, in St. Thomas's view, human reason can grasp the requirements of the natural law "only in its own capacity and imperfectly." The ease with which Edmund deceives his father into believing that Edgar wrote the forged letter suggests that Gloucester does not know the character of either of his sons at all well, and that the younger bastard has become adept at exploiting his father's weaknesses. The audience is likely to infer, for example, that Edmund's ostentatiously awkward attempt to hide the letter was devised to exploit the curiosity of a man he knows to be officious and overbearing. Given Gloucester's obvious relish in the memory of the illicit copulation that resulted in Edmund's begetting at the very beginning of the play ("yet was his mother fair, there was good sport at his making"—I.i.22–23), it is reasonable to suppose that the old man's judgment is clouded by the presence of the young man who is the living image of gratified lust.[9] When Gloucester has left the stage, Edmund sneers at his attributing disturbances in human society to dislocations among celestial phenomena—"An admirable evasion of whoremaster man, to lay his goatish disposition to the charge of a star!" (I.ii.126–28)—and it is not improbable that at least some members of a Jacobean audience would have found here evidence of superstition. But more alarming than Gloucester's predilection for astrology is his lack of self-knowledge; while he has a lucid comprehension of the King's foolish and unjust anger as a "scourge" of nature, he is blind—ominous word in relation to Gloucester—to his own:

> This villain of mine comes under the prediction; there's son against father: the King falls from the bias of nature; there's father against child. We have seen the best of our time. Machinations, hollowness, treachery, and all ruinous disorders follow us disquietly to our graves. Find out this villain, Edmund, it shall lose thee nothing, do it carefully. And the noble and true-hearted Kent banish'd! his offense, honesty! 'Tis strange.
>
> (I.ii.109–17)

While Gloucester seems to Edmund, and perhaps to us, merely a foolish old man waxing nostalgic over the "good old days," his judgment of Lear's conduct and its likely consequences is sound enough. He has insight and prudence, but they are darkened when his own pleasure, comfort, and vanity are at stake.

Lear and Gloucester, the defenders of the classical tradition of natural law, seem hypocritical and even deluded at the outset of the play; and Edmund is a far more persuasive and impressive spokesman for his self-centered but "realistic" perspective. But before the two old men are judged too severely, it is necessary to take stock, for they are easy to identify with. At least that would be Aristotle's dictum: Lear, and Gloucester in a lesser but parallel fashion, are very much "like us": they are neither absolutely good nor absolutely bad. Of course they are also, in a sense, "better" than we are; that is, they are tragic figures. Tragedy, Aristotle says, is designed to elicit pity (ἔλεος) "for the man who does not deserve his misfortune" and fear (φόβος) "for the man who is like ourselves." Hence a particular kind of character is called for at the center of a tragedy:

> This is the sort of man who is not pre-eminently virtuous and just, and yet it is through no badness or villainy of his own that he falls into the mis-fortune, but rather through some flaw (ἁμαρτία) in him, he being one of those who are in high station and good fortune, like Oedipus and Thyestes and the famous men of such families as these.
>
> (1453a)

A bit further on in the *Poetics* (1454a), Aristotle says that of the four elements of character in tragedy, "the first and most important is that the character should be good" (χρηστός).

Lear and Gloucester both correspond well to this account of tragic character. Their behavior in the first scene is embarrassingly selfish and short-sighted, and there is hardly any improvement until the climactic third act. Nevertheless, the play provides ample evidence that both have earned better reputations in the past, and that they remain capable of decency and courage and, finally, of wisdom. The action is tragic precisely because their realization of their moral failings, which suggests Aristotle's notion of "discovery" (αναγνώρισις) and is properly coupled with a "reversal" (περιπέτεια), comes too late to avert the catastrophic arc of the action (*Poetics* 1452a). Both men are basically "good," although neither comes near the luminous virtue of Cordelia. Both of them cause their own suffering and that of others not because of depraved intentions or utterly corrupt character, but because of an *error* or *piece of ignorance* arising from understandable if reprehensibly foolish vanity. In a bleak mood, Gloucester attributes his misery to "an imbecile universe"(Stampfer 10): "As flies to wanton boys are we to th'gods, / They kill us for their sport" (IV.i.36–37). Edgar's observation to his dying brother in the final scene is in strict logic an undeniable refutation of his their father's complaint:

The gods are just, and of our pleasant vices
Make instruments to plague us:
The dark and vicious place where thee he got
Cost him his eyes.

(V.iii.171–74)

Since Gloucester's moral "blindness" is the source of his personal irresponsibility and misjudgment of his sons' characters, there is even an ironic, even "poetic" justice in the loss of his eyes, as he himself admits: "I have no way, and therefore want no eyes;/I stumbled when I saw" (IV.i.18–19). But of course we find his suffering completely out of proportion to his guilt, since it arises from human frailty—vanity and sensuality—rather than malice and cruelty; and it is important to remember that Edgar utters his harsh verdict *not* to his father, but in reproof of the vicious brother with whom he has just struggled in mortal combat.[10]

Gloucester's conduct is certainly bad enough. One can only shudder to imagine what Edmund must experience in hearing his aged father crow about the "good sport" he enjoyed in begetting his "whoreson" (I.i.23–24). His obliviousness to the consequences of his indulgence in "pleasant vices" (V.iii.171) is ironically underscored in subsequent scenes by his ill-tempered and credulous rage at the suggestion that his older son may not be true to *his* natural obligations to his father. Most audiences will surely feel a great deal of disdain for Gloucester and sympathy for his illegitimate son at the outset of the play. On the other hand, Gloucester has not abandoned the bastard: he has educated him, he introduces him to a powerful nobleman at court in the first scene, and he has evidently treated him with love, even though he never lets Edmund forget his origins. More important, Gloucester, while lacking adequate self-knowledge and knowledge of his sons, shows genuine insight into the characters of Lear and Kent, and a healthy suspicion of the King's older daughters and Cornwall. Finally, when the action comes to a crisis, Gloucester displays great courage in remaining loyal not just to Lear, but to the cause of justice. At the beginning of the tragedy, Gloucester behaves contemptibly, but it soon becomes clear that he is by no means a contemptible man, and is indeed admirable in many respects.

Much the same is *a fortiori* true of Lear himself. The ritual abasement of his daughters that he stages in the opening scene is, like Gloucester's salacious reminiscing about his youthful sexual conquest, an embarrassment. Anyone who has suffered through the antics of an overbearing relative demanding to be the center of attention at a family gathering will have a sense of what Lear is doing. The difference is that he is a long-reigning absolute monarch who can demand outrageous tributes to his own vainglory. An audience in Shakespeare's England would have no difficulty understanding the apprehension of a King with only daughters about the succession to the throne, and his anxiety on this score may at least suggest an explanation for his staging of a ceremony in which he both relinquishes and seeks to retain his power and royal prestige and puts his daughters through a mortifying charade of heaving their hearts into their mouths. Once again, however, ample evidence is provided that there is—or at least has been—more to Lear than this scene might imply, that Goneril's complaint, "The best and soundest of his time hath been but rash" (I.i.295), is self-serving hyperbole. Lear has the love and respect of most of the other important characters: Albany and Gloucester and, above all, Kent and Cordelia, whose character is unimpeachable and whose regard is worth having. Both of them are apparently used to speaking freely and candidly to the King and are shocked at his behavior. Gloucester is likewise nonplussed by the turn of events, and Albany will show no predisposition to take his wife's part in Lear's confrontation with Goneril: "My lord, I am guiltless as I am ignorant / Of what hath moved you" (I.iv.273–74). When Kent returns in disguise to serve Lear in spite of his banishment, he seems to speak for many of Lear's subjects in saying to the old King, "you have that in your countenance which I would fain call master"; namely, "Authority" (I.iv.27–30). *Authority* is plainly to be distinguished from the mere raw power seized by Edmund, Cornwall, Goneril, and Regan.

Although he can with some justice claim, "I am a man / More sinn'd against than sinning" (III.ii.59–60), King Lear and the characters associated with him and with the traditional view of natural law, which maintains that objective moral norms are built into the structure of human nature and the reality of the human condition, by no means observe their own principles perfectly. Edmund, who claims that the law of nature is no more than the selfish pursuit of one's desire, has at least the virtue of relative consistency. Through the first two acts of the play, the wicked characters, the characters who follow Edmund's cynical assessment of human nature, are more vigorous and resourceful than their opponents who, when not causing their own troubles, are at best bemused and ineffectual. Having been placed in the stocks by the irate Cornwall for his assault on Oswald, "true-hearted Kent" admits the imprudence of his dealings with Goneril's steward, "Having more man than wit about me" (II.iv.42). His conduct at least provides a fairly substantial rationale for the punishment meted out by Cornwall and for Goneril's complaints about the unruliness of her father's train of 100 knights. There is some ambiguity about the extent to which the elder sisters are justified in condemning their behavior and demanding a reduction in the King's retinue. Under the very best of circumstances, however, a long-term houseguest with his own armed retainers will present a problem. The innocent characters, on the other hand, appear indecisive. Edmund manages to make Edgar's modesty and candor seem mere timidity: "A credulous father and a brother noble, / Whose nature is so far from doing harms / That he suspects none; on whose foolish honesty / My practices ride easy" (I.ii.179–82). Goneril takes the same line with her husband Albany, a "Milk-liver'd man, / That bear'st a cheek for blows, a head for wrongs" (IV.ii.50–51).

Marilyn French tells an anecdote about Robert Lowell reducing Harvard seminar students to shocked silence "by suggesting that maybe Goneril and Regan were right, maybe Lear's knights were rowdy and lecherous drunkards, and *were* disturbing the house." She goes on to enumerate the faults of Lear, Gloucester, and even Kent and complains that "these questions are not permitted within the terms of the play" (260). But not only are these questions "permitted"; they are essential to the full significance of the tragedy, which not only stages a conflict between two visions of human nature and natural law, but in fact dramatizes in the starkest terms the limitations of human knowledge of that law and the futility of man's attempt to save himself from his own worst instincts by means of moral behavior. It is not that the traditional moral vision is repudiated; it is certainly endorsed by the action of the play, and the effort to live merely according to self-interest is shown to be not only self-destructive but vile. The proponents of natural law do not, however, defeat their enemies by virtue of their superior morality. For the most part the wicked characters destroy themselves and one another along with the most virtuous characters. *King Lear* stages not just a conflict between rival versions of natural law, but the crisis of natural law with respect to its rôle in the community—an actual crisis in Shakespeare's day, as intimated by Hooker's lengthy reflection on the matter in *Ecclesiastical Polity*: "For my purpose herein is to shew, that when the minds of men are once erroneously persuaded that it is the will of God to have those things done which they fancy, their opinions are as thorns in their sides, never suffering them to take rest till they have brought their speculations into practice" (I: 139). Edmund has this in common with Hooker's Puritan rivals: a burning impatience with customary laws and practices fueled by a suspicion that there is nothing supporting them besides the arbitrary will of the established rulers. Shakespeare thus dramatizes precisely what Hooker feared: the vulnerability of social order when it is forced to explain itself. As St. Thomas concedes, since practical moral reason deals with singular and contingent affairs, "Human laws cannot possess the infallibility of the necessary conclusions of the sciences" (*Sum. Theol.* I–II.91.3 ad 3).

The intractable complexity of the issue emerges most vividly in Lear's conflict with his daughters over the number of retainers he will be allowed to keep. For Goneril and Regan, of course, the argument is a means of cruelly humiliating their father as well as a stratagem for reducing him to helplessness by isolating him. Why do you need twenty-five followers, or ten, or five, Goneril demands, since so many of my servants and my sister's are there to serve you? "What need one?" (II.iv.263), is Regan's insolent, though logical, conclusion to this economic train of reasoning. Lear's reply, while self-serving, nonetheless gropes towards an important truth:

> O, reason not the need! our basest beggars
> Are in the poorest thing superfluous.
> Allow not nature more than nature needs,
> Man's life is cheap as beast's. Thou are a lady;

> If only to go warm were gorgeous,
> Why, nature needs not what thou gorgeous wear'st,
> Which scarcely keeps thee warm. But for true need—
> You heavens, give me that patience, patience I need!
> (II.iv.264–70)

According to R.S. White, sharing in Regan's implacable logic, Lear says this "in his unregenerate state, threatened with the disbanding of his personal followers." At his point, "he speaks without the experience of true need. He is rationalising 'superfluities' " (202). Craig, however, calls it a "*pre-*philosophical view," but observes that it "is much closer to the truth than is the physiologist's view that he later espouses in the midst of liberating madness. One endlessly important respect in which human life differs from that of beasts is precisely in its being ruled neither by bare necessity nor by strict utility, and that *beauty*, in particular, is a natural human concern" (183).

As both St. Thomas Aquinas (I–II.91.2) and Hooker (I: 159–66) observe, there is a distinction between rational creatures or voluntary agents and "natural agents." Human nature transcends mere nature. Paradoxically, we truly *need* more than we *need* in strict material terms. Jonathan Dollimore gets it just backwards in asserting, "Human values are not antecedent to these material realities but are, on the contrary, informed by them" (197). This is exactly Regan's line: "I pray you, father, being weak, seem so" (II.iv.201). As rational creatures capable of choice, men and women need to have their human dignity acknowledged. And this is not altered when someone, like Lear or like Gloucester, makes very bad choices. Although they both suffer in ways that seem poetically appropriate and significant—Gloucester is blinded in order to see; Lear loses his wits in order to understand—this does not mean that their children who subject them to this indignity and anguish are justified in doing so. Goneril's complaints against her father may have merit, and her sister's logic is impeccable: "How in one house/Should many people under two commands/Hold amity? 'Tis hard, almost impossible" (II.iv.240–42). But Lear's personal retinue is part of his identity, a crucial element in his sense of self-respect; to deny him his own men is to deprive him of his sense of self, to make him, in Oswald's surly phrase, nothing but "My lady's father" (I.iv.79). That Lear has, in large measure, brought his troubles on himself and has strictly speaking no right to act like a king anymore in no way excuses his ill usage.

Natural law teaching is, moreover, not revolutionary. Law should be changed, St. Thomas says, only for the gravest of reasons (*Sum. Theol.* I–II.97.2) The fact that Lear confronts need greater than his own in Edgar disguised as "Poor Tom," who stands in for the multitude of the dispossessed and destitute, does not make Lear's own need any less. His great speech of recognition and remorse on the heath is not a renunciation of his own requirements, but the realization of his responsibility to the needs of others whom he has neglected:

> Poor naked wretches, wheresoe'er you are,
> That bide the pelting of this pitiless storm,
> How shall your houseless heads and unfed sides,
> Your [loop'd] and window'd raggedness, defend you
> From seasons such as these? O, I have ta'en
> Too little care of this! Take physic, pomp,
> Expose thyself to feel what wretches feel,
> That thou mayst shake the superflux to them,
> And show the heavens more just.
>
> (III.iv.28–36)

Lear is not renouncing royalty; he is lamenting that he has not been a better king. He is not relinquishing the "superflux"; it is that which makes alms-giving possible (see Kronenfeld 188–90).

The trouble with the natural law is that it stipulates requirements for human nature that nature cannot fulfill, and it is in providing dramatic representation of this dilemma that *King Lear* becomes a profoundly Christian play. When Lear demands love of his daughters, he is expressing a genuine need: men and women *need* to be loved. Even Edmund as he is dying takes perverse satisfaction in such love as he as elicited from Goneril and Regan: "Yet Edmund was belov'd! / The one the other poison'd for my sake, / And after slew herself" (V.iii.240–42). But as Edmund's comment shows, no one has a *right* to expect love from another individual, simply because such a requirement cannot be enforced: Goneril failed to love her husband and killed for the illicit love of Edmund. Goneril and Regan also show that love can be feigned, that it can be expressed without being willed; but Cordelia's response, which so disappoints her father's expectation, shows all that one can actually *demand* of another, even if it is so much less than what one longs for:

> Good my lord,
> You have begot me, bred me, lov'd me: I
> Return those duties back as are right fit,
> Obey you, love you, and most honor you.
>
> (I.i.95–98)

Lear's frustrated response tells us what is missing: "But goes thy heart with this?" (I.i.104). It is just the *heart* that cannot be commanded.

Of course Cordelia is the ultimate embodiment of love in the play; it is she who, unlike her sisters, when her father is in despair, will *not* "reason the need"; that is, she offers the love that one need not—that one *could not* deserve. This factor alone would cast a Christian glow over the entire tragedy despite its pagan setting, but Shakespeare is at pains to associate Cordelia with Christian virtues and preoccupations by means of a number of explicit allusions. When she is cast off by her father, the King of France describes her in paradoxical terms reminiscent of the beatitudes in the Sermon on the Mount: "Fairest Cordelia, that art most rich being poor, / Most choice forsaken, and most lov'd despis'd" (I.i.250–51). When she returns to England at the head of a French army, she disclaims any ambition in words reminiscent of the twelve-year-old Jesus when his earthly parents find him in the Temple: "O dear father, / It is thy business that I go about" (IV. iv.23–24). The unnamed gentleman who seeks to bring Lear to his daughter says, "Thou hast [one] daughter / Who redeems nature from the general curse / Which twain have brought her to" (IV.vi.205–7). We are likely at first to think "twain" refers to Goneril and Regan, but it is Adam and Eve who caused the "general curse," and to "redeem" it is the work of the Savior. All of these lines, it should be noted, are in both the Quarto and Folio versions of the text.[11]

In the end, like Christ, Cordelia is "hanged on a tree" (Acts 5.30), and we last see her dead in the arms of her grieving father, a mirror image of the traditional *Pietà*.[12] The manner of Cordelia's death is also important because she *does not commit suicide*, as she does in the principal historical and literary sources such as Monmouth, Holinshed, *The Mirror for Magistrates*, and the second book of the *Faerie Queene* (Bullough, VII: 315–16, 319, 331–34). Suicide seems a highly significant issue for Shakespeare. Hamlet's fate seems more hopeful insofar as he draws back from the suicide he contemplates expressly because of Christian scruple (e.g., I.ii.131–32; III.i.55–81), while Othello seems to affirm his own sense of damnation in taking his own life (V.ii.277–80, 343–56). Even Puck, of all improbable spokesmen, condemns suicide in *A Midsummer Night's Dream* (III.382–87).

Most important is the scene when Lear awakens to find himself dressed in clean garments in the presence of his disinherited daughter Cordelia. Filled with shame and guilt, he cannot believe that she will not spurn him:

> If you have poison for me, I will drink it.
> I know you do not love me, for your sisters
> Have (as I do remember) done me wrong:
> You have some cause, they have not.

Cordelia's reply offers what is possibly the most compelling vision of Christian charity and forgiveness in all of English literature: "No cause, no cause" (IV.vii.70–75). She does not *say* "I forgive you," thus reminding him what he owes her. Instead she wipes the slate clean as in the sacrament of penance or the divine forgiveness evoked in Psalm 32: "Blessed is he whose wickednes is forgiuen, & whose sinne is couered." The love that Lear sought to command in the play's opening scene is here bestowed freely upon him in the depths of his despair, "bound / Upon a wheel of fire" (IV.vii.45–46). This reconciliation scene is, then, a manifestation of hope for mortals who find that their own efforts to rectify the world by adhering to the law written in their hearts and exercising their own natural virtues are insufficient.

Cordelia returns to England to save her father's kingdom from her wicked sisters and to redeem him from despair. In so doing she dies. Any spectator or reader, in Shakespeare's day or ours, will almost inevitably be reminded of Christ's mission of redemption and his sacrificial death. Cordelia, however, is not Christ. She is a pagan woman who leads a French army into England, is defeated and captured, and brutally put to death by her captor. She will not rise from her grave in three days. In reminding us of the Christian Savior, she reminds us—and certainly Shakespeare's original audience—of what the world of *King Lear* did not have.

This dénouement does not, however, validate Elton's conclusion that the "implicit direction of the tragedy [is] annihilation of faith in poetic justice and, within the confines of a grim pagan universe, annihilation of faith in divine justice" (334). What happens in *King Lear* is just what St. Paul might have predicted; it conforms perfectly with his admonition to the Ephesians concerning their life before they received grace and lived in a Godless and hence hopeless world. Shakespeare looks at the pagan world of *King Lear* much as the Christian Beowulf poet looked at the world of his hero: "one thing he knew clearly: those days were heathen—heathen, noble, and hopeless" (Tolkien 71). Elton's project to undermine "the optimistic Christian interpretation of *King Lear*" (335) was thus misconceived from the outset. Christianity is a religion of *hope* in a future life founded on grace, not *optimism*, and as St. Thomas Aquinas points out, "We should not seek other goods of God [besides salvation] except in the order of eternal blessedness. Hence hope also principally has regard for eternal blessedness; other things that are sought from God it holds in a secondary regard, and in the order of eternal blessedness" (*Sum. Theol.* II–II. 17.2 ad2). Or as St. Paul puts it, "For we are saued by hope: but hope that is sene, is not hope: for how can a man hope for that which he seeth?" (Romans 8.24). Jesus Christ was tortured and brutally put to death, and His Church was sustained and expanded by nearly three centuries of martyrdom. In Shakespeare's day Christians had been martyring one another for three generations: men and women endured terrible suffering and grisly death at the hands of those who were convinced that their hope was an illusion and without tangible evidence that "the purported benevolent, just, or special providence" was "operative" on their behalf (see Elton 336). Hooker's great exposition of natural law in the 1590s was precisely an effort—futile as it turned out—to moderate some of the sectarian passion that motivated this outburst of violence and cruelty. Shakespeare's starkly tragic revision of "the unconsciously comic and pietistic old *Leir*" need not be regarded as a rejection of Christian providence and divine justice, but rather a dramatic realization that "poetic justice" and Christian hope are altogether different in kind and import.

Finally, Elton's relentless insistence of Lear's damnation—a literary critic's version of "Sinners in the Hands of an Angry God"—is as irrelevant to the meaning of the play as the question of "How Many Children Had Lady Macbeth?" "In every respect," Elton says, "Lear fulfills the criteria for pagan behavior," especially in his "total blasphemy at the moment of his irredeemable loss" (260). Elton might make a fitting addition to the company of Job's comforters: an old man who has endured insult, exposure, and mortification that have led him into madness; who has had his fondest hope briefly fulfilled and then dashed; who comes on the stage bearing his arms the body of his beloved daughter whose death he knows to be the result of his own willful folly—this man is to have his dying words and actions scrutinized for doctrinal orthodoxy according to a doctrine that he never knew. It is highly unlikely that an audience of Jacobean Christians would be thinking along these lines; if their preachers admonished them about excessive grief, it was because they knew grief very intimately. The death of Cordelia and her father's anguished demise do not erase their scene of charity, forgiveness, and reconciliation: in the tragic, pagan world they inhabit, these Christian virtues furnish a reminder of the hope of grace and redemption without altering the dreadful consequences of sin and error in that world. The fact is, Shakespeare never allows the question of Lear's salvation (or anyone else's) to arise. If he did, it is probable that his view would be closer to Hooker's "Discourse on Justification" than to the fulminations of his more severe contemporaries, and it is Hooker who has the final word:

> Let me die, if ever it proved, that simply an error doth exclude a pope or a cardinal, in such a case, utterly from hope of life. Surely, I must confess unto you, if it be an error to think, that God may be merciful to save men even when they err, my greatest comfort is my error; were it not for the love I bear unto this error, I would neither wish to speak nor to live.[13]
>
> (I: 71)

Notes

1 In the later "Four Plays," *Prose Works* I: 232–41, Swinburne seems to mitigate the severity of his view and praises Coleridge.

2 Other redemptive interpretations of *King Lear* in generally Christian terms include those of John F. Danby, Oscar James Campbell, R.W. Chambers, G. Wilson Knight, Peter Milward, Theodore Spencer, and John Dover Wilson among many others.

3 All quotations of Shakespeare's works are from Evans (*The Riverside Shakespeare*), although I am aware of discrepancies between the quarto (1608) and the folio (1623) versions. There is no altogether satisfactory text of *King Lear*, and because I wish to use evidence from both the quarto and folio, the standard conflated text simplifies the already complicated references in this essay. Other commentators on similar questions have reached similar conclusions. White, for example, follows the quarto version, but concedes that the two make virtually the same point about natural law (213–14). For an argument against the "two plays" theory, see the *TLS* review of the *Oxford* Shakespeare by Vickers.

4 *De Constantia libri duo* was first published in Leiden and Antwerp at the end of 1583 and went through numerous editions through the seventeenth century. It was translated into English by Sir John Stradling (London, 1594), and since Lipsius' work was well known to Shakespeare's theatrical colleague Ben Jonson, there is

every reason to believe that the work would have been available to Shakespeare as well. The important point is, of course, that the consideration of the guidance of divine providence in the face of dreadful evil would not have been a shocking or unusual topic for Shakespeare's audience.

5 Empson also says that "the attempts to fit Christian sentiments onto it [*Lear*] seem to me to falsify the play" (8). In addition to Empson, other skeptical accounts from around the middle of the twentieth century include G.B. Harrsion, D.G. James, John Peter, John Rosenberg, Arthur Sewell, and Judah Stampfer, who supplies the "imbecile universe" phrase cited by both Mack and Hunter.

6 For a persuasive demonstration that Lear's and Gloucester's attacks upon privilege and inequity in the middle of the play are considerably less radical or subversive than many critics claim, see Kronenfeld esp. 170–229.

7 Unless otherwise specified, I quote Scripture from *The Geneva Bible*, but I have modernized punctuation and typographical conventions.

8 All Latin translations of St. Thomas Aquinas are my own.

9 See St. Thomas, *Summa Theologia* 2–2.153.5 on "mental blindness" (*caecitas mentis*) as the first "daughter of lust" (*filia luxuriae*). In the reply to the first objection in the same article, he quotes Aristotle saying that "intemperance above all corrupts prudence."

10 Marilyn French thus misses the point in accusing Edgar of "mean-minded moralization" for this remark (259). What would have been unfeeling said to his father is properly said to the flagitious brother, who grants the justice of the remark and begins to feel stirrings of remorse. The sanctimony here is the critic's, not the character's.

11 See the parallel texts in *The Norton Shakespeare*, which is based on the Oxford edition: Q 1.258–59 = F I.i.248–49; Q 18.24–25 = F IV.iii.23–24; Q 20.191–93 = F IV.v.195–97.

12 For these and numerous other scriptural references see Milward, *Biblical Influences* 156–204.

13 "A Learned Discourse of Justification" is included in the Everyman edition of *Ecclesiastical Polity*.

Works cited

Aquinas, Saint Thomas. *De Malo*. Ed. Brian Davies. Trans. Richard Regan. Oxford and New York: Oxford University Press, 2001.

—— *Summa Theologiae*. 5 Vols. Madrid: Biblioteca de Autores Cristianos, 1961–65.

Aristotle. *The Poetics*. Ed. and Trans. W. Hamilton Fyfe. Cambridge, MA: Harvard University Press, 1965.

Asquith, Clare. *Shadow Play: The Hidden Beliefs and Coded Politics of William Shakespeare*. New York: Public Affairs, 2005.

Bell, Millicent. *Shakespeare's Tragic Skepticism*. New Haven and London: Yale University Press, 2002.

Bradley, A.C. *Shakespearean Tragedy*. New York: Fawcett World Library, 1968.

Bullough, Geoffrey (Ed.). *Narrative and Dramatic Sources of Shakespeare*. 8 Vols. New York: Columbia University Press, 1973.

Campbell, Oscar James. "The Salvation of Lear." *English Literary History* (*ELH*) 15 (1948): 93–109.

Chambers, R.W. "*King Lear*." *Glasgow University Publications* 54 (1940): 20–52.

Coleridge, Samuel Taylor. *Coleridge's Writings on Shakespeare*. Ed. Terence Hawkes New York: G.P. Putnam's Sons, 1959.

Craig, Leon Harold. *Of Philosophers and Kings: Political Philosophy in Shakespeare's* Macbeth *and* King Lear. Toronto/Buffalo/London: University of Toronto Press, 2001.

Danby, John F. *Shakespeare's Doctrine of Nature: A Study of* King Lear. London: Faber and Faber, 1948.

Dollimore, Jonathan. *Radical Tragedy: Religion, Ideology and Power in the Drama of Shakespeare and His Contemporaries*. 3rd edn. Durham, NC: Duke University Press, 2004.

Elton, William R. King Lear *and the Gods*. San Marino, CA: The Huntington Library, 1968.

Empson, William. *The Structure of Complex Words*. 3rd edn. Totowa, NJ: Rowman and Littlefield, 1979.

French, Marilyn. "The Late Tragedies." *Shakespearean Tragedy*. Ed. John Drakakis. London and New York: Longman, 1992: 227–79.

The Geneva Bible: A Facsimile of the 1560 Edition. Intro. Lloyd E. Berry. Madison, Milwaukee, and London: University of Wisconsin Press, 1969.

Harrison, G.B. *Shakespeare's Tragedies*. London: Routledge and Kegan Paul, 1951.

Hittinger, Russell. *First Grace: Rediscovering the Natural Law in a Post-Christian World*. Wilmington, DE: ISI Books, 2003.

Hooker, Richard. *Of the Laws of Ecclesiastical Polity*. 1593 and 1597. Intro. Christopher Morris. 2 Vols. London: J.M. Dent, 1907.

Hunter, Robert G. *Shakespeare and the Mystery of God's Judgments*. Athens: University of Georgia Press, 1976.

Jaffa, Harry V. "The Limits of Politics: *King Lear*, Act I, scene i." *Shakespeare's Politics*. In Allan Bloom. Chicago and London: University of Chicago Press, 1981, 113–45.

James, D.G. *The Dream of Learning: An Essay on "The Advancement of Learning" and "King Lear."* Oxford: Clarendon Press, 1951.

Johnson, Samuel. *Samuel Johnson on Shakespeare*. Ed. W.K. Wimsatt, Jr. New York: Hill and Wang, 1960.

Kronenfeld, Judy. *King Lear and the Naked Truth: Rethinking the Language of Religion and Resistance*. Durham and London: Duke University Press, 1998.

Lipsius, Justus. *De Constantia libri duo*. In *Justi Lipsi Opera Omnia*. Wessel, 1675, IV, 411–512.

Mack, Maynard. *King Lear in Our Time*. Berkeley and Los Angeles: University of California Press, 1972.

Milward, Peter, S.J. *Biblical Influences in Shakespeare's Great Tragedies*. Bloomington and Indianapolis: Indiana University Press, 1987.

—— "The Religious Dimension in *King Lear*." *Shakespeare's Christian Dimension*. Ed. Roy Battenhouse. Bloomington and Indiana: Indiana University Press, 1994: 448–57.

Neville, Alexander. "Tragedy and God's Judgments." *English Renaissance Literary Criticism*. Ed. Brian Vickers. Oxford: Clarendon Press, 1999: 125–27.

The Norton Shakespeare. Ed. Stephen Greenblatt *et al.* New York and London: W.W. Norton and Co., 1997.

Peter, John. *Complaint and Satire in Early English Literature*. Oxford: Clarendon Press, 1956.

Rosenberg, John. "King Lear and His Comforters." *Essays in Criticism* 16 (1966): 135–46.

Sewell, Arthur. *Character and Society in Shakespeare*. Oxford: Clarendon Press, 1951.
Shakespeare, William. *The Riverside Shakespeare*. Ed. G.B. Evans *et al.* 2nd edn. Boston and New York: Houghton-Mifflin, 1997.
Speaight, Robert. *Nature in Shakespearean Tragedy*. New York: Collier Books, 1962.
Spencer, Theodore. *Shakespeare and the Nature of Man*. 2nd edn. New York: Macmillan, 1949.
Stampfer, Judah. "The Catharsis of *King Lear*." *Shakespeare Survey* 13 (1960): 1–10.
Swinburne, A.C. *The Complete Works of Algernon Charles Swinburne*. Eds. Sir Edmund Gosse and Thomas James Wise. Vol. 11: Prose Works Volume I. New York: Russell and Russell, 1968.
Tolkien, J.R.R. "*Beowulf*: The Monsters and the Critics." Rpt. *An Anthology of* Beowulf *Criticism*. Ed. Lewis E. Nicholson. Notre Dame, IN: University of Notre Dame Press, 1963: 51–103.
Vickers, Brian. "By Other Hands." A review of William Shakespeare, *Complete Works*, 2nd edn. Ed. Stanley Wells *et al. The Times Literary Supplement* 5393 (11 August 2006): 10–12.
White, R.S. *Natural Law in English Renaissance Literature*. Cambridge: Cambridge University Press, 1996.
Wilson, Richard. *Secret Shakespeare: Studies in Theatre, Religion and Resistance*. Manchester and New York: Manchester University Press, 2004.

9 *Lear* in Kierkegaard

Stanley Stewart

At the age of twenty-five, the philosopher, theologian and novelist Søren Aabye Kierkegaard fell in love with a beautiful young woman, ten years his junior. Having completed his theological studies in 1840, he traveled to Jutland to visit the birthplace of his father, who had died two years earlier. This sojourn to Jutland seems to have moved him greatly. On his return to Copenhagen, the twenty-seven-year-old Kierkegaard impulsively offered his hand in marriage to Regine Olsen, the daughter of a well-to-do statesman, Terkild. Despite a certain awkwardness at first, Regine returned his affection, and since her father consented, Regine accepted, and it looked as if, in the ordinary scheme of things, the lovers would marry. But, as Kierkegaard records in his journal, events would not unfold in the ordinary way: "inwardly; the next day I saw that I had made a false step. A penitent such as I was my *vita ante acta*, my melancholy, that was enough. I suffered unspeakably at that time" (*Journals* 92).

Although Regine begged him to take her back (156), he steelily rejected her in a manner designed to make her despise him. Kierkegaardians are left to proffer a wide range of speculations as to why he broke off the engagement. Perhaps Kierkegaard feared madness, which he might have inherited from the profligacy, real or imagined, of his father. Then there was his own experience with extra-marital sex, namely, a visit which he did nor did not make to a bordello, where he did or did not get his money's worth, did or did not contract syphilis, and/or did or did not father a child, depending on whether he had, or did not have, a capable or curved penis (Garff 104–5). We should recall that most of these speculations are based on the fact that certain entries in Kierkegaard's journal are either missing or torn and hard to read.

Whatever the reason, the breach with Regine affected Kierkegaard profoundly. In his imagination, the sublimated Regine became his literary inspiration. A flood of volumes, beginning with *Fear and Trembling*, followed and were, at least in part, shaped by the failed love affair, as Kierkegaard sought to set right, in literary form, what he felt was a mistake in his relationship with Regine. In *Fear and Trembling*, he sublimated his feelings for Regine into an imagined eternal affection: "A young lad falls in love with a princess, and this love is the entire substance of his life, and yet the relation is such that it cannot possibly be realized, cannot possibly be translated from ideality into reality" (*Fear* 41). A less romantic version of their brief love is also found in "The Seducer's Diary" in which Kierkegaard attempts to portray himself as a scoundrel and thus make the break easier for the object of his affection. More important for our purpose, "The Seducer's Diary" is also a key text in Kierkegaard's critique of *King Lear*, a work that held great, even theological, significance for him. In Kierkegaard's view, *King Lear* was flawed not because Cordelia and Lear die, but because Shakespeare seemed unwilling or unable to envision a transcendent realm of religious experience.

In "The Seducer's Diary," the narrator, Johannes, claims that the "girl" he wants to seduce "was very correctly named Cordelia" (*Either/Or* 1.305). We soon learn that her name bears philosophical significance. Johannes first hears that name when one of the girls she is with, and from whom she has become momentarily separated, calls out: "Cordelia! Cordelia!" (1.336). The girls confer quietly, frustrating his effort to eavesdrop. Since he has pursued (today we would say "stalked") her in secret, Johannes is left to ponder the significance of what he has heard: "Cordelia, then, is her name!" Almost at once the name takes on a sense of familiarity: "Cordelia! It is a beautiful name!" Somehow the name fits the girl, but, to Johannes, its propriety suggests a kinship of spirit that goes deeper than physical beauty. It is a name with a literary history; and it also brings with it an important character trait: "Cordelia! Cordelia! . . . Cordelia! That is really a splendid name—indeed, the same name as that of King Lear's third daughter, that remarkable girl whose heart did not dwell on her lips, whose lips were mute when her heart was full" (1.336).

Johannes is convinced that the two Cordelias share more than a name. Cordelia even looks like her Shakespearean namesake: "She resembles her, of that I am certain" (*Either/Or* 1.336). So the physical resemblance is important. But, of course, it is in their inner composure that the two young women most resemble each other. Indeed, by comparing his young lady with Shakespeare's Cordelia, the seducer provides a hint of Kierkegaard's reverence for silence, which goes hand in hand with his disdain for idle talk. Cordelia is a model of composure, closed within herself:

> She was an enigma that enigmatically possessed its own solution, a secret, and what are all the secrets of the diplomats compared with this, a riddle, and what in all the world is as beautiful as the word that solves it? How suggestive, how pregnant, the language is: to solve [*at løse*]—what ambiguity there is in it, with what beauty and with what strength it pervades all the combinations in which this word appears! Just as the soul's wealth is a riddle as long as the cord of the tongue is not loosened [*løst*] and thereby the riddle is solved [*løst*], so also a young girl is a riddle.
>
> (1.330)

The passage turns on a pun, which does not come across in translation. Here, Kierkegaard affirms the mystery of Cordelia's silence; she remains a mystery only as long as her innermost self remains in silent repose, which is its true nature. It is in her serene silence that Cordelia imparts the paradoxical sense of a mystery that is, in essence, also the solution to the mystery. This paradox brings longing and satisfaction together in one existence. But there is the one proviso. The tongue, often purposeless speech—the chatter of the empty, everyday world—is "*løst*"—loosened, resolved—revealing what is, though mysterious, nonetheless true and beautiful. And all of this is evident in Cordelia's Christian name.

Here, in the inner thoughts of his narrator on first hearing his beloved's name, Kierkegaard registers a theme indicative of his ethical perspective on *King Lear*. I use the word "ethical" deliberately, because Kierkegaard insists on the boundaries separating the aesthetic, ethical, and religious domains. Much of *Either/Or* aims at discriminating these boundaries, but perhaps Kierkegaard's most extensive discussion distinguishing the latter two is in *Fear and Trembling*, which he began writing the year of his breakup with Regine (Garff 232). Declaring Abraham the second father of the human race, the Patriarch of Patriarchs, under the pseudonym of Johannes de Silentio, Kierkegaard affirms that Abraham's faith was for this world. He loved this world as he loved his son:

> In fact, if his faith had been only for a life to come, he certainly would have more readily discarded everything in order to rush out of a world to which he did not belong. But Abraham's faith was not of this sort, if there is such a faith at all, for actually it is not faith but the most remote possibility of faith that faintly sees its object on the most distant horizon but is separated from it by a chasmal abyss in which doubt plays its tricks. But Abraham had faith specifically for this life—faith that he would grow old in this country, be honored among the people, blessed by posterity, and unforgettable in Isaac, the most precious thing in his life, whom he embraced with a love that is inadequately described by saying he faithfully fulfilled the father's duty to love the son, which is indeed stated in the command: the son, whom you love. Jacob had twelve sons, one of whom he loved; Abraham had but one, whom he loved.
>
> (*Fear* 20)

Abraham loved Isaac; all of his hopes for posterity are in his love for this one son. In this singularity, as a parent, Abraham is at the far pole from Lear. Lear loves Cordelia in a special way, too, but not for his posterity, nor even for this world, but for a "nursery" in his old age.

Given the way in which Kierkegaard perceives the episode on Mount Moriah, Abraham's faith, tested by God, is exponentially more compelling and more terrible than it would be if Abraham, like Jacob, had other sons to make good on God's promise to Abraham that his offspring would outnumber the sands of the sea. And yet when Abraham sets off for Mount Moriah, bearing the instruction that God has spoken to his heart, he keeps silent. He says not a word to his wife, Sarah, who had waited so many years to bear a child. On its face, Abraham's silence might seem to be a moral affront, for it was Sarah whose aging womb gave life to Isaac. Further, when Abraham binds Isaac, cuts the wood, prepares the fire, and raises the knife to plunge into Isaac's breast, he is, by human standards, a moral monster. Indeed, Johannes de Silentio (note that the authors of *Fear and Trembling* and "The Seducer's Diary" bear the same Christian name) imagines him saying, before plunging the knife into Isaac's breast, that a father must love his son more than himself. Indeed, from a moral point of view, Abraham is an outlaw from human society. But for Kierkegaard, the religious domain transcends the ethical. Were this not so, the world would forever condemn Abraham. Since the demands of the ethical and religious domains conflict, Abraham cannot be understood as "a tragic hero": "He gets Isaac back again by virtue of the absurd. Therefore, Abraham is at no time a tragic hero but is something entirely different, either a murderer or a man of faith" (*Fear* 57). If the analogy between Regine, Isaac, and the princess holds, despite Kierkegaard's reprehensible treatment of Regine, he imagines that they will end up together:

> By my own strength I can give up the princess, and I will not sulk about it but find joy and peace and rest in my pain, but by my own strength I cannot get her back again, for I use all my strength in resigning. On the other hand, by faith, says that marvelous knight, by faith you will get her by virtue of the absurd.
>
> (*Fear* 49–50)

It appears, then, that Johannes shares with Abraham a suffering which goes beyond heroism and tragedy. In elucidating this point, the tragic example that comes to Kierkegaard's mind is from Greek tragedy. Agamemnon must sacrifice his daughter, Iphigenia, to propitiate the goddess, Artemis, who has deprived his ships of wind. But in Euripides, Agamemnon turns his eyes away as the priest raises the knife for the sacrifice. Kierkegaard insists that, although he "nobly conceal[s] his agony" (*Fear* 57), the true hero, Abraham, the "true knight of faith," "must raise the knife" himself (57). Here, the key term is "public," for Agamemnon suffers for his nation, to gain the help of Artemis in the Greeks' stalled military campaign. Agamemnon's action is taken in public, and for the public interest. This is what Kierkegaard means by "ethical"; the action answers to "immanent" concerns of this world. In sharp contrast, Abraham acts alone, in defiance of social values:

> Abraham's situation is different. By his act he transgressed the ethical altogether and had a higher τέλος outside it, in relation to which he suspended it. For I certainly would like to know how Abraham's act can be related to the universal, whether any point of contact between what

> Abraham did and the universal can be found other than that Abraham transgressed it. It is not to save a nation, not to uphold the idea of the state that Abraham does it; it is not to appease the angry gods. If it were a matter of the deity's being angry, then he was, after all, angry only with Abraham, and Abraham's act is totally unrelated to the universal, is a purely private endeavor. Therefore, while the tragic hero is great because of his moral virtue, Abraham is great because of a purely personal virtue. (*Fear* 59)

In the ethical realm, there can be no higher demand than that the father love his son, and, if necessary, place his son's life before his own. It follows, then, that from an ethical standpoint, the world cries out against Abraham, as if from "Isaac's loins," saying "Do not do this, you are destroying everything" (59). In this moment, Abraham's isolation from all the comforts of the world transcends all human suffering. As such, it is at the farthest possible remove from Agamemnon's plight. Agamemnon is not alone; he carries the burden of his people. Agamemnon loves his daughter as Abraham loves his son. But Agamemnon is a tragic hero because he places the welfare of his nation above his daughter's life.

We are in a position now to see that, for Kierkegaard, Abraham's agony is in even sharper contrast to Lear's suffering than to Agememnon's. It may even be doubtful that, from Kierkegaard's point of view, Lear's actions are those of a tragic hero. Lear's first cries of anguish ring out in the halls of power, and they echo through one castle after another. But his aims are not self-abnegating, in the heroic manner of Agememnon. Lear does not divide his kingdom, and "sacrifice" his throne, for the good of England. It is true that he claims such a patriotic motive, as if he divides his kingdom "that future strife/May be prevented now" (1.1.44–45).[1] His subsequent actions, however, make clear that he means to surrender only the duties, not the trappings, of kingship: a hundred knights, with squires, horses, attendants, and what is more, the deference owed to a proper king. Lear is more believable when he admits that he favored Cordelia ("I loved her most") above her older sisters, and that he planned to cast off "all cares and business" (39) of state, in order "to set [his] rest/On her kind nursery" (123–24). But more to the ethical point for Kierkegaard, Lear's demand that he retain his entourage does not exhibit paternal love for his daughters. Rather, it reiterates the self-centeredness of the test that he proposes in the opening scene. Not only is Lear enthralled by the rhetorical devices of flattery, which he believes is owed to him by his rank, but he is also a parent who dispenses his affections unfairly. He admits that, had Cordelia said anything other than "Nothing," he would have given her "a third" of the country larger ("more opulent" [86]) than the "ample third" apportioned to her sisters.

While Lear acts for his own sake, rather than for England's, Abraham acts for God's sake, to prove his faith, *and* for his own sake, in order to prove it. For Kierkegaard, the difference here is significant. Why, one might ask, if neither man's suffering is borne in the nation's interest, are the two, then, not the same? We have already seen that, unlike Abraham, Lear does not love Cordelia more than himself; and he does not love her sisters as much as he loves her. So he is not even the moral equal of Agamemnon. But neither is the Greek hero Abraham's equal. We weep for the former, but not for the latter. In the episode of his great trial on Mount Moriah, we sense the horror—the "divine madness"—of the moment, as Abraham raises the knife above Isaac, knowing that, if God wills, he must plunge it into his son's breast. Agamemnon, the tragic hero, does what he must do for the good of the many, whose tears uphold him in his suffering. In contrast, Abraham suffers alone, and in silence. What if, in his solitariness, he has made a mistake? It is no wonder that we do not uphold him with our tears:

> One cannot weep over Abraham. One approaches him with a *horror religiosus*, as Israel approached Mount Sinai. What if he himself is distraught, what if he had made a mistake, this lonely man who climbs Mount Moriah . . . what if he is not a sleepwalker safely crossing the abyss while the one standing at the foot of the mountain looks up, shakes with anxiety, and then in his deference and horror does not even dare to call to him?
>
> (*Fear* 61)

Kierkegaard once suggested that there is sound theology in *King Lear*. But when his niece expressed astonishment at his reaction to her response to *Hamlet*, she struggled to understand:

> I tried to make him take part in the matter by asking him whether he was not enthralled by that extraordinary drama, whether it did not move him in the same way. "Of course, but with me it is quite a different thing," and when I looked enquiringly at him, he added as a kind of explanation "You cannot understand that now—perhaps one day you will understand it."
>
> (*Journals* 560)

Kierkegaard regarded Hamlet as quite the opposite of Lear, more likely in fact to disguise than to show his true feelings. Hamlet was, as Lear was decidedly not, the master of "indirect communication." Specifically, he was never in love with Ophelia, but only used "his relationship to Ophelia to take the attention away from what he actually [was] keeping hidden" (*Journals and Papers* 2.206). This means that Hamlet's "reflection," the cause of his much disputed refusal to take action against Claudius, must be construed as evidence of his religious belief. What he hid from others, namely his private convictions and longings, was what was most important to him, namely, his love and fear of God. In this way, he was, as his niece might someday appreciate, like her uncle Søren, who said in retrospect:

> I could have looked for a living and as a theological student could have had one, but I could not accept it (my thorn in the flesh stood in the way), so it was decided; I understood it quite suddenly. The thing was to approach as nearly as possible to God.
>
> (*Journals* 549)

Thus, in Kierkegaard's eyes, "Hamlet had the disease of reflection but still had not even reached the point of doubting everything" (*Journals and Papers* 2.61). In this underlying but all-important belief and longing for truth lies the similarity between Hamlet and himself that Kierkegaard perceived, but refused to explain to his niece, who had become enamored of the play. Since his response to her enthusiasm for the work seemed equivocal, she inferred that he might not like it. Quite the opposite, he said, he had a high opinion of *Hamlet*, but with him it was " 'a quite a different thing.' " Hence, as we have seen, Kierkegaard's refusal to explain: " 'You cannot understand that now—perhaps one day you will understand it' " (*Journals* 560).

Kierkegaard's perception of Hamlet went to the core of his own spiritual struggle. For him, Hamlet went beyond Hegel in confronting the "*immortal* dilemma through all eternity: to be or not to be, that is the question (*Hamlet*)" (*Journals* 74). Like Kierkegaard, Hamlet suffered because he experienced "the truth of the foreboding," which entailed the "all-consuming power of original sin" to "grow into despair" (*Journals* 40). This does not mean that, in Kierkegaard's mind, Hamlet ever doubted, in the religious sense. If he entertained such doubt, even for a moment, then the play, which depends on his "reflection," makes no sense. With Hamlet, it is what he does not say—what he hides even from Horatio—that counts. In contrast, with Lear, the totality of his being is thoroughly exhausted by explanation and action (today we might say by his "acting out"). Hamlet, Kierkegaard observed, feels that no one understands his life. This is why, in the end, his wish is that Horatio, his most trusted friend, delay the solace of death, so that the world will know the truth about him: "Report me and my cause aright / To the unsatisfied" (5.2.339–40). When Horatio remonstrates, Hamlet insists: "Absent thee from felicity a while, / And in this harsh world draw thy breath in pain / To tell my story" (347–49). On his deathbed, Kierkegaard registers something of the same concern with his good friend, Emil Boesen: "It all looked like pride and vanity, but it was not" (*Journals* 550).

To Kierkegaard, Lear's suffering is palpably different from Hamlet's, as it is from Abraham's, in that it is so accessible to everyone around. Even Kent, who disagrees with Lear, can sympathize with the old king. But in his suffering, Lear demeans himself, inviting pity, as if it were an anodyne to his pain. Then and afterwards, principals from far-flung counties in England and France witness his extreme passions. Lear reviles Kent and his daughters in overblown, rhetorical figures, always with someone standing in witness. He longs for understanding, and for others to affirm his actions. And when they refuse, he lashes out, again and again, until the only audience left to hear him is comprised of fellow exiles, fugitives, a lunatic, and a fool. And even then he rages on, begging for pity:

> Rumble thy bellyful; spit, fire; spout, rain.
> Nor rain, wind, thunder, fire are my daughters.
> I tax not you, you elements, with unkindness.
> I never gave you kingdom, called you children.
> You owe me no subscription. Then let fall
> Your horrible pleasure. Here I stand your slave,
> A poor, infirm, weak, and despised old man,
> But yet I call you servile ministers,
> That will with two pernicious daughters join
> Your high-engendered battles 'gainst a head
> So old and white as this. O, ho, 'tis foul!
> (3.2.14–24)

Or fantasizing revenge:

> It were a delicate stratagem to shoe
> A troop of horse with felt. I'll put't to proof,
> And when I have stol'n upon these son-in-laws,
> Then kill, kill, kill, kill, kill, kill!
> (4.5.180–83)

Most readers and spectators know, of course, that there is a vast chasm between Lear's words and the imagined rectitude and violence of his words. Even when the harsh reality of prison at Edmund's disposal is upon him and Cordelia, Lear imagines the two of them, alone, enjoying an uninterrupted life of "chatter":

> Come, let's away to prison.
> We two alone will sing like birds i' th' cage.
> When thou dost ask me blessing, I'll kneel down
> And ask of thee forgiveness; so we'll live,
> And pray, and sing, and tell old tales, and laugh
> At gilded butterflies, and hear poor rogues
> Talk of court news, and we'll talk with them too—
> Who loses and who wins; who's in, who's out,
> And take upon 's the mystery of things
> As it were God's spies; and we'll wear out
> In a walled prison packs and sects of great ones
> That ebb and flow by th' moon.
> (5.3.8–19)

In his declining mental state, Lear unwittingly trivializes the actuality of his relinquished power, transforming his and Cordelia's arrest into a shared opportunity for a life of uninterrupted gossip. It is as if, Kierkegaard muses in *The Stages on Life's Way*, Lear would distract his daughter with banter concerning "the royal household and ask news from it" (*Stages* 264).

Regine is not merely the saintly Cordelia; she is also an Ophelia to his Hamlet. Recall Hamlet's rejection of Ophelia and then read the following passage in which Kierkegaard is trying to rationalize the suffering that he both inflicted and endured in the breakup with Regine:

> That is how things stand. With all the heroes who hover in my imagination, it is indeed more or less the case that they carry a deep and secret sorrow that they are unable or unwilling to confide to anyone. I do not marry to have another person slave under my depression. It is my pride, my honor, my inspiration to keep in inclosing reserve what must be locked up, to reduce it to the scantiest rations possible; my joy, my bliss, my first and my only wish is to belong to her whom I would purchase at any price with my life and blood, but whom I still refuse to weaken and destroy by initiating her into my sufferings.
>
> (*Stages* 197)

Kierkegaard sees himself, as he sees Hamlet, as essentially religious. *Hamlet* "is a Christian drama" in the sense that it is "a 'religious' drama" (453). Kierkegaard is like Hamlet because, in the conflict of motives within him, he transcends "purely esthetic categories" (453). In this way, his religious presentiments make him heroic: "If he is religiously oriented, his misgivings are extremely interesting, because they give assurance that he is a religious hero" (453–54). In Shakespeare, religious belief has replaced what was, in the Roman world, national allegiance:

> If Hamlet is to be interpreted religiously, one must either allow him to have conceived the plan, and then the religious doubts divest him of it, or do what to my mind better illuminates the religious (for in the first case there could possibly be some doubt as to whether he actually was capable of carrying out his plan)—give him the demonic power resolutely and masterfully to carry out his plan and then let him collapse into himself and into the religious until he finds peace there.
>
> (454)

Kierkegaard's point also applies to Lear, whose suffering never rises to heroic, self-abnegating proportions. With Kierkegaard and Hamlet, "the religious is in the interior being, and therefore misgivings have their essential significance" (*Stages* 454). In marked contrast, Lear's suffering overflows with exterior display. It is Cordelia whose inner agony is never shared. When Edmund orders father and daughter to be taken away, Lear reverts to violent figures of revenge, while Cordelia keeps a resolute, serene silence. This, for Kierkegaard, is the true sign of love.

From the outset "in the division of the kingdom," Lear overvalues what Kierkegaard considers the major symptom of social decline: meaningless social conversation, "talkativeness," "chatter."[2] Unwisely, Lear reacts with childlike credulity to what people say. Given the fact that court behavior, especially speech, is particularly contrived to advance diplomacy, his naiveté, as is evident when Kent truthfully claims that his "youngest daughter does not love [him] least" (1.1.152), is both ironic and dangerous. This faithful analysis goes hand-in-hand with his advice that Lear "[r]eserve [his] state" (149) along with his family and his peace of mind. But Lear spurns the injunction—so important in Renaissance thought—of the Oracle of Delphi: "*Nosce teipsum.*" Regan, whose paean to her father mimics her older sister's hyperbole, understands her father's weakness very well: " 'Tis the infirmity of his age; yet he hath ever but slenderly known himself" (1.1.292–93). And it happens that Kierkegaard's judgment of Lear is not far from Regan's:

> King Lear's fate can be accounted for as Nemesis. His fault is the madness with which the play begins, of summarily requiring his children to declare the depth of their love for him. Children's love for their parents is a bottomless mystery, rooted as well in a natural relationship. An event can therefore be the occasion which reveals its depth, but it is unseemly, impious, and culpable to wish curiously and selfishly to dissect it, as it were, for the sake of one's own satisfaction. Such a thing is tolerable in an erotic relationship (when the lover asks the beloved how much she loves him), although even here it is pandering.
>
> (*Journals and Papers* 2.29)

Notice the level of reprehension here. Kierkegaard is indignant, because Lear fails to grasp what most people take for granted, namely, that children love their parents. It is a fact of nature, not amenable to rational explanation. In fact, any attempt to put such a deeply rooted attachment into words would amount to a superfluity of extraneous expression. Articulation—"chatter"—is a major problem of modern life, because it misleads the credulous into believing that something of consequence is afoot. Intuitively, ordinary people understand that the feelings a child has for the parent cannot be captured by public expression, no matter how hyperbolic. And, of course, with Lear, litotes presents even greater opportunity to misunderstand. After hearing Kent's wise counsel on the love his daughters truly bear him, Lear attaches his fate, and the fate of his kingdom, to the older daughters' public, hyperbolic flourish of expression.

In marked contrast, as we read in *Fear and Trembling*, a parent's love for the child is self-abnegating; Lear's affections are not even self-effacing. While it may be harmless, on ceremonial occasions such as Lear's retirement from kingship's responsibilities, to engage in hyperbolic expressions of love, it is reprehensible for a parent to examine their content with a mind to self-gratification. Lear's insistence that his daughters articulate their love is not just "unseemly," it is "impious," pernicious, despicable. Even a lover's insistence on the beloved's verbal reassurance is a mistake, albeit one more easily forgiven than a parent's. For lovers move "unnaturally"—that is, sometimes deceptively, sometimes awkwardly, but always over a course of time—from being strangers into lovers. But children love their parents mysterious—"naturally"—from the beginning. That is why the parent–child relationship is "impermeable by verbal characterization." That is why Lear's trust in talk proves self-defeating. Even his verbal decree of exile or death for Kent holds for less than a fortnight.

For Kierkegaard, "talkativeness" is no mere solecism, like using the wrong fork at a formal dinner. More tellingly, it exhibits an enervation at the core of modern society:

> What is it *talkativeness*? It is the result of doing away with the vital distinction between talking and keeping silent. Only some one who knows how to remain essentially silent can really talk—and act essentially. Silence is the essence of inwardness, of the inner life.
>
> (*Present* 78)

Chatter fears silence, simply because it "reveals its emptiness" (79). We might expect, then, Kierkegaard to disdain the cultured conversation of the salon. Polite conversation is, in the biblical sense, "lukewarm." It is too careful, too sophisticated, too knowing, too burdened by unimportant detail. We have the sense that, from Kierkegaard's point of view, Shakespeare's Burgundy has spoken well—too well, perhaps—in Lear's court. He has performed all the niceties of diplomatic "chatter," and met every expectation of the successful suitor for Cordelia's hand. So he has every reason to suppose that he has struck a deal with the English court. All Cordelia needs to do is meet the minimal demands of polite "chatter" on the occasion of her father's retirement from public life. Her older, married sisters have shown the easy, if empty, way of talkativeness. It might be an easy way, but for Cordelia it is impossible. She cannot mimic her sisters; and it is this incapacity to perform a small imitation of speech that explains Kierkegaard's admiration of her. Indeed, to the speaker of "The Seducer's Diary," the very name, "Cordelia," suggests a rapture of silence. His Cordelia exists in a dimension beyond everyday talk. So it is that Johannes recalls how Goneril and Regan—the reader could easily add Lear and his Fool—characterize themselves by their public display of garrulity. First, there is Goneril, perhaps the most egregious example. We should remember that, for all her faults, the one that most galls her husband is her obnoxious carping. When Edgar, in disguise, fells Edmund, and everything that Goneril yearns for is at stake, she holds forth on a particular article in "th'law of war," even at the risk of revealing her treachery. Gloucester, she insists, was not obliged to answer an anonymous challenger. In fact, Albany does not even bother to refute her claim. He pays no attention to the law: "Shut your mouth, dame," he orders, "Or with this paper shall I stopple it" (5.3.44–46). Like Kent, Albany understands the vacuity of his wife's "chatter," which, from the beginning in "the division of the kingdom," aims to bring people and events into line with her desires.

It would be no exaggeration to say that, for Kierkegaard, Lear's indignant reaction to Cordelia's refusal to engage the ceremonial occasion with speech, however formulaic, in the manner of her sisters, exhibits his limited, spiritual understanding. Lear does not grasp how much his world is shaped by empty talk. Given the occasion, Cordelia's "Nothing, my lord" is the public equivalent of silence. It enrages Lear because it threatens his world, which depends on the formulae of court speech, which are geared to social rank. But, for Kierkegaard, this is precisely the existential matter exposed by Cordelia's answer, for the elder sisters' overblown sentiments are the opposite of true speech, which we hear in Kent's cryptic judgments no less than in Cordelia's stoic silence. For Kierkegaard, inwardness is the essence of love, and reticence is its human expression. Thus, Kierkegaard argues that all that is good in a person is silent:

> From the very start, everything that is good in a person is silent, and just as it is essentially God's nature to live in secret, so also the good in a person lives in secret. Every resolution that is fundamentally good is silent, because it has God as its confidant and went to him in private; every holy feeling that is fundamentally good is silent . . . every emotion of the heart is silent, since the lips are sealed and only the heart is expanded.
>
> (*Eighteen* 370)

For Kierkegaard, noise is a symptom of a deep disorder in the human soul. Indeed, for him, the first problem of modern society is that it lacks silence. The turbulence of life—its noise—sweeps a person along with the multitude into the superfluous world, away from God:

> Ah, everything is noisy; and just as a strong drink is said to stir the blood, so everything in our day, even the most insignificant project, even the most empty communication, is designed merely to jolt the senses or to stir up the masses, the crowd, the public, noise!
>
> (*Self-Examination* 47–48)

Accordingly, Cordelia is the example that comes most readily to his mind. She loves her father in the appropriate and sacred way required of a daughter. Her silence is the outward sign of her humility, of her virtue: "Nothing my Lord." Her feelings do not lend themselves to public expression.

Again, when Edmund orders Cordelia and her father to be taken away, she says nothing. Cordelia bears the knowledge of their situation alone, in secret.

In this way, in Kierkegaard's mind, Shakespeare's Cordelia is, at the core of her being, very much like the modern "tragic heroine," Antigone (*Either/Or* 1.153). As the modern counterpart of her Sophoclean namesake, Antigone exists in a world compounded of noisy, empty conversation and banal "reflection" on trivial concerns. In all other respects, the story of modern Antigone's life in the family of Oedipus and Jocasta is a repetition of the Greek tale, with this one exception:

> Everyone knows that [Oedipus] has killed the sphinx and freed Thebes, and Oedipus is hailed and admired and is happy in his marriage with Jocasta. The rest is hidden from the people's eyes, and no suspicion has ever brought this horrible dream into the world of actuality. Only Antigone knows it.
>
> (*Either/Or* 1.154)

As a young girl, Antigone learns—it doesn't matter how—this terrible secret, and, instead of the ancient, immediate, and therefore passing sorrow of her Greek antecedent, Antigone reflects upon the horror, and experiences anxiety, which, unlike the ancient sorrow, does not pass. In this way, modern tragedy has a double edge, for the two—sorrow and anxiety—exist in an inevitable dyad of the present and the not-present. In Greek tragedy, Antigone is unconcerned about her father's fate, for it is shared by the community, and understood to be an unchangeable fact, which envelops the family, but the family no more than anyone else. But now, the modern Antigone shares her sorrow with no one. She reflects upon it inwardly, for the stage of this drama is not public, but spiritual:

> Perhaps nothing ennobles a person so much as keeping a secret. It gives a person's whole life a significance, which it has, of course, only for himself; it saves a person from all futile consideration of the surrounding world. Sufficient unto himself, he rests blissful in his secret; this might be said even though his secret is a most baleful one.
>
> (1.157)

So as the world praises Oedipus as a hero, Antigone suffers, nourishing her secret of the truth in her heart. Kierkegaard's Antigone and Kierkegaard's Cordelia bear their suffering alone and in silence. And, like his Antigone, Kierkegaard's Cordelia nourishes the love she has for her father in secret.

As we know, for Kierkegaard, secrecy is a site of silence, and so of holiness. But because it exists outside the public domain of ethics, it is also, potentially, "the demon's trap" (*Fear* 88). As for the demoniacal, because he did not shrink from acquaintance with it, Shakespeare, "the poet's poet" (*Sickness* 38) "is and remains a hero" (*Fear* 105). But, Kierkegaard insists, even the greatest poet who ever lived did not speak of this horror, although he leaves the reason for this omission a mystery. As for Lear's misery, Kierkegaard thinks the explanation is obvious. Lear is forever exposing his motives, and these might arouse pity in a compassionate audience, which might even weep with him, as the world of words that he so loved strips him of the external signs of power that he once took for granted. But neither here nor elsewhere does Shakespeare touch what Kierkegaard calls "*horror religiosus*":

> Thanks, once again thanks, to a man who, to a person overwhelmed by life's sorrows and left behind naked, reaches out the words, the leafage of language by which he can conceal his misery. Thanks to you, great Shakespeare, you who can say everything, everything, everything just as it is—and yet, why did you never articulate this torment? Did you perhaps reserve it for yourself, like the beloved's name that one cannot bear to have the world utter, for with his little secret that he cannot divulge the poet buys this power of the word to tell everybody's else's dark secrets. A poet is not an apostle; he drives out devils only by the power of the devil. (*Fear* 61)

In this mix of praise and reproach, Kierkegaard questions the range, not of Shakespeare's talent, but of his vision. Shakespeare expresses "everything, everything, everything," except what is most important. That is to say, Shakespeare's chatter may fill the void of human existence, but in characters who suffer meaninglessly (i.e. Lear), he offers no consolation. In terms of spirituality, all too often Shakespeare's "everything" somehow lacks the seriousness of Cordelia's "nothing." Note his description of Cordelia in "The Seducer's Diary," which, given his thoughts on Shakespeare, reads not only as a novelized rendering of his beloved Regine, but also as a perceptive critique of Lear's youngest daughter: "She herself was hidden in herself; she herself rose up out of herself; there was a recumbent pride in her like the spruce's bold escape—although it is riveted to the earth. A sadness surrounded her, like the cooing of the wood dove, a deep longing that was lacking nothing" (*Either/Or*, 1.330). Indeed, Kierkegaard implies that perhaps Shakespeare used his literary gift to cover up the "misery" that he may have known of this "*horror religiosus*." Unlike Keats, whose view of Shakespeare's "negative capability" pragmatist John Dewey would mark out as his own, Kierkegaard regards a literary talent with an even-handed perspective on terrestrial suffering as something like "a fugitive and cloistered virtue, unexercised and unbreathed" in the rare atmosphere of man alone in the awful presence of God. Insofar as the author of *King Lear* exorcized demons, he did so by the material power of Satan.

It is one of the defining characteristics of philosophical discussions of Shakespeare—that is, discussions of those thinkers whom librarians and professors of philosophy regard as philosophers—that they cluster around certain plays. Shaftesbury thought that, of all Shakespearean plays, *Othello*, by reflecting the sexual barbarism of English women, was the one that best explained Shakespeare's unique place in the canon. Richardson was especially intrigued by the characters of Falstaff and Macbeth. Søren Kierkegaard was drawn to Shakespearean comedies and history plays, but especially to the tragedies. Kierkegaard's niece thought that her uncle was like Hamlet, whose situation he believed to be much like his own (Lowrie 1.209). She took that to mean that Kierkegaard was haunted by the ghost of his father; it does appear that his father's reputed cursing of God had a lasting effect on him. Be that as it may, surely for Kierkegaard, Shakespeare stood alone in his capacity to represent opposing impulses within a single character:

> The art of writing lines, replies, that with full tone and all imaginative intensity sound out of one passion and in which there is nevertheless the resonance of the opposite—this art no poet has practiced except the one and only: Shakespeare.
>
> (*Sickness* 157)

Indeed, in *Either/Or*, Kierkegaard's Victor Eremita virtually equates Shakespeare with Holy Writ in his capacity to imbue existence with the vitality sadly absent from the modern world:

> Let others complain that the times are evil. I complain that they are wretched, for they are without passion. People's thoughts are as thin and fragile as lace, and they themselves as pitiable as lace-making girls. The thoughts of their hearts are too wretched to be sinful. It is perhaps possible to regard it as sin for a worm to nourish such thoughts, but not for a human being, who is created in the image of God. Their desires are staid and dull, their passions drowsy. . . . Fie on them! That is why my soul always turns back to the Old Testament and to Shakespeare. There one still feels that those who speak are human beings; there they hate, there they love, there they murder the enemy, curse his descendants through all generations—there they sin.
>
> (*Either/Or* 1.27–28)

It is no wonder that Kierkegaard thinks of Richard III and Macbeth as important figures, for their sins rise to a level of grandeur. It is as if Kierkegaard recalls a passage, not from Shakespeare or the Old Testament, but the New Testament, in which he, in another place, distinguishes "an essential sin-consciousness" from the "triviality and silly aping of 'the others' that . . . can hardly be called sin, a life that is too spiritless to be called sin and is worthy only, as Scripture says, of being 'spewed out' " (*Sickness* 101). Again, he is thinking of St. John's Apocalypse: "I know thy works, that thou art neither cold nor hot: I would thou wert cold or hot. So then because thou art lukewarm, and neither cold nor hot, I will spue thee out of my mouth" (Rev. 3.15–16). The lukewarm spirit cannot be loyal to either spouse or king (*Stages* 175); nor, to Kierkegaard's way of thinking, is it possible for the true Christian to be lukewarm (*Practice* 256). Kierkegaard admires decisiveness.

In Shakespeare, as in St. John at Patmos, commitment, which is at the far pole of that bane of modernity, reflection, is what matters. This is why Kierkegaard regarded lines that Shakespeare gave Macbeth a "psychologically masterful" characterization of the way in which the works of evil "gain strength and power only through sin" (*Sickness* 106). Shakespeare does not leave Macbeth's villainy in doubt. And it is Hamlet's religious doubts that drive him to divest himself of his plan for vengeance (*Stages* 454).

More to the point of this essay, Kierkegaard's interest in *King Lear* is especially revealing with respect to his admiration of Shakespeare. Shakespeare lets the world lie as it is, with Kent willing to follow his master in a Roman death, and Edgar left to govern a world in which all of the women have either been murdered or committed suicide. It is a bleak world ("Howl, howl, howl"), but it is decidedly not one in which God decrees that Edmund murder Cordelia. Further, even Lear's cruelties toward her and Kent are his own, as the means of reconciliation are not. Similarly, Gloucester's suffering, however unjust, separates him from his household, but reunites him with his legitimate son. Like Lear, Gloucester is no Abraham on a mountaintop, ready to bear the knife to his beloved son's throat. Although he attempts to sacrifice himself, the attempt is comic. He only imagines himself at the top of a Dover cliff.

In *King Lear*, Shakespeare's view of human suffering makes no moral sense. Cordelia does not deserve what happens to her. By setting the action of the play in pre-Christian England, Shakespeare is saying, with all of his "negative capability" in play, not that "the gods . . . kill us for their sport," but that the world would not change its appearance if that were the case. Christianizers of *Lear* point to Edmund's repentance just before death, but this is the very Kierkegaardian point, which aims in the opposite direction. Edmund's rescission of his death warrant arrives too late; it does no more for Lear and Cordelia than it does for Edmund.

From Kierkegaard's point of view, in *Lear*, then, Shakespeare offers "everything, everything, everything" about human suffering, and all of it with a magisterial, diagnostic clarity. And yet, despite this "everything," Shakespeare's vision is lacking. Why? Because there is chicanery here. It is as if, like the professional magician, the poet has purchased a device, which, in turn, fabricates an illusion. So it is by a secret that the poet is able to tell secrets. The mere poet "casts out devils only by the power of the devil," and for this reason cannot be compared with prophets and apostles. As we read in *Of the Difference Between a Genius and an Apostle* (1847), Kierkegaard vigorously distinguishes between Shakespeare and St. Paul. His aim is not to deny that St. Paul could be eloquent, but only that the matter of eloquence is beside the point. It is a mistake to compare St. Paul with the likes of Shakespeare, because, when we do so, we introduce extraneous stylistic standards of comparison. St. Paul was a tentmaker, but we do not praise his accomplishments as an upholsterer on the grounds that he was a saint:

> As a genius St. Paul cannot be compared with either Plato or Shakespeare, as a coiner of beautiful similes he comes pretty low down in the scale, as a stylist his name is quite obscure—and as an upholsterer: well, I frankly admit I have no idea how to place him.
>
> (*Difference* 104–5)

Kierkegaard's point is that the comparison is silly. A serious comparison can only be seen when we recognize the juxtaposition as a joke:

> As an Apostle St Paul has no connexion whatsoever with Plato or Shakespeare, with stylists or upholsterers, and none of them (Plato no more than Shakespeare or Harrison, the upholsterer) can possibly be compared with him.
>
> (105)

The genius is bound to "*the sphere of immanence*," while the apostle belongs to "*the sphere of transcendence*" (105). With genius, even with one who is ahead of his time, there is never a serious problem—no paradox. The genius is born. If born out of his time, he may not fit in, and may even seem like a prophet. But history overtakes the genius, and society assimilates the work to which the genius was born, and to which he gives birth.

Here, however, is the secret that either Shakespeare did not know or refused to share: "It is otherwise with an Apostle" (*Difference* 107). As the designation indicates, the "Apostle is not born; an Apostle is a man called and appointed by God, receiving a mission from him." The genius might develop, nurture his talent; and that talent might have a life-altering sense of self. This is not so with an Apostle:

> Apostolic calling is a paradoxical factor, which from first to last in his life stands paradoxically outside his personal identity with himself as the definite person he is. A man may perhaps have reached years of discretion long ago, when suddenly he is called to be an Apostle. As a result of this call he does not become more intelligent, does not receive more imagination, a greater acuteness of mind and so on; on the contrary, he remains himself and by that paradoxical fact he is sent on a particular mission by God.
>
> (107–8)

The point here is that the ornaments of language—and the contingencies of historical context—play no part in the apostle's life. He does not develop a sense of God's will; it is given and obeyed, all in the same moment. In this way, the apostle is unlike the genius, who is both born with inward capabilities different from others, and, in turn, developed throughout his lifetime. In marked contrast, the apostle is called without respect to his talent or intelligence.

For Kierkegaard, this is an all-important distinction. The genius—and Shakespeare was surely one—expresses himself on the "aesthetic" level, and must therefore be judged "purely aesthetically" (*Difference* 108). Critics might argue about the particulars of that expression, its eloquence, its cleverness, its style. But the apostle speaks with "divine authority" (109), and cannot therefore demand a hearing on aesthetic grounds:

> St. Paul must not appeal to his cleverness, for in that case he is a fool; he must not enter into a purely aesthetic or philosophical discussion of the content of the doctrine, for in that case he is side-tracked. No, he must appeal to his divine authority and, while willing to lay down his life and everything, by that very means *prevent* any aesthetic impertinence and any direct philosophical approach to the form and content of the doctrine.
>
> (109)

It follows from this comparison that Shakespeare is no more responsible for the adulation heaped on him than he is for his blindness to "*horror religiosus*." Of course, modernity leaves no place for this distinction. Because of the prevailing skepticism in society, aesthetic and authoritative utterances are often judged by the same criteria. If a genius said it, then God said it. The problem here is that skepticism effectively reduces the divine to aesthetic form. Just as Lear's suffering is different in quality from Agamemnon's noble agony, so Shakespeare's tragic vision includes "everything, everything, everything" that is in the "immanent" aesthetic and ethical domains. But Shakespeare's "everything," while assimilable by society, includes "everything" except the "transcendent."

Notes

1 All citations from Shakespeare in my text are from *The Tragedy of King Lear* as printed in the Oxford *Shakespeare* (see list of works cited). Kierkegaard did not read English, and probably knew Shakespeare in the twelve-volume German translation of August Wilhelm von Schlegel and Ludwig Tieck, published in Berlin in 1839–40.

2 For an extensive discussion of this important motif in Kierkegaard, see Fenves, esp. chaps. 1 and 4.

Works cited

Fenves, Peter. *"Chatter": Language and History in Kierkegaard*. Stanford: Stanford University Press, 1993.

Garff, Joakim. *Søren Kierkegaard: A Biography*. Trans. Bruce H. Kirmmse. Princeton: Princeton University Press, 2005.

Hannay, Alastair. *Kierkegaard: A Biography*. Cambridge: Cambridge University Press, 2001.

Holy Bible: Containing the Old and New Testaments Authorized King James Version. New York: Oxford University Press, 1952.

Kierkegaard, Søren. *The Concept of Irony With Continual Reference to Socrates, together with Notes of Schelling's Berlin Lectures.* Eds. and trans. Howard V. Hong and Edna H. Hong. Princeton: Princeton University Press, 1989.

—— *Concluding Unscientific Postscript to Philosophical Fragments.* Eds. and trans. Howard V. Hong and Edna H. Hong. 2 vols. Princeton: Princeton University Press, 1992.

—— *Eighteen Upbuilding Discourses.* Eds. and trans. Howard V. Hong and Edna H. Hong. Princeton: Princeton University Press, 1990.

—— *Either / Or.* Eds. and trans. Howard V. Hong and Edna H. Hong. 2 vols. Princeton: Princeton University Press, 1987.

—— *Fear and Trembling.* Eds. C. Stephen Evans and Sylvia Walsh. Trans. Sylvia Walsh. Cambridge: Cambridge University Press, 2006.

—— *Fear and Trembling / Repetition.* Eds. and trans. Howard V. Hong and Edna H. Hong. Princeton: Princeton University Press, 1983.

—— *The Journals of Søren Kierkegaard.* Ed. and trans. Alexander Dru. London: Oxford University Press, 1951.

—— *The Point of View: On My Work as an Author.* Eds. and trans. Howard V. Hong and Edna H. Hong. Princeton: Princeton University Press, 1998.

—— *Practice in Christianity.* Eds. and trans. Howard V. Hong and Edna H. Hong. Princeton: Princeton University Press, 1991.

—— *Prefaces: Writing Sampler.* Ed. and trans. Todd W. Nichol. Princeton: Princeton University Press, 1997.

—— *The Present Age and Of The Difference Between a Genius and an Apostle.* Trans. Alexander Dru. London: Collins, 1962.

—— *For Self-Examination: Judge for Yourself.* Eds. and trans. Howard V. Hong and Edna H. Hong. Princeton: Princeton University Press, 1990.

—— *The Sickness Unto Death: A Christian Psychological Exposition for Upbuilding and Awakening.* Eds. and trans. Howard V. Hong and Edna H. Hong. Princeton: Princeton University Press, 1980.

—— *Søren Kierkegaard's Journals and Papers.* Eds. and trans. Howard V. Hong and Edna H. Hong, Asst. Gregor Malantschuk. 6 vols. Bloomington: Indiana University Press, 1970.

—— *Stages on Life's Way.* Eds. and trans. Howard V. Hong and Edna H. Hong. Princeton: Princeton University Press, 1988.

Lowrie, Walter. *Kierkegaard.* 2 vols. Gloucester, MA: Peter Smith, 1970.

Shakespeare, William. *The Complete Works of Shakespeare: Modern Spelling Edition.* Eds. Gary Taylor and Stanley Wells. Oxford: Clarendon, 1986.

Updike, John. "Foreward." *The Seducer's Diary.* Eds. and trans. Howard V. Hong and Edna H. Hong. Princeton: Princeton University Press, 1997: vii–xv.

10 The smell of mortality

Performing torture in *King Lear* 3.7

Edward L. Rocklin

For Stanley Cavell

> The scream that comes welling out of the torture chamber is thus double—the body calling out to the soul, the self calling out to others—and in both cases, it goes unanswered. Torture's stark lesson is precisely that enveloping silence.
>
> (Lawrence Weschler, *A Miracle, A Universe: Settling Accounts with Torturers* (1998): 238)

Prologue

In defending *King Lear* from various charges by critics espousing neo-classic principles, Samuel Johnson conceded that he could not justify either the death of Cordelia or the blinding of Gloucester. In the first case, Johnson was pleased to note that "Cordelia, from the time of Tate, has always retired with victory and felicity," referring to Nahum Tate's adaptation (1681), which, until well into the nineteenth century, was the basis for stage versions of the play. In what may be the single most-cited testimony to the impact of this death, Johnson remarked "And, if my sensations could add anything to the general suffrage, I might relate, that I was many years ago so shocked by Cordelia's death, that I know not whether I ever endured to read again the last scenes of the play till I undertook to revise them as an editor" (Johnson, VIII: 704). In the twentieth and twenty-first centuries, the shocking nature of Cordelia's death has been perceived as essential to the tragic design both because of its lethal impact on Lear and its heart-stopping impact on audiences, for whom it shatters the pattern of restoration the play prompts first-time spectators to expect. In addition, we have recognized the impact it would have had on those members of Shakespeare's original audiences who, knowing earlier versions of the story, would have been sure that at this point Cordelia and Lear triumph over the other two sisters.

About the second problem, Johnson confessed that "I am not able to apologise . . . for the extrusion of Gloucester's eyes, which seems an act too horrid to be endured in dramatick exhibition, and such as must always compel the mind to relieve its distress by incredulity" (703). In this case, Tate had not rescued audiences, for his version retained the blinding. But Johnson may never have had to endure this other unendurable action because the performances of *King Lear* he might have seen—and Arthur Murphy and Joshua Reynolds testify that Johnson saw the play at least once (*Johnsonian Miscellanies*, 1: 457 and 2: 248)—would almost certainly have been those produced by and starring David Garrick. And Garrick performed his own modified version of Tate, in which Gloucester was blinded offstage and by servants rather than onstage and by Cornwall (Garrick 3: 360).[1] The fact that Garrick thought it necessary to eliminate the blinding suggests that once Cordelia's death was eliminated, the shocking nature of the blinding became more foregrounded and less tolerable.

If "the extrusion of Gloucester's eyes" has in our own time come to seem horrifying yet essential to the experience of *King Lear*, one factor contributing to this shift may have been the theatrical rediscovery of Shakespeare's *Titus Andronicus*. Starting with Peter Brook's 1955 revival, a series of powerful productions have prompted us to recognize that the violence in *Lear* was anticipated and exceeded by the scenes of murder, rape, mutilation, throat-slashing, and cannibalism that permeate Shakespeare's first tragedy.[2] In the theater, moreover, the violence of the blinding can seem almost tame in comparison with some instances of modern stage violence—for example, the scene in Edward Bond's *Saved* where a baby is stoned to death in its carriage. And even the extreme instances of stage violence can, in turn, seem almost quaint when compared to the outsized yet obscenely intimate hyper-realistic violence in contemporary films. Thus whereas the blinding of Gloucester was once seen as something too horrid to be represented—A.C. Bradley wrote of "the mere physical horror of such a spectacle" (203), and Heilman acknowledged the act could seem to be "gratuitous melodrama" even as he rebutted that perception (25)—in our own time, while it is still widely considered one of the most disturbing scenes in the Shakespeare canon, it too has come to be perceived as central to the play's dramatic design and theatrical power. Indeed directors often signal the blinding's function as a turning point by placing the intermission after this scene.

This essay examines the texts and performances of this pivotal scene. First, I offer a brief articulation of the design of the first three acts. This is followed by a description of the context created by the use of torture during the reigns of Queen Elizabeth and King James. The third part traces how the action of 3.7 produces a detailed representation of the final shredding of the political, social, and personal order operating at the moment when King Lear initiates his abdication. The fourth part focuses on the most striking difference between the Quarto (1608) and Folio (1623) texts of this scene. This leads to an examination of what the scene can do in performance and, in particular, the effects created by several revivals which staged the scene in ways that served to include and implicate the spectators.

Articulating the design of *King Lear*: from "all" to "nothing"

There are a number of ways to articulate the dramatic design of *King Lear*, but for the purpose of exploring 3.7 it is illuminating to start by contrasting the first three acts of this play with the first three acts of *Hamlet*. Both plays use a royal family and the family of the chief courtier to create their double plots. And both present worlds in which the bonds that constitute the "personal, social, and political order" (Van Laan 239) are nullified by corrupting choices made by the heads of these families: Claudius, Polonius and, arguably, the Ghost, in *Hamlet*; Lear and Gloucester in *King Lear*. But this fundamental similarity points to an equally important contrast, often formulated by describing *Hamlet* as a tragedy of situation and *King Lear* as a tragedy of free will.

For its title character, *Hamlet* is a tragedy of situation, in which Hamlet confronts a world where his choices are constrained by the fact that, in murdering King Hamlet, Hamlet's uncle has unleashed forces that corrupt Denmark. Yet while Hamlet finds his life shaped by this situation, it is also true that the tragic action is triggered by the oath he takes to fulfill the Ghost's plea for revenge (1.5.111–13)—an oath which prompts Hamlet to transform himself from a mourner into an agent who can "set [the time] right" (1.5.190).[3] And it is as he seeks to perform revenge that Hamlet, licensed by his antic disposition, exposes the pervasive and still-spreading corruption created by his uncle's crime.

For its title character, *King Lear* is a tragedy of free will, in which Lear, at a moment when he faces no external compulsion, chooses to divide his kingdom among his daughters. The corruption arises not from the abdication and division but from the "love test" by which he initiates the division. If the corruption in *Hamlet* is triggered by a single pre-play act, the corruption in *King Lear* is triggered by a single word. For if Lear's purpose is to elicit public testimony of each daughter's love, he need only have asked "Which of you shall we say doth love us?" Each daughter could have professed her love and received her share of the kingdom; Cordelia's dowry would have ensured marriage to one of her suitors; and Lear's explicit intent would have been fulfilled. But Lear asks "Which of you shall we say does love us most?" (1.1.51). Whatever his intent, with the word "most" he introduces the disastrous premise that love can be quantified. Cordelia's simple but devastating question—"Why have my sisters husbands if they say/They love you all?" (99–100)—exposes the fallacy of his premise and the hypocrisy of her sisters, and drives the humiliated Lear to exile true service in the person of Kent even as he disinherits filial love in the person of Cordelia. Lear's "most" functions like the tremor that sets off an avalanche, the atom that sets off a chain reaction, the mutation that sets off a cascade of genetic changes eventually producing a new species.

Whereas the first three acts of *Hamlet* focus on the protagonist's discovery of the corruption unleashed by his uncle's murder of King Hamlet, the first three acts of *King Lear* present the process by which Lear's choice releases the forces which corrupt his world. In fact, the transforming effect of Lear's choice is instantaneous. At the end of the scene Goneril and Regan announce their intention to "do something, and that i' th' heat" (306) in order to insure that Lear cannot preserve his rights as king while abdicating his responsibilities. Their exit is followed by the re-entry of Edmund, who initiates his plan to destroy the bond between his father and his legitimate older brother, Edgar. Edmund thus begins an action which causes the descent of Gloucester, contributes to the descent of Lear, makes him the agent of Cordelia's death and thus the death of Lear, and enables him to ascend to a point where only one life stands between him and the crown. Moreover, the first two scenes also foreshadow the connection between the plots since they juxtapose the sisters with the man whose favors they will court and for whom they will die.

Whereas Goneril and Regan never articulate the principles shaping their actions, Edmund makes explicit the principles Lear has inadvertently introduced: "Thou, nature, art my goddess" (1.2.1; "Nature" is capitalized in both the Quarto and Folio texts). He does not mean the supposedly benign "Nature" Lear invokes as the goddess who sanctions the existing social order but rather that Nature which is prior to all socially created realities, including the laws which distinguish "legitimate" from "bastard" children. The premises articulated by Edmund and practiced by Goneril, Regan, and Cornwall create what Frank Kermode describes as "a world and a society conceived as purely natural, where man is wolf to man, and the human will in service of personal appetite rules conduct" (Kermode 1301).

The descent of Lear can be seen as occurring in two phases. The first phase culminates at the end of Act 2, as his elder daughters reverse the logic of the first scene: there, seeking to demonstrate they loved him "most," they were compelled to proclaim they loved him "all"; here, holding the upper hand, they bid him down to "nothing." The second phase culminates in 3.6, where Gloucester helps Lear escape capture by these same daughters who "seek his death" (3.4.153). Similarly, the descent of Gloucester can be seen as occurring in two phases. The first phase plays out in Act 2, as Edmund manipulates Gloucester into disinheriting Edgar and seeking his death; and the second phase plays out in Act 3 where, by choosing to support Lear against Regan and Cornwall, Gloucester provides the opportunity for Edmund to betray him, reducing him, like the son he wronged, to "nothing" (2.2.184). Taken together, 3.6 and 3.7 complete the process by which one world order mutates into its opposite: the blinding of Gloucester marks the moment when the hierarchic, humanly constructed order invoked by Lear, Gloucester, and Kent gives way to Edmund's predatory "Nature."

Treason and torture

In grasping the details with which Shakespeare packed 3.7, it is worth reviewing how the Tudor and Stuart regimes dealt with what they considered cases of treason, and why they resorted to torture in dealing with some of these cases. During the period from 1540 to 1603, the Tudor rulers sought to expand the statutes defining treason as a means to cope with those subjects who refused to accept either the new Protestant state religion or the restoration of the Catholic faith during the reign of Queen Mary. Charges of treason were especially common during the period when Elizabeth and the Privy Council believed the realm was under attack from Catholic Europe, in part because Elizabeth had been excommunicated by Pope Pius V in February 1570, in a bull which proclaimed that "[h]er subjects were absolved from all obedience" (MacCaffrey 328), in part because Pope Gregory XIII supported an invasion of Ireland (Guy 285), and in part because in 1584 the leader of the Dutch Protestants, William of Orange, was murdered by a lone Catholic assassin using a concealed handgun (Jardine 15–20). This conflict was also exacerbated during the years 1568–87, when the captive Queen Mary of Scotland became a focus for plots to overthrow Elizabeth. Furthermore, the Jesuit mission to England, in which the priests claimed their object was purely religious, while the regime claimed it was basically political—claims which, as Peter Lake and Michael Questier have demonstrated, could each be sustained depending on where one drew the line between religion and politics—resulted in an increase of charges of treason.[4] It was especially in dealing with Jesuits, Catholic priests, and conspirators that Elizabeth's regime resorted to torture. But using torture was problematic because, unlike European countries whose systems were based on Roman law:

> Torture has never been officially recognised in English law as a means of gaining information. The officers who tortured prisoners in the Tower were acting with the knowledge and authority of the highest levels of government—the Privy Council and the monarch—and they were able to do so because royal servants enjoyed immunity from prosecution. However, in public opinion, torture was never accepted as a fact of life. Protestants and Catholics both complained bitterly about the use of torture by regimes of the other party, praising the victims as "martyrs" and labelling [*sic*] the authorities as "tyrants" or "persecutors". Critics claimed that it was ineffective as well as cruel, and that a man on the rack would say anything to be released. From the mid-17th century onwards, torture was effectively abandoned.
>
> (Ashbee 61)

In his work on *Torture and the Law of Proof*, John H. Langbein examines the 81 surviving English torture warrants from the period 1540 to 1640, demonstrating that a substantial number of the warranted cases of torture were of people the authorities perceived as traitors because they were committed to the Queen's overthrow.[5] Langbein also demonstrates that the Tudors did not engage in judicial torture to procure evidence to be used at trial, but rather preventative torture (88–90). That is, torture was used not to secure evidence leading to convictions, especially in cases where "the statute of 1584–85 . . . made it treason for Jesuits and other priests to remain in the realm [and thereby] made apprehension tantamount to conviction and eliminated the need to torture them for evidence" (90). Rather, "[t]orture was used . . . on the chance that accomplices and wider designs might be revealed" (90). This point was made by Francis Bacon in a 1603 letter to King James in which he claimed that "[i]n the highest cases of treasons [*sic*], torture is used for discovery, and not for evidence" (Langbein 90).[6] And as Lake and Questier note, the regime used torture in its propaganda battle with the Jesuits, as in the case of Edmund Campion:

> Rather than merely kill him, the regime tried first to turn Campion into a major weapon against the Catholic cause. . . . He was racked and indeed, as he later admitted at his trial, broken under torture to the extent that he revealed some of the names of those with whom he stayed. As a number of commentators have observed, the regime's resort to torture was more likely directed toward tarnishing his reputation as a man of principle and a martyr-in-the-making than toward finding out things that the regime did not already know.
>
> (620)

It is worth noting that Francis Bacon was one of the men commissioned to interrogate prisoners designated for torture; and that among those commissioned to interrogate the Gunpowder plotters was Sir John Popham, the Lord Chief Justice, who was also named as a commissioner on five earlier occasions when torture was warranted. Langbein also points out that in his famous *Third Institute*, "Sir Edward Coke . . . concludes that 'there is no one opinion in our books, or judicial record . . . for the maintenance of tortures or torments' " (73)—and adds that Coke did not claim that torture was never used, just that it was not legally sanctioned (182). Coke would have known this fact at first hand since on six occasions he was among those commissioned to conduct interrogations using torture (Langbein 115, 117, 119).[7]

Cornwall's treatment of Gloucester as a traitor and his use of physical violence does and does not conform to historic English practice. Edmund speaks of his father's actions as "this treason" (3.5.12), and Cornwall and Regan believe that, in aiding Lear, Gloucester has become a traitor. In 3.7, Cornwall and Regan use some form of the terms "traitor" or "treason" eight times (3, 6, 21, 26, 35, 43, 85, 87), starting with Cornwall's command to "[s]eek out the traitor Gloucester" (3) and ending with Regan's gloating comment to the just-blinded Gloucester that it was Edmund who "made overture of thy treasons to us" (87). Gloucester is well aware of the risk he takes, for when he tells Edmund about the letter and announces that he will relieve "my old master" he knows that he might "die for't" (3.3.17–18). And insofar as Gloucester has sent Lear to the place where "[t]he army of France is landed" (3.7.2–3), he has committed another act which lawyers in the audience would have known rendered him a traitor by the statute of Edward III (25 Edw. III st. 5, C2), namely "to levy war against the King in his realm or to adhere to the King's enemies."[8]

When Cornwall announces the impending confrontation with Gloucester, he explains his plan in a way that prefigures the first half of the interrogation. After telling Edmund to leave because "[t]he revenges we are bound to take upon your traitorous father are not fit for your beholding" (6–7), he soon announces:

> Though well we may not pass upon his life
> Without the form of justice, yet our power
> Shall do a courtsy to our wrath, which men
> May blame, but not control.
>
> (23–26)

Cornwall acknowledges that if he wanted to execute Gloucester he would need to proceed through the phases of indictment, trial, conviction and sentence, but that his intense "wrath" means he would rather exercise his might, foregoing what might seem to be the even more satisfying revenge of a death sentence.

At first, their exchanges with Gloucester seem to indicate that Cornwall and Regan are seeking further confirmation of his guilt, yet when the Duke asks "what confederacy have you with the traitors/Late footed in the kingdom?" (43–44), he seems to be, in Bacon's words, prepared to conduct torture "for discovery, and not for evidence" (Langbein 90). In his reply, Gloucester both confesses and does not confess. He confesses he has sent the King "to Dover" (49) but in response to the thrice-asked "Wherefore to Dover?" (50, 51, 53) offers no information about the "confederacy." And, when he defies Cornwall and Regan, he does not offer the obvious answer, namely "to prevent you from murdering the King." Rather, his explanation combines compassion for the King with outrage at the actions he imagines Regan and Goneril performing:

> Because I would not see thy cruel nails
> Pluck out his poor old eyes, nor thy fierce sister
> In his anointed flesh stick boarish fangs.
>
> (54–56)

And at the end of this speech it may seem as if it is Gloucester's own defiant claim that "I shall see/The wingèd vengeance overtake such children" (63–64) —words that, as numerous critics have noted, echo not only Goneril's "pluck out his eyes" (4) from the beginning of this scene but a long skein of images earlier in the play—which precipitates Cornwall's mocking "See't shalt thou never" (65), and the act by which he "extrudes" Gloucester's eye, using a means not specified in the Quarto or Folio texts. Of course, as they begin to torture Gloucester, Regan and Cornwall validate his fear of what they would do if Lear were in their power.

At this point, Cornwall's action seems to be prompted by the failure of his effort to capture Lear and thwart the invading army. But as Stanley Cavell has argued, Regan's frustration seems to be prompted by a different objective, inferable from her comment at the end of the scene, when she directs "Go thrust him out at gates, and let him smell / His way to Dover" (91–92):

> The question is why *Regan* assumes he is going to Dover. (Her husband, for example, does not: "Turn out that eyeless villain.") We may wish to appeal to those drummed "Dover's" to explain her mind, and to suppose that she associates the name with the gathering of all her enemies. But the essential fact is that the name is primarily caught to her image of her father. In her mind, the man she is sending on his way to Dover is the man she *knows* is sent on his way to Dover: in her paroxysms of cruelty, she imagines that she has just participated in blinding her father.
>
> (281)

Cavell's analysis draws attention to another anomaly, namely that the torture is performed by members of the royal family. There is no evidence that Elizabeth I, James I, and Charles I were ever present at any act of torture, let alone that they personally tortured someone.[9] Torture was performed by the staff at the Tower or Bridewell Prison, while the questioning was performed by commissioners specified in each warrant. The nearest any representation of torture comes to anticipating Shakespeare's scene may be Anne Askew's claim that "bycause I laye styll and ded not crye, my lorde Chauncellor [Thomas Wriothesley] and mastre [Richard] Ryche, toke paynes to racke me their owne handes, tyll I was nygh dead" (Travitsky 183). Nor does Cornwall employ any of the three methods of torture prescribed in the warrants, namely the rack, the manacles, or the scavenger's daughter (Ashbee 66–70). Indeed the specific torture Cornwall employs, gouging out Gloucester's eyes, was never used as a punishment for treason by Tudor and Stuart monarchs. However, this mutilation might have reminded older members of the original audiences of one of the most notorious spectacles during Elizabeth's reign, namely the case provoked by a book called *The Gaping Gulf*, which offended Elizabeth by arguing against her proposed marriage to the Duc d'Alencon. In this case, the book's author, John Stubbs, standing on the public scaffold at the market at Westminster, on 3 November 1579, had his offending right hand chopped off by the executioner—and, famously, "put off his hat with his left hand and said with a loud voice, 'God save the Queen' " (Berry xxxvi). The mutilation shocked the witnesses who, William Camden recounted, were "Altogether silent, either out of horrour of this new and unwonted punishment, or else out of hatred of the marriage, which most men presaged would be the overthrow of religion" (xxxvi).[10] As was true in the case of Stubbs, the mutilation of Gloucester also fails to achieve its intended effect, for Regan admits that his later (off-stage) appearances arouse sympathy for the victim and hatred of his tormentors:

> It was great ignorance, Gloucester's eyes being out,
> To let him live. Where he arrives he moves
> All hearts against us.
>
> (4.4.9–11)

Cornwall's action prompts the scene's most striking anomaly, the First Servant's attempt to stop his master from completing his act of mutilation. There is no direct parallel for such an intervention in the records of the Tudor and Stuart regimes, although a remotely similar situation occurred when Richard Topcliffe, having manacled Father Robert Southwell, left him hanging, and a servant took it upon himself to let down the victim (Ashbee 73). Yet in the analysis that follows, it will become clear that the deviations from historic practice serve to intensify and clarify the experience suffered by Gloucester and witnessed by the spectators.

Violated codes, violating bodies

As his conversation with Edmund in 3.3 makes clear, Gloucester knows he faces a dilemma inherent in the logic of the hierarchic system which, while it might seem to give the ruler unlimited power, actually created reciprocal, although obviously unequal, obligations between members of that hierarchy. This dilemma could occur whenever there was a conflict between two members of that hierarchy to both of whom a subordinate figure owed allegiance. So Gloucester confronts a choice between his loyalty to his immediate patrons, Cornwall and Regan, and the man he calls his "old master."

Brought into the room, aware that he may die for saving King Lear, rendered physically defenseless by Cornwall's command to "Pinion him like a thief" (23), and hearing himself repeatedly called a traitor, in the five or so minutes that constitute the remainder of this scene, Gloucester has only his wits and his words as his weapons. As the scene unfolds, he invokes elements of the complex network of explicit codes from which his world was constructed, as well as the dozens of unspoken but powerful codes by which rulers and subjects conducted their lives. And step by step the audience shares Gloucester's discovery that he cannot gain any purchase by invoking the codes that would ordinarily protect him.

Gloucester's first appeal is embodied in his claim "You are my guests," reinforced by his plea "Do me no foul play, friends" (29), and reiterated when he says "I am your host, / With robber's hands my hospitable favours / You should not ruffle thus" (38–40). He is appealing to a code which stipulates that just as a host must take in and protect even an enemy, so his guests, even if they are his enemies, must not take advantage of the vulnerability created by the host's hospitality. "By the kind gods, 'tis most ignobly done, / To pluck me by the beard" (33–34) appeals to the imperative that members of a younger generation act with respect to their elders, rather than perform Regan's "act of extreme contempt" (*Riverside Shakespeare*, 3.7.34n).

As they question him about the "confederacy" (43) of traitors seeking to protect "the lunatic King" (45), Cornwall and Regan at first seem motivated by the same purpose that impelled the authorities to practice torture, namely to learn the names and plans of other conspirators. Hammered three times with the question "Wherefore to Dover?" (50, 51, 53), Gloucester employs a graphic analogy to grasp his plight as he admits "I am tied to th' stake, and I must stand the course" (52). In comparing himself to the bears baited by dogs at amphitheatres near the Globe, he produces a complex image of his own tormented condition. On the one hand, he sees himself reduced from human to animal status, his movement circumscribed, his body gazed at by a crowd of bloodthirsty spectators, some of whom would be treating this event not only as a "sport" but as an occasion for betting on the bear's chances of survival. On the other hand, the metaphor casts Gloucester as a powerful animal and demotes his tormentors to dogs. But insofar as the bear-baiting image also suggests Gloucester's realization that all his appeals to shared codes have failed, it also seems to prompt his decision to defy his tormentors:

Gloucester. Because I would not see thy cruel nails
Pluck out his poor old eyes, nor thy fierce sister
In his anointed flesh stick boarish fangs.
The sea, with such a storm as his bare head
In hell-black night endured, would have buoyed up
And quenched the stellèd fires.
Yet, poor old heart, he holp the heavens to rain.
If wolves had at thy gate howled that stern time,
Thou shouldst have said "Good porter, turn the key;
All cruels I'll subscribe." But I shall see
The wingèd vengeance overtake such children.
(54–64)

Because he presumes that there is a beneficent order in nature, he also believes he can objectively describe the actions of Regan and Cornwall as unnatural. Thus he claims that even the sea, the most massive, impersonal force of nature, would have shown pity to the maddened King. And he suggests that Regan's treatment of her father is an extreme aberration because even an animal as malevolent as the wolf, when caught in such a storm, would arouse the compassion she has refused to show to her own flesh and blood in the person of her father. But his most urgent appeal is to the code he supposes was created by the gods who, horrified at Regan and Cornwall's unnatural treatment of the King, will ensure that "[t]he wingèd vengeance overtake such children." While appeals to lesser codes have proved futile, and while the sense of Gloucester's impotence intensifies as each appeal fails, he maintains faith in a divine order that rewards human virtue and punishes human vice.

As Cornwall prepares his assault, Gloucester makes one last appeal which registers his sense that, while those who benefit most from these hierarchical codes have proved eager to shred them, those who might seem to benefit least may still be prepared to honor them: "He that will think to live till he be old / Give me some help!" (67). At the Globe, this appeal would have rung out to the audience as it did to the servants on stage, uniting the two groups in recognizing that no one can expect to be safe if those in power can torture subjects at will. And the spectators would have recognized that if Cornwall's servants attempted to rescue Gloucester, they would have put themselves in the same tragic dilemma that has entrapped him. It is central to the effect of this scene that Gloucester's plea initially fails, since at least some and perhaps all of Cornwall's servants "hold the chair" (65) while he puts out one of Gloucester's eyes. With the apparent failure of this last appeal, the spectators seem to witness a final shredding of the social fabric. But it is at this moment that Cornwall provokes one of his servants to intervene. And it is with this unpredictable intervention that the scene plunges into the cascade of actions which engulfs the participants, sweeping them onward to an outcome none of them desire but none can prevent. By the end of the scene, this cascade has completed the metamorphosis initiated by Lear and Gloucester in the play's opening two scenes.

On the page there is no hint that the First Servant is about to intervene, but of course the text's silence offers room for varied realizations. For example, the actor playing the First Servant might show signs of being moved by Gloucester's appeal but hold back because he simply does not believe that his master will go through with his barbaric threat:

Servant. Hold your hand, my lord.
I have served you ever since I was child,
But better service have I never done you
Than now to bid you hold.
Regan. How now, you dog!
Servant. If you did wear a beard upon your chin
I'd shake it on this quarrel. What do you mean?
Cornwall. My villein!
Servant. Nay then, come on, and take the chance of anger.
They draw and fight.
(70–77)

Thus the First Servant repeats Kent's "unmannerly" action in the first scene (1.1.45), in which Kent violates his duty to serve the King in order to fulfill what he regards as a more fundamental imperative, namely to warn him against an action which would subvert the system of hierarchic allegiances that provide the basis for the office of king. The First Servant's appeal also fails, and it is important not only *that* he fails but also *how* he fails. Regan's "How now, you dog!" invokes her understanding of the code of service, namely that a servant must behave like a creature whose only virtue is absolute obedience. Cornwall invokes the same imperative when he calls the servant "my villein" (i.e., serf): here, Wells and Taylor's choice to print "villein", rather than the form "villaine" used in both Quarto and Folio, emphasizes that Cornwall may be heard defining his servant as someone who must offer unquestioning submission. But when the First Servant responds "Nay then, come on, and take the chance of anger," his point is that by choosing to violate the code of justice, as well as the array of codes to which Gloucester has appealed, Cornwall has subverted the premises necessary to sustain his own right to command others. Stripped of the codes that govern master–servant relations, and that govern and make possible the sort of chivalric duel that Edgar and Edmund engage in during the last scene, they are now simply two men engaged in a desperate combat. But, while he fatally wounds Cornwall, the First Servant makes a lethal mistake when he does not foresee Regan's willingness to violate the gender code which defines physical combat as a male activity:

Regan. Give me thy sword. A peasant stand up thus!
[*She takes a sword and runs at him behind*]
Kills him.
Servant. O, I am slain! My lord, you have one eye left
To see some mischief on him. O! *He dies.*
(78–80)

Like Gloucester, the First Servant speaks as if he believes that the normative codes are still in operation, and he dies proclaiming what can be heard either as a confession of faith or a desperate hope. But in another instance of the bitter irony which saturates this scene, his words prompt Cornwall's riposte, "Lest it see more, prevent it," the removal of Gloucester's other eye, and the taunt "Where is thy lustre now?" (81–82). Cornwall's mockery seems to assume that, despite the wound inflicted by the First Servant, his success in removing Gloucester's second eye offers proof of the impotence of "the wingèd vengeance." Even now Gloucester retains his faith in a benign nature:

All dark and comfortless! Where's my son Edmond?
Edmond, enkindle all the sparks of nature
To quit this horrid act.
(83–85)

His plea for revenge elicits Regan's revelation that it is Edmund who betrayed Gloucester. Her words point to the intertwined series of ironic choices, in which Gloucester, having chosen loyalty to his younger son while betraying his older son, is betrayed by that younger son when Gloucester chooses loyalty to his "old master" over loyalty to that master's daughter and son-in-law. And her words compel Gloucester to realize that Edmund chose loyalty to his new patron over loyalty to his brother and his father:

Out, treacherous villain!
Thou call'st on him that hates thee. It was he
That made the overture of thy treasons to us,
Who is too good to pity thee.
Gloucester. O my follies! Then Edgar was abused.
Kind gods, forgive me that, and prosper him!
Regan. Go thrust him out at gates, and let him smell
His way to Dover. *Exit one or more with Gloucester.*
(85–92)

Gloucester's response has long been recognized as extraordinary in several ways. For one thing, as Cavell has noted, Gloucester's first two sentences record his immediate acknowledgment of his own guilt and Edgar's innocence. And this pattern, Cavell argues (272–74), is repeated when, at the end of the play's next movement, Lear recognizes Cordelia, announcing "For as I am a man, I think this lady/To be my child, Cordelia" (4.6.62–63). In both cases, these brief, seemingly prosaic speeches achieve enormous power because Gloucester and Lear acknowledge the profoundly humiliating truth that they have unjustly sought to eliminate, indeed to annihilate, a loyal child—Gloucester by proclaiming Edgar an outlaw (2.1.55–62), and Lear by declaring "for we/Have no such daughter, nor shall ever see/That face of hers again" (1.1.262–64). But Gloucester's words also offer the extraordinary affirmation of "kind gods, forgive me that, and prosper him!" In his last words in the scene, he demonstrates that despite torture and mutilation, despite his discovery of the injustice he has done to Edgar and his betrayal by Edmund, despite all that Cornwall and Regan have done to mutilate his body and break his spirit, and despite the fact that the gods have not responded to his pleas, Gloucester continues to speak of them as "the kind gods" (33).

It is symptomatic of the relentless manner in which Shakespeare works out the consequences of the initial mistakes made by Lear and Gloucester that this scene concludes with one more mandated violation of a code. For after seconding Regan by commanding "turn out that eyeless villain"—thereby insuring that Gloucester will be thrust out into the storm-filled world with even less support and in a worse condition than Lear—Cornwall concludes:

Cornwall. I have received a hurt. Follow me, lady.
Turn out that eyeless villain. Throw this slave

Upon the dunghill. Regan, I bleed apace.
Untimely comes this hurt. Give me your arm.
Exeunt [with the body].

(93–96)

From Cornwall's point of view, he is fulfilling the code which mandated not merely the execution but the obliteration of the traitor, whose body was to be dismembered, displayed, and denied the sanctification of burial. But from the point of view of the spectators, Cornwall, having sought to reduce the living servant to a dog, continues to treat him as a subhuman creature, fit only to decay in a pile of manure until nothing is left and nothing will mark his heroic act or brutal death.[11]

As this analysis reveals, the playwright composed a densely packed scene in which codes constituting the relations of parents and children, brothers and sisters, hosts and guests, masters and servants, rulers and subjects, men and women, the living and the dead, humans and gods, are all appealed to but violated by the very people making these appeals. Furthermore, in performance the scene provides twenty-first century spectators with an experience that points toward the truth about torture articulated by Lawrence Weschler, who writes that "[t]he scream that comes welling out of the torture chamber is thus double—the body calling out to the soul, the self calling out to others—and in both cases, it goes unanswered. Torture's stark lesson is precisely that enveloping silence" (238). Shakespeare's scene appears more hopeful than the "lesson" described by Weschler insofar as both Gloucester's appeal to anyone with a fundamental sense of human solidarity and Cornwall's appeal to the bond between husband and wife are answered. But in each case, the man making the appeal elicits that response only *after* he has been seriously wounded, and in both cases the reprieve is temporary. For Cornwall soon dies from his wound; and the blinded Gloucester moves toward his attempt at suicide, his stunning encounter with the mad Lear, and the offstage reunion with Edgar which elicits "the two extremes of passion, joy and grief" that shatter "his flawed heart" (5.3.188–91).

Quarto and Folio endings of 3.7

Up to this point, as many readers probably have noted, I have ignored the fact that *King Lear* is what we have come to call a multi-text play. Indeed, it was the study of the differences between the Quarto (1608) and the Folio (1623) by Warren (1978), by Urkowitz (1980), and by Wells and Taylor (1986) that became the modern starting point for re-articulating the challenges posed by multi-text plays. As these critics have demonstrated, one significant difference between Quarto and Folio texts is the ending of this scene, for whereas the Folio concludes with the final exchange between Regan and Cornwall, the Quarto continues:

Second Servant. I'll never care what wickedness I do
If this man come to good.
Third Servant. If she live long,
And in the end meet the old course of death,
Women will all turn monsters.
Second Servant. Let's follow the old Earl and get the bedlam
To lead him where he would. His roguish madness
Allows itself to anything.
Third Servant. Go thou. I'll fetch some flax and whites of eggs
To apply to his bleeding face. Now heaven help him!
Exeunt severally.
(Scene 14.97–105)

Despite the fact that it is only nine lines, this segment produces a crucial difference in the scene's action and in the audience's perception of that action. As they speak, the two servants articulate the chilling suspicion that in choosing to exercise their raw power at the expense of the system of justice, and in rejecting all of Gloucester's and the First Servant's appeals to various codes, Cornwall and Regan have shattered the basis for anyone to be constrained by such codes. The servants recognize that in such a universe nothing is forbidden and everything is permitted. At the same time, their decision to help Gloucester demonstrates that they choose to act as if the fabric of codes is still intact, and their obligation is to maintain or restore that moral order.

Borrowing a term from the language used for computer programs, we might say that readers who imagine a default performance of the Folio text will imagine an ending of the scene unrelieved by any hint of restoration. Read in this way, the scene seems to mandate that Gloucester is led offstage by one servant, that the wounded Cornwall, supported by Regan exits in another direction, and, finally, that one or two other servants drag or carry off the corpse of their comrade. In such a performance, it is only the loyalty of the wife to her husband that produces a fulfillment of a code in operation when the play begins. And even this apparently successful invocation of a code can seem equivocal, since the action hints that neither Cornwall nor Regan can presume their bond will hold if either partner comes to believe his or her self-interest might be served by violating it. Thus, the Folio text of this scene ends by intimating what Gloucester will explicitly suggest a few minutes later when he asserts "As flies to wanton boys are we to th' gods; / They kill us for their sport" (4.1.37–38). One reason why this speech has become famous is because it offers an epigrammatic expression of a primal image, but it also resonates so intensely because in performance it is incarnated before it is articulated.

Ending 3.7 in performance: open silences and audience engagements

Examining the Folio text of the ending brings into focus two other potentials whose realization can sharpen the tension between experiencing "the worst" and the hope of restoration. One potential arises from the fact that toward the end of the Quarto and at the end of the Folio text, Regan has what Philip McGuire has taught us to recognize as an open silence:

> What is an "open" silence? . . . An open silence is one whose precise meanings and effects, because they cannot be determined by analysis of the words of the playtext, must be established by nonverbal, extra-textual features of the play that emerge only in performance. Such silences are usually required by Shakespeare's words, and they occur most often during the final scene of a play.
>
> (xv)

Again, a default reading will presume that, as has been true for most of the play's performance history, Regan promptly assists Cornwall, concluding the scene with a moment in which, unlike Gloucester, Cornwall has successfully invoked an explicit code. But such a response is not mandated by the text, and in the last fifty years some productions have created stagings in which Regan does *not* respond positively to Cornwall's words. For example, in Glen Byam Shaw's production at the Memorial Theatre in Stratford-upon-Avon in 1959, the scene ended thus:

> Disregarding the usual Theobold stage-direction, *Exit Cornwall, led by Regan*, and going back to the Folio's simple *Exeunt* which allows the producer to use his imagination, Mr. Byam Shaw gave his actor an opportunity which on the first night Paul Hardwick seized with both hands. Mortally wounded, terror and pain in voice and gestures, he turned to his wife: "Regan, I bleed apace. Give me your arm." Ignoring him, almost disdainfully, she swept past to the downstage exit. He staggered back, groping for support: no one stirred to help him. Open-mouthed, staring-eyed, death gripping his heart, he faced the dawning horror of retribution as the jungle law of each for himself caught up on him and he knew himself abandoned even by his wife.
>
> (Byrne 198)

This choice has been repeated: "Similarly in the 1983 Granada TV production Cornwall fell forward across the chair in which Gloucester had been bound, and appealed in vain to Regan, who stood above him staring into the distance, apparently absorbed in a pleasing vision of a future without him" (Bratton 159). In some productions, moreover, Regan's refusal to help Cornwall occurs in a context in which her attraction to Edmund has already been non-verbally indicated, so that her choice appears particularly ruthless. When such productions place the intermission at the end of this scene, spectators witness a final demonstration of an emerging world in which pure self-interest seems to have become the categorical imperative.

A second element that directors have experimented with is the exit of Gloucester. In Quarto and Folio, Regan and Cornwall direct their servants to "thrust" Gloucester out (91) and "Turn out that eyeless villain" (94), and the Folio offers the stage direction "exit with Gloster" (Warren 1989: 95). At this point, Peter Brook, in his landmark Royal Shakespeare Company revival in 1962 (I saw this production at the New York State Theatre, Lincoln Center, in 1964) created one of his most radical effects:

> Gloster, trying to feel his way, a ragged cloth thrown over his head, stumbled into callous servants who buffeted and jostled him. With house-lights already up, the audience, forced to participate in [*sic*] wasteland, sat in the full glare as Gloster, trailing bandages, wandered upstage and out, a broken figure in a cruel, heedless world.
>
> (Rosenberg 244; also see Marowitz 114)

In productions that combine both these elements, the pattern of violating codes is extended in ways which indicate how thoroughly the fabric of the social order has been shredded.

Two more productions offer indications not only of how performances of the Folio ending of this scene may move toward something like nihilism, but how they can also realize the text so that audience members not only witness but find themselves implicated in the scene, and participate in creating a sense of a darker or lighter closure to it.

The first of these productions was performed during 1989 as part of a program known as ACTER (A Center for Teaching, Education, and Research) organized by Professor Homer Swander, then of the University of California at Santa Barbara. (The program is now known as "Actors from the London Stage" or AFTLS.) In these productions, a five-member team of actors performed an entire Shakespeare play. In this version of *King Lear*, the nature of the small company—with Geoffrey Church, Vivien Heilbron, Bernard Lloyd, Patti Love, and Clifford Rose—generated crucial effects:

> With few or no "extras" this company had no servants at the end of the blinding scene . . . to take off Gloucester, so that Clifford Rose crawled off alone (at some shows the first thing he touched was the body of the slain servant), making a whimpering sound in the process.
>
> (Dessen, "Portable Shakespeare" 9)

Critics have often noted that Gloucester's literal blindness can seem a parallel to the metaphoric blindness of King Lear, but in this performance Gloucester was, in effect, literalizing Lear's opening proclamation of his "darker purpose" (1.1.36), specifically his promise to "crawl towards death" (41). At the performances I witnessed (2 and 4 March 1989), Gloucester began feeling his way forward one limb at a time, toward the edge of the stage. As he moved nearer to what seemed like an inevitable and perhaps dangerous fall, his action meant that those sitting in the front row found themselves transformed from spectators into potential participants, confronting the question whether they should help the wounded but virtual character or the unwounded but apparently at-risk actor, or both? It was only when he touched the corpse of the First Servant that he paused, made a laborious turn, and headed off, exiting upstage left, at which point the house lights went down.[12]

Certainly if Rose's Gloucester had *not* encountered the body of the servant and *had* gone over the edge and one or more spectators had protected him, we would have felt, among other things, the unspoken but powerful sense of gratitude for fulfilling our own impulse to succor Gloucester that we can feel toward the Second and Third Servants at the end of performances of the Quarto text. Such spectators, like the Quarto servants, would have embodied the basic and, we might like to believe, difficult-to-eradicate human solidarity which makes us want to aide a helpless, victimized, wounded fellow creature. At the same time, we would also be forced to confront the fact demonstrated in the Brook production—and by the literature on torture—namely that such solidarity can, in fact, be eliminated and, in many cases, transformed into the indifference or hatred that helps make torture possible.

A second example comes from Sidney Homan who, explaining how he came to direct his own production, describes another staging of 3.7:

> The theater was . . . small, intimate, with two aisles leading to exits and thereby distributing the audience on three sides of the stage. The stage itself was raised a foot, with the first row a mere three feet from the downstage edge. In the final scene before intermission, Gloucester stood before us, blinded, blood running from his empty eye sockets and onto his robe. . . . Alone, Gloucester stood forlorn, bleeding, his eyes grotesque, red, irregular circles. Up to this point in the play all entrances and exits had been made upstage right or left; this time, violating the practice, Gloucester attempted to exit downstage. He approached the edge of the stage, his arms half-extended before him as if he were feeling for a wall. I was sitting in the second row, directly in front of him. He was now at the edge. I could see a thin line of thick tape on the rim to guide the actor. Still, even knowing it was just an illusion, the audience was concerned, as if before us were a real-life blind man, desperately seeking an exit, unaware of the one-foot drop to the floor. The actor in turn played with us, moving from side to side, each move accompanied by audience members unconsciously raising their hands to catch him, audibly expressing their fears with those "ah"s and groans real people make when witnessing an accident about to happen. We all knew it was fake, yet for the moment we were afraid. When Gloucester at last found his footing and

stepped neatly off the stage, the audience let out a collective sigh of relief. . . .

Gloucester made his way up the aisle on audience left, found the door, searched a while for the knob, opened it, and went out, the door closing behind him. Clearly, it was time for intermission, as announced in the program itself; without applauding, the audience rose in staggered groups. What was fascinating, *telling*, is that no one would exit through the audience-left door. Instead, the entire house exited through the audience-right door, unwilling to use the door just touched by Gloucester, as if it were now sacred space, something celebrated by the play's illusory world and therefore not real for us.

(Homan 2–3)

The refusal of the spectators to use the door used by Gloucester not only suggests, as Homan proposes, that they felt a sense that this door had been transformed into a different reality, but that they were also honoring the fact that, however powerful their impulse to help Gloucester might be, there was no way to cross the impermeable boundary between their world and the world of the dramatic fiction. The point, as Cavell has argued at length, is that "We are not in, and cannot put ourselves in, the presence of the characters; but we are in, or can put ourselves in, their *present*. It is in making their present ours, their moments as they occur, that we complete our acknowledgment of them" (337; but see 332–40 for the full development of this analysis). In the context of this production, the spectators' choice not to touch the door used by Gloucester was another way of acknowledging that they could only be witnesses to this torture.

I would add that at a recent production of *The Winter's Tale* at my university's studio theater, where I was inches away from the action, I was surprised to feel—and to have to restrain myself from acting on—an impulse to join the courtiers when they knelt to plead for the life of Hermione's newborn child. Arousing an impulse to intervene to save a helpless human being while prompting us to be aware of the impossibility of fulfilling that impulse is one of the powerful potentials of the dramatic medium. And when a performance creates intense realizations of this isometric tension, it compels spectators to experience both their desire to act and their impotence either to prevent or to relieve a character's suffering.

The medium of drama: actor's and spectator's bodies

Whereas readers are free to imagine the blinding of Gloucester in as much or as little detail as they find bearable, and to consider it mainly as an abstract or symbolic event, in performance the level of violence audiences must endure will be controlled by the director and the actors. The blinding of Gloucester, moreover, is a scene that reminds us with particular vividness that even as the medium of drama is the actor's body, the medium of reception is the body of the spectator. Another way to think about the interplay of stage action and audience experience is to examine the scene as inviting spectators to adopt the point of view of, and to imagine themselves in the bodies of, the participants.

That some members of the original or subsequent audiences might imagine themselves in the position, or sharing the experience, of Cornwall and Regan is not a very inviting prospect, nor have critics spoken with sympathy of Regan and Cornwall or written much from their point of view. Nonetheless, it is possible to imagine this happening, and the play itself offers a cue as to how this might happen in Gloucester's perception that "As flies to wanton boys are we to th' gods; /They kill us for their sport" (4.1.37–38). For anyone who as a child has been a small creature controlled by those large creatures called adults and discovered the corresponding possibility of having power over still smaller creatures, human or animal, will in principle have the ability to imagine what Cornwall and Regan might be doing and feeling.

It is also worth recalling that at least two other Shakespeare tragedies invite spectators to take up the view of a tormenter or would-be tormentor. One powerful instance occurs in *Othello*, where the audience is compelled to share the point of view of Iago, and, in particular, the moment in 2.3 where, after he has instigated the brawl which prompts Othello to cashier Cassio, Iago begins to plot his next maneuvers with only the spectators as witnesses. Here the question with which he begins his soliloquy, "And what's he then that says I play the villain . . . ?" (2.3.327), offers the actor an opportunity to engage his auditors directly, as if they had voiced a critique of his behavior. In the middle of his speech, he explains that he can use Desdemona to manipulate Othello because

> His soul is so enfettered to her love
> That she may make, unmake, do what she list,
> Even as her appetite shall play the god
> With his weak function.
>
> (2.3.336–39)

As a description of Desdemona, who affirms, "My heart's subdued / Even to the very quality of my lord" (1.3.250–51), the claim that she will "play the god" is a grotesque distortion. But this distortion is convincing evidence of Iago's desire precisely because he projects it onto the person to whom it least applies. The desire to "play the god" helps us understand the project of the man who claims his identity violates the law of identity when he avows "I am not what I am" (1.1.65), namely to evade the gravity created by all human relations. But "to play the god" also announces the other side of his project: to be omniscient, knowing his victims better than they know themselves; omnipotent, controlling them through his own histrionic presence; and omnipresent, taking over their imaginations with his own coercive vision. In the scenes which follow, especially the disturbing sequence where Iago drives Othello into a frenzy (4.1.1–45) and then makes him mistakenly believe that Iago and Cassio are discussing Cassio's affair with Desdemona (91–207), Shakespeare situates spectators in a position in which they may find themselves discovering whether they have the impulse to torment others.

A second instance occurs in *Hamlet* 3.3, where, after they have listened to the tormented reflections of the King (3.3.36–72), the scene invites spectators to adopt the point of view of Hamlet, who decides to postpone his revenge until he can inflict a much greater pain on the proposed victim:

> Then trip him that his heels may kick at heaven,
> And that his soul may be as damned and black
> As hell whereto it goes.
> (93–95)

During the speech as a whole, we are invited to situate ourselves with Hamlet, to feel the impulses in the muscles that begin and stop the movement to strike the King, and to share his glee at the idea of murdering the King so as to ensure his eternal torture in hell. That this *is* what Shakespeare's text and performance invite us to do is testified to by another famous response from Samuel Johnson, who wrote that "This speech, in which Hamlet, represented as a virtuous character, is not content with taking blood for blood, but contrives damnation for the man he would punish, is too horrible to be read or to be uttered" (VIII: 990). Whereas what horrified Johnson about the blinding of Gloucester was the extreme physical brutality of that scene, what he found "too horrible to be read or to be uttered" here was that Hamlet, like Iago, seeks to "play the god" in an attempt to control not merely the earthly fate of his uncle but the eternal fate of his soul—in effect, to devise something which might be called Christian revenge.[13]

In her study of *Staging Anatomies: Dissection and Spectacle in Early Stuart Tragedy*, Hillary Nunn suggests that it is Gloucester's body that commands our attention and solicits our empathy:

> playhouse viewers have little chance to take refuge from the horrible sights to come. On the contrary, Gloucester's onstage blinding demands that the spectators either participate in the scene's violence by watching it unfold before them, or hide their own eyes and thereby isolate themselves from the drama. The artificial blood shed as Cornwall puts out Gloucester's first eye no doubt rouses pity in the playhouse, and the old man's cries of desperation upon losing the second further collapse the distance between the scene and those who observe from offstage. Gloucester's desperate pleas for help, it is clear, address not so much his hovering tormentors but those beyond the walls of the imagined chamber, whether in the castle or in the playhouse. Directed at "He that will think to live till

> he be old" . . ., the writhing victim's cries seek more than sympathy; they implore spectators both within the playhouse and in the world of the play to imagine themselves occupying an aged, tormented body like his own.
>
> (172)

Going a step further, we can note that the spectators can defend themselves in two ways: they can look away, refusing to accept the role of witnesses to this crime, or they can close their eyes, in which case they imitate in their own bodies the endarkened condition represented by the actor on stage.

There is a third possible point of view open to the spectators, however, and one that for first-time spectators may initially seem the safest way to situate themselves, namely by taking up the point of view of the servants in the scene. Of course, even this choice becomes painful when Cornwall commands the servants to assist in the torture of Gloucester. And, as noted above, the fact that the servants do not respond immediately to Gloucester's plea for help means that the spectators have time to register any impulse to intervene in their own muscles *and* to become aware of their own inaction—a sensation whose pain will be diluted but perhaps not eliminated by their predetermined powerlessness to intervene.

The complex dynamics of the audience's relation with the servants in this scene can be further delineated by a powerful scene in Philip Massinger's *The Roman Actor*, written and performed in 1626. (While it is tempting to wonder if Massinger had learned from or was thinking of the blinding of Gloucester as he wrote his scene, the power of this analogy does not depend on whether the playwright remembered or was influenced by *King Lear*.) The relevance of this scene (3.2) was brought home to me when I attended three performances of the play by the Royal Shakespeare Company (2002) in the 440-seat Swan Theatre, where all the spectators sit close to the long thrust stage, and where these spectators, especially those on the first level in the U surrounding the stage, are visible to the actors and to each other. In this scene, the Roman Emperor, Domitianus Caesar, orders the onstage torture of two Senators whose loyalty to a previously executed Stoic philosopher and willingness to covertly critique Caesar's actions impels him to make an example of them. As the two senators were tortured—the text does not specify how, but in this production their backs were ripped with meat hooks—they did not appeal to anyone to intervene, but rather defied the torturers and the Emperor, promising to return as ghosts to take revenge (a promise fulfilled in the final act). Just before their speeches of defiance, and in a response which hovers between the intervention of the First Servant and the silent observation of the Second and Third Servants in *King Lear*, Caesar's slave, Parthenius—whose father the emperor had recently executed while threatening Parthenius himself with death if he tried to save his father—uttered a short but piercing aside:

I dare not show
A sign of sorrow; yet my sinews shrink,
The spectacle is so horrid.
(Gibson, III.ii.81–83)

Antony Byrne's Parthenius movingly enacted the intolerable tension between his involuntary sympathetic response to the suffering of two fellow human beings and his knowledge that any visible manifestation of this sympathy might subject him to their fate. In the Swan, moreover, we were close enough to the stage and to each other to realize that our own shrinking responses were indeed visible to Caesar, to his chief spy, Arentinus, and to the armed guards who scanned the audience for signs of dissent. The fact that the faces of the guards were hidden by metal masks also served to foreground our sense of vulnerability since their masks made them safer from the threat of inadvertent self-revelation than anyone else in the scene. Furthermore we were able to see the horror reflected in the faces of those seated across from us, even as we could sense the indrawn breath and tensed muscles of those next to us. Sharing both the situation and the response of Byrne's Parthenius offered us a compelling embodiment of the long-term dilemma confronting anyone living in the court of a tyrant. The dilemma is that either your own body will betray your dissent from the tyrant's public torture and execution of any human being who resists his whims, in which case you too will be executed; or that you will survive only by repressing these responses in an act that ultimately deforms your humanity by alienating your mind from your body, in which case you will secure your physical survival at the cost of sacrificing your integrity. Massinger's script thus creates a moment in which Parthenius and the spectators together discover that if complete suppression of the responses of one's nervous system is impossible, then dissenting from Caesar's will is a physiological inevitability, and providing a pretext for Caesar to execute you may be as inescapable as the need to take your next breath.[14]

Epilogue

If Parthenius's vivid response to watching the Senators being tortured provides a commentary on *King Lear* 3.7, it may also be illuminating to examine the response of someone who participated in torture as a member of Elizabeth's government. As noted earlier, there is no record of a torturer revolting as Cornwall's servant revolts. But the records do indicate that several commissioners asked to be excused from participation in further acts of torture (Ashbee 73). One of those commissioners was Sir Thomas Smith who, in *De Republica Anglorum* (1565, published 1583), claimed that

> Torment or question, which is used by the order of the civile law and custome of other countries, to put a malefactor to excessive paine to make him confesse of himselfe, or of his fellowes or complices, is not

> used in England. It is taken for servile. For how can he serve the commonwealth after as a free man who hath his bodie so haled or tormented? And if hee bee not found guilty, what amends can be made him? And if he must dye, what crueltie is it so to torment him before!
>
> (Heath 80)

In 1571, six years after he finished writing his book, Queen Elizabeth placed Smith on a commission to interrogate and, if necessary, torture William Barker and Laurence Bannister, servants suspected of assisting the Duke of Norfolk in the Ridolfi Plot against the Queen (Langbein 102–3; Heath 232; Dewar 125–29). Describing the work of Smith and Thomas Wilson, Mary Dewar writes that

> It is to their credit that throughout these examinations they did all they could to resist Elizabeth's pressure to use torture to extract the information from Norfolk's servants. On the 9th [of September] the Queen expressed impatience at the speed of their inquiry and ordered them to use torture against two of the Duke's agents. They did not do so and on the 15th she repeated her order to Smith in no uncertain terms: "Neither Barker nor Bannister, the Duke of Norfolk's men, having uttered their knowledge, neither will discover the same without torture . . . We warrant you to cause them both or either of them to be brought to the rack." On the 17th, Smith wrote to Burghley that they would do so not from any hope of benefiting but only because the Queen ordered it. . . . They had obeyed her only just in time. A letter from Burghley crossed theirs saying Elizabeth wanted to know why Smith had not answered her letter "authorizing him to proceed with Barker and Highford by torture."
>
> (127)

After performing this duty, Smith wrote to Burghley that "I do most humbly crave my revocation from this unpleasant and painful toil. I assure you I would not wish to be one of Homer's gods, if I thought I should be Minos, Aecus, or Rhadamanthus; I had rather be one of the least shades in the Elysian Fields" (Ashbee 73; and Dolman and Ashbee, private communication).[15] Unlike Cornwall and Regan or Iago or, at least momentarily, Hamlet, in the context of performing torture Smith apparently had no desire to "play the god" with the lives of his fellow men. In performing his task, Smith presumably could neither turn away nor close his eyes while interrogating Barker and Bannister to discover the extent of Norfolk's treason. But if he did not pursue the route taken by the First Servant in *King Lear*, it may be that, like the Second and Third Servants in the Quarto version, and like Parthenius, he found himself recoiling from the reality of torture. The fact that he felt free to ask Burghley to be excused from further duty of this kind demonstrates that Smith believed he did not serve a tyrant. And Smith would have known that the warrant which named him as one of the commissioners—it was in Burghley's hand but came directly from Queen Elizabeth—conferred on him the immunity from prosecution that made him, in this limited fashion, like "one of Homer's gods." But we might wonder if what motivated his plea was that, in acting as the good servant to the Queen, he realized that—like Kent and the First Servant in *King Lear*—he was violating a more fundamental form of service, namely adherence to the principles of the Common Law celebrated in his book. After his blinding, Gloucester perceives the world as a place where the gods torture human beings as boys kill flies, "for their sport." Smith may have discovered or rediscovered several things implicit in his own earlier words: that torture was servile precisely because it sought to reduce a free human being to a creature enslaved by pain; that those performing the torture became like Minos, Aecus, and Rhadmanthus, whose decisions could (seemingly) determine the fate not just of a body but of a soul; and that the immunity conferred by the Queen's warrant did not protect him from the deforming effects of supervising torture. Part of the power of 3.7 is that the spectators, because they are immunized by the warrant of the dramatic fiction, may experience what it is like both to "play the god" in tormenting another human being *and* to be the victim, the one who is being taught "the vulnerability of the body" and "the absolute solitude of human existence" (Weschler 238). The blinding of Gloucester thus also prepares spectators to understand the moment when Gloucester's attempt to kiss the hand of the maddened Lear provokes the reply "Let me wipe it first, it smells of mortality" (4.5.129); and the moment when Lear attempts to dissolve their existential separateness by proposing "If thou wilt weep my fortunes, take my eyes," before acknowledging "I know thee well enough, thy name is Gloucester" (172–73). Certainly the spectators are invited to perceive the double-edged irony when the blinded Gloucester describes the maddened King for whose sake he was tortured as this "ruin'd piece of nature" (130).

Notes

1 In his Cambridge edition of the play, Jay Halio notes that "The Folio text, moreover, may not have been totally eclipsed" (39) and cites evidence that not all the productions in this period were based on Tate (37–41). Richard Stock offers a perceptive analysis of the comments from Arthur Murphy and Sir Joshua Reynolds in *Samuel Johnson and Neoclassical Dramatic Theory* (212).

2 For the debates about Shakespeare's authorship, see Dover Wilson (viii–xix) and Waith (11–20). G. Wilson Knight argued that *Titus Andronicus* provided a template for the "grotesque" and the "fantastic" elements in *King Lear* (170). For an account of the emergence of *Titus*, of the Brook production, and of several notable successors, see Dessen (1989).

3 Quotations from Shakespeare's plays are from *William Shakespeare: The Complete Works*, Stanley Wells and Gary Taylor, general editors. Quotations that cite only a scene and line or lines are from the first Quarto, *The History of King Lear*. Quotations from the Folio cite act, scene, and line or lines. I have omitted added stage directions in which Wells and Taylor indicate who they believe must be the addressee of a speech or seem to mandate actions the text leaves open—as when they add (in half brackets) "*Regan stabs him again*" to motivate the dying First

Servant's final "O" (3.7.80). Although *King Lear* is a two-text play, and although I discuss the major difference between the Quarto and Folio versions of the end of 3.7, other textual differences in 3.7 do not make a difference in my analysis. When necessary, the Quarto (1608) and Folio (1623) texts are cited from Michael Warren's *Parallel King Lear*.

4 On torture and the Catholic threat, see James Heath (109–10) and MacCaffrey (chapters 27–29). For an illuminating overview of the Jesuit mission, see Lake and Questier (2000). In his essay "Richard Topcliffe," Frank Brownlow asserts that Catholic members of the original audiences would have interpreted the play as a whole, and Edmund's betrayal of his father in particular, as a covert representation of their persecution and suffering (167–71).

5 Langbein presents a chart enumerating the warrants, the purpose of the warrant, the accused, and the commissioners (81–128). Heath presents the full texts of the warrants and one government document defending its conduct (201–39).

6 Langbein points out that "The only treason acquittal in the State Trials for the century 1540–1640 is Nicholas Throckmorton's case. . . . The ease with which a case could be trumped up, for example, against Campion or Raleigh, shows how well the crown could manipulate the ordinary criminal procedure without need of evidence gathered under torture" (note 46, 192).

7 Langbein, note 6: 182. In 1606–7, the spectators watching *King Lear* had no way of knowing that they were in the middle of a one-hundred year period when torture was used with some regularity by the Tudor and Stuart monarchs, and that the use of torture was even then rapidly decreasing. In 2007, spectators at or readers of *King Lear* in the United States have no way of knowing whether the introduction of torture will prove to be a time-limited episode, as it was in England, or becomes, as Andrew Sullivan has phrased it, a permanent element of our legal or even constitutional DNA (Sullivan 20–21).

8 On the logic of Cornwall and Regan in naming Gloucester as a traitor, see G.T. Buckley, especially p. 91. The treason statute is quoted from John Bellamy, *The Tudor Law of Treason* (1979) by Karen Cunningham, *Imaginary Betrayals* 8. As Cunningham notes, the statute of Edward III "had redefined treason . . . from behavior to thought, from a physical to a mental action, and from an overt into a covert violation of royal prerogative, extending his control over even the 'imaginings' of subjects" (7).

9 While the Tudor and Stuart monarchs did not personally supervise torture, James I did, in one famous instance, arrange a complex drama in which three of the men convicted in the 1603 treason trials were led, one by one, to the scaffold and, one by one, temporarily dismissed; and then were reunited and informed that the king was suspending their executions. This drama was also watched, but could not be heard, by Sir Walter Raleigh, who was himself scheduled to be executed three days later. For an account of this event and of its possible relation to *Measure for Measure*, see Bernthal (1992).

10 For Stubbs, see Berry (1968). The passage from Camden comes from Camden's *Annals, or the historie of the most renowned and victorious Princesse Elizabeth, late Queen of England*, translated R.N. (London, 3rd edn. 1635), 239. Although gouging out Gloucester's eyes might seem unmotivated by any legal concerns, Hillary M. Nunn notes that under medieval English law "a maiden's rapist should 'lose his eyes which gave him sight of the maiden's beauty for which he coveted her. And let him lose as well the testicles that excited his hot lust' " (Nunn 173; she is quoting Jay Halio's "Gloucester's Blinding" [1992] 221–23).

11 In terms of Shakespeare's practice in his tragedies, the intervention of the First Servant repeats an effect the dramatist had recently rehearsed in *Othello*. In that play, Emilia attacks Othello for his folly for murdering Desdemona because he (falsely) believes his wife has been unchaste. And her vehement indictment of

Othello surely functions, like *Lear*'s First Servant, to articulate the outrage of the spectators.

12 I would like to thank Alan Dessen (who directed ACTER from 1994 to 2000) not only for sharing his own recollections of this production with me but also forwarding a request for further information to Vivien Heilbron, who had performed Regan. Ms. Heilbron consulted with Bernard Lloyd (King Lear and Cornwall) and Clifford Rose, and shared their recollections with me as well. The other two members of this production were Patti Love and Geoffrey Church.

13 For a fuller analysis of this scene see Rocklin (2007).

14 For a fuller analysis of the design of Massinger's play and its realization in this production, see Rocklin (2006). This paragraph is adapted from that essay.

15 A short version of the second passage from Smith appears in Ashbee (73). Brett Dolman and Jeremy Ashbee have supplied material omitted in Ashbee's published essay. I want to thank Dolman, Curator (Collections), Historical Royal Palaces, and Ashbee, Head Properties Curator of English Heritage, for sharing their knowledge of the process by which torture was authorized and performed in this period, for demythologizing some later accounts of torture in the Tower, and for supplying material on Sir Thomas Smith.

Works cited

Ashbee, Jeremy. "Torture in the Tower." *Prisoners of the Tower: The Tower of London as a state prison, 1100–1941*. Eds. David Wilson, Brett Dolman, Sebastian Edwards, and Jeremy Ashbee. Hampton Court Palace: Historic Royal Palaces, 2004: 61–75.

Bernthal, Craig. "Staging Justice: James I and the Trial Scenes of *Measure for Measure*." *Studies in English Literature* 32 (1992): 247–69.

Berry, Lloyd E. (ed.). *John Stubb's Gaping Gulf, with Letters and Other Relevant Documents*. Folger Documents of Tudor and Stuart Civilization. Charlottesville: The University Press of Virginia for the Folger Shakespeare Library, 1968.

Bradley, A.C. *Shakespearean Tragedy*. 1904; New York: Meridian Books/St. Martin's Press, 1960.

Bratton, J.S. (ed.). *Plays in Performance: King Lear by William Shakespeare*. Bristol: Bristol Classical Press, 1987.

Brownlow, Frank. "Richard Topcliffe: Elizabeth's Enforcer and the Representation of Power in *King Lear*." *Theatre and Religion: Lancastrian Shakespeare*. Eds. Richard Dutton, Alison Findlay, and Richard Wilson. Manchester: Manchester University Press, 2003: 161–78.

Buckley, G.T. "Was Edmund Guilty of Capital Treason?" *Shakespeare Quarterly* 23.1 (Winter 1972): 87–94.

Bullough, Geoffrey. *Narrative and Dramatic Sources of Shakespeare*. Volume VII: Major Tragedies. London: Routledge and Kegan Paul; New York: Columbia University Press, 1973: 269–420.

Byrne, Muriel St. Clare. "*King Lear* at Stratford-on-Avon, 1959." *Shakespeare Quarterly* 11.2 (Spring 1960): 189–206.

Cavell, Stanley. "The Avoidance of Love: A Reading of *King Lear*." *Must We Mean What We Say?* 1969; Cambridge: Cambridge University Press, 2002: 267–353.

Cunningham, Karen. *Imaginary Betrayals: Subjectivity and the Discourses of Treason in Early Modern England*. Philadelphia: University of Pennsylvania Press, 2002.

Dessen, Alan C. *Shakespeare in Performance: Titus Andronicus*. Manchester: Manchester University Press, 1989.

—— "Portable Shakespeare: Exigencies and 'Magic' in Five-Actor Productions." Unpublished manuscript, June, 2003: 16 pages.

Dewar, Mary. *Sir Thomas Smith: A Tudor Intellectual in Office*. London: Athlone Press, 1964.

Evans, G.B. and J.J. Tobin (eds.). *The Riverside Shakespeare*. 2nd edn. Boston: Houghton, 1997.

Garrick, David. *The Plays of David Garrick 3: Garrick's Adaptations of Shakespeare, 1744–1756*. Eds. Harry William Pedicord and Frederick Louis Bergmann. Carbondale and Edwardsville: Southern Illinois University Press, 1981: 301–90.

Gibson, Colin (ed.). *The Selected Plays of Philip Massinger*. Cambridge: Cambridge University Press, 1978: 95–179.

Guy, John. *Tudor England*. Oxford and New York: Oxford University Press, 1988.

Halio, Jay. "Gloucester's Blinding." *Shakespeare Quarterly* 43.2 (Summer 1992): 221–23.

Hanson, Elizabeth. "Torture and Truth in Renaissance England." *Representations* 34 (Spring 1991): 53–84.

Heath, James. *Torture and English Law*. Westport, CT: Greenwood Press, 1982.

Heilmann, Robert Bechtold. *This Great Stage: Image and Structure in "King Lear."* Baton Rouge: Louisiana State University Press, 1948.

Hill, George Birkbeck (ed.). *Johnsonian Miscellanies*. 2 vols. 1897; New York: Barnes and Noble, 1970.

Homan, Sidney. *Directing Shakespeare: A Scholar Onstage*. Athens, Ohio: Ohio University Press, 2004.

Jardine, Lisa. *The Awful End of Prince William the Silent: The First Assassination of a Head of State with a Handgun*. London: HarperCollins, 2005.

Johnson, Samuel. *Johnson on Shakespeare*. Ed. Arthur Sherbo. *The Yale Edition of the Works of Samuel Johnson*. Vol. VIII. New Haven: Yale University Press, 1968: 702–5.

Kermode, Frank. "Introduction to *King Lear*." *The Riverside Shakespeare*. 2nd edn. Eds. G.B. Evans and J.J. Tobin. Boston: Houghton, 1997: 1297–1302.

Knight, G. Wilson. *The Wheel of Fire: Interpretations of Shakespearean Tragedy*. 4th edn. Cleveland and New York: Meridian Books, 1962.

Lake, Peter and Michael Questier. "Puritans, Papists, and the 'Public Sphere' in Early Modern England: The Edmund Campion Affair in Context." *The Journal of Modern History* 72.3 (September 2000): 587–627.

Langbein, John H. *Torture and the Law of Proof*. With a new Preface. 1976; Chicago: University of Chicago Press, 2006.

MacCaffrey, Wallace. *Elizabeth I*. London: Arnold, 1993.

McGuire, Philip. *Speechless Dialect: Shakespeare's Open Silences*. Berkeley: University of California Press, 1985.

Marowitz, Charles. "Lear Log." *The Tulane Drama Review* 8.2 (Winter 1963): 103–21.

Nunn, Hillary M. *Staging Anatomies: Dissection and Spectacle in Early Stuart Tragedy*. Aldershot: Ashgate, 2005.

Pechter, Edward. "On the Blinding of Gloucester." *English Literary History* 45 (1978): 181–200.

Rocklin, Edward L. "Placing the Audience at Risk: Realizing the Design of Massinger's *The Roman Actor*." *Acts of Criticism: Performance Matters in Shakespeare and*

His Contemporaries. Eds. Paul Nelsen and June Schlueter. Madison, NJ: Fairleigh Dickinson University Press, 2006: 144–58.

—— " 'That his heels may kick at heaven': Exploring the Gielgud / Burton *Hamlet*." *Staging Shakespeare*. Eds. Lena Cowen Orlin and Miranda Johnson-Haddad. Newark, DE: University of Delaware Press, 2007: 133–56.

Rosenberg, Marvin. *The Masks of King Lear*. Berkeley, Los Angeles, London: University of California Press, 1972.

Scarry, Elaine. *The Body in Pain: The Making and Unmaking of the World*. New York and Oxford: Oxford University Press, 1985.

Shakespeare, William. *Titus Andronicus*. Ed. John Dover Wilson. Cambridge: Cambridge University Press, 1968.

—— *Titus Andronicus*. Ed. Eugene M. Waith. New York and Oxford: Oxford University Press, 1984.

—— *William Shakespeare: The Complete Works*, Gen. Eds. Stanley Wells and Gary Taylor. Oxford: Clarendon Press, 1986.

—— *King Lear*. Ed. Jay Halio. Cambridge: Cambridge University Press, 1992.

—— *The Riverside Shakespeare*. 2nd edn. Eds. G.B. Evans and J.J. Tobin. Boston: Houghton, 1997.

Stock, R.D. *Samuel Johnson and Neoclassical Dramatic Theory: The Intellectual Context of the "Preface to Shakespeare."* Lincoln: University of Nebraska Press, 1973: 209–12.

Sullivan, Andrew. "The Abolition of Torture." *The New Republic* (19 December 2005): 19–23.

Tate, Nahum. *The History of King Lear*. Acted at the Duke's Theatre. Reviv'd with Alterations. London: Printed for E. Flesher, and are to be sold by R. Bentley, and M. Magnes in Russel-Street, near Covent-Garden, 1681.

Taylor, Gary and Warren, Michael (eds.). *The Division of the Kingdoms: Shakespeare's Two Versions of "King Lear."* Oxford: Clarendon Press, 1986.

Travitsky, Betty. *The Paradise of Women: Writings by Englishwomen of the Renaissance*. New York: Columbia University Press, 1989.

Urkowitz, Steven. *Shakespeare's Revision of "King Lear."* Princeton: Princeton University Press, 1980.

Van Laan, Thomas F. *The Idiom of Drama*. Ithaca and London: Cornell University Press, 1970.

Warren, Michael J. "Quarto and Folio *King Lear* and the interpretation of Albany and Edgar." *Shakespeare: Pattern of Excelling Nature*. Eds. David Bevington and Jay L. Halio. Newark: University of Delaware Press, 1978: 95–107.

—— *The Parallel King Lear, 1608–1623: Parallel Texts of the First Quarto (1608) and the First Folio (1623)*. Berkeley: University of California Press, 1989.

Weschler, Lawrence. *A Miracle, A Universe: Settling Accounts with Torturers*. With a New Postscript. Chicago: University of Chicago Press, 1998.

11 Some *Lears* of private life, from Tate to Shaw

Christy Desmet

Between 1660 and the 1760s, as Michael Dobson writes, Shakespeare became England's "national poet." Since that time, "Shakespeare has been as normatively constitutive of British national identity as the drinking of afternoon tea, and it is now probably as hard for any educated Briton to imagine not enjoying the former as it would be to imagine forgoing the latter" (Dobson 7). But while Shakespeare himself became a cultural touchstone for England, *King Lear* seems not to have played a particularly prominent role in the national project between 1660 and the end of the nineteenth century. As R.A. Foakes writes, *King Lear* has come down to us through a Romantic paradigm that located "the tragedy within the mind of Lear, and tended to reduce the external action to a domestic drama centered on the Old King's quarrels with his daughters" (Foakes 47). Outside this dominant paradigm, however, there exist domestic versions of the play that, by exchanging Charles Lamb's drama of intellect with an emphasis on family dynamics—in particular, the daughter's role within the family—address issues of social concern and national character.

Nahum Tate's revision of *King Lear* (1681), which supplements family tragedy with a romance between Cordelia and Edgar, underwrites later versions of the story as domestic drama. Amelia Opie's *Father and Daughter* (1800) and more explicitly, the melodrama by W.T. Moncrieff based on the novel (1820), rework Shakespeare's play as a story about the Lear of private life to address broader cultural concerns—in particular, the relation of home and nation. At the end of the century, Henry Irving and Ellen Terry's production of *King Lear* at the Lyceum Theatre rehabilitates the figure loathed by Lamb: Lear as a senile patriarch balances the father's tragedy against an emerging counterplot with the daughter as its heroine. One of Irving's later projects, the melodrama *Waterloo*—written by Arthur Conan Doyle and starring Henry Irving (first performed in 1895)—re-situates the Irving–Terry *Lear* within a more conservative national politics that relegates the daughter's story once again to the social background from which she had gradually emerged in literature of sentiment. Finally, reacting against both *King Lear* and *Waterloo* in *Heartbreak House* (written during the First World War but not performed or published until 1919), George Bernard Shaw reworks *King*

Lear as an elegy for England, chronicling the demise of empire, but also holding out the possibility of national renewal through the creation of a family composed purely through affective bonds, with new father-lovers for different daughters.

Although varied in their gender and cultural politics, these dramas of father–daughter estrangement and reconciliation cohere as a genre by their concentrated focus on three moments from the Shakespearean text: the reunion of father and daughter after the heath, including Lear's dawning recognition of Cordelia and the exchange of blessings between them, ratified by copious, healing tears (4.1); Lear's final vision of Cordelia, followed by the breaking of his heart (5.3), which in some instances is assimilated to the previous scene; and between these two pivotal moments, Lear's appeal to Cordelia to retire with him into an hermetically closed relationship within the confines of prison, which repeats the topos of mutual blessing:

> We two alone will sing like birds i'th' cage.
> When thou dost ask me blessing, I'll kneel down
> And ask of thee forgiveness, so we'll live,
> And pray, and sing, and tell old tales, and laugh
> At gilded butterflies, and hear poor rogues.
> (5.39–43)[1]

In anthropological narratives about the family, as Lynda E. Boose writes, the daughter is, paradoxically, both extraneous to the internal regulation of the family and crucial to the establishment of relations with other kinship groups. If the traffic in women that undergirds civilization depends on the circulation of daughters, and if "the prohibition of incest is essentially a mechanism to control internal family sexuality so that outward exchanges can take place, then the incest taboo would seem to have a special applicability to one particular pair": the father and daughter (Boose 19). Father–daughter incest was of concern throughout the nineteenth century and, of course, became a repeated trope in Freud's emerging theory of psychoanalysis. Several of Freud's female patients had sickly or diseased fathers; the patient "most comparable" in her material circumstances to the "Cordelia of private life" was Anna O., whose " 'profoundly melancholy phantasies' started from 'the position of a girl at her father's sick-bed,' " the fantasies and symptoms and illness emerging from the experience of "nursing her terminally ill father" (Freud, *Standard Edition* 9–20, cited and discussed by Willbern, 84). Freud also analyzed *King Lear* in terms of the love/death connection in "The Three Caskets" (1913), arguing that in *King Lear*, Shakespeare translates the mythic pattern of the hero's sexualized choice among three women into the King's incestuous embrace of death through a choice among daughters.

After Tate, appropriations of *Lear* as a story of private life generally repress or translate the incestuous dream at the heart of Shakespeare's play into a more decorous register. The dynamics of love and desire in these versions of the story engage more specifically with what Stanley Cavell identifies as Lear's "avoidance of love," which is rooted in his failure and refusal to "acknowledge" Cordelia. Cavell begins with Paul Alpers's observation that in *King Lear*, imagery related to sight has less to do with the acquisition of self-knowledge than with ordinary uses of the eyes "to express feeling, to weep, and to recognize others" (Cavell 45). Arguing against the Romantic notion that Lear experiences an internalized progress toward self-knowledge, Cavell instead interprets Lear's simple recognition of Cordelia in Act 4 as his climactic achievement of insight—an insight achieved not through metaphysical speculation about justice and the nature of humanity, but through the ordinary act of seeing, and therefore acknowledging, his daughter Cordelia.[2] While Cavell admits that the love Lear feels ashamed of and seeks to avoid may be incestuous—"it is at least incompatible with [Cordelia] having any (other) lover" (70)—he sees Lear's effort to retreat with Cordelia to prison as a move at once to bring his love into the open and to avoid the gaze of others.

Appropriations of *King Lear* that focus on the Lear of private life, however, conclude generally with the recognition scene, where the father recognizes his daughter and acknowledges her as a daughter by noticing the wetness of her filial tears. In reconstructing *King Lear* as a drama of benevolent recognition between father and daughter, however, these appropriations must contend with the powerful Romantic objection to staging *Lear*, most famously articulated by Charles Lamb; this revulsion against the physical experience of Shakespeare's play may itself be seen as a desire to "avoid" recognizing the indecorous decrepitude and sexuality that characterize the father–daughter dyad of *King Lear*, which in turn produces a powerful desire on the part of *Lear*'s consumers—whether readers or audiences—to retreat into the kind of privacy that Lear himself finally achieves at the end of Shakespeare's play, and that the appropriations discussed below reject as the proper conclusion to the daughter's odyssey back to her paternal home.

Tottering old men

Charles Lamb, most famously, argued that the passions of *King Lear* are too big for the stage:

> The greatness of Lear is not in corporal dimension, but in intellectual: the explosions of his passion are terrible as a volcano; they are storms turning up and disclosing to the bottom that sea, his mind, with all its vast riches. It is his mind that is laid bare. This case of flesh and blood seems too insignificant to be thought on; even as he himself neglects it. On the stage we see nothing but corporal infirmities and weakness, the impotence of rage; while we read it, we see not Lear, but we are Lear,—we are in his mind, we are sustained by a grandeur which baffles the

> malice of daughters and storms; in the aberration of his reason, we discover a mighty irregular power of reasoning, immethodised from the ordinary purpose of life, but exerting its powers, as the wind blows where it listeth, at will upon the corruptions and abuses of mankind.
>
> (Lamb 298–99)

Lamb's essay is most commonly taken as a diatribe against stage machinery and the actor's mediation between Lear's mind and the reader, but the "corporal infirmities" that offend Lamb suggest an affective as well as a technical dimension to his disapproval. Lamb as reader, like Lear himself, seeks "refuge from the malice of daughters and storms." Distaste for filial malice is a steady undercurrent in Lamb's critique and seems to be the source of his image of Lear as a debilitated human being—"an old man tottering about the stage with a walking-stick, turned out of doors by his daughters on a rainy night" (298)—and an object of pain and disgust. Even Cordelia is not exempt from Lamb's censure. Although he does not fault her for stubbornness, as Coleridge does, he also disapproves of the fact that in Tate's *King Lear*, "it is not enough that Cordelia is a daughter, she must shine as a lover too" (299).

In his critique of *King Lear*, Lamb returns repeatedly to a sense that when seeing rather than reading a play, privacy—both that of the King and of the audience—has been violated. There is something indecorous in watching, rather than contemplating, the "living martyrdom" that Lear has experienced, of watching his feelings be "flayed" in full public view (Lamb 299). Lamb compares these feelings of embarrassment to those elicited by paintings of Adam and Eve naked. That the painters themselves are shamed by such biblical nudity is confirmed by the "awkward shifts that they have recourse to, to make them look not quite naked; by a sort of prophetic anachronism, antedating the invention of fig-leaves" (300n). Seeing what ought to be hidden—the decrepit body of the patriarch and the imposing femininity of the actress, not to mention the hard-edged virtue of Cordelia turned to sentimental romancing and the boisterous lust of the bad daughters—are what bother Lamb. Sex, the body, and the affective power of both on stage are exorcised only by the more restrained "delight" of reading Shakespeare in privacy.

Love and empire

Sex, the body, and the affective power of both on stage are also evident in the play Lamb had reviled in his essay on Shakespearean tragedy: Nahum Tate's Restoration adaptation of *King Lear*, which first was performed in the season of 1680–81 and maintained a powerful presence both on stage and in the literary imagination well into the nineteenth century. Tate's version not only expanded greatly Cordelia's role, but it also developed a love interest between her and Edgar; their honorable attachment stands in contrast to the adulterous adventures of Goneril, Regan, and Edmund, which also are more elaborated in Tate's version.[3] Cordelia begins Tate's play as Edgar's true beloved, whom Lear is about to marry off to Burgundy. This alteration to the Shakespearean plot strengthens Cordelia's motive for resisting her father's command and translates her dominant mood from moral intransigence to romantic despair. In a rushed conference before the commencement of the trial scene, the lovers exchange laments. To the request that she "cast back one pitying look on wretched *Edgar*," Cordelia replies:

Alas, what wou'd the unhappy *Edgar* with
The more Unfortunate *Cordelia*;
Who in obedience to a Father's will
Flys from her *Edgar*'s Arms to *Burgundy*?
(Tate, Act 1, p. 60)

This sounds more like Hermia and Lysander at the start of *A Midsummer Night's Dream* than it does the denizens of *King Lear*. Indeed, in Tate the aside spoken by Cordelia before her bold response to Lear's demand for oratorical proofs of love—"Nothing" (1.1.85)—becomes the daughter's rejection of paternal authority in affairs of the heart: "Now comes my Trial, how am I distrest,/That must with cold speech tempt the chol'rick King/Rather to leave me Dowerless, than condemn me/to Loath'd Embraces!" (Act 1, p. 69). But while Tate's Cordelia joins such Shakespearean comic heroines as Hermia, Imogen, Miranda, and Perdita in fighting the father's tyranny, she also is careful to assert her freedom from taint or blame: "Some comfort yet 'twas no vicious Blot/That depriv'd me of a Father's Grace" (Act 1, p. 70). Whether the "blot" she denies is filial disobedience or sexual impropriety remains unclear. To complicate matters further, both Cordelia's chastity and her sexuality are emphasized by Edmund's libertine desire to rape her.

In Tate's version of the heath scene, Cordelia and her attendant join Lear, Kent, and Edgar on the stormy heath, where Edmund watches from a distance. This non-canonical scene was a particularly powerful one; the "Grand Procession of Shakespeare's Characters" in Garrick's Shakespeare Jubilee (1769), for instance, included a tableau of " 'Edgar in the mad dress with a staff, King Lear, Kent, Cordelia,' all together amidst 'Thunder and Lightning' " (Dobson 223). Cordelia's role in this scene also has a pronounced effect on Edmund. Determined to succor the King, Cordelia vows to her attendant Arante:

What have not Women dared for vicious love,
And we'll be shining Proofs that they can dare
For Piety as much; blow Winds, and Lightnings fall,
Bold in my Virgin Innocence, I'll flie,
My Royal Father to Relieve, or Die.
(Act 3, p. 79)

Cordelia's formulation collapses filial piety with virgin innocence. This combination of virtues, however, excites Edmund's lust, who decides that he will go to the heath:

> Where like the vig'rous *Jove* I will enjoy
> This Semele in a Storm, 'twill deaf her Cries
> Like Drums in Battle, lest her Groans shou'd pierce
> My pitying Ear, and make the Amorous Fight less fierce.
> (Act 3, p. 79)

While Edmund's idea of rape here seems more indebted to *Titus Andronicus* than *King Lear*, the scenario of a sexualized woman wandering through inclement weather in search of her father, combined with a masculine lust for the dutiful daughter, will find expression later in Amelia Opie's *Father and Daughter*.

Further problems are created by Tate's choice to have Cordelia turn her banishment into a love test for Edgar. The baseness of Burgundy, she reasons, "Draws suspicion on the Race of Men, / His Love was Int'rest, so may *Edgar*'s be" (Act 1, p. 70). She resolves to test the constancy of Edgar's love, and should he prove loyal, "cold *Cordelia*" will "prove as Kind as he" (Act 1, p. 70). Perhaps such caution is sensible for a daughter exiled from the patriarchal home, as Edmund's projected rape confirms, but this Cordelia's penchant for coquetry lost her support in the nineteenth century. Including Tate's version in the Variorum volume for *King Lear*, for instance, H.H. Furness wrote that "Cordelia, true to the fashionable propensity of the last century, at once becomes coquettish, and thinks that she must test Edgar's love by coldness" (Furness 469). The whiff of coquettishness in Cordelia's character will be transferred as well to later appropriations of the story that have Cordelia elope with a libertine.

Nahum Tate's *King Lear* also retains and highlights the affecting reunion between Cordelia and Lear when he awakes from madness and recognizes her. Tate introduces the stage direction "LEAR *a Sleep on a Couch*; CORDELIA, *and* ATTENDANTS *standing by him*" (Act 4, p. 89), which will be used in the visual arts and production through the time of Henry Irving and Ellen Terry.[4] Retained as well in this tightened version of Shakespeare's scene are Lear's effort to kneel before Cordelia and her countering request that Lear hold his hands in blessing over her. This scene, too, will figure heavily in subsequent variations on the play. Tate, most famously, also introduces an extra-textual scene, in which Lear's fantasy about his future life with Cordelia in prison is staged as a tableau of "LEAR *asleep, with his Head on* CORDELIA's *Lap*) (Act 5, p. 94). William Blake painted the scene in 1779 (Figure 11.1). The realization of such intimacy, raising as it does overtones of incestuous love or, at the very least, an "unnatural" reversal of parent–child roles that Lear had sought at the beginning, is not represented in the appropriations discussed below, although it haunts subsequent texts in a powerful way. In Tate, Cordelia

Figure 11.1 Lear and Cordelia in Prison (*ca.* 1779) by William Blake. By kind permission of ARTRES.

sanitizes the scene by thinking about Edgar, and Lear adds a further diversion by waking up and killing two of the officers sent to dispatch them.

As C.B. Hardman notes, by the mid-1670s the Royalist vision of nationalism had shifted its emphasis from "restoration to succession by presenting the story of a royal family whose internal divisions nearly destroy an empire" (Braverman 117, quoted and discussed by Hardman 917). Tate's *King Lear* achieves this shift of focus from monarch to family by replacing the tableau that dominates the conclusion of Shakespeare's *King Lear*—a *pietà* in which Lear holds the dead Cordelia in his arms—with the sight of Edgar leading his sightless father by the hand onto the stage (915). A second Aeneas, the true son conducts the aged father out of Troy en route to a "second Birth of empire" in Rome (Tate, Act 5, p. 95). A nation destroyed, King Lear's England, is transformed into a nation reborn by substituting for the father–daughter dyad a national "family" of refugees who live on to rebuild the empire.

Tate's love plot concludes in a way that subordinates the lovers to the demands of empire yet makes them a crucial part of that political rebirth. Having already reconciled and pledged their troth on the heath, Cordelia and Edgar are reunited, and Lear gives her to Edgar in marriage, although he insists that it is Cordelia who shall reign as monarch. Edgar readily agrees to the love match: "Divine Cordelia. All the Gods can witness/How much thy

Love to Empire I prefer!" (Act 5, p. 96). Lear himself retires to a hermit's cell in the venerable company of Gloucester and Kent. In this way, both father and daughter privilege the private life, but in ways that support nation and empire. The *Lear*s of public and private life come to support one another. The same might be said for the appropriation of *King Lear* to be discussed next, Amelia Opie's post-revolutionary *Father and Daughter*; in this novel, however, the family becomes the antidote to a failed politics of nationhood, rather than the natural expression of the nation and its regeneration.

The prodigal daughter's return

Even before W.T. Moncrieff had turned Amelia Opie's *Father and Daughter* (1800) into a stage melodrama as *The Lear of Private Life*, the novel betrayed distinct Shakespearean influences. This story recounts what might have happened if Cordelia had been seduced away from the paternal house, rather than ejected from it. At the beginning of Opie's tale, Agnes Fitzhenry and her father constitute a peaceful father–daughter dyad, the state imagined by Lear himself in Act 5 of Shakespeare's play: "Agnes Fitzhenry was the only child of a respectable merchant in a country town, who, having lost his wife when his daughter was very young, resolved, for her sake, to form no second connexion" (Opie 3). Fitzhenry, like another Prospero, serves as both father and mother to his young child; and she, in turn resolves not to marry, but "to live single for my father's sake" (4). According to Opie's narrator, who is quoting Elizabeth Inchbald, "love, however rated by many as the chief passion of the heart, is but a poor dependent, a retainer on the other passions—admiration, gratitude, respect, esteem, pride in the object" (5, discussed by Tong). Love for both husband and father is therefore grounded in "gratitude," the principal filial virtue in dispute between King Lear and his daughters. Agnes, however, is not perfect; she overestimates her ability to read the character of others and suffers as well from lack of self-knowledge. Agnes, in other words, is marred by that touch of "pride" some writers found in Shakespeare's Cordelia. But she is also marked by the sheltered innocence—indeed, sexual vulnerability—that others found in Shakespeare's Ophelia. *Father and Daughter*, in fact, may follow the structural pattern of *King Lear*, but it refers more often and more explicitly to *Hamlet* through allusions and citations. It is as if Opie's novel, in anticipation of Mary Cowden Clarke's imaginary biography for The Rose of Elsinore (1851–52)—who also grew up in the country and was plagued from an early age with unwanted romantic advances—must gradually come to "recognize" its principal affinity with *King Lear*, the most patriarchal of Shakespeare's tragedies.

In Opie's tale, Clifford, an officer of the guards and a shameless rake, sets his sights on Agnes, methodically alienating her from her father and then luring her away from Fitzhenry's paternal care. When Agnes bridles at her father's objection to a supposed marriage with Clifford, the father, borrowing his mood from *Hamlet*'s ghost, shows a "countenance more in sorrow than in anger" (Opie 7) and tries to reason his daughter out of her determination to pursue an inappropriate, and amorphous, connection with Clifford. The ensuing events will be familiar to readers of Samuel Richardson's *Clarissa*. Eloping with Clifford, Agnes finds herself not in Gretna Green but in London, sequestered without marriage in an apartment as an "acknowledged mistress" to Clifford; eventually, she gives birth to a boy. When Clifford finally convinces Agnes to leave her private refuge and attend a performance at Drury Lane, she fortuitously overhears two gentlemen discussing Clifford's imminent marriage to a city heiress and recognizes, to her shame, the depth of his betrayal. She also learns that her father, whom she had thought remarried, suffers in his health.

During her long, cold, penitent escape from Clifford and her prodigal journey home through a fierce winter storm, Agnes encounters in the dark wood outside her native village a furtive, manacled lunatic—a metaphoric conflation of King Lear and Poor Tom—and discovers, to her horror, that this lunatic is her own father, who straight off threatens to strangle the baby because he has been screaming with fright. "I do not like children," the figure declares, "[I]f you trust them, they will betray you" (Opie 29, echoing Lear's sentiments about the ruin daughters bring to their fathers [3.4.67–70]). In a poignant reunion, Agnes kneels to the father, who in turn fails to recognize her, initiating a motif of expiatory blessings—an obvious legacy of *King Lear*—that Agnes and Fitzhenry exchange throughout the remainder of the text, as she reunites with him and seeks to cure his insanity. After the keepers recover Fitzhenry, and Agnes's child nearly dies of cold, she seeks refuge with cottagers and, overcome with guilt and remorse, threatens to commit suicide in the manner of Goneril, by stabbing herself with a knife. But once reinstalled in her hometown, Agnes commits herself and her child to a life of penitence and humble industry, visiting her father daily until he is released from Bedlam, an institution that his benevolence had helped to build. Agnes takes Fitzhenry into her home and continues nursing him until, in a final crystallization of the structural homology the book shares with Shakespeare's *King Lear*, the father recognizes and forgives his daughter and then dies.

Throughout the long process of Agnes's attempt to cure Fitzhenry, Ophelia and Hamlet, rather than Cordelia and Lear, remain the allusive center for Fitzhenry and Agnes as they struggle toward their Shakespearean destiny of recognition and death. Mr. Seymour, who had first shut his door in Agnes's face, defends Agnes to the aptly named Mrs. Macfiendy: "If heart-felt misery, contrition, and true penitence, may hope to win favor in the sight of God, and expiate past offences, 'a ministering angel might this frail one be, though we lay howling' " (Opie 61). Besides the poignancy of foreshadowing Agnes's death in Laertes's justification of Ophelia's suicide, we see the tendency for characters in this novel to see Agnes as the doomed and damned lover rather than as a prodigal daughter. Fitzhenry and Agnes themselves remain caught in the *Hamlet* paradigm for most of the novel. At their first meeting in the forest, the father tells Agnes, "I had a child once—but she is dead, poor soul" (Opie 29). As they roam the grounds of the asylum later in the novel, Fitzhenry offers to show Agnes his daughter's supposed grave, alternately showering his present companion with anxious pity ("Poor thing! Poor thing!") and mourning his imaginary daughter ("She is dead, for all that" (51)); his lament echoes Ophelia's song in the mad scene:

> He is dead and gone, lady,
> He is dead and gone;
> At his head a grass-green turf,
> At his heels a stone.
> (4.5.29–32)

The unspoken sin that must be confronted by both father and daughter, promiscuity, also resonates with Ophelia's mad visions. In the forest, Fitzhenry had confided, in response to Agnes's sympathetic inquiries after his lost daughter, that "They said she ran away from me with a lover—but I knew they lied—she was good, and would not have deserted the father who doted on her" (29). What Agnes has already accepted and Fitzhenry slowly comes to accept is the bleak fate of romantic lovers in ballad. Agnes's fate has been that of Ophelia's improvident maid:

> To-morrow is Saint Valentine's day,
> All in the morning betime,
> And I a maid at your window,
> To be your Valentine.
> Then up he rose, and donn'd his clothes,
> And dupp'd the chamber-door;
> Let in the maid, that out a maid
> Never departed more.
> (4.5.47–54)

It is Agnes who turns the relationship away from the scenario of *Hamlet*'s doomed lovers to the broader moral canvas painted by *King Lear*. She takes Fitzhenry into her home, where they enjoy a peaceful, secluded life, walking in the garden and tying up drooping flowers. Fitzhenry, of course, is still mad, and the grandson's occasional satire of his behavior reminds us that neither father nor daughter achieves Lear's projected bliss of companionship.

Like Cordelia nursing Lear back to health in Shakespeare's play, Agnes tends her father patiently, day after day, for an entire year: "Not for one moment, therefore, would she leave his bedside, and she would allow herself neither food nor rest, while with earnest eyes she gazed on the fast sinking eyes of Fitzhenry, eager to catch in them an expression of returning recognition" (Opie, *Father and Daughter* 89–90). One day, awaking from a nap, Fitzhenry achieves a moment of Lear-like recognition, and cries, "My child? Are you there? Gracious God! Is this possible?" (Opie 90). He forgives

Agnes, they exchange stories, and, with his final breath, Fitzhenry blesses his daughter; she, falling into a "state of stupefaction" (91), soon dies and is buried with him.[5] In the coda to Opie's rewriting of *King Lear*, the rake Clifford, now a lord by virtue of his second marriage, sees the funeral, learns Agnes's story, and, in a rush of emotion, abducts his young son Edward, who, as it turns out, has proven to be his only heir. Although Opie makes it clear that Clifford's repentance remains at bottom a selfish impulse, he nevertheless is allowed to maintain custody of the boy until Clifford's own untimely death, brought on by guilt and dissipation.

For Opie, it seems, the price of a father–daughter apotheosis is the return to patriarchy, the daughter's absorption into the story of male succession. Nevertheless, as Roxanne Eberle argues, Agnes does not suffer the inexorable and ruinous slide into sin that characterizes the "harlot's progress"; she lives for six years after her seduction, works her way back into the respect of her society, and has a final reconciliation with the father she betrayed. By ending the tale with Clifford's agony and eventual demise, "Opie's tale—even as it disciplines its sexualized heroine—simultaneously addresses the sins of seducers, fathers, and even 'respectable' men" (Eberle 104). But while Eberle detects the persistence of a radical, feminist politics in Opie's post-Jacobian writing, the myth of England as a nation that underwrites the recovery of *King Lear* by the nineteenth-century theater does not survive intact the heroine's death in *Father and Daughter*. The critical eye that Opie casts on father figures—on Clifford as a representative of the army, on Clifford's own father, who uses his son to build the family fortune, and even on Mr. Seymour, whose respectability involves a too precise concern for public opinion—suggests, as Joanne Tong writes, that the nation of fathers "vanish[es] in the novel's conclusion, which spells the end of the patriarchal family and unsettles the future of the nation." As women such as the faithful servant and the staunch friend Catherine Seymour take on the responsibility of paternal support for Agnes (Tong; Eberle 99), patriarchy itself is seriously compromised: Agnes's middle-class family is gone, Clifford himself dies, and the child, Edward, faces an uncertain future—despite his projected absorption into an aristocratic family—caused by his status as a bastard.

While Opie herself would go on to imagine a family based on mother–daughter relations in *Adeline Mowbray; or, The Mother and Daughter*, others were happy to repeat and rework the story of Agnes Fitzhenry in a variety of media. Of the many adaptations of *Father and Daughter* that followed, W.T. Moncrieff's *The Lear of Private Life! Or Father and Daughter* (1820) most explicitly develops the connection between Opie's plot and *King Lear*. The play, which ran at the Royal Coburg Theatre, London, in April of 1820, starred Junius Brutus Booth as Fitzhenry (now called Fitzarden, possibly with an additional Shakespearean pun on Arden), while Mrs. Barrymore was Agnes.

Moncrieff capitalized not only on *Father and Daughter* as a parent text, but also on the revival of *King Lear* in 1820 after a ten-year absence from the stage—still in Tate's version—by both Junius Brutus Booth (who played Lear on his nights off from the Royal Coburg Theatre) and Edmund Kean at Drury Lane Theatre.[6] Kean was noted for the explosive power of his madness; Richard Henry Dana writes that "the violent and immediate changes of the passions in Lear, so hard to manage without offending us, are given by Mr. Kean with a spirit and fitness to nature we had not imagined possible" (*The Idle Man*, p. 35, reprinted in Furness 441).[7] The material bequeathed to Moncrieff by Opie, by contrast, focused on Fitzhenry's long, protracted melancholy, a life of sketching tombs with Agnes's name on them, punctuated by wild ravings. And, of course, the play had to end with the recognition scene, as prescribed by Opie's novel.

For key scenes in the play, Moncrieff remains quite faithful to the letter of Opie's text. Act 2, scene 3, the meeting of father and daughter in the forest outside Agnes's natal village, remains close to Opie's language as well as her plot; so too does Act 3, scene 3, the meeting of father and daughter in the lunatic asylum. What is different in Moncrieff's version is the social construction of the society that surrounds and sustains Agnes and Fitzarden as they reconcile with one another. In Moncrieff, the line between the aristocratic libertines of London and the solid villagers of Agnes's home is firmly, even crudely drawn. Alvaney (the Clifford figure) plans the elopement with cool efficiency; he maneuvers Agnes into a midnight assignation on her balcony, to which he arrives with rope-ladder and post-chaise at the ready. The aristocrats whose company Alvaney frequents in London are both salacious in their desire to see his lovely mistress and insouciant about his plans to marry for money. The scene in which Agnes discovers her lover's perfidy is even more painful than the experience of Opie's Agnes at the Drury Lane Theatre. In Opie, Agnes's shrieks of agony are incorrectly and unkindly treated as signs of drunkenness by her fellow theatergoers. In Moncrieff, by contrast, Agnes suffers the ignominy of being secreted behind a screen, as if she were in a Restoration comedy, where she overhears the news of Alvaney's impending marriage and then rushes forward to expose herself to the collective gaze of the libertines.

By contrast, the village of Agnes and Fitzarden is both healthier and more comfortingly comic than that of Opie. There is no Mrs. Macfiendy here; nor are there unscrupulous military men. Instead, Fitzarden has in place a strong system of local charity that gives relief to widows and sustains, with gratitude, the army veteran. An added subplot features Meriel and Gilbert the Bachelor. Gilbert may not be overly industrious, but unlike the aristocrats of London and unlike Alvaney, he is eager and ready to marry, and has been thwarted in this effort only by lack of a "portion," which the sudden recovery from death of a miserly aunt frustrates once again during the first act. Fitzarden generously offers to provide the portion, although this kindness is prevented when Agnes's elopement is discovered. When Agnes returns, Gilbert and Meriel selflessly turn their attention to supporting and serving her.

The whole village ethic, it seems, is based on simple benevolence. Whereas Lear complains that "How sharper than a serpent's tooth it is/To have a thankless child! (1.4.265–66) and Opie cites Inchbald's belief that love is grounded in "gratitude," in *The Lear of Private Life*, both generosity and love are bestowed freely and unconditionally. Blessings are requested and given frequently, much more so than in *King Lear* and more so than in *Father and Daughter*. Fitzarden's offer of a marriage portion to Gilbert, like all of his charitable acts, comes with no strings attached. The villagers not only take Agnes back into their collective bosom, but, in a final, stunning alteration of Opie's plot, Agnes's friends arrange her marriage to the repentant Alvaney. After a brief moment of railing against her seducer, Agnes accepts the man who had ruined her and had driven her father mad. She is rewarded by Fitzarden's concluding recognition of her as "my long-lost child, my much loved erring and forgiven Agnes" (52). Fitzarden's spontaneous expression of both love and forgiveness concludes the play, and the final tableau groups together Fitzarden, with Agnes embracing his knees, Alvaney, Gilbert, and Meriel. Father, husband, and child—Agnes emerges from her trial with a complete family and is fully reintegrated into her wholesomely rustic community.

Within the framework of Opie's tale, Moncrieff produces a critique of the English class system, subordinating the harlot's return and redemption to a celebration of a long-vanished rural England where community, not class, determines social relations, and society is sustained by an idyllically feudal alternation of willing work and festival. Moncrieff's play, produced at the Royal Coburg Theatre in 1820, was part of what David Worrall has described as a politically radical artisan drama, which flourished in the non-patent theaters between 1797 and 1830:

> Wherever one looks in these few hundred square yards of London's theatreland in 1819–20 hard by the Theatres' Royal Drury Lane and Covent Garden, one comes across specific radical ideologies in close conjunction with a non-patented drama, which is visibly experimenting and enlarging its treatment of social, racial, and sexual issues.
>
> (226)

Moncrieff's substantial oeuvre includes dramas such as *Reform; Or John Bull Triumphant: A Patriotic Drama* (1828) and *Giovanni in London; or, The Libertine Reclaimed* (1817). Within this context, *The Lear of Private Life* suddenly seems quite public, even political. It continues Opie's critique of gender politics even as it takes up issues of class in the English nation. Finally, as a reworking of the combined family and romantic drama initiated by Tate's revised *King Lear, The Lear of Private Life* puts Shakespeare back into the public sphere, this time with a very different political slant.

Mad king and motherless daughter

While the phenomenon that I have been calling the "*Lear* of Private Life" —governed by a dialectic between public and private sphere, home and nation—crystallized with Moncrieff's play of that name, a rather late manifestation of its ethos can be found in Henry Irving's 1892 production of *King Lear*. Irving's depiction of Lear as a fond, foolish old man carries over into his performance as Corporal Gregory Brewster in Arthur Conan Doyle's potboiler, *Waterloo*, which reconstructs the senile old man as a national war hero.

Irving himself described his concept of Lear as an attempt to "combine the weakness of senility with the tempest of passion" (Irving, "Four Favorite Parts" 929, quoted in Hughes 117).[8] Clement Scott, in his account of Irving's first-night performances at the Lyceum, offers this sympathetic description:

> A tall, gaunt, supple, and kingly figure, the thin and attenuated body weighed down with a swathing load of regal garments. A splendid head, indeed, with finely cut features; the restless eyes; the yellow parchment skin, set in a frame of snowy-white hair and silvered straggling beard; and, of course, those eloquent hands which have been so often discussed, and so frequently described.
>
> (348)

Irving's Lear, in this account, is majestic—Scott compares him to "Moses at Mount Sinai, or Noah at the hour of the flood" (349)—but also fragile: "We see him at his entrance with the Court, tottering down a steep incline in an ancestral castle, half-supported, and leaning on the gold scabbard of a broadsword, which serves as a staff" (348). The tottering old man repressed by Charles Lamb thus returns to the stage, decades later, in the person of Henry Irving.

Playing Lear as an old man, Irving highlights the private over the King's public self. Irving's archaic England, in fact, is an empire in ruins. As his introduction to the acting version of the play states, he placed the action in pre-feudal times, at "a time shortly after the departure of the Romans, when the Britons would naturally inhabit the houses left vacant" (Irving, *King Lear* 1). The idea of Lear and his daughters inhabiting abandoned houses is vaguely gothic, and Hawes Craven's sketches for the production generally depict the *dramatis personae* as being dwarfed by the architecture of their sparsely furnished dwellings. At the same time, the landscape seemed idyllic to Clement Scott: "It is a fanciful England, no doubt, but certain it is that the Romans must have quitted the loveliest of lands, and that the Britons that supplanted them were mighty men and warriors of heroic stature, much like a species of Viking" (Scott 346).

Whether or not the Roman ruins signify on a grand scale the ruin of King Lear's mind, as Alan Hughes suggests (139), the lasting impression given by Irving as Lear is not one of sublimity, or even the pathos of creeping madness, but the father's restored love for his daughter. Scott writes that "[t]here have been wild Lears, Bedlamite Lears, Lears frenzied from the outset: here was a Lear who, from first to last, emphasized the chord of human affection" (345).

Edward Dowden's essay, contemporaneous with the production, declared as well that the theme of *King Lear* is "love made an alien and an outcast; the temporary triumph of unnatural hate; the onset and victory of love" (Dowden, quoted by Hughes 121). A tragedy of love requires two people, and to the extent that the play did succeed, as Scott realized, it depended on the interaction of Irving's Lear with Terry's Cordelia: "Without such an ideal Cordelia as was found last night in Miss Ellen Terry, such a Lear might have been considered a rash and hazardous experiment. But the artist knew where he had posted his reserves" (346).

We can infer some idea of how Irving and Terry interacted as King Lear and Cordelia from the two Ford Maddox Brown paintings that inform its staging and sets and from Brown's series of pen-and-ink drawings of scenes from the *King Lear* story. Irving knew these works of art well. In "Cordelia's Portion" (1866), a print of which hung in Irving's dressing room (Meisel 418), the King is white-haired with a long beard; he slumps in his throne, seemingly unconscious of the tumult around him, while other figures throng about him. Cordelia, her hand pressed to her cheek in dismay, stands apart to the side, leaning for support on an emotionally expressive King of France. On the floor lies the map, now forgotten as the drama of Cordelia's banishment unfolds. Lear slouches away from his daughter; Cordelia is upright, but drooping in the direction of her father. Together, they form the focus of Brown's composition, with the other characters posed around them as a dramatic frame. The series of sketches that Brown made chronicling the play's narrative offers a further gloss on the semiotics of posture in this painting. Cursing his bad daughters in the first sketch, Lear rears back away from them. In two subsequent mad scenes, in which the King cavorts with his Fool, the two figures are separated, but engage with one another in an energetic dance. In the fourth sketch, as Lear awakes from his sleep, he rises toward Cordelia, and she reaches downward and toward him. The series of four sketches is framed as a movement from rejection to reconciliation. In the last of the sequence, Brown adds a subtitle in which Cordelia, standing at the foot of her father's bed and awaiting "anxiously the effect of her presence on him," utters "the touching soliloquy that begins: 'Had you not been their father, these white flakes/Had challenged pity of them' " (quoted in Meisel 425; referring to 4.7.30–31). The musicians summoned by the doctor to wake Lear with music stand clustered together in the background. Lear and Cordelia, who occupy the foreground, are separate but formally responsive to one another. Lear is asleep and unconscious, but Cordelia, despite her sternly erect carriage, leans toward him with her arms outstretched in silent supplication.

While the art of Ford Maddox Brown influenced directly Henry Irving's conception of King Lear as a character, reconstructing Ellen Terry's contribution to the tragedy of father and daughter is a bit more complicated. In her *Memoirs*, originally published as *The Story of My Life*, Terry had relatively little to say about Irving's *King Lear* or her own performance in the role of

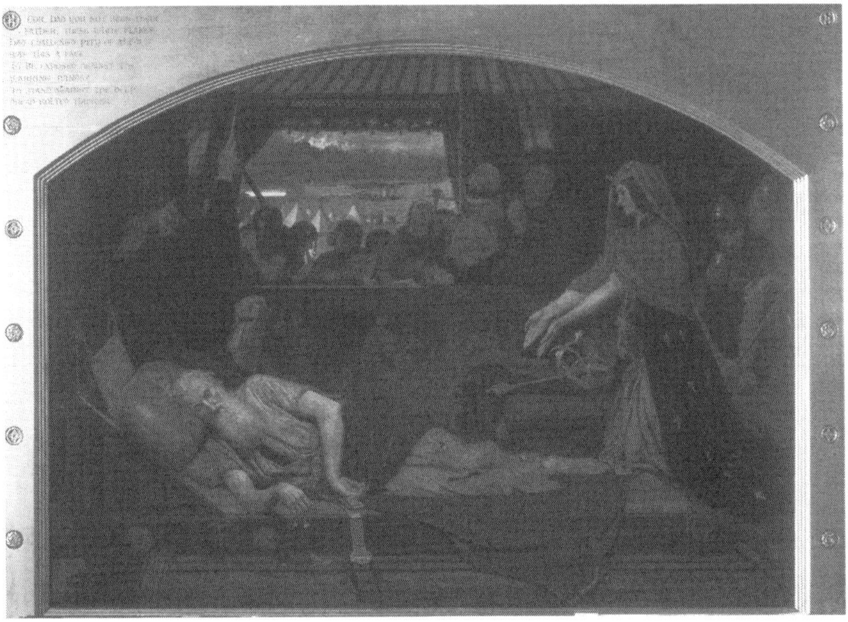

Figure 11.2 Lear and Cordelia (1848–49) by Ford Maddox Brown. By kind permission of ARTRES.

Cordelia; the reason given was that these plays, having been produced in the 1890s, were still too close in memory to permit generalizations. In her *Four Lectures on Shakespeare* (1912), however, Terry does discuss Cordelia as one of Shakespeare's "pathetic" women: "Perhaps some of you have a daughter, who like Cordelia is extremely reticent, loves you dearly, but never gushes. Perhaps there is a daughter here who knows exactly what Cordelia means when she says her love 'is more richer than her tongue [*sic*.]' " (153). Terry's lectures, performed after her career as an actress was over, were in part reading performances, and to illustrate Cordelia's character she chose a generous selection from the recognition scene. Her final comment is: "Kind and dear princess! Still waters run deep!" (156).

Terry's further startling contrast between Cordelia and Cleopatra is perhaps an indication of her close engagement with Anna Jameson's *Characteristics of Women* (originally published in 1832). This was a text that Terry owned and annotated and one that clearly influenced her understanding of Cordelia. (In Jameson's text, the analysis of Cleopatra as a historical character immediately follows that of Cordelia as a character of the affections.) Jameson's Cordelia is a secular saint, "ready prepared for heaven" (Jameson 273); "There is in the beauty of Cordelia's character an effect too sacred for words" (262); she is governed by the "purest and holiest of impulses" guided by two of the "sublimest principles of human action—the love of truth and the sense of duty" (263). Balancing Jameson's encomium for Cordelia's character, however, is a long and thoughtful refutation of the notion that Cordelia's "modest pride" might be a character flaw, a form of "harshness or obstinancy" (260): in her assessment, Cordelia shows merely "a natural reserve, a tardiness of disposition" (267). Jameson scrutinizes carefully those small gestures that reveal the depth of Cordelia's emotion—her gentle sighs and tears, but also her terse, but loaded criticisms of the sisters. Like Terry, Jameson dwells on the recognition scene, quoting extensively from it (271–72). Finally, the strength that Jameson attributes to Cordelia is evident in her extended analogy between Shakespeare's dutiful daughter and Antigone.

What, then, actually transpired between Henry Irving and Ellen Terry in the Lyceum version of *King Lear*'s recognition scene, which is so central to the experience of the Lear of private life? A sketch of the scene from the *Illustrated London News* (3 December 1892) confirms that Irving and Terry played the scene very much according to the scenario sketched out in Brown's painting of Lear and Cordelia. While other figures are grouped around Lear's bed, the King rises from it, with one hand clenched and the other supporting him on the pillow, to stare directly at his daughter. Cordelia leans in toward the bed, her hands outstretched in supplication, as they are in the Ford Maddox Brown painting (Figure 11.2). Graham Robertson remembers the scene in this way: "I can still see him, weary and half dazed, sitting up on his couch and staring at the daughter he had banished as she bent tenderly over him. 'You are spirit, I know—when did you die?' " (Robertson 167–68, discussed by Meisel 428). Terry apparently generated real tears; Irving tasted them with appreciation (Rosenberg 290).

Jameson, while she had constructed Cordelia as a figure of transcendent femininity, also insisted on her integrity as a character. Had Cordelia never even known her father," Jameson writes, "she would not have been less Cordelia, less distinctly *herself*" (275, discussed by Lootens 101).[9] Terry's Cordelia is even more individualistic and less generally transcendant than the Marian saint of Jameson. Anticipating one strain of twentieth-century feminist criticism, which understands Cordelia as a "motherless daughter," Terry writes in her *Memoirs*:

> How many times Shakespeare draws fathers and daughters, and how little stock he seems to take of *mothers*! Portia and Desdemona, Cordelia, Rosalind and Miranda, Lady Macbeth. Queen Katherine and Hermione, Ophelia, Jessica, Hero, and many more are daughters of *fathers*, but of their mothers we hear nothing. . . . Of mothers of sons there are plenty of examples. Constance, Volumnia, the Countess Rousillon, Gertrude; but if there are mothers of daughters at all, they are poor examples, like Juliet's mother and Mrs. Page . . . I often wonder what the mothers of Goneril, Regan, and Cordelia were like! I think Lear must have married twice.
>
> (Terry, *Memoirs*, 162)

That the motherless daughter need not be asexual is confirmed by Terry's explicit linking of Cordelia to Desdemona as a woman who has "plenty of character" (Terry, *Memoirs*, 161). But having already experienced the loss of one parent, she reaches out to the other with a deep knowledge of human mortality.

Waterloo and *King Lear*

No direct connections link Henry Irving's production of *King Lear* with his sensational appearance as Corporal Gregory Brewster in Arthur Conan Doyle's *Waterloo* (first performed 1894)—in fact, Irving's performance as King Arthur intervenes between them—but Brewster and Lear were two in a series of old men played by Irving near the end of his career. In his diary, Bram Stoker, Irving's manager and the author of *Dracula*, noted that at the conclusion of *Waterloo*, "all laughed and wept. Marvellous study of senility" (Stoker 1:249). The combination of tears and senility evoked by the comment irresistibly recalls Irving's *King Lear*. In this one-act play, Brewster is managing rather badly as an aged bachelor, and the play opens when his niece Norah arrives to care for him. Brewster himself is woolly, and although his elderly ills do not exactly include *hysterica passio*, Corporal Brewster downs suitable amounts of paregoric, a treatment for diarrhea (King, Appendix A, *A Story of Waterloo* 6). Norah proves to be no Cordelia. She worries about the butter and bacon but can muster only the most anemic of romantic attractions to one of Brewster's visitors; she is neither the intensely committed daughter of Shakespeare's play, nor the romantic heroine of Tate's *King Lear*. But Brewster remains, in a manner of speaking, every inch a King. The portrait of him in military uniform that hangs over the fireplace contrasts the martial dignity of his past with the old man's present decline. But the reiterated reverence of a string of military visitors who troop through Brewster's door for the duration of the play re-establish him as a national hero.

At the climax of this one-act melodrama, Brewster has a vision. Having described himself as an impatient "straggler" in his original regiment, the Scots' Guards, the other members of which have passed on to become a celestial army, Brewster apparently slips into death but suddenly staggers once more to his feet to proclaim, "The Guards need powder, and, by God, they shall have it!" (King, Appendix A 259). As Norah and the attending Sergeant rush forward, Brewster subsides into his chair (like Irving as Lear), and the Sergeant portentously announces, "I think that the 3rd Guards have a full roster now" (259). With the subordination of Cordelia (both Norah and Ellen Terry as prototype), the father (as Lear, Brewster, and Irving) can be recuperated as a national hero. In this way, in *Waterloo* Irving re-produces King Lear as an exemplar of English military virtue whose apotheosis is achieved at the expense of the figure of Cordelia as English saint.

Bringing down the house

George Bernard Shaw hated *Waterloo* with a passion and wrote a scathing review of it ("Mr. Irving Takes Paregoric," Appendix B in King 260–63), but that did not stop him from writing his own version of Shakespeare's *King Lear. Shakes vs. Shav* records the following conversation, in which Shakes asks tauntingly, "Where is thy Hamlet? Couldst thou write *King Lear*?" Shav responds confidently, "Aye, with his daughters all complete. Couldst thou have written *Heartbreak House*? Behold my *Lear*" (Shaw, *Shakes vs. Shav* 278). *King Lear* looms behind *Heartbreak House*, but can be glimpsed only intermittently, in an oddly refracted manner. First of all, the patriarch's catastrophic mistake, the division of his kingdom, has never really occurred. One daughter, the aptly-named Ariadne, fled the father's house twenty-three years earlier; and although her father claims the privilege of heartbreak for himself —"You left because you did not want us. Is there no heartbreak in that for your father?" (141)—once the prodigal Ariadne has crossed her father's threshold, she makes no real move to leave nor he to banish her. The second daughter, Hesione, is not sacrificed to the gods' wrath, as was her Trojan predecessor. Instead, she presides over Heartbreak House with complete insouciance, if limited efficiency. Captain Shotover, the ancient Lear figure, also survives comfortably, if sardonically, amid a never-ending stream of unwanted "retainers," who arrive at his doorstep with great regularity throughout the play. He himself still controls the patriarchal home, as Stanley Weintraub points out: "I keep this house," the Captain tells Ellie; Hesione merely "upsets it." He seeks to "attain the seventh degree of concentration; she invites visitors and leaves me to entertain them" (Shaw, *Heartbreak House* 46; Weintraub, "*Heartbreak House*"). The placid kingdom of Captain Shotover exerts a fascination for strangers that nearly equals the fascination his daughters inspire in men; lost and "damned" souls flock to Heartbreak House—"this silly house, this strangely happy house, this house without foundations" (Shaw, *Heartbreak House* 140)—and fly like moths "into the candle" (Shaw, *Heartbreak House* 148).

As a tragicomedy of private life, *Heartbreak House* sets the sexual/social games played by its denizens against a backdrop of lost empire. Ariadne's husband still labors abroad for England's glory; Captain Shotover reminisces about his adventurous youth on the sea; but in the modern world, such heroism (and, incidentally, the colonial exploitation upon which they are built) are no longer possible. The Captain's black wife, left behind with the empire, is just a memory. In Shakespearean terms, what England has lost in the era of Heartbreak House is *Othello*'s penchant for hyperbolic adventures. What attracts Ellie to the figure of Othello are his exotic stories of travel and travail:

> Don't you think it must have been a wonderful experience for Desdemona, brought up so quietly at home, to meet a man who has been out in the world, doing all sorts of brave things and having terrible adventures, and

> yet finding something in her that made him love to sit and talk with her and tell her about them?
>
> (Shaw, *Heartbreak House* 60)

To this, Hesione responds drily, "Do you indeed? He was jealous, wasn't he?" (59). Jealousy may be in short supply at Heartbreak House, but Othello's other problem, compulsive storytelling, or lying, is present in abundance; Hector Hushabye, for instance, has to fashion fictional adventures for himself that he recounts to the eager naif Ellie. England, in Shaw's play, has become all about money, but even this solid commodity proves to be a chimera, as Alfred Mangan's reputation for wealth is based on economic sleight-of-hand; the "industrial Napoleon" of the public's imagination merely gets by on "traveling expenses" and "a trifle of commission" (Shaw, *Heartbreak House* 133).

More to the point of this article, *Heartbreak House* also undoes the foundational family relationship of Shakespeare's *King Lear*. Until the very end of the play, the foregrounding of father–daughter relationships that had characterized *Lear* in the second half of the nineteenth century is displaced completely by a focus on men and women, the making of marriages and the adulterous accommodations of their continued existence. A disruptive asymmetry characterizes the romances of *Heartbreak House*. Ariadne and Hesione both have husbands, and both also dally with extramural lovers. No single Edmund, however, commands the adulterous affections of these women. Everyone flirts, or "fascinates," indiscriminately, and the most charismatic, if feckless, man in the play is Hector Hushabye, an Albany figure emptied of leadership qualities and moral center. Ellie, although not officially a Shotover daughter, has not two, but three beaus: Hector himself under an alias, the industrial "boss" Mangan, and, ultimately, Captain Shotover. She epitomizes the most objectionable qualities of Nahum Tate's Cordelia, as defined by Lamb: "It is not enough that Cordelia is a daughter, she must shine as a lover too" (Lamb 299). As Cordelia, Ellie also has multiple fathers; her biological father, Mazzini Dunn, is marrying her off to Mangan for financial security; Captain Shotover mistakenly links Ellie to Billy Dunn, the pirate-robber who, in Act 3, appears as a burglar; and finally, the Captain himself, who functions as a paternal mentor for Ellie.

The social disjunctions in the family patterns of *Heartbreak House* produce a moral miasma. Within the *Lear* paradigm, Hesione and Ariadne should function as the King's "demon daughters" (Shaw, *Heartbreak House* 127). Ellie, although technically not a Shotover daughter, stands in for Cordelia, the good daughter. Her father says of Ellie what Terry said of Shakespeare's good daughter in *King Lear*: that she has a strong character, which he attributes to her reading of Shakespeare (93). But in *Heartbreak House*, the allegorical distinction between good and bad daughters does not hold up. Not only are Hesione and Ariadne more "fascinating" than fiendish, but Ellie, as a Cordelia figure, has a home-grown toughness that derives from her acute awareness that she is a daughter without a dowry. Not so deluded to think that she is "herself a dowry" (*King Lear* 1.1.242), Ellie defends her shameless manipulation of Mangan on the grounds that "every woman who hasn't any money is a matrimonial adventurer" (98). Her sentiments, although realistic, are a far cry from Cordelia's expressed contempt for Burgundy's cautious insistence on a dowry: "Since respects of fortune are his love, / I shall not be his wife" (1.1.149–50).

Lear's journey to self-knowledge, the solitary experience of the Romantic hero as envisioned by Lamb, is never realized in Shaw's remake of Shakespeare's play. The seventh degree of concentration, which Captain Shotover pursues diligently, turns out to be just a rum-induced calm. Captain Shotover himself explains why deep self-knowledge is impossible for the elderly: "[Y]ou are young: you sleep at night only, and sleep soundly. But later on you will sleep in the afternoon. Later still you will sleep even in the morning; and you will awake tired, tired of life" (Shaw, *Heartbreak House* 119). While the Captain slips into the dreams of second childhood, Ellie feels her own dreams "dashed to pieces" and seeks marriage to a rich old man. The soul, the foundation of self-knowledge, in the end, proves too expensive for Ellie: "Old-fashioned people think you can have a soul without money. They think the less money you have, the more soul you have. Young people today know better. A soul is a very expensive thing to keep: much more so than a motor car" (116).

By the end of *Heartbreak House*, the role of King Lear suffering on the heath is assumed unwillingly by Mangan, in spite of his expressed wish for nothing more than a quiet life and the "last word" (Shaw, *Heartbreak House* 104). Mangan is the only visitor to Heartbreak House who makes any effort to leave; while Ariadne remarks that he will certainly be uncomfortable without his luggage, Ellie offers Mangan a chance to play Lear on the heath: "It is a heavenly night: you can sleep on the heath. Take my waterproof to lie on: it is hanging up in the hall" (105). In the play's final scene, Mangan makes one final effort to strip away the games and lies that structure relationships within Heartbreak House: "Let's all strip stark naked. We may as well do the thing thoroughly when we're about it. We've stripped ourselves morally naked: well, let's strip ourselves physically naked as well, and see how we like it. I tell you I can't bear this. I was brought up to be respectable" (136). Mangan's great scene is interrupted, however, by Ellie's surprise announcement of her marriage to Captain Shotover.

Ellie marries the Captain as her "spiritual husband and second father" (Shaw, *Heartbreak House* 138) in a gesture that Lagretta Lenker calls "spiritual incest." While the Captain believes that there can be no blessing on his happiness (139) and therefore no climactic reunion of Lear with Cordelia, Ellie's reconstruction of the family successfully nudges the play away from tragedy toward comedy, so that the nation, although reduced to a ship of fools guided by a drunken skipper, is superfluous to happy life. A Learesque, O, reason not the need, is Shaw's response to Shakespeare. Rejecting the notion of Providence that had justified the nation's sense of its own importance and privilege, Shaw's England is restored by becoming hermetically sealed, made safe from the horrors of the World War I by a violation of the incest taboo on which civilization is founded. That retreat is far from the idyllic village of Moncrieff or even the melancholy beauty of Irving's stage sets. The justice rendered at Heartbreak House is random, its peace reduced to mere boredom. When Heartbreak House comes under a zeppelin attack, Shotover calls out eagerly, "Stand by, all hands, for judgment" (146). The only victims of the attack, however, are Billy Dunn the burglar and Mangan the boss. No one else is touched, and all hope that the zeppelins will "come again tomorrow night" (149). The house, although on weak foundations, still stands, and only the poor clergyman must seek a new place to sleep.

In *Shakes vs. Shav*, when Shav claims that *Heartbreak House* is his own *King Lear, "a transparency is suddenly lit up, showing Captain Shotover seated, as in Millais's picture called North-West Passage, with a young woman of virginal beauty"* (278). Millais's painting (Figure 11.3) features a retired sea captain, who sits in his chair brooding about the north-west passage to Asia. His daughter, seated at his feet, extends to him a comforting hand. This is the dream of nation and empire that, in response to war, Shaw renounces in *Heartbreak House*, the same pre-Raphaelite image of a pastoral England

Figure 11.3 The Northwest Passage (1874) by Sir John Everett Millais (1829–96). By kind permission of ARTRES.

with global reach that informs Henry Irving's prehistoric *King Lear*. Shaw's revamped sea Captain, sleeping quietly on Ellie's shoulder, has no great recognition, no lingering ambitions, no epiphany—just the "happiness of yielding and dreaming instead of resisting and doing, the sweetness of the fruit that is going rotten" (120). This is not much, but as Shaw implies, it is sufficient for the early twentieth-century Lear of private life.

Notes

1 All references to *King Lear* are to the Conflated Text in *The Norton Shakespeare*, ed. Stephen Greenblatt *et al.* (New York: Norton, 1997).
2 For a particularly coherent account of Lear's journey toward self-knowledge, following the Romantic paradigm, see Jorgensen.
3 Jean Marsden discusses how an emphasis on pathos, like the foregrounding of the Restoration actress's body, became a subtle source of titillation in plays rewritten to accommodate the advent of actresses on the stage (*Re-Imagined Text* 30). Although Tate's *King* Lear appears during the period in which "she-tragedies," or tragedies of helpless women, become ascendent, his Cordelia remains too faithful to her Shakespearean prototype to make the play conform to this emerging genre or to participate in its emerging discourse of family and empire.
4 Tate's 1681 version of *King Lear* was revised in turn by George Colman (1768), David Garrick (1773), and John Philip Kemble (1808), but the play remains substantively that of Tate well into the nineteenth century (*King Lear*, ed. Foakes 85). Doris Adler notes that Colman took out the love interest between Edgar and Cordelia, but remarks as well that his version was less popular and durable than Tate's (Adler 53).
5 No reason is given for Agnes's collapse, but Joanne Tong suggests that the vehemence of Agnes's reaction recalls the scene of her attempted suicide.
6 Junius Brutus Booth opened as Lear at Covent Garden on 18 April 1820; Edmund Kean opened as Lear at Drury Lane Theatre on 24 April 1820; and *The Lear of Private Life* opened at Royal Coburg Theatre on 27 April 1820. George III, on account of whose madness the play had been banned from the stage between 1798 and 1820, had died in January of that year.
7 The text is still basically that of Tate, filtered through Garrick and Kemble. The Shakespearean conclusion of the play, involving the deaths of Cordelia and Lear, was not restored by Kean and R.W. Elliston until 10 February 1823 (Odell 2: 151–52, 154).
8 For some time, the character of Lear had been treated as a document in madness, and it was from this perspective that Irving chose to play the King. A summary of the medically-oriented discussion of Lear's madness can be found in Furness's Variorum *King Lear*, 412–17.
9 For Jameson's contribution to the canonization of Shakespeare's female characters, see Lootens, Chapter 3, 77–115.

Works cited

Adler, Doris. "The Half-Life of Tate in *King Lear*." *The Kenyon Review* 7. 3 (Summer 1985): 52–56.

Boose, Lynda E. "The Father's House and the Daughter in It: The Structures of Western Culture's Daughter–Father Relationship." *Daughters and Fathers*. Eds. Lynda E. Boose and Betty S. Flowers. Baltimore: Johns Hopkins University Press, 1989: 19–74.

Braverman, Richard. *Plot and Counterplots: Sexual Politics and the Body Politic in English Literature, 1660–1730*. Cambridge: Cambridge University Press, 1993.

Cavell, Stanley. "The Avoidance of Love: A Reading of *King Lear*." *Disowning Knowledge in Seven Plays of Shakespeare*. Updated ed. Cambridge: Cambridge University Press, 1987: 39–123.

Corrigan, Robert W. "*Heartbreak House*: Shaw's Elegy for Europe." *Shaw Review* 2.9 (1959): 2–6.

Cowden Clarke, Mary. *The Girlhood of Shakespeare's Heroines*. 3 vols. London: W.H. Smith and Son, 1850; reprint, New York: AMS, 1974.

Dobson, Michael. *The Making of the National Poet: Shakespeare, Adaptation, and Authorship, 1660–1769*. Oxford: Clarendon; New York: Oxford University Press, 1992.

Dowden, Edward. *King Lear. Illustrated London News*, 11 December 1892.

Eberle, Roxanne. *Chastity and Transgression in Women's Writing, 1792–1897: Interrupting the Harlot's Progress*. Houndsmill, Basingstoke, Hampshire: Palgrave, 2002.

Foakes, R.A. Hamlet *versus* Lear: *Cultural Politics and Shakespeare's Art*. Cambridge: Cambridge University Press, 1993.

Freud, Sigmund. *The Standard Edition of the Complete Psychological Works of Sigmund Freud*. Eds. James Strachey *et al.* 24 vols. London: Hogarth and The Institute for Psychoanalysis, 1953–74.

—— "The Theme of the Three Caskets." *Standard Edition of the Complete Psychological Works of Sigmund Freud*. Eds. James Strachey *et al.* 24 vols. London: Hogarth and The Institute for Psychoanalysis, 1953–74, 12: 290–301.

Furness, Horace Howard. *King Lear*. Variorum Edition. 9th edn. Philadelphia: J.B. Lippincott, 1880.

Hardman, C.B. " 'Our Drooping Country Now Erects Her Head': Nahum Tate's *History of King Lear*." *Modern Language Review* 95.4 (2000): 913–23.

Hughes, Alan. *Henry Irving, Shakespearean*. Cambridge: Cambridge University Press, 1981.

Irving, Henry. "Four Favorite Parts." *English Illustrated Magazine*, 10 (September 1893).

—— *King Lear: A Tragedy in Five Acts, by William Shakespeare, as arranged for the Stage by Henry Irving*. London: Nassau Steam Press, 1892. Readex microprint, English and American Drama of the Nineteenth Century.

Jameson, Anna Brownell. *Characteristics of Women, Moral, Political, and Historical*. 2nd edn. London: George Routledge and Sons, n.d.

Jorgensen, Paul. *Lear's Self-Discovery*. Berkeley, University of California Press, 1967.

King, W. D. *Henry Irving's Waterloo*. Berkeley: University of California Press, 1993.

Lamb, Charles. "On the Tragedies of Shakespeare." *The Complete Works and Letters of Charles Lamb*. Eds. Bennett A. Cerf and Donald S. Klopfer. The Modern Library. New York: Random House, 1935: 289–93.

Lenker, Lagretta Tallent. *Fathers and Daughters in Shakespeare and Shaw*. Westport, CT: Greenwood, 2001.

Lootens, Tricia. *Lost Saints: Silence, Gender, and Victorian Literary Canonization*. Charlottesville: University Press of Virginia, 1996.

Marsden, Jean I. *The Re-Imagined Text: Shakespeare, Adaptation, and Eighteenth-Century Literary Theory*. Lexington: University Press of Kentucky, 1995.

Meisel, Martin. *Realizations: Narrative, Pictorial, and Theatrical Arts in Nineteenth-Century England*. Princeton: Princeton University Press, 1983.

Moncrieff, W.T. *The Lear of Private Life! Or, Father and Daughter*. London: T. Richardson, 1828. Readex microprint, English and American Drama of the Nineteenth Century.

Odell, George C.D. *Shakespeare from Betterton to Irving*. 2 vols. New York: Charles Scribner's Sons, 1920.

Opie, Amelia. *The Father and Daughter: A Tale*. Boston: S.G. Goodrich, 1827.

Robertson, W. Graham. *Life Was Worth Living*. New York: Harper, 1931.

Rosenberg, Marvin. *The Masks of King Lear*. Berkeley: University of California Press, 1972.

Scott, Clement. *From* The Bells *to* King Arthur: *A Critical Record of the First-Night Productions at the Lyceum Theatre from 1871 to 1895*. London: Jack Macqueen, 1896.

Shakespeare, William. *King Lear*. Ed. R.A. Foakes. Arden Shakespeare. Walton-on-Thames: Thomas Nelson and Sons, 1997.

—— *The Norton Shakespeare*. Eds. Stephen Greenblatt *et al.* New York: Norton, 1997.

Shaw, George Bernard. *Heartbreak House. The Works of Bernard Shaw*. 31 vols. London: Constable and Company, 1930, 15: 43–149.

—— "Heartbreak House and Horseback Hall: Where Heartbreak House Stands." *The Works of Bernard Shaw*. 31 vols. London: Constable and Company, 1930, 15: 3–41.

—— *Shakes vs. Shav. Shaw on Shakespeare: An Anthology of Bernard Shaw's Writings on the Plays and Production of Shakespeare*. Ed. Edwin Wilson. New York: E.P. Dutton, 1961: 276–79.

Stoker, Bram. *Personal Reminiscences of Henry Irving*. 2 vols. New York: Macmillan, 1906.

Tate, Nahum. *The History of King Lear*. In *Adaptations of Shakespeare: An Anthology of Plays from the Seventeenth Century to the Present*. Eds. Daniel Fischlin and Mark Fortier. London and New York: Routledge, 2000: 66–96.

Terry, Ellen. *Ellen Terry's Memoirs*. Preface, Notes, and Additional Biographical Chapters by Edith Craig and Christopher St. John. New York: Putnam's Sons, 1932.

—— *Four Lectures on Shakespeare*. Ed. with an intro. by Christopher St. John. London: Martin Hopkinson, 1912.

Tong, Joanne. "The Return of the Prodigal Daughter: Finding the Family in Amelia Opie's Novels." *Studies in the Novel* 36.4 (Winter 2004): 465–83.

Weintraub, Stanley. "*Heartbreak House*: Shaw's *Lear*." *Modern Drama* 15 (1972–73): 255–65.

—— *Journey to Heartbreak: The Crucible Years of Bernard Shaw, 1914–1918*. New York: Weybright and Talley, 1971.

Willbern, David. "*Filia Oedipi*: Father and Daughter in Freudian Theory." *Daughters and Fathers*. Eds. Lynda E. Boose and Betty S. Flowers. Baltimore: Johns Hopkins University Press, 1989: 75–96.

Worrall, David. "Artisan Melodrama and the Plebian Public Sphere: The Political Culture of Drury Lane and its Environs, 1797–1830." *Studies in Romanticism* 39.2 (Summer 2000): 213–27.

12 If only

Alternatives and the self in *King Lear*

Jeffrey Kahan

> Where would be the foundation of *morals*, if particular characters had no certain or determinate power to produce particular sentiments, and if these sentiments had no constant operation on actions? And with what pretense could we employ our *criticism* upon any poet or polite author, either natural or unnatural, to such characters, and in such circumstances?
>
> (David Hume, *An Enquiry Concerning Human Understanding* (1748): 65)

In *The Morality of Shakespeare's Drama Illustrated* (1775), Mrs. Elizabeth Griffith suggests a solution to the play's troubling finale. If the point of tragedy is to reward virtue and to punish vice, then *King Lear* is a failure, so far as both the just and the unjust are punished alike. However, if the point of tragedy is to stir in the reader and in the audience pity and fear (Catharsis), then "surely no Play that ever was written can possibly answer both these ends better than this performance, as it stands in the present text" (351). This is a clever evasion of a critical issue in Shakespeare's play. Rather than answering why Shakespeare violated classical rules of justice in *King Lear*, Griffith argues that *in*justice itself is a rooted classical aesthetic. Thus, Shakespeare, whether he is morally just or unjust, is always classically correct. Even with this loophole, there remains one passage that continues to trouble Griffith. Gloucester's lament that:

> As flies to wanton boys are we to th' gods;
> They kill us for their sport.
>
> (4.1.37–38)

Griffith writes: "This is a most impious and unphilosophic reflection. Poor Gloster seems, by this expression, to have rather soured, than softened, by his misfortunes; which his attempted suicide afterwards proves still further." Of Lear's own angry sentiments, his questioning of divine justice, Griffith says nothing, though her commentary upon Gloucester's "impious" lines above obviously has some bearing: "Such a sentiment must certainly surprize us, in Shakespeare, when uttered by a person of so good a character as Gloster—It could not so offend in the mouth of Edmund, though better not spoken at all" (365).

Griffith argues that Shakespeare himself could not have espoused such a sentiment, and, if he had to do so for purely dramatic purposes, he should have carefully placed these sentiments in the mouth of a villain, such as Edmund. Her choice is far from accidental. Giving these lines to Edmund would have restored Shakespeare's ethical universe. The sense of divine indifference in the lines themselves would have been negated by Edgar's chivalrous conquest of Edmund, and his certainty that "The gods are just" (5.3.161). The fact that Shakespeare did not place these words in the mouth of a villain, to say nothing of Lear's equally unhappy last moments, collectively threaten to throw Griffith's entire project—of "placing [Shakespeare's] Ethic[al] merits in a more conspicuous point of view" (Preface, IX)—into chaos. If the gods in *King Lear* kill for sport, then all you have is moral chaos—the heath as universe.

Reviewing this same "impious" statement, Wordsworth offered a solution to the ethical dilemma of Gloucester's declaration and, by extension, of the play: "I very much doubt whether Sh.[akespeare] would have allowed any but a Heathen character to utter this sentiment" (Furness IV.i.37cf). This is not so much a retort to Griffith as a continuance. Injustice triumphs in *Lear* because Lear wanders not in Judeo-Christian clarity, but in pagan fog. It's not clear if Wordsworth is accusing Shakespeare himself of harboring impious religious sentiments here, but his reading does offer a workable solution to the play's moral dilemma. Judeo-Christian values work in a simple enough paradigm: good versus evil, God and his angels versus Satan and his minions. That's not Lear's world.

Certainly, Gloucester's reference to "gods" suggests a pagan universe, and while Judeo-Christian critics have dwelled at length on Lear's suffering into truth and Cordelia's Christ-like virtues, few critics have explored the way Gloucester's and Lear's laments fit into any sort of pagan mythos. Attempting to do so is fraught with difficulties. Paganism, like "fast food," allows for choice: Roman, Greek, Norse, Celtic, etc. Even if we were to limit the mythological selections to books accounting for Shakespeare's supposedly small Latin and less Greek, we would, as catalogued recently by Robert S. Miola, still fill a good-sized library. Not that this knowledge does us much good. Shakespeare doesn't devotedly follow any theological system; he deliberately mixes things up. But even mix-ups have their virtues. Paganism allows for pantheism. That means more choice. You might insult one god but insulting them all is difficult, if not impossible. In *The Iliad*, Agamemnon insults Apollo, but Zeus stands by the Greek king. Closer to Lear's agonies with Cordelia, consider Book 24 of the same work. Priam has just watched his son Hector die, in part because the gods themselves turned away Hector's lance before it could ever harm Thetis' son. The fair fight has been fixed, and Priam knows it. Yet he still has to prostrate himself before Achilles, and beg for his son's corpse:

> I am wretcheder, and beare that weight of miseries
> That never man did . . .
>
> (2.4.249–50)

Or, as Lear would say:

> I am a man
> More sinned against than sinning.
>
> (3.2.59–60)

If this makes Priam impious, he can take some solace in knowing that he's not the only one upset with his lot. Achilles has just lost his friend Patroclus, and worse yet, has been told by his mother that the gods have already planned out his imminent death. His crime? He's destined to become famous, but only after his death, and the gods feel that, when dealing with fame, there's no time to start like the present. Achilles, while not happy with his fate, philosophically explains the sad state of human affairs to the old king:

> Sit
> And settle we our woes, though huge, for nothing profits it.
> Cold mourning wastes but our lives' heates. The gods have destinate
> That wretched mortals must live sad. Tis the immortall state
> Of Deitie that lives secure. Two Tunnes of gifts there lie
> In Jove's gate, one of good, one ill, that our mortalitie
> Maintaine, spoile, order; which when Jove doth mixe to any man,
> One while he frolicks, one while mourns.
>
> (24.466–72)

Achilles recognizes that a man's life cannot be measured by ethical absolutes. Stuff happens. It is pointless—"nothing profits it"—to label a person or an action as good or bad. Similarly, Lear seems to wander in a world too complex for ready-made ethics. Lear's is an erratic world where "men are / As the times" (5.3.30–31), a hurly-burly where a good daughter says bad things and bad daughters say good things, where fools utter wisdom and wise kings act like babies, where Gloucester's blinding is pointless—even when his eyes worked, he was unaware of what was going on around him. The only sane thing Lear can do is go insane, for what drives him mad is his inability to deal with a world that leaves him utterly bewildered. *King Lear* is a statement of the unknowable glimpsed in acts that are, at least to the characters within that world, unintelligible.

The chaos of *King Lear* is not really chaos, since it is so obviously patterned throughout Shakespeare's canon. In the comedies, people meet, fall in love immediately, then just as quickly fall out of love. Girls dress as boys to seduce straight men, mechanicals are turned into beasts of burden; your little girl dies; twenty years later, you bump into her shearing sheep. Your wife is lost at sea, joins a monastery and never thinks of writing home to let you know she's alright. The Pope pops up in one play, Soothsayers in another, the Roman god Jupiter and a bunch of ghosts speak to you in your sleep; Rumour and Time pop in for a quick conflab; English fairies serve an Amazonian queen; Danish witches dance with a Greek Goddess. It's a dreamscape where nothing is but what is not; where landlocked countries meet the sea, where trees walk and daggers float and men are not born of women, where heroes surrender to cowards, where kings walk as beggars and beggars think they are lords, where princes party with pickpockets, where clowns dig graves and husbands kill their wives over lost rings or worse, misplaced linen.

If this mélange is perplexing, we can at least say that it is certainly not pantheistic. Wordsworth might be right in thinking that the author of Lear's world is not always Christian in his thinking, but Shakespeare is not a pagan either. He's not burning incense to Pan or sacrificing hecatombs to Poseidon. He's moved beyond paganism *and* Christianity: Lear does not call upon the gods or expect them to answer as do Achilles or Priam or the Biblical prophets. Rather, the people of Lear's world have to reinvent themselves, as the Olympians themselves do—in *The Metamorphosis*, Zeus takes the shape of a bull, a swan, even rain; in *The Iliad*, Venus disguises herself as an old woman; in *The Aeneid*, Cupid cloaks himself as Aeneas' son, Ascanius. Likewise, Edgar masquerades as Mad Tom and then a variety of yokels to aid his father; the protean Edmund plays the dutiful son, the faithful lover, the loyal soldier.

These characters trudge through the mire of life not with their eyes fixed upon a beacon of rock-solid principles but with only short-term situational ethics to help them along. Consider Lear's demand to know which daughter loves him best. Of course it's a silly test, but it has a fair and practical solution for the situation, one that Cordelia's sisters ace and Cordelia fails. There is a simple enough lesson here. Life does not always call for candor. If Cordelia doesn't know that, then the girl needs to grow up. Other tests in the play are a bit more abstruse. Think of the Quarto version: Lear creates a so-called mock trial in which he prosecutes his daughters for ingratitude. To Lear, the trial is real; to Lear's entourage, he's merely shouting at three foot-stools. Crazy? He may seem that way, but we haven't walked in his boots, and until we are ready to imagine ourselves as Lear, to role-play Lear even as we watch him, we're unlikely to understand his actions in this scene.

We might reason that Lear enjoys his mock-trial, but still reject his pleasure therein as a poor consolation prize. His triumphal jubilance in the mock-trial is disagreeable to us because it is "false," whereas Edmund's familial, sexual, and martial victories seem "real." There is no doubt that Griffith and other critics through the ages, including Coleridge and, more recently, Danby and Matthews have worried that Shakespeare has made Edmund a little too smooth and a little too successful. (That the villain has many triumphs could hardly be otherwise in a tragedy.) The key to his success is not his excesses (i.e. too much charisma, cruelty, avarice, cunning or some other characteristic), for Edmund is never any *one* character for very long. Edmund worships Nature, which changes season-by-season and day-by-day. To be at one with Nature, Edmund has to be equally polymorphic: bold, admirable and resolute as well as furtive, worthless and perfidious. Not surprisingly, Edmund's triumphs are as fleeting as his personae. Moreover, given that Edmund wins the war and loses his life, we may ponder whether his gains are any less illusory than Lear's. In this regard, the play is neither joyous nor gloomy. One character may express encouraging thoughts one moment, discouraging thoughts in another, one may say something that seems lucid or mad, but each statement is no more authoritative or less transient than another. In *King Lear*, people take pleasure where they can and hope that their gains are real and lasting, but hope is not the same as certainty.

Often, it seems that Shakespeare is not merely testing the limits of his characters' ability to change with the times, he's also testing our ability to bend our normally rigid ethical norms. In *Measure for Measure*, we want Angelo to be punished with something a bit more severe than an unhappy marriage, yet the same fate for Lucio seems somehow too harsh. In *Merchant*, we're on Antonio's side, but we are also made to feel that Shylock has been cheated by the Venetians. Sometimes murdering the king or emperor is alright (*Titus*), sometimes it's not (*Macbeth*); rape is abhorrent in *Lucrece*, yet something akin to rape—here over-narrowly defined as not knowing the identity of your sexual partner, without which the sex cannot be mutually consensual —is sometimes justifiable (think of the bedtricks of *Measure for Measure* and *All's Well*).

While situational ethics within Shakespeare are by design, his own plot choices do not always meet with our approval. Sometimes, like Griffith, we wish Shakespeare would have written otherwise. Why did Shakespeare kill Cordelia? Even if we put Shakespeare aside for the moment and blame Cordelia's death on Edmund, the act is senselessly violent. Edmund has already secured power. Cordelia is the youngest of three, so her claim on the crown could only be legitimated—lovely word—by a Richard III-esque blood-bath. Killing Lear makes some sense, killing Albany makes still more, but killing Cordelia, the Queen of France, and, by so doing, raising the ire of the king of that puissant power, is not just nasty, it is a strategic blunder. But Edmund, while ruthless, has never been motivated by sheer logic. His acts smack not just of expedience but of malice.

What bothers us is not Cordelia's death, but that she dies by a commixture of motiveless malice and comic ineptitude. What with all *Cymbeline*-ian explanations, Edgar, Albany, and Kent simply seem to have forgotten that she's at Edmund's (lack of) mercy—"Great thing of us forgot!" (5.3.211). We could accept her death, were it to have some meaning and function beyond closure, but here it's executed with artistic callousness. After all, as Stephen Booth notes with some perspicacity, her death follows hard upon a comforting reconciliation with her father, a moment that certainly looks and feels like a happy ending. Watching father and daughter kiss and make up, the audience gathers "itself mentally in preparation for leaving a theatre where a play has formally concluded while its substance is still in urgent progress" (22). The car keys are out. We're ready to go home. But Shakespeare shatters our expectations.

Some would counter platitudinously that the death of Cordelia is an artistic triumph because "life doesn't imitate art." For that we can be grateful. After all, if there were a pay-off for pain, we'd all be, like Titus, chopping off our hands. Then again, we might respond that art should at least imitate art, that within the confines of a drama in which we have forged real—"real" in the sense that we are emotionally invested—ties, we have a right to expect some respect for the sanctity of life, especially in deference to the outcome of our friends. That Shakespeare kills off his characters with malice is not as bad as imagining that Shakespeare has some malice for *us* (Bradshaw 87). He raises our hopes and then dashes them, and not just here. Why does the king of France have to die at the end of *Love's Labour's Lost*? It serves no purpose but to thwart a perfectly happy ending. We're irritated that Shakespeare refuses to follow his source and have Hector killed by that bulk Achilles. Why doesn't Juliet awake from her sleep in time to save Romeo? Can't they both live in exile, even if in Baz Luhrman's film that exile is a dusty trailer park?

It is not merely that Cordelia is killed. As Booth points out, "Literature abounds in instances in which virtue miscarries—Little Eva, Little Nell, Little Emily, little Macduff, the little princess in the Tower" (111). Yes, Cordelia has to die, but, even within the bounds of his other tragedies, Shakespeare had a variety of more palatable options. Shakespeare might have staged it akin to Romeo and Juliet's demise. Lear comes on carrying his daughter, dies of a broken heart; Cordelia then revives, sees her father and dies. Or, he might have done it along the lines of *Othello*: Lear carries her in, she revives, forgives her father for starting all this mess, then dies, prompting the king to kill himself. The difference between these plays and *Lear* is one of expectation. Since in *Romeo and Juliet* the plot-turn depends upon playing dead *and* we know it's a tragedy *and* we're in the fifth act *and* she's lying there *and* Romeo has poison, we expect it to all go wrong. Having plotted Desdemona's death, Othello's and our own surprise is merely that she awakens long enough to forgive him. With respect to the fact of her death, it is both expected and, occurring as it does in the fifth act, necessary to a neat close. But the death of Cordelia is not the sacrifice of an innocent victim, nor is it presented with poetic justification. Indeed, given that in Act 4, scene 6 Lear awoke thinking that he was dead, might we not here also expect in Act 5, scene 3 for Cordelia to do the same?

Shakespeare could have easily made the change, as he made so many others. After all, that's why there are two texts of *Lear*, because Shakespeare wanted to rework what he didn't get right. In the final scene of the Quarto text, Cordelia is just plain dead. But in the Folio, Cordelia is allowed something akin to a Desdemona-last-breath moment:

> This feather stirs. She lives. If it be so,
> It is a chance which does redeem all sorrows
> That ever I have felt.
>
> (5.3.240–43)

Critics often dwell on the passage to gauge Lear's sanity. Perhaps we should be gauging his imaginative capacity. It is a mistake to think that in the Quarto Lear dies facing stark reality while in the Folio he dies in fantasy, as if fantasy itself were a break from what has come before. In both Quarto and Folio, Lear lives in daydream. As G.G. Gervinus points out, "King Lear, in the extremity of age and desolation, looks back upon a time when he was 'every inch a king', when enemies fled before his sword . . . 'when he stared, the subject quaked' " (622). These dream-like reminiscences, are, given his reduced circumstances, somewhat deflated: "They flattered me like a dog, and told me I had white hairs in my beard ere the black ones were there. . . . They told me I was everything; 'tis a lie, I am not ague-proof" (4.5.96–98, 104–5). We might, therefore, think that Lear has disabused himself here; that he gets that he has lived (past tense) in fantasy but is now waking to reality, but the speech itself is preceded by Lear's fading and flashing memories of better times, of hunting, or raising armies, of setting passwords for a camped army:

> *King Lear.* Nature's above art in that respect. There's your press-money. That fellow handles his bow like a crow-keeper. Draw me a clothier's yard. Look, look, a mouse! Peace, peace, this piece of toasted cheese will do 't. There's my gauntlet. I'll prove it on a giant. Bring up the brown bills. O, well flown, bird, i'th' clout, i'th' clout! Whew! Give the word.

Within three lines, he confuses Gloucester with Goneril—"Ha! Goneril with a white beard?"—and about a hundred lines later Lear will speak again with seeming "Reason in madness" (4.5.171). He'll argue that life is about pain and folly, and that it would be a great idea to equip his long-lost cavalry with sound-proof hooves:

> *King Lear.* When we are born, we cry that we are come
> To this great stage of fools. This' a good block.
> It were a delicate stratagem, to shoe
> A troop of horse with felt. I'll put 't in proof . . .
>
> (4.5.178–81)

If Lear has one insight into his dilemma or allows us one insight into our own, it is that clarity and madness, "matter and impertinency mixed" (4.5.170) are matters of perspective. Lear's life is filled with the stuff dreams are made on. Raised as a king, you might think that the skies thunder on your command, and that you are infallible, that you are born to be the theme of tribal songs, to win wars, fight giants and sack some Troy-like citadel with silent, if not wooden, horses. But Lear learns that his reality is not the same as everyone else's, and he encourages Gloucester to "see" the world from alternative perspectives:

> A man may see how this world goes with no eyes; look with thine ears. See how yon justice rails upon yon simple thief. Hark in thine ear: change places, and, handy-dandy, which is the justice, which is the thief?
>
> (4.5.146–50)

Take away the crown and suddenly you can go cold and hungry like everyone else. Change places and "A dog's obeyed in office" (4.5.154–55). No matter that Gloucester has lost his eyes; what he really needs is to see life through the eyes of others.

Encouraging others to see life from a variety of perspectives is part of the play's design. When Edgar convinced his father that he is on the edge of Dover Cliff, that the sea is raging below him, that there are people milling about in the distance, Gloucester, in his mind's eye, sees everything and thinks it completely real. We know, as does Edgar, that even within the world of the play he's not really in Dover, but that does not make his attempted suicide or his miraculous survival any less authentic an experience, at least to Gloucester. Indeed, Edgar wonders whether his father might actually be dead, not from any bona fide fall but from his belief that his imaginative plunge was all too real:

> And yet I know not how conceit may rob
> The treasury of life, when life itself
> Yields to the theft. Had he been where he thought,
> By this had thought been past.—Alive or dead?
>
> (4.4.42–45)

Edgar's question concerning his father—"Alive or dead?"—resonates in Lear's revival, in which the king is unable to distinguish whether he's living or lifeless, whether he's in England or France, whether he is surrounded by loyal subjects or ministering angels:

> You are a spirit, I know. Where did you die?
>
> (4.6.42)

> Where have I been? Where am I?
>
> (4.6.45)

> Where did I lodge last night[?]
>
> (4.6.61)

> If you have poison for me, I will drink it.
>
> (4.6.65)

Am I in France?
(4.6.69)

Lear is asking for his cue. Should he play the king or the refugee, the fool or the wise man, the tyrant or the victim, the man or the spirit? Once he has those prompts, Lear transforms not into what he has been—indeed, he asks that *that* Lear be forgotten—but into a character he thinks his daughter will love:

You must bear with me. Pray you now, forget
And forgive. I am old and foolish.
(4.6.76–77)

That Lear asks his daughter for direction is itself a remarkable reinvention of the self. From the first, Lear has given the orders and has established how his subjects, above all Cordelia, should act around him. He has taken comfort in the thought of spending his remaining years with Cordelia: "I loved her most, and thought to set my rest/On her kind nursery" (1.1.123–24). When, in Act One, she violates that scripted fantasy, Lear begs Cordelia to consider revising her part:

Nothing will come of nothing. Speak again.
. . .
How, how, Cordelia? Mend your speech a little
Lest you mar your fortunes.
(1.1.90, 94–95)

Speak again, get it right, take it back, he importunes. Similarly, we catch Lear sometimes regretting, sometimes wondering aloud what he would have done had he been able to do it all over again:

I did her wrong.
(1.5.25)

I have ta'en
Too little care of this.
(3.4.32–33)

Given that he has grown adept at role-play, Lear, when faced with Cordelia's death, reacts in the only way he knows—by imagining an alternative ending in which father and daughter can finally talk, if only she would "stay a little" (5.3.246):

Ha?
What is't thou sayst?—Her voice was ever soft,
Gentle, and low.
(5.3.246–48)

Lear may be standing before Edgar, Kent and Albany; he might be holding a dead Cordelia in his arms, but, in his mind's eye, he's playing in an alternative and equally authentic reality with his daughter.

We need not wonder what they are talking about. Lear already has the rough outlines of the plot in hand:

> We two alone will sing like birds i' th' cage.
> When thou dost ask me blessing, I'll kneel down,
> And ask of thee forgiveness; so we'll live,
> And pray, and sing, and tell old tales, and laugh
> At gilded butterflies, and hear poor rogues
> Talk of court news, and we'll talk with them too—
> Who loses and who wins, who's in, who's out,
> And take upon's the mystery of things . . .
> (5.3.9–16)

In a world where role-play constructs quiddity, Lear simultaneously occupies two worlds. In one, he's in a blissful domestic arcadia, where no one ever dies, and the worst thing that ever happens is some courtly indignity; in the other, winners and losers are starkly determined by life and death:

> She's gone for ever.
> I know when one is dead and when one lives.
> She's dead as earth.
> . . . now she's gone for ever.
> (5.3.234–36, 245)

Our pathos is heightened because, like Lear, we have see the world through the guts of a king and a beggar, and, like Lear, we want things to turn out well. If Lear has to do so in a dream hardly any of us can share in, so be it. But it is by no means certain that Cordelia, even when reconciling with Lear in 4.6, shares in her father's fantasy. Few would envy Cordelia spending eternity in a cell with Lear, staring at tree moths and listening to courtly tittle-tattle. If Lear thinks this is a great life, we might wonder how long it would take for Cordelia to shatter that fantasy. Recall that in the sources, a despairing Cordelia hangs herself. If death is preferable to despair, maybe Cordelia is better off dead.

Certainly, Shakespeare can't imagine them being happy together. His later plays confirm that fathers and daughters just don't get along. In *Pericles*, father and daughter, separated by distance and years, accept that remaining apart is perhaps best for everyone. As soon as they are reunited, Pericles marries his daughter Marina off to Lysimachus, Governor of Mytilene. In *The Winter's Tale*, Leontes is reunited with his entire family for all of 25 lines before he breaks them up again by informing Hermione that Perdita is to marry Florizel and, doubtless, live in faraway Bohemia; in *Cymbeline*, father and daughter don't respect each other, and the king tries to marry her off as soon as he can; in *The Tempest*, where we might argue for a healthy father–daughter relationship, Prospero ships off Miranda with the first prince that comes wafting by.

The difficulties of a healthy father–daughter relationship were well known to Shakespeare—he lived it. His daughters grew up in Stratford-upon-Avon; he, a virtual stranger, lived in London. He never taught them even the rudiments of reading and writing. Both daughters, like their mother, were lifelong illiterates and signed their documents with an "X." Even in retirement, Shakespeare could not bridge the gap in years and experience with his family. Drawing up the will his own daughters could not read, Shakespeare apparently rewarded the daughter that loved him best. His youngest daughter, Judith, got £150. That's not nothing, but, considering Shakespeare's possessions, this amount—even factoring for inflation—is close to nothing. As for his eldest daughter, Susanna, she received what sounds like the portion of the kingdom Lear gave to his eldest, Goneril:

Shakespeare's Will: To Susanna	*King Lear's Will: To Goneril*
I Gyve Will Bequeth and Devise . . . all my barnes, stables, Orchardes, gardens, landes, tenementes and herediaments . . . unto my daughter Susanna Hall and her heires for ever.	Of all these bounds even from this line to this, With shadowy forests and with champaigns riched, With plenteous rivers and wide-skirted meads, We make thee lady. To thine and Albany's issues Be this perpetual. (1.1.63–67)

Of course, some might argue that discussing Shakespeare's art is one thing, extrapolating from his art to discuss his life is another. Yet, these passages are not without their correspondences, and even the most conservative of critics might find it uncomfortable to deny Shakespeare the very same empathetic quality that they so regularly attribute to centuries of audiences the world over. If, in writing these late plays, Shakespeare was working out his own situation, imagining and rehearsing scenarios in which he—like the wandering or alienated kings and princes of his own plays—longed for reunion and reconciliation with his daughters, then it is clear that Shakespeare saw himself as Lear and expected no happy ending for himself. Griffith accuses Shakespeare of writing "impious and unphilosophic" passages best left unread. Yet the function of philosophy is to explore the truths and principles of being. In Shakespeare, that exploration takes place in role-playing games in and through which we can safely imagine, rehearse and expand upon the repertoires each of us needs in life. There is no right or wrong answer here but imagining that makes it so. Shakespeare is a thoroughly postmodern philosopher.

Works cited

Booth, Stephen. *King Lear, Macbeth, Indefinition, and Tragedy*. 1983; rpt. Christchurch, New Zealand: Cybereditions Corporation, 2001.

Bradshaw, Graham. *Shakespeare's Skepticism*. Ithaca, New York: Cornell University Press, 1987.

Chapman, George. *Chapman's Homer*. Ed. Allardyce Nicoll. Princeton, New Jersey: Princeton University Press, 1998.

Furness, Horace Howard. *King Lear: A New Variorum Edition*. Twelfth Impression. Philadelphia and London: J.B. Lippincott and Co., 1908.

Gervinus, G.G. *Shakespeare Commentaries*. Translated by F.E. Bunnett. Revised Edition. London: Smith, Elder, and Co., 1883.

Griffith, Elizabeth. *The Morality of Shakespeare's Drama Illustrated*. 1775; rpt. London: Frank Cass and Company, Ltd.; New York: Augustus M. Kelly, 1971.

Hume, David. *An Enquiry Concerning Human Understanding*. Ed. Peter Millican. Oxford and New York: Oxford University Press, 2007.

Miola, Robert S. *Shakespeare's Reading. Oxford Shakespeare Topics*. Oxford and New York: Oxford University Press, 2000.

Shakespeare, William. *William Shakespeare: The Complete Works*. Gen. Eds. Stanley Wells and Gary Taylor. Oxford: Clarendon Press, 1986.

—— "Shakespeare's Will." *The Bedford Companion to Shakespeare: An Introduction with Documents*. Ed. Russ MacDonald. Boson: Bedford, 1996: 35–38.

Notes on contributors

Jean R. Brink is Professor Emeritus in the Department of English at Arizona State University. She is currently a Research Scholar at the Huntington Library. Author of *Michael Drayton* (G. K. Hall, 1990), she is working on a biography of Edmund Spenser.

Paul A. Cantor is Clifton Waller Barrett Professor of Romanticism, Shakespeare, and Comparative Literature at the University of Virginia. He is the author of several Cultural Materialist studies, and several studies of Shakespeare and pop culture.

Tom Clayton is Regents Professor in the Departments of English and Classical Studies at the University of Minnesota. He is one of the chief architects of the Quarto/Folio revisionist school.

Cyndia Susan Clegg is Distinguished Professor of English at Pepperdine University, Malibu. She is the author of several studies on Elizabethan and Jacobean censorship.

Christy Desmet is Professor of English at the University of Georgia, Athens. She is an expert in appropriation and performance, and a co-editor of the Routledge collection, *Shakespeare and Appropriation* (1999).

R.A. Foakes is Professor Emeritus at the Department of English, UCLA. He is the editor of *King Lear* for Arden (1997) and the author of *Hamlet Versus Lear* (Cambridge, 1993).

Jeffrey Kahan is Associate Professor of English at the University of La Verne in California, and completed his PhD at the Shakespeare Institute, University of Birmingham. He is the author of *Reforging Shakespeare* (Lehigh, 1998) and *The Cult of Kean* (Ashgate, 2006) and editor of *Shakespeare Imitations, Parodies and Forgeries, 1710–1820* (3 vols. Routledge, 2004).

Richard Knowles is Dickson-Bascom Professor in the Humanities at the University of Wisconsin-Madison. He is editor of the *King Lear* Variorum (forthcoming).

Edward L Rocklin is Professor of English at California State Polytechnic University, Pomona, California. He is the author of several performance studies and has published *Performance Approaches to Teaching Shakespeare* (NCTE, 2005).

Stanley Stewart is Professor of English at UC Riverside. He is editor of *The Ben Jonson Journal* and currently writing a book on Shakespeare and philosophy.

R. V. Young is Professor of English at North Carolina State University. He is co-editor of *The John Donne Journal*.

Index

Note: page numbers in italics denote illustrations

Abraham 280–2, 283
Achilles–Hector 193, 352–3, 356
Ackroyd, Peter 56
ACTER program 313
acting companies 158, 161, 170–1
actresses 147, 348n3
Addison, Joseph 90n20
Adelman, Janet 52, 91n34
Admiral's Men 171
Aeneid (Virgil) 354
Agamemnon 281, 282, 295, 352–3
Agate, James 48, 50
Albany 60–1, 192; and Edmund 193; and Gloucester 192; and Goneril 268, 289; justice 234; named for prince 60–1, 172, 180; played by Shakespeare 4; Quarto/Folio texts 115; taking initiative 198–203
Aldridge, Tom 73
Alexander, Peter 185
All is True 156
Allen, Woody 82
All's Well That Ends Well 355
Alpers, Paul J. 47, 328
alterations, authorial 105–6, 138–9, 179
anti-Christian readings 254, 257–9
Antigone 290
Antony and Cleopatra 15
Aquinas, St Thomas 261, 263–4, 269, 270, 273
Arcadia (Sidney) 12–13, 89n16, 128, 212
Arden edition 64, 164, 184
Aristophanes: *The Clouds* 231
Aristotle: catharsis 195; *Poetics* 184, 186, 258–9, 266; *Politics* 240; tragedy 127
Armin, Robert: additions 138, 139; as Fool 4, 56–7, 76; influence of 88n4, 89n11; writings 11–12, 56–7, 89n14
As You Like It 13, 211
Ashbee, Jeremy 301, 304, 305, 319
Ashton, J.W. 55
Askew, Anne 304
Attewell, Hugh 5
Atwood, Margaret 84–5
Auberjonois, Rene 73

Bacon, Francis 302
Balakirev, Mily Alexeyevich 85
Bannister, Jack 19
Bannister, Laurence 320
Bantam edition 124
Barber, C.L. 55
Barge, Gillian 76
Barker, William 320
Barksted, William 5
Barnes, Barnabe 173
Barnes, Clive 73
Barroll, Leeds 135, 136
Barry, Ann 29
Barrymore, Mrs. 336
Bate, Jonathan 46
The Beatles 85
Bell, Millicent 257, 258
Bentley, G.E. 5, 140
Berger, Harry Jr. 55, 60
Berlioz, Hector 85
Berry, Ralph 57
Berryman, John 40, 41–2
Bethell, S.L. 46
Betterton, Thomas 15, 55
Bevington, David 185
Bickersteth, Geoffrey L. 46
Birmingham Post 71
Blackfriars Theatre 138–9, 142, 173
Blake, William 331, *332*

Blayney, Peter: alternative texts 155, 159; authorial revison 179; copyright 161; Folio 67, 178; *King Lear* as exception 173–4; printing of plays 131, 165–6, 171, 172–3; Quartos 66, 129, 162
Blethyn, Brenda 76
blinding 91n37, 189, 322n10
blindness 267, 270, 313–14
Bloom, Harold 90n27, 184, 185–6, 201, 248n2, 250n18
Blount, Edward 177
Boaden, James 36
Boesen, Emil 284
Bond, Edward 80–1, 84, 298
Boose, Lynda E. 327
Booth, Junius Brutus 336–7
Booth, Stephen 57, 91n36, 355–6
Boswell, James, the Younger 34, 35, 38
Bottomley, Gordon 80
Bowers, Fredson 48, 156, 157
boy actors 5
Bradbrook, M.C. 45
Braddock, William 167
Bradley, A.C.: on Cordelia 43, 46, 56, 256–7; on Edgar 53; on Edmund 45, 51–2; on Fool 56; on Gloucester 43, 58, 298; on Goneril and Regan 53–4; redemption 45–6, 254; texts available 69
Brandl, Alois 56
Brayne, Margaret 3
British regime 242–3
Brook, Peter 54, 70–1, 298, 313, 314
Brooks, Douglas 37, 68
Brown, Ford Maddox 340, *341,* 342
Brown, Ivor 44
Bryant, Michael 77–8
Buc, George 136, 161, 163, 169–70, 174
Bullough, Geoffrey 211
Burbage family 2–4, 11, 173
Burghley, Baron of 320–1
Busby, John 134–5, 165–6, 167, 174
Bussy, Dorothy 92n56
Butter, Nathaniel 134, 165–6, 167, 174, 175, 177
Byrne, Antony 319

Calderwood, James L. 58
Cambridge edition 124, 162
Camden, William 304
Campion, Edmund 302
Capell, Edward 7, 33, 34, 146
Carr, Robert 227, 228
Carroll, William C. 53
Carter, Thomas 45
Case, R.H. 40
Casson, Lewis 126
catharsis 195, 351
Catholicism 220, 301, 322n4
Cavell, Stanley 51, 59, 297, 304, 309, 315, 328
censorship 136–7, 163
Chaillet, Ned 74
Chamberlain's Men 171
Chambers, E.K. 126, 127
Chambers, R.W. 45
Chapman, George 171
Charles II 14, 15, 16
Christian IV 226–7
Christian readings 46–8, 253–4, 262–3, 275n5
Church, Tony 71, 77
Clark, William G. 38, 39
Clarke, Mary Cowden 333
Clive, Kitty 19
Coke, Edward 302
Coleridge, Samuel Taylor 4, 18–19, 51, 218–19, 254, 329, 354
Colie, Rosalie 209
Collier, John Payne 37–8
Colman, George 25–6, 64, 348n4
compositors 131–2, 133, 141
Condell, Henry 33, 40, 66, 105, 127, 149
convention 244–6, 247–8, 270–1
Cook, Judith 74
copyists 107–8
copyright 161, 175, 177
Cordelia: banished 231–2, 271–2; Bradley on 43, 46; death of 187, 195, 204n10, 225, 234, 297, 355–7; and Edgar 25–6, 54–5, 147, 255, 330, 332–3; feminist reading 52; and Fool 56–7; forgiveness 219, 272; and Lear 116, 219, 236, 265, 285–6, 327–8, 331, 359–60; Quartos 122n8; redemption 254–5, 272, 273; sacrifice 46; saying nothing 289–90; sexuality 330, 331; suitors 226, 249n7; Tate's version 253; virtue 266; *see also* Cordella
Cordelia's Dad 85
Cordella 9, 11, 213–17, 223, 225; *see also King Leir*
1 Corinthians 107
Cornwall: Brook's version 71; and Gloucester 240, 302–8, 310; named for prince 60–1, 180; and Regan 312–13; retribution 187; wounded 189–90

Cox, Brian 77
Craig, Gordon 60, 270
Craig, Hardin 128
Craig, Leon Harold 259
Crane, Ralph 141
Creighton, Charles 61
Cymbeline 89n16, 355, 360–1

Daborne, Richard 104
Dana, Richard Henry 337
Danby, John F. 52, 62, 63, 259–60, 354
Daniel, P.A. 39
Dasent, Arthur Irwin 15–16
Davenant, William 15, 146
Davies, Thomas 19
Day, John 173
decorum 19, 198, 201, 226–7
Dekker, Thomas 167, 171
Dessen, Alan C. 313
Devereux, Robert 220, 228
Dewar, Mary 320
Dewey, John 291
The Division of the Kingdoms (Taylor and Warren) 64, 162–3
Dobson, Michael 90n17, 326
Dollimore, Jonathan 258, 270
Doran, Madeleine 39–40, 65, 128, 129, 130–1
Doren, Mark Van 59
Dowden, Edward 340
Downes, John 146
Doyle, Arthur Conan: *Waterloo* 326, 339, 343
Draper, J.W. 61
Driscoll, James P. 47
Dryden, John 15
Dudley, Robert 220
Duthie, George Ian 39, 46, 65
Dutton, Richard 127–8, 159
Dyce, Alexander 38

Eagleton, Terry 53, 86
Eberle, Roxanne 336
Edgar: Bradley on 53; coming to power 244–5; and Cordelia 25–6, 54–5, 147, 255, 330, 332–3; duel with Edmund 193, 243–4, 266–7, 308; and Edmund 16–17, 189; and Gloucester 267, 309, 358; just gods 352; loyalty 192–4; as Poor Tom 231, 238, 239–41, 247, 270–1, 358–9; Quarto/Folio texts 115, 116; retribution 187; suffering 188–9; taking initiative 198–203
Edmund: and Albany 193; as bastard son 16–17, 189, 233, 260; Bradley on 51–2; and Cordelia 16; death of 271; duel with Edgar 193, 243–4, 266–7, 308; and Edgar 16–17, 189; and Gloucester 308–9; human nature 264, 268; from *King Leir* 9–10; Nature 259–60, 264, 300, 355; as proto-capitalist 63; and Regan 20; retribution 187; successes 354–5
Edward VI 220, 222
Eliot, Michael 77
Eliot, T.S. 209
Elizabeth, Princess 179
Elizabeth 1 221, 301, 320
Elliston, Robert 26, 70
Elton, William R. 47, 59, 257–9, 273–4
Empson, William 46, 55, 256–7, 275n5
Ephesians, epistle to 263
Erne, Lukas 128, 133, 134
Evans, Henry 173
Evening News 70
Everett, Barbara 46, 129, 258
evil 47, 180–1, 209, 236, 238, 243
Eyre, Richard 77–9

Faerie Queene (Spenser) 14, 210, 224–5, 272
fair copy 104–5, 129–30, 133, 135, 142–3, 164
faith, crisis of 46–8
Father and Daughter (Opie) 79, 326, 331, 333–8
father–daughter relationship 287–8, 328, 345, 360–1; *see also* incest; patriarchy
Feather, J.P. 12
Felperin, Howard 59, 87–8
feminist reading 52
Firth, Colin 82
Fisher, Thomas 176
Fletcher, John 65
Flynn, Barbara 77
Foakes, R.A. 62–3, 67, 68, 164, 165, 203n2, 326
Folger edition 124
Folio texts: as authorative 65, 145, 149; cuts/additions 121, 140; Doran on 39–40; omissions 136–7, 156; playbook 135–45; and Quartos 31, 64, 104, 108–16, 144–5, 146, 177–8; Restoration period 31–3; topicality 178–9

Fool: Armin 4, 56–7, 76; Brook's version 71; Bryant 77–8; and Cordelia 56–8; and Lear 241–2; Macready on 29–30; mock-prophecy 140–1; omitted 15, 26, 64; playbook 138; played by woman 30; Quarto/Folio texts 114–15; as social commentator 115; sources 11–12; truth 89n12
forgeries 35–8
Forrest, Edwin 22, *24,* 25
Fortin, René 47
foul papers 104–5, 133, 157, 160, 164
Frederick, Elector Palatine 179
French, Marilyn 268–9, 275n10
Freud, Sigmund 327
Frye, Northrop 47, 53
Furness, H.H. 37, 331
Fuseli, Henry 85, *86*

Gambon, Michael 74
Garber, Marjorie 68
Gardner, Helen 53
Garrett, Davidson 84
Garrick, David 19–20, 64, 298, 330–1
Genette, Gerard 228n1
Geoffrey of Monmouth 13, 210, 272
Gervinus, G.G. 357
Gibson, Colin 318–19
Gielgud, John 48, *50*
Gildon, Charles 18
Globe Theatre 2, 124, 139, 165
Gloucester 58–60; as adulterer 189, 233, 265–6, 267; and Albany 192; "As flies to wanton boys" speech 254, 266, 293, 311, 316, 321, 351–2; blinding of 10–11, 44, 58, 116, 189, 190, 192–3, 254, 270, 297–8, 300, 302–8, 315–19; Bradley on 43; Brook 71; despair 254; empathy for 317–18; James I 172; loyalty 267, 302–3, 305–8; natural law 265–6; Quarto/Folio texts 115–16, 117; servants' kindness 189–90, 318; and sons 58–9, 308–9, 358; subplot fitted in 128; treason 239
God 256
Godard, Jean-Luc 82, *83*
gods 244, 255–6, 267, 321, 352–3
Goldberg, Jonathan 59, 68
Goldberg, S.L. 46
Goneril 53–4; and Albany 268, 289; blinding of Gloucester 303–5; Brook's version 70–1; cursed 232; development of character 111–12, 218–19; evil 236; garrulity 289; humiliating father 269–70; in *King Leir* 9–10; love 271; motivation 300; Nature 264; retribution 187; trial of 238–9
Gonorill 209, 213–17
Gordin, Jacob 79, *80*
Grady, Hugh 61
Granville-Barker, Harley 45, 60, 76, 91n40, 126, 127
Greenblatt, Stephen 55, 59, 63, 121–2n1, 257
Greene, Robert 210
Greg, W.W.: fair copy 133; *King Leir* 211; Maguire 65; on Pavier 174; Quarto 39, 40–1, 129–30, 157–8, 176
Gregory XIII, Pope 301
Grey, Catherine 221, 222
Grey, Lady Jane 222
Griffith, Elizabeth 351–2, 354, 361
Gunpowder plotters 302
Gurr, Andrew 61, 125, 127, 135, 136–7, 161, 172
Gwyn, Nell 15–16

Halio, Jay L. 67, 91n37, 162, 165, 203n2, 321n1
Hall, H.T. 60
Hamilton, N.E.S.A. 38
Hamilton, Victoria 78
Hamlet: cuts 140; Horatio 69; Kierkegaard on 283–4; and *King Lear* 299–300; length of 126; sold 133; spectators 317; variants 107–8
Hardman, C.B. 332
Hare, David 59–60
Harington, John 224, 226–8
Harris, Arthur John 90n21
Harrison, Thomas P. 211
Harsnett, Samuel 128
Hart, Alfred 125, 126, 127
Hayward, Sir John 223
Hazlitt, William 20, 53
Heartbreak House (Shaw) 326–7, 344–8
Heath, James 319–20
Heilman, Robert B. 59, 298
Heinemann, Margot 61
Heminge, John 33, 40, 66, 105, 127, 149
Henry, Prince 179, 180
Henry IV 109, 245
Henry V 176
Henry VIII 221, 222
Henry VIII 156
Henslowe, Philip 5, 210
Herbert, William 40
Heywood, Thomas 160, 166–7, 168, 171

Higgins, John 210
High Noon 193–4
Hinman, Charles 66
Hittinger, Russell 261
Hobbes, Thomas 260, 262, 264
Hobson, Harold 71
Holderness, Graham 62, 68, 122n8
Holinshed, Raphael 13–14, 210, 272
Holloway, John 30, 46
Holly, Ellen 73
Holm, Ian 77, 79
Holmes, Martin 56
Homan, Sidney 314–15
Honigmann, Ernst 141–2
Hooker, Richard 176, 261, 262–3, 264, 269, 270, 274
Hopkins, Anthony 60
Hordern, Michael 76
Horton, Priscilla 30
Howard, Thomas 227–8
Howard-Hill, T.H. 66–7, 142, 177
Hughes, Alan 339
Hughes, Ted 13
human nature 246–7, 262–3, 268, 271
Hume, David 351
Hunt, Leigh 21, 25
Hunter, G.K. 185
Hunter, Robert G. 47, 256
Hurt, John 77

Iliad (Homer) 193, 194, 352–3, 354
Illustrated London News 342
incest 54–5, 327–8, 331–2
Inchbald, Elizabeth 333, 338
Ioppolo, Grace 105, 122n2, 122n8
Ireland, William-Henry 35–7
Irving, Henry: cuts to text 43, 147; in *King Lear* 48, *49,* 339, 340, 342, 348; Stonehenge set 30–1; and Terry 326, 331, 340, 342; in *Waterloo* 339, 343

Jaggard, William 141, 174–6, 177, 178
James, D. G. 62
James I (and VI): accession to throne 226; interest in supernatural 180–1; *King Lear* 65–6; King's Men 161, 172; sons 61, 172, 180; succession 220–2, 221–2; torture 322n9; Union 179, 181, 226
Jameson, Anna 341–2
Jennens, Charles 146, 203
Jerrold, Douglas 25
Jesus Christ 273
Job 46, 274
John, Saint 292
John Bull 30
Johnson, Arthur 176
Johnson, Gerald D. 174–5, 176
Johnson, Samuel: Cordelia's death 297; on Gloucester 58, 297–8; justice 184–5, 186–90; on Pope 33, 34, 65; on Tate 18, 210, 253
Jones, James Earl 71–3, 78
Jonson, Ben 65, 105, 126
Jorgensen, Paul A. 57–8
justice: arbitrariness 234; gods 244, 352; Johnson 184–5, 186–90; natural 236–7, 239–40, 267; poetic 186–7, 198; power 311; pragmatic 186–90; self-destruction of evil 243; in universe 209, 351–2

Kahn, Coppélia 55
Kahn, Paul 48
Kean, Charles 30, 42–3
Kean, Edmund 4, 22, *23,* 26, 337
Keats, John 84
Kemble, John Philip 20–2, 72
Kenrick, William 33–4
Kent: disguised 191–2; from *King Leir* 10–11; and Lear 284–5; loyalty 190–2, 198, 268; Quarto/Folio texts 115–16, 117, 179, 190; Servant 307; in stocks 113, 268
Kermode, Frank 300
Kettle, Arnold 52, 63
Kierkegaard, Søren: Abraham 280–2, 283; *Eighteen Upbuilding Discourses* 289; *Either/Or* 280, 290, 292; *Fear and Trembling* 278–9, 280–1, 287–8; on *Hamlet* 283–4, 292; on *King Lear* 279–80, 282–3, 286–7, 293; on St Paul 293–5; Regine (Olsen) 278–9, 286, 291; religious/ethical domains 281; "The Seducer's Diary" 279–80, 288, 291; *Self-Examination* 289; *Sickness Unto Death* 292; silence 287, 288; *The Stages on Life's Way* 286
Kiernan, Victor 30–1, 61
Killigrew, Thomas 15
King, Tom 19–20
King James Bible 107
King Lear 1, 184; and *Hamlet* 299–300; James I 65–6; and *King Leir* 7–11, 208–9, 226; played/printed versions 42–5, 70, 90n27, 124–5, 126, 140–1, 147; playing time 126–7; topicality

171–2, 178–9, 209, 224–8; *see also* Folio texts; Quartos
King Lear's Wife (Bottomley) 80
King Leir 5–11, 128, 136, 209–11; ending 119; political contexts 219–24; succession of king 222–3; suggested authors 210; topicality 224–8; *see also* Cordella
King of Texas 82
kingdom divided 172, 217–18, 220–1, 237–8
King's Men: Blackfriars 138–9; Globe Theatre 165; Jaggard and Blount 177; James I 161, 172; printing plays 141, 167, 173, 176–9; publishers 170–1
King's Theatre 15
Kirby, Ian J. 48
Kirschbaum, Leo 39
Knight, G. Wilson 44, 46, 57
Knights, L.C. 91n34
Knowles, Richard 67, 109, 110
Knutson, Roslyn 171, 172–3
Korol Lir (Kozintsev) 81
Kott, Jan 1, 46
Kozintsev, Grigoriy 81, 198, 204n8
Krige, Alice 74
Kronenfeld, Judy 60, 62
Kurosawa, Akira 81–2
Kyd, Thomas 210

Ladder of Year (Tyler) 84
Lake, Peter 301, 302
Lamb, Charles 17–18, 42, 50, 77, 326, 328–9, 346
Lanchester, Robert 73
Langbein, John H. 301–2, 322n5, 322n6, 322n7
Lange, Jessica 82
Lascelles, Mary 48
Lear: begging for pity 285; brutality 239; Burbage 2–4; and Cordelia 116, 219, 236, 285–6, 327–8, 331, 359–60; damned 273–4; death of 194–5, 197–8; deepening of character 111–14; and Fool 57–8; in his dotage 48–50, 57–8, 321; identity 270; incest suspected 54–5, 91n35, 327–8; killing soldier 234; nature/art 357; paganism 232; Passion of Christ 47; revenge fantasies 285; self-knowledge 265, 268, 346; suffering 2–3, 45–6; understanding 270, 289, 357–8; on women 241; *see also* love test
Lear, Charles Bernard 85
Lear (Bond) 80–1, 84
Lear in Private Life (Moncrieff) 333–8
Leggatt, Alexander 61, 71, 76, 77
Leigh, Jennifer Jason 82
Levin, Harry 14
license for performance 158–9, 169–70
Lindsay, Robert 77
Lippincott, H.F. 12
Lipsius, Justus 256, 274–5n4
Longfellow, Henry Wadsworth 25
Lord Chamberlain 125
Lord Chamberlain's Men 161
Lord Mayor 125
Lothian, John M. 45
love 271, 299, 331–2
love test 208–9, 213–14, 218, 226, 237, 267–8, 354
Love's Labour's Lost 356
Lowell, Robert 268–9
Lownes, Humphrey 176
loyalty: Edgar 192–4; Gloucester 267, 302–4, 305–9; Kent 190–2, 198, 268; natural law 264
Luhrmann, Baz 73
Lynch, Stephen J. 48

The Mabinogion 13
Macbeth 355
McClure, Lucas 85
McCowen, Alex 71
McGuire, Philip 312
Mack, Maynard 44, 46–7, 255, 256
McKern, Leo 77
McKerrow, R.B. 156–7
MacLean, Hugh 60
McLuskie, Kathleen 55, 58, 63
Macready, William Charles 25–30, *27, 28,* 70, 147
Maguire, Laurie E. 65, 159
Mallet, Gina 73
Malone, Edmond 34, 36–7
manuscripts 105, 131, 158, 159, 168–9
Marcus, Leah 65–6, 172
Marlowe, Christopher 210
Marowitz, Charles 70
Marsden, Jean 348n3
Martin, William F. 48
Marx, Steven 46
Mary, Queen of Scots 220, 221, 222, 301
Mary Tudor 221, 222
Massinger, Philip 65, 318–19
Master of the Revels: censorship 163; fair copy 129–30, 135; ideal text 127, 143; King's Men 161; license for performance 134, 136, 158–9

Matthews, Richard 52, 354
Maugham, Somerset 80
Measure for Measure 355
Melchiori, Giorgio 127, 150
Mendonça, Barbara Heliodora Carneiro de 14
The Merchant of Venice 6, 355
Middlemass, Frank 76
Middleton, Thomas 173
A Midsummer Night's Dream 179, 272
Millais, John Everett 347
Miller, Jonathan 74, 76
Milton, John 107
Miner, Valerie 84
Miola, Robert S. 352
Monck, Nugent 126
Moncrieff, William 79
Moncrieff, W.T. 326, 333, 336–8
Montaigne, Michel Eyquem de 128
Montgomery, William 156
morality 259–60, 293–5
More, Thomas 261
Moriarty, W.D. 140
Morrissey 85
Mortimer, John Hamilton 85, *87*
Mueller, M. 211
Muir, Edwin 52, 53
Muir, Kenneth 44, 64, 65, 147, 185, 186, 204n6, 211
Murphy, Arthur 298
Murphy, John L. 44
Myles, Robert 3–4

natural law: crisis of 258; divine providence 260–1; Gloucester 265–6; Hooker 262–3, 264, 269; human nature 271; loyalty 264; redemption 253–4
nature: art 356, 357; convention 244–6; Edmund 259–60, 264, 300, 355; Goneril 264; human art 246; justice 231–7; political order 231–2, 234; sympathetic 187–8
neoclassical tastes 14–15, 16–17, 146, 297
neo-Puritanism 20–2
Neville, Alexander 255–6
Nevo, Ruth 46
New Arden edition 124, 186, 204n6
New Bibliographers 156–7, 159–60
New Historicists 257
New Oxford Shakespeare 184
New Variorum series 149, 200–1, 203
The New York Post 22
Noble, Adrian 74
Norton Shakespeare 106, 109, 121–2n1, 124
Nottingham Guardian Journal 71
Nowottny, Winifred M.T. 30, 44
Nunn, Hillary 317–18, 322n9

Odell, George C.D. 22, 26, 29
Oedipus the King 194
Okes, Nicholas 105, 131–2, 133, 134, 165, 166, 167
Old Corrector 37, 38
Olivier, Laurence 48, 76–7
Opie, Amelia: *Father and Daughter* 79, 326, 331, 333–8
Orgel, Stephen 68, 106, 122n5, 126
Ornstein, Robert 47
Orwell, George 46, 62, 69, 91n39
Oswald: on Albany 199; and Kent 268; from *King Leir* 9–10; and Lear 270; loyalty 190, 192; proto-capitalist 60; retribution 187; source for 214–15
Othello 316–17, 322–3n11, 344–5
Oxford Clarendon Press 211
Oxford edition 32, 124, 146, 163–4, 186

paganism 232, 254, 273
Papp, Joseph 71–3
Parsons, Robert 220
Pascal, Blaise 256
patriarchy 55, 336
Patterson, Annabel 91n38
Paul, Saint 264, 273, 293–5
Paul's Boys 173
Pavier, Thomas 40, 174–5, 177
Payne, John Howard 20
Peat, Derek 88
Peele, George 210
Pelican edition 124
Penguin edition 124
Pepys, Samuel 15, 16
Pericles 156, 190, 195, 360
Perillus 10–11, 223
Perret, Marion D. 48
Petti, Anthony 168
Pfeiffer, Michelle 82
Phelps, Samuel 30
Philips, Robin 73
Pius V, Pope 301
plague 135, 136, 139, 171
playbook 135–45, 159
playhouses 135, 136, 171
playing times 125–6, 147
Poel, William 90n22
political approach 61–4

political order 231–2, 234, 238
Pollard, Alfred W. 39
Pollard, Graham 156–7, 158, 159
Pope, Alexander 31–3, 34, 35, 64–5, 124, 145–6
Popham, John 302
postmodern revisions 64–88
Prince's Company 173
Prince's Men 167
printed plays 122n3, 164, 171, 172–3
printers 106, 109, 121, 130, 131–2, 167
promptbooks 143, 158, 160
Protestantism 220, 222, 301
public/private spheres 338–43
puns 107–8
Puritans 220, 224, 262, 269

Quarto, First 38, 128–35, 162–5; Albany 119; Cordelia 119–20, 122n8; and Folio 104, 108–9, 110–16; Gloucester/Edmund 117; Goneril/Albany 118; Greg 41; as ideal text 148–9; Kent/Gentleman 116–17, 118; lineation 132–3, 168; manuscript source 39–40, 105, 167–9; as performance text 65; as printer's copy 144; publishers 165–7; and Quarto, Second 157; setting of 66; Stone on 64
Quarto, Second 40, 64, 66–7, 144–5, 157, 174–7
Quarto, Third 145
Queen's Men 5, 167, 173, 210
Questier, Michael 301, 302
Quilligan, Maureen 55

Rackin, Phyllis 60
Ragan 9–10, 209, 213–17
Raleigh, Walter 224, 249–50n10
Ran (Kurosawa) 81–2
Raphael, D.D. 195
Rasmussen, Eric 140
Raworth, Robert 167
redemption 45, 253–4, 273
redistribution of wealth 205n15
Redman, Amanda 77
Regan 53–4; Brook's version 70–1; and Cornwall 312–13; development of character 111, 112–13, 218–19; and Edmund 20; evil 236; and Gloucester 304–8; in *King Leir* 9–10, 209, 213–17; and Lear 269–70, 287; love 271; motivation 300; retribution 187; trial of 238–9
Regency period 22
Reibetanz, John 44
Renaissance period 2, 106, 128
Restoration period 14–19, 31–3, 147, 203n3
resurrection scene 190–1
revisionist hypothesis 104, 128–9, 147–8
Reynolds, Joshua 298
Ribner, Irving 46, 59
Richard II 223–4
Richard III 6
Richardson, Samuel 334
Richardson, William 45–6, 291–2
Ridley, M.R. 65, 146
Ridolfi Plot 320
Rigg, Diana 77, *78*
Ringler, William A. Jr. 56
Riverside edition 124, 131, 184, 185, 248n1, 306
Roberts, James 133
Roberts, John 175–6
Robertson, Graham 342
Roche, Thomas P. Jr. 47
Romans, epistle to 263
Romeo and Juliet 73, 106
Rose playhouse 5
Rosenberg, Marvin 86, 313
Rousseau, Jean-Jacques 261, 262
Rowe, Nicholas 31, 145, 155, 200
Rowley, Samuel 167, 171
Rutter, Carol 54
Ryan, Kiernan 63, 104

sacrifice 46, 280–2, 283
Salgado, Gamini 56
Sanders, Julie 82, 84
Saunders, Laura 85
Saunderson, Mary 16, 55
Schlegel, A.W. 45, 48, 58
Schoff, Francis G. 47
Schücking, Levin 126
Scofield, Paul 70, 71, *72*
Scott, Clement 339, 340
scribes 135–6, 141, 142–3
Sellars, Peter 82
Seneca 255–6
Shaftesbury 291
Shakespeare, William: and daughters 361; early works 5–11; playing Albany 4; revision 15, 177–8, 179
Sharma, R.C. 52
Sharpe, Ella Freeman 62
Shaw, George Bernard 147; *Heartbreak House* 326–7, 344–8; *Shakes Versus Shav* 347

Shaw, Glen Byam 312
Shebbeare, John 19, 79
Sher, Anthony 58, 74, *75*
Siddons, Sarah *21*
Sidney, Sir Philip 228; *Arcadia* 12–13, 89n16, 128, 212
Siegel, Paul N. 45–6
silence 287, 288–9
Simkins, Michael 77
Simkins, Stevie 194
Singer, Samuel Weller 38
Sir Thomas More 105, 131, 156
Sisson, C.J. 47
Skulsky, Harold 52
Skura, Meredith A. 211
Smidt, Kristian 127, 128–9
Smiley, Jane 82, 84
Smith, Thomas 319–21
Socrates 231
Somogyi, Nick de 68
Sophocles 290
Sorvino, Paul 73
source materials 1, 2–5, 211–12; *see also* *King Leir*
Southwell, Robert 305
Speaight, Robert 254–5
spectators 314, 315–19, 322n7
Spencer, Theodore 259
Spenser, Edmund 228; *Faerie Queene* 14, 210, 224–5, 272
Stafford, Simon 171
stage directions 108–9
stage machinery 70, 329
Stampfer, James 48
Stampfer, Judah 255
Stanley, Ferdinando 222
Stationers' Company 160–1
Stationers' Guild 155
Stationers' Register 134, 165, 167, 170, 210–11, 223
Stattel, Robert 73
Steevens, George 35, 38
Stern, Jeffrey 55
Stern, Tiffany 89n9
Stewart, Patrick 82
Stoker, Bram 343
Stone, P.W.K. 64–9, 65
Stonehenge set 30–1, 70, 77
Stoppard, Tom 81, 106, 121
storm scene 26, 232, 241
Stroup, Thomas B. 56
Stubbs, John 304–5
succession to throne 219–20, 235–6
suffering 45, 188–9, 255–6, 293–5
supernatural 180–1
Sutton, James M. 179
Swan Theatre 318–19
Swinburne, Algernon Charles 54, 61, 254

Tarlton, Richard 4
Tate, Naham: Cordelia 56, 193, 329–30, 331; Edgar–Cordelia 147, 330, 331, 332–3; Johnson on 210, 253; revisions 1, 14–19, 54–5, 64, 146–7, 203n3, 253, 262, 326
Taylor, Gary: conflated text 165; *The Division of the Kingdoms* 64, 162–3; *Henry VIII* 156; multiple texts 310; Quarto/Folio texts 65, 122n7; Shakespeare's revisions 65–6, 177–8; *see also* Oxford edition
Taylor, Joseph 5
The Tempest 15, 361
Tennenhouse, Leonard 53, 55, 63
Terry, Ellen 326, 331, 340–1, 342–3
texts: acted versions 42–5, 70, 90n27, 124–5, 126, 140–1, 147; acting companies 158; alternative 155, 159; authority 155–6, 157, 160; conflated 64, 106, 149–50, 164–5, 185; evolution of 108, 124, 125; ideal 127, 143; manuscripts 105, 131, 158, 159, 168–9; multiple 106, 107, 157–8, 310–15; parallel 68, 185, 196; Renaissance period 2, 106, 128; two-texts 163–4, 185
Thackeray, William Makepeace 42
The Theater 2
The Theatrical Review 26
Theobald, Lewis 33, 34, 146, 200–1
A Thousand Acres 82
Tilney, Edmund 161, 170
Timon of Athens 43
Titus Andronicus 6, 44, 89n15, 298, 331, 355
Tolstoy, Leo 58–9, 210
Tong, Joanne 336
Topcliffe, Richard 305, 322n4
topicality 171–2, 178–9, 209, 224–8
torture: Catholicism 322n4; gods 321; James I 322n9; neoclassical taste 297; spectators 314, 322n7; state use of 298, 319–21; treason 300–5
transcripts 141–2
Traversi, Derek 46
treason 239, 300–5
Trewin, J.C. 70

trial scenes 91n40, 234–5, 244, 249n4, 354–5
Tutin, Dorothy 77
The Two Gentlemen of Verona 211–12
Two Noble Kinsmen 156
two-texts hypothesis 163–4, 185
Tyler, Anne 84
Tyndale, William 107

Union of Parliaments 179, 181, 226
Unities of Action/Place/Time 14–15
Urkowitz, Steven 64, 66, 89n9, 192, 205n23, 310
Ustinov, Peter 73

verse irregularities 143–4
violence 44, 71, 298

Walker, Alice 39
Walkley, A.B. 90n19
Warner, Deborah 77
Warren, Michael: Albany 179; *The Division of the Kingdoms* 64, 162–3; Edgar 192; Kent 179, 190; multiple texts 64–5, 106, 310; *Parallel "King Lear"* 203n2; parallel texts 68
Warton, Thomas 26, 34
Waterloo (Doyle) 326, 339, 343
Watts, Cedric 258
wealth, redistribution of 205n15
Webb, Alan 71
Weis, René 185, 203n2
Welby, William 166
Welles, Orson 54, 60, 71
Wells, Stanley: conflated text 165; on Gambon 74; *Henry VIII* 156; *King Leir* 211–12; mock trial scene 91n40; multiple texts 310; Quartos 67, 185; *see also* Oxford edition
Welsford, Enid 11–12
Wentworth, Peter 224
Werstine, Paul 158, 160
Weschler, Lawrence 297, 310
West, Timothy 77
White, R.S. 261, 263, 270
Whitefriars Boys 179
Wiles, David 56
William of Orange 301
Williams, George W. 46
Wilton, Penelope 76
wind-machine 26
Wingate, Charles E.L. 29, 30
The Winter's Tale 191, 246, 315, 360
Woffington, Peg 29
Wolverhampton Express and Star 71
Woods, Leigh 19
Worde, Wynken de 155
Wordsworth, William 352, 354
Worrall, David 338
Wright, William Aldis 38, 39

The Yiddish King Lear 79, *80*
The Yorkshire Tragedy 156